US ACCORDING TO THEM

US ACCORDING TO THEM

Stateside Portrayals of Puerto Ricans
and Their Culture, 1898–2010

Ligia T. Domenech

University Press of Mississippi / Jackson

The University Press of Mississippi is the scholarly publishing agency of
the Mississippi Institutions of Higher Learning: Alcorn State University,
Delta State University, Jackson State University, Mississippi State University,
Mississippi University for Women, Mississippi Valley State University,
University of Mississippi, and University of Southern Mississippi.

www.upress.state.ms.us

The University Press of Mississippi is a member
of the Association of University Presses.

Copyright © 2025 by University Press of Mississippi
All rights reserved
Manufactured in the United States of America

∞

Library of Congress Control Number:2024050014
Hardback ISBN: 9781496854605
Trade paperback ISBN: 9781496854612
Epub Single ISBN: 9781496854629
Epub Institutional ISBN: 9781496854636
PDF Single ISBN: 9781496854643
PDF Institutional ISBN: 9781496854650

British Library Cataloging-in-Publication Data available

DEDICATED TO

Michael D. Franz, who patiently put up with the endless research, writing and editing hours, and who never failed to encourage me to work on this project and many others.

Samuel Silva Gotay, who motivated me to follow this line of research.

Ignacio Rivera Cordero, who cleverly provided the title for this book.

Marcia Rivera Hernández, who corrected my writing and encouraged my spirit.

Malena and Paloma Sandoval, for whom I write this book in the hopes that they continue the resistance against colonialism.

That strange blend of the commercial traveller, the missionary, and the
barbarian conqueror, which was the American abroad.
—OLAF STAPLEDON (1886–1950) IN *LAST AND FIRST MEN* (1930)

The Yankees are interested in the cage, not the birds.
—PEDRO ALBIZU CAMPOS (1891–1965) IN A SPEECH (1930S)

CONTENTS

Introduction 3

Chapter 1: "Oh, Dear Lord, Why Didst Thou Ever Inspire Me to Go to Puerto Rico to Teach?": About the Selected American Authors . 19

Chapter 2: "They Considered Them Conquered Animals": On How Colonialism Permeates All 36

Chapter 3: "Living from Hand to Mouth": On the Poverty of Puerto Ricans 60

Chapter 4: "Neither Aliens Nor Americans": The Convoluted Politics of the Colony 77

Chapter 5: "We Think We Are Better Than Other People": On the Onset of the Relationships Between Colonizers and Colonized . . 92

Chapter 6: "From the Yellow Pine of Castile to the Mahogany of Africa": On the Racial Types and Social Classes 112

Chapter 7: "Song, Laughter and Mañana": On the Myth of the Lazy Puerto Ricans 128

Chapter 8: "Lust Was Written in the Very Faces of the People": On the Morality of Puerto Ricans 140

Chapter 9: "Known by Their Fruits": On Violence, Illegality, and Policing 157

Chapter 10: "The Body Was There but Not the Soul":
On the Puerto Ricans' Religious Practices 170

Chapter 11: "A Poor Specimen of Manhood":
On Matters of Health and Death 191

Chapter 12: "Satan Himself Would Dance If He Could Hear Them":
On Puerto Rican Entertainments 218

Chapter 13: "We Iss One Happy People": On Puerto Ricans' Values
and How They See Life 243

Chapter 14: "People Who Will Always 'Be There'":
On Puerto Ricans' Relationships with Family, Friends, and Strangers . . 260

Chapter 15: "Those Indescribable Eyes": Puerto Rican Women 276

Chapter 16: "Bright-Eyed Little Fellows": Puerto Rican Children 297

Chapter 17: "They Want Rice and Beans First":
Food, Drinks, and Smokes 315

Chapter 18: "Dear Me! What a Busy, Noisy Place!":
On Commerce and Animal Treatment 336

"To Be Born in Porto Rico Is, for Me, a Privilege": Conclusion 356

Appendix 1: General Nelson A. Miles Proclamation 361

Appendix 2: Bibliography of Analyzed American Authors 363

Appendix 3: American Authors' Informative Table 369

Notes 385

Works Cited 409

Index 421

US ACCORDING TO THEM

INTRODUCTION

HISTORICAL BACKGROUND

By the end of the nineteenth century, Puerto Ricans had been colonized by Spain for almost four hundred years. By then, Spain was a declining empire with only two colonies left in the Americas: Cuba and Puerto Rico.[1] But that was about to change. After becoming involved in the Cuban-Spanish War in 1898 and actually winning it, the United States substituted Spain and acquired Puerto Rico as a colony from which to extract desired raw materials (sugar, tobacco), and that provided a new colonial market which they would force to buy American[2] production. The acquisition of Puerto Rico also provided the United States with a strategic location to establish coal bases to supply their merchant and military ships.

On July 25, 1898, US forces disembarked in Guánica, a town located in the south-west of Puerto Rico. Three days later, General Miles issued a proclamation, claiming that the American forces were coming to protect Puerto Ricans (see appendix 1). But the timing of the following events clearly revealed what the invasion was all about. After the proclamation, Miles passed on the control of all civic affairs to General James H. Wilson, who then appointed Colonel F. A. Hill as a collector with orders "to seize the Customs House and its receipts."[3]

From Guánica, US soldiers kept moving to conquer many other towns until the armistice was declared on August 12, 1898. In total, some 15,472 American soldiers participated in the invasion, and they came with their wagons, horses, mules, rations, weapons, ammunition, and other war supplies.[4] To the surprise of the invading forces, many Puerto Ricans received them joyfully, expecting them to bring them freedom from Spanish imperialism and unaware that they were about to experience a mere exchange of empires. The naiveté of Puerto Rican politicians regarding the intentions of the US government in 1898 was evident in expressions published around the time of the invasion, such as this one from *La Democracia* of July 4, 1899: ". . . a people constituted on a basis so free and democratic cannot bring forth tyrants. . . . the offsprings of these who signed the Declaration of Independence can't do less than give liberty to our people . . ."[5]

The so-called "Spanish-American War" lasted only four months. Ironically, what US Secretary of State John Jay called "a splendid little war" allowed the United States to become an empire just 123 years after they fought British imperialism, as they acquired Puerto Rico and Guam with no intention of constitutionally incorporating them ever into the United States. The whole Puerto Rican Campaign lasted only seventeen days. The US forces suffered only three deaths and forty injured, while Spain suffered seventeen deaths, eighty-eight injured, and 324 prisoners of war.[6]

Puerto Rico, which had just elected its first autonomous government while under Spain and which was economically self-sufficient with no foreign debt, was now to be colonized by the United States, which acquired it under a new status: an unincorporated territory, the colonial status that the Island still has. Puerto Ricans, since then and to this day, became subject to the plenary powers of the US Congress (under Article IV of the US Constitution). The prophecy of Puerto Rican patriot Ramón Emeterio Betances was fulfilled: "If Puerto Rico does not act fast, it will forever be a United States colony."[7]

The acquisition of Puerto Rico was completed on December 10, 1898, with the signing of the Treaty of Paris, which, among other dispositions, ceded the Island to the United States. It was followed by two years of US military government and then by over 120 years of a still ongoing US colonial government. During this time, the US colonial government attempted the Americanization of Puerto Ricans through its educational, political, economic, and legal system. It was fundamentally unsuccessful.

The acquisition of Puerto Rico as a colony in 1898 prompted the interest of a variety of sectors of the United States (military personnel, news correspondents, wealthy investors, missionaries, politicians, scientists, and potential tourists) who wanted to know more about Puerto Rico and its inhabitants, and about their potential utility for them. Some of them visited the Island and then wrote about their experiences while there for the benefit of others who planned to visit in the future. Decades later, other Americans visited the island to explore the "effects of American civilization" on Puerto Rican society. This book is about the books they published.

ON THIS RESEARCH

Years ago, I read *The American Presence in Puerto Rico,* which included a short essay by Eugene V. Mohr titled "Language, Literature & Journalism," where he briefly discussed several books written by Americans who lived in Puerto Rico for different periods of time and under different circumstances. The reading of this short essay kindled my interest in this theme and thus activated almost fifteen years of intermittent research of every possible such book that I could find. Some books I received as gifts from friends and mentors, many I bought, others I got as interlibrary book loans, and finally, I got access to a large amount through hard-to-find books' Internet sites. I read every single book I found. In the meantime, I kept teaching, publishing, and presenting on multiple unrelated history themes in Puerto Rico, the United States, Cuba, Chile, and Uruguay. I kept taking notes from the books I found, fueled by my natural curiosity and passion for research.

The research for this book turned into a fascinating opportunity to see Puerto Ricans, including myself, as if in a mirror, although a distorted one, through the eyes of foreigners. This is what I expect to share with the American and Puerto Rican readers, hoping that it will help us all to better understand how American colonialism has pervaded American-Puerto Rican relationships and has nurtured stereotypes of ourselves that, sadly, many Americans, and even Puerto Ricans, have adopted as true without questioning.

Few researchers have paid attention to these accounts authored by common Americans who visited Puerto Rico. As Puerto Rican intellectual René Marqués once wrote:

> . . . it is very rare to hear or read a personal report on Puerto Ricans coming from a North American visitor who is neither a public relations official (read political propagandist) on the payroll of the colonial government, nor a hypocritically smiling congressman from Washington, nor an opportunistic New York politician, nor a "good will" visitor on a well-paid vacation in one of our luxury hotels, nor a Point Four "tourist" carefully selected and subsidized by the Department of State in Washington, nor one of those rich, young girls, with bourgeois vulgarity and pretentiousness, from Sarah Lawrence, on her offensive annual "poverty vacation" on our island (Go to your own Deep South, young girls!), nor that "generous friend of Puerto Rico" with thousands of dollars invested in the absentee economy of the island for his own profit.[8]

The research for this book was difficult and time-consuming. Reading it will probably be also difficult for any Puerto Rican. Reading demeaning portrayals of your own people and your own country is not a pleasant experience. There were times in which I just cried, others in which I ranted and raged over the frequent allusions to Puerto Ricans using terms generally employed for animals. But it was never boring, and many other authors presented more balanced views of us. Most often, I felt extremely proud of my people and my culture. I think that my deep and unyielding sense of humor helped me go through my readings. In any event, I consider it an advantage to be a native Puerto Rican since my knowledge of the culture that the selected authors tried to describe gives me the ability to relate to their findings and a deep understanding of the system of symbols and values that the foreigners tried to make sense of. For example, I know exactly what this American soldier is referring to in this amusing remark: "It seemed strange that one could yell or shout at a Porto Rican to stop, without any effect, while if you but knew how to make the little hissing sound—'tsc'—like escaping steam for instance, he would stop in his tracks as though he has been shot" (Rossiter [1900?]).[9]

Of the 132 texts I analyzed for this book, thirty-one were published between 1898 and 1899. This reflects the high level of interest in the United States regarding the development of the Spanish-American War that was created by the American "yellow press." Of these thirty-one books, six were authored by military officers and another fourteen by US newspapers' war correspondents.[10] Most of these authors were direct witnesses of their stories.

After the war ended, the interest shifted to knowing more about the new possessions acquired as a result of the war. Many of those books document the so-called "progress" of the Island since the US invasion. Between 1900 and 1910, thirty-three books were published, many of them by missionaries and other travelers. Another seventeen were published in the 1910s decade. Afterward, the interest seemed to fade until the 1950s when the fast industrialization program established there briefly turned Puerto Rico into a so-called "showcase of development and democracy." The wide scope of this research confirmed that the colonizers' prejudices and biases do not change through time in any substantial way. The following table illustrates the increase in publications based on our sample:

Table 1.

Published books by period	
1898–1900	31
1901–10	34
1911–20	17
1921–30	9
1931–40	7
1941–50	7
1951–60	9
1961–70	5
1971–80	3
1981–90	2
1991–00	4
2001–10	4

The book titles tell us that, since the beginning of American colonialism, different sectors in the United States (missionaries, politicians, investors) had different projects for the transformation of Puerto Rico, and they frequently made reference to those expectations: *The Remaking of a Culture*; *The Waiting Isles*; *Uncle Sam's Modern Miracles*; *Island of Promise*; *An Island Grows*; *Citizens of Tomorrow*; or *Kingdom Building*. But this positive/hopeful intention of transformation was not shared by all. As early as 1904, Leo S. Rowe used this title: *The United States and Porto Rico, with Special Reference to the Problems Arising Out of Our Contact with the Spanish-American Civilization*. And then, when the success of the Americanization of Puerto Ricans didn't materialize, we found in the 1930s to early 1960s negative titles such as: *Dynamite on Our Doorstep*; *Workshop U.S.A. The Challenge of Puerto Rico*; *Puerto Rican Paradox*; *The Stranger is Our Own*; or *White Elephants in the Caribbean*.

The selected authors discussed all kinds of themes that are not the subject of this book, such as history, politics, economic activities, flora, fauna, climate, literature, science, arts, etc. Each author became the final authority on what to include and what to leave out of his/her writing. Since the selected authors were writing for other Americans, with their books they helped create a general American opinion regarding their new "subjects." Accurate or not, these books contained perceptions of Puerto Ricans and their world that became the "general knowledge" about us in the United States.

ON THE CREDIBILITY OF THE WRITERS

These books were never intended to be read by Puerto Ricans: they were written in English and mostly published in the United States for an American audience. This implies an honesty in their reporting that Puerto Rican readers might find interesting, even though they are frequently offensive. In the eyes of their American readers, they provide a truthful account of a cultural encounter under unequal circumstances. And they are truthful in the sense that what they wrote was what they understood as true at the moment from their biased perspective. Since I value these sources for their accounts only, I do not evaluate the authenticity of the narrations, considering them all as the truthful perspective of the onlooker, even when I disagree with their interpretations about the observed. This practice is commonly seen in similar studies: "Many other historians and anthropologists are less willing to abandon a belief in the ability of the observer to portray, record, or analyze another culture and the actions of its members, however imperfectly, in a manner that allows us to cross that barren but mysterious beach that separates cultures and peoples from each other..."[11]

According to another analysis, until the technological advances in transportation, science, and health, as well as an increase in Europeans' affluence, allowed easier, safer, and more affordable traveling (around the second half of the nineteenth century),[12] those called "armchair anthropologists" based their theories on materials collected by informal travelers with other purposes (missionaries, government employees, adventurers).[13] An example is philosophers John Locke and Jean Jacques Rousseau who relied on information provided by such travelers, less educated than themselves.[14] Since these informers had the real experience of being in a foreign place of interest, their texts were considered credible sources of information regarding what they saw there.

Who were the target audience of our American authors? Mostly members of the new American middle class who "grew from 756,000 in 1870 to 5,609,000 in 1910" made up of "the managers of the economy, the devotees of urban social reform, the arbiters of national culture, the conspicuous consumers, the hustling climbers," as defined by historian David Leviatin.[15] This curious new class fueled an economy and a culture that, influenced by travel literature, had an interest in "acquiring information about foreigners living in 'strange' places."[16] They were avidly interested in having a "vicarious adventure" since the distance prevented them from having to experience the foul odors and vulgar sounds of the lower classes as they read about these subjects from the comfort of their middle-class homes. In effect, "looking at the misfortune of others—even the picturesque and romantic images . . . helped the members of the new urban middle class to distinguish and define themselves" as progressive and prosperous.[17]

With only three exceptions,[18] all of the selected authors analyzed in this book had no formal training as anthropologists,[19] sociologists, or ethnographers. Therefore, they lacked the scientific knowledge to understand in-depth the conducts they observed. Most were amateur recorders of a group of people they just met, "implicit ethnographers," as Stuart Schwartz called them, or "spontaneous anthropologists," according to John Cuisener.[20] Lacking historical, political, and economic context, their writings reflect their racist and classist attitudes as well as their romanticism, exoticism, and puritanism, and reinforced within the general population the imperial policies that they seldom criticized.[21]

The lack of familiarity of the selected authors with the Puerto Rican (and, in most cases, the Latin American) "imaginative universe" is what prevented them from "grasping what people are up to" and "adequately interpret what are the acts they observe signs of."[22] For example, two American authors (Fowles and Boyce) concluded that Puerto Ricans saluted with the word "Adiós," which they correctly translated to one of its meanings: "good-bye." But in Puerto Rico the term can also be used to express surprise or just as an interjection, which can be an appropriate use in a salutation situation. When this author incorrectly claimed "good-bye" as its only meaning, he concluded that Puerto Ricans were either odd or ignorant: "The form of salutation in Porto Rico is 'Adios.' Literally translated, this means 'Good-by.' Whenever a child meets you and wishes to open a conversation he usually begins by saying, 'Good-by.' All over the island I was greeted with smiles and 'Good-bys'" (Boyce 1914, 443).

Travelers' tales are not superior nor inferior to those of an ethnologist's or an anthropologist's: they are just different and serve different purposes. Different also were the two cultures that sort of "bumped into each other" since 1898, and neither Puerto Rico nor the United States were the same after that moment: one becoming recolonized by an Anglo-Saxon culture, and the other becoming a modern empire. Regarding this, Albert Memmi established: "The colonial relationship . . . chained the colonizer and the colonized into an implacable dependence, molded their respective characters, and dictated their conduct."[23] The deep-seated differences between Americans and Puerto Ricans were graciously expressed by a pair of American writers:

> Everything on the island is done in the wrong way, and in order to do anything right it must be done wrong, as contradictory as this statement seems. To move forward is to move backward, but the Porto Rican boatman rows with his face towards the bow, as he says, to see where he is going. Articles that we would carry in baskets or boxes are here moved in bags, and vice versa. The Porto Rican gentleman beckons with the same movement we should use to drive a person away. . . . in their style of architecture . . . [houses] are constructed so that the front of the house faces the alley, at what we should call the rear, and the backside fronts the streets. (Browne and Dole 1907, 1398)

ON THE IMPERIAL/COLONIAL CONTEXT OF THE BOOKS

According to Frantz Fanon, the logic of colonialism lies in the denial or distortion of the history and past of the colonized.[24] By the end of the nineteenth century, Puerto Rico had existed as a Spanish society for almost four hundred years. Puerto Ricans had a defined culture and identity separate from the Spaniards. On the other hand, the United States had less than 125 years of having an identity separate from the English. Nevertheless, some American authors denied the existence of a Puerto Rican history and culture previous to the US invasion: "Of Porto Rican history it may be said that it has been so uneventful as to escape notice. No complete historical work upon the subject exists in any language" (Hamm *Porto* 1899, 71).

Portraying Puerto Rico as an ahistorical place implied that Puerto Ricans were still in their "savage state," still in the process of developing a sense of identity. The logical inference was that Puerto Ricans would, therefore, be open to being civilized and assimilated by the Americans, a process that was expected to flow without problems. In general, the Puerto Rican possession was portrayed as a *tabula rasa* where Americans could easily write a brand-new history without having to consider the past.

Because of their lack of knowledge about Puerto Rico, American observers frequently tried to explain what they observed using multiple theories popular at the time in the United States. Prominent among these are theories explaining the Puerto Rican temperament through the Island's racial composition or its tropical climate. A review of some of those theories follows.

According to historian-philosopher Tzvetan Todorov, racialism, which is the doctrine regarding human races, is an ideological movement born in Eastern Europe in the eighteenth century.[25] This doctrine considered human races as similar to animal species, and was against the "interbreeding" of different races, thus denying what has happened throughout history: the continuous combination of human genes that cancels the idea of "pure races." These ideas, highly questioned today, were very popular in the Western world until the 1950s. Many racialists see the world as divided by races and see races in terms of a hierarchy, with some (white, Nordic) superior to others (Black, Asian). As becomes evident, this doctrine helps to justify the subjugation of the "inferior races" by the "superior" ones.

Ideas regarding the influence of climate on the personality of people were likewise popular in the nineteenth century and were supported by the writings of Enlightenment thinkers such as Montesquieu.[26] An American war correspondent documented in 1899 that the tropical climate had an effect on Puerto Rican laborers: according to him, nature makes inhabitants of tropical lands lazy and then gives them a fruitful land so that they actually don't need to strain so much:

> Nature is really a very kindly old dame . . . in countries where more than a certain degree of active physical exercise becomes injurious, she interposes a disinclination for exercise. . . . in hot climates she makes men lazy. . . . Along with this disinclination for energetic work, she pours out a lavish bounty which makes energetic work quite needless. . . . Porto Rican heat saps the energies, both physical and mental. The physical disinclination is accompanied by a mental indifference. (Robinson 1899, 186–87)

Another example of environmental determinism applied to Puerto Ricans is the research work of Australian geographer Dr. A. Greenfell Price in the

West Indies, *White Settlers in the Tropics*, where he intended to find "why the white races, particularly the northern races, have in general failed to colonize the tropics."[27] After visiting Puerto Rico in 1933, he concluded that "many white groups and individuals abhor heavy labor in tropical climates and that this fact greatly impedes white settlement."[28]

Surprisingly, as late as 1934, a highly respected Puerto Rican intellectual, Antonio S. Pedreira, brandished both racial and climate theories to explain Puerto Rican culture. Pedreira affirmed that the reason why Puerto Ricans go fast through childhood and mature before they should is because of their race: "This rush to be a man we inherited from the race."[29] And then he basically attributed to the Island's climate a lot of "defects" of Puerto Ricans, in a tone as harsh as that of some of the American authors we analyzed:

> ...because of our geographical position, we live in permanent anguish... the destructive storms... the undesirable earthquakes. Tremors and storms... the drought... the inclement rains... forcing the landowner to think daily of his failure. This defeatist attitude is present in our general compliance and is an important artery of our pessimism. The climate melts our will... The heat matures us before our time and before time it also decomposes us. From its unnerving pressure on men comes that national characteristic we call lethargy... a kind of inhibition, of mental drowsiness and lack of assertiveness. It is following, without stifling, comfortably and routinely, the course of life, without change or worry, nodding our aspirations and squatting in front of the future.[30]

But there were also philosophical constructions behind the perspectives of our selected authors. An obvious one is "the myth of the noble savage," which is based on the idea of the innate goodness of all humans, which is only altered by civilization.[31] Under this premise, the purest, most candid, generous, and honest people will be the less civilized, who should be seen with a benevolent lens. Many American travelers saw Puerto Ricans as "noble savages," finding them sweet and amusing, generous and not materialistic, living in a primitive society which, to an extent, reminded them of what they had learned about the beginnings of the development of the United States in the 1600s. These writers saw themselves as the civilized who were to update Puerto Rico's development.

Todorov analyzed the 1503 *Mundus Novus* letter in which Amerigo Vespucci described the society of the "savages" discovered in the New World, and he identified in it five characteristics that, coincidentally, permeate many of the descriptions made by our selected authors: "lack of clothing; absence of private property; no hierarchy or subordination; no sexual prohibitions; no religion."[32] In the case of our authors, we might change the words used: naked children;

generous sharing of every resource; no racism; sexual freedom; no practice of religion. An American journalist provided a good example of this when describing the almost "paradisiacal" life of the Puerto Rican peasant:

> . . . while during whole months of the year he may not earn a single centavo, he still has his little plot of vegetables on the hill; then, if worst comes to worst or the landowner turns him out, he may live on the profusion of fruits and roots of the forest . . . yet he needs but the merest rags to cover his nakedness, for on no day in the year it is colder that our mildest autumnal weather. Shoes are a useless burden to his bare and sole-leather-lined feet, which have trodden the rocky, briary trails in their nakedness from infancy; and a hat, if he must have it, he makes in his own house from the grass grown around the doorway. . . . As a story-book life of primitive simplicity, in which the human needs are few and readily met with a minimum amount of labor, it is idealistic, but as an existence for civilized man it is a horrible fantasy. (Dinwiddie 1899, 155–56)

In the eighteenth century, European Enlightenment ideas inspired liberal imperialists who believed that it was their duty to share the glory of European civilization with "the 'primitive' peoples still living in 'darkness.'"[33] The idea was that colonized peoples needed European intervention in order to modernize and that, eventually, all peoples in the world would adopt the European civilization, thus becoming perfect. Most of the American missionaries sent to the Island adopted this doctrine, establishing schools, hospitals, and orphanages in Puerto Rico, many of which still survive. And an American politician visiting the Island in 1906 applied these "redemptive" imperialist lenses not only to Puerto Rico but to all the West Indian islands:

> Studied geographically, the whole West Indies would seem to be a part of us. Millions of natives, in whom we show little humane or philanthropic interest, inhabit them. They are waiting for the civilizing, Christianizing influences of the United States. If the duty of the nation is to uplift and support the weak, what an opportunity the West Indies, under our direction, would afford. . . . In these fair islands—at our very door, there is sufficient opportunity for "National Altruism" to gratify the most unselfish spirit. . . . I believe the United States would be benefited if it could, in some honorable way . . . assume control of the West Indies. . . . the West Indies might be absorbed and, in course of time, be made as truly a part of the United States politically as they now are geographically. (Moore 1907, 407–10)

Another philosophy that nurtured this "civilizing mission" was the Manifest Destiny theory. This theory became very popular in the United States in the late 1840s after a journalist named John O'Sullivan used it in an article published in 1845 in which he claimed that the country was justified to keep expanding to the West by taking control of the Native Americans' lands because it was its "manifest destiny," as recognized by "Providence," to possess the whole continent. As argued by Dr. Samuel Silva Gotay,[34] even though constitutionally, Church and State were separated, in practice, the idea of the United States as a Puritan Christian Nation persisted, creating, in 1898, an "imperialist theology." As such, the concept of Manifest Destiny is directly connected to American Puritanism, which, through Reverend John Winthrop's words in 1630, proclaimed that the United States was "the city upon a hill" mentioned by Jesus in the "Sermon of the Mount"[35] as "the light of the world" that cannot be hidden. Winthrop's interpretation gave the United States a "holy leadership" to become a model society. It is also related to the spirit of the Monroe Doctrine, as announced in 1823 by US President James Monroe, when he proclaimed the hegemony of the United States over the Western Hemisphere, leaving the rest of the world under European hegemony.

This idea of a holy mission of conquest and "civilization" of the "uncivilized" was immediately adopted by politicians who added that it should not be limited to the conquest of all of North America. This theory, therefore, turned into a sacred task the fulfillment of the American greed for lands to control. In fact, David Spurr, who has studied the rhetoric of colonialism, analyzed how the colonizer portrays himself as a redeemer of those he oppresses: ". . . without our intervention . . . these indigenous populations would still be abandoned to misery and abjection . . . massive endemic diseases . . . would continue to decimate them; . . . their minds would still be degraded by . . . superstition and barbarous custom; and they would perish from misery in the midst of unexploited wealth."[36]

The theory was influenced by the contemporary publication of *Democracy in America* (1835), a book by French diplomat Alexis de Tocqueville, who spent nine months studying American society and who described the country as "exceptional" or different, a term that was later considered as "American exceptionalism," the idea that the United States is inherently special and unique among the nations. This was interpreted by many Americans as them being better than other peoples; as a war correspondent explained: "Americans are superior to all other races because they and their ancestors have had liberty and plenty, and the universal application of this principle will make all nations great" (Olivares, *Vol. 1* 1899, 362).

We can add to these factors the concept of Social Darwinism, the result of Herbert Spencer's application of Darwin's law of natural selection to human societies in the late 1800s. Darwin's law of natural selection implied that random and spontaneous traits, when they best fit an organism to survive, will be genetically transferred to other organisms, thus maximizing the species' fitness to survive. Social Darwinists added the concept of "the survival of the fittest," wrongly applying it to individual survival instead of to group survival, to particular nations' survival rather than to mankind's survival.[37] Spencer explained that naturally, only the most suitable nations survive and that, naturally also, the stronger and most civilized nations are expected to dominate the weakest and less civilized ones. He also alleged that intelligence is developed naturally in colder climates and that the tropics degenerate all races, lending superiority to Nordic, Anglo-Saxon societies. Due to the fast process of industrialization in the second half of the nineteenth century, Americans began to see this as evidence that they were inherently more "advanced," as well as more intelligent and able than other less industrialized peoples.[38]

And to these ideas, all very popular in the United States right before the US invasion of Puerto Rico, we can add a Christian justification for American imperialism expressed by Congregational Reverend Josiah Strong in his influential book *Our Country: Its Possible Future and Present Crisis* (1885), where he stated that American white people had the duty to "lift up" inferior inhabitants of other nations throughout the world through the imposition of their moral superiority over them. He said then that "the world is to be Christianized and civilized" by those who had "the majesty of the numbers and the might of wealth."[39] It shouldn't be surprising, then, that so many of the selected authors, raised within such a philosophical background, sprinkled their memories about Puerto Ricans with imperial arrogance and civilizing zealousness.

Finally, and closer in time and context to the US invasion, is the ideology of the "White Man's Burden," which stated "that whites were obliged to raise so-called savages up to the highest level of civilization they could attain," which, of course, would never even get close to that of the colonizers.[40] This ideology led to Rudyard Kipling's poem *"The White Man's Burden"* (1899) regarding the US colonization of the Philippines as part of its heritage as an imperial power.[41] The poem depicted the colonized as "half devil and half child": immature and helpless, but at the same time dangerous and evil. An American journalist used a different set of words to convey the same idea: "The task that lies before the American people is one that will tax their energies and good will to the utmost. A mass of human minds lies dormant in these beautiful islands, waiting for the light of intelligence to lift it into a new existence" (Olivares, *Vol. 1* 1899, 287).

The perspective of the American authors studied here is never based on an equal relationship between observers and observed, even when an author expressed sympathy towards Puerto Ricans. They simply could not shake off the fact that they represented, on a variety of levels, the empire in their interactions with the colonized and that the only possible relation between those two was one of subordination of the colonized. As an author confirmed: "... as a rule the American underestimates and looks down upon the natives...." (Verrill 1914, 134).

Those who realized this troublesome position frequently defended themselves by stressing the difficulties of their life on the Island: the insidious climate and pests, the threat of illnesses, and the distrust of hostile populations.[42] Others embraced their imperial advantages and proclaimed their pleasures while there, such as having cheap servants and an inherent authority. These last realized that in the colony, they were not mediocre anymore; that only in the colony were they admired.[43] Only a few opened their minds to a new understanding of life, like Everett W. Lord, who candidly wrote: "... when we took Puerto Rico we were fired with the noble purpose of giving the people of the island 'what was good for them'. It took some years for us to learn that our conception of what is good is not necessarily identical with that of other people" (Lord 2004, 15).

Is it ever possible for the American visitor to describe objectively what he experiences with Puerto Ricans? It has long been studied the difficulty that the foreign observer has while trying to describe the characteristics and actions of "natives." JanMohamed's "Manichean allegory" proposes that the colonizer's culture and ways are absolutely right, good, and superior, and the colonized culture and ways are absolutely wrong, evil, and inferior; there are no middle points, no reconciliation: only a clash between the two.[44] In such a viewpoint, all the "evil" characteristics and customs attributed to the natives are expressed, not as a result of their history, but as naturally determined by their immutable "race," their "basic nature," thus giving birth to stereotypes about natives that are then widely popularized. In Albert Memmi's words: "It is what it is because they are what they are, and neither one nor the other will ever change."[45]

A series of hand-picked adjectives used to describe the colonized end up cornering the colonizer into a contradiction as he/she assigns to the colonized conflicting, but still "evil," characteristics: "[The colonized] is depicted as frugal, sober, without many desires and, at the same time, he consumes disgusting quantities of meat, fat, alcohol, anything; as a coward who is afraid of suffering and as a brute who is not checked by any inhibitions of civilization, etc."[46]

Albert Memmi theorized that the systematic devaluation of the colonized can lead to the "most absurd accusations" toward the colonized and to disfavor them in any possible comparison:

> The colonized's devaluation thus extends to everything that concerns him: to his land, which is ugly, unbearably hot, amazingly cold, evil

smelling; such discouraging geography that it condemns him to contempt and poverty, to eternal dependence.

. . . Ethical or sociological, aesthetic or geographic comparisons, whether explicit and insulting or allusive and discreet, are always in favor of the mother country and the colonialist. This place, the people here, the customs of this country are always inferior . . ."[47]

An example of this attitude can be seen in this description in which an American reverend considers that "everything" is smaller in Puerto Rico:

The observer is especially impressed with the smallness of everything. Travelers often speak of Porto Rico as a country in miniature. Many of the hills are hardly more than knolls . . . The mountains,[48] with one or two exceptions, would hardly be called by so dignified a title were they in the neighborhood of our mighty Rockies or Adirondacks. . . . And the gardens, the trees, the rivers, and the lakes . . . all are of diminutive size. The Porto Ricans themselves . . . not so large nor so rugged as the people of the northern and colder climates . . . (Seabury 1908, 20)

PUERTO RICO VS. PORTO RICO

The readers will also notice that some of the books' titles we examined name the Island "Porto Rico," while others call it "Puerto Rico." This is not a typographical error. When the US forces invaded the island, they called it "Porto Rico," a new phonetical version based on their pronunciation of "Puerto Rico." Therefore, all official US Administration documents referred to the island as "Porto Rico" up to the year 1932 when, while Theodore Roosevelt Jr. was Governor of the Island, the US Congress approved a resolution presented by then Puerto Rican Resident Commissioner Félix Córdova Díaz, and officially accepted "Puerto Rico" as the name of the Island.

ORGANIZATION OF THIS BOOK

This book is organized into eighteen chapters, each focusing on an aspect of the descriptions made by American authors about Puerto Ricans and different aspects of their culture. The themes are discussed chronologically within each chapter.

Each chapter's title includes a representative citation from that same chapter. A works cited section contains all the sources reviewed for this analysis. Three appendices are included, and appendices 2 and 3 might be of particular interest to researchers since they provide, respectively, a separate bibliography of the 132 reviewed books and a table with general information regarding most authors and coauthors.

WHY READING THIS BOOK?

Even though the selected authors' observations are heavily tinted by an imperialist perspective of dominance over those they observed, they are still valuable. Knowing how they saw us might help us Puerto Ricans to do some introspection on ourselves as a people through the eyes of outside observers who are not always sympathetic. And the judgments made by the American authors about Puerto Ricans sometimes tell us more about the authors themselves than about us Puerto Ricans.[49]

These authors recorded, sometimes in great detail, many Puerto Rican customs and attitudes. Some Puerto Rican readers will find, like I did, that many of the things we nowadays do every day without even thinking about them are not new at all. This can develop a reflection on those cultural traits and practices that we keep to this day: why do we keep them? In which ways are they still either useful or meaningful to us as *puertorriqueños*? Just to provide an example, their reading helped me understand the origin of my odd ideas of distance: "The distance was reckoned by the natives as about two miles, in other words, about four times a good American mile. The natives had no more idea of distance that they had of time" (Oliver 1901, 148).

Unfortunately, we are still a colony of the United States. We are still judged from the outside in many ways, and we are constantly fed conceptions of ourselves that come from the eyes of the empire's representatives. As Edward Said explained, the not-white "other" is considered inferior, something to be judged, disciplined, and corrected.[50] The white colonizer retains forever a colonial privilege just for the fact of being; the other side of this is that the nonwhite colonized is condemned to daily humiliations in this subordinated relationship in which, according to Memmi: "Even the poorest colonizer thought himself to be—and actually was—superior to the colonized. . . . he needs only show his face to be prejudged favorably . . . the colonized . . . have more faith in his word than in that of their own population. . . . Even his dress, his accent and his manners are eventually imitated by the colonized."[51]

Frantz Fanon once suggested that the effect that colonialism consciously pursued was "to drive in the natives' heads the idea that if the settlers were to leave, they would at once fall back into barbarism, degradation, and bestiality."[52] We have heard enough of this nonsense. Many wounds have been inflicted on our people, and some of them are finally exposed here. This book can provide a template from which we can identify those foreign conceptions of ourselves that are not based on a deep understanding of our culture but instead are just intended to keep imposing on us a low self-esteem and a psychological dependency that allows the empire to control our behavior and secure our support of colonialism.

Chapter 1

"OH, DEAR LORD, WHY DIDST THOU EVER INSPIRE ME TO GO TO PUERTO RICO TO TEACH?"

About the Selected American Authors

Even before the US invasion, American businessmen used to travel to Puerto Rico by steamships, the only way available at the time. Once the acquisition of the Island was completed, many other Americans came for different reasons. The trip took, at the time, around four days. The service between New York and Puerto Rico was provided by "two lines of steamships, the New York and Puerto Rican—and the Red 'D' lines, maintaining a weekly service with the Island, leaving New York at noon on Saturday and arriving at San Juan . . . on the following Wednesday or Thursday."[1] After five days in Puerto Rico, during which the ships toured the Island's coasts, they returned to New York.

Who were the writers of the books used as sources in this book? They are widely diverse: American writers, US soldiers who came to fight in the Spanish-American War, correspondents of US newspapers and journals, missionaries, scientists, teachers, academics, federal and local government officials, children's books writers, travel writers, curious travelers and even some who married Puerto Rican women. Indeed, most of the selected books (124) were written by independent writers, and eight were coauthored. Most authors were writers (thirty-four), missionaries/mission officers (twenty-eight), journalists/photographers (twenty-four), soldiers (twelve), English teachers (five), and other educators (seven). There was also a mix of government officers (eleven), tourists (two), scientists (five), and men who married Puerto Rican women (two), besides two (two) anonymous books.

Some of these authors traveled for work-related purposes, others for adventure, and others for both. They all found themselves in a different society that they tried to make sense of with whatever tools they had in their cultural and/or academic backgrounds. How did they achieve that?

The traveler acts as an intermediary between two opposing spaces, which he connects with each other: he travels through an unknown territory, writes about what he sees and transmits it to a distant reader, with whom he shares a code (linguistic, but also cultural) and with whom he creates a complicity in the face of that strange culture he describes. The traveler always resembles a spy: he observes and writes down, accumulates information about a distant society and transmits it to a culturally close and geographically remote audience, which ignores what that culture is like and is curious about it.[2]

Before discovering that Puerto Ricans were far from wild people, an English teacher candidly expressed her feelings when she knew she would go to Puerto Rico to teach:

As I reread the folder, I became nervous, in fact, panicky. There would be so many things to face bravely—and first among these would be the Puerto Ricans. Any picture on any folder is enough to make one believe Puerto Rico is inhabited by wildmen.... I looked heavenward and mumbled: "Oh, Dear Lord, why didst thou ever inspire me to go to Puerto Rico to teach? Why didst thou pluck me from safe Chicago to set me down in a Spanish-speaking wilderness? (Dean 1944, 9, 11)

Many American authors, after getting a glimpse of Puerto Rico and Puerto Ricans, felt compelled to challenge the widely spread stereotypes that common Americans had about West Indies inhabitants:

... that they were hot, pestilential, peopled by negroes, subject to earthquakes and hurricanes, and that their sole contributions to the world's wealth were sugar and rum. As to their appearance, a few rude woodcuts come to mind: pictures of half-naked negresses dancing to the strum of banjos in rubbish-littered, squalid streets; of broad-hatted, besashed, fierce-whiskered horsemen holding menacing whips above black minstrel-like laborers; of frantic people, rushing through a chaos of flashing lightning, inky clouds, and flying, shattered trees ... how little we really know of the world beyond our narrow sphere of daily life. (Verrill 1917, 2)

Others, after visiting the Island and witnessing the conditions of exploitation in which poor workers lived there, wanted to denounce them to their fellow Americans. A clear example was A. G. Dana, whose first edition of *Porto Rico's Case, Outcome of American Sovereignty, 1898–1924, 1925–1928* was heavily criticized as "an unjustifiable attack on the present Federal Administration at Washington." This forced him to publish the second edition with a page titled "*A Presidential Apologia*," clarifying that the book was not meant to be political but economic and that the generous American representatives in Puerto Rico "have simply been misled by incomplete data and false promises." He wrote about the reason for writing the book: "This pamphlet was not written for personal profit, but to secure justice for a suffering people. Any money made on sale of copies beyond cost of same will be turned over to the Bureau of Tuberculosis at San Juan, in aid of indigent patients" (Dana 1928, title page).

These Americans, according to René Marqués, felt guilty of imperialism, even if unconsciously, and this is reflected in them taking one of two extreme positions towards Puerto Ricans: either "the aggressive arrogance of the 'superior' man who must prove to himself the validity and morality of his position"; or the "benevolently condescending" one with a "human concern to help the weak or 'inferior' person" economically.[3] But many of the examined American authors showed no guilt, embracing instead American imperialism: their contact with the newly acquired subjects only emphasized their sense of superiority and clouded their views of the relationship between colonizers and colonized:

> My journeys in recent years to every quarter of the globe, and to all our outlying possessions, have confirmed my belief that the United States is not only the world's best country to live in, but that colonies or territories coming under its ownership or protection are more justly treated and rapidly developed than are the similar possessions or dependencies of any other nation. (Boyce 1914, vii)

The studied authors tended to describe what they perceived as different, interesting, and sometimes bizarre. Each one chose what piqued their curiosity or interest. An American governor commented: "I had found in myself a genuine curiosity to know everything about this strange, lovely, stricken land" (Tugwell 1947, 83). But we can identify recurring themes such as the washerwomen, the food, the death-related practices, the naked children, etc. The authors experienced an extension of their known universe, and they felt compelled to share those experiences with other North Americans who could not travel to the Island. As Dr. Aida L. Morales Tejeda articulated it regarding romantic travelers of the nineteenth century who wrote about Santiago de Cuba, who "venture into subjects that are not covered by other documentary sources": "... travelers ... describe the human types and different social strata that inhabited it [the city], ways of life and customs, the social relations of its inhabitants and its most varied cultural manifestations."[4]

Most of these authors had only brief contacts with Puerto Ricans, ranging from a few days to a few months, but they still saw themselves as authorities in everything Puerto Rican and expected to provide in their books a complete analysis of Puerto Ricans. As editor, H. A. Phillips wrote after a ten-day visit to Puerto Rico, his was "a hand-book and a head-book of the peoples, their problems, their human nature and mental make-up, their raison d'être and their destiny" (Phillips 1936, xiv).

Several authors supported their views on texts written by previous visitors, which they accepted as being truthful. Particular is the case of José de Olivares, who wrote based on a group of correspondents sent to the Island; this explains why, in his book, we can find completely contradictory sections. But for many American authors, it was very important to be considered truthful and, unbiased, and as accurate as possible in their depictions of what they saw. Of course, we understand that complete accuracy is impossible, so theirs are what Stuart Schwartz called "imperfect approximations to reality." To validate their observations, these authors frequently clarified in their respective introductions and prefaces that they directly witnessed the things they will narrate:

> The present book has been written with the aim of presenting all the important facts and figures in regard to Porto Rico without bias, prejudice, or exaggeration. In its preparation, nothing has been taken for granted and nothing included in the work which is pure hearsay. The author has personally visited the island, has lived in its various cities and villages, has toured the roads from end to end and from coast to coast, and has mingled and talked with all classes and conditions of people, both native and American, from the Governor to the lowliest peon.... no statement or information has been included which has not been personally investigated.... In the following pages Porto Rico is described as found by the author and as seen through his eyes ... (Verrill 1914, xvii)

Only two female Americans, a journalist and a teacher, writing over one hundred years apart, recognized their bias, although it was allegedly in favor of Caribbean peoples:

> To a certain extent, my opinions are unavoidably colored by my impressions.... my feelings are strongly in favor of the tropical countries. (Hamm *America's* 1899, v)

> I cannot presume to capture the essence of that which is Puerto Rican.... As I write with my prejudiced pen, keep in mind that all of us write with

such a pen, given our respective individual biases, rearings, educations, and experiences. (Tavenner 2010, 23–24)

The last one, M. H. Tavenner, shared with her readers a general catalog of biases that Americans still had about Puerto Ricans as recently as 2010:

Some might say Puerto Ricans routinely and illegally gamble on, and are likewise entertained by cockfights.... Some think Puerto Ricans pretty much live on rice and beans. Others report that these people will typically house three generations and extended family, under one roof. U.S. citizens also have the perception that Puerto Rican men typically have a wife, and at least one mistress. And that the Puerto Rican people accept and even expect this behavior. Others believe Puerto Ricans are knife-wielding and temperamental, unreliable and lazy. Furthermore, some of us imagine that they have little respect for law ... or that they routinely freeload off of the American taxpayer. (Tavenner 2010, 30)

Even though they wrote their books as individuals, they carried over their shoulders their own culture, with its prejudices and preconceptions of what was "right" and what was "wrong." They faced these foreign peoples from *their* North American culture and judged everything they saw based on *their* cultural standards. For example, this cavalryman ascribed to Puerto Rican poor peasants' feelings of jealousy of the neighbor's goods that are more compatible with his US society (individualism, competitive drive, and "keeping up with the Joneses" attitude) than with the sense of sharing commonly seen in Puerto Rican peasants' communities by the turn of the century: "Just as soon as a native is able to support a pig, he is looked on enviously by his late fortunate neighbors, as a Broadway beggar looks on the swell aristocrat in his automobile" (Oliver 1901, 94).

The case of Dr. Bailey K. Ashford is particularly interesting because he referred to himself as Puerto Rican when participating in international conventions and congresses.[5] On the other side of the spectrum is teacher Wenzell Brown, who presented a virulent attack on Puerto Ricans and about whose book was written: "That such a book might be written by an insecure persona surrounded by an unknown language in an unfamiliar cultural milieu is not surprising."[6]

FEMALE AUTHORS

Most of our selected authors are men. Certainly, for a long time, they were the only ones able to travel freely. Nevertheless, twenty-two of the 132 selected books were written by women alone (without coauthors), and two were written by women as coauthors.[7] Four of these were children's books. Most female writers were missionaries (eight). The rest were educators (six), writers (five), or journalists (three). While in Puerto Rico, these women enjoyed their white privilege at all times in their relations with Puerto Ricans, with the sole exception of Corrine Dean, an African American English teacher.

I found accurate what has been concluded before: that women travelers "provide serious, detailed social information, detailed descriptions of diet, childcare ... the everyday ..." as well as "details of clothing, accounts of domestic life, or the inclusion of romantic episodes" with a "strong emphasis on the personal ... conversations, and chatty accounts of incidents involving people she meets on her journey rather than specific analysis."[8] Probably the best example to illustrate this detailed style of writing is Margherita A. Hamm, one of the first women to cover a war from the front lines, who discussed almost every possible theme in her books.

Marion Blythe is another example: this newlywed missionary published in the form of detailed letters to her mother-in-law back in the United States. She expressed in her book a soft heart for the poverty-stricken Puerto Ricans she encountered:

> Last night we went to a country meeting station. . . . It brought the tears in spite of myself. . . . I just wanted to buy every old woman there a new dress, send all those hungry looking young men off to college, and gather all those sweet little brown-eyed children, yes, and the black kinky ones, too, into my arms and take care of them the rest of my life. (Blythe 1911, 21–22)

We also have the sweet case of English teacher Corinne Dean, who found herself in quite a predicament as she was asked for marriage by a Puerto Rican young man in love. The cultural differences made it impossible for her to understand the young man's feelings until they were openly expressed:

> ... the Puerto Rican's ability to resist is surpassed only by his ability to persist. . . . The point is I found myself one fine morning betrothed to a fine young man. And I must say I was utterly taken aback. I met him ... about five months before I had planned to leave Puerto Rico for study in Europe. He was a wonderful pal. . . . The type of man you don't want to marry and whom you don't want to marry anyone else. We went everywhere together ...
>
> [In a conversation with María, a Puerto Rican friend:] "But I haven't done anything. I merely went places with him."

"Yes, but you went only with him. Why did you go with him, and no one else, for two months?"

Truthfully, I replied: "Because I liked him more than anyone else—for two months."

"Well, if you like him more than anyone else, why don't you want to marry him?"

In a land of clear-cut emotions such a question is perfectly logical. Down there they don't spoil love by rationalizing it. You love, or you don't love and it shouldn't take you a decade to find out. Love is supposed to come with the suddenness and force of an explosion (and with much the same results). No dawdling along and sounding yourself out to know if the explosion has hit you or not; no mental meandering on "can this be the real thing?" No pondering on how marriage and a career will mix. (Dean 1944, 95–97)

Miss Dean had to ask advice from Puerto Rican women to get herself out of the unwanted situation without hurting her suitor's feelings, something she attained by asking her father to oppose the relationship in writing: "Papá heard from me and I explained in full. Dutifully he sent the letter refusing to give my hand in marriage. . . . Papá did not consent and therefore for Alberto to ask my opinion would have been superfluous, unnecessary, and above all not customary" (Dean 1944, 102).

Being able to get closer to the families they proselytized among, female missionaries and teachers had the opportunity to have deeper intercultural experiences than any other American authors. And they recorded them in their writings. An unidentified female missionary shared a sweet/sad anecdote she experienced with a little Black Puerto Rican:

Among the missionary teachers in our new possession, was one fair-headed, sweet-faced woman. . . . She noticed one day that a little black girl kept very close to her and finally asked the child why she clung to her so. "You are so white, señorita," she answered, "I thought that perhaps if I kept real close, some of the white would rub off on me.'" . . . The child was lovingly told how her heart could be white as snow though her skin must be always black. (Johnston 1905, 152–53)

SOLDIERS

The occupation forces of the United States were a total of 15,472 men between July 25 and August 2, and they arrived in different waves. The Commander in

Chief of the operations was General Nelson A. Miles, supported by Major Generals John R. Brooke, Guy V. Henry, and James H. Wilson, and Captain Francis J. Higginson (from the Navy).[9] Their forces were divided into four brigades: the Garretson Brigade, with regiment volunteers from Illinois and Massachusetts; the Schwan Brigade, a regiment of regular infantrymen; the Ernst Brigade, with regiment volunteers from Wisconsin; and the Haines Brigade, with regiment volunteers from Ohio and Illinois. The soldier-writers included in this book belonged to them.

Most soldier-writers wrote for their ex—fellow combatants. Their stories are full of everyday anecdotes of the campaign: some heroic, some comical. Their patriotic stories frequently highlight the bravery and sacrifice of their fellow soldiers and the cleverness of their commanders. Their observations tend to be more imperialistic in tone, which is not surprising since they were actually conquering land for the US Empire. Many of their books are accompanied by photographs they took while in Puerto Rico.

JOURNALISTS

Many journalists who wrote about Puerto Rico were war correspondents who accompanied different groups of soldiers as they moved through the Island. They covered the war for their respective newspapers and magazines, thus providing their American readership with their first glances at Puerto Rico and Puerto Ricans. Because of this, many of the early stereotypes were created by them and repeated by the following authors.

Once the occupation was over and the soldiers returned home, fewer journalists were interested in Puerto Rico. One of the most renowned was Frank G. Carpenter, who came to the Island right after the invasion and published several news articles about his views and experiences regarding Puerto Rico.[10] He returned in the 1920s while visiting all of the Caribbean and recorded his experiences in a book which is included in this analysis.

MISSIONARIES

The years between 1890 and 1916 have been considered the era of the most aggressive American missionary work, a time for the propagation of American cultural values and the imposition of religious values they considered superior.[11] Missionaries promoted educational and health projects, but both areas of endeavor were also "tools of empire" in which foreign-made "solutions" were imposed on the colonial subjects with no feedback from them. In the end, all their reforms did little to improve the lives of the majority of Puerto Ricans.

Even though some of the missionary-writers have never been to Puerto Rico, we included them because their books are anthologies of the writings made by others who have been in Puerto Rico and gave testimony of their experiences there through letters or short articles. Memoirs are also common among these zealous writers. These books were commonly used in mission study classes.[12]

In the American missionaries' books, we frequently find an explanation of why these books were written: typically to familiarize their American brethren with the work being done in Puerto Rico, to entice young Americans to serve as missionaries, to highlight the need for the gospel among Puerto Ricans, to showcase the accomplishments attained in Puerto Rico with the donations of church members in the United States, and to elicit future funding for their Puerto Rican missions: "The purpose of this book is to familiarize our people with the past and present of the islands, and to show what has been accomplished and what it is hoped to accomplish through the missionary agencies sustained by American Protestants" (Grose 1910, xii).

Most missionaries who worked in Puerto Rico had good intentions toward Puerto Ricans, but they had imperialistic attitudes that interpreted the colonized as lesser, incompetent, and primitive. As a matter of fact, some of the harshest criticism of Puerto Ricans and their culture came from missionaries. They wanted to help them, but they could not see Puerto Ricans as equals; instead, they burdened Puerto Ricans with heavy stereotypes that precluded an egalitarian relationship. In 1910, H. Paul Douglass, Secretary of the American Missionary Association, opened his book with a summary of the challenges that missionaries confronted in Puerto Rico. His enumeration clearly shows how these missionaries projected themselves as superior in culture, religion, and societal values:

> In the occupancy of Porto Rico, the Association confronts for the first time in Home Missionary experience, four problems:
> First: How to establish an American Christian civilization out of Latin materials, with men of Spanish blood and heritage.
> Second: How to establish an evangelical type of faith in a land ruled for four centuries by a decrepit and incredibly bigoted form of Roman Catholicism.
> Third: How to establish a free and democratic church in a society essentially without a middle class.
> Fourth: How to furnish staunch and inspiring leadership in a land historically lacking in great personalities. (Douglass 1910, 5)

Missionaries were also the authors who most frequently presented Puerto Ricans as people with a potential to change and become "civilized," and for obvious reasons: "For, if Puerto Ricans were ineducable, missionaries would be hard pressed to justify their civilizing project."[13] Female missionaries, in particular, had a closer look at Puerto Ricans' poverty as they visited their shacks to proselytize. They frequently benefited from the curiosity of Puerto Ricans who have not frequently seen Americans so close:

> In this little house live an old grandmother, her two daughters, and I have never counted the grandchildren. I was urged to take a seat on the hammock . . . I accepted it with fear and trembling. . . . Several children outside left their play and came to see "La Americana." We read a portion of the Word and had prayer, and by that time quite a number of women had gathered about the door, and we entered into conversation with them and distributed some tracts, and gave all an invitation to attend our services in the church. (Mills et al. 1908, 202)

The missionaries' testimonies are full of passion. They evidently felt a part in a higher mission of transformation of a people and expressed their ideals for the future Protestant society they envisioned for Puerto Rico. Moreover, as they wrote for their brethren, they tried to promote the missionary intervention in Puerto Rico with both human and monetary resources. This, of course, presented a permanent temptation to exaggerate the level of "savagery" of Puerto Ricans as a way of rationalizing their presence there and also "to explain the frustrations they experienced in making converts, and to win support from mission societies at home."[14] They were immersed in a transformation of Puerto Ricans with all their hearts, and sometimes the transformations they "performed" were quite tangible, as was the case of the following Puerto Rican girls:

> [Regarding a girl interned in the Presbyterian Hospital where she received donations from the United States:] There are so many new things to learn—how to dress, for instance, for never before had Carmita so many clothes to put on—all these things, especially the little red shoes, are delightful, but the crowning pleasure is her beautiful doll, sent to her, so she is told, by some unknown little friends in "The States." (Crowell 1907, 2)

> I spent two days last week . . . dressing some little colored girls for the Christmas festivities. . . . By noon on Thursday, everything was ready and three of the dirtiest but most expectantly happy girls you can

imagine came over to dress for the school exercises . . . We began by giving them the first tub bath they had had in many a long day, I am sure, and they were surprised that we put soap all over them, for they said it was necessary only for their hands. Then we combed and puffed their hair and tied it with big black bows and they felt like princesses, I know. They were worried about their bare feet, however . . . Then, to their perfectly entranced vision, I produced the shoes and stockings. (Blythe 1911, 115–16)

Still, a few were humble enough to recognize that they had a lot to learn from Puerto Ricans, too:

Many sincere and lasting friendships were formed with the Puerto Rican people during those first few months when we had to rely heavily upon them for our very existence. As we worked side by side with the people of the community, we appreciated the many fine qualities which they possessed and felt at times that perhaps we had more to learn from them than they from us. (Holsinger 1952, 25)

GOVERNMENT OFFICIALS

As the US government began to consider all the potential benefits to be obtained from their newly acquired colony, they began to rely on the many travelers to the island for accurate information. But, these accounts, although useful, lacked statistical information vital for planning. A series of economic studies followed, as well as all sorts of censuses and inventories of resources. Although official accounts of government officers were not considered in this analysis, I included some of their memoirs whenever they included personal anecdotes and experiences of the writers, as well as their personal assessments of Puerto Ricans and their customs.

These travelers usually came to the Island for extended periods of time while they occupied their governmental positions. They frequently wrote memoirs in which they included experiences with Puerto Ricans, which are part of this study. We must keep in mind that they came with an agenda that might include or not the assimilation or "reform" of Puerto Ricans and their most "primitive" customs, such as cockfighting and toddler nudity. In this regard, what they wrote about Puerto Ricans intended to call attention to what needed to be "reformed" and can be easily related to the concept of "anthropology of domestication."[15] They perceived, judged, and then hoped to transform the natives by imposing on them their American way of life.

TEACHERS

When, as part of the Americanization policy, in 1905, the American Commissioner of Education for the Island, Samuel M. Lindsay, ordered all classes (but for Spanish as a Second Language) to be taught in English, the agency realized that they needed to import teachers, since very few Puerto Rican teachers were fluent in English. This need was satisfied by a group of idealist American teachers, some of whom wrote books that are included in this selection.

One of these authors, Everett W. Lord, as assistant to the Commissioner of Education, was in charge of appointing nine hundred American teachers in five years (1902–1907). The recruits were mostly young college graduates from New England and the North Central states.[16] Probably unbeknownst to them, they were paid more than double the salary of Puerto Rican teachers: "The native teachers in graded schools are paid $30 a month.... American teachers in the graded schools are started at $75 a month" (Boyce 1914, 444). More importantly: their salaries were paid from the colonial budget.

These teachers probably felt highly motivated in this crusade to share their knowledge with these kids, who they perceived as ignorant and primitive. As a travel writer expressed it: "The only inducement Porto Rico offers to instructors from "the States" is an appeal to the love of adventure" (Franck 1920, 282). Some of their observations reveal the important cultural differences between them and their students as they became obvious in the classroom, where misunderstandings led to comical, but at the same time dramatic, episodes.

Wenzell Brown, an English teacher who tended to portray everything Puerto Rican as negative, began his story with a terrifying description of the teaching experience in Puerto Rico made by a fellow teacher while they were both sailing to the Island:

> "Look," he responded, "I don't know if I want to tell you fellows anything about Puerto Rico, because nobody will believe me I if tell the truth about the place. Nobody ever does.... Puerto Rico is going to seem crazy as hell to you, and most of you aren't going to like it.... you're going to be sent to tiny towns up in the mountains or along the coast. You'll find these towns unbelievable dirty. Most of the people you meet will be diseased and poverty-stricken, and they'll hate your guts because you're an American. They'll follow you about the streets yelling at you. They'll take you to court every time they get a chance. They'll spread malicious gossip about you and make life miserable for you. You won't like their food because they serve rice and beans every meal. But you'd better not say anything about it. You'll think their houses are dirty and you'll squirm when you see the kids in your classroom digging in their

hair for lice and cracking them between their fingers. By the time you've been there a couple of months, some of you will be ready to leave for home. You'll be damn glad to leave the Island ... (Brown 1945, 11–12)

An interesting anecdote is that of a teacher who wanted to leave almost as soon as she arrived in Puerto Rico, only to later change her mind and embrace the experience on a deeper level. Her story is told by Everett W. Lord:

> One of the best of my teachers in Bellows Falls decided that she wanted to teach in the tropics, but after one day in San Juan she was a little doubtful. The sight of naked children and the apparent disregard of conventions shocked her immeasurably. To her dismay, I had to send her to a little city in the interior. ... As she had no Spanish, she naturally met with some difficulties at first, especially in getting food that appealed to her Vermont taste. She liked Puerto Rican coffee, however, when well sweetened with native brown sugar; but when she found that the half inch of apparently undissolved sugar in the bottom of her glass of coffee was in reality not sugar, but a mass of black ants, she refused to take even coffee. After only three days of suffering she wrote me that she was returning to San Juan to take the next boat "back to civilization." I wired her peremptory orders to stay until Christmas, agreeing to release her then; but at Christmas time the perfection of the climate held her, and she consented to remain till the end of the year.... The end of the year came: she left with jubilation: and as soon as she reached Vermont cabled me for an appointment for the next year. This lady spent some ten more years as a teacher in Puerto Rico, and then retired with the keenest regret. Many others had a similar experience. (Lord 2004, 20)

A similar experience happened with then nun, M. H. Tavenner, who came almost against her will but who, over time, learned to love Puerto Rico and Puerto Ricans:

> I was a nun then, a Sister of St. Francis of Syracuse, NY, sent to Puerto Rico to teach English. . . . . . . only because of my vow of obedience, I moved to Puerto Rico. I was not at all happy about going to Puerto Rico. I endured three months in Puerto Rico, then I left the convent. (Tavenner 2010, 21–22)
>
> I can only hope you discover a nation so impossible to capture in words; so resilient in nature; so diverse in thinking; so unique in character, that one must step back and be amazed, intrigued, perplexed, and often—amused. (Tavenner 2010, 34)

Some of these male and female teachers found love in Puerto Rico: "Many of our young women were besieged with offers of marriage, and while few of them chose to accept Puerto Rican husbands, many romance developed between American young men in the government service, or in business, and American teachers" (Lord 2004, 26).

But the adjustment to a different culture remained a challenge for many American teachers for a long time:

> We still heard stories of continental teachers, however, who left the island after their first year of teaching or didn't even make it through the first year. One of them told me, "I think it may be harder to adjust now than it was when you first came down [in the 1950s]. When you get here it all <u>looks</u> so much like the United States, but, as soon as you get a little bit below the surface, you're in a different world. You can't understand anything that's going on. Nothing works the way it's supposed to." (Cooper 1994, 154)

CHILDREN'S BOOKS

The popularity of children's books in the United States had its boom by the end of the nineteenth century, right when imperialist ideas were also booming. A coincidence? Certainly not. This literature was promoted right when the United States needed it as a way of "imperial indoctrination" of future generations. This literature was directed to white, middle and upper-class American children, and its purpose was "to instill feelings of patriotism, national pride, and exceptionalism; racial, eugenic and cultural superiority; and political and economic domination."[17]

Seven of the selected books were written to present to American children the theme of Puerto Rico, its people, and its culture. Of these, five were published soon after the US invasion to present the "new possessions" (George, Seabury, Kellogg, Wade, and Winslow), and two were published in the 1960s to showcase the fast-economic industrialization of Puerto Rico (Schloat and Rollins). Probably the most comprehensive of these teacher's renderings of Puerto Ricans and their cultures is that of Marian George, who visited the Island briefly. These books were published in the United States for American children and contained many stereotypes that emphasized negative traits: "Here and there is a village full of shops and <u>drinking booths</u>, and much frequented by the city people on afternoons and Sundays.... The streets and houses of San Juan are <u>dirty, and crowded</u> with a somewhat <u>thriftless</u> population" (Kellogg 1898, 222. Underlining by Kellogg).

White American children were taught about a Puerto Rican "other" that was typically uncivilized and inferior to them, thus fostering their nationalism as they could feel smarter, healthier, moral, virtuous, and empowered. In general, the authors of these books showed Puerto Rico either as a ward of the United States in need of guidance from its new mentor or, in the 1960s, as a very modern country with unlimited progress to be expected in its future, thanks to American imperialism. This children's literature has been aptly described as a "white children's burden."[18]

Even though I couldn't find evidence of some of them ever visiting the Island (Kellogg, Wade, Seabury, Winslow), they still wrote as if they had witnessed life in Puerto Rico. It is obvious from what they wrote that even if they were never there, they did research sources who had visited the island. Some acknowledged that: "... the author has availed herself of the records of the most reliable travelers and writers of recent years" (Kellogg 1898, 5).

Their young readers were encouraged to think of Puerto Rican children as their "neighbors," "cousins," or "brothers." Their purposes are more or less stated in some of these books:

> Do you know what people mean when they speak of "Our New Possessions"? What are they? Where are they? Why are men, in the streets, in the shops, everywhere, talking about them? Why are the newspapers full of articles in regard to them? Why are our lawmakers at the capital devoting so much time and attention to them? Can you tell? (George 1900, 1)

Probably due to space restrictions, but also in order to portray Puerto Ricans as a *tabula rasa*, they typically disregarded the history of Puerto Rico previous to the US invasion: "Porto Rico has no prolonged or varied history, no exciting historical periods" (Seabury 1905, 6).

Mary Hazelton Wade, considered "one of the most prolific and popular imperialistic turn-of-the-twentieth-century American children's authors" (Wade 1902, 13), wrote her *Our Little Porto Rican Cousin* (1902) for the series "Our Little Cousins" that has been reckoned as "arguably her most imperialistic of all."[19] No other of our selected authors better exemplifies the imperial indoctrination of American children through the denigration of Puerto Rican people and culture. Unfortunately, her books were very popular with her contemporary educators and parents, which resulted in multiple editions and printings of her books. Disturbingly, Wade's books "are experiencing a renaissance in the twenty-first century on Evangelical homeschooling websites," thus reproducing these imperialistic views of Puerto Ricans and many other "others."[20]

This Boston teacher used baseless stereotypes to give the impression of Puerto Rico as a big Antebellum Southern plantation with Black servants, spicy[21] and fried food, laziness, neglectful parents, and ignorance galore. Wade frequently criticized Puerto Rican parents for their "neglectful" parenting, as they allegedly allowed their kids to smoke (something hard to believe in an *hacendado* family) and go to cockfights (she called them "the cruel pleasure") with their father, while they prevented them from washing with soap, or learning math or grammar:

> ... old Juana prepares a bath for him. She does not bring any soap, for his mother believes it spoils the skin, but the bath is scented with Florida-water ... (Wade 1902, 13])
>
> I fear you will think them rather backward in arithmetic and other grammar-school studies, but their parents do not see the need of knowing as much of such things as do American fathers and mothers. (Wade 1902, 21)
>
> After this second breakfast is over, cigarettes are served, and, would you believe it! our little Manuel, as well as his mother and older sister, joins in a smoke. Such is the custom of his country that even children of three or four years use tobacco. It is no wonder then, that as the boys and girls grow up, they have so little strength. We are no longer surprised that Manuel does not care much for active play. (Wade 1902, 25)

As expected, Wade's book ends with the promise of an upcoming complete Americanization of the protagonists:

> It seems strange to the children to see the red, white, and blue of the American flag floating over the city...." But this new flag means friendship, you know, Dolores," says her brother. "The poor will not be taxed so much as they used to be, and the good Americans will not allow any other people to harm us.... I want to get acquainted with my American cousins in their own land, our own land, now." (Wade 1902, 106)

THIS CHAPTER

Since most of the selected American authors were common men and women, it was frequently hard to find general information regarding them and the reason for their travel or stay in Puerto Rico. Only those of some renown were easily researched. In appendix 3, we share what our research revealed about them in a table format.

A diversity of American authors visited Puerto Rico for a variety of reasons and met and interpreted their colonial subjects using their American culture as a template. Surprise, sympathy, pity, empathy, and disdain characterized their writings. Many tried hard to be unprejudiced, but that proved to be impossible. Even when their intentions were good, their colonizers' eyes would create a distortive view of Puerto Ricans and their culture that would spread through the years and would impact the colonial policies and practices of the United States in Puerto Rico. Journalists and children's book writers had the largest audiences; missionaries were the most passionate. But all of them contributed to defining who Puerto Ricans were for generations to come both in the United States and in Puerto Rico.

Chapter 2

"THEY CONSIDERED THEM CONQUERED ANIMALS"

On How Colonialism Permeates All

Of all the American authors here reviewed, it is the American governor and economist Rexford G. Tugwell who best-defined colonialism and its effects on Puerto Ricans:

> That is what colonialism was and did: it distorted all ordinary processes of the mind, made beggars of honest men, sycophants of cynics, American-haters of those who ought to have been working beside us for world betterment—and would if we had encouraged them. Economically it consisted in setting up things so that the colony sold its raw products in a cheap market (in the mother country) and bought its food and other finished goods in a dear market (also in the mother country); there was also the matter of foreign products to be carried in American ships. In that sense Puerto Rico was a colony just as New York and Massachusetts had been colonies.... Puerto Rico was just as badly off. And relief was something which the Congress made Puerto Rico beg for, hard, and in the most revolting ways, as a beggar does on a church step, filthy hat in hand, exhibiting sores, calling and grimacing in exaggerated humility. And this last was the real crime of America in the Caribbean, making of Puerto Ricans something less than the men they were born to be. (Tugwell 1947, 42–43)

With or without noticing it (there is no way to prove one or the other), American authors collaborated with the imperialist plan of the United States for Puerto Rico. In general, they created a picture of Puerto Ricans as really nice people, very backward and uncivilized, who were incapable of governing themselves without the "guidance" of the United

States but who were able to learn the American culture and values. Still, they would not see themselves as imperialist, as illustrated in the musings of Tugwell:

> I was, to begin with, taken by surprise to find that Puerto Ricans felt themselves badly treated by the United States. This was true of nearly all of them whether they had reasons or merely feelings about it. And all alike spoke often and bitterly of our policy. Sometimes I heard of Yankee imperialism in such terms of hatred as could only originate in a penetrating fear.... Anyone could tell that this issue was alive and, perhaps, growing. I sometimes felt like looking over my shoulder when I was talked to in this way to see whether someone else was not being addressed. I didn't know any imperialists. Even American businessmen with export businesses didn't seem to me to fit the descriptions I heard. (Tugwell 1947, 37)

In 1920, an American travel writer considered Puerto Ricans as "primitive and simple" and "naïve," although already changing: "The island has a less grasping, less materialistic atmosphere than Cuba, it is less sinister, less cynical, more naïve, its people are more primitive and simple, though industrial oppression and American influence are slowly changing them in this regard. Their naiveté is often delightful" (Franck 1920, 282).

Since the beginning of the colonization, the Spanish conquerors called the Native inhabitants of Puerto Rico "jíbaros" or "gíbaros." The word was Indian in origin and named one of the groups into which the Caribe people were divided.[1] Later, the Spanish used that name for mestizos (the product of the union of white people and Indians) and Black enslaved people who escaped to the mountains to flee servitude. Eventually, the name was used to refer to all *criollos* (born in Puerto Rico of Spanish descent) or Puerto Ricans who lived a rustic and "primitive" lifestyle in the rural mountainous part of the Island. It seems to be pity the feeling that Dr. Bailey K. Ashford argued these Puerto Rican workers instilled in him:

> To-day, through the oiling up of our data ... we are enabled to comprehend why the jíbaro is so ignorant of the world about him, why he is so gullible, so lacking in initiative, so dependent on others. His history is plain. His world became smaller and smaller until it was limited to the confines of his plantation, because his physical forces were too depleted to carry him out into the world which, small as it is, is Puerto Rico. Yet this is the man of whom we have to make a citizen, a man with a vote

and a say in the affairs of the Island.... He is neither a degenerate nor a fool. He is a man deserving of our warmest pity and of our most merciful treatment. (Ashford 1934, 92)

The colonized is understood as inherently dirty and polluted, carrying in himself the possibility of polluting the colonizers unless they were protected by the representatives from the empire. The white colonizers saved the colonized from themselves: "The first thing the United States did when it took Porto Rico was to begin the work of improving conditions so that nearly a million of dirty people crowded on the island at that time could live longer, and that our white American officials might escape death in doing their duty" (Boyce 1914, 431).

The case of English teacher Wenzell Brown is particularly illustrative of the loathing he constantly expressed towards Puerto Ricans in his book. The reader can easily feel the hate and scorn, and it becomes clear that the author selected everything negative to write about. For example, while in his classroom at the Juan Morel Campos School in Ponce, students began to laugh with him, and this is how he chose to describe the children's laughter:

Suddenly... I broke into laughter. Sixty kids roared with laughter.... It was my first experience with mass laughter in Puerto Rico. The laughter of these youngsters bore no relationship to the laughter of American boys and girls. This was high-pitched, almost hysterical.... The kids... seemed unable to stop. The laughter of a frightened people, a hungry people, a dissatisfied people, can be a horrible thing. (Brown 1945, 31)

The colonized will never be accepted as an equal by the colonizer, and if he tried to be treated as one, the colonizer considered that either disrespectful or simply foolish, an object of ridicule. What this missionary calls here "newly fledged politicians" were, in actuality, highly educated Puerto Ricans with vast experience in politics, such as José de Diego, Manuel Zeno Gandía, and Luis Muñoz Rivera. In his view, as a colonizer, everything Puerto Ricans did was incompetently performed unless done "the American way":

Notwithstanding this simplicity of mind, the Porto Rican has a sublime confidence in himself. He thinks he can do things as well as any man living.... a young man or a young woman with scarcely an elementary education wants a certificate to teach.... The newly fledged politicians want either independence or statehood at once—they know more about government than any of the United States officials.... Workmen as a rule perform their tasks in a most slipshod, careless manner. The carpenter mutilates the wood, the painter splashes paint over everything in the vicinity of his brush ... Under proper instruction, it has been shown that the Porto Ricans are apt scholars. The carpenter soon learns to do his work with precision and skill.... If the people could only be brought to see their need of instruction instead of having such a high estimate of their own abilities, progress would be made much more rapidly. (Fowles 1910, 48)

This inequality between colonizers and colonized, Americans and Puerto Ricans, inherently contained a superiority and an inferiority. In effect, Americans in Puerto Rico boasted on their nationalistic pride and righteousness based on their "material wealth, democratic institutions, free public education and the advancement of technology."[2] Whenever the colonized did something in a different fashion from the colonizer, that way of behaving was inherently wrong:

Fundamentally, we were different from the Spanish Americans, and by saying this I am not saying that we are either better or worse.... The difference of which I have spoken is evident in everyday life, the ordinary small amenities. For example, we would say on meeting a man merely, "How do you do? A Spanish-speaking Puerto Rican, with far greater courtesy, would, in addition, ask. "¿Cómo está su estimada esposa y su distinguida familia? [How is your estimable wife and your distinguished family?] If he is of the old school he will close a personal letter with q.b.s.m.—quien besa su mano [who kisses your hand].... A Puerto Rican orator turns phrases in the ordinary address which our people would consider flowery. (Roosevelt Jr. 1937, 115)

The Americans acted as if they were dealing with a primitive, unorganized, racially inferior people rather than with a poor but proud Euro-American national group.... Hardly any consideration was given to what the Puerto Ricans felt...... by and large, the American is impatient with Puerto Rican culture which, measured by his own standards, seems inferior.... most American visitors seem to approach Puerto Rico with an air of condescension and a desire to prove to the Puerto Rican as well as to themselves that they as Americans are superior. (Petrullo 1947, 134–35)

Even the reactions of Puerto Ricans to films were analyzed from an otherizing perspective and qualified as odd. The American observer deemed the Puerto Rican sensibility as faulty:

> The patrons [at the cinema] are not altogether responsive to the same situations that appeal to continental audiences. There is more laughter than sentiments in the love passages, less satisfaction in the triumph of virtue and downfall of vice, more applause for poor heroes than for rich ones, and little reverence for the very sentimentality which seems so real to them in their own lives. Villainous oppressors are hissed in melodramatic fashion, but the villainous poor seem to get off lightly.
>
> [At a specific movie titled *Ramona*] The audience ... clapped with equal enthusiasm at the onset of the villainous raiders and of the noble heroes. They equally "guyed" the love scenes and were untouched by the most touching episodes, apparently indifferent to sentiment, love, sorrow, or religion. (White 1938, 327–28)

Frequently, what is written as praise ends up condemning Puerto Ricans. For example, even though in 1947 Puerto Rico already had very renowned scientists, such as Agustín Stahl, Isaac González Martínez, Carlos E. Chardón and Juan A. Rivero, to mention just a few, an American anthropologist considered Puerto Ricans unfit for science and only capable of "sentimental" things like art and religion: "Besides, the Puerto Rican is not made for science and technology; his Latin soul is cast in a different mold from that of the American. He can appreciate and value highly what is derived from a higher sensitivity (art) or through revelation from God (religion). These higher perceptions are denied to the less refined souls of the Americans" (Petrullo 1947, 148).

Soldiers and ministers and several other American authors infantilized Puerto Ricans. This is very common in colonizer-colonized relationships. If the colonized is a child in the eyes of the colonizer, he/she will always need the guidance and control of the colonizer since children cannot take care of themselves. Also, infantilizing the colonized allows the colonizer "to feel secure ... because it restores the moral balance" in his favor:[3]

> Great numbers of the Porto Ricans gave one the impression that they were simply grown up children, with all a child's natural affection and trust, and it always seemed to The Corporal that we had assumed a great responsibility, and must be careful to live up to the promises made them by General Miles upon our landing ... (Rossiter [1900?])

> ... young and old are all children.... There were a half dozen swells from Arecibo ... getting ready for a dance at the Alcalde's. I happened to have a little souvenir flag in my pocket, and pinned it to one of them.... He was as pleased as a child ... (King 1929, 82)

> One generalization is that . . . the Puerto Rican is still living in racial and political immaturity. This expresses itself in countless ways. . . . This Puerto Rican is as sensitive as a child to misjudgment, actual or imagined. (White 1938, 348–49)

Several American soldiers emphasized the submissive attitudes of the Puerto Ricans they met as they moved from town to town: "[At the Plaza of Guayama] . . . Men cheered and women cried; children ran like wild creatures, shouting as loud as their little throats would permit, "Vivan los Americanos." . . . They kissed the hands of their deliverers and fell at their feet to worship them" (Creager 1899, 156–57).

And some American soldiers clearly took advantage of the Puerto Ricans who received them so generously, as they considered it appropriate to pay them for their services with hard bread or biscuits that were part of their rations ("hardtacks") and which often got infected with insects or were stale before reaching the battlefront.[4] Soldiers used to complain that they had to soak them in liquid to prevent damaging their teeth while eating them: "The natives brought us everything we wanted, and I used to get my washing done in exchange for a few hardtacks" (Edwards 1899, 96).

But a travel writer in 1914 realized that Puerto Ricans were not that submissive and respectful and that they, indeed, made fun of Americans. This awareness, as the following quote reflects, turned into fear of the colonized's contained rage towards the colonizer:

> Political orators say one thing to the American and quite another thing when addressing an audience of Porto Ricans. They take delight in insulting us. Call them into account afterward and they say that they did not mean it, that their oratorical exaggeration was responsible. Yet the apology is made privately and the ignorant mass of the people are not undeceived. Nearly every American I met said that he would have to leave the island by the first boat were it given independence. (Boyce 1914, 415)

Dehumanization of the Puerto Rican colonized was also very common. An American travel writer quoted from the American Chief of the Insular Police regarding his way of classifying Puerto Ricans based on the shape of their feet, a system he would have never used to classify his own people. His descriptions sound as if referring to animals:

> "We divide the people of Porto Rico into four categories for purposes of identification," said the American chief of the Insular Police, "according

to the shape of their feet. The minority, mostly town-dwellers, wear shoes. Of the great mass of countrymen, those with broad, flat feet, live in the cane-lands around the coast. The coffee men are over-developed big toes, because they use them in climbing the steep hillsides from bush to bush. In the tobacco districts, where the planting is done with the feet, they are short and stubby. It beats the Bertillon system[5] all hollow." (Franck 1920, 257)

Social worker Knowlton Mixer also commented on this physical feature: "... the coffee farms of the high altitudes are ... generally at an angle of 30° or 40°, [and] require such tenacity on the part of the worker that he has developed a big toe of abnormal size and strength as a result of his generations of clinging perseverance" (Mixer 1926, 115).

Even the description of the poor Puerto Ricans' huts frequently emphasized on them being uninhabitable by humans, a comment that implied that whoever lived inside these places must not be human, but animals:

> ... we can look into the houses as we pass on the street; it seems impossible that human beings can exist in such quarters. (Wilcox [1918?])

> The ramshackle, tumble-down, dilapidated, dry-goods-box dwellings of the poorer people in Porto Rico looked more as if they had been put up for temporary chicken coops than for the use of human beings. (Jordan 1922, 149)

Yet other American writers, more callous and clearly visualizing Puerto Ricans of the lower classes as less-than-human beings, compared them, their surroundings, and their actions to those of animals. This is a common phenomenon of colonialism pointed out by Albert Memmi, Frantz Fanon and Aimé Césaire:

> How can an elite of usurpers, aware of their mediocrity, establish their privileges? By one means only: debasing the colonized to exalt themselves, denying the title of humanity to the natives, and defining them as simply absences of qualities—animals, not humans.[6]
>
> The colonial world is a Manichean world. . . . the settler paints the native as a sort of quintessence of evil. . . . At times this Manicheism goes to its logical conclusion and dehumanizes the native, or to speak plainly, it turns him into an animal. In fact, the terms the settler uses when he mentions the native are zoological terms.[7]

> ...the colonizer...in order to ease his conscience gets into the habit of seeing the other man as an animal, accustoms himself to treating him like an animal, and tends objectively to transform himself into an animal.[8]

As Memmi expressed it: "The extraordinary efficiency of this operation is obvious. One does not have a serious obligation toward an animal...."[9] Furthermore, once Puerto Ricans are categorized as animals, "then clearly there is no meeting ground, no identity," and their differences are so vast that "the process of colonizing the natives can continue indefinitely."[10] Here, I include, underlining them for emphasis, the examples of animalization of the colonized that I found:

> ...the children naked, and their parents in rags <u>squatting like apes</u> in the front of the shack.... Men or women followed by children creep out in the morning and hunt their breakfast of bananas or fruit <u>just as a pig will hunt</u> its breakfast of acorns. (Edwards 1899, 250)
> ...the dwelling places of the peons are as bare of furniture and the common conveniences and comforts of life as the stables in which an American farmer shelters his horses.... The masses...were ignorant and debased, and lived with less comfort than the domestic animals on an American farm.... at night they bunched together like shivering pigs on the dirt floors of their miserable hovels, without beds or covering... (Olivares, *Vol. 1* 1899, 302, 332)
> ...the [peasant] women squatting on their heels when the rush of domestic duties is over, and chattering together like so many parrots... (Hannaford 1899, 249)
> ...the lowest type of Porto Rican. He was black, dirty, lazy, ignorant, immoral, naked and diseased.... They did not live in houses, but existed more as the lower animals.... as it was dangerous to get near them on account of disease, the soldiers remained away from them as much as possible. (Creager 1899, 211)
> ...there has been shown over and over again a willful malice, by a certain type of volunteers, resulting in ordering and cuffing the natives about, as if they considered them conquered animals instead of human allies and friends. (Dinwiddie 1899, 150)
> [About malnourished children:] They resembled a troop of monkeys, as they squatted on the ground with the most solemn expression, and so totally unchild like that they were a pitiful sight.... the peons...were treated just like beasts, both when living and dead. (Oliver 1900, 159, 175)

[As a group of soldiers made hungry kids do "stunts" in exchange for discarded morsels and hardtacks held in front of them as if they were dogs:] [In Aguadilla] They overran the camp like a lot of flies on a piece of fly-paper as soon as we commenced to eat. We hugely enjoyed the stunts we made them go through with before we gave them a single morsel . . . the man . . . held a hardtack temptingly in mid air. (Oliver 1900, 200)

. . . half a score of naked children . . . with their protruding stomachs,—the result of living entirely on fruit and vegetables,—look like moving barnacles.[11] (Browne and Dole 1907, 1401)

. . . the jíbaro . . . a man who <u>had descended almost if not quite to the level of the beasts</u> . . . procreating, with no thought of morrow . . . (Ashford 1934, 97)

. . . <u>the people breed like rabbits</u> . . . (Ickes 1953, 504)

A Puerto Rican psychiatrist, Dr. Guillermo González, has studied the colonial phenomenon and confirmed that the colonizer considers everything Puerto Rican as "inferior" when compared with anything from the United States.[12] More importantly, he detected, "Subordination and fear of and dependence of the colonizer are immersed in this personality." A sense of inferiority and self-incompetence are, therefore, to be expected in a colonized person, as Aimé Césaire described: "I am talking about millions of men in whom fear has been cunningly instilled, who have been taught to have an inferiority complex, to tremble, kneel, despair, and behave like flunkeys."[13] This submission or servility has been identified by Albert Memmi as part of what is called the "colonized personality" and was noticed by an American journalist: "Puerto Rico can hardly claim to be cosmopolitan, in the face of its supervening local pride. . . . That curious admixture of uplifted pride and an inferiority complex manifests itself sometimes by undue boastfulness and sometimes by quite unnecessary apologetics" (White 1938, 324).

In the specific case of Puerto Ricans, their "docility" has been widely discussed by Puerto Rican intellectual René Marqués. He believed that it originated from the fact that Taíno Indians and Africans were made docile by the Spanish through forced labor and abuse and that the Spanish settlers themselves, being modest laborers, had already learned docility in Spain.[14] Indeed, Kal Wagenheim commented on Marqués concept of "docility": "René Marqués refers to . . . the "docility" [which] . . . emanates from the mix of respect for order, the smallness of the island (which decreases the options available to change that order in force), and a long-time colonial dependency" (Wagenheim 1970, 215).

In a characterization of the Puerto Rican *jíbaro*, a team of medical doctors (one American, one Puerto Rican) depicted him pretty much as the epitome of the colonized: childish, lacking assertiveness, with low self-esteem, and distrusting authorities. Writing in 1911, they reported that the *jíbaros*' mistrust is related to Spanish colonization as if Puerto Ricans were free from colonialism at the time:

> . . . he shrinks from the stranger and lapses into stolid silence when brought face to face with things that are foreign to his life. He does this because he has been made to feel that he must do all that he is told to do by established authority, and he knows that this authority never takes the trouble to look for him unless it expects to get something out of him; because he is suspicious of outsiders, having been too often led astray by false prophets and disappointed by broken promises; because he realizes that he is not a free agent anywhere save in the mountain fastnesses. In other words, he seeks liberty in his home, freedom from the constant repression of those he recognizes as his superiors and exemption from a repetition of deceptions that have been so often practiced upon him. He has always been made to stay strictly in his class, in the "jibaro" class. Frequently, when he tries to express himself he is laughed down, frowned down, or growled down. "Tu eres un jibaro" is not a term of reproach exactly, but it means, "You are not in a position to express yourself for you are only a mountaineer. You know nothing of our world; you are still a child. Your place is under the shade of the coffee tree; the mark you bear is clear to everyone; you are a "jibaro." . . . All the Porto Rican people are kindly and they love their "jibaros," but nevertheless they treat them as though they were children. And the jibaro loyally follows his educated, emancipated fellow citizen, perfectly satisfied to be guided as the latter sees fit.
>
> Care must be taken in deducing facts from questioning a group of jibaros even in the most unimportant matters. They are tremendously suspicious and generally let someone amongst them who is "leido" (one who has established a local reputation for worldly wisdom) speak for them. One can be pretty sure that the rest will say "amen" to all of his remarks. It is said that this deep suspicion of a strange investigator proceeds from the methods employed by the Spanish "guardia civil," or rural guard, to run down those suspected of unfaithfulness to the administration, petty infringement of law, etc. (Ashford and Gutierrez 1911, 13–14)

A reverend commented on the Puerto Ricans being "too submissive and long-suffering," and an anthropologist categorized Puerto Rican history as "placid." Others saw Puerto Ricans as lacking a spirit for rebellion. They obviously ignored the Taíno Indian rebellions,[15] multiple slave revolts during the nineteenth century,[16] and the 1868 Grito de Lares rebellion against Spanish oppression:[17]

> Although the blood of different classes mingles freely in their veins, they have never been a rebellious or a warlike people. No general insurrection has ever occurred in the island. If any criticism can be brought to bear upon them, it is that they have been too submissive and long-suffering under Spanish rule. They have never shown a warlike spirit towards the people of other islands, and they are, on the whole, orderly and docile, peaceable, industrious, considerate of one another's welfare. (Seabury 1908, 46)
>
> There are certain principles which color the behavior of a Catholic society . . . There is perhaps less reliance on oneself, and less rebellion, except in innocuous fields, than in a Protestant community. Church discipline is stronger, and reliance on authority is greater. . . . there is a greater tendency to lean on someone else for a solution of one's problems than there is in Protestant societies. On the whole, there is a strong preference for the status quo rather than for rebellion. (Petrullo 1947, 128)

Even though Puerto Rico has had revolutionary movements and organizations, at times very active, such as the Nacionalistas in the 1930s and the Macheteros in the 1970s-1980s, most Puerto Ricans suffer their colonial ordeals in apparent passivity.[18] This has been attributed to a fatalistic view of life: life is controlled by supernatural forces, and people should accept their fate, good or bad, without complaint.[19]

Economist Victor S. Clark, who visited Puerto Rico as director of a Brookings Institution's study, recognized that the "degree of submissiveness to misfortune" and the "helpless fatalism" with which the Puerto Rican *jíbaros* accepted illness and suffering "with little attempt at alleviation," was difficult to understand "to an outside observer."[20] He theorized it might result from "widespread illness," "the background of slavery and feudalism," "the extreme poverty," or "the terrific impact of the periodic storms that carry all away with them and make human effort and ingenuity seem like naught." And to illustrate his point, he provided the experience of one of the members of his staff:

One day while climbing a steep mountain side along one of the many footpaths that always lead to a jíbaro home, one of the members of the survey staff stopped to rest in front of a little hut. On the doorstep sat a middle-aged woman. In front of the hut two barefooted children were playing. After talking with the woman for a while he noticed that within the house, stretched on the floor, was the body of a dead man, with newly lighted candles burning at his head. The woman on the doorstep at length remarked: "I am now poorer than ever. My husband is dead." Then, after a pause, "Won't you come in and rest? I will make you a cup of coffee."[21]

In the 1950s, an American Catholic priest saw this passivity in a similar light:

He [the Puerto Rican] has learned from folklore, from family and neighborhood gossip, from the tales of the older men, how people cope with troubles. He has for the most part learned to bear with troubles with resignation and dignity. If faith lives in his head, as it does in so many, he has learned to face trouble with a wonderful sense of God's Providence. "Si Dios Quiere," "If God wills it," is as common a phrase on Puerto Rican lips as is the phrase on American lips: "Somebody ought to do something about it." (Fitzpatrick 1996, 142)

Much later, around 1969, a Mennonite missionary analyzed Puerto Rican fatalism, comparing it to the American view on life:

The traditional Hispanic philosophy of fatalism came into direct conflict with the prevailing American middle-class value system which believed strongly that man is master of his own destiny and that he can through his own efforts improve his human existence on this earth. It is not difficult to understand why a people who live under the constant threats of devastating hurricanes might develop a fatalistic philosophy since each year they may become victims of circumstances wholly beyond their control.... An expression commonly heard among Puerto Ricans today as in the past is "si Dios quiere" (if God wills). This expression might be interpreted to mean a deep faith in God, or it might mean a surrender to the forces at work in one's environment. The Puerto Rican "jíbaros" (country folk) used to say, each day that man digs in the soil he is brought one step closer to his grave, which is a reflection of a fatalistic outlook on life. (Holsinger 2013, 160–61)

And in 1970, an American journalist commented on Puerto Ricans' fatalism:

... one value often ascribed to Latin cultures is "fatalism," the belief that life is controlled by supernatural forces that one should be resigned to misfortune or rejoice when some divine decree, perhaps in response to prayer, brings good fortune.... The impoverished (and sometimes the wealthy) Puerto Rican will often say Acepto lo que Dios me mande.... This stoicism chains a man to his destiny. (Wagenheim 1970, 210–11)

Humor, or "relajo," is a self-protective tool related to this fatalism: if we cannot solve it, we can still find something funny about it and get a laugh out of it. This stoic humor, expressed even under the saddest circumstances, was frequently interpreted as callousness or has been used in expressions such as "happy in poverty" or "happy colony" to refer to Puerto Ricans (see chapter 3). Indeed, even in the worst times of the Great Depression, Puerto Ricans still experienced their extreme poverty with generosity and humor, as described by New Deal photographer Jack Delano and by American journalist Kal Wagenheim:

> I had seen plenty of poverty during my travels in the deep South, but never anything like this. Yet people everywhere were cordial, hospitable, generous, kind, and full of dignity and a sparkling sense of humor. Wherever we went, no matter how dire the poverty, we were welcomed into people's homes and offered coffee.... people who were living in a slum area called El Machuelito, where living conditions were infrahuman. Even here, the unquenchable sense of humor of the people was evident in the jokes they told about their own misery. This is one: A man comes home from work and sits down to dinner. He looks at the plate before him and says: "What's the matter, woman, no meat today?" And she replies, "Oh, yes, there is. It's under that little grain of rice on your plate." (Delano 1997, 72)

> ... the word "relajo" ... means joking, goofing-off, fun-making, disorder, a tendency not to take "serious" things seriously. A mild form of el relajo occurred in 1968 when Governor Ferré visited the state penitentiary and a pickpocket deftly stole his handkerchief. A week later, the Governor's handkerchief was returned. It was embellished with drawings of seven coconut palm trees (his party's symbol), three United States flags, and two of Puerto Rico's. A card accompanied the stolen object, with a poem from the prison's drug addicts, thanking him for the visit.... In Puerto Rico, el relajo is a strong form of defense ... against the grayish color that often permeates life in the "developed" countries. (Wagenheim 1970, 219–20)

Puerto Rican historian Loida Figueroa attributed this Puerto Rican fatalism, as well as what she called Puerto Rican "uncertainty," to a colonial history of being attacked by Carib Indians and French, English, and Dutch pirates and buccaneers, as well as by hurricanes, which made Puerto Ricans feel vulnerable unless under the wing of a world power.[22] But even this so-called "impotent fatalism" has also been attributed to a more plausible cause: over five hundred years of Spanish and American colonialism and exploitation of Puerto Rico's workforce and natural resources.

Colonialism can also explain why Puerto Ricans "see their lives as being influenced by powerful others who are beyond their control":[23] the answer is "because they are." As a colony, Puerto Ricans have been denied the right to self-determination. This, of course, promotes the feeling that we are not in control of our own destiny, which makes Puerto Ricans feel impotent to change our colonial reality at the same time that fatalism allows us to keep on with our everyday lives without constant aggravation. As Frantz Fanon explained it: "A belief in fatality removes all blame from the oppressor; the cause of misfortunes and of poverty is attributed to God: He is Fate. In this way the individual accepts the disintegration ordained by God, bows down before the settler and his lot, and by a kind of interior restabilization acquires a stony calm."[24]

An American journalist called Puerto Rico *"Our Orphan Island,"* and in 1940 described his impressions of it pointing to the abandonment of Puerto Ricans to their own fate during the Great Depression:

> I saw, in short, misery, disease, squalor, filth. It would be lamentable enough to see this anywhere. . . . But to see it on American territory, among people whom the United States has governed since 1898 . . . is a paralyzing jolt to anyone who believes in American standards of progress and civilization. . . . We do not use the term "colony," which is too imperial for American taste; but a colony is what the island is, more or less. (Gunther 1940, 423–24)

This Caribbean fatalism comes with a dose of stoicism. In 1920, an American travel writer noticed the stoicism with which poor Puerto Ricans endured their poverty and even spoke about it without the shame he would have expected from an American poor:

> For all their abject poverty these hapless people are smiling and cheerful, sorry for their utter want, yet never ashamed of it, convinced that it is due to no fault of their own. That is a pleasing peculiarity of all the huddled masses of Porto Rico. They are quite ready to talk, too, on closely personal subjects that it is difficult to bring up in more urbane circles, and to discuss their condition in a quaintly impersonal manner, with never a hint of whining. (Franck 1920, 267)

Encompassed in Caribbean fatalism is the notion that life must be lived day by day since nobody knows what tomorrow might bring. People enjoy what they can when they still can since tribulations and death are always nearby: "... tendency is to live for the present, and to take little care for the future through a system of saving and economy. The average manual laborer saves nothing and makes little effort to accumulate property" (Fleagle 1917, 73–74).

Another American author of the 1920s, trying to explain how Puerto Rican laborers got involved in labor strikes, pointed to their "natural inert state," their "lack of foreplaning," and their "docile nature," mocking their newly exercised class consciousness. He seemed to imply that their only motivation to strike was opportunistic:

> But the ranks of Porto Rican workmen. . . . Held down for centuries to almost the level of serfs, they have little notion of how to use . . . the strike. . . . Inert by nature and training, they plod on until some outsider agitator comes along and tells them they shall get higher wages if only they will follow his leadership and quit work, with no funds to support themselves in idleness or any other preparation. It is the old irresponsibility, the lack of foreplanning common to the tropics. Then . . . they strive to keep on good terms with their employers by telling them that only the fear of violence from their fellows keeps them from coming to work, being so docile by nature that they would not hurt even the feelings of their superiors. (Franck 1920, 273)

In 1945, an American teacher wrote that his Puerto Rican elite friend, Cecilian Cofresí, explained with the following words the complexity of the thought processes of the colonized:

> You don't understand, Nick. Love and hate, pain and joy, are all very close. That's why you've never understood Puerto Rico and my fierce love of the country that has brought me so much sorrow. We live too closely together in this crowded little Island. We're always hurting each other and destroying the beauty of the land. We beat up false passions, fling ourselves into abysses of misery, welcome abuse. That is the way of a frustrated, self-doubting people. (Brown 1945, 146)

Even to this day, the inferiority complex inculcated by the colonial experience of over five hundred years is studied by mental health specialists. Such is the case of what has been called "*the pendejo phenomenon*." In Puerto Rico, a "pendejo" is a very nice person who has no self-value and allows other people to disrespect and abuse him/her without doing anything about it. Nobody has to call you "pendejo" since we label ourselves as such. In therapy, professionals have identified that when someone feels that he or she is a "pendejo (a)" this affects "the person's sense of dignity, capacity, and respect which are three of Puerto Ricans' highly cherished values.... To be taken for pendejo is a traumatic event..."[25] This psychological phenomenon results in "feelings of worthlessness and powerlessness" that make people accept being degraded or utilized while "keeping all the anger and frustration to themselves." In our effort not to be treated as "pendejos" again, we assume defensive attitudes against criticism. Biascoechea-Pereda's analysis identifies this phenomenon in the Puerto Rican "jíbaros" as "evasive nature, their benevolent demeanor toward their own kind, and a deep-rooted distrust after centuries of false promises and unfulfilled offerings."

One American journalist saw Puerto Rican fatalism as part of the Spanish heritage and opined that it was related to the Puerto Ricans' "inferiority complex" that made them susceptible to criticism, giving a clear example regarding their command of the English language:

> Spanish influence on the Puerto Rican character shows up primarily in his emotional pattern and cultural mores. Like the Spaniard, he is inclined to be fatalistic. Though death is always just around the corner and he treats it with proper respect, he is not unduly oppressed by it. He is perhaps overly sensitive; manifestations of this are evident in his inferiority complexes when his education, physical size, color and honor are questioned. It shows in his susceptibility to criticism, in the ease with which he may be slighted. Any condescension of feeling of superiority is quickly sensed and resented.
>
> The Puerto Rican who knows English would rather converse with you in English than put up with your poor Spanish. If you find yourself in such a situation don't insist on using Spanish, even though you think his English is poorer than your Spanish. You will thus give his ego a boost, eliminate one sensitive point in his inferiority complex, and contribute to your own better public relations. (Hancock 1960, 20)

This "susceptibility" and defensive attitude regarding criticism was associated with the colonial experience by American educator and philosopher, Dr. Theodore Brameld, who added:

> The manner in which defensiveness is expressed in everyday behavior was exemplified in a number of ways. Common replies to the greeting "¿Cómo está?" ("How are you?") were said to be "Estoy defendiéndome" ("I am defending myself") or "Ahí luchando" ("Struggling

along"). Again, it is characteristic not to oppose openly any persons who are regarded with suspicion or doubt, especially if they are persons of authority. Rather, the procedure is more commonly to wait till one discovers what they themselves think, and then to agree with them ... (Brameld 1959, 195)

To Dr. Biascoechea-Pereda, through the "pendejo" phenomenon as a defense mechanism against imperial aggression and subordination, Puerto Ricans "reenact their deep-rooted fears of annihilation as a people, and project their doubts about their worth.... There remains a feeling that we are not "good enough," that we are "flawed" one way or another. The pendejo phenomenon reveals this fear of being exploited and harmed by people who place themselves above."[26] Regarding this defensive attitude of Puerto Ricans, an American anthropologist provided an example:

Before the intransigent and critical attitude of the American, the Puerto Rican has become hypersensitive. He is forever on the defensive.... Any allusion to "primitiveness" in Puerto Rico meets with the same response. [In a discussion of magic] an American, in the course of the conversation, asked of the Puerto Ricans present if there was any trace of African magic left among the Negroes of Puerto Rico.... The reaction was again violent. Of course not, was the answer. The Negroes of Puerto Rico had forgotten all about the occult. Yet later, when the excitement has died down, these same individuals began to tell stories of magic and spiritism which apparently are believed in extensively throughout the island in spite of the preaching against both by the Catholic Church. (Petrullo 1947, 137)

An emotional and volatile character was also ascribed to Puerto Ricans in 1984:

The gaiety of Puerto Ricans is very real and spontaneous. They laugh and joke with each other easily.... Equally, they are quick to get into passionate rages. They get excited over arguments. Their "dignidad" is quickly offended. Over drinks in a bar, a knife may be pulled out quickly. A fight can ensue over a triviality.... there is little mass violence. (People on strike usually carry their pickets around in smiling fashion).... experts thought that much of the individual violence rose out of the present confusion about national identity. (Samoiloff 1984, 161)

And the concept of the "ay bendito" did not escape several American authors who had longer stays in Puerto Rico and did their best to understand it. Their interpretations of its meaning depended on the context: a way of postponing dealing with an uncomfortable situation, a "passive noncooperation," or a way of showing commiseration with others:

> An exclamation—literally, "Oh, blessed"—with many uses ranging from expressing mild interest to great indignation. To illustrate the sense in which it is usually used: should you complain that, for instance, a certain government employee is lazy, illiterate, incompetent, dishonest and a little weak in the head, it is not unlikely that the person to whom you complain (if he is a Puerto Rican) will agree entirely with your estimate and then say, "But ay bendito! he has ten children! He must have a job!" (Tugwell 1947, 74, footnote)

> Puerto Ricans are a sensitive people, who avoid direct confrontations if someone's feelings may be injured. Doing things a la buena . . . is the preferred method to settle any dispute. Resistance to someone else's views is usually via the "pelea monga" (literally, a relaxed fight) of passive noncooperation, rather than a direct counterattack. A directly negative reply to some requests is also avoided when possible. One rarely says "no" or "yes." Instead, one says, "Let's see" and lets the matter drop, trusting that the hint has been caught. There is also a soft-hearted sentimental attitude, which some people call the ay bendito complex. Ay bendito . . . serves as a handy lubricant for potentially abrasive situations. . . . The ay bendito is also a favorite tactic employed with traffic policemen. . . . the sentimentalism of the ay bendito ameliorates much personal conflict and makes possible many small favors and amenities . . . (Wagenheim 1970, 213)

Taking into account this "pendejo" attitude, it is not a surprise that Puerto Rican political leaders have in the past tacitly accepted the collective role of lower-class Puerto Ricans as guinea pigs for an array of scientific and social experiments. American scientific research began regarding hookworm disease treatments in the 1910s and went through to research regarding the use of Agent Orange defoliant in the 1960s[27] in the Luquillo Tropical Forest.

The idea of the colony itself being a political experiment was expressed by the following American in 1916: ". . . in Porto Rico. None of the political experiments of the United States has proved more successful" (Jones 1916, 98). But it was in the late 1940s and throughout the 1950s when the Island was presented to the world as a model for Third World economic development and a "showcase for democracy" in opposition to socialist Cuba. The conception of Puerto Rico as a "social laboratory" came originally from the American governor of

Puerto Rico Rexford G. Tugwell (1941–1946), whose idea of more state-owned industries and substitution of exports was later abandoned by Puerto Rican governor Luis Muñoz Marín in favor of the attraction of American private investors through tax breaks and other incentives.

In the 1950s, American social experiments in Puerto Rico made their boom when American scientists such as Clarence Senior, Harvey S. Perloff, Henry Wells, and Carl J. Friedrich created models for the economic development of Puerto Rico and the control of its population growth through massive female sterilization and the testing of birth control pills on unsuspecting Puerto Rican women: "In what has for many Puerto Ricans become a notorious example of the arrogance of American colonialism, Puerto Rico in the 1950s became the chief testing ground for the birth control pill."[28]

In the colonial relationship, characteristics that are considered good for the colonizers turn into either ridiculous or evil when exhibited by the colonized. Even though Americans are widely known for their patriotic zeal, they either mocked the colonized's love for their homeland, considering it "inordinate," or simply acknowledged it as another "problem" with Puerto Ricans:

> The Porto Rican is inordinately fond of his birthplace. Send him to the most distant part of the world and he is sure sooner or later to come back to his beloved Borinquen. Emigration from the Island can reach even a moderate success only when entire families are sent. The letters of Puerto Rican soldiers . . . were filled with wails of homesickness . . . (Franck 1920, 278)

> . . . that took me longer to understand. They desperately wanted you to love Puerto Rico. Insecure, they were supersensitive to any possible slight to the island or themselves. Even those who had never been to the States, where their friends and relatives had tasted their first racial and ethnic prejudice, could not ignore the patronizing attitude of many continentals on the island, mostly government officials or, more recently, businessmen. (Cooper 1994, 28)

Only a few American authors with long stays in Puerto Rico commented on Puerto Rican's proud nationalism as a positive force: "There is a quieter, gentler nationalism, which permeates every corner of the Puerto Rican consciousness. It is not so much against America—or against anything—it is for Puerto Rico" (Wagenheim 1970, 257).

In 1947, American anthropologist Vincenzo Petrullo published the results of a field study he conducted in Puerto Rico for the first Puerto Rican colonial governor, Jesús T. Piñero. From page one, he commented on a latent chip-on-the-shoulder attitude he observed, a hypernationalist love for their land and their people, which made them extra-sensitive to criticism and incapable of looking for a better future somewhere else:

> But there is no peace in the Puerto Rican soul.... Instead of a contented people with easy-going ways, the visitor will find soberness, self-consciousness, and a startling sensitiveness to anything even remotely connected with the subject of Puerto Rico. The Puerto Rican act as if they nursed a passionate grievance against the world.... It is not an uncommon experience for the visitor of a few hours to hear a Puerto Rican ask him if the island isn't the most beautiful spot on earth. To the Puerto Rican this is almost a creed... His island is the world—the most beautiful and most perfect—and there is, occasionally, a tendency to believe that the Puerto Rican people are the most precious, too.... The Puerto Ricans love what they have, their land and their people.... The fact is that Puerto Rico has never appeared to be important to anybody but the Puerto Ricans, and to those few continentals who have been charged with its government.
> ... Puerto Rico, the small, crowded, pleasant prison of its people, provides somewhat the same sort of security that a wild animal discovers in his cage after years of imprisonment.... They do not want to leave their island and their people to seek their fortune in foreign parts.... Rice and beans and codfish in Puerto Rico are preferable to steak or chicken on the mainland or elsewhere. They love their island and they love their own people. Separation from their homeland causes them actual distress. And so they ... crowd themselves ... being content with less if necessary, in preference to leaving their small, confining, and frustrating birthplace for an unknown fate in some other land. (Petrullo 1947, 1, 10, 32)

Remarkably, even though many American authors mocked the hypersensitivity to criticism of Puerto Ricans, they strongly resented any opinions that Puerto Ricans had about Americans. American journalist Trumbull White implied that the opinion of an American regarding Puerto Ricans was appropriate but that the opinion of a Puerto Rican regarding Americans was not:

> This Puerto Rican is as sensitive as a child to misjudgment, actual or imagined. He does not want to have the things the stranger does not like indicated to him in response to his question, "How do you like Puerto Rico?" The question is more rhetorical than inquisitive. He really wants nothing except those things that permit compliments. But oddly

enough ... he maintains the ready habit of telling what he does not like about things American.

Over and over I enjoyed such as experience as this: I sat with a young Puerto Rican of brilliant education, unqualified ability, and devotion to the island and the people. He told me things of the utmost interest and value about Puerto Rico, and how Puerto Ricans think and react.... But interpolated with what he was telling me about Puerto Rico and its heart and soul and manner of thought, he would interrupt himself to tell me with particularity how continental North America acts, thinks, and reacts in all circumstances.

But North Americans were my people, with hundreds of years of Anglo-Saxons in England behind my background, nearly as many centuries in New England and the Middle West, to establish them and their attitudes which I inherited understandingly, as he and his had been in Spain and Puerto Rico. I knew the high percentage of error he was making when he told me all about how Americans think and act under varying circumstances, with the same dogmatic avowal of accuracy that he claimed and possessed on behalf of the Puerto Ricans.

In rueful protest more than once I interrupted him with frankness: "I give full respect and confidence to the accuracy of what you assume to know about Puerto Rico and the Puerto Ricans. Why will you not realize that I know better that you do about the Americans of New England and the Mississippi Valley ... that I know how haplessly you misinterpret the governing spirit, the motivation, the public opinion and reaction of those Americans in the mass; and that you have got them wrong?" But it did no good, and he will have the eternal advantage over me in his own mind that he not only knows all about Puerto Rico, but all about the United States too, although he has had little opportunity to learn the latter.... Humility of judgment and of information regarding the things that move men elsewhere was rarely to be found. As one unhappy American commentator phrased it ... "You can always tell a Puerto Rican—but you can't tell him much." (White 1938, 349–51)

In the same line of thought, Trumbull White mocked the resentment Puerto Ricans expressed when they acknowledged that Americans didn't care nor were interested in them. He used sarcasm to convey that Puerto Ricans believe that their Island is a "prize possession" that Americans should "admire and covet" like a child would his "most treasured toy":

> The one thing that is more disquieting to Puerto Ricans than any other single detail when once they realize it is the all but complete indifference

of the people of the United States to the island of Puerto Rico.... In their own consciousness, the island to which they are so devotedly and justly attached has all but the same universality of interest among the people of the continental North as among themselves. It deserves that degree of interest, ergo it must command that degree of interest. What comes to their eye as spectacular outgivings ... must be the subject of discussion in every household on the mainland!

They cannot realize that this indifference, based on lack information though it may be, is an entirely kind one. Too many Puerto Ricans feel that they must translate the explanation of the American attitude into terms of conscious political purposes, primarily selfish.

The beauteous island which all the world would naturally admire and covet, the rich potentialities resultant from its ultimate prosperity, the people who are justly to be so prized for their racial worthiness, and every manifestation of man and nature, unite in Puerto Rican estimates to make the island the same prize possession to the continental United States which it is to themselves. Believing this, it is not strange that they interpret everything under that concept when they look for motivations. It parallels the child's concept of his own most treasured toy as a coveted object for seizure by any sturdier youth whose predatory instincts are unrestrained. (White 1938, 351–53)

In reality, colonialism frequently generates contradictory feelings on the part of the colonized toward the colonizer. It is, then, a love-hate relationship when the natural love for the homeland is confronted with the image that the empire portrays of the colony: a land that could not be able to survive or progress without the "help" of the empire. This paradoxical thinking was described by the last American governor:

In any colonial situation the emotions of the governed toward the government are mixed. The Spanish and Puerto Rican landlords wanted the conservatism and order which came from the kind of outside rule they were getting; but all the same they had enough local feeling to resent interference. They exhibited the most amazing inconsistencies. They seemed, at times, when their pride was involved, to be at one with the most radical independentistas. Puerto Ricans could take care of their own problems; they did not need any outsiders to tell them what to do, and so on. At the same time many of them advocated statehood, or belonged to the political party which advocated it; and they were sending their sons, and even some of their daughters, to American institutions for education. (Tugwell 1947, 38)

As should be expected, most American authors avoided the discussion of American imperialism altogether. Still, over time, the theme was harder to avoid as calls for independence became louder in Puerto Rico. Then, a few American authors ventured to portray American imperialism as benevolent, compared to Spanish imperialism. They could not fathom why any Puerto Rican would feel offended by American imperialism:

> Porto Rico . . . is beginning to think it would like to get out—but I suspect that is rather fashionable talk than real desire. I can't imagine why Porto Rico should want to get out. The island pays no taxes to Uncle Sam. It has its own local government—supervised by an imported American governor, to be sure, and by a handful of other assistants, but not in any oppressive way. It has nothing to worry about—and after so many centuries of worrying and fighting to keep out of other people's hands, I should think the present situation would be a relief. At least America isn't Old Spain. . . . After all, Uncle Sam has done a creditable work in Porto Rico, not changing too many things, not meddling too much, but keeping the place in line. (Marden 1921, 164–65)

But it was the last American governor, Rexford G. Tugwell, who deeply reflected on American colonialism and how it prevented Puerto Ricans from living healthy and prosperous lives:

> . . . the lowly folk of all sorts . . . felt that they were not getting anywhere under American rule except into deeper trouble. They seemed always to have hard work—with the paradox that often they had no work and were then worse off—little food, more sickness and no fun. They desperately wanted something more, not something very different, perhaps, but just more to eat and more fun. Even I, a casual and official visitor, carefully shown around by the insular elite, discovered that. And it was a disturbing discovery, so deep, so powerful, and so bitter it seemed. What was the colonialism which produced this resentment and distrust? No Governor was responsible, though any Governor might seem to personify it . . . It was the system. How many Americans any more are quite clear in their minds what their Revolution was about? Have they forgot the meaning of "taxation without representation"? (Tugwell 1947, 40–41)

American anthropologist Vincenzo Petrullo concluded in his 1947 book that although Puerto Rico was far better under the United States than it was under Spain as colonizer, and that many Puerto Ricans were dissatisfied with the relationship and wanted to decide by themselves their language, education, culture, etc. He believed that the United States had an undeniable responsibility for the economic problem of Puerto Rico and held that, since assimilation failed, it should be abandoned. His plight has relevance even today:

> For most Americans Puerto Rico is another Latin American country which, in some fashion, is making trouble for the United States. Even tourists ..."Oh, the Puerto Ricans—they are niggers and pretty dirty, aren't they?"... Puerto Rico is as close as it can be to open rebellion. It is to the credit of the Puerto Rican people that they are trying to obtain consideration of their problem without having recourse to acts of violence. [Puerto Rico] is a political and economic liability rather than an asset. The two million Puerto Ricans have not been assimilated, and we have not solved their economic, social, and political problems. All Latin America resents our sovereignty over the island.... In all probability the Puerto Ricans would make better citizen and could absorb more American culture if the attempts to force them to do so were abandoned. (Petrullo 1947, 155, 160, 168)

THIS CHAPTER

American colonizers never saw themselves as such. Because of that, they were unable, with few exceptions, to understand the bitterness of Puerto Ricans towards the United States. Unwittingly or not, they unleashed their imperialistic values while on the Island, as evidenced in their descriptions of Puerto Ricans as inferior, childish, or even beastly beings worthy of pity. While enjoying their imperial position, they still feared the contained rage of their subjects.

Puerto Ricans internalized the contempt of their new colonizers and became submissive and overly sensitive to criticism from American outsiders. Living in a world in which adversity was beyond their control, they assumed a fatalistic perception of life, seasoned with Caribbean stoic humor, to protect themselves from despair and desolation. Life became a one-day-at-a-time event of collective survival that has been successful to this day as assimilation has proven to be unsuccessful and Puerto Ricans' love for their Island and for each other prevails.

Chapter 3

"LIVING FROM HAND TO MOUTH"

On the Poverty of Puerto Ricans

In contrast with their descriptions of a lavishing nature on the Island, American authors alluded to the poverty of Puerto Rican laborers by using a variety of grim descriptions. But . . . what were the causes for the perceived poverty?

In 1896, seventy-seven percent of Puerto Rican exports consisted of coffee (sold in Europe or to Cuba), mostly produced by small coffee planters.[1] The largest landowners were the "hacendados" who kept their workers as "agregados": peasants who were given the use of a small piece of land to live on in exchange for their employment with the landowner. The Island's working force was made up of mostly free, independent, and dispersed farmers and artisans surviving out of subsistence agriculture, smuggling, and "loosely communal and cooperative neighborhood networks."[2] It is painful to read the way in which a Presbyterian clergyman summarized the economic state of Puerto Rico at the time of its acquisition by the United States, as it evidences the healthful state of Puerto Rico's economy:

> James S. Harlan, who has been in Porto Rico the last two years as attorney-general of the island . . . reported to have spoken as follows to a Washington, D. C., daily paper: "The government is out of debt, and has a surplus in its treasury of more than $500,000. If Congress will leave Porto Rico alone for the next twenty years, the people of the United States will be astonished at the result. Porto Rico will be the garden spot of the country, supporting a well-to-do community of intelligent, peace-loving, and patriotic people." (Stoddard 1903, 240)

But this promising reality rapidly changed: independent farmers soon became sharecroppers and wage workers. At the time of the US invasion, around fifty percent of all Puerto Ricans worked in the coffee industry.[3] Now, as a territory of the United States, Puerto Rico lost its preferential access to

European and Cuban coffee and tobacco markets, and the US markets did not favor Puerto Rican coffee, preferring the Brazilian one. This happened right after an 1897 international drop in the price of coffee due to overproduction. Additionally, the US colonial government approved measures that further impoverished Puerto Rican small landowners.

First of all, the US military government decided to modify the exchange rate for the Spanish provincial currency to merely 60 cents per dollar, in effect devaluating it. At the same time, it also froze all local credit and increased taxes on land properties. Even after a civil government was established in 1901 (Foraker Act), the colonial government kept approving legislation that served to secure more and more agricultural land for American sugar investors. One example is the 1901 Hollander Act, which launched a tax on movable and immovable property, a tax on inheritance, and the imposition of new tariffs.[4] G. H. Hollander, treasurer of Puerto Rico, declared "that the aim of the project was to force native landowners, too poor to cultivate their farms, to abandon them or sell them to others more fortunate."[5] The government appraisals of the coffee land further devaluated it at a time when only American investors had the capital to buy land at excellent prices if paid with dollars. At the time, there were no formal banking institutions, so there was no other way to obtain local loans than from other *hacendados* and businessmen, so the large *haciendas* struggled to survive.

In a colony, the most essential value of the people is their land because it is tangible, it feeds them, and above all, it gives them dignity.[6] But now, while the *hacendados* and small landowners were forced to sell their plots of land to stay afloat, the majority of landless agricultural workers found themselves jobless and homeless, too, and misery and starvation haunted them.[7] This worked perfectly for the US capitalist investors who, besides monopolizing the best agricultural lands, secured a large reservoir of cheap labor. In 1928, an American author compared what had been done in rural Puerto Rico with what had been done to the Northern Native Americans, but without any compensation at all: "Not unlike the Indians in the United States, these rural people have been elbowed off the land, their natural habitat.... For the Indians, everything has been done, cash payments, huge land reservations, education, occupational training, hospitals, etc. For the Porto Ricans, we have done nothing, and there is very little land of consequence available on which to establish them" (Dana 1928, 39).

Then, about a year after the US invasion, on August 8, 1899, the Island was battered by a very strong hurricane: San Ciriaco. Every major hurricane that hit the Island was a traumatic experience, as an American missionary recognized: "The mention of the word "tormenta" (hurricane) strike terror to the hearts of the Puerto Ricans because the term literally means death and destruction" (Holsinger 1952, 33–34). San Ciriaco wrought twenty-eight hours of nonstop rains and winds of over one hundred miles/hour. Besides causing the deaths of around 3,400 people and leaving homeless twenty-five percent of the population, it destroyed ninety percent of all coffee trees, thus ruining that year's harvest. For new coffee trees, it will take three to five years to produce a harvest. The coffee industry recovered around 1904, but by then, the US sugar investors had already capitalized on the acquisition of land, and sugar became the primary export product.

The hopeless existence of the coffee peons was described by Dr. Bailey K. Ashford in his autobiography. Ashford commented on what Dr. Wickliffe Rose, director of the Rockefeller Sanitary Commission, witnessed in 1908 as he rode on horseback all over the Puerto Rican mountains:

> Rose saw the poor mud-stained laborer degraded by his disease [uncinariasis] and literally submerged in the monotonous routine of coffee culture, living from hand to mouth; his children starving and sick; and his wife, no better off than he, working a bit in the coffee grove and a listless bit more in the bare shack.... He talked to the plantation owner and found that only a tithe of his workmen were worth their salt—with a wage pitifully low, it is true—because the owner hadn't the heart to turn his half-starved people off, sick as they were. He personally verified their ragged clothes, their lack of shoes, and their docile, animal-like constancy in the work of the amo, or master. He talked with the jíbaro and found a man who had descended almost if not quite to the level of the beasts, stumbling about by day over the slippery mud of the coffee plantation, sleeping cold and wet at night without bed or bed covering, eating what he could get—a fare limited principally to a mess of rice and beans, with codfish and tubers—and procreating, with no thought of morrow, no thought of here-after, no thought of the future of his sons and daughters, not even a thought of a freer, better life.... (Ashford 1934, 97)

In contrast with the reality of the Puerto Rican agricultural laborers, between 1899 and 1910, sugar exports increased from 61,000 to 285,000 tons.[8] By 1920, three large US sugar companies owned fifty percent of all the sugar land as well as forty-three percent of sugar production.[9] Puerto Rico's economy became dependent on the export of three cash crops: sugar, tobacco and coffee (in that order), and on the import of basic foodstuffs and manufactured goods to supply its population's consumption needs.

Dr. Bailey K. Ashford, who lived and worked in Utuado and married a Puerto Rican, had the same impression of several Puerto Rican historians regarding the relationship of coffee *hacendados* with their peons as a paternalistic one, in which they actually took care of their peons' needs:

... the educated country squire; the very cream of Puerto Rican citizenry ... with an intelligent sympathy for the country folk who practically formed his family. ... absolute honesty prevailed, together with an intense longing to better the condition of the laborer. ... over half of these planters were paying a wage to invalids, whose living expenses they were sustaining out of human pity and without hope of return. In numerous cases, the planter was wittingly conducting his business at a loss so ruinous as to threaten him with foreclosure—for mortgages lay heavily on almost all of these plantations. (Ashford 1934, 89)

But this social system in which the *hacendado* cared for his workers and helped them in times of need was shattered, and large and modern sugar mills that produced refined sugar, called "centrales," became the norm. The relationship of the workers with their jobs changed dramatically. First of all, many coffee workers had to abandon the mountains and move to the coastal lands where sugar was harvested. Sugar *centrales* belonged to American owners located in New York, Boston, and Philadelphia, and their managers and technicians came from Louisiana and other Southern states.[10] This is why they were called "absent corporations," as their profits were removed from the Puerto Rican economy. In these absent corporations, there was no longer loyalty toward the employers, and the workers lacked protection in times of need. All this economic growth did nothing to alleviate the misery of the poor in Puerto Rico; in effect, it deepened it. Several American authors, like this missionary, realized this and were honest enough to describe the reality as they understood it:

The cultivation, manufacture and exportation of sugar ... gives the appearance of prosperity to the island. The truth about this trade balance is that the money made in the sugar business is made by outside investors. Little but the meager wages of the laborers stay in Porto Rico. The huge profits go to the Continent, the marking is for the most part done abroad, and even the banking in many cases is transacted in New York City. Porto Rico suffers from Absentee Landlordism in its acutest form. No good is done by sentimentalizing about the situation ... (James 1927, 30)

By 1926, the unemployment rate was around thirty percent; there were new roads, but most peasants went around barefooted; there were more hospitals than ever before, but child mortality was one of the highest in the hemisphere. In the cities, new filthy slums served as homes of workers in overcrowded huts. Undernourished men, women, and children suffered anemia, uncinariasis, and intestinal parasites and died in large numbers due to tuberculosis. Then, on

September 13, 1928, Puerto Rico was hit by one of the worst hurricanes in its history: San Felipe, with winds of over 160 miles/hour and some thirty inches of rain in two days. Around two thousand died, and thousands lost their dwellings. In the face of the emergency, the US Congress refused to provide hurricane relief unless Puerto Ricans paid interest on the funds expended there, as well as third mortgages on the destroyed lands.[11]

The situation worsened in 1929 when the Great Depression in the United States added to the misery of the Puerto Rican poor. Some New Deal programs arrived to the Island, but they were too little, too late. While the sugar corporations' earnings kept growing, the agricultural workers saw their income decline dramatically as their working days became longer: "The average wage was 11.1¢ an hour in 1932 and by 1933 it had dropped to 9.6¢. Weekly income dropped from $3.80 to $3.55 even though the average number of hours increased..."[12] As the undersecretary of the Department of the Interior Oscar Chapman recognized in a broadcast to Americans on October 10, 1934: "the sugar industry, while yielding handsome returns to the stockholders of corporations... benefitted the Puerto Rican people little."[13]

Desperation led to the worker unions' agitation as they engaged in multiple violent strikes, mostly in the sugar and tobacco industries but also in the needlework industry.[14] Politically, the anti-American Nationalist Party grew in popularity, and independence became a goal for many oppressed workers who, with the help of trade union education, began to hold big American corporations accountable for the dramatic worsening of their quality of life. An American photographer described the situation: "I had seen plenty of poverty during my travels in the deep South, but never anything like this" (Delano 1997, 72).

Even when the New Deal programs reached Puerto Rico and funds were assigned for the Island's economic reconstruction, the empire only provided meager funding. After offering $150 million, they reduced it to $75 million and, in 1935, they ended up announcing only $37 million.[15] But this only netted $16 million for Puerto Rican people, which represented much less per capita than the amounts secured for any other state, territory or possession of the United States.

The entrance of the United States into World War II in 1941 provoked a serious scarcity of food and medicines in 1942 as the Island was part of a massive German submarine blockade that came close to giving victory to the Germans.[16] After this was sorted out, Puerto Rico began to supply rum to the United States, and the living standards of the poor showed some improvement, but malnutrition persisted as inflation kept raising.[17] Puerto Ricans kept working hard as usual, but the benefits of their work were taken away from their pockets and, furthermore, from their Island. As an American governor stated in the late 1940s: "many who know Puerto Rico well enough are not interested in her welfare but only in exploiting her for their own profit" (Tugwell 1947, 3).

Poverty in Puerto Rico remained rampant until the late 1940s when the colonial government began Operation Bootstrap, a program to fast-forward the industrialization of the Island. The idea behind it was to attract American investors to establish their factories in Puerto Rico. The no-strings-attached enticements offered were: full tax exemption from federal and local taxes for ten years, rent-free facilities with utilities included, free training of employees, free access to the US markets, and a cheap and abundant workforce.[18] None of these were made available to local investors.

In the early 1940s, a Mennonite missionary witnessed the lack of hope in the eyes of some La Perla slum dwellers:

> "They are friendly—unusually friendly. Almost all of them smile and answer our greetings with a cheery "adios" as we pass by. Once in a while we find a man or a woman from whom the squalor and dirt and the misery in which they have lived so long, have finally erased the last vestige of human response and left them with deep lines in their faces and a hopeless, ejected look and blank state indelibly stamped upon their countenances. It is only to these few that this kind of life have meant a living death. The others live and breathe, and have their joys and sorrows, ambitions and aspirations, like the rest of us, though they have little to draw from and hardly more than bare essentials to keep body and soul together. They call their shabby board boxes, homes. (Holsinger 1952, 163)

Operation Bootstrap created new job opportunities, but it provoked the decadence of agriculture, and the new jobs still paid low salaries. The Popular Democratic Party (PPD in Spanish) that governed the Island from 1948 to 1968 enforced an Agrarian Reform that limited the latifundia owned by American corporations, but these absent American agricultural investors were eventually substituted by the new group of absent American industrial investors. As a result, Puerto Rico was as dependent on American investors as before. Nevertheless, besides the slum dwellers, a middle class emerged in the urban centers.

Writing in 1960, an American journalist discussed the "success" of Operation Bootstrap, emphasizing the "transformation" of the Island as he made exaggerated claims:

> The old familiar symbol of the mañana spirit, the peon dozing against a wall with his sombrero resting on his chin, is no part of the scenery. Nor are there the beggars, the afflicted mendicants, or the shoeshine boys

who lounge in hordes on the sidewalks of many Latin American cities. Everyone in these streets seems to be going somewhere—and they are. Energy, purpose, and determination are in the very atmosphere. Energy is, in fact, the most obtrusive characteristic of the island.... Houses, hotels, factories, schools, and new streets and highways are a-building everywhere you look. (Hancock 1960, 12–13)

Slum dwellers abandoned the countryside as agriculture lost its impetus, hoping to find better opportunities in the industrial transformation that politicians promoted. But, not enough industrial employments were created, and life in the foul city slums became the only option for many. To make things more difficult for them, the modernization of the Island was made so quickly (in about twenty years) that their set of values became obsolete, as an American journalist noticed:

The poor, uprooted from a strongly structured environment where one knew how to act by conditioning since infancy, have been thrust into a new situation, without the patron, without the neighbors... without the old taboos, and with a frightening dose of anonymity.... It is bewildering for any adult to have his cultural underpinnings removed without something equally strong being put in their place.... The real trouble comes when he tries to transmit the old ways to his children, in an environment where these ways make little sense or cannot be enforced. The hostility and rambunctiousness of many of the children of the urban poor appear to be a direct consequence of the landslide of the old values.... The city child soon learns that while docility and respect may work in the hills, to survive in the slum one must be tough and brash. (Wagenheim 1970, 216–17)

One of the goals of Operation Bootstrap was to reduce unemployment by controlling the so-called "overpopulation" in Puerto Rico, which was accomplished through massive emigration to the United States, massive sterilization of one-third of Puerto Rican women, and the promotion of oral contraceptives which were tested on unsuspecting Puerto Rican women.[19] With fewer people living there, the level of unemployment became manageable. Sadly, Puerto Rican migrants and women made the personal sacrifices that made possible the industrial development of Puerto Rico.

Signs of the failure of Operation Bootstrap and its fast-track industrialization became more evident in the Puerto Rican way of life during the late 1960s and were summarized by an American journalist:

> . . . there are a number of ominous cracks in what has been hailed as "The Showcase of the Caribbean." Over half of Puerto Rico's families are still poor. . . . income distribution is inequitable . . . price levels surpass those of New York City. Classrooms are overcrowded, and many children attend less than a full day. . . . In rural areas, as many as 40 per cent of the children drop out before sixth grade. . . . Today, most middle-class Puerto Ricans live in suburbs far from their jobs. They fight through nerve-jangling traffic jams twice daily and feel the constant pressure of keeping up the payments on the house, car, TV set, washer, and so forth—bought on easy, high-interest credit. Another large chunk of the populace . . . living in . . . culture of poverty, have seen progress pass them by. . . . they live in urban shanties . . . surviving on meager relief payments and odd jobs. (Wagenheim 1970, 6–8)

Indeed, the collapse of the so-called "Puerto Rican miracle" became undisputable in the 1970s when, to prevent social unrest, the Federal Food Stamps program was implemented in Puerto Rico, which was just a breath of fresh air for many struggling families. Since more than forty percent of Puerto Ricans qualified to receive this aid, over time, a welfare culture developed among them and extended over generations. This federal aid, as well as federal funds allocated in block grants to agencies for health services for the poor and educational programs, veterans' pensions and services, Social Security payments, and emergency aid, etc., have since then been wrongly interpreted by many Puerto Ricans as a "generous gift" from the US government that they should be grateful for, instead of as what they really are: part of the obligations that the United States has to have regarding its citizens.[20] From this point of view, in actuality, Puerto Ricans have always been discriminated against, as they receive lower federal benefits per capita than continental US citizens.

Besides promoting a culture of dependence in their largest colony, these US federal remittances were not (and still are not) destined to promote the economic self-sufficiency of the people but to alleviate poverty. These funds artificially sustain the Puerto Rican economy. They keep the money moving and maintain the local demand for consumer goods, but they do not stimulate local production and, in the end, only benefit the producers of goods in the United States. Billions of dollars in federal funds are given to individuals to spend in shopping malls to sustain jobs in the continental United States. Banks would also rather lend money to facilitate Puerto Ricans' buying of cars and personal goods than to finance local businesses.

As a response to the economic crisis that Puerto Rico faced at the time, in 1976, the US Congress allowed Puerto Rico to offer a new incentive to attract

US corporations' investments: the Internal Revenue Service Code § 936, which allowed their subsidiaries in Puerto Rico to repatriate their earnings to the United States tax-free. This, in fact, attracted American capital for many pharmaceutical and other companies, but its effect on creating jobs was not as expected. At some point, only sixty percent of Puerto Ricans worked and paid taxes. By 1996, the IRS Service Code was no longer applicable in Puerto Rico, and in less than twenty years, the Island, after decades of money-grubbing colonial governments and of surviving on the selling of hedge funds, finally accepted that it had a $70 billion debt it could not pay.

The US Congress then moved to further increase its power over the Island by imposing an unelected Financial Oversight and Management Board to control Puerto Rico's economy. The Board's efforts have been directed toward securing the payment of the debt to the US investors and to establish a "visitor economy" with ". . . a downsized state and many fewer Puerto Ricans living on the island. In their place would be tens of thousands of 'high-net-worth individuals' from Europe, Asia, and the US mainland, lured to permanently locate by a cornucopia of tax breaks and the promise of living a five-star resort lifestyle inside fully privatized enclaves, year-round."[21]

"THEIRS IS A 'CHEERFUL' POVERTY": WHAT AMERICANS HAD TO SAY

Most descriptions of the poverty conditions in which Puerto Rican laborers managed to survive were very detailed and ended in some declaration that the places where they inhabited were "unfit for human habitation." This has been interpreted as having a further implication: if the places where they lived were not fit for humans, then *they* cannot be human: "if human existence under such conditions was unbelievable, then in the final analysis, the humanity of these inhabitants was suspect."[22] This tendency among colonizers to animalize the colonized was discussed in chapter 2. This description of the town of Sabana Grande exemplifies many others:

> There is a suitable proportion of the very dirty-looking little stores which are common to such villages. There is the same general air of decay which characterized the average Porto Rican village. . . . long rows of rough and badly built shanties, which give the greater portion of the town the appearance of being utterly poverty stricken. Yet the people of the place do not look any more dirty, ragged, or hungry than a great man of their compatriots in other places. (Robinson 1899, 94)

There were multiple examples of descriptions of malnutrition, but the authors typically reported it without connecting it to the extreme poverty of so many Puerto Rican workers. The fact is that within the United States's capitalist society, the reality of poverty has been either denied or ascribed to individual failures of the poor, such as "mental deficiency, bad health, inability to adapt to the discipline of modern economic life, excessive procreation, alcohol, insufficient education."[23] Furthermore, "The structure of the society is hostile to these people" whom they see as "lazy people" who "just don't want to get ahead."[24]

Several nineteenth-century writers simply denied the existence of poverty in Puerto Rico, one claiming there was no hunger in Puerto Rico. This is understandable because maybe accepting the reality of poverty implied looking for the origin of that poverty or ascribing responsibility to the US colonial government's policies in Puerto Rico, something they were not prepared to do. Some seemed to suggest that the extreme poverty in which many Puerto Ricans lived was a sort of "choice," as if they did not need more food or clothing than they had and actually preferred the "simplicity" of their poverty and a vegetarian lifestyle. In the United States, a myth had already been created: "Conventional wisdom . . . stated that blacks could physically survive on less food than whites could. This myth was used to justify the perpetuation of dramatic inequalities," and it allowed governmental aid institutions to give less welfare help to Black families than to white ones.[25] The same logic was applied to Puerto Ricans:

> The habits and necessities of a large proportion of the rural population are extremely simple and limited. A little rice, a very little flour now and then, a few beans, and a constant diet of bananas, plantains, bread-fruit and vegetables, supply their physical requirements; a few yards of cotton cloth for the adults and nothing for the children furnish all that they seem to require in the way of clothing, while a few boards and a plentiful stock of plantain and palm leaves afford material for the humble dwellings . . . (Olivares, *Vol. 1* 1899, 348–49)

The most explicit defense of the theory of "fake poverty" in Puerto Rico was that of Frederick A. Ober, who provided a detailed but devoid-of-evidence explanation of it. He falsely claimed that the US military colonial government had provided well for Puerto Ricans without receiving any gratitude from them. According to Ober, it is not possible for Puerto Rican peasants to starve because nature provides them for free all they need: the materials for their miserable thatches; native woods for fire to cook; fruits and vegetables for their vegetarian diet (which he portrays as optional); and a few animals they can hunt for meat (if they had any ability to do so). Clothes are minimal also.

Therefore, to him, Puerto Ricans claim to be poor just because they come from "a long line of paupers":

> ... at the expense of our government. The Puerto Ricans were fed from our overflowing granaries, they received millions of rations gratis, and, after that, millions of dollars were returned to them which had been received as duties on their goods. Still it is not a matter of record that the islanders ever murmured a single expression of thanks!
>
> ... the laboring classes, which comprise the bulk of Puerto Rico's population and which were the recipients of charity from the United States ... reside mainly in the mountain districts, but their mouthpieces, the native politicians ... readily reached the ears and the purses of sympathetic Americans. ... they dispatched carefully-coached delegations of emaciated men and barefoot women to San Juan, there to beard (sic) the governor in his castle. ... To one who knows the island and its almost limitless resources, this story of starvation seems false on its face ...
>
> ... the gibaro, or peasant laborer ... is the present representative of a long line of paupers extending through centuries ... let us show how nearly impossible it is for him to starve, or even to suffer severely, save through his own fault. In the matter of habitation he is content with the merest shelter from the elements. ... The gibaro's house costs him nothing but a little labor. ... For the simple utensils used in his domestic economy ... the calabash, the fruit of which is converted into vessels of various sizes, such as dishes and water bottles, plates and spoons, while the yagua of the royal palm furnishes tubs for washing clothes in, cradles for the babies ...
>
> The first necessity, fuel for fire (for culinary purposes only), lies in the fields or woods, or near their door. An iron pot has been begged, borrowed or stolen, and no other kitchen utensil is actually necessary except a knife, which is supplied by the machete, universally carried by the peon. ... The only expense for garments is incurred by the adult members of the family, and probably does not aggregate $5 a year. ... The average Puerto Riqueño is a vegetarian, perforce; yet there are certain indigenous animals ... that would yield him at least a taste of flesh on occasion, were he possessed of any skill at all as hunter or trapper. (Ober 1904, 229–36)

Others blamed Puerto Ricans for their own misery due to their alleged "laziness" or for their personal inability to save money, which is quite offensive considering that they barely subsisted on the meager wages they received:

The regular wage-day on the plantations is at the end of the week, but laborers are permitted to draw their earnings daily if they choose. They are improvident in the extreme, and often have to obtain advance orders on the stores when they come to work in the morning, in order to get food for the same day's breakfast ... (White 1898, 399)

Few authors recognized that the problem was more income inequality than mere poverty, although some still blamed Spain for these conditions as if honestly believing that American colonialism was better than Spanish colonialism:

Nine-tenths of the people of Porto Rico are miserably poor. Their rude huts, scattered over the country, are meaner than the mud hovels of Egypt ... All the property of the island is owned by a few families. It is estimated that at least 700,000 of the 890,000 population live from hand-to-mouth, never knowing one day what they are going to have the next.... These conditions are due entirely to the evils of the Spanish system of government ... The island is marvelously fruitful, and capable of sustaining a population at least twice as dense as that now in existence. (Olivares, Vol. 1 1899, 299)

The depiction of a "happily poor" population was quite common in the reviewed books. Though they recognized the precarious life conditions of the poor in Puerto Rico, they pointed to the happiness of the people, thus giving the impression that Puerto Ricans somehow enjoyed their lives of constant struggle for survival. A Baptist minister had the audacity of referring to their "'cheerful' poverty," evoking the old European Enlightenment concept of the "noble savage": "The relief is that there is no suffering from the cold, and that the people do not appreciate their filthy, unmoral, and degraded state. Theirs is a 'cheerful' poverty. These untaught poor, who are not immoral but unmoral, not evil at heart but ignorant of anything better" (Grose 1910, 186).

Nevertheless, when American authors faced the death of children due to starvation, the truth of poverty was too obvious to be ignored or hidden: "I saw three corpses yesterday of victims of starvation. They were children of about five to ten years of age and their throats were very little bigger than my two fingers. It was a frightful sight" (Edwards 1899, 156).

Brigadier General Leonard Wood reported on the first plan to promote the emigration of poor Puerto Ricans in order to lower the poverty levels on the Island, a recurrent practice of the US federal government and the colonial government on the Island throughout the years, and to this day. Wood also implied that Puerto Ricans who don't emigrate are just lazy, and then explained the importance of the defense of the "right to emigrate" of desperately poor

Puerto Ricans, as if for them, emigration was a real option, and disregarding the tremendous trauma implied in abandoning your family and friends to venture in an unknown land. Then he affirmed that Puerto Rico had enough poor people, so these migrants not only "will never be missed" but will also be substituted by capitalist and energetic investors, presumably Americans:

> Heretofore emigration has been almost unknown. These islanders are essentially a home-loving people, and remarkably attached to their native land. . . . it would not seem to occur to these simple peasants that by moving over to the next township they might find employment. Many of them would prefer to remain in idleness until some one solicited their services. A few potatoes and bananas will sustain life, and clothing is a luxury in this climate. . . . Laborers are wanted in Hawaii to work in the sugar fields and in Cuba for the iron mines. Good wages were offered, and many were persuaded to emigrate.
>
> Most of them have gone to Honolulu, and a few to Santo Domingo. The Federal faction [in local political parties] has called on the insular government to prevent their emigration. This has not been attempted because, in the first place, it is the privilege of every person to emigrate if he chooses so to do . . . The humblest bare-footed peon . . . has the same right to expatriate himself if he chooses as does the millionaire. And, in the second place . . . They will never be missed in making up the census returns of the next decade. Porto Rico has plenty of laborers and poor people generally. What the island needs is men with capital, energy, and enterprise to develop its latent industries. (Wood 1902, 325–27)

In the 1950s, when colonial governor Luis Muñoz Marín realized that the fast-track modernization and the industrialization of Puerto Rico were raising the level of unemployment and political unrest, he decided to follow the advice of urban planner Harvey S. Perloff and, to solve the then-called "population problem" by embarking on a campaign to promote the emigration of Puerto Ricans to the United States, mostly to New York. Partially subsidized, cheap, and frequent flights were provided, and between 1945 and 1970, one-third of the population (around one million) migrated.

Around seventy percent of the migrants were between fifteen—and thirty-nine-years-old: the most productive Puerto Ricans. They made the sacrifice of working in the United States on the worst jobs available (due to their lack of proficiency in the English language, low education level, and skin color). Their sacrifice allowed the economic progress of the Puerto Ricans who remained on the Island. At the time, an English teacher soon realized that in Puerto Rico,

"Nueva Jork was the generic name for all the continental United States," and commented about Puerto Ricans' migration:

> Puerto Ricans might spend their forty-five dollars to fly to Nueva Jork, but no one had any intention of staying. They certainly didn't want to live there; all they wanted was to earn enough money to buy a house for their family or start their own little colmado. This is why even my students who had lived in the States knew very little English. Why bother learning it when you were only going to be gone from the island for a few months or a year at the most? It only took forty-five dollars to fly back. (Cooper 1994, 27, 29)

By 1970, Puerto Ricans were already "frequent flyers," something that provided a still palpable and familiar atmosphere to the Isla Verde Airport:

> Puerto Ricans are among the most "flying happy" people in the world.... Puerto Rico's airport has a distinctly local flavor. It has been the scene of colossal traffic jams, since huge delegations of friends and relatives often congregate to welcome or see off a traveler. (Wagenheim 1970, 123–24)

More recently, the economic bankrupt of Puerto Rico, added to a devastating Hurricane Maria (October 2017), a series of earthquakes, and the COVID-19 pandemic, all in the decade of 2010–2020, resulted in a massive exodus in which 11.8 percent of the population left their beloved island in an effort to find a better future, mostly in the United States.[26]

"THE PROCESSION OF PITIFUL, REPULSIVE MENDICANTS": THE ISSUE OF THE BEGGARS

Beggars have been a normal part of life in cities for millennia, and giving alms to beggars has been an important part of Judaism and Christianity since their onset. Nevertheless, the dramatic labor shortage caused by the Black Plague in Europe changed that benign view of beggars. And then, with the Industrial Revolution and the rise of industrial capitalism, beggars began to be seen "as threats to the social order and national prosperity."[27] At this point, beggars became a reminder of the downside of a wage-dependent economy and became "people not deserving of aid," while poverty transformed into "a moral failing" as the US government declared that "able-bodied beggars were in the wrong and should be punished."[28]

In his book about poverty in the United States, Stephen Pimpare stated that the concern in the United States during the nineteenth century was that giving any assistance to beggars "would strengthen workers' bargaining rights in the labor market," and explained: "If you had nothing other than the awful, dangerous job in the factory, you're gonna take it."[29] This capitalist logic looks for the convenience of the industrialists who, in order to keep wages at their lowest, need to have available a larger number of potential workers than job opportunities. By blaming beggars for their failure, a capitalist society abjures their responsibility regarding abject poverty. These ideas were part of the "common knowledge" of Americans in the nineteenth century and, being so important for capitalism, persisted over time.

Puerto Rican beggars caught the attention of many American authors as an unpleasant sight from the very beginning. A US soldier narrated how poor Puerto Ricans begged for leftovers, disgusting food, or any food at their camping sites. Hardtacks were happily given away by the soldiers because they detested them. Two American soldiers clearly animalized the beggars as they explained how soldiers threw the food at them in Dantean scenes:

> Always at mess times a row of natives, old men and women, young ones, and children were ranged along the wire fence behind the kitchen, eager for any scrap of food that one might throw them. "Look here!" they cried in their pimping voices. "Look here! Look here!" They balked at nothing. Even the hard black things in the rice didn't quench their enthusiasm, and bits of hardtack were gifts from heaven. (Cammann 1899, 127)

> [The poor children] . . . waited for some morsels of food to be tossed at them. . . . Their elders would stand at the hut doors watching them. Just as sure as a youngster brought back a can full of slops—canned beef, potatoes, hardtack and coffee all in one, the father or mother, but more often the latter, would grab it, disappear through the door and a moment later hand the empty can to the youngster, who knew his little game as he came toddling up the road for another can full. These children were the source of so much merriment amongst us. . . . Of course, we did not give the bacon to these hungry natives as we ate this with great relish, but the canned meats of which there seemed to be an endless supply in Mayaguez, we gave of them freely. . . . the canned meats . . . the foul, greasy appearance, sickening odor and nauseating taste. The natives evidently had never tasted anything so good, for they seldom ate meats . . . (Oliver 1900, 159–60)

The penal code adopted by the US colonial government in Puerto Rico in 1902, basically a translation of the California Penal Code, made it a misdemeanor for any adult to involve a child younger than twelve in begging.[30] The following comment was made by a female American missionary and is well-aligned with the Protestant/Puritan view of poverty as a shameful condition, but her choice of harsh words to describe the sight of Puerto Rican beggars in San Juan is still shocking: "Shameless beggary in the streets of San Juan has been prohibited. Horrors of deformity creeping from door to door or dragged in carts by interested relatives or friends are not so much in evidence as formerly, when, especially on Saturday morning, it was difficult to keep one's footing on the yard-wide sidewalks because of the procession of pitiful, repulsive mendicants" (Johnston 1905, 171).

Many American authors seemed mystified by the fact that Puerto Rican beggars and their supporters had developed a very well-organized system for the collection of alms:

"In the cities of Porto Rico there is one day of the week when the beggars are expected to go about asking alms. This has always been the custom, and it is so well established that our Governor General has sanctioned it under American rule. The day is Saturday. On this day every merchant and business man expects a call from the beggars, and puts a pile of 'centavos' . . . on his counter or desk. The beggars come in one by one. They each take one coin, and no more, and then depart, blessing the giver." (F. G. Carpenter as quoted in Olivares, *Vol. 1* 1899, 301)

The American colonial government in Puerto Rico soon began their effort to change the Puerto Ricans' perceptions of beggars, as they considered them losers and lazy people. Charity institutions were established to keep those with ailments out of the streets, but Puerto Ricans insisted on their old views of beggars as unfortunate people and felt pity for them. As Albert Memmi stated, the colonizer manages to portray all of the colonized's positive character traits, such as his/her compassion for the less fortunate, as negative traits, as this American journalist did in 1938:

In these cities of the continental United States there are no blind or crippled or diseased on fixed station in the post-office corridors, begging from the line-up at the stamp windows, or blocking the doorways or the steps as one attempts to enter. . . . But Puerto Rican begging is not a transient surrender to dire necessity at a time of exceptional economic disaster. . . . whether from the needy or the prosperous, there is no existing sense of shame and humiliation in the fact of beggary. . . . beggary apparently accepted by the entire population as a natural, inevitable fact.
. . . When the subject is raised for discussion . . . The inquirer is reminded that the needy are always with us, that charity is kind, that alms

giving brings blessings alike to those who give and those who receive, that poverty is the fixed lot in life for a multitude who has no escape, and that mendicancy should not cease if the habits of mercy and charity are to be preserved.... Their beggars are bad advertising. They know that, but they don't do anything about it. (White 1938, 343)

In contrast, in 1944, an American teacher staying at a Puerto Rican family house reported on the strict moral code of the beggars she encountered in Humacao: "Ave María por Dios," a pitiful voice rang out.... I gave the nickel to the haggard old woman. Conscientiously, and without asking if it were necessary, she gave me four cents change" (Dean 1944, 47–48).

THIS CHAPTER

Before the US invasion, Puerto Rico had a healthy economy, but the incoming American sugar and tobacco investors made sure that the new colonial government supported their interests through local currency devaluation, freezing of credit sources, and new land taxes. Soon, American sugar investors hoarded Puerto Rican lands as small landowners were forced to sell theirs. But American investors also required a large reservoir of cheap labor, so a large portion of Puerto Ricans would be kept under the poverty level through meager salaries and discriminated against whenever federal reliefs were granted.

The profits created by Puerto Rican workers were taken to the continental US while Puerto Ricans endured, almost on their own, misery, illness, malnutrition, earthquakes, and hurricanes. It was never about the needs of the Puerto Ricans. The natural and human resources of the colony have been plundered shamelessly for over a century. When industrialization was promoted in the 1950s, the capital was also American, and exploitation continued, even though some level of progress became available for the new middle class. But when it only replicated income inequality, now in an urban setting, Puerto Ricans were blamed for it: they were "too many." So, through the active encouragement of emigration, sterilization, and contraception, frequently under unethical pretenses, some Puerto Ricans sacrificed for the progress of the rest.

American authors described the malnutrition they encountered but denied the existence of poverty, saw poverty as a "choice," and described it as "cheerful." To them, misery was the fault of Puerto Ricans, who were "lazy" and "squandered" their meager wages. But they were the harshest when describing their encounters with beggars, who they saw as shame-deserving, while Puerto Ricans saw with pity and treated with dignity. Though US imperialism fomented their poverty, it was not willing to assume responsibility for it.

Chapter 4

"NEITHER ALIENS NOR AMERICANS"

The Convoluted Politics of the Colony

The relationship between common Puerto Ricans and the Spanish colonial government was affected by hundreds of years of abandonment of the colony by a distant empire, which led the islanders to fend for themselves through vigorous contraband. Getting Puerto Ricans' needs supplied in an illegal fashion for so long sharpened Puerto Ricans' shrewdness and malice to deceive or bribe Spanish government agents. These qualities "persist and are transferred to any situation where a demonstration of cunning mates with the hidden pleasure of winning one over the government."[1] So, in Puerto Rico, the government is commonly seen as "the enemy of the people."

Nevertheless, as a result of the Cuban Independence War (1895–1898), Spain recognized the political autonomy of Puerto Rico on November 25, 1897, through the Autonomic Act of 1897, which organized Puerto Rico's government with the highest level of participation of local politicians ever attained in its history, up to this day (with full representation in the Spanish Courts and only annullable by the Puerto Rican parliament). A few months before the US invasion, the new autonomic government was organized, but its Parliament only met for a little more than a week before the US invasion brought Puerto Rico back into colonial status.

When the United States acquired Puerto Rico with the December 1898 Treaty of Paris, it became an unincorporated territory, a new category created for the new acquisitions (including Guam and the Philippines). Under this category, the new United States Empire made no promises of a future statehood for these territories, a position they have kept. Instead, Puerto Rico was to be governed perpetually and with unlimited ("plenary") powers by the US Congress, as established in the US Constitution's Territory Clause (Article IV).

After the US invasion, Puerto Ricans lived under a military government until 1900. Four military governors were in charge of transforming the Spanish colony into an American one. These two years of ruling by decree were used by the young empire to dismantle the Spanish order and give form to the new colonial regime based on the American model of government and values. The military government rapidly implemented some progressive concepts like trial by jury, the right of habeas corpus, civil marriage, and divorce. They also began to work in sanitation brigades to deal with the sewage problems of several cities. But they also implemented censorship as when Governor G. V. Henry decreed that "Publication of articles criticizing those in authority and reflecting upon the government or its officers will not be allowed."[2]

Since the very beginning, mistrust permeated the attitude of the US government towards Puerto Ricans. The War Department was assigned jurisdiction over Puerto Rico, and its Secretary from 1899 to 1904, Elihu Root, was convinced that, even though the elite was very talented, Puerto Ricans were not ready for self-government because of them having a different culture and values, a high level of illiteracy, and an extreme poverty.[3] So, the general consensus in Washington was that Puerto Ricans would need tutoring on self-government. A few American authors agreed with this consensus after almost a decade of US colonial government:

> The Porto Ricans are anxious for a larger measure of self-government immediately.... The Americans resident in Porto Rico have the same point of view that I have: it would not be the part of wisdom for us to surrender the Government entirely into their hands, since they are of different civilization, not looking upon matters of Government in the same light as the Anglo-Saxon.... They really have no conception of the true meaning of equality and liberty. (Boyce 1914, 414–15)

On May 1, 1900, as a result of the approval by the US Congress of the Foraker Act, a civil government was inaugurated by Charles W. Allen, the first of a series of civil American governors appointed by the American president that culminated with Rexford G. Tugwell (1941–1946). This colonial civil government instituted a nonreligious coed educational system free for all children, but the Puerto Rican elites were dismayed as they were left without citizenship and were offered precisely what Americans had fought against in their own Independence War: taxation without representation. Besides this, all laws approved by the Puerto Rican legislature needed to be approved also by the US Congress.

Puerto Ricans were allowed to occupy some positions in the colonial government, but never as "equals" since they remained "under the direct supervision of the American governor, the US Congress, and the US President."[4] Even Protestant missionaries insisted that Puerto Rican politics were "mendacious, corrupt, and proof that the Puerto Rican body politic required cleansing, disciplining, and lifting to a higher moral plane."⁵ The possibility of granting US citizenship has been considered by American politicians and congressmen since at least 1909. In 1914, an American explorer favored such political measure, but not as a recognition of Puerto Ricans' capacities; instead, he thought it might be a way to give some "decent" standing to Puerto Ricans who have been obedient and loyal to the United States despite being impoverished and mismanaged by its imperial power:

> Although it would probably be unwise to grant full citizenship to all the native Porto Ricans, a vast number of the people are as intelligent, as capable, and far more versed in the duties of citizenship than the majority of Americans. At any rate, we owe to these people to give them some standing; they welcomed us with open arms when we delivered them from Spanish misrule; they have obeyed our laws, have been loyal, peaceful, and true, and yet to-day they find themselves at the mercy of sharpers and grafters, . . . not United States citizens, but merely "people of Porto Rico,"—a race and nation apart, ruled by aliens, mismanaged, and with an executive assembly wherein the majority are Americans; but on the whole steadfastly patriotic, true to the flag, and ready to send their young men to fight for the very people and the very administration which has robbed them of their chief source of revenue and reduced them from affluence to poverty. (Verrill 1914, 137–38)

In August 1914, the Panama Canal, under the control of the United States, became operational. Puerto Rico's geographical position in the Caribbean Sea made the Island a principal point of access to the canal and, therefore, assigned to it a central role in its protection from future enemies of the United States. With no say from Puerto Ricans, they became the center of the future geopolitical planning in the American empire. As a pair of American missionaries stated in 1916: "No spot under the American flag is of greater interest to the American people than that little island gem, guardian of our Panama Canal" (McLean and Williams 1916, 101).

Several American authors recognized the way the American government had disrespected Puerto Ricans and their culture by refusing to provide them with citizenship. Once again, Verrill commented:

> We have given them much,—for which they are keenly grateful,— but we have robbed them of much that was dear to their hearts. They welcomed us with open arms when we came unbidden to their land; they have proved loyal, law-abiding, worthy, and yet we have failed to

treat them as equals, or even as equals of the colored inhabitants of the United States or the black and brown people of Hawaii. We have refused them citizenship—the right to rule and govern, or even to have an audible voice in their own island. No wonder they are more or less aloof, no wonder they chafe and feel injustice done to them, for they are neither aliens nor Americans, but merely "people of Porto Rico." Like their island they are legally neither one thing nor the other, neither "fish, flesh, fowl, or good red herring." (Verrill 1917, 260)

Eventually, about a month before the United States entered World War I, on March 2, 1917, the US Congress approved the Jones Act, imposing, among other dispositions, a second-class US citizenship and a Bill of Rights on all Puerto Ricans. Citizenship unilaterally applied to all Puerto Ricans ended up becoming a priority only after the US Congress adopted a bill to organize its largest territorial government, the Philippines,[6] and when the proximity of war with Germany made it necessary to secure the loyalty of all Puerto Ricans in case of a possible German invasion of the Island. Ironically, "the US military wanted to prevent what happened to Spain in 1898 happening to them in case of a German invasion to the island."[7]

The reaction on the Island to the imposition of US citizenship took many American politicians by surprise. Puerto Rico's Resident Commissioner in the US Congress, Luis Muñoz Rivera, clearly expressed the rejection of this citizenship project in his testimony there on February 26, 1914: "If you wish to make us citizens of an inferior class . . . if we cannot be one of your States; if we cannot constitute a country of our own, then we will have to be perpetually a colony. . . . Is that the kind of citizenship you offer us? Then, that is the citizenship we refuse."[8] On their part, the Puerto Rican legislature unanimously approved a resolution sent to the US Congress on March 27, 1914: "we firmly and loyally maintain our opposition to being declared, in defiance of our express wish or without our express consent, citizens of any country whatsoever other than our own beloved soil that God has given us as an inalienable gift and incoercible right."[9]

Other congressional acts followed: in 1947, allowing colonial governors to be elected by Puerto Ricans; and in 1950, allowing Puerto Ricans to have a local constitution approved by the US Congress. Still, Puerto Ricans were not allowed to vote in presidential elections and remained in most matters under the sole jurisdiction of the US Congress, where they had only one representative without voting rights. Each congressional act has only reinforced this colonial relationship. To this day, the US Congress remains the ultimate source of power in Puerto Rico. The general assumption was, and still is, that Puerto Ricans are not capable of self-government.

"REPUBLICS DO NOT THRIVE IN THE TROPICS": WHAT AMERICANS HAD TO SAY

One of the first American theories to explain why Puerto Ricans were not capable of governing themselves was that it was "due to the profuse racial mixing in the Island and to the 'enervating effects' of a tropical existence."[10] Predictably, the American authors we studied followed the same line. But, once the new civil colonial government began to operate, resentment became evident among Puerto Rican legislators who felt that Puerto Rican progress was being hindered by the excessive power concentrated by American colonial authorities. For Leo S. Rowe, professor of political sciences, Puerto Ricans could be trained for self-government as they were afflicted by an "arrested development" and an "enervating" climate:

> The situation on Porto Rico . . . was not the contact of a primitive with an advanced civilization, but rather the meeting of two civilizations, one of which was suffering from the consequences of arrested development. . . . Porto Rico had derived from Spain the sciences, the arts, and mode of life of an advanced people, but had suffered from the effects of complete isolation from outside influences.
>
> To all these conditions must be added the enervating effect of the climate. The energy and assertiveness which are as necessary to the maintenance of civil and political rights as to the attainment of industrial success, have little opportunity for development under the conditions that prevail in the tropics. . . . the fact that in our new possessions we must secure the active support of the native population, involves a relative lowering of efficiency. This is not due to any inherent defect of the native, nor does it necessarily involve any reflection upon his ability, but is simply a recognition of the fact that the has not been trained to participation in public affairs. (Rowe 1904, 143, 145–46)

Rowe kept going, providing the most detailed descriptions of the passionate Puerto Rican political atmosphere by any of the studied authors:

> . . . political feeling, although vigorous and aggressive, is not without appreciation of a point of view other than its own. . . . After four centuries of repressive measures . . . The full force of the people's pent-up energy was thrown into political agitation. . . . the importance of political belief was exaggerated far beyond its real significance and soon became a kind of religion, with all the fanaticism and intolerance. . . . Party division in Porto Rico arouses an intensity of personal

antagonism, which produces irreconcilable conflicts in the community, not only arraying families against each other, but often breaking family ties.

Amusements are stamped as Federal or Republican according to the party affiliation of those taking part in them. In some of the towns, the public concerts and promenades were, by tacit agreement, frequented on certain evenings by members of one party, and on others by members of the opposite party. At bottom, this is due to a failure to realize that the politics of a community occupy a relatively unimportant place in the sum total of activities. In the United States the excitement of a campaign period disappears immediately after the election. The minority cheerfully submits to the rule of the successful majority. . . . Not so in a country like Porto Rico . . .

Instead of an incidental and relatively subordinate interest, it has become a kind of religion, with its array of fanatics and martyrs. Members of the same political faith are referred as coreligionists. The minority, instead of acquiescing in the rule of the majority, attempts wherever possible to hamper and to clog the machinery of government. . . . Party affiliations mean a far closer personal relationship than they do in this country, just as party differences mean a far greater personal estrangement. (Rowe 1904, 108–10, 233)

In 1914, an American journalist understood that it would be hard to convince elites that the lower classes' votes had the same value as theirs and to convince the lower classes themselves of the equal value of their votes:

The United States has had a difficult task in getting Porto Ricans to govern themselves in the light of the American idea. The Porto Rican of the upper class, when he speaks of popular government, means government by his class. He never considers the masses. They are chattels. It requires much repetition before he gets the idea of these men having a voice in government equal to his own. . . . On the other hand, the peon of Porto Rico, having always been a practical chattel of some landowner, can not grasp the idea that he is to have anything to do with the government. He has never had any voice, has never expected any. He is hard to awaken. (Du Puy 1914, 114)

The first Marshall of the Federal Court in Puerto Rico, Edward S. Wilson, saw in a positive light the "sentimental politics" he witnessed there. To him, the personalism in politics actually propended a familiar atmosphere that was "a good sign."

No people are more easily swayed by gentle sentiments or drift away more smoothly from their influence than the Porto Ricans. It often happens that political antagonisms rise to blood heat and end in an embrace.... I recall to occasions, where factional bitterness was intense, and in a few minutes after, the chief combatants hugged each other in fervid fraternity, on public platforms, before great audiences, which wildly cheered the affectionate scene. It is a favorite experience in Porto Rico. The people like it. They are fond of sentimental effervescence, and it is a good sign. (Wilson 1905, 63)

A Mennonite missionary, writing around 1969, coincided with this vision of personalism as an attribute of Puerto Rican politicians that brought them closer to their constituents:

The successful politician in Puerto Rico seeks those opportunities which put them in direct contact with their constituents, and these contacts seemingly do not become burdensome to them because they enjoy the feel of personal relationships. In my experiences I have found that Puerto Rican government officials from the Governor down never hesitate to socialize with persons who come to their offices on business matters, even though they were extremely busy and pressed for time. (Holsinger 2013, 162)

Wilson supported the assumption that Puerto Ricans were not able to undertake self-government citing racial and climate theories:

That race has never succeeded in maintaining a real republic.... They are contentious, inconstant, wayward, and when disappointed, spitefully protest against majority rule. Besides, republics do not thrive in the tropics. There is something in the sun that neutralizes the self-governing instinct of the people. There is something in the physical conditions of the tropics that does not contribute to the formation of strong, well-poised character, and that fact makes a republic difficult if not impossible. (Wilson 1905, 146–47)

For the most part, Puerto Rican politicians were declared "unfit" for democracy by American authors who agreed that Puerto Ricans needed tutoring on democracy:

... the politician, if he cannot have his way, either resigns his position or sulks, refusing to take any part in the deliberations of the body of which he is a member.... The Porto Rican is by nature and training of an uncompromising temperament. This is especially manifest in his politics. There are numerous fights and riots during political campaigns and at election times. Although peaceable by nature, he cannot tolerate an opinion differing from his own ... They have not yet learned to submit gracefully to majority rule.... Men of one party frequently will not speak to those of the other. Hatreds are intense and led to riots...... in 1900 a number of clashes occurred which resulted in bloodshed. (Fowles 1910, 49)

An American journalist and frequent visitor of the Island identified a politicization of Puerto Rican journals. He described his worries regarding the limiting effect of political partisanship in Puerto Rican newspapers, which, in his opinion, were totally polarized:

Unhappily, the effort to maintain the rudimentary relationships of detachment between news and opinions does not seem so vigorous or constant in the papers of Puerto Rico. Puerto Rico is politically minded, politically self-conscious, to a degree and with an intemperate zeal far beyond what we commonly meet elsewhere in the United States. One result of this condition is that the newspapers of Puerto Rico are read almost exclusively by their partisans....

[One of his friends from a Puerto Rican newspaper told him:] "Why have a newspaper to support our cause, and then use that paper to give the opposition the breaks, and our valuable space?" ... The daily papers are all crusaders.... To attack the others is always easy. To an extent not customary in continental American papers, the Puerto Rico dailies give conspicuous prominence to interviews, and particularly to written communications from the party heads....... papers would print supporting letters and interviews upholding their own side of the subject, and not give equal space to letters in reply, demolishing the editor's point of view! (White 1938, 286, 289–91)

Corruption, here understood as "the violation of one or more of the obligations imposed by the regulatory system in order to obtain a benefit additional to that of the position held," results in a loss of public patrimony and/or an injury to public function or integrity, but it also harms those members of society who are originally meant to benefit from such resources and public function.[11] American authors were impressed by the amount and variety of corruptive schemes devised by Puerto Rican politicians:

> The legislature and native insular officials are by no means free from intrigue, graft and dishonesty. Towns with $100,000 incomes spend half of its salaries to the mayor and his colleagues. Teachers were forced to pay ten per cent of their wages into political funds. . . . Even the post-offices are said to be corrupt with local politics. . . . So long as there is a great apathetic, illiterate, emotional mass of voters self-government can be no more than a farce. . . . No Anglo-Saxon party leader can hope to keep pace with the suave machinations of Spanish-American politicians. They can think of more tricks overnight than he can run to earth in a week. (Franck 1920, 290)

As bureaucracy became politicized, patronage became entrenched. In the colony, power became more personalized around the governor figures and their select cronies, and party loyalty became the way to connect to power, to positions and promotions, and to government contracts, among other benefits. To prove their loyalty, government officials were more willing to break the rules. This "fondness for bureaucracy" is still a source of criticism in Puerto Rico.

> To hold office has been, and still is, the ruling passion in Porto Rico. Besides good pay, leisure, authority, social distinction, it meant an opportunity to exploit one's self in many ways, not always directed by motives of a lofty patriotism. Consequently, offices were numerous and useless employees sat around by the hundreds . . . There were assistants and underlings to every sinecure. . . . These favors distributed by party chides made the question of leadership the most serious political issue. . . . the habit in Porto Rico, was for those in authority to oppress those whom they disliked, and make of office-holding a purely personal and selfish matter . . . (Wilson 1905, 64–65)

Corruption in the conduct of elections and the everyday provision of governmental services was identified by many American authors, some of whom attributed it, once again, to poor Spanish administration of their colony, disregarding the fact that nepotism and influence peddling were also common in the United States. The nepotism issue, in particular, should not be surprising due to the small size of the population and the high value given to family ties in times of need. Even to this day, having a relative or a friend in a high government position is crucial to getting a position in the colonial government:[12]

> . . . we had established in every municipality a school board, a "Junta Escolar," elected by the voters of the town. The board was given charge

of school buildings and of nominating, from certificated lists, many of the local teachers.... Then we discovered that teachers were often assessed a considerable sum as a contribution to party funds, and ... we never succeeded in wholly preventing the collection of these political assessments.... Nor could any of the board members understand why the daughter of the alcalde, or the son of the local "jefe" should not, as a matter of course, be given a teacher's certificate without the formality of passing an examination. (Lord 2004, 34)

[Regarding elections:] ... And it was rumored that in some sections the same gang of peons might go to the polls two or three times in one day, voting under different names supplied by the particular "jefe" who brought them in from the country.... the Governor ... called on nearly every American official for special service ... and assigned them to supervise the election of some town or district.... I was surprised to find over eight thousand names on the list—twice as many as could reasonably be entitled to vote.... when, standing out from the Spanish, I noticed many common English names I was puzzled, for there were almost no American residents in the district. And I was intrigued when I came to several strange names, such as "Holeproof stocking," "Eastman Kodak," "Ivory Soap," "Scott's Emulsion," and "Gillette Razor." Altogether, several hundred names appeared to have been copied out of American magazine advertising pages by someone whose knowledge of English was so slight that he took any capitalized words for names.... Strange to say, not one of them appeared.... (Lord 2004, 36–37)

As time passed and the local elites realized that the political control of the colony was not going to be entrusted to them, nationalism strengthened and began to be expressed as discontent with the American colonial government. The campaign for local elections of 1920 exemplified "an intense pro-independence excitement," which was later toned down by the offer of a Commonwealth status in the US Congress (Campbell Project of 1922).[13] But when that project died in Congress in 1924, Puerto Rican political leaders once again claimed liberty using the visit of aviator Charles Lindbergh on February 3, 1928 as a platform. In the reception of Lindbergh in San Juan, the Speaker of the House of Representatives José Tous Soto sent what American journalist A. G. Dana considered a "somewhat ambiguous" petition that was anything but "ambiguous" to the American people:

"... to your country and to your people you will convey a message of Porto Rico not far different from the cry of Patrick Henry—'Liberty or death!' It is the same in substance.... The message of Porto Rico to your people is: Grant us the freedom that you enjoy, for which you struggled, which you worship, which we deserve and you have promised us. We ask the right to a place in the sun of this land of ours, brightened by the stars of your glorious flag." (As quoted in Dana 1928, 7)

The despair caused by the Great Depression in the 1930s only fed the independence flames. The Nationalist Party, founded in 1922 and headed by prominent Pedro Albizu Campos, voiced the discontent. The elections of 1932 were extremely violent as riots, rock-throwing, and the use of firearms, sticks, and knives made the news; ironically, the least physically violent party was the Nationalists, who chose to verbally attack colonialism instead.[14]

Nevertheless, American teacher Wenzell Brown connected the activities of the Nationalist Party with the violent anti-Americanism that manifested in the 1930s. Due to the fact of his evident racism, he developed an obsession with mulatto Nationalist leader Pedro Albizu Campos. This personal involvement with events in Puerto Rico further biased his opinions on what he observed:

> ... the black-shirted thugs who walked the streets in gangs.... Their ambition was to seize the government and set up a black dictatorship in the Island. The organization was strictly fascist and wore all the trappings of the fascist gangs in power in Italy and Germany.... Most of Albizu's followers were colored boys.... The inarticulate rage of the Negro against the white burned beneath the false banner of nationalism. Representatives of fascist powers helped to feed the flames. (Brown 1945, 70–71)

The theme of political corruption has been constant through time. In the late 1940s, the last American governor described Puerto Rican politicians:

> The Puerto Rican políticos were on the whole not men whose distinguishing characteristic was a disinterested patriotism; they were hard, slick manipulators, without the least sense of guilt about a thoroughly demoralized Government.... But it would be a mistake to leave it at that; these bosses were supported by a vast love for Puerto Rico among the common folk, which no cheapening by fake political oratory and no betrayal could destroy. It was rooted in the island's hills and valleys, indestructible, native in the deep sense, and incredibly persistent. (Tugwell 1947, 82)

The widespread rejection of Puerto Rican colonialism became evident on March 8, 1945, when, in response to the onerous Tydings Bill, which proposed the granting of independence to Puerto Rico with only a twenty-year transition period in trade, independence activists surprised the US Congress with a document listing the Puerto Rican officeholders who supported the Tydings Bill. An American writer described what Puerto Rico was meant to become if the project was approved: "An abandoned orphan stepchild of nations, a waif and stray of the world; a lonely White Elephant of the Caribbean left amid tropical plentifulness to starve!" (Phillips 1936, 157). Even though Puerto Rican politicians were aware that the purpose of the bill was to punish them with a harsh independence deal, the numbers of those who supported the Tydings Bill were staggering: eleven of the nineteen senators, twenty-two of the thirty-nine representatives, and forty-two of the seventy-three mayors supported the Tydings Bill for independence. In all, fifty-seven percent of all democratically elected representatives in Puerto Rico had the independence project that was meant to scare Puerto Ricans with the possibility of independence.[15] Taken aback, Senator Millard Tydings soon retired from his project.

It was in 1948 when, for the first time, Puerto Ricans were allowed to elect their governor, which was Luis Muñoz Marín. He remained in office throughout the 1950s and only retired in 1964. According to a Mennonite author, the 1948 elections were as eventful as usual:

> There were speeches galore and arguments everywhere.... There were charges of bribery and various attempts at chicanery. One image that sticks in my mind is the trucks and buses that carried people to the polling places. These vehicles had brooms fastened to the front bumpers to sweep away any nails that the opposition party might have scattered on the road to prevent voters from getting to the polling places on time. (Luke Birky in Falcón and Lehman 2014, 54)

In the 1950s, Luis Muñoz Marín and his Popular Democratic Party (PPD) coalesced with the US government to enact a US Congress-approved constitution for the Island that allegedly ended colonialism and changed the official name of the Island to "Commonwealth of Puerto Rico" or, in Spanish, "Estado Libre Asociado de Puerto Rico," an obscure and contradictory term that translates as "Free and Associated State of Puerto Rico." With this approval, both the federal and the colonial governments falsely claimed before the United Nations that, due to this new "status," Puerto Rico was no longer a colony. The whole deceptive process once again activated the Nationalist Party under Albizu Campos's leadership, which organized an armed rebellion in 1950 and a series of attempts on the lives of the colonial governor (1950), the American president (1950), and members of the US Congress (1954).

Since, in the 1950s, the independence movement was still strong, the 1952 elections were held under martial law and intense repression. However, the Independence Party candidate was favored with nineteen percent of the votes and was the second-largest party.[16] Notwithstanding the facts, and up to these days, a majority of the leadership of the now decadent Popular Democratic Party (PPD, in Spanish) refuses to accept that Puerto Rico remains a colony. The importance of this denial was identified by an American journalist in 1960: "Never say 'colonial' in Puerto Rico where the term is, understandably, anathema" (Hancock 1960, 4).

In 1960, Earl Parker Henson, then consultant for the colonial government, penned *Puerto Rico, Land of Wonders*, an ode to the "Estado Libre Asociado," to Operation Bootstrap (see chapter 2), to the Popular Democratic Party, and to Luis Muñoz Marín, who he presented as a messianic figure:

> ... that relatively small Caribbean island—formerly a colony of the United States, but now its enthusiastic voluntary partner.... was beginning to give Uncle Sam a fine reputation ... because the Puerto Ricans have rolled up their sleeves and are making their island over.... In less than a decade Puerto Rico has become a showcase for U.S. decency in handling one of the world's former outstanding colonial problems....
>
> Before 1940 Puerto Rico was a colony, an "agrarian" society ... It was bankrupt financially and, to all appearances, psychologically and spiritually as well. Everybody could see and feel the suffering ... Then "the man" appeared. He stirred his people out of their lethargy, taught them political awareness and morality, and promised to set them on the tortuous upward road to their own salvation. (Hanson 1960, 9, 11)

In his absurd effort to portray Luis Muñoz Marín and the PPD politicians in the best possible light, Hanson tripped over his own contradictory statements regarding corruption. He goes from affirming that there was no corruption before Muñoz's government to mentioning that there was elections-related corruption right before it, all to end up proclaiming the end of all governmental corruption under the PPD:

> Puerto Rico's politicians have always been among the most honest to be found anywhere, as far as money is concerned. Virtually all of them, during and since the Spanish regime, maintained high moral standards in financial matters involving their personal integrity; every one of them died poor. The island has never experienced great scandals involving large-scale graft as opposed to petty pilfering ...

Nevertheless, before Muñoz Marín changed matters in 1940, elections were riotous displays of cynical dishonesty. Votes were bought openly and shamelessly and all the more easily because the men who sold them needed the money for their hungry families.... false registration, the use of floaters, the enlistment of the dead—were employed by the various parties with enthusiasm.

... the capitalist investors and potential investors who now flock to the island are almost unanimous in praising the Puerto Rican officials for honesty, hard work, dedication, and eagerness to serve.... no favors can be bought. Except for occasional petty pilfering on a municipal level, there is no bribery or other financial corruption in the government. Having been in close contact with Puerto Rico since 1935, I venture to say that the island has by far the most consistently honest government in the Western Hemisphere. (Hanson 1960, 66, 199)

Already in the twenty-first century, an American educator confirmed the importance and pervasiveness of politics in the everyday life of Puerto Ricans, as well as the festive atmosphere around election time that reflects a banalization of the whole process and its consequences in a colony where decision-making is ultimately minimal:

When the elected political party is voted out of office there are major upheavals in government. Many lose their politically related jobs and others take them. Puerto Ricans on the island take their politics seriously.... attendance at the polls is extremely high. Puerto Ricans are not only passionate about their politics, but they take their elections just as seriously.... I've never seen political parades like I saw in Puerto Rico. They consist of long lines of cars, blaring music, and megaphones blasting political messages. Often the people are walking alongside the caravans, passing out their literature as the entourage of cars and people winds through the residential side streets. Puerto Ricans ... like to march and carry banners.... These events often have a carnival type of atmosphere. In the United States ... We seldom use a parada (parade) of vehicles of loud obnoxious sound, winding through the neighborhood ... (Tavenner 2010, 176–78)

THIS CHAPTER

The US invasion reversed the autonomic government that Puerto Rico was inaugurating in 1898. From then on, the political relationship between the new empire and its Caribbean colony would be founded on mistrust. The general premise was that Puerto Ricans were not (and are still not) ready for self-government. The reasons varied over time: their culture, their mixed race, their illiteracy level, their poverty, their "enervating climate," the bad influences of Spain, etc. Puerto Rican politicians were deemed as corrupt, temperamental, fanatic, and lacking moral standards, and a decree was proclaimed: "republics do not thrive in the tropics."

Over time, Puerto Rico was governed through a series of congressional acts that did not change the colonial status of the Island in any meaningful way, as they all served the imperial needs of the United States and ignored the needs and wants of Puerto Ricans. And when Puerto Ricans protested against colonialism, their efforts were violently suffocated.

Chapter 5

"WE THINK WE ARE BETTER THAN OTHER PEOPLE"

On the Onset of the Relationships Between Colonizers and Colonized

BEFORE THE US INVASION

After its independence was attained from England in 1783, the United States of America began to have contraband commercial relations with Puerto Rico, then a Spanish colony. Both this commerce and its natural resources (sugar, tobacco) were highly coveted by the new American government, which began to consider ways to acquire both Cuba and Puerto Rico. Following a commercial agreement, the commerce of the United States with the Spanish colonies in the West Indies became official in 1795.[1] After Spain signed the Cédula de Gracias in 1815, an American consul arrived in Puerto Rico; by 1823, Puerto Rico acquired most of its imports from the United States; and by 1851, the Island exported forty-two percent of its goods there (and only 6.75 percent to Spain).

Several attempts by the United States to acquire Cuba and Puerto Rico through diplomatic negotiations were rejected by Spain, but this did not diminish their interest in acquiring the islands. They knew it was a matter of time and patience. Even before the Spanish-American War ended, and four days before the invasion of Puerto Rico, the US Government expressed in a press release published by the *Oakland Tribune* what their ominous intentions were for it: "Puerto Rico will be kept.... That is settled, and has been the plan from the first. Once taken, it will never be released.... Our flag, once run up there, will float over the island permanently."[2]

"WITH OPEN MOUTHS AND STARING EYES": THE US INVASION

In July 1898, the US invading army was gladly surprised by the joyful reception they received as they arrived in most towns. Aside from the Spanish-born minority and its loyalists, most inhabitants had great expectations from this invasion. The Puerto Rican elites expected to increase their business through the American markets and investors and to increase the level of autonomy recently conceded by Spain. The rest of the population wanted to be liberated from the oppression of those same local elites that exploited them every day in their sugar, coffee, and tobacco *haciendas*. Some Puerto Ricans have heard that the United States was a country of freedom and legal equality and expected just that for themselves. Naively, the Puerto Ricans received the Americans believing in their promises.[3] Indeed, a pair of American writers noticed that after the Spanish surrender, many Puerto Ricans shouted their expectations clearly: "... the people were wild with joy, and as they danced in glee at their emancipation from Spanish thralldom, they shouted: "¡Viva los Americanos! ¡Viva Puerto Rico libre!" (Browne and Dole 1907, 1460).

On their part, American soldiers were dumbfounded as they witnessed a war turning into a "big picnic," an idea that might have originated in war correspondent Richard Harding Davis's early book where he complained about how in the United States, the Puerto Rican campaign was unfairly regarded "as something in the way of a successful military picnic, a sort of comic-opera war, a magnified field-day ..." (Davis 1898, 296). Other Americans openly joked about it:

> The fourth town to surrender ... Juana Diaz ... Couriers announced the coming of the Americans to the people of the town, and a brass band came out to meet them. The vast majority of the citizens assembled on the outskirts of the town and as the American volunteers appeared the band played "Yankee Doodle" and other patriotic American airs, while the people cried: "Vivan los Americanos." ... A large number had presents of cigars, cigarettes, tobacco and various fruits which they loaded upon the soldiers, and many insisted upon taking the visitors to their homes. Everywhere, the American flag was waving. In the public square ... the crowd shouted: "Death to the Spaniards!" (Hall 1898, no page number)

> We had been through this triumphal entry business several times before; but I, for one, never grew tired of it. It was for all the world like being in the procession of a great circus. The sidewalks, balconies, windows, and roof-tops were packed with wide-eyed humanity, of all ages and conditions, hues, sizes, and degrees of beauty. At every street corner, and in every square, great crowds of the lower classes rent the air with vivas and bravos, regulating their enthusiasm by the size of the guns that swung past them. [In Mayagüez] ... At one corner a richly dressed

old woman threw handful after handful of small silver coins among us. In several places we trod upon great quantities of flowers thrown in out path by peasant girls. (Herrmann 1900, 67, 69)

A very interesting reception event was recorded by soldier Karl S. Herrmann from Wisconsin. As his brigade was parading from Calle Mirasol to Calle Candelaria in the town of Mayagüez, the band began to play "The Stars and Stripes Forever." Then on a balcony, "a beautiful young girl, tears streaming from her eyes, leant far out over the rail, and waved a crudely made Old Glory over the ragged ranks below" (Herrmann 1900, 68–69). Overwhelmed by emotion at the sight, the soldiers removed their hats, "and for the first time that day we split the heavens for a cheer, lustily and long. The outbreak was infectious, and from every side the clamor swelled and burst till it seemed as if the universe had vaulted into mad tumult at the touch of a girl's hand." He identified the girl as Catalina Palmer and commented that she later married an American lieutenant.

Another curious moment happened as General Brooke entered Caguas with his entourage, which included American war correspondent Trumbull White and his wife. No cheers welcomed the group until the Puerto Ricans noticed Mrs. White:

Then a murmur ran through the crowd that thronged each side of the street and filled every porch and doorway and window. "Una senorita Americana," "An American lady," and Mrs. White, who accompanied me, was the object upon which every eye was focused. Probably few of them ever had seen an American woman before and she was quite as much interest to them as even the general of the army. (White 1898, 349)

But their reception was not always that joyful. Occasionally, the troops committed excesses that changed the whole tone of the arrival of the US Army into town, and there was a sense of distrust emanating from some American soldiers who couldn't believe the generosity shown by Puerto Ricans could be sincere:

The reception of the Americans in Coamo was not as cordial. . . . Many of the people were on the streets and some shouted welcomes, but there was a much greater reserve than in places previously occupied. This was due, in great measure, to the misbehavior of some of the American soldiers who first entered the town. Some of them went into the stores and eating houses, seized what they wanted, and went off without paying for it. The result was that the stores soon closed, and it was not possible for anyone to buy a thing to eat. . . . the officers could not be identified. (March 1899, 429)

. . . there has been shown over and over again a willful malice, by a certain type of volunteers, resulting in ordering and cuffing the natives about, as if they considered them conquered animals instead of human allies and friends. This conduct, in a few towns, has thrown the volunteers out of touch with a people who, from habit, at least . . . are inclined to show courtesy and graciousness to the military. (Dinwiddie 1899, 150)

After these bad experiences, the invasion army established an important practice that several authors commented on: soldiers were required to pay in cash for all food or resources received from Puerto Ricans. This practice undoubtedly eased the relationships between American soldiers and locals, but the American shoppers still distrusted the good intentions of Puerto Rican businessmen on a regular basis:

Say "quiero" and the name of the thing wanted; then say "cuanto," and produce all the money you have, and permit the one with whom you are dealing to help himself to all he wants; then take your purchase and your departure, saying, "muchas gracias" (many thanks). This latter expression serves a double purpose. It gives the dealer an idea you are thanking him for what he has done for you; but it is in reality your expression of gratitude to a beneficent Providence that, out of your little store of wealth, that dealer has left you even a few centavos. (Robinson 1899, 59)

The elite classes, being either Spanish or *criollos*, were not enthusiastic at all about the US invasion, as revealed by the following testimonies. Sometimes, the American troops responded to the local elite's derision with violent attitudes:

Others shouted that the "Americano was mucha Bueno," but we noticed that the better class eyed us with stolid indifference, or frowned on us, but they, the well dressed, were so few and far between. . . . The aristocratic community were very much in the minority. Most of their houses were tightly closed and not a sign of life within or without, with a few exceptions, and the ultra-swell citizens looked down at us disdainfully, just as if to say—"Pouff, Yankee pigs, begone!" . . . This anti-American feeling on the part of the better class was so unexpected and so entirely in contrast to our San German conquest that we were nonplussed for the moment, but we recovered from our astonishment and removed our hats and smiled at the bevies of Senoritas gathered on the balconies in the immediate neighborhood. These young ladies only laughed derisively at our salutations or glared scornfully down at us. Our tattered appearance ... doubtlessly caused their ridicule, mingled with the feelings too, perhaps, that we were usurpers. (Oliver 1901, 98, 122–23)

During the actual invasion, most American authors described the locals either as submissive or indifferent. According to Frantz Fanon, the natives bypass the colonizers through their "belief in fatality," which allows them to "remove all blame from the oppressor," attributing to "God" all their misfortunes and their poverty. This allows them to bow down before the colonizers in "a stony calm."[4] We can only imagine the experience of these young American volunteer soldiers, many probably of humble origins, having, all of a sudden, the opportunity to feel like rulers:

> ... soon we were on the right side of the natives and had a small army of kids to fetch milk and eggs. All one had to do was to yell "Tokio" or "Teodor" or whatever the name of his special kid, and the milk or eggs would be ready for breakfast.... we lived high in our town of Aibonio, and were monarchs on all we surveyed. (Rossiter [1900?], 66)

> [At Guayama:] Men cheered and women cried; children ran like wild creatures, shouting as loud as their little throats would permit, "Vivan los Americanos." Their happiness knew no bounds and no one attempted to restrain their demonstrations.... They kissed the hands of their deliverers and fell at their feet to worship them. (Creager 1899, 156–57)

To encourage the good feelings of Puerto Ricans towards the invasion forces, three days into the campaign, on July 28, 1898, General Nelson A. Miles signed and made public a proclamation in which he, representing the United States, offered to protect and foster Puerto Ricans and to bring them "liberty," "justice," "humanity," "order," "liberal institutions," "prosperity," and an "enlightened civilization" as they "hoped a cheerful acceptance" of the US government by all Puerto Ricans.[5] Regarding this decision, General Miles wrote in his memoir:

> Before landing I was aware of the fact that there existed considerable disaffection among the people in the southern portion of the island and, as our force was so much inferior to the Spanish I deemed it advisable to encourage this feeling, and also to impress the people of the island with the good intentions of the American forces. (Miles 1899, 299)

Remarkably, we did find some aggressive reactions from American soldiers towards their gracious hosts right after General Miles's proclamation was made public. An American soldier seemed to believe Puerto Ricans should be forced to obey Americans through violence:

> Nor is it at all certain that the average inhabitant of Puerto Rico is worth cuddling, protection, prosperity, "and the immunities and blessings" accorded him by his new rulers. A thick, stout cudgel or a bright, sharp axe will be more effective than honeyed words in helping him cheerfully to assimilate new ideas; though no one will believe it here at home until the hurrah is all over and some of the truth gets into general circulation. (Herrmann 1900, 34)

A war correspondent observed that Puerto Ricans were impressed by the large horses that the soldiers rode because, as discussed in chapter 18, Puerto Rican horses were a lot smaller but sturdier than those brought by the US military. The tall Americans and their weapons, as well as the extravagant amount of supplies they carried and their heavy-looking uniforms, were likewise identified as awe-striking elements:

> ... large horses by the hundreds was something which they had never seen before. The people stood in crowds, with open mouths and staring eyes to see load after load of our big army horses and mules brought ashore by the lighters. Our tall and brawny soldiers were a type of men which they did not know. Our field-guns were new to them. The tons upon tons of supplies gave them a wholly new idea of national resources. (Robinson 1899, 34)

"AMERICANO MUCHO BUENO": GETTING ACQUAINTED

Right after the US invasion, some authors, under the protective cloak of writing for Americans only, embraced American imperialism and clearly stated the colonial intention and its inequality basis in an almost callous way:

> Porto Rico is and shall remain our very own. We have got her and we will keep her. The island is the best in many ways of the West Indies ... As to contiguity, those pleasant Danish islands, always for sale, are in the neighborhood.... The people of Porto Rico are of mixed races, and it is probable it will take them some time to assimilate Americanism even under the weighty expression of military authority.... Some of them may think reading certain interpretations by eloquent men of our Constitution, that it is a part of the contract implied when we took them

in charge that they are to soon have a call to be heard in our general government. We have firmly but kindly to make known to them that they are mistaken. The people of Porto Rico, we are sure, will contentedly remain with us, partake of the bounty of our good will, consent to the investment of our capital in the improvement of the island, and be taught by us . . . (Halstead, *Pictorial* 1899, 36–37)

The future exploitation of the hard work of the Puerto Rican lower classes for the benefit of American investors was clearly in the mind of American authors since the very beginning and kept being blatantly exposed as time passed: "The dense population promises abundant labor for many years, and producers will thus feel secure against outside competition. It will, of course, be no place for laborers from the United States, but for families of moderate means . . . Porto Rico will be the Mecca" (Olivares, *Vol. 1* 1899, 312).

Some American soldiers soon learned some Spanish in order to fulfill their needs at town stores, and they made Puerto Ricans laugh at their faulty utterances. Relationships between Americans and Puerto Ricans were commonly affected by language barriers and frequently illustrated Puerto Rican humor, as the anecdote of this English teacher:

One day I used a story of a small boy who went out into the woods to shoot partridges. I looked up the word in my Spanish dictionary and found it as chocha. . . . However, in Puerto Rico it is the coarsest of words for the female sex organs. . . . it took me three or four tries before I realized that something was seriously wrong. I went to Mrs. López with my problem. . . . From that time on my fate was sealed. I was known simply as Señor Chocha. As I walked along the streets at night, I would hear my newly acquired name shouted in feminine voices from balconies. The taxi drivers hurled it at me as they passed. . . . Over the walls of my house were chalk scratching announcing: "Señor Chocha viva aquí." . . . Worst of all, a letter was sent to the Department of Education stating that I had used "vile and obscene" language in my classroom. (Brown 1945, 120–21)

Right after the invasion ended and Puerto Rico became a US colony, as he reported on the Ceremony of Flags' Change in San Juan, a war correspondent reported the first fears of a not-so-welcome reaction from Puerto Ricans:

It was all a quiet affair. There was no excitement, and but little enthusiasm. . . . Here and there a native showed the new national colors, and a few householders and merchants displayed the American flag. Here and there one got an ungracious look; here and there a merchant was neither very alert nor very courteous in attending to the wants of an American customer. (Robinson 1899, 222, 225)

American soldiers noted how the attitudes turned colder as Puerto Ricans realized that they would stay after the invasion. The imperialistic tone is evident in their recollections:

That this [their enthusiastic reception] was only ephemeral was shown after a few weeks, by the diminution of respect felt and shown the Americans, when the novelty of the situation had worn away and they began to discover that the Americans were not there to entertain them or to enable them to spend the rest of their days in idleness, good-natured though they be.... "Americano mucho Bueno" is pleasant but cheap, and "Americano" will become to the populace "mucho malo" just so soon as Uncle Sam sits down to stay. (Edwards 1899, 110–11)

For a good many reasons I shall be glad to get out of Utuado. The natives here are getting too fresh.... They need a more dominant hand. When we got on the island, they were the ideal of subserviency; now they cheat us and steal from us. (King 1929, 89)

The violent behaviors and imperialistic attitudes of the American soldiers were commented on here and there but were dismissed as actions that would be a source of laughter in the United States, and that were overblown by "serious-minded Puerto Ricans":

In spite of the general good behavior of our soldiers there are some lamentable incidents of rowdyism. They were due entirely to the fun-loving disposition of our volunteers, and were not intended to be disrespectful or hurtful. At home they would have been dismissed with a smile or a laugh, as belonging to the ordinary run of camp life and the ebullient spirits of "young America." But they were viewed in a different light by the serious-minded Porto Ricans. (Olivares, *Vol. 1* 1899, 358)

[As a group of American soldiers arrived to a cockfighting pit:] The price of admission was usually a couple of centavos. We troopers never paid anything, but just walked by the box-office, and if the native made any objection would simply say, "Collect from Uncle Sam." The reference was sufficient. (Oliver 1900, 219)

An early incident regarding an elite family in Ponce was published in two local papers. A prominent physician there complained because his family, particularly his young daughters, were being accosted by a group of American soldiers to such a level that he was considering abandoning the Island:

> Said he: "In the past my family have always been able to attend mass, to walk on the plaza on a Sunday evening, and to sit out on their porch, which is on the second floor, without molestation of any kind from any one; but now my daughters cannot even sit at their own windows without being subjected to insult, much less go on the streets. Consequently my family are prisoners within the walls of their own home and it is my firm intention to remove them to a country where such things do not prevail." (Olivares, *Vol. 1* 1899, 359)

The American correspondent commenting on this case dismissed the complaint as "over-sensitive" since the soldiers' actions were just flirtation welcomed by the pretty daughters of the physician because "they all flirt." Besides, young men of Kentucky would never act improperly with women. He then concluded that Puerto Ricans must be jealous of the Kentuckians. Olivares' justification is quite telling:

> But there is a suspicion that this gentleman was over sensitive.... Some of the "insults" and familiarities that he so strenuously objected to were nothing more than innocent flirtations with his pretty daughters. In this particular the soldier boys were not entirely without encouragement, for one of our staff writers asserts that "the native women of the upper-middle class . . . they all flirt, and their feelings seem to be hurt if the men do not deliberately stand still and stare at them." . . . it was some of the boys of the 1st Kentucky Regiment that gave the offense, and no one in this country would ever dream of attributing anything but the most chivalrous courtesy to a Kentuckian. They were no doubt doing their utmost to please the girls and manifest their devotion to the fair sex. But their motives were misconstrued. Jealousy doubtless had much to do with the matter. (Olivares, *Vol. 1* 1899, 359)

In 1917, zoologist A. Hyatt Verrill described in detail the deep rift between the two cultures that forced Americanization was already fomenting. Besides the issue of the language, he perceived the rejection of the uppity attitudes of some Americans:

> But do not imagine because the island is an American colony that you will feel thoroughly at home in Porto Rico. Do not delude yourself with

the idea that you will be able to converse in English with everyone you meet, and don't go to Porto Rico puffed up with the importance of being an American citizen and expect to lord it over the natives, white, black, or brown. You will find Porto Rico as foreign, as strange, as incomprehensible in many ways as any European country.

... Moreover, you will find that with all our shortcomings as colonizers, Porto Rico is governed for the Porto Ricans, and he who goes about figuratively dressed in the American flag is looked upon with contempt and ridicule by Porto Ricans and resident Americans alike. You will not be in Porto Rico for long, ere you learn that the Porto Rican—white or colored—looks upon the Anglo-Saxon race with much the same feelings that the Anglo-Saxon regards the Latin and the man of color, and that to enter their social life, their homes—to get a real insight of the Porto Rican character—is as difficult a task for the American as for the rich man to enter the portals of Paradise. (Verrill 1917, 258–59)

As time passed, the American culture began to have an effect on Puerto Rican culture, and not in the most positive way, at least judging by the view of this young American missionary living in Aguadilla in 1907:

There is a class of all-sufficient, self-satisfied, swaggering Americans who always take it for granted that things American are necessarily the best, and they are no special ornament to Porto Rico.... what I see here is the shattering of much that is good and the substituting of much that is bad. The massive stone structures that the tropic dwellers knew so well how to build are giving way to flimsy American dwellings, pine boards and varnish are replacing polished mahogany and marble, the notes of the guitar and the serenade are now seldom heard and screeching phonographs fill up our Sunday afternoons. (Blythe 1911, 157)

"A MOST DELIGHTFUL AND HEALTHFUL WINTER RESORT": THE FUTURE

The vision of Puerto Rico as a future winter resort for Americans' enjoyment has been in the minds of several authors since the very beginning of colonialism there. Unfortunately, this was resurrected around 2008 when the federal government, as well as the colonial one, began to take steps towards turning Puerto Rico into a sort of "American Bahamas," a winter resort for the rest and entertainment of the rich.

This vision became evident when facing a financial crisis with a $70 billion debt, the colonial government in Puerto Rico decided to raise the taxes paid by Puerto Ricans while offering American and other foreign multimillionaires (through Act #20 of 2012) a guarantee of no capital gains taxes and a mere four percent tax rate on their businesses, as long as they moved to the Island with their investments and committed to creating jobs in Puerto Rico. This, in effect, has been named a "visitor economy" where rich foreigners come to spend their winters at Puerto Rico living in "five-star resort lifestyle . . . fully privatized enclaves . . ."[6] But as we can see, such a plan was only a modern version of the initial dreams of these early American visitors:

> The general healthfulness of the whole island gives rise to the belief that it will become a splendid winter resort in the future under the Stars and Stripes. . . . it will probably be the land of refuge when snow and sleet chase the rich from their homes in the great cities of the North. (March 1899, 460)

> Porto Rico in a very few years will chiefly stand to most of Americans as a charming pleasure resort, and above all a delightful place of winter residence. . . . The time is coming when Porto Rico will be a veritable Mecca for winter tourists, and health-seekers, of nearly every type. . . . Discriminating observers predict its destiny to be a great orchard and garden-patch for supplying the cities of the United States. (Hannaford 1899, 240, 245)

> Puerto Rico will, in a few years, be an ideal winter resort. The island is now a paradise, and when American customs, capital and cookery are introduced, and large hotels erected, it will be flooded with tourists. Just as the Bahamas are crowded every year so will Puerto Rico be a haven of rest for those who desire quietness and ideal scenery. (Oliver 1900, 214)

Then, after a decade or more, the view of Puerto Rico as a "winter resort" was less frequently found, but still in many minds: "The Porto Rican have taken hold of sanitary improvements with enthusiasm . . . and Porto Rico has become a most delightful and healthful winter resort. A new race of Porto Ricans, sturdy and energetic, is coming to the front" (McLean and Williams 1916, 109).

After the first years of contact, the relationship between Puerto Ricans and Americans, between colonized and colonizers, began to be looked upon as "difficult" and hostile, a hostility some American authors attributed to the racial differences, thus validating the colonizer's discourse of their superiority. Another source of conflict was what many US administrators complained about: the purported "lack of gratitude" of Puerto Ricans as they assumed that "what the United States touches she makes holy."[7] From that perspective, the Puerto Ricans were meant to be "forever indebted" to the United States and to Americans, a colonialist expectation that will crash with the colonial experience as seen from the Puerto Ricans' point of view:

> [In Barranquitas:] Here in this little Federal town I am, more than anywhere I go, a persona non grata.... It is saddening to be in a disliked minority, and to have children run from one, and hide, or call out saucy words at one. Some day it will be different. (Duggan 1920, 158)

> It is a civilization of one climate directing that of another. Difficult, indeed, is the task of bringing into harmonious action and destiny, two peoples that are unlike. Centuries will not accomplish it.... The Latin-Indian flavor will outlast centuries. (Wilson 1905, 127)

> In no other part of the Americas does one experience such antipathy to the United States and everything American as in Puerto Rico, nor does one hear such slanderous remarks against any people as against the Puerto Ricans by the Americans.... The continental Americans demand gratitude, adulation, and praise, but they receive suspicion, scorn, and hate. (Petrullo 1947, 142)

In the late 1930s, Wenzell Brown, an American teacher, included in his book countless hard-to-believe stories in which his students, as well as other Puerto Ricans, known and unknown, allegedly told him that they wanted to kill Americanos like him. Since he particularly despised members of the Nationalist Party, he frequently made them the "aggressors" in such stories. In one of his stories, he claimed to have felt threatened by several Puerto Ricans as he walked through the business district of San Juan. This author was extremely biased against Puerto Ricans, and his expressions actually illustrate the hatred *he* felt towards them, as he pointed out every unwholesome detail surrounding his "horrific experience":

> [As three beggars approached him:] ... I walked rapidly away, but they kept pace with me, alternately begging and heaping me with abuse. The boy grasped my coat ... I finally stepped on him. He let go then, screaming that I had killed him. A little crowd gathered about. I heard the word Americano and the threatening tone behind it.
> For refuge, I sought out a restaurant ... the waiter brought me the Coca—Cola I ordered. The glass was streaked with dirt and greasy

fingerprints were visible on its surface. He placed the glass upon a red-checkered tablecloth that was stiff with stains of food and drink.... this man came over to me. He was dressed in a torn, starched white suit and wore a battered straw hat. His skin was dark and deeply wrinkled. His eyes were brown beads of evil. Two yellow teeth projected like fangs from his lower jaw. The rest of the empty mouth was a bright red. "You are a stranger in Puerto Rico."..."It is beautiful. You think so?" "I just got in. I haven't seen enough." "Oh, so you don't like Puerto Rico." The evil face was thrust close to mine, so that saliva spattered across my face. "I didn't say that. I only said-." "Yes, but that is what you mean, I know." "Not at all. What I have seen is very beautiful." "Ah, that is better. Maybe you like to drink toast to Puerto Rico." "I'm sorry. I don't feel like drinking. I just got in and-." "So I was right. You are enemy of Puerto Rico." "Not at all. Okay, if you want to drink, I'll be glad if you'll have one on me." The little man sat down. "That is better."

[After drinking rum which "I managed to get it down":] "Now we will drink to the Republic." As if by magic, two more glasses were on the table.... and this time a bottle was brought to us. [Brown tried to refuse more rum.] "Drink," commanded the Puerto Rican and looked at his hand held beneath the table. In the hand was a razor with a straight, shiny edge. I looked to the waiter for help, but he stood stolidly at the counter, his face a mask of dull hostility. So I gulped the drink and then got to my feet to leave. The waiter blocked my passage. "Six dollars, please."... "But it can't be." "Six dollars," the man repeated loudly. His hand slipped to the heavy knife on the counter. I paid and got out. (Brown 1945, 16–18)

Undoubtedly, for those who came for longer periods of time, like English teachers, their adaptation to the new environment turned into a big challenge. In the particular case of an English teacher in Mayagüez, the rejection he experienced among the elite almost became fatal, as he ended up attempting suicide by slitting his wrists, after which he was sent back to the United States:

Dick said he thought people were staring at him, and undoubtedly they were. We were very conspicuous, so obviously not natives, and if people stare at you and then speak in a language you can't understand, it is easy to be paranoid. Though people may not be talking about you, how can you be sure, if you don't understand what they're saying? (Cooper 1994, 142)

A few American authors attributed the difficult relations between Puerto Ricans and Americans to some Americans who have been known by the term "ugly Americans" in reference to Americans living in foreign countries "whose behavior is offensive to the people of that country":[8]

> The relations between the American and the native workers are close, cordial, and brotherly, and friction is rare. As a professional gentleman engaged temporarily in Porto Rico said to me, it is the ill-bred, contemptuous, noisy, boastful type of American, commonly in Porto Rico as a commercial exploiter, who keeps the water of ill-feeling boiling. (Grose 1910, 217)
>
> One hears a great deal about the ill-feeling of the natives against Americans. As a matter of fact, there is a certain amount of this feeling, especially in certain sections, but the feeling is against the American Government and Americans as a people and not against Americans individually. . . . many of the officials we have sent out to Porto Rico have been men of little principle or ignorant, prejudiced, dissipated, or in other ways a disgrace to their country and their flag, and totally unfit to handle local conditions or affairs. (Verrill 1914, 136–37)

Even Wenzell Brown acknowledged, in his return trip to the Island in 1945, that a negative first reaction of Puerto Ricans toward Americans was easy to turn around and become a welcoming experience if the American made the effort and communicated in Spanish:

> [As he walked in San Sebastián:] Sometimes small boys would throw stones at me from the hillside, or the jíbaros would stare at me sullenly as they passed. Then I learned the magic key to their friendship—one simple word, "Buenos—good," a word of greeting and kindly regard. . . . The boys stopped throwing stones and brought me gifts of oranges and quenepas. . . . The jíbaros walked along with me, answering my questions concerning the names of trees and flowers; they took me to their houses to show me babies or a litter of kittens. (Brown 1945, 167)

In general, American authors never looked to Puerto Ricans as their equals. As representatives of the empire, they were at all times conscious of their "superiority" and expressed that position in their writings. Governor Theodore Roosevelt Jr. was candid enough to recognize this fact but only considered the arrogant attitude of Americans as "objectionable" if openly shown:

> We have one besetting sin in common with many other peoples, including the British. We think we are better than other people. Anyone who does things in different fashion from us is either comic or stupid. We

regard being a foreigner in the nature of defective moral attribute. A little proper pride is good for a people and far from objectionable. What is objectionable is showing it. Naturally this does not make us popular. In our case it has been the cause of endless friction between our country and the Spanish-American republics, whose people are both proud and sensitive. (Roosevelt Jr. 1937, 83–84)

The 1930s were a tumultuous time in the relations between the United States and Puerto Rico. A series of workers' strikes in the sugarcane, tobacco, and needlework industries was paired with a proindependence fervor that became evident in the colonial elections. The Nationalist Party and its leader, Pedro Albizu Campos, represented those who no longer believed that independence could be attained peacefully. At the time, an American writer tried to explain the friction as a result of too much "kindness" on the part of the empire:

Most Americans on foreign shores—officials or otherwise—become Mr. Fixits, missionaries by social profession. The Yankee traders follow the flag, lured by concessions. On first acquaintance we become warmly personal, and then paternal. . . . A flare-up follows the coddling. We become as cruel as we were kind. Perhaps the marines are called in to give the natives a beating. . . . and go about thereafter with an injured air and growing animosity. . . . We are so kind, and when they take full advantage of our kindness we are so cruel. We do not know how to treat simple children, especially foreign mixed or black children. It is a difficult job for which we are totally unfitted. (Phillips 1936, 155, 159)

In the 1940s, an American teacher, in telling the story of a coworker, realized that even the perception of generosity on the part of an American broke down prejudice and was immediately reciprocated with affection. After a student stole a pen and a pencil from Hilda, a teacher, the boy told her she should come to his house so that his mother could tell her that the pen and pencil were his. Hilda considered the proposition thinking that "his mother would probably agree that the pen was his; not because the mother was innately dishonest, but it was considered right to do wrong to Americans, who as a group were insulting and rude to the Puerto Ricans." During her visit, Hilda realized that the boy had convinced his mother that the teacher had actually given him the pen and pencil as gifts. This followed:

Tears stood in the grateful mother's eyes as she took Hilda's hand and said: "Vd. no es como las otras Americanas (You aren't like the other Americans) Vd. es muy buena, muy simpática (you are very good, very nice). . . .

Hilda didn't get all the words but she knew she had won their enduring friendship because of her "gift" to their son. (Dean 1944, 56, 60)

After over two decades of direct contact, but still showing an imperialist mindset, this American social worker began to see the potential of using Puerto Rico's Latin American culture as a bridge to reach Latin America:

Porto Rico is the natural meeting ground for Latin and Anglo-Saxon America and in this lies our opportunity to strengthen the bond between the continents, not through the Americanization of the Island, but by making it the center of exchange of knowledge between the peoples, the binding link in the chain of good will uniting two continents. (Mixer 1926, xv)

"IT IS AS UN-AMERICAN AS EVER": AN UNSUCCESSFUL AMERICANIZATION

Since the US invasion, and as expected, the US colonial government embarked on an Americanization campaign on multiple fronts, especially the schools. Its goal was not to prepare Puerto Ricans for joining the Union in the future but "to teach young Puerto Rican school boys and girls to love, support, and advocate for US colonialism on the island and to imagine themselves as members of the United States."[9] Along with the English language came American culture and industrial capitalism. Education was expected to create a force of obedient workers who would become eager consumers of American goods:

The American idea of advancing a people to a higher plane of living is to create a want within the breasts of that people. If it can be caused to want any given thing badly enough, it will find a way of acquiring that thing. So Uncle Sam figures that by educating these youngsters, he will create within them a desire for better living. He tries to plant always in their minds the advisability of the ownership of a bit of land, the benefits of work, the possibilities of farming, the need of participation in government. All this comes with the attendance of the American school . . . (Du Puy 1914, 113)

This process of Americanization was formally and actively implemented in Puerto Rican public schools from 1900 to 1949 when the US colonial government in Puerto Rico finally realized that the aggressive program was not bearing fruit. Between 1900 and 1948, most primary education was performed solely in English,[10] but this never turned Puerto Ricans into Americans, not even close. Leo S. Rowe, a political science college professor, envisaged the impossibility of successfully imposing an undesired Americanization on Puerto Ricans unless it was done through a slow process of education:

> ... the sovereignty of the United States was extended over a people speaking a different language, whose traditions were far removed from our own and who have been denied the invigorating influence of active participation in the affairs of their country.... We are in a sense strangers in their midst.... They have and will retain a mode of life and a standard of activity which is quite different from our own and which we cannot hope radically to change.... In Porto Rico we have come into the midst of a people foreign to us in manner of thought and distinctly European in their institutional life. For nearly four centuries the Roman law ... a highly centralized administrative system ... and the Roman Catholic Church....... it is evident that it cannot be changed at a stroke without seriously endangering the entire social fabric of the island.... if, in our contact with foreign civilizations in the West Indies, we show a harsh, unbending spirit, this feeling of distrust will develop into an abiding hatred, which will block effectually the fulfillment of our mission on the American continent. (Rowe 1904, xiii, 13–15, 18–19)

In 1914, an American explorer foresaw the absurdity of the imposition of English as the "official language" on a Spanish-speaking island, although he proposed an English-only solution:

> Although English is,—according to theory-, the "official language," yet those who speak it are few and far between.... Even the policemen in San Juan cannot speak the "official language" ... English is supposed to be compulsory in the schools, but comparatively few scholars ever learn their English, save in a parrot-like manner.... they will not and do not use the language if it can be avoided. If we are bound to Americanise the Porto Ricans, why stop halfway? Why not carry on all official business in English and make all documents in that language ... ? ... Moreover, although English is the "official tongue," we do not require native officials or employees to speak it. (Verrill 1914, 13–15)

But three years later, Verrill changed his opinion and summarized the absurdity of Americanization up to then, realizing that there were lessons to learn from Puerto Ricans:

In many ways Porto Rico has been Americanized, yet, save on the surface, it is as un-American as ever.... our schools have educated thousands of Porto Rican children ... but in speech, manners, many of their customs, and home life they are still Spanish to the core. And this is as it should be. We cannot expect the traditions, blood, ties, inheritance, and civilization of centuries to give way, to be tossed, aside and revolutionized, in a score of years or less. The Porto Ricans are of a different race than ourselves, and we should not be misled into thinking that any Latin will ever become Anglo-Saxon in ideas, thoughts, manners, or ideals—we cannot graft the palm upon the pine,—and, truth to tell, we could learn much to our own benefit and advantage from our Porto Rican neighbors. (Verrill 1917, 259–60)

During the 1920s, American authors already pointed to the superficial nature and outright futility of the Americanization process in Puerto Rico:

Porto Rico manfully strives to be American, but is as Spanish as a tortilla still.... unless you remember some of your Spanish, you may at time find it difficult to make your wants known in the island, despite the fact that the American occupation dates back more than a score of years. I cannot conceive how it happens, but in this prolonged period our country has done precious little to Americanize the island beyond making the place sanitary and compelling the shops to close on Sundays.... A Porto Rican here and there will claim to speak English—but in most cases he doesn't really, and often only pretends to understand because that is agreeable to you. (Marden 1921, 21, 147–48)

In 1944, an American teacher expressed her frustration with the absurdity of forced Americanization in public schools. In her view, the result was that students couldn't learn either English or the other subjects taught to them in that language:

Teaching in Puerto Rico was the most difficult and perplexing task I had ever encountered. It wasn't the children's fault. They were very bright and willing. Unfortunately the United States Government had ordered all text books and teaching from the sixth grade up to be in English. American teachers who were assigned to the sixth grade and up, had the dubious pleasure of not only breaking the little ones into the mysteries and intricacies of the sixth grade (remember fractions?), but also into the intricacies and inconsistencies of the English language. The American teachers didn't understand Spanish and the Puerto

Rican children didn't or sometimes wouldn't understand English. (Dean 1944, 69)

American anthropologist Vincenzo Petrullo got it right, as he was able to perceive the relationship between resistance to the English language and the colonial experience:

> ... the Puerto Rican child carries a burden far greater than any child on the continent. It is pulled in two directions by two different cultural traditions and two languages.... English is largely a schoolroom language for most of the Puerto Rican children, with little or no opportunity to employ it in everyday situations outside.... outside the schoolroom the Puerto Rican derives his intellectual food from Spaniards and Latin Americans. One suspects that the difficulty experienced by the Puerto Ricans [to learn English] may spring largely from the out-of-school reminder that English is a "must" imposed by a "tyrannical power." (Petrullo 1947, 68, 70–71)

Writing in 1993, this UPR—Mayagüez Campus's English teacher finally realized that Puerto Ricans would not learn the English language, even though he couldn't understand the element of resistance in this unconscious act:

> ... In later years, unfortunately, we got students who were convinced that they <u>couldn't</u>, learn English.... In 1993, when this is being written ... we realized that we were facing a much bigger challenge than we had realized. It was clear that no matter what we tried to do, it was not going to help much in solving the overall problem of English learning in Puerto Rico. (Cooper 1994, 69, 71–72)

More effective than the formal Americanization effort has been the arrival of modernity and, with it, of television programming from the United States portraying the "perfect lives" of implausible characters as well as the American consumerist propaganda with its newly conceived "needs." Eventually, cable TV and the internet magnified the effect of that consumption-oriented propaganda and introduced American values into Puerto Rican homes. A travel book's author commented in 1973: "History is still taught as it is in Pennsylvania, or Ohio, from the Yankee point of view. Only now are children being taught something of their own considerable heritage.... Thanks to TV, films, and advertising, they have had many Yankee ways grafted onto their own" (Rand, A. 1973, 49).

After almost 125 years of American colonialism, Puerto Ricans living on the Island proudly retain their language and culture. In 1991, then governor Rafael

Hernández Colón recognized in the US Congress that only twenty percent of Puerto Ricans spoke English.[11] In 2011, the US Census reported that eighty-five percent of all Puerto Ricans do not speak English "very well," and in 2013, it was reported that fifty-four percent of Puerto Rican public school children were not fluent in English.[12]

THIS CHAPTER

In 1898, the United States became a modern empire. For Puerto Ricans expecting full independence, or at least more autonomy than under Spain, the invasion was a big fiasco. The original enthusiasm for the US invasion soon crashed with reality, and promises proved empty. When Puerto Ricans realized that a new empire had taken over, and as American soldiers and others showed rowdy, rude, and uppity attitudes, they showed resentment. But, the US government kept on with their plan to get the most out of the Island's abundant cheap labor and fertile lands. Meanwhile, the dream of Puerto Rico as a winter resort for rich Americans began to come true.

For all these years, the US colonial government of Puerto Rico has been trying to elicit American patriotism from Puerto Ricans with little success. They have added American holidays and celebrations with American-style parades, marching bands, and baton twirlers, as well as constant displays of the American flag and other American symbols, but little of this has been effective. Evidently, after almost four hundred years of Spanish colonialism, Puerto Rican culture was already strongly and proudly defined as a separate culture from that of Spain by 1898.[13] Otherwise, it would not have been able to survive all the efforts made by the US colonial government to substitute it.

Chapter 6

"FROM THE YELLOW PINE OF CASTILE TO THE MAHOGANY OF AFRICA"

On the Racial Types and Social Classes

Although "race" has already been recognized as a fictional concept created by humans,[1] during the eighteenth and nineteenth centuries, racial conceptions and categories were widely discussed and were part of the ideology of the American authors hereby studied.[2] But American racial definitions will contrast with Puerto Rican ones. In the United States, "a black is any person with any known African black ancestry," a policy known in the South of the country as "the one-drop rule" since it meant "that a single drop of 'black blood' makes a person black."[3] This strict definition is unique to the United States and was "used to buttress the castelike Jim Crow system of segregation" in the South.[4]

In Puerto Rico, on the other hand, a person is considered Black if most of his/her physical characteristics are those common in a Black African person, mostly in terms of skin color, lips' size and shape, nose shape, and hair texture.[5] So, what matters in Puerto Rico is how the person looks (their phenotype) instead of the person's genealogy (their genotype). Also, in Puerto Rico, between the white and the Black, there is a continuous hierarchy of racial types, including such terms as "trigueño," "colorao," "grifo," and "jabao," with at least nineteen different racial categories.[6] Each of these racial categories is the subject of "the differential awarding of value, preference, social prestige, and opportunities."[7] At the same time, the terms "negro," "negra," "negrito," and "negrita" ("black" or "blackie") are common terms of endearment for Puerto Ricans of any skin color.[8] As an American journalist noticed: "In the Spanish Caribbean... 'black' in a certain sense is 'beautiful.' The word 'negro' (black) is often used as a term of endearment" (Wagenheim 1970, 17).

According to the 1899 US Census of Puerto Rico, 589,426 (61.8 percent) of its inhabitants were recorded as "white," and 363,817 (38.2 percent) were recorded as "colored." Considering these numbers, at the time, Puerto Rico had a larger percentage of white people than seven of the then forty-two US states: Virginia (61.6 percent), Florida (57.5 percent), Alabama (55.1 percent), Georgia (53.5 percent), Louisiana (49.9 percent), Mississippi (42.3 percent), and South Carolina (40.1 percent).[9] This explains why so many American authors considered Puerto Ricans "mostly white."

Happening just thirty-three years after the end of the US Civil War, the invasion of Puerto Rico itself was tinted with racism from its very beginning. During the invasion, General James Wilson specifically refused to include Black soldiers in the occupation army, requesting exclusively the "best American whites"; in this request, he was later joined by the Protestant churches, which excluded Black missionaries from their missions in Puerto Rico.[10]

After the US colonization, white skin and blue eyes became the ideal of beauty for many Puerto Ricans who, probably associating these characteristics with the superiority they provided to the person, praised babies who looked like an "americanito." This was grasped with surprise by an American anthropologist doing family research in rural Puerto Rico, who made this note:

> The woman of the house was telling of a family who had moved . . . The woman of the house was obviously Negroid and her visitor seemed white to me, but she remarked in the former's presence that the new family had such pretty children because they all had blue eyes, blond hair, and very white skins. The visitor said she wished her children had been as pretty as these, but unfortunately they had been "ugly and dark" as she was. To me, the woman was far from dark and could easily have "passed" in any white community. The Negroid hostess agreed emphatically with her visitor.[11]

American authors found themselves in deep waters when they tried to apply to Puerto Ricans the homogeneous racial categories of common use in the United States. In 1919, Texas congressman James Slayden established his view of Puerto Ricans: "We are mainly Anglo-Saxon, while they are a composite structure, with liberal contributions to their blood from Europe, Asia, and Africa. They are largely mongrels now."[12] Their templates didn't seem to fit in Puerto Rico, and they felt confused about what they had observed. The censuses said something, but their eyes told them something different; they couldn't easily decipher the categories for many Puerto Ricans who were not clearly either white or Black. This confusion is revealed in their descriptions of Puerto Ricans:

> The market people are almost as varied in color as the goods they sell. It makes a weird combination when three or four young peasant women

with flashing eyes, erect carriage, and well-rounded figures form a group and begin to chat. The yellow arm resting upon the bronze shoulder, the black hand patting the olive back, the copper fingers arranging the ruddy red hair around the white face, compose an off study in the variations of color. (Hamm, *Porto* 1899, 117)

[In Adjuntas:] The school next claimed our attention, and from what we saw the scholars were attentive and disciplined, though ranging in color from the yellow pine of Castile to the mahogany of Africa. (Cammann 1899, 247–48)

The racial classifications in the studied books vary. Authors frequently emphasized the presence of "white peasants" and disregarded the Black and mulatto presence in the mountains. Some clarified that the Black people and mulattos lived only on the coasts, which made them more visible to American visitors, even though they were far less than the white people: "To the casual visitor the colored element in Porto Rico seems to be a far more important factor . . . due to the tendency of the negroes to congregate in the coast towns. . . . As soon as one penetrates in the interior, the preponderance of whites becomes evident, the laborers of the coffee plantations almost exclusively being white" (Rowe 1904, 102–3).

Some American authors used statistics, like the 1887 Census,[13] to prove the predominance of white people in Puerto Rico, and some authors went further, insisting that the "African race" was disappearing:

. . . the pure-blooded African, black as the ace of spades, and ordinarily of magnificent physique. Few of these people are to be seen, though there is a colony at one end of the island. . . . But the African race is declining, and will eventually either disappear or be amalgamated with the white race. Whether this will produce a higher or a lower type of humanity is a question for the sociologists to settle. . . . The majority of the peons are whites, although there are many mulattos, and not a few negroes. They have good faces and are naturally intelligent. (Olivares, *Vol. 1* 1899, 287, 297, 299)

As late as the 1930s, American authors, like this missionary, insisted that the majority of the population of Puerto Rico was white: "I went to this island in the belief that it was honey-combed with negroes. I discovered, however that . . . one can travel through the interior of the island and seldom see a black face. In fact, I can safely say that the real native of Porto Rico is a blonde with blue eyes" (Harris 1932, 15).

Other authors, although just a few, celebrated the variety of tones of Puerto Ricans, as did war correspondent Margherita A. Hamm. Hamm showed that she paid careful attention to the variety of tones she observed in Puerto Rico, which she described with extensive detail, covering every possible skin tone:

> Owing partly to nationality and partly to the climate the complexion of the Porto Ricans is a trifle darker than that of the Spaniard, Portuguese or Italian. Probably the admixture of red and black blood has something to do with it; but the fact remains that they show greater varieties of brunette skin than any other people in the New World. Beside the orange-yellow of the mulatto there is a curious red-orange which is very striking. When this is combined with the reddish hair of Spain it makes a color scheme which is picturesque and novel if not beautiful. Young girls of this red-orange tint present a startling appearance when attired in low-cut evening dress of white silk or of black silk and velvet. The coloring is so intense that an ordinary brunette seems a sallow gray by contrast, and a northern blonde to be suffering from anemia. Another type which is very beautiful has an oval face and Spanish features in the outline, but Carib in the delicacy; soft brown eyes, a warm olive skin, and Spanish red hair. . . . The Moorish type is quite common, especially where there is a dash of African blood. This serves to make the eye darker, to give the corner a bluish tinge, and to change the pearly Spanish teeth into the whiter ivories of the Ethiop. To an outsider this Moorish type is lovelier than the so-called Spanish blonde, but the natives themselves seem to prefer the latter. Another complexion undoubtedly expresses physical degeneracy. It is a sodden brownish-gray which suggests ecru color in some faces, mouse color in others, and a long standing liver trouble in others. It is usually accompanied by small muscles, hollow shoulders and a bowed-in waist. . . . Some handsome types are produced by the crossing of natives with stronger-built blonde types of the northern races. This union tends to produce light-colored brunettes with brown hair, gray eyes, and fine physique. They are to be found chiefly in San Juan, Ponce, and Mayaguez. (Hamm, *Porto* 1899, 66–68)

And then a smaller group actually emphasized the Blackness of Puerto Ricans of all social classes:

> The people are dark in color, for even the Porto Ricans of the better class have a tinge of Negro blood in their veins, while the lowest classes show strong traces of Indian blood. (March 1899, 452)

The Puerto Rican will tell you that only 30 per cent of the island is colored.... Some place the figure with colored blood as high as 85 per cent. Such a statement angers the Puerto Rican.... The Puerto Rican with colored blood denies it hotly and is insulted by the term "colored." At the same time, he is insulted at any slur at the Negro. As he does not admit he is a Negro, he must conceal the real reason for his resentment under the subterfuge of being discriminated against as a Puerto Rican. (Brown 1945, 196)

Adding to these intricate racial definitions, in Puerto Rican society a Black person can become "white" since: "... money, 'good manners,' a 'respectable' lifestyle, and stylish dress could 'whiten' a person."[14] As is common in colonies: "The cause is the consequence; you are rich because you are white, you are white because you are rich."[15] Indeed, in Puerto Rico, a rich person is frequently called "a blanquito" ("a whitey") irrespective of the person's skin color, and a lighter-skinned mulatto can be accepted as "white" by members of the elite. Some American authors struggled to explain this:

If a man was upper class, the Puerto Rican knew the man would be "white," although interestingly enough, some of the "white" people in the upper class were darker than people who were not called "white." If a man were lower class, the Puerto Rican knew he might be of any color. (Fitzpatrick 1996, 146)

[When he was invited to a dance at the Yacht Club in Ponce] ... it was repeatedly told me that no Negroes or persons of colors were allowed in the club. I needn't worry.... I could not help noticing, since the subject had come up, that there were people who I was quite sure could not "pass" in Alabama or Mississippi. [The author mentioned this to another American teacher and] He laughed and explained that what they meant was that no <u>poor</u> Negroes could belong to the Yacht Club, or most fraternities. "There is a saying in Puerto Rico that as you get richer your skin gets lighter." (Cooper 1994, 57, 61)

An American missionary affirmed that the "persons of mixed blood" made a tremendous and "pathetic" effort "to be classed as whites," with a description that reminds us of so many Puerto Ricans who still go through the same efforts with the same purpose:

One of the pathetic features connected with the people of mixed blood is their desire to be considered white.... By a generous use of face-powder, by skillful dressing of the hair, by talking disparagingly of persons of negro blood, by explaining their own dark complexion as due either to the sun or to Indian blood, or to a dark-skinned Spaniard, they try to avoid suspicion themselves . . . (Fowles 1910, 60)

Frequently, the authors claimed that there was neither racial segregation nor racism in Puerto Rico. Such a perception was confirmed in 1930 by a Brookings Institution's research that concluded: "Race lines are not as strictly drawn in Porto Rico as on the mainland. Intelligent, educated, and forceful colored men and women are found in all walks of life, where they associate without apparent discrimination with whites."[16]

Although American authors were correct about the absence of racial segregation in Puerto Rico, they failed (probably due to the brief nature of their encounters with Puerto Ricans) to identify a racial prejudice that was, in fact, there. Clearly, their reference was the strict racial segregation that was strong in the United States since 1896, when the US Supreme Court legitimized, in its decision on *Plessy v. Ferguson*, that racial segregation laws for public facilities were constitutional as long as the segregated facilities for white people and Black people were equal in their quality, equality never provided and also never required except on paper. So, as they witnessed popular activities in which Black people, mulattos, and white people shared spaces devoid of conflict, their conclusions make sense.

In Puerto Rico, racism coexists, to this day, with intermarriage and racial confraternity, even though parents tend to resist the marriage of one of their offspring with a darker person and insist on the importance of "enhancing the race."[17] Black faces are just recently being seen in TV programming, banks, higher-class social clubs, beauty pageants, and elite schools. As a Puerto Rican writer explained: "racial prejudice seeps into the polite and democratic precincts of Puerto Rican society through the curious rejections and sudden exclusions of black Puerto Ricans."[18]

Even though it was not the kind of hateful and violent racism that Americans were probably used to witnessing in the United States, there was different access to opportunities for people of different skin colors. In Puerto Rico, racism does not generally imply hate. Here are some examples of how American authors understood the relationship between races in Puerto Rico, mostly in comparison with race relations in the United States:

. . . Puerto Ricans are considerably less color conscious. . . . On the whole, in Puerto Rico there has been a lack of any deep-seated racial prejudice which might have kept the Negroes and whites apart. . . . The Negro is not discussed in terms of fear, special virtues, or special faults.

He is simply a Puerto Rican, and is judged according to his individual merits. As a result, there are no race riots, no lynchings, no overt discrimination. He is given the same educational opportunities as any other Puerto Rican.... He lives where he pleases.... There is no self-consciousness on either side. (Petrullo 1947, 17, 20)

The students in the private schools, which were expensive, had lighter skins ... than the students in the public schools.... Bank teller had lighter skins than público drivers. But there was no absolute line drawn on the basis of race; it was family and money. Another Puerto Rican expression was that "Everyone has a grandmother in the kitchen" ... For most of them, their first experience with real racism was when they lived in or visited the States, and to most of them it came as a shock. They simply did not, or sometimes would not, understand the, to them, perfectly arbitrary distinctions that most Americans made on the basis of race. (Cooper 1994, 58)

Only a few American authors were able to perceive the social limits in the relationship between Black people and white people and the hidden racism of Puerto Ricans, and its relation to social class divisions, as they became explicit regarding the entrance into the local Casinos, which were not gambling spots, but more like the "social club" concept of the United States in which parties and other recreational activities were held for members and their guests exclusively, and which required the payment of annual or monthly charges:

In the schools, as everywhere else, the blacks and whites get along most amicably. A black man, the same as a white man, can occupy any position his intelligence or wealth may secure for him. Those with negro blood may even visit with some of the best white families. There is only one place where the color line is drawn. In every town there is a club known as the Casino, about which the social life centers. No one with negro blood is permitted to become a member of the Casino. (Boyce 1914, 444)

I gathered that the Negroes were a people somewhat apart in Puerto Rico, but less drastically so than on our mainland.... they seemed at an economic, or class, disadvantage compared to whites ... Some Puerto Ricans I have met have been critical of our race prejudice, but have not—or so it has seemed to me—taken corresponding note of their own class prejudice ... (Rand, C. 1958, 48)

In Puerto Rico's lower classes, the everyday reality was multiracial, and men of all races "worked, gambled, made music, and bet on cockfights together" while women of all races "mingled in the city's marketplaces, shared washing spaces at the rivers, and gossiped as they worked."[19] Since they also lived close to each other, multiracial sexual relationships and marriages were common. Of course, none of this was acceptable to the Puerto Rican white elite.

During the 1950s and 1960s, as hundreds of thousands of Puerto Ricans were encouraged by the colonial government to migrate to the United States, mostly to New York, in order to alleviate the high level of unemployment, they became confronted with a racial atmosphere that considered them "Black people" regardless of their physical appearance or economic status, and which they resisted. This was commented on by a few American authors:

> . . . if he travels to the United States . . . only too often he meets with a suspicion that all Puerto Ricans are colored, and if he shows negroid traces he may find himself humiliated by such incidents as being refused hotel accommodations. The Puerto Ricans who have moved to New York have been made color-conscious. This tendency to apply against the Puerto Ricans the prejudice which so many American communities express toward the Negroes is deeply resented. . . . It makes for bitterness against the country . . . (Petrullo 1947, 22–23)

"THERE IS BUT LITTLE CASTE OR CLASS FEELING": ON SOCIAL CLASSES

As anthropologist Jorge Duany established through his research, "Puerto Rican society is stratified in both class status and color gradations."[20] Frequently, social class and economic situation have more weight than skin color to establish the opportunities and challenges that a child will face in the future. As an adult, the selected occupation and family connections also influenced how a person saw himself/herself and how others saw him/her.[21]

In general, four social classes were identified by most of our American authors of the first decades under US domination; journalist Charles Morris presented them in most detail:

> The natives of the island are usually divided into four classes,—those who consider themselves the superior class, and rejoice in the name of Spaniards; the peasant class, usually called "gibaros"; the mestizo class, of mixed blood; and the blacks. During the period when Porto Rico was

a penal colony, many of the military men who formed the colonial garrison married and settled in the island, and it is their descendants who now constitute the upper or Spanish class. Some of these are wealthy and all of them proud, filled with Spanish opinions and prejudices, and manifesting all the stateliness of deportment of the Spanish grandee. From this class come most of the merchants, planters, and professional people of the island.

The lower class of whites constitute the small farmers in the country, and many who in the cities manage to support life by any labor that comes to their hands.... The black and colored population forms, with the gibaros, the laboring class of the island. They are in a minority, have been well treated, and seem thoroughly content with their lot.... There is a reason for this in the relations of equality existing between the whites and the negroes. (Morris, *Our Island* 1899, 190–91)

As usual in other places, too, the Puerto Rican elite was a closed social group whose members shared frequent social reunions. In the case of this Colegio de Mayagüez English teacher, he was accepted by the town's elite:

It was certainly a closed society. Before the end of the first semester, I could recognize almost all the faces of the people attending these dances ... No invitations were necessary for these parties or dances, because everybody knew everybody else and teachers at the Colegio, particularly the continentals, were very conspicuous. People you had never met before would start a conversation with you and within a few minutes it was obvious that they knew where you lived, what you were teaching and whether you preferred rum or Scotch. (Cooper 1994, 56–57)

The Puerto Rican-born white elite reunited the tradesmen, the *hacendados* who produced mostly coffee, sugar, or tobacco, the professionals, and the governmental administrators.[22] In general, they cooperated with the colonization of the Island because their interests matched those of the American elites. For sure, they did not identify with the poor Puerto Ricans: the workers and peasants.[23] Social classes were clearly defined based mostly on the level of richness or poorness of each person or family but with no direct animosity between classes. This was clearly perceived by some American authors:

Just as there is little or no race prejudice there is but little caste or class feeling. The high Spanish officials, military and naval officers, look at themselves as the aristocracy. Next to them are the large plantation owners and wealthy merchants, that is to say, the Spaniards. Then come the Spanish minor officials and the wealthy natives. Below these there are the middle classes, two-thirds farmer and one-third shopkeeper, and below these the laboring classes. (Hamm, *Porto* 1899, 69)

Interestingly, even though *hacendados* were rich, they usually had no capital beyond their land. Because of that, they had to rely on the tradesmen for credit, which allowed them to pay for the seeds, the labor, and other expenses associated with their agricultural production. When the harvest time arrived, the *hacendados* paid back the tradesmen with their crops, which they then sold in foreign markets for a profit. But whenever the crop was affected by one of the frequent hurricanes, floods, or droughts, a smaller harvest meant that the *hacendado* became indebted to the tradesman who might end up owning the *hacienda*. In such a system, therefore, even though they shared the social class, the real economic power lay on the tradesmen.[24] Indeed, after the US invasion, as the colonial government favored sugar and tobacco production over coffee, many coffee *hacendados* lost all their money; their social fall was discussed by an American missionary as she perceived it in Aguadilla:

> . . . there is something exceedingly pathetic in the shifting of scenes that is taking place in this little land. . . . . . . I have seen the wife and the daughters of a once wealthy plantation owner reduced to a mere shack of a dwelling, where they eke out a pitiful existence by making lace—a genteel but profitless occupation. . . . Their poverty has never affected their innate gentility or their dignity of bearing or their position in society. Their very presence is queenly and their pride unbroken, though they enjoy only the most meagre comforts of lie, the plainest of food, and the cheapest of clothing. Their patrician blood is as pure as it ever was and money cannot buy social recognition in Porto Rico, nor the loss of money rob them of the place bequeathed them by noble sires. (Blythe 1911, 155–56)

The Puerto Rican peasants were the lowest social class, the ones that had no land or any property beyond an occasional animal, such as a pig, a cow, a goat, or a few hens. They had no chance of progress regardless of how much effort they put into doing a good job in any of the Island's agricultural productions (coffee, sugar, tobacco, etc.) Historian Fernando Picó described the male peasant's life: "He worked hard, ate poorly, got sick often, had little access to medicine, and died young."[25] After the US invasion, most moved from working in coffee production in the mountainous part of the Island to working in tobacco (also in the mountains) and sugarcane production (on the coasts).

Regardless of their working places, their hard work was exploited every day, and their efforts and sacrifices allowed both the local and American elites to enjoy a life of privilege and abundance they could not even dream about.

Right after the US invasion, Americans visiting the Island struggled to understand how Puerto Rican elites of San Juan could live so close to the poorer classes without feeling disgusted. In the United States, even to this day, the inequality between the haves and the have-nots is spatial, as they occupy different living spaces altogether because of the neighborhood informal segregation. But class differences, although not violently confrontational, existed, and an American soldier seemed baffled at the elitist treatment of a servant by a local member of the elite:

> At the end of a ride of over twenty miles from Utuado to Arecibo, the gentleman from San Juan with whom I was riding, stopped and spoke to a native standing by the roadside with a trunk. When asked if the native was in trouble he replied: "Oh, no; that is my servant bringing my trunk to the station." The servant had walked that distance with the trunk on his head over a mountain trail, and no more was thought of it than would be of an express company here taking a trunk to the station. (Edwards 1899, 240)

On the other hand, the familiarity and commitment between servants and their masters captured the attention of this female author, who singled it out:

> ... the servants, as a class ... are models of rectitude. A man-servant will die in defense of his master or his master's guest, and a maid-servant will sit up cheerfully every night for a week to serve as a nurse for a sick visitor within the home. Wages are very small, and, in fact, many servants work for their food and clothing. ... When servants become sick and old they are not thrown out into the street, as it must be confessed is the custom of the more cold-blooded commercial communities of the North, but are cared for and attended to with as much solicitude as if they were aged members of the family. There is no prettier sight than an old retainer of a Porto Rican family. He glories in his weary days of service, in the virtues and accomplishments of his master and master's relatives, in the pedigree of his master's race, in the house, grounds, or plantation beyond it. (Hamm, *Porto* 1899, 96)

By the 1950s, as the modernization of the Island was fully in progress through the opening of hundreds of factories, an emerging middle class was identified by a college-level English teacher in Mayagüez who also commented on the elite students at the CAAM, establishing comparisons:

> The students were assigned to sections, in theory at least, by their abilities in English. The morning class was filled with the graduates of private schools, which meant money. One of them, who lived in Las Mesas, was regularly driven to school in a chauffeured Cadillac. More money meant better clothes, jewelry and elaborate hair-dos, and though by continental standards they were overdressed for the school room, they certainly looked good. They were lively, talkative, socially secure, and flirted outrageously with their English teacher, another new continental.
>
> My girls, being from public schools, were not quite lower class, or they never would have finished high school, but they were on the lower edge of the middle class which was just beginning to emerge at this time. This also meant that they tended to be darker-skinned, although it was impossible to draw any clear line. There were plenty of beautiful dark-skinned girls around, but not many in my class. The real problem was that they were insecure, timid and afraid to smile. (Cooper 1994, 25)

In 1970, Kal Wagenheim presented a more accurate depiction of the tribulations of the new middle class as it became entangled in a culture of indebtedness to sustain their "standard of living": "Most families spend in excess of their incomes. Credit cards, revolving charge accounts, and loans for vacation trips are now common in Puerto Rico" (Wagenheim 1970, 120). Wagenheim also provided a portrait of the Puerto Rican elite class and its activities by the end of the 1960s:

> For business and relaxation, the wealthy travel often to the United States. They may have a second home or small farm in the countryside; some... involved in... paso fino horses. Others maintain yachts... or swim or play tennis at private clubs, or join the clubs of the more prestigious hotels...
>
> The children of the upper class attend private schools; many of them study abroad. They have larger church weddings and receptions, the costs of which are usually exaggerated.... As women grow older and raise a family, they become active in civic, cultural and charitable organizations in much the same way as their wealthy American counterparts. The men still congregate with the same "crowd" for business luncheons.... Puerto Rico's upper class are known as blanquitos... by the poor, many of whom are also white. (Wagenheim 1970, 186, 188)

"A SON OF THE SOIL": THE *JÍBARO*

Although the *jíbaros* constitute neither a race nor a social class per se, they are a collective that was understood by the Spanish colonial government as an inhabitant of the mountainous center of Puerto Rico. They were perceived as ignorant but also as shrewd.[26] As the basic laborer in the coffee and tobacco plantations and later also in the sugarcane cutting, several American authors became interested in the *jíbaros* and described their values, attitudes, and appearance. These medical doctors portrayed them as hard workers surviving under harsh life conditions:

> [The jíbaro] . . . is a squatter and does not own the land upon which he builds his modest house, nor does that house cost him anything save the trouble of building it. . . . The food of the jibaros is poor in fats and the proteids are of difficult assimilation, being of vegetable origin, as a rule. . . . The jibaro, mountain bred, avoids the town whenever possible, avoids the genteel life of a higher civilization to that of his own. He instinctively tucks his little hut away in the most inaccessible spots; he shrinks from the stranger and lapses into stolid silence when brought face to face with things that are foreign to his life. He does this because he has been made to feel that he must do all that he is told to do by established authority, and he knows that this authority never takes the trouble to look for him unless it expects to get something out of him; because he is suspicious of outsiders, having been too often led astray by false prophets and disappointed by broken promises; because he realizes that he is not a free agent anywhere save in the mountain fastnesses. . . . The jibaro is respectful and obedient, fearful of the law and never defiant of his superiors; he is generous to a fault, sharing with any wayfarer his last plantain; he is devoted to his family and to his friends. . . . Care must be taken in deducing facts from questioning a group of jibaros even in the most unimportant matters. They are tremendously suspicious and generally let someone amongst them who is "leido" (one who has established a local reputation for worldly wisdom) speak for them. . . . In spite of this lack of knowledge of the world above him he has one quality which is his ever ready defense, his astuteness. (Ashford and Gutierrez 1911, 12–15)

Other American authors, like this travel writer, disparaged Puerto Rican *jíbaros* as lazy, primitive, backward elements who needed to be modernized, even against their will, if necessary:

The "gibaro" is a happy, careless, child of Nature. His peasant ancestors in sunny Spain were not unmindful of the delights of "dolce far niente," and their descendants are past-masters in the art of loafing.... Their manner of living is not far removed from a primitive state. Their cabins are the crudest kind of dwellings.... A plantain grove, or a clump of coffee trees, affords sufficient subsistence. Like the early Borinquenos, they display a disinclination to exertion unless it be in the pursuit of amusement, and find their chief enjoyment in swinging in their hammocks, twanging a guitar, and puffing a long, home-made cigar. They have a passion for gambling.... The "gibaro" is above all things a son of the soil. Confined to the city he would pine and die. He loves the free life of the country-side with its good-fellowship and utter absence of all conventionality.... As a plantation laborer the "gibaro" is intermittent.... He is self-supporting and law-abiding.... Hope has been expressed that education may in time raise the "gibaro" to the status of the American farmer, and so it may—in time; but there are serious difficulties in the way of such a consummation.... The "gibaro" cannot conceive of anything better than his own life, with which he is perfectly satisfied, and it would be difficult to persuade him that it could be improved upon. (Forbes-Lindsay 1906, 97–99)

But over time, the *jíbaro* became a symbol of Puerto Rican pride. In 1940, the profile of a *jíbaro* with a traditional straw hat became the symbol for the Popular Democratic Party (PPD, in Spanish), a populist party that dominated local elections from 1940 to 1968, thus consolidating the *jíbaro* image as the symbol of all Puerto Ricans.[27] Thus, in his 1947 memoirs, the last American governor described the *jíbaros* as people full of dignity who would never whine about their problems or ever expect to receive more than they deserved:

Their bellies may be empty, or relatively so, for the killing day they have to put in, but if you stop one of them on the road or talk to him in the field, you do not find him feeling sorry for himself. You find him full of the ancient wisdom unlettered men always have, and full of mental contrivances for getting the best of his difficulties. Or perhaps, because half-starved or sick, he is merely numb. But he doesn't ask to have guaranteed more than the usual minimum of goods which, just as a human being, he thinks due him. (Tugwell 1947, 42)

To emphasize the proverbial wisdom of Puerto Rican *jíbaros*, Governor Tugwell included in his memoirs the following anecdote narrated by a Puerto Rican military man:

> ... two scientists—weather-bureau men ... who came to Puerto Rico in 1918, just after the disastrous hurricane and tidal wave, to study the effects of the storm and to gather reports of its character in progress. They stayed for a while at a mountain finca and rode out daily, accompanied by a local jíbaro as guide, on inquiring journeys into remote districts. One bright blue morning, as they prepared to leave, their guide for the day objected; there would, he said, be a severe storm presently and they would better wait until it had passed. The scientists, who after all were weather men, had another look at the innocent sky, consulted each other in a look, and decided that this was absurd. They went on their way. They were, however, drenched within an hour and had a really difficult time with suddenly deep streams and slippery trails. When finally they got back, they asked their country friend how he had known. "That, senores," he had said, "is simple. The donkey went under the mango tree. That, as everyone knows, means that a storm will come soon." "Everyone," General Esteves reported one of the investigators as saying, "but us. Perhaps we'd better retire from a country where the donkeys know more than the scientists." (Tugwell 1947, 118)

Over time, and as there were less and less *jíbaros*, the connotation of the word "jíbaro" began to change. Modernity made obsolete many of the core values of this class, as Kal Wagenheim analyzed in 1970:

> Today, the word "jíbaro" has two meanings. Among the urban poor ... is a hick, an ignorant, naive man, not to be emulated. But the Puerto Rican who has "made it" ... often likes to describes himself as a jíbaro at heart ... a solid person. ... To Puerto Ricans who has successfully moved to the city ... the jíbaro is ... the honest man, the man with both feet firmly planted on the soil, the man whose lack of schooling does not deprive him of a native shrewdness and wisdom ... (Wagenheim 1970, 218)

THIS CHAPTER

American invaders and visitors discovered that, in Puerto Rico, their strict racial definitions made no sense. There, they encountered a society with racial prejudice but without racial segregation, racial conflicts, or racial hate. They insisted on describing the inhabitants as "mostly white" in comparison to other Caribbean islanders, partly to secure support from continental Americans for the colonization, Protestant evangelization, and "civilization" of the promising Puerto Ricans.

Within the Island, racial differences provided different economic and social opportunities, but it was not until they migrated to the United States, where they were treated as despised racial minorities, that Puerto Ricans were confronted with their own "racialization." After suffering racial aggression, many realized that they would never be treated as equals by the American government or its people.

Chapter 7

"SONG, LAUGHTER AND MAÑANA"

On the Myth of the Lazy Puerto Ricans

The trait of laziness has been assigned to colonized people all over the world whenever colonizers needed an excuse or justification for their control and privilege. But it also justifies their exploitation. Albert Memmi explained the usefulness of the myth of the "lazy native" for the colonizer:

> Nothing could better justify the colonizer's privileged position than his industry, and nothing could better justify the colonized's destitution than his indolence. The mythical portrait of the colonized therefore includes an unbelievable laziness, and that of the colonizer, a virtuous taste for action. At the same time the colonizer suggests that employing the colonized is not very profitable, thereby authorizing his unreasonable wages.[1]

The control that first the Spanish Crown, and then the American absent corporations, had over the most cherished thing for the Puerto Rican peasant: the land, and over the industry that employed him, further fed in him a known colonized attitude "where work is not seen as a personal benefit. As a consequence, an attitude of resentment is inappropriately transferred toward work. The problem then stops being the colonizers and becomes work itself."[2] On this, a few American authors commented:

> Porto Rico is a land of perpetual sunshine ... of poverty in the extreme, where work is considered a disgrace and self-indulgence is the order of the day. (Guernsey 1903, 122)

> ... there is considerable truth in the complaint that the jíbaros now are interested only in money. They no longer have any real love for the land, or any sense of responsibility to it ... since [the soil] neither belongs to them nor gives them a satisfactory livelihood. (Petrullo 1947, 143)

Already in the eighteenth century, the Puerto Rican elite complained about the "idleness, laziness, indolence, and sloppiness" of the lower classes.[3] According to historian Gervasio García, the Puerto Rican elites of the late nineteenth century kept complaining about the peasants' "laziness" and "lack of will." They already enjoyed and thrived in a racist and colonial society, and García sustained that this is why these elites supported the invasion.[4] But this Puerto Rican elite, so severely criticizing the *jíbaros* for being "lazy," was soon disparaged by American writers for their lack of "working ethics." This is not surprising since American Puritanism considered time "as a precious gift from God which has to be used. There is no greater sin than to waste the time."[5]:

> The Porto Ricans have not yet learned the dignity of labor.... Their ideas ... disdain the appearance of work. The gentleman and the lady do not work themselves—they merely direct their servants. To carry a package on the street is indicative of either poverty or lack of breeding.... To do any kind of housework cannot be considered by the lady of the house. She sits in the parlor dressed in loose garments and spends much of the day in idly rocking to and fro in a rocking chair. When she goes out shopping, she is either accompanied by a servant who carries her small purchases, or she hires a boy to carry them for her.... A woman in good social standing is not expected to do any work that can be done by a servant.... The merchants ... object to performing work that can be done by an employee.... menial tasks are for common workmen.... The farmer ... mounts a horse and rides around telling his laborers what work must be done. (Fowles 1910, 51–53)

A review of the working conditions prevalent in the coffee milieu during the last half of the nineteenth century reveals that, at the time of the US invasion, sixty percent of Puerto Rican laborers worked in coffee production, as analyzed in Fernando Picó's thorough review.[6] Coffee production was conducted in small and medium-sized lands where the labor came from the owner's family and from the "agregados." These *agregados* were landless Puerto Ricans who were allowed to live on the landowner's property in exchange for their labor, as well as that of their wives and offspring. Also known as "arrimaos" or "peones," they were the majority of the rural area inhabitants.

In most cases, the *hacendados* owned stores known as "tiendas de raya," where they sold all kinds of necessities, from rice and beans to gas, clothes, and machetes. They usually paid their laborers with valueless tin tokens or vouchers that could only be redeemed in their stores, where the *hacendados* also received a profit on every sale.[7] This system chained the laborers to a specific *hacienda* since, as long as they had debts in that store, they could not move, and because they only had a place to live within the confines of that *hacienda*. Besides this, which clearly shows exploitation, the work itself was a hard one; the coffee trees had hidden perils within their branches: wasp nests, albayaldes (*Wasmannia auropunctata*, a small fire ant that has a very painful and long-lasting bite), and plumilla moths (*Megalopyge krugii*, a very small "flannel moth" endemic of Puerto Rico. With the movement of the coffee tree limbs, its larvae fall onto the coffee-pickers; among its long white hairs, there are thorns provided with a liquid that causes pain and burning of the skin).[8]

According to Picó, even three-year-olds engaged in this work for which their families were paid per almud, a measurement based on a large cracker can that was equivalent to about five gallons or 18.9 liters. The families worked between ten and twelve hours per day at harvest time, and they commonly earned less than one peso per day since the *hacendados* paid merely cents per almud (fourteen cents in 1917).[9] With such low wages, it is not a surprise that the laborers barely ever ate meat or drank milk, resorting to plantains and roots to survive. This reality of coffee workers' lives contrasts the bucolic description made by these American writers:

> . . . the little army of coffee-pickers may be seen coming out of the odd-looking thatched-roof huts on every hand, some with gray heads and wrinkled faces, others with hair that vies in hue with the raven; some moving with quick, elastic steps, others trudging laboriously toward their scene of toil; some mere children clad at the most in a single strip of faded cloth, others with raiment, though sadly torn and tattered, speaking a kinder word for human decency; some bright-eyed, comely girls, stopping now and then to whisper a secret to a companion or to cast shy glances at some dusky swain, some with snatches of song on their lips, others with low murmurs of discontent, all carrying slung over their shoulders by a band a small basket to hold their pickings, or with these home-made utensils balanced upon their heads, as they swing carelessly along. Altogether it is hard to match this train for its rare mixture of pain and pleasure, of peace and poverty . . . (Browne and Dole 1907, 1412)

Why would an exploited worker want to work more efficiently every day? What difference will it make if he/she does not receive at least a reasonable part of the benefit of his/her hard labor? Some American authors suggested that Puerto Ricans were hard workers whenever they received fair remuneration and that low remuneration engendered poor-quality performance on their part:

However, the at first sight apathetic and weak jíbaro, when roused to exertion or when stimulated by personal interest or passion, can display remarkable powers of endurance. Notwithstanding his reputation of being lazy, he will work ten or eleven hours a day if fairly remunerated. (Van Middeldyk 1903)

The "jíbaro" . . . While he is accused of working only four days a week, it must be remembered that he has no incentive beyond providing for a day-to-day existence. The landed proprietors do not permit the peons to own real estate, and they can be dispossessed from their wretched huts on short notice. What incentive is there . . . ? (Boyce 1914, 421)

A nation founded on Puritan-Calvinist values, the United States society of the nineteenth century looked down on all activities that distracted people from working. The Puritan work ethic was based on "the calling," meaning that each person had a calling from God to perform a particular vocation and that his/her devotion to those duties was a measure of his/her devotion to God, as well as evidence that the person has been "selected" by God to be saved.[10] Added to this was the fact that Puritan-Calvinists believed that the entire society had to obey their rules and work hard every day because if just one person disobeyed, that sole person could bring calamities to the whole society as a punishment from God. So for many of our American authors, as shown in other sections of this book, dancing "wildly," flirting, gambling, cockfighting, or even laying in a hammock for a siesta were all evidence of idleness or laziness and, therefore, inappropriate behaviors. As a war correspondent put it: "Industry also has much to do with the morality of a nation. Idleness promotes degeneracy and crime. Busy peoples have always possessed the highest standards of morality" (Olivares, *Vol. 1* 1899, 362).

The low level, at least according to US standards, of cultivated lands for commercial purposes, as well as the "contentment within poverty," was attributed to the "apathy" of Puerto Ricans, who had "low aspirations" improper of American capitalism: "This limited cultivation is in a measure due to the lack of energy and ambition on the part of the native people. But beyond that and operating as a factor in the apathy of the natives, has always stood the lack of encouragement to greater activity" (Robinson 1899, 133).

American authors sometimes went to ridiculous extremes as they pointed out "Puerto Rican laziness." Such is the case of war correspondents Albert G. Robinson: "Men, women, and children appear to occupy the bulk of their time in eating mangoes . . ." (Robinson 1899, 39), and Margherita A. Hamm who, when discussing the possibility of Puerto Rican elite women riding bikes, sentenced: "It is not probable, however, that this healthful sport will ever prove really popular in Porto Rico. It requires too much energy and industry from the riders" (Hamm, *Porto* 1899, 133).

Many American authors, like this missionary, ranted about the inefficiency of Puerto Rican laborers and considered reprehensible their work habits:

> How to keep a washerwoman was one of the problems of housekeeping in Porto Rico.... she could never be depended upon to return on Monday to begin the week's wash. Sometimes the whole week will go by and the woman would not come. Always having some, to her mind, perfectly good excuse. After a while Mrs. Jordan hit upon the happy expedient of keeping back on Saturday a part of the pay for the week's wash till the next Monday morning.... This worked like a charm. (Jordan 1922, 158)

And if the typical peasant was accused of perennial laziness, much more so was the Puerto Rican oligarch:

> Everywhere throughout the length and breadth of the city is this languorous, sedentary element emphasized, personified.... The average denizen of San Juan is a silent, but most eloquent, exponent of habitual somnambulism. He appears to be perpetually wrapped in slumber. I have sometimes thought his ambulatory hours, if anything, the more restful, because therein he never need so much as dream of having to work.... I took occasion to inquire of a certain scion of this insouciant aristocracy what he considered the most violent tax on his exertions... he replied: "Acostarme en la noche y levantarme en la manana"- climbing into bed at night and crawling out in the morning. (Olivares, *Vol. 1* 1899, 257)

Over time, different American missionaries concluded that the reason why vocational schools were not successful in Puerto Rico was because "manual labor" and "education" were opposite terms there, as Puerto Ricans allegedly understood that the only role of education was precisely to avoid manual labor:

> Vocational schools, which were emphasized in the earliest public school policy... have been completely abandoned.... The reason for this abandonment is interesting and throws a flood of light on the Porto Rican character and situation.... The Porto Rican idea of education is entirely academic. Schooling is supposed to prevent the necessity of manual labor and to look toward the professions.... the normal American respect for labor will be slow in impressing the Porto Rican, if he never has the

opportunity to see the average American, self-respecting in his daily toil. (Douglass 1910, 22–23)

In the eighteenth century, Fray Iñigo Abbad y Lasierra posited that Puerto Ricans' indolence responded to the fertility of its land, which made it unnecessary to work too hard in order to obtain basic needs. The idea of the effect of climate on people was commonly discussed in Europe during the eighteenth-century Enlightenment by thinkers such as Charles de Secondat Montesquieu, who insisted that because nature is bountiful in hot climates, it renders men indolent and passive since all their needs are easily satisfied with the plentiful fruits of earth; in a similar fashion, since in cold climates food is scarce, men there are forced to be more self-reliant and to work more.[11] This position is also frequently found in the studied books, where they blame a prodigal tropical nature for the "laziness" of Puerto Ricans. As Abbad y Lasierra, many American authors implied that Puerto Ricans lived comfortable lives, in abundance and without needs, "choosing" to sustain their families on plantains and breadfruits, when in reality, they lived in constant poverty and usually could not afford even the simplest medical care. Some proposed education on the "benefits" of the accumulation of property will help:

> Life for both sexes and all grades in Puerto Rico is a rose, a kiss, and a cigarette; song, laughter and mañana. The island is, unequivocally, a Paradise; and, if I remember rightly, dwellers in paradise are not expected to labor. These people amply fulfil the expectation. (Herrmann 1900, 37)

> The climate and geographical condition of Porto Rico have never provided the laborer with any incentive to economize, inasmuch as he has no need for providing against a period of cold, and Nature produces some form of plant or vegetable food throughout the entire year. Clothing and lodging may be of the simplest and still prevent much suffering and with physical weakness caused by disease, the tendency is to live for the present, and to take little care for the future through a system of saving and economy. The average manual laborer saves nothing and makes little effort to accumulate property. Incentive must be provided through education which will accustom the countryman to the idea of accumulation of property in a small way . . . (Fleagle 1917, 73–74)

But this alleged "laziness" of the Puerto Rican peasants had more to do with the difference between Latin American and US American cultures (one communal, with a carpe diem attitude, and the other individualistic and based on fierce competition), and with the different stages of capitalism of the two economies (one precapitalist[12] and the other industrial capitalist) than with a moral defect or racial inferiority on the part of Puerto Ricans. Puerto Rican peasants living as *agregados* in the *haciendas* had access to small plots of land where they worked to develop subsistence agriculture, harvesting plantains, breadfruits, mangos, bananas, avocados, and edible roots, as well as to raise hens, goats or pigs for their daily sustenance. For a capitalist system, this kind of independent life was a threat because capitalism needs large numbers of cheap wage workers whose surplus can turn into capital and who can be turned into avid consumers of all kinds of goods. As a result, the independent and simple way of life of the peasants was attacked:

> On the whole, Puerto Rican society was not capitalistically minded. Capitalism demands a particular discipline of thrift, and acceptance in ... the Jewish—Protestant tradition. [In Puerto Rico] the tendency was to spend what was earned. ... The cultivation of the art of living was far more important than the business of living, so work naturally took second place. ... Satisfaction of the spiritual needs of man took precedence over the physical. (Petrullo 1947, 129)

Historian G. García agreed that the attitude of Puerto Ricans toward work was a result of them living in a precapitalist economy.[13] Long before the US invasion, there were complaints made by different contractors regarding the absenteeism of Puerto Rican workers and their "nomadic" lifestyle. In essence, what they didn't have was a capitalist working discipline. García explained:

> Workers, accustomed to the irregular pace of agricultural work, can hardly adopt strict labor discipline. The intermittent and seasonal work in the sugar plantations creates attitudes and work habits that clash with ... [those of the] industrial worker. ... [The workers] had other options besides [their] salary, such as working on the small property, which would allow them to supplement their wage income.[14]

In 1927, though, an American missionary valued this same lack of capitalistic drive for the acquisition of material goods, deeming it "refreshing." Having lived in Puerto Rico for thirty years, he understood the Puerto Rican lifestyle:

> It is refreshing to find a people whose standard of success is not accumulation of material property, and who will put up with all kinds of political inconvenience provided they are able to live in comfort with family and friend; yet, on the other hand, it is disappointing to see so few

native leaders develop. Of good ideas and theories there is not dearth, but the will to put them into effect is lacking. (James 1927, 16)

José de Olivares, who was writing to report on the investment opportunities available in Puerto Rico, also went against the current and praised the laboriousness of Puerto Rican workers:

> Americans who have employed them say that they are excellent workers, and that they are glad to do all they can to earn their money. They work from sunrise until sunset, and are as reliable as the average American workmen. Some trouble is had as to the numerous holidays and feast days which have been customary, but the most of the men will do to their work irrespective of these, asking for Sunday only.... As laborers and mechanics they excel those of many of the more favored nations. It is a fact that the Porto Rican masons, blacksmith, etc. are superior in their various branches to similar workers in nearly every part of the civilized world.... The people, as a rule, are industrious and willing to work if given an opportunity; and in every instance those employing them speak in terms of commendation of their faithful earnestness. (Olivares, Vol. 1 1899, 299, 332, 345)

Armed with science to prove their point, in 1911, a pair of physicians, an American and a Puerto Rican, debunked the image of a lazy peasant laborer, instead describing how much they contributed with their labor despite their anemia (due to uncinariasis or hookworm disease), their malnourishment, and their dismal poverty:

> Thus the poor laborer, his earning capacity cut down by his disease, with employment which is at the best very irregular, with his sick wife and children for whom he has to buy "iron tonics" that cost all that he can rake and scrape together, without money for clothes, much less for shoes, with a palm-bark hut not too well protected against the damp cold of the grove in which he lives, with not a scrap of furniture save, perhaps, a hammock, and, worst of all, with a miserable diet lacking in proteids and fats, lives from day to day, saving nothing, knowing nothing of the world beyond his plantation, working mechanically simply because he is not the drone he has been too frequently painted outside of Porto Rico, but without any object save to keep on living as generations have done before him.... nevertheless ... with an average of 40 per cent of hemoglobin and two and a half millions of red corpuscles per cubic millimeter he has labored from sun to sun in the coffee

plantation . . . the sugar estate . . . the tobacco fields . . . other industries and commercial enterprises. He is a sick man and deserves our highest respect and merits our most careful attention as a vital element in the economic life of the island. (Ashford and Gutierrez 1911, 17)

An American missionary cited General Roy Stone, who participated in the US invasion of Puerto Rico and who gave "high praise" to Puerto Rican laborers despite their lack of proper nourishment:

Having had occasion to employ many thousands of laborers on military roads during the war, General Stone says he has rarely found more willing or effective workers in any country, although the men appeared to be scantily fed and stunted in growth. He believes that with regular employment, good wages, nourishing food, better homes, some education, and hope for a future, the Porto Rican "jibaros" (peon or peasant class) will be as good laborers as one could find anywhere. (Grose 1910, 178)

As Puerto Rican peasants were exploited and paid meager wages, which kept them poor and malnourished, they had no motivation to exert themselves beyond what was necessary to keep their jobs and survive. But there was a contradiction between the interest of the Puerto Rican workers and the interests of the American capitalists:

At grammar school and high school I had been taught that this little island is overflowing with the proverbial milk and honey but that its natives are too lazy to garner this vast harvest. Imagine my surprise [after spending several months in Puerto Rico] that the Porto Rican stevedore, for example, does twice as much work as the wharf worker of the United States and receives only two dollars per day as against the American stevedore's daily wage of ten dollars. . . . The average Porto Rican native is like the American hobo who tramps wearily past prolific orchards, his palate craving the oranges and grape fruit and his eyes welling with tears at the sight of shot-gun-toting caretakers. Mr. Big Business owns everything . . . (Harris 1932, 5)

Many elements of Puerto Rican culture were brandished in these books as evidence of Puerto Ricans' laziness, among them the profusion of holidays:[15]

The villagers are a happy, light-hearted class, and spend their evenings and numerous holidays merrily. Every saint's day is a holiday, and their number has now been increased by the addition of the Fourth of July,

Washington's Birthday, Thanksgiving, and others of our national holidays... (Olivares, *Vol. 1* 1899, 371)

The people of Puerto Rico have 200 holidays or feast days in their calendar. They are always ready to welcome new ones, however... (George 1900, 35)

An American journalist commented briefly on the Puerto Rican custom of being late: "... by this time one knew that eight-thirty meant an hour later, at least in P.R" (Marden 1921, 206). A Mennonite joined him in his opinion: "One beautiful morning in June... [a group gathered for a trip on horseback]... Plans had been made to start by 9:30, but in typical Puerto Rican manner we waited until almost 11:00 before all of the borrowed horses had been brought to La Plata.... Even fire trucks in Puerto Rico are sometimes late for appointments" (Holsinger 1952, 166, 183).

And a young American missionary complained about the slowness of construction in Puerto Rico, which she explained as the pace of any and all Puerto Rican work, including housework. Yet, she recognized that Puerto Ricans were very talented:

> ... we have come about to the conclusion that we would rather live in a shack than to go through such an upheaval of affairs as the building of a house requires in Porto Rico. We began it some three months... but it is only begun. Porto Ricans have their own way of doing things and there is no use to trying to change it. If you give them time enough they will produce a pretty good thing in most any line, but they do not know how to work under pressure.... Tomasa [her latest cook] has left me, life in an American household having been too strenuous for her and life, at the pace she set, being too slow for me. (Blythe 1911, 149, 177)

Another omnipresent theme in American authors' books used as evidence of Puerto Ricans' "laziness" is the siesta or napping. It is evident that most of them struggled to understand its logic: "Business in Ponce, as in other towns on the island, ceased at eleven o'clock in the morning, and the people slept or rested until three in the afternoon, when business was resumed.... They had an aversion for work, but were always ready to earn a centavo, provided they could do so and not lose their noonday siesta" (Fiala 1899, 92–93).

American authors sometimes considered the apathy and laziness of Puerto Ricans somewhat contagious and "in the air," like a virus that will spread to Americans living in Puerto Rico:

... the education of a race to persistent day in and day out labor, would be no simple matter.... Even those who go to the island, either in search of a livelihood or for fortune-making, will speedily fall into the ways of the place and, more or less consciously, adopt the local "mañana" as an object of worship. Whatever may be the result of increased contact between these people and ourselves ... one thing is quite certain, and that is that any settlers on the island will soon drop into the prevalent indolence. It is in the air and in the life.... It is not the intense heat, for, measured by the thermometer, the heat is not so very intense, and in most places it is tempered by a breeze which elsewhere will doubtless be refreshing. But it is hardly so there. The air is dull and heavy, and one grows listless.... One might in time become used to it all and find life there as pleasant as it is anywhere. But before he reaches that point he will land in the clutches of potent, implacable, irresistible "mañana." (Robinson 1899, 161–62)

H. A. Phillips, who visited Puerto Rico for ten days in the 1930s, claimed to have changed his whole sense of time and, having some sort of epiphany, adopted the lay-back attitude of the natives after a bath at the Coamo Springs:

The bath had made a West Indian youth of us. We were filled with rocking-chair pep and had learned the precious meaning of mañana! We had thrown off that North American incubus and maxim, which dings our ears and rowels our souls from morn to night like an alarm clock, "Time is money! Time is money!" The time clock had stopped. We went completely native in that respect. Coamo Springs is that sort of place. We had caught the tempo of the country, and a few days later pushed on slowly, rolling the delightful scenes under our sightseeing palate; stopping overnight when and where we saw fit. (Phillips 1936, 147)

Some of what the American authors considered "laziness," in reality, responds more to what has been the Puerto Rican fatalism, as discussed in chapter 5. As colonized, Puerto Ricans frequently succumb to the belief that they lack personal power or control over their fate. Surrounded by natural disasters like hurricanes and earthquakes capable of destroying all material wealth in a few minutes or a few hours, their accumulation doesn't make sense, even if it might be accessible. In such a cultural milieu, you learn to enjoy every day whatever you have, as this Presbyterian missionary basically described:

"Take no thought for the morrow" is one Biblical injunction that they certainly know how to keep. No matter whether there is a cent in the house or not. If you have had supper, why work yourself all up into a pet and get indigestion by worrying about breakfast? They can lie down and sleep the sleep of the just, feeling perfectly confidently that they will, some way, get some bread and coffee from some source in the morning. They just go on and get more fun out of life than the multi-millionaire ever dared dream of, and as for the simple life, they easily out-Wagner Wagner.[16] (Blythe 1911, 99)

Writing in 1960, an American journalist debunked the myth of the lazy Puerto Rican, explaining what it was all about: "Puerto Rico is a relaxed island. Relaxation is philosophy of life. This is no siesta-land. The Puerto Rican is not the cartoon Latin American, with a sombrero pulled over his eyes, sleeping lazily in the midday sun. He works hard, but he relaxes gracefully" (Hancock 1960, 26).

THIS CHAPTER

As has happened in other colonial relationships, the colonizers accused Puerto Ricans of being lazy and apathetic in order to justify their domination and the low wages paid to them. Besides, they could not understand the relaxed way of life prevalent on an Island where the maxim "work dignifies" does not apply. The colonizers thought that a bountiful Nature provided no incentive to work hard; in reality, it was preposterous to expect Puerto Ricans to enjoy toiling for the benefit of American capitalists. Contrary to imperial assumptions, Puerto Ricans proved to be talented, hard workers, and some Americans residing in Puerto Rico ended up understanding the benefits of enjoying life at its most.

Chapter 8

"LUST WAS WRITTEN IN THE VERY FACES OF THE PEOPLE"

On the Morality of Puerto Ricans

As with any other culture in the world, Puerto Rican culture had moral codes that were transmitted through the family, the school, the neighborhood, the church, etc. Nevertheless, as representatives of a "moral empire," very few American authors recognized that Puerto Ricans, especially those of the lower social classes, had any morality. As has been defined by Frantz Fanon, "The colonial world is a Manichean world" in which the colonizer "paints the native as a sort of quintessence evil": its society lacks values, but, more important, "the native is declared insensible to ethics" so he is "the enemy of values, and in this sense, he is the absolute evil."[1] The customs, traditions, and general behavior of the natives are "the evidence" of their depravity and poverty of spirit. The moral superiority of the colonizers was attributed by an American missionary to Puerto Ricans lacking the "noble ancestry" of Protestant leaders as well as to their "tropical climate":

> The people of the United States point with great pride to the sturdy, religious character of the founders of their nation. The Puritans of New England, the Dutch of New York, and the Quakers of Pennsylvania . . . Porto Rico has no such noble ancestry. The Spaniards who came to this Island were soldiers, adventurers, politicians, merchants, priests and convicts. . . . Their object was to secure money, no matter what means were employed. . . . In view of the ancestry of this people, and the laxity of morals that is induced by a tropical climate, and the corruption of the spiritual leaders . . . it ought not to be surprising if we find there . . . conditions which in our country would be considered shockingly immoral, but which in Porto Rico can scarcely be considered as anything more than non-moral . . . (Fowles 1910, 95, 98)

As expected, the missionaries were the ones who most frequently mentioned morality issues. We should keep in mind that their interpretation of the native Puerto Ricans as promiscuous gave missionaries a justification for their conversions. If Puerto Ricans were not able to care for themselves, they would need to be "guided" and "taught" how to be "decent" Americans. Even though one of them wrote, "The morality and habits of these people are not to be judged by New England standards" (Stoddard 1903, 243), for most of these authors, the moral standards of the United States became the model through which all other moralities should be measured.

What these authors ignored was that Puerto Ricans had their own informal system for regulating moral conduct (or lack thereof) within their communities: gossiping. Since towns in Puerto Rico were small, most people knew of each other's lives, especially within the same social classes. Men and women of all classes "invested a great deal of energy in patrolling one another."[2] Through gossip, slander, and mockery, they kept everybody on track regarding their morality and honor. "Falling in someone else's tongue" was widely feared, and this threat helped the community to regulate itself morally. Those who disobeyed the moral codes paid for it by becoming subjects of scorn or being ostracized, especially if they were female.

At the time of the US invasion, and up to at least the 1920s, female honor in Puerto Rico was "based on the maintenance of a woman's virginity and sexual fidelity, which, once lost, was only reparable by marriage to the conquering male," but Eileen Suárez Findlay established that this principle was not absolute because its strictness depended on the social position a woman had regarding her wealth, lineage and race.[3] Still, being a virgin was not enough: in order to be considered honorable, a woman had to have a good reputation. So, it was more important to be considered a virgin than to actually be one. By the same logic, if a virgin woman was rumored to be "lost," she would lose her honor, and marrying would be almost impossible for her.

Did these restrictions on virginity apply to women of all races and all classes? Not really. White elite women were presumed respectable; white poor women were sexually suspicious; Black women were presumed disreputable.[4] The loss of virginity could make it impossible for an elite woman to marry, but that was not necessarily the case for the lower classes.

In this context, Puerto Rican men, especially those of the elite, regulated the moral conduct of the members of their families, especially the women. As an author commented about elite women, they "are strictly secluded and have little freedom" (Ober 1899, 169). Besides being a good provider for his family and having a reputation of trustworthiness, a man's honor required him to be able "to protect the women of the family from the sexual incursions of other males ... especially ... darker and poorer than themselves."[5] This duty of preserving women's honor was found in all social classes and sometimes ended up in fights or death.

Still, there was an additional resource to keep the honor of the family's teenage girls of the higher classes: the chaperone or duenna. Many American authors discussed the role of these family friends or older siblings who accompanied teenage girls on their outings in order to prevent them from being "too close" to young men, thus keeping their virginity and reputation intact until marriage. As we can see, elite teenage girls and women were subjected to strict sexual surveillance by their family members, chaperones, and virtually the whole community, all zealously protecting their virginity and reputation. As an American soldier stated: "if the men wished to see the señoritas it must be in the presence of the señora" (Edwards 1899, 252). As a corollary, we have to surmise that, in the meantime, all young men were devoting all their energy to trying to circumvent the security systems around their chosen ones.

A female war correspondent widely commented on the duties of a "duenna" presenting her in an almost cartoonish fashion:

> In regard to public sports women can only go to a place with an escort, who must be her father, grandfather, uncle, brother, son, or else a duenna. Wealthy people employ a duenna, while those not well-to-do hire one whenever necessary. The average duenna is a hideous old maid or widow, and sometimes a poor married woman. She is ugly, plainly dressed, tireless, sleepless, garrulous, suspicious, and always hungry and thirsty. She takes a particular pleasure in preventing wicked men from coming too near her charge, and preventing her naughty charge from winking and otherwise encouraging wicked men. She has two ideas, one is that every man has a mad desire to carry off each woman he meets, and each woman has a mad desire to be carried off; and second that it is her duty to get everything possible out of her position.
>
> ... She is not exactly venal, and in many cases will spurn a bribe unless it is diplomatically given, but she will accept cigars, cigarettes, coffee and wine at all hours of the day and night.... She is not such a bad creature altogether, and is invaluable as a gossip or cicerone. She knows every scandal that has occurred in her native city from the time of her childhood.... She knows the name and fortune, prospects and pedigree of very eligible young man and woman in the province.... When she comes from poor stock she invariably announces herself as being the illegitimate descendant of a duke, count or captain-general. When she comes from a good family she wearies you with long tales of its grandeur,

estates and achievements. The duenna system is woven curiously into native life. (Hamm, *Porto* 1899, 128–29)

A war correspondent portrayed the duenna as a necessary control for the "señoritas": "During the week the señoritas are kept under rigid restriction, never permitted to walk abroad alone, and constantly watched by parents and duennas, as if expected to rush to the bad if allowed the smallest opportunity" (Olivares, *Vol. 1* 1899, 353).

And although the surveillance relaxed a little during the courtship, the couple was still closely observed during their dating period: "According to the etiquette of Spain, which prevails in Porto Rico, a young man cannot engage in conversation with his sweetheart upon the street. He dare not call upon her expecting to find her alone, and in case there is another man paying attention to her, he is not supposed to interfere" (Olivares, *Vol. 1* 1899, 353).

In the early 1950s, an English teacher in Mayagüez observed the chaperone system while at a Lion's Club dance and discussed its rationale in detail:

> I had been told, repeatedly . . . that though the chaperone system was beginning to break down in San Juan and even in Ponce . . . it was still rigidly enforced in Mayaguez. . . . As the evening progressed, it was evident that the chaperone system, as advertised, did in fact exist. The girls spent most of the evening dancing, but, after each dance, her partner returned her to the seat she came from, surrounded by other females. There was no sitting with or talking to boys between dances, with the exception of couples . . . who were considered more or less engaged.
>
> The rationale behind the system, shared by most Latin American countries, was that there was no way that a young man and young woman, if left alone together, could possibly restrain themselves from having sexual intercourse. Any normal man would try to seduce any female he could, and there was nothing the female could do to stop him, so she simply had to let him have his way. It was no fault of hers, or his, but simply the way human beings are created. Only the presence of another, older person could keep the inevitable from happening. This was the "conventional wisdom," and even if not literally believed by everyone, it was part of the social structure. Any man who did not take sexual advantage of a girl given the opportunity must be abnormal, a pato, a homosexual. This, of course, put a good deal of pressure on the young men, starting at a fairly early age, and while they strongly defended the system, ostensibly because it protected their sisters, it also made it possible for them to talk macho without continuously having to prove it, either to themselves or to others. (Cooper 1994, 48, 50–51)

But regarding the elite's moral practices, Kal Wagenheim pointed to the important changes that modernity and industrialization effected on them:

> In preindustrial days, the typical family followed the Latin American (and old European) stereotype: papá was boss, no questions asked.... The children respected their father, but la madre was adored, and any insult, no matter how indirect, of the mother, was (and is) considered the supreme offense, to be answered by violence. Family protection of a young daughter's virginity amounted to an obsession. After marriage ... The wife was idealized, sometimes revered, as a second mother by her mate.... At social gatherings in the home, after the usual salutations, males would usually congregate to discuss politics, sports, or business, while the women, off in another corner, talked about family matters. Young girls led sheltered lives; boys were more pampered and encouraged to explore. Even today, when a girl is born, although she is the light of her father's eyes, he will accept mild kidding from his friends, who call him a chancletero[6] ... maker of useless things ... They may cast mild aspersions on his virility, his machismo, if he is unable to produce a male heir.
>
> These relationships had been altered ... but they have not disappeared. Women have been "liberated" to the extent that they travel more, contribute their wages to the household's welfare, and are more "vocal partners" than before; the image of the madre sufrida ... stuck at home, is slowly fading.... Today, middle-class women may drive a second family car ... but they will rarely venture out at night without the husband. The man is now somewhat a tamer macho although ... still asserts his freedom with the ritual of viernes social ... where, on payday, he may linger with "the boys" for drinking and socializing.... In the city, the custom of chaperoning has relaxed. (Wagenheim 1970, 189–90)

Things, indeed, began to relax by that time. In 1970, a travel book's author wrote: "Everyone is conservative and formal compared to the United States but girls do date, wear bikinis, and belong to consciousness-raising groups" (Rand, A. 1973, 50).

Regarding the lower-class members, a general stereotype was shared by most American authors: they are more sexual in their appearance and behavior, had multiple sexual partners throughout life, as well as many children, and preferred living in consensual relations rather than marrying. Part of the expectation of immorality in the lower classes was attributed to them living in too-close quarters:

> ... it is a common sight to see six or eight persons, or even more, living in a wretched hut barely large enough for two. There can be no privacy

in such an arrangement, and the conditions would seem to produce a scale of morality but little above that of animal life; and yet there is no apparent lack of modesty among the people, and strangers always note their urbanity and politeness. (Olivares, *Vol. 1* 1899, 330)

A US geographer provided in 1914 his own explanation for the moral deficiencies of the inhabitants of "tropical America" in what we will consider today as pseudoscience:

> ... it is due partly to the low standards of the natives themselves, partly to the mode of dress among the women which constantly calls attention to their sex, and partly to the free open life which naturally prevails in warm countries.... a missionary of a small and extremely devout sect, a most austere man.... Speaking of Central American in general, he said: "When I am at home in the United States I feel pure and true, but when I come here it seems as if lust was written in the very faces of the people." His experience is that of practically all northerners.[7]

"TAKEN AWAY": ON ELOPEMENTS

In the nineteenth century and probably, in some cases, up to the 1960s, seduced girls or young women in love left their homes in the middle of the night to join their boyfriends. This event was called a "rapto," a word that, in English, can be translated as abduction or kidnapping, but in Puerto Rico's case, the female left her home voluntarily. The next day after the eloping, people gossiped that the girl "was taken away" ("se la llevaron"). The young couple "secretly agree upon the occasion to elope," and the young man secretly arranged "with a relative (or, rarely, a trusted older friend) living in another village or town, and arranges hospitality for himself and his wife-to-be for a two—or three-day period."[8] After having sex, they were considered a couple in a free union, and they returned to their town and moved to their own place as soon as possible. Although the practice was more common in the lower classes, the elite young women also "were taken" now and then.

"CASADOS, CASADOS": MARRIAGE

Before the US invasion, the Catholic Church, protected by the Spanish colonial government, controlled the social institution of marriage. Therefore, marriage was not interpreted as a social contract between two parts but as a Catholic sacrament or sign of grace exclusively provided by priests. As happened with many services provided by the Catholic Church, it implied a monetary charge that most Puerto Ricans of the lower classes couldn't afford:

> The exorbitant fees charged for the marriage ceremony made it practically impossible for the laboring classes to pay it. The priests charged ten dollars for the simple marriage service, sixteen dollars for a more elaborate service, and twenty-five dollars or more if the persons were in better circumstances. Since the ordinary laborer received about thirty cents a day as his wages, it will be seen that to accumulate such a fee was out of the question. (Grose 1910, 201)

According to an American missionary writing in 1916, these were the statistics regarding marriage at the time of the US invasion: "A census . . . in Porto Rico soon after the American occupation . . . one-third of the people living as husband and wife acknowledged that they were not married, and one hundred and forty-eight thousand six hundred and five illegitimate children were reported" (Hough 1916, 75).

The Catholic Church considered all marriages indissoluble unless declared null by the pope, another expensive canonical procedure. When a married couple decided to separate, if an annulment was not granted by the pope, they were still married and, therefore, were unable to remarry if they wanted to remain members of the Catholic Church. All of this changed with the US invasion because the US Constitution established a secular government. Under the new circumstances, marriages became a civil contract between two, performed in the presence of a representative of the state licensed to do so. The lawful age for marriage was changed from fourteen years old for males and twelve for females (Civil Code of 1889) to eighteen for males and sixteen for females (Civil Code of 1914).[9]

The Catholic Church lost its privilege and control over marriages, and priests were put in the same level of authority to perform them as judges, rabbis, pastors, etc. The Protestant pastors immediately began to offer to perform marriages for free, making them accessible to the poor, so their frequency increased. Beyond officiating marriages for free or for any donation, the ministers required formal marriage to couples prior to them joining their religious communities: "The first difficulty came in regard to the mixed domestic relations of those who desired to unite within the Church. The missionaries insisted upon a straightening out of the family relations, and thousands of marriages took place, with no charge. This fact produced a profound impression" (Grose 1910, 211).

Additionally, in 1902, the colonial government recognized the right to divorce, providing married women the means to end unsatisfactory marriages. This was soon used by a considerable number of women.

The higher classes were the ones who most frequently married at the time of the US invasion. Indeed, when in the lower classes, a couple married, they were described as "casados, casados," to emphasize that this was a real marriage.[10] An American writer commented in 1908 on the infrequent countryside weddings, providing a detailed description of such events:

> A far more pleasant sight is the country wedding. . . . previous to the American occupation, weddings were of the quaintest simplicity. Very seldom did either of the contracting parties possess suitable garments, or the money to purchase them. The alcalde, or village major, with kindly foresight and at the same time a keen eye for business, was ready to loan the bride and groom clothing . . . old-fashioned and ill-fitting . . . Thus arrayed, the pair proceeded to the alcalde's office, where the civil marriage service was performed. Then came the religious ceremony at the hands of the village priest, after which the pair mounted an ox-cart, and accompanied by neighbors and friends, whose numbers were continually increasing, they rode in state to their new home. (Seabury 1908, 36–37)

"THEY LOVE AND MATE LIKE THE BIRDS": CONCUBINAGE

Even with the possibility of an affordable marriage and divorce, many lower-class women accepted to live with a man without marrying him because they were poor and couldn't afford to live on their own, especially if they already had children from a different man. As Suárez Findlay explained, they exchanged sex and domestic labor for the financial support of the male.[11] On their part, the men were willing to share their income in exchange for control of the women's sexuality. If the relationship ends, the woman and her children usually return to her parental home or find another man to live with. These unions were considered respectable in the community as long as the woman was sexually faithful to her partner; they were understood as permanent and as binding as legal marriages and will keep being the norm for the lower classes beyond the 1940s:

> While the statistics of birth show that 48 per cent are illegitimate, this fact is attributed to the excessive expenses which the church has thrown around the marriage ceremony, rather than to a criminal disposition. The people are poor and unambitious; their social relations are not exacting, and being unable to meet the expenses of the wedding ceremony, they love and mate like the birds, and are said to be singularly true and devoted in their domestic relations. (Olivares, *Vol. 1* 1899, 287)

Yet a few American authors disagreed and blamed the common practice of concubinage for a heavy amount of social, economic, and even physical problems:

> It may well be that these unions do not involve immediate moral degradation for either the man or the woman, and yet their ultimate effect must be the lowering of the moral tone of the community. The uncertainty and instability introduced into the family relationship react most unfavorably on the status of the children, and especially upon their training. Parental authority is weakly asserted and the feeling of parental responsibility sadly undermined. The children of these unions soon throw off the restraints of home influence, and are left to their own resources. Lasting and irreparable harm is thus done to the morals, economic efficiency, and the physical vigor of the population. (Rowe 1904, 111–13)

In both married and consensual couples of the upper or lower classes, domestic violence incidents were a possibility. Since there was no institutional protection for battered women, most women addressed their situation silently as long as the men were good providers for the family. As is still common these days, abused women handled their men's violence the best way they could, trying to appease men in order to keep domestic harmony.[12] This might explain why there was little success in the promotion of formal marriages. In 1947, an American anthropologist theorized that women of the lower class who preferred consensual relations rather than marriage did so because that empowered them in the relationship:

> The woman [under Spain] occupied a place of honor in the home, but was completely under the domination of the husband, did not participate in public life, and generally occupied an inferior position before the law. In the hills . . . marriage was of the consensual type. . . . Attempts to put an end to the custom had failed. The resistance came from the women, who felt that so long as they had no legal ties with their husbands they were free, and consequently the latter had no real authority over them. . . . Since poverty and despair often led to family abuses, she felt safer if she could abandon her mate at will and without incurring the disfavor of the priest. . . . There is also the fierce pride of the women, who are free, and will bear children for their men as long as they behave. There are neither church vows nor civil laws to interfere with their dignity and rights as human beings. (Petrullo 1947, 128, 142)

The side-effect of concubinage was the so-called "illegitimate child," one born of parents not legally married to each other. In the Puritan society of New

England, where the United States was born as a nation, the "model of family as the central economic unit necessarily problematized ... children born out of wedlock."[13] Beginning in the seventeenth century, laws were passed to punish parents of bastards in an effort to stop the practice.

The high proportion of Puerto Rican children born out of wedlock troubled both the Catholic and the Protestant Church representatives, but it was mostly used as a weapon to attack the Catholics for the "weakness of their morals."[14] Under the Spanish colonial government, an illegitimate child could become legitimized through the marriage of the parents or through a Spanish Crown's decision. Under the US colonial government, of course, only the marriage of the parents would do.

An American missionary discussed what he understood was a huge predicament for both illegitimate and "natural" children who, for different reasons, were "denied a real home":

> In the eyes of the law, there is the "natural" child and the illegitimate child. The "natural" child is a child born out of wedlock but recognized and registered by the father. This child has a legal standing. The father supports it and grants it a minimum percentage of his estate. As a rule the child lives with its mother. Later, should the father marry, the natural child has the humiliation of seeing his half brothers and sisters enjoying social recognition and prestige in which he too ought to share. . . . society rejects him. If it accepts him at all it is on an inferior level . . . Frequently his father turns his back upon him and pretends that he does not know him. (James 1927, 26)

It was in 1952 when illegitimacy was eradicated in Puerto Rico by means of a law that was approved unanimously.[15] This fact was commented on by an American journalist: "Illegitimacy has been legally outlawed. One of the first laws enacted by the Popular Democratic Party declared that every child was legitimate. At birth every child is registered with a father's and a mother's name." (Gruber 1960, 150).

"BOYS WILL BE BOYS": MACHISMO AND HOMOSEXUALITY

Machismo, the obsession of many men with the continuous assertion of their virility[16] that makes them "display physical strength, bravery, and dominance over his wife and children," was, and many will argue that still is, a part of Puerto Rican culture at the time of the US invasion.[17] The macho should have a strong character and protect the honor and welfare of his extended family, but frequently, the image of the macho is enhanced by his having extramarital affairs, and women are expected to tolerate such behavior. The woman's only power comes from learning how to manipulate the man so that he believes he is the boss while she gets what she wants.[18] A journalist commented:

> "Machismo" has always been a great feature of Puerto Rican men. This is the show of their manhood. They will fight each other with knives if they are angry enough. There have been reports of killing over what may seem trivial affairs to outsiders. Very often it will be over a woman. Not to have more than one woman is almost a sign of lacking virility. (Samoiloff 1984, 161–62)

In the United States, machismo, labeled as "the only Spanish word that every North American knows," also existed (and still exists), even if it is more frequently denied.[19] American machismo, also called "toxic masculinity," is associated with the lone cowboy image of a self-reliant, iron-willed "loner" who disregards the consequences of his acts.[20] But this overlooks an American form of machismo that many Puerto Ricans consider even more "machista" than any of their own: the still widespread practice of women changing their last names after marriage in order to adopt those of their husbands. This actually stems from a ninth-century English common law doctrine that assumed women as property and without an independent legal identity.[21] In Puerto Rico, the practice for elite women used to be to add their husbands' last names to theirs: "full matri-patri title, thus: Señora Juana Fernández Ramírez de Fulano ..."[22] This practice was generally abandoned around the 1980s. An American author misunderstood this and wrongly advised her traveling readers:

> Remember that Puerto Rico follows the Spanish system of family names.... Inherited from the tight formal world of Spain, the system was designed to help you place people by telling exactly who their parents were ... When a woman marries, she keeps her mother's name[23] and adds her husband's name, prefaced by "de." (Rand, A. 1973, 51)

Many Americans of the end of the nineteenth century accepted the "machismo" stereotype as a "Hispanic trait" but not as part of their own culture. This American soldier made this claim implying that women did most of the domestic work for their "worthless" husbands:

> ... the women were far more industrious, whether taking in washing from the "high" families in and around town, or cultivating the meagre vegetable patches in the rear of their huts.... The lords and

masters lounged around and allowed their far better halves, and other members of their usually large families, to do the manual labor in the most approved Indian fashion, while they smoked the eternal cigarette, guzzled the poisonous sugar rum, attended cock-fights and were in fact as worthless a lot of human beings as one would wish to see. (Oliver 1901, 159)

An American travel writer identified in 1920 a still common "machista" practice of many Puerto Rican women who give control of their salaries to their husbands or partners, who then give their wives or partners an allowance for their expenses. In the reported case, the couple was not even married, a fact that further disgusted her American employers: "The cook of an American missionary family openly gave all her wages, except what went for the rent of her hovel, to her 'man,' who was married to another. It was not that he demanded it; there is little of the 'white slave' attitude in Porto Rico, but she was proud to do so and it is costumbre del país" (Franck 1920, 287).

"Decent behavior" expectations were different according to the sex of the young person, in a "double standard of sexual morality," observed by an American priest:

Typical of the Latin tradition, a double standard of sexual morality has been common in Puerto Rico. The girl is carefully protected, regularly chaperoned. The family feels deep responsibility to bring her safely to marriage as a virgin. As a wife she is expected to be close to the home, protected by husband and relatives, faithful to her husband. . . . More liberty is accorded to the boy. Sexual liberties outside of marriage are not considered a "problem" in the American sense of the word. Premarital relations with prostitutes or "bad" women are more openly accepted than on the Mainland, and outside interests during marriage are tolerated, often openly admitted. Illegitimate children have generally been openly and honorably acknowledged. . . . These outside interests of the man are never considered "morally good;" they are tolerated as "humanly expected." (Fitzpatrick 1996, 144)

Homosexuality was an absent theme until the early 1950s when Jim Cooper, an English teacher at the Mayagüez Campus of the University of Puerto Rico (CAAM), described how Mayagüez was already then considered a hub of homosexuals (a conception still widespread in the 1980s). Cooper also explained two categories of homosexuals: the teenage houseboys hired to have sex with both parties of a heterosexual married couple and then young men, married or not, who, in effect, were either "temporary homosexuals" or bisexuals. The last ones were somewhat accepted, and their masculinity was not questioned, as long as they acted "the male role in the situation," Cooper also emphasized the hypocrisy of the whole situation:

> We had certainly heard stories about Ricardo [his landlord] being homosexual, but then we've heard the same stories about almost every other male in Mayaguez. From the day I arrived I had learned that homosexuality was one of the most popular, if not <u>the</u> most popular, topics of conversation in Mayaguez.... It was giggled about, made fun of, brought into almost any conversation on any subject, but no one seemed shocked by it. It was not felt to be a threat to anyone. It was a very complex situation, filled with hypocrisy and inconsistencies and extremely difficult to try to understand.
>
> Nobody tried to pretend that overt homosexuality did not commonly occur in Mayaguez, but it was always shrugged off as a joke. If you didn't take it seriously there's no problem. Boys will be boys. They did not, as many mainlanders do, feel that homosexuality was a disease which can spread, which can be caught, and so boys and men must be protected from it. It is the loose women you must beware of. They could upset the system.... the Puerto Rican words were pato (duck) or maricón.
>
> On one level, there were the houseboys.... Houseboys were school dropouts from poor families and ranged in age from about twelve to eighteen.... in Mayaguez it was assumed that they were, for that period of their lives at least, homosexual. If you were to believe rumors and gossip, and that was all I had to go on, the male head of the household regularly had sex with the houseboy as well as his wife. It was the women in town who originated and repeated this gossip....
>
> On another level, it was known and accepted that the sons of the middle class families were sleeping with one another; it was a normal phase that young men went through. They would outgrow it when they married and started their own families, as most of them did.... Husbands, too, aside from houseboys, might well have a fling with a younger man, usually, as with the wives a la izquierda, one with darker skin. They were no threat. After all, men are by nature insatiable for sex and there was almost no chance that this could change into anything more than a strictly sexual liaison, and they don't last long. Let him have a little fun if he wants to.... That was also the myth, clung to tenaciously, that your son or your husband or your brother always took the male role in any homosexual encounter.... As long as you are acting the male role in the situation, whatever that may mean, your virility and manliness are not called onto question....

They were not angry at Ricardo [who produced travesty shows in the outskirts of Mayagüez], we learned, because of what will be called today his sexual preference, but because he was not dealing with it the socially acceptable way. Why didn't he marry one of their daughters and raise a family in downtown Mayaguez? He would be free to spend their evenings and weekend any way he wanted. (Cooper 1994, 124–28)

"UNA MUJER A LA IZQUIERDA": INFIDELITY

In the nineteenth century, Americans came to understand adultery as a very serious public offense with public consequences. Its meanings transcended the home sphere, turning it into "the sexual betrayal of a spouse, a violation of the Seventh Commandment, a crime in most jurisdictions, and the basis of divorce."[24] This perspective did not stop the practice, but it moved Americans to further conceal it to avoid legal, religious, and communal consequences.

In Puerto Rico, although men of all classes expected "their" women to be faithful, they reserved for themselves the right to have as many partners as they wanted. The women who engaged with them in sexual affairs either were already disreputable or were willing to become such because they expected to get some material advantage from the relationships, especially if they were with wealthy men.[25] Interestingly, the unfaithful men never lost social prestige because of their open infidelities, as some American authors noticed:

> It is not considered extraordinary for a (middle or upper class) husband to take a mistress, and there are frequent indications that it is accepted as a matter of course. Neither the man, his wife, nor his mistress loses caste, though it would be a horse of a different color should a wife take a lover. Those who are repulsed by this practice may be able to conceal any outward signs of shock by remembering that it is more honest to admit that such relationship exist, as the Puerto Ricans do, than to attempt to conceal their existence, as certain mainlanders do. There is little hypocrisy in the Puerto Rican make-up. (Hancock 1960, 24)

Several American authors, at different points in time, considered a defect of Puerto Rican women the kindly way in which they accepted their husbands' infidelities:

> We know of a friend, a Puerto Rican woman of perceptions and position, to whom the knowledge of her faithless husband's life and his paramour was no secret. Neither it was a secret to any one else, and her

tolerance of the situation was likewise known to all. Her high resolve was that she "would not release him and let the other woman have the satisfaction of getting him!" There seemed to be no repugnant shock to her in the fact that she continued . . . to take triumphant satisfaction in the fact that she was feeding her own misery through a false concept of personal pride. Her American women friends could not understand her tolerance of the situation and her proud resolve to endure by such logic. Her Puerto Rican women friends understood, and approved! (White 1938, 340)

Less judgmental was the position taken by this American missionary when asked to help a woman in a very peculiar distress:

It was New Year's Eve, our children were all tucked in bed and Verna and I were starting to get ready to go to bed as well, when there was a knock on our door. There was a woman we knew fairly well. . . . We invited her in. She was very upset and asked for help. Her problem was that her husband had "una mujer a la izquierda" (a mistress) and to add insult to injury, he had chosen to spend the night with his mistress and took his wife's pig as a gift to the mistress. It was her pig and she wanted it back, now, tonight. And she wanted me to go with her to retrieve the pig. Verna and I tried to calm her down and persuade her to go home to her children and we'd see what could be done in the morning. But she could not be dissuaded. If I would not go with her, she would go alone. . . . I agreed to accompany her to retrieve her pig. It was around 10 p.m. She knew exactly where the mistress lived. . . . She untied her pig and we carried that little pig one and a half or two miles . . . toward her home. (Luke Birky in Falcón and Lehman 2014, 57–58)

In the early 1950s, English teacher Jim Cooper discussed in detail what he still observed in Mayagüez at the time:

. . . there still existed at that time in Puerto Rico, among the rich, the practice of a man having wives and families a la izquierda (on the left). . . . This was, though not technically legal, a form of socially accepted polygamy, and no secret was made of the arrangement. On the contrary, there was, of course, a certain amount of prestige in a man letting people know that he could support two or three households. . . . The second or third wives, I found later, were always from lower class families that the first wife, and, consequently, usually although not necessarily would have darker skin. The wives were aware of one another but did not associate with one another. The children normally played together when young, since their houses might well be in the same barrio or neighborhood, although the first wife's house would almost certainly be bigger and newer. Her children probably went to private schools too, and it was rare that the father would send all of his children to college, but, of course, if he had the money... why not? (Cooper 1994, 96–98, 133)

Only men were allowed the largesse of mistresses. Women were expected to be one hundred percent loyal, especially in the elite class. A married woman was observed by many sets of eyes in her community, and it was very important that she did not give any cause for rumors: "Once married, the women avoid being seen alone with other men, because for a husband to be cuckolded... or even for there to be suspicion of such a thing, is serious affront to his dignidad...".[26] (Wagenheim 1970, 211)

"LIBIDINOUS NATIVE WOMEN": PROSTITUTION

Prostitution in Puerto Rico probably began with the colonization in the 1510s, and by 1526, Emperor Carlos V authorized a prostitutes' house in San Juan.[27] After the US invasion, the American Protestant missionaries joined the local elites in their attempts to remove prostitutes from their sight, frequently urging authorities to halt the practice through arrests. This finally was granted in 1918 when two hundred women were arrested and charged with practicing prostitution near the Las Casas US military base. Yet the reason was not to make a moral statement but to protect American soldiers stationed there: about fifty percent of them suffered some venereal disease.[28] These women were examined vaginally without their consent. Of course, this did not eliminate prostitution in Puerto Rico since, for many poor women there, it was a lot more profitable than cleaning houses: a cleaning lady worked twelve hours a day for ten dollars a month, while a prostitute could earn twenty dollars or thirty dollars a night.[29]

Only one American soldier made a comment that seemed to allude to Puerto Rican prostitutes in Utuado, probably because these themes were not considered appropriate for a war memory: "We received two months' pay... Taps were ordered late, and some of the men spent the evening (and a little money) with libidinous native women on the hill" (King 1929, 120).

An American physician who married a Puerto Rican woman commented on his work with prostitutes in Manatí during World War II:

> ... it became my duty as municipal doctor to examine the Manatí whores on Saturday mornings.... The Puerto Rican "puta" was very

poor, very young, in her early teens, and very clean and neat.... they were the breadwinners of the family.... The war did not bring the whores to Manatí. Manatí was famous for its whores long before Pearl Harbor Day. (Flax 1995, 45–46)

And an English teacher received the following advice from a Puerto Rican he met at the ship that was taking him to the Island: "The little man ... was the most amiable.... He spoke some broken English ... 'The girls of Puerto Rico, they iss so beautiful.... Very cheap, too. Fifty cents, maybe twenty-five. Oh, You will have good time in my beloved Puerto Rico'" (Brown 1945, 15).

As "the embodiment of sexuality and of all that is associated with sexuality—disease as well as passion,"[30] these sexualized women were coveted by American tourists who applied to them a double-moral standard, according to this anthropologist:

> ... the American censures the Puerto Rican for the latter's sex morals.... He dwells on the peculiar morals of the jíbaros and, because prostitution flourishes in Puerto Rico, he tends to attribute moral looseness to all Puerto Rican womanhood.... Were he better acquainted with Puerto Rican culture, he would know that ... prostitution flourishes so well in Puerto Rico because of the poverty and the economic dependence of the woman. [About the areas dedicated to prostitution, the tourist] ... is not shy about going to these places, but the next day he is likely to discourse on the low morals of the Puerto Ricans. (Petrullo 1947, 139)

THIS CHAPTER

Most American visitors saw themselves as morally superior to Puerto Ricans, especially to those of the lower classes. As in the United States, women's reputations were of paramount importance, but Americans tended to ascribe a proclivity for immorality to Puerto Rican ones when they opted for open marriages that empowered them. The definition of "decent behavior" was culturally determined and the American and Puerto Rican ones remained incompatible and frequently still do. This became evident particularly in the divergent understanding of homosexuality (an aberration vs. a normal phase of adolescence), adultery (a crime vs. a natural inclination of men), and prostitution (a social offense vs. a livelihood). Evidently, their different religious traditions affected how each society defined immorality.

Chapter 9

"KNOWN BY THEIR FRUITS"

On Violence, Illegality, and Policing

"BETWEEN SPANISH AND PORTO RICANS": HOW AMERICAN SOLDIERS ENDED UP PROTECTING THEIR ENEMIES

The last census before the US invasion was made in December 1897, and showed the presence in Puerto Rico of 19,565 Spanish-born residents, who represented two percent of its total residents.[1] But that small representation had an enormous influence in the Spanish colonial government and in the commercial scene, particularly in animal husbandry, in the production of coffee and other foodstuffs, and in trading houses. They tended to be very conservative and were generally resented by Puerto Ricans because of their privileged status.

Since the US invasion began on the southern coast, where the Spaniards were less numerous, there they suffered more derision from the locals as the invading forces took control of towns like Guánica, Ponce, Yauco, etc. This tension between Spaniards and locals was identified by several authors:

> Someone in the crowd had the temerity to shout "Viva l'Espanola." He was pounced upon by a dozen natives and somewhat roughly handled before his friends could rescue him from their violence and hustle him away to a place of safety. . . . The people were so excited and high-strung on that memorable morning, that they would have stopped at nothing to show their thankfulness at the deliverance from the despotism of the Spanish soldiery, who were hated by all classes, except the few higher officials and aristocrats who catered to them, knowing that in so doing they were insured against any mob violence, which only needed a spark to inflame, to a white heat, the passions of the masses caused by generations of misrule and militarism. (Oliver 1901, 122)

After the armistice was signed, something unexpected by the Americans happened: frequent violent actions were taken against Spanish storeowners and farm-owners, mostly perpetrated by members of rebellious groups then called "partidas sediciosas" or seditious bands.[2] They were also called "los tiznados" (blackened or sooty) because, to avoid capture, they blackened their faces with charcoal. These groups were mostly numbered by native small landowners and farmworkers who took advantage of the war and the US occupation to take revenge on those they perceived as their oppressors.

> The natives are becoming very unruly—they have confused justice with retaliation, and the Spanish coffee plantations are in constant danger of fire and plunder. There is already an organized band called the Black Hand, of great strength throughout this whole section, that burns, plunders, and murders almost nightly. We mount details on native ponies, and accomplish something in the way of restraint. . . . Arecibo is getting pretty hot. There was a riot there yesterday—people were shot and wounded. The trouble is all between Spanish and Porto Ricans. (King 1929, 106, 122)

The "tiznados" usually burned the accounting ledgers where their victims kept records of their debts. Eventually, they also attacked the properties of "criollos" (Puerto Rican-born of Spanish descent). These bands set homes, businesses and warehouses on fire, and looted stored food. One of the most known was "the Black Hand Society": "The society known as the "Black Hand," similar to the old Ku-klux of the South, whose warning symbol was the impress of the hand in black on the door, was the terror of the island" (Edwards 1899, 235). Facing the situation, American soldiers, who came to the Island to fight the Spaniards, ended up having to protect them and their properties from the Puerto Ricans' retaliatory attacks.[3]

> While occupying the barracks, the natives brought in many Spanish subjects, making very expressive gestures towards the throats of their prisoners, evidently expecting us to treat the Spaniards as the Spaniards had always treated the Porto Ricans. We finally were obliged to get out guards to protect the prisoners. (Rossiter [1900?])

But, controlling the natives' animosity against the Spanish proved tricky. On October 9, 1898, a Sunday afternoon, an American soldier narrated how "a private quarrel between a Spanish soldier and a native of Arecibo over a woman ended in the shooting and killing in cold blood of five natives" by the soldier "and some comrades," while the natives were "armed only with machetes" (Edwards 1899, 226). But then things escalated:

> Within two hours after the shooting, from every by-way and road came crowds by the hundreds, armed with the ever-present machete, flocking towards town, gesticulating and yelling, vowing death to the Spaniards and destruction to the city. What promised to be a terrible calamity of ravage and fire was averted only by the timely arrival of Company E . . . The comandante proclaimed martial law, closing every store and shop in Arecibo, and cleared the streets . . . The natives . . . finding themselves debarred from entering the city and foiled in their plan of revenge by violence to Spanish soldiers, had resorted to the subterfuge of burning the haciendas in the neighborhood of Arecibo. Sunday night, fourteen were burned, the following evening twenty-one, and an equal number on Wednesday night . . . as a defiant message to the departing army of their hatred and contempt for them. (Edwards 1899, 226, 233)

"AND THE FIGHT BEGINS IN EARNEST": COLONIZED VS. COLONIZED

Once the violence against the Spanish elite in Puerto Rico subsided, the deep-seated frustrations of Puerto Rican laborers exploded in other forms of violence. Murder and suicide rates almost tripled between the late 1920s and mid-1930s.[4] Not only did suicide rates rise by about fifty percent during the Depression years, but alcoholism also resulted in brawls, serious injuries, and sometimes death. During the 1930s, there was a rise in sexual crimes and child neglect, with a doubling of the number of rapes.

Violence and colonialism are intrinsically related. As Frantz Fanon explained: "The colonized man will manifest this aggressiveness which has been deposited in his bones against his own people" by attacking his fellow colonized men.[5] This reflects, he posits, the hostility of the colonizer's world "which spurns the native, but at the same time, it is a world of which he is envious." Fanon also explained:

> While the settler or the policeman has the right the livelong day to strike the native, to insult him and to make him crawl to them, you will see the native reaching for his knife at the slightest hostile or aggressive glance cast on him by another native; for the last resort of the native is to defend his personality vis-a-vis his brother.[6]

Certainly, several American authors commented on the frequent fights in which many countryside dances ended and which were widely documented by historian Fernando Picó in *Los Gallos Peleados*. In Puerto Rico there is even an expression to refer to them: "la fiesta terminó como el Rosario de la Aurora" ("the party ended up as the Rosary of the Dawn").

> No dance is a success unless it ends in a general free-for-all fight, and when it starts each man rushes to the corner, secures his machete, and stands at bay. Then the women are all driven into another room, and the fight begins in earnest. It is not a two-man affair, for every one in the crowd takes sides with one or the other of the two original belligerents. The light is extinguished, and every one slashes right and left, several men usually being seriously wounded and perhaps killed, and all the participants gashed more or less. As soon as the fight is over, every one who is able to do so apologizes to all the rest, declaring that it was all his fault, and the company separates with expressions of the utmost good feeling. Those who escape severe injury are usually arrested by the police, but when taken before the judge they simply stare in an idiotic way, and answer, "I do not know," to every question put to them. (Church 1898, 36)

Interestingly, aggressive behavior was not fostered by parents, according to the study *Tropical Childhood* published by David Landy in 1959. Landy observed that fighting was not condoned, even in self-defense situations, as the parents asked their children, if they were attacked by another child, to run back home and let them know so that the father could handle the situation. Typically, if a child fought at school, the parent would take the child home and would "punish him, whether or not it is his fault, since his orders are not to fight under any circumstances but to run home."[7]

Probably to establish a contrast with the Philippines, who resisted colonialism in a bloody war against the US invaders from 1899 to 1902,[8] several American authors writing right after the US invasion remarked on the good nature and nonviolent behavior of Puerto Ricans:

> Crime, however, is not excessive. . . . The Porto Ricans are polite, sociable, kind-hearted and patient. Their disposition inclines them to be just to all men, and they are not easily driven to violence. . . . one can travel all over Porto Rico in perfect safety, and be received everywhere with generous hospitality by this kind-hearted and grateful people. . . . They are generally a peaceful and law-abiding people, and while there is unquestionably some lawlessness, and some minor offenses, they do not

exceed, if they equal, the number of similar offenses committed in our States of a like population. (Olivares, *Vol. 1* 1899, 287–88, 345)

A few American authors accepted that Puerto Ricans of the lower classes could be violent, but not as much as American criminals:

> The life of the poor people in the towns.... They fight in the streets and kill each other now and then. There is less virtue in this class, and a great propensity for small pilfering.... there is small difference between their sins and those of our own desperately poor class. In fact, in the weighing, it could be shown that the advantage lies with the Puertorriqueño ... he is less profane and less apt to do desperate deeds. He is a mild criminal at his worst ... not nearly so bad as the burly, fearless, vicious ruffian of American cities. (Dinwiddie 1899, 165–66)

But by the late 1920s, American authors had stopped insisting on the idea of a "crimeless" Puerto Rico. Red Cross officer Knowlton Mixer recognized "the great prevalence of petty crime and the tendency to disturbance of the peace on slight provocation" (Mixer (1926), 193). He also documented how local laws were ignored, and property crimes had become frequent: "Carelessness in complying with local laws and municipal ordinances is almost universal.... in San Juan ... cars parked in front of places of amusement in the evenings are likely to lose everything that is removable.... it is so deftly done that it is extremely difficult for the police to catch the offenders" (Mixer 1926, 195).

In 1927, an American missionary who had lived thirty years in Puerto Rico attributed Puerto Rican violence to the emotional and passional nature of Puerto Ricans, which he contrasted with American emotional detachment:

> ... a more fundamental difference between the Porto Rican and the North American. These islanders, like the rest of their race are fundamentally emotional while the continental is unemotional. By his virtues and his vices, we find that the Porto Rican is far more influenced by the great emotional instincts of life,—love, hate, fear, joy and sorrow than the American. They are an impulsive people. In one small town there have been within a year three attempts of assassination, two of which were successful.... an infuriated brother ... [to show] his disapproval of his sister's sweetheart ... shooting him as he came from the theatre.... a young man who shot and killed his best friend over a dispute as to the merits of their revolvers.... a boy who fatally stabbed his opponent in a game of dominoes in which a wager of three cents was at stake. (James 1927, 20)

Nevertheless, the 1945 description of a crime of passion by Wenzell Brown speaks louder about the violence in the description than in the narrated act itself. It is obvious that Brown wanted his readers to come to the conclusion that Puerto Ricans were savages and that there was no rule of law there. It is no surprise that in the 1950s, Brown became a popular pulp fiction writer if we pay attention to the gory description of the events he witnessed in Ponce:

> At the plaza's edge the sound of screaming reached me. Then there was a clatter of running feet, the sharp explosion of a gun.... a bullet whined into the roadway, ricocheted, and buried itself in a tree.... He was a slight man, tall for a Puerto Rican, and neatly dressed.... Then he fell forward with a motion horrible in absurdity.... Then he crumpled again. By this time, the man who was chasing him was upon him. He was a short, stocky man with a dark and brutal face. He stood above the other man and emptied his revolver into the thin back.... The dark man began to kick him. He kicked at the head and neck—long, hard, vicious kicks. There was the snap of bone and meaty impact of the boot against flesh.... The thin man's head was nearly severed from his body.... A crowd was gathered, but no one interfered. Now a policeman arrived and took charge. They had to pull the dark man away from his victim.... far worse than the hate was the look of triumph, the sense of pride, that followed it.... Later on I learned that this man received no punishment for his crime. His claim was that his victim had seduced his sister three years previously, then to escape retribution had fled to New York. The brother had sworn to kill the alleged seducer if he ever returned to Puerto Rico. On this day, the victim had come back to Ponce.... Friends of the brother ran to inform him. "It was a crime of passion," said the Puerto Ricans, "and should not be punished too harshly. Besides, it is the duty of a brother to protect the fair name of his sister." That was the end of the matter. (Brown 1945, 27–28)

But another American missionary wrote in 1932, once again, about the peaceful Puerto Ricans and compared them favorably with the disrespectful and disobeying Americans. After acknowledging that most property crimes responded to poverty, she commented on the absence of kidnapping cases in Puerto Rico, which is valid to these days, and on "honor slayings," which she seemed to condone since they were perpetrated to "protect the honor of their women":

> Murder and other crimes involving gross violence are few and far between, and highway robbery is almost unknown. Kidnapping is un-

thinkable. Most cases requiring the attention of the police have to do with reckless driving and petit larceny. Moreover, a check-up on the latter cases shows that the persons involved are food-filchers and penny-snatchers who are goaded to crime by economic circumstances.... As for crimes due to prohibition enforcement.... There are bootleggers, to be sure; but no racketeers and no highjackers.... Nor does one find there the utter disrespect for law and order that threatens the foundations of society in continental America.... And as for murders, most of these are "honor slayings".... Other types of murder are rare, despite the fact that Porto Rico punishes with neither the hangman's rope nor the electric chair. Moreover ... the "honor slaying" ... would continue under any punitive system. Porto Ricans have a high regard for their women and the assassination of womanhood's betrayer or defiler is but a part of an "unwritten code." (Harris 1932, 17–18)

As expected, after a process of fast-track industrialization and modernization lacking cultural and social gradual adaptations, by the end of the 1960s, the Island was much more dangerous than ever before. Interestingly, an American engineer acknowledged that the first bank robbery and the first attempted holdup of a bank messenger were actually perpetrated by continental Americans:

The alarming increase in crime, especially in the San Juan area, is a negative aspect of modern culture changes.... When Puerto Rico began to import good things from the United States, bad things came with them. The island's first bank robbery occurred in 1958, followed a few weeks later by the first attempted armed holdup of a bank messenger.... the fact that both crimes seem to have been committed by one or more continental Americans did little to assuage the sorrow. (Hanson 1960, 297)

Drug trafficking and drug use also entered into the picture with modernity and became a serious problem by the 1980s:

About ten or fifteen years ago, there was no drug addiction on the island. Now it is rife as well as the high crime rate that accompanies it. Much of the drug trade is brought in from New York and Miami. The forty per cent unemployment rate among the young, also contributes to the crime rate. Today in San Juan and its suburbs, every house has "rejas," iron grillwork to keep out burglars. In the countryside, it is different, and doors do not have to be locked. (Samoiloff 1984, 171)

And in 2010, an English teacher justified the lack of respect for authority and law that was in her list of common American biases regarding Puerto Ricans:

> If you are aware of all the poor examples of exemplary leadership Puerto Ricans have endured over the past five centuries, you will be more likely to understand their apparent lack of respect for authority.... Perhaps I should say that there are many Puerto Ricans who are cynical regarding authority.... Who respects hypocrisy in any form? ... so many Puerto Ricans I have known personally seem to have their own personal preferences regarding standards of conduct, and don't always feel obliged to conform to authority, the expectations of others, or to the law. "Big Brother" of government and/or The Holy Roman Church seem to rarely intimidate the Puerto Ricans.... Yet I believe they remain far, far more Puerto Ricans who **are** law—abiding. (Tavenner 2010, 33)

BOOTLEGGING AND "LA BOLITA"

According to the anthropological research of Sydney W. Mintz and Morris Siegel, rural Puerto Ricans had a "predilection ... for doing things illegally ... where something can be to one's advantage, one does it, illegal or not, especially where there is a strong need and tacit approval of the community."[9] Examples given at the time were "illegal slaughtering ... illegal rum ... illegal lottery." Even to this day, most Puerto Ricans will probably agree with this statement, even if its causes elude them.

The Prohibition, the legal ban on the manufacture, sale, or transportation of any alcoholic beverages in the United States from 1920 (Eighteenth Amendment) to 1933 (Twenty-First Amendment), was established in Puerto Rico earlier than in the United States because the 1917 Jones Act that declared that all born in the Island were considered US citizens, also mandated the holding of a referendum in Puerto Rico to determine if the Prohibition will be enforced there.[10] Missionaries and others supported the Prohibition that began in Puerto Rico in 1918. The only access to alcohol was through illegal sources, and many poor Puerto Ricans jumped at the opportunity of supplementing their meager incomes through the production of home-distilled rum called "pitorro" or "ron caña" made from the molasses of sugarcane.[11] On occasion, it became the livelihood of entire households. The activity was so popular that, despite police harassment, it became an example "of mass-based, illegal economic activity."[12]

The Insular Police tried to enforce the Prohibition through the frequent pursual of offenders. Between 1923 and 1933, there were three and five thousand infractions per year.[13] But bootlegging proved impossible to control as "... the men outside may down a nip of "cañita" ("clandestine cane rum") to combat the cool night air" (Wagenheim 1970, 161).

Another illegal practice that became persistent was the underground lottery called "la bolita" or "el bolipul." This system was associated with the government's official lottery. Usually, on "a Tuesday or Saturday night, illegal numbers-game sellers will be making their rounds, collecting bets placed on credit at an earlier time."[14] People bet money on three-digit combinations of numbers, and if someone's numbers coincided with the last three digits in the winning number for the official lottery (of six digits), the person won. The advantages of this system over the official lottery were that the prize was received immediately after the lottery, and that no taxes were paid over it. Both men and women sold "la bolita," an illegal activity that is still very much alive in Puerto Rico nowadays. Even though just during the late thirties, the Insular Police reported over fifteen thousand infractions for illegal gambling,[15] only one of the selected writers commented on it: "Despite all this legal access to betting, Puerto Ricans love to play clandestine games of chance, such as 'la bolita,' the small-time version of the lottery ..." (Wagenheim 1970, 226).

The almost total absence of comments regarding both bootlegging and "la bolita," which are still illegal and still very popular, supports the thesis that both practices were and still are pretty much hushed about, so only Kal Wagenheim, who married a Puerto Rican and therefore had an insight perspective on Puerto Rican culture, was able to come in contact with these themes.

"A RATHER LIGHT-WEIGHT LOT": POLICE AND MILITARY FORCES

During the US invasion, public order was enforced in Puerto Rico by the US military forces: regular troops plus eight US volunteers' companies. When the invasion concluded, the American military government in Puerto Rico organized the "Insular Police of Porto Rico" in February 1899. This force substituted the Spanish Guardia Civil de Puerto Rico, founded in 1837, and its 313 members were commanded by Colonel Frank Techner.[16] In August 1899, the municipalities were allowed to organize their Municipal Police forces. But in 1902, under the American civil government of Puerto Rico, most of the Municipal Police forces were incorporated into the Insular Police,[17] which then patrolled on foot, on horses, or on bicycles.[18]

All Insular Police members had to be citizens of Puerto Rico, between the ages of twenty-one and forty, not less than five-feet-six inches in height, weighting not less than 130 pounds, physically sound, of good character, and capable of reading and writing.[19] Vacancies in the highest ranks of officers were filled by the American governors exclusively with Americans, as Puerto Ricans were relegated to subordinate and rank-and-file positions.[20] Besides enforcing law and order, the Insular Police guarded all the prisons and also the prisoners while working outside the prisons. Over time, they were also used to control "electoral violence and labor agitation," as well as bootlegging and gambling.[21] A war correspondent made fun of Adjuntas' police consisting of a chief and twenty under him:

> They are a rather light-weight lot, and a fair specimen of the Bowery tough would probably have but little trouble in doing up a half-dozen or so of them in the course of an evening, without breaking his gait. . . . They were not stalwart six-footers—these police. That sort does not grow here. I doubt if any one of them weighed a hundred and twenty pounds, and a diet of plantains, beans and rice does not make men of brawn and muscle. (Robinson 1899, 74, 83)

But this American soldier recognized a local policeman's politeness in contrast with New York policemen: "A native policeman strutted past. . . . I greeted him with a 'Buenos noches, senor,' and he politely returned the courtesy. Imagine saying good night to a New York policeman! What would be the consequences? Probably a 'G'wan now and stop yer gab, if yez don't want ter be run in. See'" (Oliver 1900, 195).

In 1906, as US President Theodore Roosevelt visited Puerto Rico and spoke in Caguas and Cayey, this Republican representative witnessed this:

> A detachment of native troops was stationed nearby one of the towns and their natty appearance impressed us. They looked to be much superior to the unkempt natives. I inquired about the serviceability of the native soldier and the Governor [Beekman Winthrop, 1904–1907] said they were brave, honest and faithful. They were all right, he said, when they had a leader in whom they had confidence—if they trusted the leader they would follow him anywhere. . . . Their weakness was in overestimating their authority amongst the other natives, but the latter generally looked up to them. They were assisting materially in promoting "the American idea" amongst the islanders. (Moore 1907, 47)

When, during World War II, Puerto Ricans volunteered for military service, they discovered they were accepted but not trusted with any meaningful missions. American governor Rexford G. Tugwell commented on the racism that motivated this lack of trust in the capabilities of Puerto Ricans as soldiers:

None of those roving young mariners in the Caribbean in 1942 was Puerto Rican. The Navy still would not take them. But the Army was, somewhat reluctantly, shaping a different policy. It would be foolish to contend that there was not a prejudice in the Army against Puerto Ricans. The Continental officers, of course, maintained that it was an attitude based on facts. The facts cited were that Puerto Ricans were largely not only illiterate but natively unintelligent; that they would not fight since they were faintly disloyal; and that the educated among them made poor officers because they would not lead instead of drive. On the whole the Army was against Puerto Rican recruiting . . . and it was intended to confine this service to garrison duty at inactive posts.

. . . It was found, as time went on and the new techniques of jungle training and bush fighting were developed, that Puerto Ricans were not such bad soldiers after all, that, indeed, they had some qualities which were unique and valuable for the purposes now developing. But the reluctance of the continental army men to accept them as equals left a resentment which would never be altogether overcome. This sense of injury led to a far less enthusiastic service than might have been secured. (Tugwell 1947, 365–66)

Tugwell also described Puerto Rican soldiers:

As for the soldiers themselves, they often came to camp barefoot, straight from bohíos with dirt floors and no furniture; they were unaccustomed to any sanitary facility or to tools other than the universal machete; they might never have touched a machine of any sort, or even have moved a vehicle with wheels. They had, in fact, stepped out of the Middle Ages into a mechanized army. No wonder it took a long training to bring them into functioning in their newly aseptic, rigidly disciplined, mentally demanding life. (Tugwell 1947, 367)

"CARRYING THE GUN FOR THEIR GUARD": PRISON SYSTEM

Local prison guards were scorned as cowardly by an American soldier in 1899:

The native guards were timid to a degree, and under no circumstances would they appear in time of trouble alone. They moved about in twos and threes, or as many as could get together. The absolute terror of the guards of the jail in Arecibo of being left alone to guard a desperate criminal who had been captured by our soldiers, was laughable. They had faith neither in the bars of the jail nor in the webbed fetters by which he was held, but begged piteously for a United States guard, assuring the major that "he always got away." (Edwards 1899, 239–40)

In his 1914 evaluation of the system of vigilance in La Princesa prison (in Old San Juan), A. H. Verrill considered it superior to American prisons. He also commented on the trustworthiness of the inmates:

The guards and prison-keeper are courteous and obliging . . . Here the prisoners enjoy far greater liberty and better treatment than in our Northern prisons or jails. The whole building is spotlessly clean and neat . . . nowhere is there an appearance or the depressing effect of being behind barred windows and bolted doors. . . . The prisoners are kept busy, the trusties being sent out to work on the roads, and the others being employed in the tailor and shoe shops, kitchens, bakery, etc. The women prisoners do the laundry work; a large exercise ground is provided, and the boys and young men and women are given instruction in a well-equipped school. . . . They are well fed, are happy, contented, and healthy . . . many of the inmates are better off in jail than in their own houses, and they show no disposition to escape. . . . It is not unusual to find a party of convicts returning from work and one of them carrying the gun for their guard, while now and then a prisoner is dispatched on a message for a considerable distance without guards of any sort. (Verrill 1914, 40–42)

In 1960, an American journalist once again commented on the relaxed atmosphere prevailing in the Puerto Rican prisons that she visited:

This is a relaxed land, and even the prisons are relaxed. Prisoners can leave prison walls every day to work in Ayuda Mutua, in the mutual self-help houses. . . . The families paid the prisoners twenty-five cents and gave them lunch. Life is relaxed inside the prison gates too. Every three months, prisoners who are not repeaters of felony crimes, are allowed to go home to their wives and families for fifty-two hours. In the huge white concrete prison in Río Piedras, I walked through the carpentry shops where teachers from the Department of Education were training the prisoners. (Gruber 1960, 145–46)

THIS CHAPTER

The colonized society is a violent one. First, the violence came from Spanish authorities and then from American ones. The colonized receives direct or indirect violence from the colonizer and sometimes, unable to respond directly without getting in serious trouble, reflects that violence instead towards his fellow colonized. The emotional and passional spirit of the Puerto Ricans was frequently interpreted as a predisposition to criminal conduct, and socially sanctioned "crimes" such as bootlegging and "la bolita" became forms of resistance against the economic inequality that kept the poor poor. In the end, Puerto Ricans proved to be as law-abiding as any American.

Chapter 10

"THE BODY WAS THERE BUT NOT THE SOUL"

On the Puerto Ricans' Religious Practices

Religion is a well-known resource that helps empires establish their oppressive systems with the acquiescence of the colonized. This is explained by Frantz Fanon in the context of Catholicism: "The colonialist bourgeoisie is helped in its work of calming down the natives by the inevitable religion. All those saints who have turned the other cheek, who have forgiven trespasses against them, and who have been spat on and insulted without shrinking are studied and held up as examples."[1]

As a Spanish colony, the only religion accepted in Puerto Rico was Catholicism. Spain's principle of union of Church and State was transferred to all their colonies. The Catholic Church was financially supported by the Spanish State and held prestige and protection from any other religions. Nevertheless, the Catholic Church in Puerto Rico was elitist and urban, leaving to their own the mountain *jíbaros* and the poor. Besides the number of priests assigned to the Island being insufficient, "Puerto Rico's mountainous topology, and its few and dangerous roads meant that thousands of rural or isolated parishioners seldom saw a priest."[2]

This "disassociation between the Catholic clergy and the masses of workers" was studied by Fernando Picó, who identified some of its manifestations: the institutional racism of the Catholic Church in Spain; its rejection of expressions of popular religiosity like the altars of saints in homes, the devotion to unsanctioned apparitions of Virgin Mary, and the Three Kings' wakes; its support to repressive measures taken by the government; and the excessive amounts charged by the clergy for burials, the anointing of the sick and marriage ceremonies.[3]

Regarding the excessive charges required by the Catholic clergy for the administration of the sacraments, several American Protestant missionaries explained how they alienated the poor:

The poor in this island are not "good Catholics" because, as they admit, they "cannot afford it." "Dollars are scarce" is the reply to the question, "Why is not your child baptized?" "I have no fine clothes," is the excuse for not attending church on feast days. "Why do you bury your wife like a dog, without having mass said to her?" is another question asked, which has brought the piteous answer, "Because I have living mouths to feed and the dead do not hunger." (Johnston 1905, 150)

Another way in which the Catholic Church "abandoned" the Puerto Ricans was by always siding with the Spanish monarchy and its authoritarian and repressive colonial policies and opposing all liberal reforms requested by Puerto Ricans.[4] Even if they considered themselves Catholic, most poor peasants only visited Catholic churches on special holidays or celebrations. Their everyday spiritual needs were, thus, served by alternative belief systems such as Spiritism (also called Spiritualism) and Santería.[5] *Santería* is an Afro-Caribbean religion born of the syncretism or combination of Catholicism and Yoruba religion. Also known as *Regla de Ocha*, it worships African divinities through their equivalent Catholic saints and the Virgin Mary's apparitions. It is popular in Cuba, Brazil, and Puerto Rico. Spiritism (*Espiritismo*) is a secular philosophy based on the belief in reincarnation, the existence of parallel worlds, and the communication between incarnate and disembodied spirits.

In their religious ideas, many Puerto Ricans comingled the belief in the powers of spells, evil eye, and witchcraft with the belief in the powers of images, medals, or scapulars of Catholic saints and virgins.[6] The Catholic saints were particularly dear to many Puerto Ricans who developed quasi-personal relationships with their favorite ones. They asked for favors from their saints (such as a healthy baby, the cure for an illness, a good harvest, etc.), and if conceded, they paid them with devotion or specific vows.[7] Indeed, a Mennonite missionary commented:

Some of the country people attend Catholic religious gatherings only several times a year, and the smattering of religious belief which they receive from the church is closely coupled with superstitions passed down from generation to generation. Some of their religious beliefs show superstitious characteristics that were probably inherited from their Indian ancestors.... Their religious devotion to a saint is often far more pagan and superstitious than religious and sacred. (Holsinger 1952, 37)

A few Christian missionaries wrote about this abandonment of the Catholic Church's role as a moral guide for Puerto Ricans. Some concluded that the institution of so many holidays promoted "laziness" and associated the church with entertainment:

> The Sabbath[8] day was desecrated, it being the chief market and business day of the week, and a day for gambling, cock-fighting and the like. Indolence was encouraged by teaching the people to observe forty holidays annually, connected with which were many superstitious ideas.... The immorality of the priests and the ignorance and superstitious doctrines fostered by the church combined to make it practically impossible for a small percentage of the people who came in contact with the Catholic Church to be able to grasp the spiritual significance of the religion of Jesus Christ. As a result, great numbers of the men have drifted into utter indifference and unbelief concerning all spiritual realities ... (Mills et al. 1908, 186–87)

Other missionaries pointed out the lack of physical presence of the priests in the lives of rural Puerto Ricans as all churches were located in the center of the towns:

> Although 82 per cent of the population was rural, the [Catholic] priests built no rural churches, nor did any of them locate in remote communities. The people of the mountains received little or no religious instruction except as they might go into the towns for an occasional feast day or, more rarely, for a baptism or marriage. The dead were buried without a religious service, and couples were mated without the sanction of church or state. Witchcraft prevailed. (Morton 1949, 9)

In 1899, journalist William Dinwiddie painted a picture of a decadent Catholic clergy, blaming it on the coalition of Church and State under Spanish law, which, by sustaining them, provided no motivation for their active involvement with the communities they were supposed to serve:

> ... the real weakness in the ecclesiastical system of the island ... lay in the fact that the church and state leaned upon one another in close association . . . their representatives are directly dependent upon a civil government for their support.... The life of the clergy seems to have been one of idleness and almost complete indolence in the past; they have never been active factors in an effort to ameliorate the depressed condition of the people; they have never been educators.... There have been, of course, exceptions to this rule.... (Dinwiddie 1899, 203–5)

American authors accused Catholic priests of living in open concubinage, gambling, and other corrupt actions. According to American missionaries, with their bad example, the priests promoted the immorality of Puerto Ricans:

> We are looking for a site to build on L.... The priest is a wicked, unscrupulous man. Conscience doesn't trouble him apparently in the least. I never heard a man, even in Spanish, that can swear more freely than he. He is a gambler; I saw him at it, before I knew he was a priest. He lives with a woman, and has a family of her. He never preaches of course, says Mass sometimes. All his time is given to gossiping and fooling the people about the Protestants. (Douglass 1910, 49)

Another source of conflict with American Protestants was the Catholic ideal way of life: a humble existence with detachment from earthly goods, where people work just enough to fulfill their personal needs and nothing more: "Work is for man, not man for work."[9] Protestant missionaries clearly stated that the Catholic Church in the United States was more "enlightened" than the one in Puerto Rico thanks to the influence of Protestantism: "The Catholic Church of Porto Rico is very different from the church of the same name in the United States, which ... has been enlightened by one hundred years of contact with aggressive, spiritual Protestantism" (Mills et al. 1908, 186).

In the United States, although there was a constitutional separation of Church and State, in reality, they were attuned perfectly. We have to remember that the US Constitution was written, for the most part, by men with a puritanical view of life. As Max Weber analyzed, the Puritan/Calvinist emphasis on avoidance of idleness and embracement of hard work in order to stay safe from sinning and in rejection of mundane activities and spending made this Protestantism the perfect match for a capitalist-based nation.[10] Together, modern industrial capitalism and Puritan Protestantism will follow the American flag into the Island[11] with the mission of bringing to Puerto Ricans a new vision of life "based on the continuous pursuit of profit, on the equivalence of time/credit and money, and on the promotion of values such as punctuality, commercial and industrial spirit, and the production and investment of capital."[12]

"WOMB TO TOMB": CATHOLIC RELIGIOSITY BEFORE AND AFTER THE US INVASION

The first known report about the state of religion in Puerto Rico was made by Catholic Father Thomas E. Sherman, the son of the famous General

Tecumseh Sherman, who, after a three-month tour through the Island, wrote to Governor-General John R. Brooke. This document became a source of information consulted by many of the American authors during the first twenty years of US colonialism in Puerto Rico. Sherman reported that, even though in every town there was a "large and handsome" Catholic church, they were "very poorly attended" and that most men were just "Catholic in name," concluding that "Religion is dead on the island" (As reported in Edwards 1899, 247).

An American missionary also mentioned a separate report that was decisive for American Mission Boards, although most books on this topic do not mention it:

> In the fall of 1898, even before the Spanish flag had been taken down ... W. H. Sloan, a Baptist missionary from Mexico, at his ... own expense was touring the island and preaching to the people by the roadside. He wrote back to New York of the eagerness of the people to hear and the slight hold that the Roman Church had upon their hearts. . . . Clearly, here was a call to the church of Christ in the United States, to enter Porto Rico and give to the people what our Government could not give, Christian institutions, to take the place of those that were crumbling in ruins. (Detweiler 1930, 22–23)

Several American authors commented on how they evaluated the level of faith of Puerto Ricans right after the US invasion:

> While the priests and nuns of Porto Rico all seemed to be truly good and noble, and doing their utmost, yet one somehow got the feeling that there was very little true religion. The body was there but not the soul. This is simply an impression and may be a wrong one. And possibly a Porto Rican might form the same opinion of us with equal justice. (Rossiter [1900?])

Similar criticism of the lack of spirituality and real practice of Catholicism on the part of Puerto Ricans was brought by an American missionary after twelve years of American colonial government there:

> Religion in Porto Rico, as taught by Roman Catholicism, was a matter of formality, attending mass and confession, joining in the religious processions and observing the forty or fifty "fiesta" days by refraining from labor, giving due reverence to the priests, conforming to certain customs when within the church walls. No schools, no Sabbaths, no real homes, a profligate priesthood supervising religion—what wonder that

the people came to have little respect for such a religion, and as far as the men were concerned abandoned church-going and all pretense of loyalty to the organization. (Grose 1910, 207)

But it was an American English teacher at CAAM, Mayagüez, who, in the early 1950s, made the most detailed attempt to explain the possible reasons for the lack of spirituality and practice of Catholicism, beginning with the lack of authority of American priests and nuns in the eyes of the Puerto Ricans:

> When I first came to the island I assumed that the population was overwhelmingly Catholic. . . . But though there was the traditional Catholic church on the central plaza of all the towns, usually across from the city hall, the churches were usually closed or, if open, looked empty. They were well kept up, were certainly not deserted or abandoned, but you never saw any people going in and out, even when the doors were open. I soon found out that most Puerto Ricans are Catholic in name only, if that. In asking other students the same question, I found out that most of them said they were Catholics, but that this had very little or nothing to do with the church they attended. The only students, it turned out, who went to church regularly, attended the Pentecostal churches.
>
> I asked one of the continental teachers about this, since I knew he was a very devout Catholic and attended church every Sunday. He was upset and discouraged about the status of the Church on the island. He said that the Catholic churches were almost empty on Sundays, that all the priests and nuns were from the mainland and, as an example, said that one of the things which most annoyed him every week was that the priest will always go on at great length that it was a mortal sin to eat meat on Friday, that they should _not_ eat meat on Friday. On the way out, he said, any Puerto Ricans who were there would turn to him and say. "But that doesn't apply to us, you know. We have a special dispensation. _We_ can eat meat on Friday." . . . Their attitude toward divorce; birth control and sterilization were the same. Those things didn't apply to _them!_ Besides, what did that priest know? He wasn't even a Puerto Rican! There were, in fact, no Puerto Rican priests at that time . . . (Cooper 1994, 111–12)

Regardless of their attendance, or lack thereof, to Catholic Mass, most Puerto Ricans showed respect for all kinds of religious celebrations, as was noted by this journalist, who highlighted this in comparison with the lack of respect in a hurried and money-centered American society:

The people, no matter what they believe, treat these events with profound courtesy, and uncover themselves, standing in silence until the affair has gone by. Often the traffic of a business street will cease for a few minutes out of respect, it may be for a marriage procession, a funeral, the carrying of a relic to a sick-bed, or the celebration of the anniversary of some saint. There is a certain vague pleasure in this courteous treatment of religious ceremonies which is in marked contrast with the fierce business turmoil of the great American cities, where nothing is ever permitted to interfere with the mad pursuit of the flying dollar. (Hamm, *Porto* 1899, 120)

In 1897, only twenty-one percent of the Catholic priests were Puerto Rican.[13] The few Catholic priests and nuns who did not return to Spain after the invasion were soon joined by American priests and nuns. The few Spanish and Puerto Rican priests and nuns who remained had to accept new realities: they would follow orders from the Catholic Church in the United States. With the separation of Church and State, the colonial state will not support them anymore; their Church will be forced to surrender many buildings and other properties to the colonial government; and their Church will lose privileges such as their monopolistic control over cemeteries, marriage ceremonies, civil registry, and public education, among other.

An American Protestant missionary pointed to the new need to ask for alms that Catholic priests and nuns had to engage in once the government no longer supported them, a situation that probably was quite humiliating for them. The account also illustrates the fierce competition for parishioners between Protestants and Catholics on Puerto Rican soil:

The Roman Catholic nuns go about daily, begging from house to house and from store to store, for money to sustain their convents, putting generally "the Holy Sacrament," or "Blessed Souls" as the objects for their charity.... If a servant answers their rap at the door she is keenly questioned, and if she has the courage to overcome her superstitious fears of these black-robed, mysterious women, and boldly tell them she is a Protestant, she is bitterly reproached and reprimanded, and ordered to go to the parish priest and confess, on penalty, if she refuses to do so, of being forever condemned with the Protestants. (Johnston 1905, 171)

These traumatic years of adaptation were a true challenge for the first American Catholic bishop in Puerto Rico, German-born William Blenk, who, after the first five years (June 5, 1905), reported that "the power of the church to do good has been destroyed."[14] In this period, Puerto Ricans who lived in the rural areas of the Island resorted to popular religious expressions that they learned from their mothers, aunts, and grandmothers to express their faith in god: "home altars, memorized prayers . . . and devotion to the saints."[15] The group recitation of the rosary became a substitute for the unavailable Catholic mass, especially during special crises such as upcoming hurricanes or serious illnesses of loved ones.

As they managed their new reality, Catholic priests and nuns also had to compete with the zealous Protestant missionaries for the trust and support of the Puerto Ricans. A war correspondent, quoting from a colleague of the *New York Sun*, provided this disparaging view of Sunday Catholic services in Puerto Rico:

> The manner of keeping Sunday would be apt to shock our New Englanders of Puritan descent. . . . ["] . . . giving Sunday mornings to church and Sunday afternoons to pleasure. In Ponce the merchants are not willing to close their stores for the religious observances of the day, but hold that it would be wholly wrong to mar the hours of pleasure by business attentions. . . . The priests have not been paid since the arrival of the American army. It was the Spanish custom to pay them from the customs receipts. Colonel Hill has refused to give them any money since he has been in charge of the custom-house, and has told them that hereafter their people will have to support them voluntarily. . . . Under existing laws, they are taxed for the support of the church. ["] (Hall 1898)

Something that surprised many American authors was the fact that Sunday was a day of entertainment in Puerto Rico. In 1899, Frederick Ober commented how on Sunday morning, from 8:00 to 9:00 a.m., the San Juan municipality held its lottery: "two perspiring black boys turning a crank attached to an immense wooden globe within which, as it is hollow, were the tickets" (Ober 1899, 177). After that came the bullfights and the cockfights in the suburbs. Baptist minister Howard Grose emphasized the lack of respect towards the "day of rest" or Sabbath:

> . . . the Roman Church had no word to say against the common vice of gambling, or the degrading sport of cock-fighting. Indeed, Sunday was the day for sports and all forms of recreation. Our missionaries have to work against the fact that there is no Sunday properly speaking in Porto Rico. Sunday morning is the chief market time of the week, and the crowds are in the market-place, not in the churches. . . . Sunday afternoon was the regular time for cock-fighting exhibitions. . . . Sunday evening is given to the "bailes," or balls, which last far into the night, with

forty dances or more in the night's program. This is the time also for the promenades in the plazas and the band concerts. When the great annual carnival comes, with its ten days of festivities, the closing feature is a grand parade of masqueraders on Sunday afternoon. Instead of teaching the people to keep the Sabbath day holy, the Church sanctioned the turning of it into the chief pleasure day of the week. (Grose 1910, 206–7)

In the 1940s, Sundays allowed an American doctor to eyewitness from his balcony the arrival to the Catholic Church of Puerto Ricans, mostly women, who had made promises to God, Jesus, the Virgin Mary, or some saint to dress in a religious habit, a particularly unattractive garb, for a determined amount of time (or for life) if their loved ones came safe from World War II or sorted some illness.[16] Since Puerto Rican women are well known for their care in dressing up, this was a real sacrifice.[17] The religious habit was described by Dr. Herman J. Flax, an orthodox Jew:

Since our balcony was on the second floor, we were not privy to first-hand gossip, the real stuff, but had to be content with people watching. Sunday was the best time, because the whole family passed by on their way to and from church, dressed in all their finery. There were penitents with bowed heads and secret promises, dressed in their conspicuous costumes. These looked like a monk's robe, either brown or white, gathered at the waist and knotted with a white cord belt that terminated in two or four, hand-like balls, hanging loosely down the side. They never changed this garb until their problem was solved.... During the Forties, the number of robbed individuals, usually females, increased enormously [because of WWII]. It was obvious that the wives wanted their husbands back safely, the girls their lovers and mothers their sons. I wish to make clear that this was not a penitent's punishment. It was a promise, a vow, made to God, to the Virgin Mary or to some Saint not to remove the garment, the sack-cloth, until a stipulated period of sacrifice, or "suffering" was completed. (Flax 1995, 20)

In 1970, an American journalist provided a panoramic of the practice of Catholicism in Puerto Rico. He pointed out how, regardless of the level of faith, or its lack thereof, on the part of a Puerto Rican, his/her everyday conversations were spattered with references to the Virgin Mary and God:

But the prevailing mood is a kind of "womb to tomb" Roman Catholicism, with little practice in between. Christianity permeates even daily conversation. It is common in the countryside for a child, when entering or leaving the home, to request a "bendición" ("blessing") from the father, who will respond, "May God and the Virgin bless you." In planning a matter as casual as meeting for lunch the next day, many Puerto Ricans will add, "Si Dios quiere" ("God willing"). Common expressions of surprise are "Ay virgin!" and "Ave María!". . . . Even more frequent, to express or plead for compassion, is "Ay bandito!" which is short for "Bendito sea El Señor" ("Blessed be The Lord")

Almost all homes in Puerto Rico, from mansions to shacks, are adorned with pictures of Christ, crucifixes, or figurines of saints. Children are taught to fear "el Diablo" and to respect "Papa Dios" ("Father God"). People often cross themselves when passing in front of a church. Each year, towns and villages celebrate festivals honoring their patron saint. Periods such as Holy Week, or between Christmas and Three Kings' Day (Epiphany) feature many masses and processions. When a new business opens, be it a mammoth bank building or a humble laundromat, the ubiquitous priest appears, with holy water and a blessing. But Puerto Rico's Catholicism is hardly orthodox; it is often mixed with personalistic saint worship, spiritism, and superstition. (Wagenheim 1970, 160)

The overall presence of religious symbols and expressions was also highlighted by a former Catholic nun in her analysis of Puerto Ricans' religiosity in the twenty-first century:

When empathizing with someone's misfortune, the phrase, "ay bandito" means "oh, what a pity" or "oh, my goodness." Disbelief or frustration is often expressed by saying "Ave Maria Purisima," "Hail Mary, the most pure one" and upon receiving bad news or when in need of God's help, Puerto Ricans declare "Dios mio!" or "my God!." . . . Even among Protestants, the presence of a home altar, religious symbols, a Bible opened to a favorite passage, or an image of Christ knocking on a door are also common practices. . . . Overall, Puerto Ricans are a very religious people, despite the fact that many attend mass/church only on major holy days. (Tavenner 2010, 129–30)

"VISITING FROM HOUSE TO HOUSE": THE FULL ENTRANCE OF PROTESTANTISM

As explained, Spanish Catholicism was protected and financed by the Spanish government, but by the end of the nineteenth century, a liberal government in Spain accepted the tolerance of Protestantism to a certain level. Because of this, in 1873, the Anglican Church was allowed to conduct public services in the city of Ponce, as long as their brethren entered through a side door and no bells were tolled.[18]

Right after the US invasion in 1899, American Protestant leaders from four denominations met in New York City and literally divided a Puerto Rican map into four regions, assigning a region where to proselytize to each denomination: Presbyterian, Methodist Episcopal, Congregational, and American Baptist. The regions of San Juan and Ponce were open to all denominations, and in 1900 other denominations were incorporated into the agreement: Disciples of Christ, United Brethren, Christian Missionary Alliance, and Lutheran Church. Soon after, missionaries followed, bringing with them money to build schools and hospitals. Interestingly, the Protestant churches decided to exclude Black missionaries from their missions in Puerto Rico, maybe echoing the refusal of General James Wilson to include Black soldiers in the occupation army going to Puerto Rico.[19]

By 1913, there were twelve different Protestant denominations in Puerto Rico, with 107 American missionaries and two hundred Puerto Rican "collaborators" serving in five hundred organized congregations with a total of 13,355 members.[20] A positive side effect of their arrival was the speeding of the alphabetization of Puerto Ricans since these Protestant religions, as opposed to Catholicism, encouraged the reading of the New Testament. The schools, orphanages, and hospitals established by Protestant churches also improved their penetration in the central mountainous part of the Island. As a Disciples of Christ minister explained:

> The services were different, consisting of reading and writing as a great majority could not write their names. It was line upon line and precept upon precept. . . . It was a new experience for them and attracted attention because of the fact they were learning to read. . . . Much of our time was given to this teaching for a number of years until the public school could do it for us. . . . This approach was very helpful, because they thought we had come to change their religion. When they saw we wanted them to learn first it was something that no one else had done before so they said to themselves they are our friends. (Carpenter 1960, 33–34)

Missionaries reported about the state of religion in Puerto Rico as a promising one, although these reports actually tended to describe more auspicious expectations than what reality granted because these books were used to entice donations for the mission work:

Says Bishop James H. Van Buren, "... The poorer people hear the Gospel gladly, and come in great number to listen to any one who can speak to them in their own language. They are eager to have their children attend the mission schools. Never was there an opportunity more rich in its invitation and possibilities, than Porto Rico presents to-day." (Johnston 1905, 139)

In his seminal book about American Protestantism in Puerto Rico, Dr. Samuel Silva Gotay discussed how American Protestant missionaries came with the intention of converting Puerto Ricans to "the real Christianity," as opposed to the Catholic Christianity they had received from the Spanish. They came to morally transform the population by educating them on the Protestant culture and ethics that they considered a requisite for Puerto Ricans to become "citizens of the United States."[21] An American soldier expressed how he saw the role of Protestant churches in the process of controlling the newly acquired colony: "When our zealous missionaries have succeeded in leading them into the confines of other creeds, we shall have all the excitement we want in Puerto Rico, and the part of our army stationed there will have no lack of exercise" (Herrmann 1900, 35).

To the surprise of Catholic authorities, many Puerto Ricans did respond to the efforts of the Protestant missionaries, especially in the countryside, where the peasants had felt "abandoned" by the Catholic Church for a long time and now welcomed the horseback missionaries who came looking for them. The Protestant missionaries and their morals came to fill the vacuum created by the priests' absence: "I road with our mission workers for days up into the mountains and down to the playas, where I preached ... There are Protestant churches in every city and town on the island; also in the mountains are many chapels ..." (Mathews 1912, 4).

Their novel way of proselytizing, right on Puerto Ricans' doorsteps, was welcomed by the many who, being taught to be polite with visitors, respectfully received at their modest homes the Protestant missionaries who displayed interest in their lives:

Visiting from house to house is one of the chief means employed to gain acquaintance with the people, grow familiar with their homes, and come close to their hearts.... The children run to meet the visitor, an American lady in such quarters being a novelty, and inside the wretched rooms the mothers put down their irons and leave their tubs to entertain the welcome messenger, while an eager crowd of unkempt children gathers at the door.... The women eagerly take the Spanish tracts, though few of them can read. Sitting upon a box or broken chair the deaconess reads to the interested groups that gather about, and they tell her of their bare and bitter lives. Looking into their faces she thinks of the poverty and oppression and the superstition under which they have long been bound.... The confidence with which people come in their trouble, to the Protestants, marks the estimate in which they are held, compared with the Romish priests. (Johnston 1905, 145–46)

Still, the task of convincing Puerto Ricans to join Protestantism was not that easy. Real challenges, according to these American missionaries, were the powers Puerto Ricans traditionally assigned to the Virgin Mary and the saints and the authenticity of the shown devotion: "It costs these dear creyentes a pang to give their idea of Mary's power with her Son. Much less it costs to look with disfavor upon confession to priests, and even to doubt the value of the propitiation of saints. But the beautiful, tender, sorrowing 'Mother of God' makes strong appeal to their hearts" (Duggan 1920, 94).

Another challenge identified by American missionaries was the religious names that Puerto Ricans, as well as many other Latin American parents, gave (and still give) to their offspring, such as "Jesús"[22] or "Juan Bautista" ("John the Baptist"), which are never used as such in the Anglo-Saxon tradition, as that was interpreted as blasphemy:[23]

Even the names of these people make the missionary's task more difficult. Often a child is named for the patron saint of the day on which he was born and in addition will usually have some Biblical cognomen added. Popular names for the girls are Resurrección, Concepción, Asunción.... The chief carpenter's [of a mission building] name was Jesús while his peon's name was John the Baptist. The new missionary... had to invent nicknames for the men. (James 1927, 39)

The early success of the Protestant missionaries was reported by many American authors. Some even attributed their success precisely to the warnings against them made by the Catholic priests, which made Puerto Ricans more curious about their services. Also, the singing in Spanish attracted many Puerto Ricans who felt alienated from the Latin chants of Catholic masses:

Mr Wood... hold services weekly in a rented store front.... It was not too bad, they had the habit of going to the place as a store, so came to the church as usual. In the start it was slow because the folks had lost faith in religion.... We began to grow when the Roman Church through the priest began to fight us. It stirred up good interest. People liked it....

The songs were committed to memory one line at a time and oh how they did sing.... You would think that you were in a Pentecostal meeting if you were to attend. The Latin wants to express himself differently to what we do. They want something of their own.... They have converted the Guitar, Maracas and hand clapping, etc. and you would hear some hallelujahs and glorias in the services. (Carpenter 1960, 33, 36)

However, many converts embraced Protestant Christianity in their own way, blending it with other spiritual practices popular in Puerto Rico. This, of course, alarmed the mission boards. Spiritism became a common theme of American missionaries and other authors because of its popularity:

"Spiritism" is very prevailed both in Porto Rico and Cuba. It is spiritualism and more. It has its mediums, its table tipping, knockings, etc. and has arrayed itself to a considerable extent in a Christian garb. There are numerous organizations for the propagation of this faith. They teach the repeated reincarnations of human spirits until at length perfection shall be attained.... It is estimated that a third of the population are adherents of this system. At first they thought that we, who placed so much stress upon spirituality and the insufficiency of ceremonies as means of salvation, were essentially like themselves and were ready to join our churches. They soon found, however, the radical differences between us and fell away, though some have come to a knowledge of the truth. (Morehouse 1904, 24)

It is common among amateur observers of a new and unknown religious expression to associate it with the devil, sorcery, or witchcraft: "... it has often been shown that when two civilizations come into contact the lesser is always accused of sorcery by half-studied and ill-informed judgments of the greater."[24] Indeed, many authors discussed the religious practices of Puerto Ricans, labeling them as "sorcery," "fetishism," or "heathenism." Also, Freethinkers were considered a small but negative force in Puerto Rico by Protestant missionaries because of their anticlerical positions. They became a target for Protestant proselytism:

The purely negative side of the religious life of Porto Rico is expressed in the rationalism and indifference of the Island. The rationalists or freethinkers (libre pensadores) theoretically believe in material conception of the universe. They profess to have nothing to do with anything that savors of the spiritual.... As an organization they are small in numbers, but they have many semi-adherents throughout the Island....

Cheap Biblical criticism appears every week [in their periodical papers]. Those that are indifferent to any kind of religious appeal form the largest section of the population of the island.... It is among these honest doubters that the Protestant Churches do their most effective work. (James 1927, 41–42)

And there were some locals who used violence or threatened it to express their discontent with the new Protestant services that endangered the world as they knew it: "Much opposition has been encountered in the opening of the first Protestant service in many districts. Sometimes the house in which the meeting was held has been stoned, and the lives of those inclined to attend the meeting threatened; but the people are learning under the American Government, that it is perfectly safe to attend..." (Mills et al. 1908, 208).

Another serious problem confronted by the Protestant missions was the difficult adaptation of their American missionaries to the tropical climate, the food, and other new conditions they faced while in Puerto Rico. The seriousness of this issue is illustrated by several American missionaries:

For an all year residence Americans find the climate enervating, and need frequent furloughs to get the brace of our northern ozone. The American missionaries ought to come home once in two or three years. (Grose 1910, 173)

... of all the home-mission fields in Latin America, Porto Rico has been the most severe on the health of the foreign worker. This is not altogether due to the climate, but is the result in large measure of overwork, to which the missionaries have been driven by the dense population.... The fact that Porto Rico is a small island naturally brings the missionary into close touch with his people; they have not far to go to find him in order to pour their troubles into his ear. There is a constant pressure and appeal that is not known in other countries. (Detweiler 1930, 33, 35)

The cultural and religious differences between Puerto Ricans and American missionaries became particularly obvious regarding the celebration of the Christian Holy Week and Easter. Marion Blythe, a young missionary then living in Aguadilla (which she called Doquiere), described the lack of "holiness" in the way Puerto Rican Catholics celebrated them. As she shared her vivid description of the celebrations, she also showed her class prejudice when she called the lower classes "the least intelligent" or "the street rabble." Blythe also gave particular attention to the early morning Holy Saturday celebration of the Meeting Procession (*Procesión del Encuentro*) and the Judas' races (*Corridas de Júas*),[25] which, to her horror, were understood by some as the main part of the Easter celebration:

> Our idea of Easter is quite foreign to the people here. They do not think of it as the day of Christ's resurrection primarily, nor do they feel any of the freshness and sweetness and newness of life that is attached to the day in our land. The days of the Holy Week seem to us to be anything but holy. If you ask the average Porto Rican of the least intelligent classes—and they far outnumber the higher classes—what Holy Week is, they will tell you that it is a week of holidays and processions ... and in many towns the majority of the people give little or no attention to them, while in others there is little else to be seen or heard. Here in Doquiere [Aguadilla] all is comparatively quiet during the earliest part of the week. On Thursday, the day of the crucifixion ... the bells are tolled.
>
> Friday, the day of burial ... is the day of horrors to us. At three o'clock the burial procession leaves the Catholic church. First comes a large gilded casket which contains a more than life-sized wax figure of the body of the Christ, which can be seen through the glass front of the casket. This is placed upon a splendid gilt bier which is borne on the shoulders of men. Then comes a procession of priest and people ... Then we see a large figure dressed in black, carrying in her hand a black-bordered handkerchief. It is Mary, mourning for the death of her Son. There are groups of altar boys bearing candles, groups of girls and groups of women ... the procession ... is led by the town band and followed by the street rabble. They pass through the principal streets of town and then return to the church.
>
> On Saturday, all is quiet. Even the bells are not rung. But early on Sunday morning ... the clanging of bells and the shouts of the rabble in the streets, for on the plaza there is another demonstration in honor of the glorious resurrection day. Two processions are formed. One is headed by an image of Christ, and the other by an image of Mary. These two divisions move in opposite directions around the city square until they meet, when the images are made to bow to each other. This is Mary greeting the risen Christ. Then another figure appears.... It is an effigy of Judas, who has betrayed his Master. It is sometimes carried and sometimes mounted on a horse. It is seized by the mob, torn limb from limb and carried out of the city, and often the luckless horse ... is cruelly treated, and the scrabble continues until they have banished the traitor Judas from their midst. [A Sunday school boy of hers described in a class what Easter days stands for:] "It's the day they run Judas out of town." (Blythe 1911, 193–95)

Another Catholic celebration mentioned by a few American authors was the Fiestas de Cruz, celebrated every May in commemoration of an earthquake on May 3, 1797, in which a group that prayed around a big cross were not hurt.[26] It consists of a sung rosary that includes nineteen special songs in front of an altar of a large cross adorned with candles, flowers, and ribbons:

> "La fiesta de Cruz" is a quaint religious festival which lasts for nine days during the month of May, at which time also the Southern Cross constellation is at its highest point in the sky of Porto Rico. In the open air or indoors a small cross is erected upon an altar with nine steps. This altar is adorned with flowers, tapers, and cherished relics.... voices intoning litanies and chants written for the occasion ... while reverent figures kneel about it singing. (Van Deusen and Van Deusen 1931, 178)

Judging by their own appraisals, Protestant missionaries had an enormous success that their numbers did not confirm. Since their books were written for their religious communities in the United States, they presented their accomplishments somewhat enlarged. Since as early as 1907, Protestant missionaries were already boasting about the almost "miraculous" transformation and regeneration they had already inspired in Puerto Ricans:

> Men who were given to drinking rum have become total abstainers. Gamblers have been changed into honest men ... Great changes have taken place among men and women with respect to the kind of language they use and to truthfulness of speech.... Porto Rico is rapidly being regenerated, and her children will soon be as intelligent and as moral as those of any other part of the Great Republic. (Fowles 1910, 125)
>
> ... visitors from the north ... come expecting ... small groups of people brought together by all sorts of inducements. They are greatly surprised to see the enthusiasm, spontaneity, and interest of the Porto Rican in his church.... The greatest influence of the evangelical churches in Porto Rico is in the country.... The country services of the evangelical churches are the only opportunity for worship the "jíbaro" or peasant has. In many instances people walk over ten miles each week across mountain and stream to some preaching center.... The cottage service is very popular, and often is the only kind of service that can be had. With his customary generosity the Porto Rican will offer the use of his house for "los protestantes" even though he is not a believer. (James 1927, 58–61)

But by the 1920s, we also find more down-to-earth missionary testimonies that recognized their lack of success in converting Puerto Ricans to Protestantism:

> It is true that the majority of the people have deserted the priests and the churches that long held imperial sway over them, and that the old regime is waning in its influence, but is not true that this majority, or even a major fraction of it, have responded to the appeal of a vital spiritual religion.... Such is not the case.... In large measure they stand unrelated to the evangelical movement. (Drury 1924, 21–22)

After a few years, the competition for souls led the missionaries to accept more and more compromises, and eventually, they realized that the future of Protestantism in Puerto Rico depended on the development of local ministries. They decided to ordain Puerto Rican ministers, a factor that attracted many poor Puerto Ricans.[27] This confronted them with the challenge of instructing Puerto Rican preachers according to the cultural expectations of American Protestantism. The clash was inevitable because styles depended too much on cultural traits and because most of the Puerto Rican ministers came from the lower classes, and their preaching styles alienated the elites. The expressions by American missionaries regarding the lack of education and culture of Puerto Rican ministers clearly denoted the prejudice of the Americans:

> The salvation of Porto Rico . . . depends upon the development of a native ministry.... These simple and practical beginnings have developed a remarkable corps of Porto Rican evangelists.... It is, however, increasingly manifest that the development of a stable and intelligent church life requires more adequately trained workers. While the Porto Rican has a native gift of speech, he frequently lacks in self-restraint and in genuine thoughtfulness.... All the faults of the first disciples are found in these men. Finally, most of them were converted too late ever to acquire a thorough-going education. The relative failure of Protestantism to reach the more cultivated classes in Porto Rico is partly due to the rudeness of many of these devoted evangelists. (Douglass 1910, 38–40)

Charles S. Detweiler also commented on the clash between the local idea of a preacher and his duties and the American one. In Protestantism, and definitely in missionary work, manual work was welcomed and encouraged as a way to remain humble, but Puerto Rican preachers had as a model the Catholic priests who scorned manual work and were considered part of the local elite:

[About the students at the Theological Seminary in Río Piedras] . . . Most of them had come from the humbler classes, and this was a step upward into a higher social class. If we asked one of them to sweep the halls or mop the floor he considered it a degradation; it subjected him to the danger of being considered a peon, when in reality he held himself to belong to one of the professions. How could we succeed in changing this attitude of mind, so unworthy of the Christian ministry? . . . Boys who live in the towns and wear shoes have never been accustomed to manual labor, and therefore, it is no easy task to get them to wield a pick and hoe in the hot morning sun. . . . Of course they were rebellious in having to undertake that kind of work; they had come to Rio Piedras to study for the ministry and not to learn agriculture. (Detweiler 1930, 47–48)

A Disciples of Christ missionary tried to explain the difficult relationship between native and foreign Protestant leaders:

. . . between the missionaries and nationals. Although an excellent relationship had prevailed, there was a tendency for the missionaries to feel sometimes that the nationals were not altogether frank with them, and for the nationals to feel that the missionaries thought themselves superior. This situation resulted in a tendency to form a little bloc excluding the missionaries.

. . . the placing of control in the hands of the Puerto Ricans revealed hitherto latent capabilities for the carrying of responsibility. . . . Puerto Rican Disciples believe in prayer, and they pray with an earnestness, constancy, and confidence that are lacking in the prayer life of their more sophisticated northern neighbors. . . . Puerto Rican Christians believe in God as a personal, living, working, loving Father. . . . . . . the most outstanding feature of the Protestant church in Puerto Rico . . . is the excellence of the native leadership. . . . No sophisticated, cold, formal Anglo-Saxon type of worship will find favor in Puerto Rico. (Morton 1949, 57–58, 71, 87, 108)

Besides this, native pastors received lower salaries than American ones, and some complained accordingly as soon as they realized the discriminatory practice:

. . . in training Porto-Rican pastors . . . the difficulties that had to be surmounted in making possible this achievement. There were periods of great tension, when waves of anti-Americanism swept over the island and illy affected the hearts of the pastors towards the foreign missionaries. In their poverty they were tempted to believe . . . that they were discriminated against in matters of salary because of their race. There is a difference in the salary paid to the foreign missionary and the local pastor that can be justified on several accounts . . . (Detweiler 1930, 36)

Pentecostalism arrived in Puerto Rico in 1916 and has been growing since then, with a special expansion after the 1950s.[28] This Protestant religion is characterized by a fundamentalist interpretation of the Bible, a belief in the second coming of Christ, an emphasis on faith healing, a full-immersion baptism, a high degree of emotional participation in the "cultos" or religious meetings, and an active seeking of possession by the Holy Spirit manifested in "speaking in tongues" or glossolalia.[29] These churches are one hundred percent native Puerto Rican in the sense that they are autonomous from American Pentecostals, self-sustained, and have one hundred percent Puerto Rican leadership.[30] Their success, particularly among the lower classes in Puerto Rico, has been attributed to their native leadership, but also to the high level of emotional satisfaction and catharsis and to the opportunities for direct participation and leadership that they provide to its members. Only American journalist Ruth Gruber mentioned Pentecostalism:

Today almost anyone with a Bible and enough faith can become a lay leader and open a new church. In Puerto Rico the lay leader, with or without education, is an important figure in the hills and in the towns. Bishop Davis explained why Pentecostals were making the deepest inroads in this once monolithically Catholic country. "The Puerto Rican men and women have a greater, deeper desire for some kind of religious experience than most other people. They are sitting ducks for anyone who has something exotic to offer. Catholics ritual . . . is too disciplined, too controlled, for the people who want to give vent to their emotions. . . . the Pentecostals . . . are equivalent of the Holly Rollers. It is a truly native church. It doesn't depend on outside direction or help." (Gruber 1960, 156)

In 1960, an American journalist recognized the poor results of over sixty years of Protestant proselytizing and even questioned the sincerity of some adhesions:

Recent studies in the field show that despite the traditional hold of the Catholic Church and 60 years of proselytizing by the Protestant sects, organized religion has a superficial hold on many "puertorriqueños." . . .

At heart these are pagan, and while they may not worship idols, they do practice voodoo, table rapping, séances, and spiritual psychography.... Their belief in spirits and ghosts... in many represent the only religion experienced even though they may outwardly profess membership in some established church.... But the Puerto Rican is no fool. We recall watching a missionary at work some years ago in a hill village near Juncos. He had a large barrel of crackers on one hand and The Good Book in the other and as long as he handed out crackers he had an audience. (Hancock 1960, 23)

THIS CHAPTER

American Protestant religions came to Puerto Rico in tandem with American imperialism and this served to secure the acquiescence of the colonized with the new circumstances. Even though most Puerto Ricans professed to be Catholics, they also believed in spirits, superstition and magic. Abandoned for centuries by a Catholic religion that was urban and elitist, they joyfully received the horse-riding missionaries, at least until cultural differences and inequalities became evident. Only Pentecostalism, with its one hundred percent native leadership, proved to be successful, mostly within the lower classes of the Island beginning in the 1950s and to this date.

"A POOR SPECIMEN OF MANHOOD"

On Matters of Health and Death

In a colonial setting, biopolitics come into play: the colonizers pay special attention to sanitation and health as these will be fundamental for the steady supply of a productive workforce, as well as for the safety of the colonizers living in the colony. Typically, the foreigners attributed health problems to the Puerto Ricans and their alleged cultural "failures," and these issues were presented as disconnected from the economic and political problems of the Island. This way the writers avoided confronting the colonial practices their country was responsible for. In *The Rhetoric of Empire*, David Spurr commented: "... social problems in health and sanitation, unemployment, or population growth come to be associated with individual filth, indolence, and sexual promiscuity.... the individual is both cause and emblem of a more general degradation."[1]

As suggested by Spurr, American authors usually blamed Puerto Rican cultural practices and genetics for the Puerto Ricans' poor health and early deaths, as if colonialism and the poverty it imposed on the colonial lower classes had nothing to do with them, even though it was widely known at the time that, for example, highly contagious diseases, like tuberculosis, thrived in overcrowded living conditions, and that anemia was associated to poverty, hunger and lack of medical care.[2] Somehow, every health issue seemed to them to be caused by the Puerto Ricans' "bad habits" and their "failings," such as "overcrowding in houses" or "lack of muscular exertion." Most American authors made a great effort to evade the obvious relationship between poverty and illness:

> ...a sure cure for the bronchial and lung problems of the natives may be found in a little healthful physical exercise, to which your Porto Rican at present is a perfect stranger. The lack of muscular exertion, together with the effects of the everlasting cigar or cigarette, and the enormous amount of strong coffee consumed daily, have left the Porto Rican a poor specimen of manhood. (Rector 1898, 45)

> There are fewer elderly persons in Porto Rico, proportionally, than there are in the United States. Only 2.6 per cent . . . live to be seventy years old. This is due mainly to the fact that so many people disobey the laws of health, eat little nourishing food, live in ill-ventilated houses and fail to enjoy the pleasures of a wholesome and buoyant life. (Seabury 1908, 166)

Obviously, it is absurd to discount as a major reason for many health issues in Puerto Rico the real hunger and undernourishment that Puerto Rican laborers faced every day during the first half of the twentieth century, which was then more prevalent than at any time in the nineteenth century.[3] Hunger and malnutrition were not a natural misfortune, a choice, or a fact of life but the direct result of the brutal exploitation of Puerto Rican laborers under US capitalism. Only a few American authors recognized that poverty and malnourishment were behind the sickly appearance of Puerto Rican peasants, as did this missionary:

> The cities have excellent doctors and good hospitals. For the person who has sufficient money, good medical and surgical care are available. . . . The average life span in Puerto Rico is twenty-one years less than in the continental United States. . . . Tuberculosis is still one of the greater killers in Puerto Rico. . . . Were it not for excessive poverty, ignorance, and the lack of adequate medical care, tuberculosis will be rare in Puerto Rico. (Morton 1949, 38)

This American rural sociologist realized that the control of anemia and malaria was necessary, not to enhance the quality of life of Puerto Rican workers, but to increase the "economic conditions," which in actuality meant to increase the surplus that the foreign investors extracted from Puerto Rican workers: "With a large proportion of the country people sick from anemia and malaria, and with tuberculosis as prevalent as it is at the present time, the weakened vitality will not permit strenuous or continued work sufficient to improve economic conditions to any great extent" (Fleagle 1917, 83).

By the late 1920s, smallpox and yellow fever were controlled, but not so tuberculosis and general infant mortality. Many of the authors of this period kept referring to the distressing life conditions of Puerto Rican workers as if the US corporations and the US colonial government were unrelated to them:

> In talking with leading physicians I was told that tuberculosis claims more lives in Porto Rico than any other disease. It is especially prevalent in the cities and towns. I did not marvel at it, because of the manner in

which many of the people live. To bring it home to you, let me picture it in this fashion: Take your small woodshed on a hot August night, board up the one window, close and bolt the door. Then make six or eight people pass the night in that small space. The result is inevitable. Where one falls a victim to tuberculosis, it follows that almost without exception the others are doomed. (Boyce 1914, 437)

As discussed in chapter 3, low wages, adding to the rise in the cost of imported foodstuffs and to the catastrophic effect of San Felipe hurricane's devastating force, worsened an already dramatic situation. Governor Theodore Roosevelt Jr. described the situation in a 1929 article titled "The Children of Famine": "I have seen mothers carrying babies who were little skeletons. I have watched in a class-room thin, pallid, little boys and girls . . . trying to study on only one scanty meal a day, a meal of a few beans and some rice."[4]

An American writer of the 1940s ended up appalled by the unhealthy conditions in which poor Puerto Ricans lived:

I plodded through the streets of San Juan, and I took a brief trip or two into the countryside. What I found appalled me. I saw rickety squatter houses perched in garbage-drenched mud within a few miles of the new United States naval base. I saw native villages steaming with filth—villages dirtier than any I ever saw in the most squalid parts of China. I saw the smoke of burning refuse near San Juan harbors—and smelt it—a scene that is a shame and disgrace to the United States. (Gunther 1940, 423)

"THEY NEVER BATHE": PERSONAL CLEANLINESS

Puerto Ricans' emphasis on body cleanliness was reported in at least two studies in the 1950s and 1960s. The first quote is from a 1955 study on Puerto Rican families and fertility, and the second one is from a 1956 study on Puerto Ricans' childhood:

Careless about the home and its surroundings, lower class individuals are extraordinarily fussy about personal cleanliness and particularly about secretions or body products . . .
 . . . there is almost a general phobia of bodily filth . . . lower class mothers worry about their children looking clean . . . just like middle— and upper-class mothers . . .[5]

Several American missionaries also made a point about the high level of cleanliness in Puerto Ricans' bodies and clothes as observed in all social classes: "The Puerto Ricans are proud and sensitive. Their little homes may be made of palm bark and covered with grass, but they will be floored—and the floors will be spotless. Clothing may be simple and sometimes scant; it may be patched and darned; but, like their bodies, it will be clean" (Morton 1949, 6).

This journalist pointed to the different fragrances used by Puerto Rican elite women, mentioning two classics that our grandmothers still favored: "agua de Florida" (Florida water by Murray & Lanman) and "alcoholado" (a mixture of alcohol and natural extracts such as bay rum, menthol, and eucalyptus):

> Some rich scent is added to the bath of every woman who can afford it. The favorite preparation is Florida water, which is imported from the United States, England, France and Germany, as well as from other islands of the Antilles. Next to that is the native bay rum, of which the finer qualities are exceedingly pleasant. The third is cologne, both the standard article and such varieties as violet, jasmine, lilac, and jockey club cologne waters. (Hamm, *Porto* 1899, 122)

Other authors made the opposite observation, sometimes making outrageous statements such as the claim that Puerto Ricans never bathed. Others criticized the lack of sophisticated toiletry implements in elite homes:

> The people are for the most part lazy and dirty. They never bathe, and they always wear the same clothes. (March 1899, 452)
>
> [About elite homes] Bad soap is found everywhere, and a single comb and brush seem to meet the needs of the family. One seldom sees manicure sets, though the powder-puff and rouge are in evidence in every well-conducted house. The lack of toilet articles, dressing-stands, chiffoniers, and pier-glasses is painful to those who are familiar with the profusion of implements of dainty toilet. (Dinwiddie 1899, 149)

"TEN CENTS FOR EVERY RAT": SANITATION

In December 1898, the US Army embarked in a large sanitary campaign directed by the federal Public Health Service (PHS).[6] Their priorities were to secure adequate waste management and water supplies, and to establish the compulsory registry of diseases.

One of the first measures taken by the US colonial government was to create sanitation brigades in the larger cities, like Ponce, where open sewage represented a serious health hazard.[7] Indeed, in July 1900, Ponce had an excessively high mortality rate of 123 per every one thousand inhabitants, mostly of people between thirty—and forty-five years old suffering from either anemia or gastrointestinal diseases.[8] Over time, American authors commented on the lack of proper sanitation in Puerto Rican towns:

> The unsanitary condition is another source of trial and suffering. When the Americans took possession of Porto Rico they found nearly all the towns without sewage, and garbage and all forms of filth in the streets. (Mills et al. 1908, 207)
>
> First the filth; never, I thought, had I seen so little evidence of that civic or personal pride which shows itself in property care and cleanliness. Refuse lay along the streets and the well-dressed citizen walked over and through it with no apparent consciousness of its presence. (Tugwell 1947, 73)

But Old San Juan was sometimes described as a clean place, even in comparison to Washington, DC:

> ... the business and residence section of San Juan could entitle it to be called a marvelously clean city. I know no city in the United States except Washington which compares with it in the cleanliness of its streets.... the paving is kept in the best condition.... The streets are on such an incline that ... the frequent showers of rain wash all the dirt off and down into the bay. (White 1898, 369)

There was a bubonic plague officially recognized in 1912 that provoked panic in San Juan, where most of the infected lived (fifty-one out of fifty-five).[9] Thirty-six died (sixty-five percent), and its origin was never identified. In 1914, a few American authors discussed how the bubonic plague of 1912 was controlled through the extermination of rats, through new laws mandating the raising of all wooden house floors above the ground (to prevent the entry of rats), and through efficient waste management:

> A short time ago the island was visited by an epidemic of Bubonic plague, but it was soon under control, and a war of extermination was waged upon the rats ... [that] have been practically exterminated. Cocoanut trees throughout the island were provided with bands of tin to prevent the rats from seeking refuge among the leaves and nuts; all vessels were compelled to place large iron circles or discs about their hawsers and were removed to open water during the

night; traps, poison, and the mongoose were brought into play . . . (Verrill 1914, 139–40)

Forty trappers worked in San Juan alone with 3,000 rat traps. They put out six or seven hundred pounds of poison. Twenty-five thousand rats were examined in the San Juan laboratory. A rat-catcher is paid seventy-five cents a day and a bonus of ten cents for every rat he brings in. (Boyce 1914, 434)

In 1917–18, the living conditions of the working class further deteriorated as many families lost their male providers who were compulsorily sent to serve in the US Army during World War I, but also because the salaries of those soldiers took a long time before being received in Puerto Rico. Then, on October 11, 1918, the northwestern part of the Island suffered the destructive San Fermín Earthquake (measuring 7.1 on the Richter scale) and its tsunami, together causing around one hundred deaths and millions of dollars in losses. At the same time, the mistakenly called "Spanish flu" worldwide pandemic generated in Puerto Rico between October 1918 and February 1919 some 260,000 contagions and around eleven thousand deaths.[10] This influenza epidemic was mentioned by two American authors, one of whom blamed Puerto Rican doctors for its terrible death toll: "Doctors seldom go into the country, but let the sick be brought in to them, whatever the stage of their illness. More than ten thousand, chiefly of the hut-dwelling class, died of "flu" during the winter of 1918–19, largely because of this inertia of physicians" (Franck 1920, 284).

An American explorer emphasized in 1914 the enhancement in sanitary conditions after the US invasion:

When the Americans took possession of Porto Rico it was one of the dirtiest, filthiest, and most unsanitary of countries. Lack of adequate water supply, carelessness, and an utter ignorance and disregard for the simplest rules of hygiene and sanitation had made the island a menace to human health, life, and comfort. . . . To-day Porto Rico is one of the cleanest, the most sanitary, and the healthiest countries . . . Drainage and sewerage are excellent, a pure water supply is maintained, and garbage, rubbish, and similar things are removed daily. (Verrill 1914, 139)

Yet, in 2010, an English teacher was surprised by the lack of sanitation and the decayed buildings she witnessed in Puerto Rico, probably a sign of the economic and social crisis the Island was beginning to experience at the time and discussed in chapter 3: "I noticed throughout the island that many of the streets and neighborhoods were dirty, even trashed. . . . Many of the buildings on Puerto Rico need to be knocked down or restored. Too many are abandoned and left as eyesores" (Tavenner 2010, 195–96).

"THEIR EFFICIENCY WAS LESS THAN 50 PER CENT": THE HOOKWORM

One of the selected authors, Dr. Bailey K. Ashford, a US Army Medic who accompanied the occupying forces, was the physician who identified hookworm infection or *uncinariasis* as the cause of the loss of iron that studies revealed in a large proportion of Puerto Rican peasants. Working with Puerto Rican Dr. Pedro Gutiérrez Ingaravidez, they realized that Puerto Rican laborers' anemia was the result of them getting infected with hookworms (*Necator americanus*) as its larvae entered their bodies through their bare feet. Once inside, the larvae traveled to the mouth through the blood, and once there, it was swallowed by the host. From there, the larvae traveled to the intestines and attached themselves to the intestinal walls, where it caused chronic blood loss and, therefore, iron-deficiency anemia. When the worms produced eggs, these left the host through the feces, which, due to the lack of latrines, were deposited in the soil, where the cycle began again. At the time, according to the 1899 US Census, in the rural districts of Puerto Rico, eighty percent of the homes had no access to a latrine, being forced to "resort to the fields."[11] Ashford and Gutiérrez explained why the affliction was so prevalent among coffee pickers:

> The picking of the coffee is all too frequently done in the pouring rain . . . The vast majority of the pickers . . . are barefooted. They work from a little after dawn to near dark, and are thus employed for about three months . . . Here, in this shade . . . the ripening ova give raise to an infinity of nests of active larvae . . . The result is that uncinariasis has its great breeding place in the coffee plantations of Porto Rico, and here a barefooted people pollute the soil and are infected and reinfected by it until the life of every man, woman and child is punctuated by a vast number of reinfections . . . (Ashford and Gutierrez 1911, 11)

In 1904, Ashford began the antihookworm drive in the coffee-producing towns of Utuado, Aibonito, and Lares, and most of the funding was provided by the Rockefeller Foundation's campaign to eradicate hookworm in Latin America. At the time, around fourteen thousand Puerto Ricans had died of this affliction.[12] Remarkably, the solution the researchers proposed was not to build latrines for the poor peasants, nor providing them with free shoes or hygiene education to prevent reinfection, but instead focused on prescribing medicine to kill the worms. Furthermore, the prescribed medicine, *thymol*, was considered dangerous in Europe, but was nevertheless used in Puerto Ricans "although other treatments were known and available at the time."[13] It is not a surprise, then, that hookworms continued affecting Puerto Ricans through the 1920s.

> ... in Puerto Rico ... people were actually dying in large numbers from it. Moreover, the working class were really invalid.... their efficiency was less than 50 per cent of what it should have been for men of their size and stature...... in the South of the United States the disease caused only laziness ... in hardly any place except Puerto Rico do people ever die of such a disease.... The degree of intensity of the disease is based on the density of population plus, of course, the unsanitary habits and ignorance of the victims. (Ashford 1934, 76)

In 1914–16, some missionaries dramatized the effects of the hookworm disease on Puerto Rican peasants and thus debunked the laziness myth regarding Puerto Rican workers:

> [After the US invasion:] The Porto Ricans were stigmatized as "lazy and incompetent" by the first American settlers, but when it was found that not less than eighty per cent were affected with the dreaded tropical anemia, or "hookworm," the marvel was that they had enough vitality to work at all. Pallid and bloated or emaciated men, women, and children were seen at every step ... (McLean and Williams 1916, 109)

Eventually, the Anemia Commission pushed for the approval of a law requiring every home to build a latrine. Its enactment was accompanied by medical visits to country stores where Puerto Rican men gathered in order to receive information about the hookworm disease and its prevention. But all of this proved to be insufficient since old customs prevailed, as the following anecdote of Dr. Bailey K. Ashford with the mayor of Aibonito made evident:

> ... we found that in the rural towns of Puerto Rico a small coterie gathers in front of the drugstore in the cool air of starry nights. To this Atheneum repair the molders of local opinion—the town doctor, the priest, the apothecary, and, above all, the militant political leader.... Everything was discussed at those reunions, and everything was settled at them.... Similar groups of men could be seen squatting in a circle in front of the country store in every far-away barrio. There it was that public opinion was formed. [In Aibonito] ... I stood before the

community council in front of the country store, I announced that the Legislature had made a law requiring every home to be provided with a latrine ... I returned about six weeks later [the Alcalde informed him that every house had a latrine. Ashford asked to see the alcalde's latrine and they walked a long distance from the house. So, he asked the alcalde:] "... do you mean to tell me that you walk this distance every time you want to use a latrine—you, much less your wife and your children? "Why, of course not," said he. "The law requires us to have one, and there it is," proudly pointing to a rude structure of palm bark, "but neither my wife nor myself believe in these things, as they produce constipation. And besides, it's a nasty thing to have near a house. But the law requires it, and everybody else has one, too." (Ashford 1934, 69, 71)

The medical procedures of the Puerto Rican hookworm-anemia campaign had been analyzed as a colonial intervention on the natives' bodies intended "to restore order and mediate dispossession and economic decline" and to "save white civilization ... in other 'tropical' countries."[14] Their approach did not intend to improve their patients' social status or to enhance their economic situation, but to keep them in their social class as peasant workers in the mountains:

Education will transform this jíbaro into something much better or much worse, for he will not remain content as he is when he can read, write, and see the world with his own eyes. In this education the respect he bears his more fortunate compatriots, the power for good they have over him, and the confidence he reposes in them must be preserved. The labor he must perform to enrich the island must be dignified by his employer and by himself, or else the hills will be deserted and the "jíbaro" will become a vicious hanger-on of towns.... He considers himself a ward of his employer and of those placed on authority over him. He does not care to accept any responsibility for the simple reason that he has always been made to feel that he is not a responsible person. Therefore, how can we blame him when we find him without shoes, knowing that by wearing them he will protect himself against a dangerous infirmity; without bacon and corn; without household furniture; with but one room for his entire family. (Ashford and Gutierrez 1911, 14–15)

Even though at the beginning the campaign seemed to be interested in the social context of the disease, at the end it centered on "medicalizing jíbaros' malnutrition and hunger." Its ultimate goal was "promoting worker productivity and economic development" as healthier workers will yield more profits to capitalist investors.[15] Indeed, Ashford and his Puerto Rican research partner, Pedro Gutiérrez, sided with the coffee planters rather than with the poor laborers when they stated: "The heaviest load he [the planter] has to carry is the infirmity of his laborers, their almost universal anemia, and the ignorance of the class of labor upon which he has to depend" (Ashford and Gutiérrez 1911, 16).

Though the Anemia Commission acknowledged that malnutrition was an important factor in the devastation of uncinariasis in Puerto Rico, where it was considered a pandemic, Dr. Ashford seemed to consider himself incapable of correcting this:

> ... there was evidently another factor to be considered ... chronic malnutrition, or ... "nutritional unbalance." People had enough food to eat; in fact, they ate inordinate quantities of food ... but the people could be said to be on the very point of starvation for such vital elements, especially meat.... We also had to leave the correction of glaring nutritional defects in the jíbaro's daily ration for that happier day when he could more or less choose his food. Even to-day his inadequate ration cannot be changed. He still lacks money to buy the obviously necessary elements of diet. (Ashford 1934, 77–78)

The theory behind the Rockefeller Foundation was: "Disease is the supreme ill of human life, and it is the main source of almost all other human ills—poverty, crime, ignorance, vice, inefficiency, hereditary taints, and many other evils."[16] The problems were not social, but medical; the solution was not enhancing the living standards of the sick, but curing the individual. This credo became the new norm and put an end to the previous medical practice in Puerto Rico, which emphasized on social medicine. Trujillo-Pagán analyzed that "by focusing on the hookworm instead of the social context in which infection occurred, doctors shifted the attention away from economic and class oppression and implicitly blamed the patient for his/her suffering." The exploitation of the poor laborers, their malnutrition and poverty, the inequality of Puerto Rican society, all were therefore arbitrarily ruled out as contributors to hookworm anemia.

"A PITIABLE AND DISGUSTING SIGHT": LEPROSY

One of the diseases that captured the attention of the US health authorities was leprosy. Even though its prevalence was low (only seventy-one cases were identified by military authorities out of 950,00 inhabitants),[17] it was considered a public health issue because most leprosy sufferers were vagabonds and beggars, something considered disgusting by Americans, as expressed in 1914: "The lepers, which are usually in evidence and are a pitiable and disgusting sight in many tropical communities, are safely and comfortably isolated on an island in the harbor" (Verrill 1914, 140).

The mentioned island was Isla de Cabras, an islet of one mile by an eighth of a mile, separated from San Juan and Cataño by natural barriers of rocks and rough surf that further isolated it. In 1876, the Spanish colonial government turned it into a hospital and a maritime quarantine station. In 1900, under the US colonial government, it was turned into a leprosarium:

> There are a number of lepers scattered throughout the country, and Uncle Sam is doing all he can to gather them together and isolate them. The lepers are very secretive, and it is very difficult to find out just who they are. The poor herd together to such an extent that the danger of contamination is great, and so the Government has chosen this island as the exclusive home of the lepers.... it is believed that the leper colonies will be largely self-supporting. The Government ... will give the lepers houses and will supply them with seeds and farming tools and will stimulate them in every way to form a society of their own." (Olivares, Vol. 1 1899, 283)

By 1920, the leprosarium's facilities became uninhabitable, with leaking roofs over patients' beds, an inoperable cistern that was the sole source of clean water, and moisture-collecting cement floors. But, only the pressure of the Protestant organization American Mission for Lepers was able to pressure enough the US colonial legislature to provide in 1919 for a new leprosarium in a forty-acre site in Trujillo Alto, which began operations in 1926 with forty-six patients.[18]

"CREATURES IN REGIMENTS AND BATTALIONS": PESTS

Frantz Fanon explained how pests and illnesses become a metaphor for the indocility of the colonized which the colonizers came to tame: "Hostile nature, obstinate and fundamentally rebellious, is in fact represented in the colonies ... by mosquitoes, natives, and colonization is a success when all this indocile nature has finally been tamed.... the draining of swamps and a native population which is nonexistent politically and economically are in fact one and the same thing."[19]

Mosquitoes[20] were frequently mentioned as the cause of fevers or just as an endless annoyance: "In August a suffocating heat reigns throughout the day, and at night it is useless to seek for coolness ... the mosquitoes, buzzing about the ears by day and night, perplex and annoy by their stings, while the fevers of the tropics attack Europeans with sudden and irresistible violence" (Halstead, *Triumphant* 1899, 60).

As happens in all Caribbean islands, Puerto Rico has an abundant number of cockroaches. Indeed, a 1998 study identified fifty-eight species, including a native one called *Nublatella borinquensis*.[21] However, the most common one in Puerto Rican households is the *Periplaneta americana*, originally from Africa, which seemed to "terrorize" American visitors due to its large size (around 1.5 inches) and capacity for short flights.[22] A young missionary wife seemed to find these cockroaches particularly offensive and even disrespectful:

> Every creeping thing that creepeth upon the earth seems to be running at large here.... when we arrived ... Harry found a snake in his suit case ... And the roaches! I have never before believed that they could develop to such mammoth proportions nor that they could marshal such hosts in one night. The kitchen looks innocent enough by daylight, but if I suddenly appear with a lamp at night I am greeted by a vision of these creatures in regiments and battalions, lined up on the stove, the table and the shelves...... at sight of a lamp they break ranks and flee to the most remote and unheard-of cracks and crevices ... (Blythe 1911, 35)

All kinds of insects, mostly associated with poor sanitation or simply with tropical weather, are discussed as the cause of illness and death, or at least annoyance. Some are not identified by their names, but by the aggravation they inflicted. But many American authors seemed convinced that somehow these pests were less annoying for the natives:

> Rats and mice are responsible for many noises at night, in these old houses.... The hot little loft of our cottage, under the zinc roof, is infested with bats, which flutter and flap and squeak above the ceilings all night long. Sometimes a spider ... creeps out of a crack in my room—but all of them are perfectly harmless, as are the small brown lizards that run over.... (Duggan 1920, 25)

> The most formidable among these pests are centipedes, scorpions, tarantulas,[23] mosquitoes, ants, ticks, and wasps. Intolerable as these are to strangers, the natives, having always been accustomed to them, appear to be but little annoyed by their presence. (Baldwin 1899, 11)

> One enterprising and annoying insect, the chigoe or "jigger" [nigua],[24] is able to bore a hole through the sole of a shoe and attack the foot. (George 1900, 65)

"WHEN AVOCADOES ARE PLENTIFUL": AN OMINOUS NATURE

The possibility of earthquakes captured the attention of some authors long before the strong 1918 earthquake that caused important damage on the west coast of the island. This author described how Puerto Ricans knew that an earthquake was about to happen:

> Earthquakes are somewhat frequent, but not violent or of great consequence. The natives foretell them by noticing clouds settle near the ground for some time in the open places among the mountains. The water of the springs emits a sulphurous odor or leaves a strange taste in the mouth; birds gather in large flocks and fly about uttering shriller cries than usual; cattle bellow and horses neigh, etc. (Halstead, *Pictorial* 1899, 62)

American journalist Ruth Gruber was in Puerto Rico in 1963 when a hurricane was expected to hit the Island. She was surprised by the relaxed attitude of Puerto Ricans:

> Yet despite the fear, most people were joking. One man coming out of a supermarket, his arms loaded with bundles, said, "Don't worry. No hurricane with an American name ever hits Puerto Rico." Some of the more pleasure-loving people, with the psychology of a soldier's last fling, decided to eat, drink, and be merry before Edith [the hurricane] struck. Some prayed, some sang, some danced, some made jokes, some argued, some fought, some stole, some sat remembering all the superstitions their grandmothers had learned from their grandmothers, but most stayed awake waiting for the hurricane to lift off their roofs . . . (Gruber 1960, 149)

Writing much later, in 1970, an American journalist reported on the bizarre atmosphere he observed whenever an upcoming hurricane was announced to the general public, and which was still observed at least until Hurricane Maria devastated the Island in 2017:

> [The] . . . advance of approaching storms. It has almost developed into a national pastime. . . . Puerto Ricans dutifully charted it on their maps, after having boarded up windows and taken other precautions. . . . Folkloric superstition in Puerto Rico . . . contends that when avocadoes are plentiful, there will be no hurricanes. (Wagenheim 1970, 27–28)

"THE HIGHER THE FEVER THE MORE RUM I DRINK": HOSPITAL CARE

The first medical missionary in Puerto Rico, Dr. Grace W. Atkins, arrived in 1901 sent by the Presbyterian Woman's Board of Home Missions.[25] After her, other medical missionaries followed and they frequently joined religious Puerto Rican physicians to provide part-time and/or sporadic services in makeshift dispensaries and clinics or in churches, missionaries' houses, and sugar mills. Even though they offered their services free of charge, they had to ask their Puerto Rican patients to pay for their medicines, even if the payment could be made in fruits, eggs or services. As expected, the missionaries also provided their patients "sermons, prayers and religious pamphlets," as well as invitations to church services.[26]

When the Protestant missionaries realized that their efforts were insufficient for Puerto Rican needs, they invested in the establishment of hospitals: the Presbyterian Hospital in San Juan (1904), the Presbyterian Rye Hospital in Mayagüez (1904), the Episcopalian St. Luke's Hospital in Ponce (1907), and the Congregational Ryder Memorial Hospital in Humacao (1914).[27] Except for the Rye Hospital of Mayaguez, which closed after the 1918 earthquake, all the others are still operating, sometimes with new names, like the Ashford Presbyterian Community Hospital in San Juan. A Congregational missionary described the difficulties poor patients sorted to arrive at the Ryder Memorial Hospital in Humacao in search of the *"Americano medico"*:

> Every once in a while we notice among the pedestrians, men with a hammock slung on poles, the ends of which they support on their shoulders. We discover that the hammock holds a sick friend or relative, and the little group is on its way to Ryder Memorial Hospital, Humacao. . . . we pity both patient and friends, as we think of the weary miles to travel on foot over mountains and streams before they can reach the help they need so much. However, they are gladly enduring all the discomfort because they are confident the "Americano medico" will give back health and strength to the sick one and make life worth living again. (Wilcox [1918?])

A missionary commented on the system of bartering established by the Presbyterian Hospital of Santurce in order to get payment from poverty-stricken patients. Following Protestant ethics, this author advocated that even poor patients should pay for their medical services:

> People come from surrounding towns to be treated. If able to pay, they are charged moderate fees, the lowest being ten cents. If too poverty-

stricken for this, medicine and care are given freely. Most of the patients have a self-respecting wish to pay for service, the principle having been clearly inculcated from the beginning. Those who have no money often bring vegetables, fruits, and other eatables and usables. One of the first cases made payment by bringing a chicken, and some bamboo sprouts to plant on the hospital grounds. (Johnston 1905, 181)

In contrast, others simply refused to allow family members to receive medical attention at hospitals. After taking an old lady named Paula to the Tricoche Hospital in Ponce, without her family's consent, the nurse informed this American missionary: ". . . that Paula's relations had come to her and carried her back to their house in a hammock. They were "ashamed" of what people were saying of their letting their aunt go to the hospital . . . [She died three days later] . . ." (Duggan 1920, 23).

According to some American authors, modern healthcare was not readily accepted by all. Many Puerto Ricans of all classes resisted the foreign physicians' advice or couldn't understand its purpose if it contradicted local cultural assumptions. Many preferred to follow the medical advice of their friends, "curanderos," spiritism's mediums, or known local druggists:

> . . . many medical men do not listen with as much patience as they might, to the detailed list of complaints which the countryman has to offer. As a consequence, the countryman buys a bottle of medicine which has been recommended for him by a friend, or perhaps by the druggist, who often serves as a consulting physician in the smaller towns. If the medicine makes him feel better, he becomes a firm believer in its power to cure. . . . He recommends the medicine to his friends as a sure remedy for all their illnesses, and probably makes of it a household remedy, to be used by all members of the family when they feel indisposed. (Fleagle 1917, 95)

> . . . among the unenlightened country people there were formerly innumerable superstitions, which have persisted with characteristic tenacity. . . . The countryman in olden times had too great a faith in the powers of the "curandero," a kind of medicine-man. His diagnoses were intentionally alarming, for he knew that if his patient was ill, he would be delighted if pronounced "very" ill. He designated the ailments with such remarkable names as "buzzings," "twistings," "witches," "evil eye," and so on, and ordered strenuous treatment by the employment of charms and incantations and strong medicines derived from natural herbs. . . . Though the ministrations of the "curanderos" are now strictly

forbidden by law, many poor country people still consult them—perforce! in a country where there is but one doctor to about 6,800 people, outside of San Juan and Ponce.... Remedies derived from herbs run literally into the hundreds. (Van Deusen and Van Deusen 1931, 174–75)

Home-made remedies were commonly favored over a doctor's prescription since there was a lot of respect for the elders who recommended them. Some of these remedies seemed to include a tint of magical thinking embedded:

Blood-poisoning and infections of various kinds are very common. For their cure the countryman will drink the soup of boiled ants' nests (comejen) and place on the infected part a mixture of olive oil, tobacco and nutmeg. Should the children of the family develop colds, the countryman will make bracelets of small unripe lemons and place them on the wrists of his children. For severe nervous diseases the ignorant farmer will take a watermelon, cut a hole in one end and place in it his rings and everything he has that passes as jewelry. He will then cut a smaller hole in the other end and catch the water as it passes through. This water when taken is supposed to quiet the distraught nervous system. (James 1924, 43)

In the early 1940s, Mennonite missionary and director of the Puerto Rico Reconstruction Administration (PRRA) Justus G. Holsinger quoted from comments made by Puerto Rican peasants to PRRA social workers regarding why they did not visit health clinics when ill. Some of the comments make a lot of sense, at least to another Puerto Rican. He concluded that "the beliefs of many country people are a combination of superstitions, religious fatalism, ignorance, and mistrust of strangers":

The best medicine for a headache is to take some sage leaves and put them over your forehead. It is better than any aspirin or other medicine for it cures the ailment even if it comes from a spirit."..."I would rather let my daughter die, than call a doctor. I know they will say that she is anemia (sic) without even seeing her." "I can't believe that a doctor who works for a sugar central has any pity for children of the poor." "I have a medicine for all diseases; a bath in the river, blue soap and rum. When I feel as if I'm going to catch a cold, I take a bath and get well. When I have a sore or wound I don't use mercurochrome or iodine. I rub it with blue soap instead and get cured. As to malaria and all types of fever, my only medicine is rum. The higher the fever the more rum I drink. Next day I don't even remember that I was ill." "The best treatment for colics, evil eye, infraction of glands, and spasms is to call a person who knows how to bless." "I had a child with rickets, but we treated her with coconut oil and she got cured." "I have a good many children. That one over there is enrolled in school; but he is dying. I have been unable to take him to the doctor; but since I believe in God, everything will come out well. (Holsinger 1952, 39–40)

For decades, most Puerto Rican peasants accepted Western medicine just as one of many treatment options, keeping the practice of visiting the "curandera" (who heals using herbal treatments) and the "santiguadora" or sanctifier (who heals through rubbing the affected part of the body as they pray), and giving birth at home with the help of the local "comadronas" (midwives).[28] Many still visit *curanderas* and *santiguadoras* these days. As a pair of physicians explained in 1911: "The jibaro is equally superstitious and very quickly impressed by a supernatural explanation of any phenomena he can not understand. The more outlandish the explanation of a disease, the better he likes it, and for this reason, the "curandero" or local charlatan is so popular and powerful in the mountains" (Ashford and Gutierrez 1911, 14).

Lacking the scientific knowledge that would have explained many childhood afflictions, most Puerto Ricans were prone to accept magical explanations for their children's ailments. Some of these explanations are of ancient origin, such as the belief in the damaging "evil eye" ("mal de ojo"), which refers to a curse transmitted through the malicious glare of an envious person.[29] Its "antidote," used in Puerto Rico to this day, is a pendant in the shape of a fist made in jet or black coral, although nowadays, many are made just of black plastic. It was explained by an American journalist: "There is still considerable fear among the uneducated of 'el mal de ojo' ('the evil eye'). The greatest concern is for attractive infants, who are the object of stares from covetous strangers. To ward off this threat, some parents adorn the child with a bracelet known as the 'asabache' . . ." (Wagenheim 1970, 165).

For generations, Puerto Ricans were taught, and they taught their own children, that babies' heads had to be covered during the nighttime if they ever had to be taken out of the house. Supposedly, the night air or "sereno" could turn the baby's eyes into crossed eyes. Apparently, it "affected" adults too, judging by this reference: "Invariably, there was a woman [a seriously ill patient] with a parasol contraception held over the head to keep the 'sereno' (night dew) off the face, because this was very dangerous to the patient's health. Babies were swaddled in so many layers that it was impossible to understand why they didn't asphyxiate" (Flax 1995, 62).

Another "affliction" of cultural interpretation mentioned by an English teacher was the so-called "pasmo," which seems to be a sort of partial paralysis resulting from the sudden exposure to cold air while the person is sweating. It was described as early as 1582 by the Spanish governor of Puerto Rico, Juan de Melgarejo, in a memoir requested from him by King Felipe II: "mueren . . . muchos hombres de solo beber un jarro de agua estando sudando."[30] In this case, it was cleverly used by one of the students of this English teacher at CAMM, Mayagüez, as an excuse for skipping a test:

> One day a very serious student, and a reasonably good one, asked to be excused from a test because his girlfriend was sick and he was so worried about her that he couldn't study. I asked him what the problem was.
>
> "She's half paralyzed. She can't move her right side at all. Her left side is fine, but she's is paralyzed right down the middle . . . I've just been to see her at the hospital and I'm very worried about her."
>
> I stared at him for a moment, and, perhaps sensing disbelief in my expression, he went on, "The same thing happened to my grandmother. She's paralyzed right down in the middle too. She's been in the hospital for three days. I'm just too upset to study."
>
> I continued staring at him, hoping for more.
>
> "You know what usually causes this, don't you?" I shook my head.
>
> "It's when you stare in the refrigerator so that you get chilled and then go over to a hot stove. It's going from cold to hot too fast. But my girlfriend would never do that."
>
> When I continued saying nothing, he added, "I think it's something that's going around."
>
> I excused him from the test. (Cooper 1994, 87)

Interestingly, when Puerto Ricans actually visited the health clinics to get medical services, other cultural issues came into the picture:

> Conducting a medical clinic and opening a hospital among rural people of Puerto Rico carried with it many unusual problems and experiences that a medical staff would hardly encounter in the States. . . . Teaching patients to spit into a basin rather than following the common practice of spiting on the floor was one of the first problems. When the hospital was finally opened strict discipline was necessary to get some patients to understand that smoking in hospital rooms was absolutely forbidden. To get people to conform to an orderly and systematic clinic system was indeed a problem . . . Not being able to converse with the people made it even more difficult to maintain order. Fortunately most Puerto Ricans are extremely patient and do net get in a hurry. Had the several hundred waiting clinic patients shown the degree of impatience characteristic of

most Americans, some days would probably have ended in riots. (Holsinger 1952, 76, 83)

The tale by an English teacher who, in 2010, visited a Puerto Rican hospital for services she never got, speaks loudly about the worsening of the Puerto Rican public health system as a result of a combination of its privatization in the 1990s, the economic recession of 2008, and the increasing indebtedness of the Island's government. Indeed, in December 2015, Puerto Rico's health system was considered "on the verge of collapsing," crippled by the condition of the US colonial government: "a growing debt standing at more than $70 billion, a poverty rate of 45%, and more than 12% unemployment."[31] Ex-nun and educator Mary H. Tavenner narrated her ordeal:

> ... we drove to Centro Medico in Rio Piedras. I was not impressed with the medical care. Pregnant mothers were sitting on the floor waiting for appointments with the clinic doctors. It seemed so disrespectful to me. I guess I found it so shocking because I have never seen anything like that in our United States hospitals. The long wait was also making us unhappy as we were there by 8:00 AM as directed. After a few hours of waiting ... we returned ... (Tavenner 2010, 203)

"BEARING ON THEIR SHOULDERS A COFFIN": THE BURIAL OF THE DEAD

In an island stricken by poverty, malnutrition, and disease, death was commonplace. Regarding this theme, Catholic Father Thomas E. Sherman's report to General Brooke was quoted by several American authors as an authority: "Deaths occurred amongst the natives in numbers that are simply appalling. From three to nine funerals passing on the same road during a single morning was not unusual" (As quoted in Edwards 1899, 248).

Puerto Ricans' vision of death is influenced by the conceptions of death of the Taíno Indians, the enslaved African people, and Spanish Catholicism. For the Taíno Indians, there was a continuation between the living and the dead in which physical death was just a step; death was just the transition from one existence to the other.[32] The Taíno believed that their dead never abandoned them; they just turned into part of nature in a spiritual way, being represented by the stone "cemíes." Death was understood as continuity and renovation.

On their part, enslaved African people went through their tough lives with the idea that, after death, they would return to the other side of "the big waters" (a reference to the Atlantic Ocean that separated them from their African homelands.) to see Africa and their relatives there again.[33] So, for them, death was to be celebrated, as it was the end of slavery. The living ones envied the dead ones, said goodbye to them, and asked them to give greetings to their friends and family still in Africa.

Finally, for Catholics, death is a reality of human nature that should be accepted stoically since there is no way out of it: it should not be feared because it is part of the trip to the next life stage. What will happen after death, for Catholics, depends on their actions regarding performing charitable activities, their use of the sacraments that give "the grace of God," and their compliance with penitence for their sins. The outcome of Catholics' lives can be changed, and every person is responsible for their after-death situation.[34] But the Catholics' final destiny is also affected by the actions of family members and friends who can have masses in their honor and pray for their souls to the saints and Virgin Mary, who can then intercede for them before Jesus. This belief system, therefore, supports an attitude of serenity, consolation, and companionship at the time of death. The death of the Catholic is accompanied, consoled, in the presence of heavenly and earthly intercessors that can "entrust you to God."

The American vision of death was very different from that of Puerto Ricans. The United States has been defined by experts in bioethics as a "death-denying society . . . that cannot accept death as anything but defeat," and, being a highly competitive society, they are extremely afraid of death.[35] It is very difficult for an average American to even talk about the possibility of his/her own death, and the theme is considered very solemn and serious. This solemnity, in contrast with the matter-of-fact attitude of Puerto Ricans, was illustrated by an American soldier:

> [Three soldiers] were seated on the door steps of the old church at Coamo enjoying their breakfast, when quickly and silently four natives appeared around the corner, bearing on their shoulders a coffin, which they unceremoniously dropped in the midst of the breakfast, while they rang the bell for the "Padre." That was too much for even the volunteers,[36] and they gathered up their belongings and found another breakfast place in short order. (Rossiter [1900?])

The American Calvinist Protestant tradition understands that every human's after-life destiny is prefixed by God since "the beginning of time." It supports an imperious individualism: you can do nothing to change your final destiny because it is predetermined. Once you are dead, your family and friends can do no masses or prayers to help you get a better afterlife. The death of the Protestant is individual and without the protection of his/her community or family.[37]

In Puerto Rico, to this day, Catholic death rituals include the congregation of the dead's relatives and friends to mourn together and to show "their respect for the dead person" in a wake service (a "velorio") that can be held in a funeral home or at the dead's home, and that lasts until the body is taken for burial at the cemetery.[38] In the 1900s, women, forbidden to accompany the dead to their burial site, expressed their mourning accompanied by their children in the wake. Even these days, it is frequent for some close relatives of the dead to cry and scream during wakes and burials.[39] A few American missionaries commented on the wake services in Puerto Rico:

> The last minutes of the dying person are accompanied by great manifestations of pain and sorrow by all the family. The night following the death, the Catholic Rosario is conducted in which prayers are offered to the various saints in behalf of the soul which has just entered purgatory.... The spirit of sympathy for relatives who have lost loved ones is similar to that found among rural people in America a generation ago when funerals drew overflow crowds to churches. When death visits a rural family in Puerto Rico, almost every acquaintance assembles at the home for the Rosario ... (Holsinger 1952, 37–38)

> [After the first death of a child in the Disciples of Christ's girls' orphanage in Bayamón, that of a four-year-old girl:] Mrs. Fullen wrote of the first death in the orphanage: "... It is the custom here for the people to scream and cry when the angel of death has laid his hands on any of their loved ones, but I had talked to the girls as best I could and taught them why they should not do this." (Morton 1949, 22–23)

In 1970, an American journalist updated the concept of "velorio" as he experienced it:

> In rural villages, a person near death will be visited by friends and relatives, who maintain a night-long "velada" ("vigil"); the women pray inside the home; the men, after paying their respects, will often sit outside chatting, where they are served black coffee, soda crackers, and cheese. The night after death, a "velorio" is held, and much the same ritual is celebrated, although the men outside may down a nip of "cañita" ("clandestine cane rum") to combat the cool night air. Drunkenness or loud talk in such occasions is deplored ... (Wagenheim 1970, 161)

Because of their malnutrition, the overcrowded and unsanitary conditions in which they lived, and the lack of proper medical care, infant mortality was high among the Puerto Rican poor. According to the 1899 Census, the life expectancy was just 18.1 years.[40] The burial process for an infant or a child was particularly interesting and confusing for American authors. This is not a surprise because, again, the cultural background of a person affects his/her vision of the death of a child. Congruent with what their visions of death were since the Middle Ages and up to 1965, Catholics considered the death of unbaptized children as a blessing for the child: since they have not committed any sins, their souls went to live in Heaven, in a place called "limbo" where, although they could not see God, they will live in "natural happiness" and will not be punished.[41]

On their part, enslaved African people celebrated the death of their children in a festive wake or "baquiné" where the whole community gathered to rejoice over the "little angel's" death, which, instead of being seen as a loss, was seen as a gain: the dead child was spared a life of suffering.[42] The death of a child whose expectations in life were so limited by poverty was not regarded as a loss but as a gain for the family. On the other hand, for Americans, the death of a child is as solemn as that of an adult: a profound, difficult, and painful experience that is also experienced as the death of the parents' dreams for that child.[43]

Probably few American authors had the opportunity to attend a death ritual in which the Puerto Rican poor "celebrated" the death of a small child as a return "to its place among the heavenly hosts."[44] That will explain why only two of them, both Protestant missionaries, referred to this event. Here is one of those accounts:

> The death of small children, especially in the country districts, was formerly, and is still, to some extent, made the occasion of feasting and even merriment, with the accompaniments of singing and dancing. . . . "The little angel," as they consider the child to be, is laid, in its best frock and with a crown of flowers, before a species of rude altar made of rough boards and adorned with fresh flowers. Lighted candles and tinsel decorate the center of the room . . . The mother, with eyes swollen from much weeping, makes pathetic attempts to smile a welcome on the guests who come to celebrate the entrance of "the little angel" into a better world. (Seabury 1908, 35–36)

In what was described as "a strange experience," a group of American soldiers used their military might to halt a funeral procession in which the voice level of the group was "too lively to characterize any sorrow by any means." Since language barriers prevented mutual understanding, a suspicious officer ordered the opening of the casket, which exposed a ghastly scene:

> ... a strange experience was gained by those in the road. It was the first time for them to witness a Porto Rican funeral procession. The corpse in this instance was a small child; the casket which contained the remains was a rude wooden box and the bier was the shoulder of the father. Several half-dressed natives followed on behind jabbering away in their native tongue at a rate too lively to characterize any sorrow by any means.... the party was halted. They made a series of incoherent exclamations and doubled themselves up so hysterically in making signs that the officers in charge of the advance asked them in the wordless language to open the box. They did so and there were exposed to view a sight which none who witnessed it will ever forget.... they saw the half decomposed body of the child.... the funeral was permitted to proceed ... (Creager 1899, 147)

A young missionary attended, with her missionary husband, the funeral of the young daughter of one of their congregation's families. She seemed shocked by the naturalness with which death was accepted:

> We have just returned from the funeral of a little daughter of one of our Presbyterian families ... We went to the house and Harry sat down in the front room where we gathered the friends of the family, including ever so many children who chattered and played about, and seemed perfectly accustomed to the occasion. I went with the women into the next room where the child lay on a canvas cot, covered with a white veil.... None of the family except the father was present, and after the services, he took her with his own hands, placed her in the casket, and, after the other members of the family had come in for a moment to see her, he closed the casket ... and nailed it shut. Then we followed it to the cemetery, the father taking charge of everything.... Children acted as pallbearers and carried the casket all the way to the place of burial.... Through it all the people talked and visited. Death is so common here that even the children seem to have no awe for it. (Blythe 1911, 89–90)

Many American writers commented on the process of burial in Puerto Rico, especially right after the US invasion. They pointed out how class differences influenced the burial ritual. In Catholic burial processions of the turn of the century, the body of the dead was accompanied to the cemetery by as many men as possible; women and children did not participate:

> A funeral in Porto Rico is as simple and unpretentious as it can be made. The rank or circumstances of the family who suffers loss by the death of

a member, may be judged in watching a procession to the cemetery. The poorer are carried to their last resting place by their friends and sometimes on the heads of a couple of sturdy peons. The next class, or middle class will enjoy the luxury of a cart, and the higher class will resort to the extravagance of a hearse. In no case do the women or children attend the funeral of a native or a Spaniard. (Rector 1898, 130)

Elite funerals were described in 1899 in a way very similar to that still seen in many towns of Puerto Rico: "Some of the funerals of the wealthy are functions of great solemnity and ostentation.... At the church, a solemn ceremony takes place ... and then the march to the grave proceeds, to the murmuring chant and the direful tolling of bells. At the grave is gathered half the city, and employed orators extol the virtues of the deceased ..." (Dinwiddie 1899, 212).

The burial of a person was not the end of death ceremonies for Puerto Rican Catholics. For the next nine consecutive nights, which are called "la novena" ("the ninth"), family members, neighbors and friends of the deceased (mostly older women dressed in black, white or purple) met in the deceased family's home to offer rosaries for the dead.[45] The rosary is a long and repetitive prayer[46] in which a conductor guides the others in a call-and-response fashion. The conductor is usually a mature woman who have memorized the order of the prayers of the rosary and is not supposed to be paid for her service.

Subsequent rosaries were held on the yearly anniversaries of the death for at least seven years.[47] The *novena* is believed to help the soul of the deceased to find its way to heaven with the forgiveness of all his/her sins, and after the rosary the attendants were served refreshments while they frequently engaged in conversations regarding the positive qualities of the deceased.[48]

The purpose of the prayers of the "Rosario de Difuntos" (Deceased's Rosary) is directly related to the Catholic belief in the eventual resurrection of all Catholics once Jesus returns to earth. Its purpose is to ask god, the saints, the Virgin Mary, and the souls of the previously dead to intercede for the newly deceased so that his/her sins can be totally forgiven and the deceased can resurrect at the end of times.[49] Beyond the religious significance of this process, in practical terms it helped the family and friends of the deceased to deal with their loss through their accompaniment, and it gave them the feeling that there was still something they could do to ease the suffering of their loved one. Few American missionaries mentioned this practice of the rosary: "'It is the custom here' ... when one is in mourning not to go outside of the house for at least nine days after the death, except to the cemetery" (Duggan 1920, 14).

The habit of a year of mourning for dead family members during which people (mostly women) dressed in black as an external confirmation of their suffering, was commented in a somewhat exaggerated fashion by a young American missionary: "... some little colored ... were wearing black for their mother—for even mere babies are put into deep mourning, no matter how remotely connected the deceased relative may be" (Blythe 1911, 115).

"UNCEREMONIOUSLY THROWN INTO A PIT": THE CEMETERIES

After the US invasion and occupation, the municipalities in Puerto Rico began to claim control of the cemeteries, which, until then, belonged to and were administered by the Catholic Church. The Catholic Church insisted on keeping them because they depended on the collection of fees paid by those who buried their dead there. They also refused to allow non-Catholic bodies (such as those of free-thinkers, masons, suicides, atheists, heretics, and Protestants) to be buried in them, considering their land as "blessed soil."[50] The municipalities insisted that the sanitary issues in the cemeteries, as well as the cities' growth, required them to take over the administration of the cemeteries.[51]

After multiple lawsuits, in 1901, the Catholic Church retained control only of cemeteries built one hundred percent with the Church's funds. Cemeteries built with public funding will be civil in nature and administered by the municipalities.[52] All parochial registries of births and deaths became civil.

Several American authors of the first decade after the US invasion used as their reference regarding the burial facilities in Puerto Rico the cited report of Catholic Father Thomas E. Sherman. The report described the cemeteries' practices as "barbarous":

> In places corpses are thrown into shallow graves, sometimes without boxes or casket. The cemeteries are too small and frequently crowded. ... An incident which happened in Utuado, while the regiment was in camp there, was the burial of a woman, who unfortunately was too tall for the space prepared for her. The problem was solved by amputating her legs at the knees, interring her by sections.[53]

Father Sherman's observations were later confirmed by other American authors right around the time of the US invasion of Puerto Rico, pointing to the different burial practices according to the social class of the deceased:

> They were treated just like beasts, both when living and dead. ... Upon the death of a native of the peon class, the body is enclosed in a rough wooden box and dumped in the cemetery. The cemeteries were so

thickly populated with their denizens that the coffin was barely covered with earth. The severe rain storms washing away the earth left the bodies to decompose under the heat of the sun. Every cemetery which I saw on the island, and I examined several, had a specially constructed pit where the bones had been thrown to make room for other bodies. It was a revolting sight to look into one of these pits and see human skulls grinning at one, the bones and other refuse all jumbled into one confused mass. (Oliver 1900, 175)

Since in the United States most cemeteries are not walled, but open to the sight of passers-by, which to some Puerto Ricans might seem "creepy," An American soldier was surprised by our walled cemeteries, and struggled to make sense of them: "The most curious place is the cemetery.... From outside there is nothing to be seen but the high gray wall" (King 1929, 79).

After fifteen years under the US colonial government, changes were made in the disposition of the bones of the people whose family members couldn't afford their monthly payments to the cemeteries, but these changes were only sanitary, and the bones were still removed:

[At the cemetery of Old San Juan:] As long as the rent is paid the corpse is allowed to occupy its resting-place in peace, but if in arrears it is unceremoniously thrown into a pit or trench with scores of others.... In the old Spanish days the skeletons of such unfortunates could be seen in a great confused mass of bones, and prowling dogs often carried the bones hither and thither, while the stench at night was terrible. Nowadays, the bones are covered with earth and disinfectants, and are hidden from public view. (Verrill 1914, 36–37)

THIS CHAPTER

The colonial relationship mediated the understanding of Puerto Ricans' health issues, which were blamed on local cultural practices and beliefs, and barely ever associated to their exploitation and abject poverty. Although medical missionaries worked hard to improve the health of their patients, they were a minority, and lower-class Puerto Ricans kept their trust in their local healers and pharmacists. The treatment of the uncinariasis that weakened Puerto Rican laborers was never accompanied by an intention of enhancing their living conditions, but only to medicate them and bring them back to work. Health education was not considered an option, since it might empower them.

In the same fashion, as cultural interpretations of pests, natural phenomena, and especially death, differed culturally and made it difficult for American authorities to understand Puerto Ricans' reactions to them, the colonizers insisted that *their* points of view were the only correct ones and, through their legislation, dismissed centenary cultural practices that they never even bothered to comprehend.

Chapter 12

"SATAN HIMSELF WOULD DANCE IF HE COULD HEAR THEM"

On Puerto Rican Entertainments

Puerto Ricans are well known for their "joie de vivre" or zest for life. Sociologist Haroldo Dilla Alfonso have pointed to "that proclivity of Puerto Rican society to turn any incident into a cause for celebration."[1] There is a local expression that says that Puerto Ricans "would not miss even a doll's baptism" ("no se pierden ni un bautismo de muñecas"). This is partly true, but it is not an absolute; poverty will make it hard for many Puerto Ricans to enjoy life that happily. Nevertheless, the common use of music and dancing to vent frustrations and despair gave outsiders the erroneous impression of a never-ending happiness: "'Fiesta' is an ever-present and glorious reality to the Porto Rican. Feasting and merry-making lie so close to his heart that no excuse is too slight to permit indulgence in them. Undoubtedly, this love of pleasure induces improvidence, but it is a charming improvidence . . ." (Van Deusen and Van Deusen 1931, 162–63).

This Puerto Rican love for "fiesta" became evident to almost every American author: "If there is any one thing the Porto Ricans seem to love above anything else, it is a fiesta. To pass a holiday without a fiesta of some kind is worse than going home and finding that when you get there the cupboard is bare" (Blythe 1911, 184).

"PARTY, PARTY, PARTY": ELITE'S ENTERTAINMENT

Most of the dancing and partying of the elite class was done in the towns' casinos, where only members and their guests were allowed to participate. In the casino dances, the elite families allowed their offspring to mingle under their watchful eyes, and frequently, it was there where future couples met. The *quinceañera* parties, to celebrate the turning of a girl into a "señorita" as she becomes fifteen years old, and the debutante dances, where the elite girls were "presented in society," were also held in the casinos which every town had. Since these spaces were exclusive for the elite, they left out the Black people, which made American authors understand them as "segregated spaces" even though, in reality, it was class segregation more than racial segregation what was in place there:

> The Casino is the apex of the social life of the Island. Every town, even though it be not more than a group of huts in the mountain, will maintain its casino. To be a member of this group is the social ambition of the youth of the town. It is however exclusive, by reason of its color line and by its prohibitory fees, and is really the only institution in the Island's social life that does not recognize the social equality of the negro. In spite of protests from one or the other excluded parties the casino maintains its exclusive feature and sets the pace for the smart set of the community. (James 1927, 27)

Dancing was a very important social event in Puerto Rico. It was the way in which young people could get physically closer to each other, even under the zealous eyes of chaperones and other family members. One such event at the Mayagüez Lions Club in the 1950s was described in detail by an American English teacher:

> Most of the young people were there in groups, but there were a few couples, who sat on the side of the room with the girls, their older married sisters and mothers. I was at first surprised that there were no older men around, but, on thinking about it, I decided that getting rid of your daughters is women's work. While there were chairs, and even a few tables, on the men's side of the room, most of the men were standing about in groups talking loudly to one another, with drinks in their hands.... By this time the dancing has started, and there was certainly no shyness or stiffness on the dance floor. These kids were having fun and looked like they might have been extras in a Carmen Miranda movie.... Not only were the girls dressed in brilliant colors, but the boys' open necked sports shirts were all like the ones the press used to make fun of President Truman...
>
> ... I am amazed at how fast, on the surface at least, I became acclimatized to life there. What amazes me even more is how I survived. Day after day, week after week: dance, dance, dance, party, party, party. And, apparently, I also met my classes, at least most of the time (Cooper 1994, 48–49, 55)

According to Margherita A. Hamm, in 1899, the elite enjoyed their plentiful free time in card games and elite sports, including cricket (mostly a British sport), but she attributed to the hot climate and lousy genes the poor performance of the locals compared to American and Englishmen:

> The favorite parlor games of cards are ombre, quadrille, siete y mitad, baccarat, piquet, solo, and sometimes, though rarely whist. Other games are draughts, dice, chess, lotto and backgammon. Young men of the well-to-do class imitate young Englishmen and indulge in hunting, fishing, fencing, tennis, steeple chasing, and a few go so far as to play cricket and indulge in mild athletics, but the best native athlete I ever saw would not be a match for the average Vassar graduate. It is partly the climate and partly hereditary indolence which make all exercise and activity unpleasant. (Hamm, *Porto* 1899, 98)

The elite also frequented the theaters:

> In every large community there is a theatre, and at least once a month there is a praiseworthy performance. Sometimes it is an operatic or concert company.... Sometimes it is a dramatic troupe, or it may be some strolling vaudeville artist, a prestidigitator, a panorama, a phonograph, a kinetoscope, educated dogs or a set of acrobats. The natives love amusement, and patronize entertainments so generously that companies can do as well in towns of 1,000 population as they do in American cities of 10,000. The American circus is very popular... (Hamm, *Porto* 1899, 115)

By the 1930s, the elite entertainments included new activities and sports popular in the United States, such as horse racing, boxing, and golf:

> Nearly every urban community has one or more moving-or talking—picture theaters.... There are excellent hippodromes in the Island where horse-racing is enjoyed. As a love of chance is inherent in the Latin character, horse-racing vies with the recently legalized sport of boxing in attracting interest amongst the Islanders. Miniature golf and tennis are games much in favor; and baseball, basketball, and volley-ball teams have been organized in all the principal towns. There are several fine golf courses. Sea-bathing is a strictly summer sport, "which is indulged in with safety from barracudas and sharks only in the months which do not have an "r" in their names," according to local belief. (Van Deusen and Van Deusen 1931, 167)

"A MOST UNEARTHLY NOISE": PUERTO RICAN MUSIC

Music is a very important part of Puerto Ricans' lives. It's hard for us to conceive any sort of activity to be held without music playing a part. This was easily grabbed by American authors over time:

> Porto Rico's love of music is . . . one of the many points in her favor. As a rule, the people have good voices, and sing with pleasing effect, alone and in chorus. Every city, every town, and every little hamlet supports its band of musicians. Concerts are given twice a week in every important plaza throughout the island. All the people attend these concerts . . . (Seabury 1908, 48)

> Hunger and sickness were the daily lot, but it was not un-relieved misery, for one thing they possessed—music, or if not music, at least noise. . . . Thousands of radios blasted music played, horns blew. I have been in hundreds and hundreds of Puerto Rican houses. No matter how poor the people, how hungry, how sick, they still have a radio. I cannot think of a single exception. . . . [When the author suggested a fellow to sell his radio to buy food and medicines] "But then I would lie here in silence," said the old man, his voice raised with horror at the thought. (Brown 1945, 100)

> The people of Puerto Rico respond to music. They like to sing and dance. . . . A party without music and dancing is described as "demasiado hablao" (too talky) or as a gringo fiesta. (Wagenheim 1970, 246)

And music was so important in Puerto Rican culture that as soon as new schools began to be opened, Puerto Ricans asked for musical instruction:

> Lovers of music by inheritance and endowed with special aptitude for it, the people have demanded that the schools provide this instruction. . . . with the creation of school bands. . . . The bands generally play at all school exercises, athletic meets, school celebrations, and in the public plazas certain evening each month. . . . The extension of the moving-picture shows throughout the island has given the schoolboys the opportunity to market their musical ability. In a number of towns the music at these shows is furnished entirely by schoolboys who have learned to play in the school bands. (Verrill 1914, 205–6)

Marion Blythe, a young missionary, couldn't make sense of the music called "aguinaldos,"[2] a Christmastime lyrical composition with a chorus, where something is offered or requested: a song, music, food, drinks, money, or a place to dance:

> The latter [the aguinaldo] . . . is sung in a chant-like strain that is at once catchy and monotonous, and there seems to be an endless chain of stanzas to it. . . . when I ask what the Aguinaldo is, they say it is a present, which means, I have learned, that I am expected to give something to the singers. I have listened to groups of children who have ventured up to our door, and to the more respectable people among us, too, as well as to beggars, and, although they all seem to know what they are saying, it is beyond my powers as a linguist to make rhyme or rhythm out of it. Our milkman . . . has caught the strain and an Aguinaldo goes with every quartilla of milk he dispenses. (Blythe 1911, 185)

Some Puerto Rican musical instruments were particularly annoying for American authors. Such is the case with the "güiro" or "güícharo," an Arawak percussion instrument made out of a dry hollow gourd where parallel notches are cut. It is played by rubbing metal tines along those notches and makes a rasping sound:

> The instruments were somewhat similar to those used in American bands except the drum or "guichara" which was a long gourd shaped species of calabash, which had been plucked while green and in the surface of which had been cut a number of small circular grooves which had become almost as hard as flint when the instrument had ripened in the sun. It was "played" by rubbing a hard stick across the grooves, thus making a most unearthly noise, but which served as a very good chronometer for the other performers. (Creager 1899, 233–34)

In general, Puerto Rican music was not esteemed by most American authors who cataloged it as "weird," "discordant," "primitive," "noise," or even "inspired by the devil":

> They are very fond of dancing, and have considerable musical talent of a certain kind. They make their own musical instruments, most of them being stringed affairs somewhat resembling a guitar. They also compose their own music, and when a native orchestra busts forth into melody the very atmosphere and the leaves of the trees become animated, and Satan himself would dance if he could hear them; and perhaps he can,

for some of the music sounds as though inspired by him—a veritable reproduction of the wail of a lost soul disappearing into the fiery depths. (Church 1898, 35)

"NO STATESIDE GIRL HAD EVER DANCED WITH ME LIKE THAT": DANCING

In a colonial context, dance has been analyzed as an acceptable form for the colonized to "exorcize" themselves from the violence (either the "in-your-face" kind or the more subtle "microaggressions") exercised against them by the colonizers. Frantz Fanon explained this perspective:

> On another level we see the native's emotional sensibility exhausting itself in dances which are more or less ecstatic.... The native's relaxation takes precisely the form of a muscular orgy in which the most acute aggressivity and the most impelling violence are canalized, transformed, and conjured away. The circle of the dance is a permissive circle: it protects and permits. At certain times on certain days, men and women come together at a given place, and there, ... fling themselves into a seemingly unorganized pantomime, which is in reality extremely systematic, in which by various means ... may be deciphered as in an open book the huge effort of a community to exorcise itself, to liberate itself, to explain itself.... There are no limits—for in reality your purpose in coming together is to allow the ... hampered aggressivity, to dissolve as in a volcanic eruption.[3]

Dancing to the rhythm of drums was an African tradition that crossed the Atlantic with the enslaved African people and, in Puerto Rico, became an integral part of the cultural expressions in plantations and sugar mills. In the coastal areas where they worked and concentrated, African descendants danced the "bomba" in all kinds of celebrations: weddings, birthdays, christenings, Catholic feasts and end-of-harvest festivals.[4] The *bomba* dance is performed in Puerto Rico either by a lone dancer or by a couple who engage in a performance with at least two large hand-beaten drums, while participants sing in a call-and-response fashion. At least one of the drums have to be higher pitched (the "repicador") and it is this drummer the one that engages in a rhythmical dialog or challenge with the dancer (or dancers) in which each side tries to choreographically impose their style on the other.[5]

Although several authors depicted negatively the Puerto Rican *bomba* dances, they pointed to their sensuality as their offending quality. This is expected from a Puritan-based society that condemned dancing as an activity that "breaks all the Ten Commandments of God."[6] The *bomba* dances were held on Sundays, and American authors coincided with Puerto Rican elites describing them as "wild." But the local elites' rejection of *la bomba* had more to do with its African origins. Indeed, the word *bomba* means "drum" or "drumbeat" in Ashanti ("mbomba" in Angola and "nbomba" in Congo).[7] "One often hears at night from the negro quarters the barbaric notes of the 'Bomba,' the favorite dance of the colored people, which harks back to darkest Africa. Bands are forever playing somewhere in the offing . . ." (Mixer 1926, 109).

But all kinds of dancing were commented on, especially the balls that were held in the casinos and other social clubs. The Puerto Ricans' fondness for dancing, as well as their rhythm, were noticed, and comparisons were made with American dancing styles: "Porto Ricans, like all southerners, are very fond of dancing. . . . Frequent balls are given for . . . organizations in hotels and private halls. . . . The modern dances are performed with more grace and rhythm and somewhat less syncopation than is the habit in the north . . ." (Mixer 1926, 110).

Interestingly, an American English teacher in the early 1950s discovered the sensuality of Puerto Rican dancing while attending a Mayagüez Lion's Club dance. When he got a Puerto Rican girl to dance with, Cooper happily realized that Puerto Rican bolero dance was quite erotic for his American point of view:

> Finally, when they played a very slow bolero I thought I could manage, I approached a girl. . . . She let me onto the dance floor, pressed herself tightly against me, and off we went. And I understood . . . why there was no cutting in or switching partners on the dance floor. No Stateside girl had ever danced with me like that. While it wasn't exactly a sexual act, it was as close as you could get to one in a few minutes fully clothed on a public dance floor. The bragging manner a student assumed when, in discussing a girl he said, "I've danced with her," now made sense too. No wonder any and all social occasions were turned into dances. (Cooper 1994, 51–52)

An American soldier enjoyed the sight and sounds of waltzes coming from a downtown home and began dancing with a lamppost; similarly, a young American missionary wife found herself entranced by Puerto Rican music almost to the point of dancing, having to make an effort to contain herself:

> . . . the strain of the beautiful "Blue Danube" was wafted to my ears. As I came abreast of the house from which the music came, I saw through

the open windows, a room full of young people dancing and merrily enjoying themselves.... I unconsciously moved my feet, one, two, three, one, two, three, with a lamp-post for a partner. (Oliver 1900, 196)

[Hearing the orchestra's music:] Before I knew it, I caught myself beating time with one foot while my missionary foot said, "Don't! It isn't becoming to you!" (Blythe 1911, 173)

For elites, dancing meant private social events where young men and women got an opportunity to meet under the vigilant eyes of their parents and others, as well as an occasion for all to display their best outfits and dancing talents. A detailed description of their dances and attires was provided:

Billiards and dancing are universal. Private billiard parties are more frequent than in American cities. Every man, woman and child appears to be a master of round, square and fancy dancing. Those who are fashionable favor the styles in vogue in Paris, while the great middle classes still retain their love for the bolero, fandango, cachuca, and the rustic bailes or country dances of the old country. Their dancing parties are pretty pictures. The gentlemen are attired in white and black clothes, the regular attire being a black silk or alpaca coat, white linen shirt, vest and trousers, patent-leather shoes, and sometimes in place of a waistcoat they wear a broad silk sash. Officers wear handsome tropical uniforms, and ecclesiastics the neat and artistic robes of the church. The priest never dances the round dance, but may take part in a quadrille. The women range from black and white combinations in their dress to delightful bursts of lace and varicolored silk and satin. Black or white dresses which disclose the arms, shoulders, bust and back, but are lined elsewhere with white or many-colored satin, are more numerous than any other single style, and embroidered linen or silk is also in vogue. The bolero jacket, the most graceful of the articles of raiment here, is worn by nearly all the señoritas. (Hamm, *Porto* 1899, 98–99)

"THE MOST IMPORTANT HOLIDAY OF THE YEAR": CHRISTMASTIME

Regarding Christmastime, Puerto Ricans, as previously said, boast about being "the loudest, the merriest, the longest of them all."[8] But it was not always that long. In 1955 it was calculated as consisting of sixteen days, if we don't count the holiday extensions called "octavas" (an eight-day extension until

January 17) and "octavitas" (another eight-day extension until January 24): "a total of almost sixteen days of partying, dancing and singing during which people eat, dances, loves and drinks in excess."[9] This is probably the happiest time of the year for all Puerto Ricans, regardless of their economic situation, because beyond the gift-giving tradition, it offers plenty of occasions for sharing time, music, food, and drinks with family, friends, neighbors, and coworkers:

> By far the most important holiday of the year is the Christmas season. . . . The Christmas spirit begins to effervesce early in December and bubbles on through to January 6 . . . it extends a week or two for the octava de reyes and the octavita. Puerto Rican hospitality glows brightest during the Christmas season; it is a time for visiting and eating and drinking heartily . . . (Wagenheim 1970, 222)

Not many of our American authors mention the Christmas traditions of the Island, probably because, as foreigners, they were not invited to join. But those who stayed longer enough and who mingled enough among Puerto Ricans, mostly missionaries and teachers, did comment on the celebrations. One example is the Van Deusens, a lawyer and an English teacher who spent over twenty years in Puerto Rico and who reported on the Misa de Gallo, a special Catholic mass celebrated at midnight on December 24:

> The coming of Christmas ushers in a season of merry-making. "Noche Buena" (Christmas Eve) is celebrated by the "Misa de Gallo," an impressive and melodious Midnight Mass . . . a chorus, either mixed or of young girls alone, which breaks forth into a joyous rendition of Spanish Christmas carols accompanied by the "güícharos," castanets, "maracas," and tambourines. (Van Deusen and Van Deusen 1931, 178)

Being a Catholic country, Puerto Rico has a long tradition of Christmas celebrations. For the sugarcane workers, since it coincided with the "zafra" or sugarcane cutting season, this was the best time of the year as they were employed and receiving a salary (as opposed to the following terrible six months of the "tiempo muerto" when most were laid off).

Once the Americanization process was ongoing, American traditions began to be implanted through the colonial school system. The most prominent and shocking change in the Christmas tradition was the introduction of Santa Claus, with his snow sled and reindeer that made little sense on a tropical island.[10] Up until then, Puerto Ricans commemorated the birth of Jesus and, more importantly, for the children, the Three Wise Men visited all houses to deliver gifts to all well-behaved children. This big change was depicted by an American missionary:

> There are some of our own people here who are convinced that America is the only sensible country in the world and that our ways are, as a matter of course, always the best. Before they came here to improve things, the Porto Ricans knew little and cared less for our pagan idea of Santa Claus.... The children here know that Christmas day is the day on which the infant Jesus was born, and some one asked a little girl who Santa Claus was and she said that he was the saint of the Americanos. (Blythe 1911, 181–82)

Blythe broadly explained the "Día de Reyes" or "Three Kings' Day" as she understood it from her Sunday school students. She also mentioned another tradition: the Three Kings' "trullas,"[11] in which a group of country musicians visited homes and stores singing Christmas *aguinaldos* as one of them carried a wood-carved representation of the Three Kings. In return for their songs, they received whatever monetary collaboration their audience was able to give them. Blythe ended up criticizing the lack of Christian piety during the holiday as she described the other, more common "trullas de a pie" ("on-foot trullas") that the lower classes enjoyed as they accompanied a group of musicians singing *aguinaldos* from home to home where they danced, sang, drank and ate through the night and to the next morning:

> ... the great day of days to the children is January sixth: "Three Kings' Day" they call it, which they claim is the day when the three wise men came from the East with gifts for the Child Jesus.... our southern children keep Three King's Day, which day expands into a week. And such a week! Every home is a stir with preparations, another new outfit of clothes come into being for every member of the family, work is suspended for another week, as old and young, rich and poor, one and all join in the preparation for the reception of the three kings who, according to long accepted tradition, are to come from Greece, India and Ethiopia, respectively, the first of these being mounted on a white beast, the second riding a bay, and the third, a black one.
> The whole island is on holiday and the country roads ... are lined with happy peasants who carry boxes containing the images of the three ... to which you are expected to make at least a copper offering.... The day, however, has quite lost its religious significance ... and it is considered as little more than a grand holiday for all.... There are country house parties where beer—another American improvement (?)—flows like water,

and dancing continues all night, and there are barbecues and bonfires and eating and drinking and dancing to the music of the wichero[12] ... We also hear rattle-bones and an occasional guitar which heads some serenading party and the Aguinaldo fills the air and is on everybody's lips. (Blythe 1911, 183–85)

The Christmas "asaltos"[13] were also mentioned: "Christmas.... We had what were called 'asaltos' (sic), where you'd go from house to house, and people had guitars and there would be lots of singing. They'd knock at your door, and you were supposed to be ready for them. Of course, they let everybody know there was going to be an asalto (sic)" (Mildred Grub-Acosta in Ezratty 1986, 164).

Beyond the traditional *trullas* or *asaltos*, Christmas parties were also part of the seasonal gatherings. These depended on the monetary possibilities of the hosts, of course, but the gay atmosphere was always there and is preserved to present times:

> ... as we approached ... we could hear from a distance that the party was already in full swing.... The little wooden house was bursting with people—some making speeches, others reciting poetry, and everyone dancing, singing, drinking, and eating roast pork and all sorts of sweets I have never tasted before. In one corner, a group of country musicians kept things lively on native instruments. I was introduced to everyone and immediately made me feel as one of the family. They knew I didn't understand Spanish, but it didn't seem to matter. We communicated anyway. People kept serving me food and drinks and when the girls asked me to dance, they couldn't understand when I tried to explain that I didn't know how to dance. Impossible! In Puerto Rico, everybody can dance! The warmth, cordiality, and generosity of everyone made an indelible impression on me. I didn't yet know that I would find the same characteristics everywhere on the island. (Delano 1997, 73)

Marion Blythe also commented on the gifts that the Three Kings brought to all children, rich or poor, on the night of January 5:

> On the evening of the fifth of January, baskets ranging in quality from the pathetic little home-made tissue-paper affair of the shack dweller to the larger and more elaborate silk and gilt creations of the wealthier homes will be hung around the houses, or, better still, left in the gardens or on the front door-steps to receive the offerings of the never failing three kings who come in the night to fill their baskets as certainly and mysteriously as our Santa comes to fill our stockings. The

children are too excited to sleep late in the morning, but they bound from their beds—that is, in cases where a kind Providence has provided beds—or, if not, they pull themselves off from an old home-made hammock, a canvas cot, a straw mat on the floor, or even a bare floor. Their own thought is of their baskets, the Aguinaldo and the nightly visit . . . (Blythe 1911, 186)

This missionary, who spent thirty years in Puerto Rico, explained why, in his view, Santa Claus had no chance to substitute the Three Kings:

Christmas day in Porto Rico did not mean much to the children. The youngsters have their festivals on the 6th of January, Three Kings Day. This holiday celebrates the coming of the Wise Men. Before retiring the children will fill baskets with grass and place them in conspicuous places so that the Wise Men in their search for the infant Jesus will see them and in return for fodder for their beasts, will leave presents for the children. The coming of Santa Claus with the Americans could not introduce much in the way of amusement. (James 1927, 28–29)

"FOR THE AMUSEMENT OF THE POPULACE": CARNIVALS, FESTIVALS AND "FIESTAS PATRONALES"

Protestant churches opposed carnival celebrations, considered "hideous." They also protested the Patronal Feasts, Catholic celebrations—gambling included— in honor of saints associated to each of the towns in Puerto Rico, because the Protestant churches were against the separate worship of saints, because they vetoed the money and time invested in them, and because of the so-called "immoralities" the people engaged in during the celebration.[14] For Protestants, the worship of Catholic saints and the Virgin Mary was considered a display of idolatry.

Following a Catholic Spanish tradition, each Puerto Rican town had a patron saint which was supposed to protect it from evil and to intercede with God in favor of the town's inhabitants in exchange for their worship once a year during ten days (including the day of the patron saint).[15] During those days, the townspeople engaged in a variety of activities both religious and secular. The religious ones included a Catholic mass, a procession and a "diana" (musical ensemble's procession very early on the morning of the saint's day); and the secular ones included music, dances, gambling in "picas," children's rides such as the merry-go-round and the Ferris wheel, youth promenading in the town's plaza, and fireworks, typically at the town's central plaza.[16] Participants tended to use new clothes on these days of feasting. A few American authors referred to these celebrations called in Spanish "fiestas patronales": "Each town has its patron saint, and saint days are celebrated over a period of anywhere from a day to a fortnight, by festivities in the church and in the town plaza, which is decorated with strings of triangular banners and colored lights, and where pleasure booths with varied attractions are set up for the amusement of the populace" (Van Deusen and Van Deusen 1931, 177).

An American reverend provided a very detailed description of the St. John's[17] (San Juan) Festival in the capital city in 1908 as a fun-filled time in which different social classes participated, but where only the higher classes were protagonists of the celebration, leaving to the poorer classes the role of mere spectators:

> The festivals of the church are national gala days. Especially is this true of St. John's Eve, June 27, and the days preceding. The festivities . . . last for more than two weeks. . . . . . . the great parade to be held on the day . . . devoted to the patron saint of San Juan . . . a procession of men, women and children on horseback, all in fantastic dress, passes through the streets. . . . Social distinctions are forgotten. . . . Those who do not wholly disguise themselves appear on the street in fancy costume. . . . At night, bonfires are kindled on the corners of the streets. It is a time for all kind of jokes. . . . For three days all the houses are thrown open. Lemonade and other refreshing drinks are offered to all who are thirsty. People with masks and without enter freely into these open houses, but no property is ever disturbed.
>
> In connection with the St. John Festival is held . . . the Feast of Flowers . . . a poetical contest. . . . The successful rhymes are printed in all the papers and are read aloud . . . To the writer of the finest poem of all is presented a natural rose. The lady upon whom he bestows this rose becomes queen of the feast. . . . She sits upon a flowery throne from which she distributes all other prizes . . . for the second best poem is a rose of gold; the third in rank . . . a rose of silver. (Seabury 1908, 50–53)

But the St. John's Festival was celebrated in a different way by the lower classes, who spent the eve of St. John's Day at the beaches and practiced magic rituals to get luck, as described in a travel book of 1984:

> Everyone in the island takes part in "San Juan Bautista" day. Families crowd into whatever vehicle is available to take them to the beach. Decorative lights and platforms for musicians are erected. Many younger people put up tents intending to stay all night. Food and drinks are

bought for late supper. Then at midnight everyone goes into the water fully dressed. The ritual is to walk in backwards into the water three times. This is to bring "suerte," luck, for the whole of the coming year. (Samoiloff 1984, 180)

Another celebration, identified only as "St. Peter's Day and Carnival," was described in detail as one in which Black Puerto Ricans participated much more:

St. Peter's Day and carnival ... Dressed in grotesque fashion, people go from house to house, filling the air with music of a more or less absurd character. Masked balls are given. Ridicule of everybody and everything is regarded as allowable. The negroes are very boisterous in their antics. They romp and caper and contort their bodies into all sort of shapes. The "cake walk" is a mild performance compared with the pranks of these people. Their gayety lasts for several days, and ceases only when the participants have exhausted all new forms of amusement and are completely tired out. (Seabury 1908, 53)

A young American missionary portrayed the carnival as she experienced it in Aguadilla in 1907. She points to the "natural" segregation of races during the celebration and to the "perfect order" all participants kept during it, at least according to local customs, to which even the Presbyterian congregation adhered:

It took us two weeks to get ready for the carnival and two weeks more to get over it.... No one was left unentertained nor did any one seem to be bored.... On Friday evening the whole town was on the plaza ... The air was filled with gay colored paper serpentinas, yards and yards long, thrown by the practiced youth, carrying love's tender missives and twining them about the objects of their desires as they passed.... Everybody, young and old, rich and poor, high and low, had a good time; only the darker brothers, in conformity to an unwritten but well understood law, were obliged to walk only on the outside of the plaza, while the white and more favored people held sway down the centre walks. Those who preferred to do so sat in rocking chairs which could be hired for ten cents each. Although all classes and kinds of people participated in the events of the evening there was little or no need for police, for perfect order seemed to reign. Should such a thing occur in the United States I am sure the press will unite with the clergy in proclaiming that the world was coming to an end or that the millennium was about to dawn ... (Blythe 1911, 137, 139–41)

"IT SEEMED A KIND OF SOCIAL TREADMILL": PROMENADING AT THE PLAZA

Following the Spanish towns' tradition, every Puerto Rican town had its plaza around, which gathered the most important buildings of the town, particularly the Catholic Church and the City Hall, usually facing each other at the extremes of the plaza. The plaza was the center of town life and the gathering place for special celebrations of both the church and the government. At the time of the US invasion, plazas were the quintessential gathering places for all urban social classes, even though class distinctions were clearly made. Sundays, in particular, were special days at the plazas since the towns that could afford it had musical bands playing while elite youth promenaded at the music's rhythm in order to see and be seen:

> ... Sunday night the attendance is larger and more attention is paid to dress. It becomes a sort of dress parade for the better class of people. The band plays, and the throng moves back and forth, up and down, up and down, the length of the plaza. Others sit in rented chairs along the sides and ends, and watch them as they walk.... To me it seemed a kind of social treadmill ... a sort of general public reception at which everyone met everyone else, with the opportunity for a chat if it was wished, a dignified bow, or a cold shoulder. (Robinson 1899, 53)

The promenade was used by the elite youth to become somewhat acquainted, though at a distance, with their potential future partners. Girls and young women promenaded in one direction, and the males did so in the other direction, so they kept seeing each other's faces as they kept promenading. We can imagine how important gestures might have been in order to show that liking was mutual. Only formal couples, with the approval of their respective parents, were allowed to promenade together, side by side, but without holding hands. Since the older generations sat around them in for-rent rocking chairs, all eyes were set upon them.

The tradition was kept for some time after the US invasion, and it was documented by American authors, one of whom identified racism regarding the promenading:

> On Sunday night, which happens in our case to be in the Carnival season, the populace disported itself in the main plaza, marching about as the band played. No negroes were allowed to promenade—and whenever the police perceived a dusky person with kinky hair in the procession, he, or she, was gently but firmly removed and put on the sidelines.

It appeared that kinky hair was the test. No less dusky parties whose hair was straight seemed to pass muster all right. (Marden 1921, 152)

In the early 1950s, an American teacher deemed Ponce as the cultural bastion of the plaza promenades, but with a little new touch: the option of couples walking together (and touching) without formal permission from the parents:

Ponce prided itself on preserving its Spanish colonial charm and customs, including the weekend promenade of young men and women around the central plaza, the men in one direction, the women in the other. After a ritual exchange of smiles and, on the men's part, often very suggestive comments about the young ladies, a young man could, if given a nod of approval, change directions and walk around the plaza with an arm around the girl's waist. (Cooper 1994, 85)

"TRUSTING TO FICKLE DAME FORTUNE": GAMBLING

Since their first stake at government in 1649 England under Oliver Cromwell, the Puritan ideals legislated against gambling because it led to a waste of time that should be spent in working or praying. These ideas traveled to the United States and in New England they turned even stricter and any gambling was condemned, not because it was considered evil per se, but because Puritans opposed all idleness.[18] Facing the roughness of American wilderness, every hand was necessary for their survival and any activity that distracted people from their hard work was banned. Hence, as early as in 1631 the Massachusetts Bay Colony passed an anti-idleness statute that outlawed the possession of cards, dice or gambling tables, even in private homes.[19] For them, the "get-rich-quick appeal" mocked "capitalism's core values: disciplined work habits, thrift, prudence, adherence to routine, and the relationship between effort and reward."[20] These Puritan ideas permeated the laws and institutions of the United States.

As part of their moral mission, American Protestant missionaries zealously fought against every instance of gambling available to Puerto Ricans. This was a tough mission to embrace since gambling was socially acceptable by the Spanish colonial government in Puerto Rico, which in 1814 instituted the Royal Lottery to increase its funds and looked the other way regarding gambling and cockfights.[21] As a missionary censured:

The Porto Rican is an inveterate gambler. . . . The poor will throw dice for their last penny and will then go hungry. . . . When the Catholic

Church has special need for money, it gets up some sort of a raffle.... Everywhere the spirit of gambling seems to have taken hold of the people and become a part of their life.... Anything that can be turned into a game of chance meets with favor. Throwing dice, playing with cards, dominoes or checkers, are only interesting as money is placed on the game. Betting on the cockfights is the most popular form of gambling. (Fowles 1910, 53–54, 63)

Taking the Protestants' side, the new Penal Code of 1902, in its Article 291 specifically banned all lotteries and raffles, considering a misdemeanor any engagement in them. Nevertheless, as happened with many other intents of regulating Puerto Ricans' entertainment, it was habitually disobeyed.

For the Puerto Rican elite class, gambling was a source of excitement, but for the poorer classes, it represented the possibility (no matter how remote) of earning enough money to fix a run-down shack, buy medicines for a family member, invest in a pig or a cow, or maybe just to buy shoes for the kids. This hope sustained their spirits through the tough times they lived in. Nowadays, the dreams have changed, but the hope of winning extra money through gambling persists. Gambling of some sort, according to most American authors, was widespread in Puerto Rico and common to all social classes:

> The Puerto Rican is an inveterate gambler. He will bet all of his hard earned money, his shack, his wife, even his soul on the turn of a card or a favorite game-cock. He is a game, or I might say a philosophical loser, for he will be consoled when the cards, or whatever he may be betting on, do not favor him by continuing on with his play, trusting to fickle Dame Fortune for a lucky strike on the next bet.... I never saw a native bet more than a peso (fifty cents American money) in all the time I was on the island, and usually it was no more than from one to ten centavos. (Oliver 1900, 218)

During the US military occupation, there is an account of a sort of "gambling festival" shrewdly organized by the natives right after the American soldiers got paid a much-waited-for two-month salary:

> ... the night that we were paid off [after two months]. Monte tables and roulette wheels were set up all over town. It seemed as if every native owned either one or the other, or a pair of dice, or some kind of gambling device whereby we could be relieved of our money in the shortest time possible.... Soldier and native commingled and the drunken shouts and brawling reminded me of those Tampa days, only

the noise seemed to be multiplied a hundred fold for the games were all held out in the open air, very few private games being held in the houses. The torches with which every table was provided lent an uncanny appearance to the motley crowd of crazed gamesters as they shouted their bets on a card or on some number on the wheel, or the ha ha in short, rasping tones from a group of excited, crap shooters. It was impossible to sleep that night for the whole town seemed to have gone mad. The officers . . . did not interrupt them unless a man became too unruly . . . The games were not all run by the natives. A few soldiers combined their funds into a lump sum and founded a bank. (Oliver 1900, 169)

Many activities not usually associated with gambling, such as kite flying, became a gambling opportunity quite frequently, as this American journalist noticed:

When I first visited this island [in 1899] I was surprised to see so many men and boys flying kites. The strings of the kites had been soaked with glue and dusted with powdered glass, and each flyer tried to cut the string of his opponents' kite by making his own rub against it. When one of the glass-dusted strings touched and ordinary cord, it sawed through it like a knife, and the kite thus loosened sailed away or dropped to the ground. It seemed odd to me that the people should be so excited by these kite fights, until I learned that every man and boy has a bet on some kite, and that varying sums, from pennies to dollars, changed hands each time the kite strings were cut. (Carpenter 1930, 268)

Another one of these activities in which sometimes money or other goods were (and still are) betted was playing dominoes. This was an entertainment for adults, as noticed by some American authors, and is still a favorite entertainment at the beach or the plaza and in any kind of gathering:

. . . a boy who fatally stabbed his opponent in a game of dominoes in which a wager of three cents was at stake. (James 1927, 20)

Actually, the island's favorite participant sport hinges on chance but in combination with skill and friendly confrontation. It is dominoes. In parks, cafes, and private homes, the endless silent battles continue night and day. Do not ever make the mistake of telling a Puerto Rican, "I used to play dominoes when I was a kid." Here, it is a very adult pastime. (Rand, A. 1973, 126)

Modernity brought a new form of gambling: the casinos (mostly for tourists), the government-run lottery, and horse racing:

> A casino can be in a hotel and only in a hotel . . . Alcoholic beverages cannot be consumed or served in the casino, although free coffee and soda pop can be provided. There can be no entertainment, no slot machines, no under 18, no sports clothes. . . . casinos became legal in 1948. . . . Residents have not flooded the casinos. They find them too stuffy and expensive. Local gambling instincts are amply catered to by the lottery, the racetrack, and the prominently located Agencia Hipica, legal horse parlors. (Rand, A. 1973, 123, 125)

"BULL FIGHTING WITH NO FIGHTING": BULLFIGHTS

Bullfighting began in Puerto Rico during Spanish colonization and became a Sunday entertainment. The shows were open for women and never ended with the death of the bulls. A "plaza de toros" (bull pit) opened in Puerta de Tierra, San Juan, in 1893.[22] An American soldier gave an account of a very disappointing bullfight:

> The only bullfight that I personally witnessed took place in a natural Amphitheatre of great scenic beauty, near the romantic town of Aguadilla. The arena was defined by stone walls about five feet in height and the adjacent hillsides were utilized in seating the thousand spectators. There were but few women present, and these were of the lower class. [The bulls refused to fight even after being prodded for an hour] . . . so finally, the master of ceremonies announced that the slaughter would be postponed, as the intended victim was too inconsiderate for proper sport. The gazing crowd seemed to take this ending in good part, and slowly dispersed, chatting and laughing in excellent humor. (*Greater America* 1900, 22–24)

Somehow, some Americans wrongly understood that bullfights were already in decline in 1899:

> Bull-fights have never gained a foothold in the island. . . . The only reason given is that the people have always been too poor to indulge in the expensive luxury of importing any of the distinguished matadors from home, such experts being indispensable when it is desired to raise bullfighting above the level of mere brutality. (Dinwiddie 1899, 175)

In 1944, an American teacher seemed disappointed with the violence-free version of bullfights the colonial government was trying to promote:

> Bull fighting was to be permitted again—but with reservations. The reservations were that there was to be no bloodshed, that no one was to get hurt. The picadors were not to pique too hard, the riders were not to ride too hard; the horses were not to hurt each other, the toreador was not to hurt the bull, and I suppose they had the bull under contract not to hurt the toreador. In other words there was to be bull fighting with no fighting. (Dean 1944, 66)

Bullfights were celebrated in several baseball parks until 1965, when the "Plaza de Toros España" was inaugurated in Isla Verde, mostly for the benefit of tourists. But after the Animal Protection Society complained, this venue closed in 1971 and with this, the shows ended in Puerto Rico.

"LIKE BEDLAM LET LOOSE": COCKFIGHTS

In the United States, the state of New York approved in 1866 its first law against animal cruelty, which, in its Section 2, specifically banned all activities "for the purpose of fighting or baiting any bull, bear, dog, cock, or other creature," considering them misdemeanors.[23] The philosophy behind animal advocacy in the United States rested on the Christian notion that in Genesis 1:6 humans were granted control and stewardship over all animals, which was then interpreted as a moral responsibility to protect animals. By 1900, cockfighting was illegal in forty states, and the policy was unilaterally extended to Puerto Rico by its civil colonial government on March 10, 1904. The ban established a fifty dollar fine and/or a month in jail as punishment for violators. In the eyes of Puerto Rican "galleros" ("cockers"), this imposition disregarded their cultural heritage and was seen "as imperialism by another name."[24]

The discourse of animal advocates was framed within the "white man's burden" philosophy discussed in the introduction. They intended to "enlighten their brethren of color abroad with a gospel of kindness" to put an end to the "spectacle of homosocial alterity and ruin."[25] This approach ignored the deep bond developed between cockers and birds as the animals were raised with special diets and care, becoming the symbol of hope for their owners. It also ignored the social relationships fostered around cockfighting and the deep roots of this form of entertainment for many Puerto Ricans who considered it a "sport." On the contrary, American authorities in Puerto Rico reasoned cockfighting was "a catalyst to idleness, permanent poverty, Catholic fatalism, and wholesale violence to birds and men."[26]

Puerto Ricans offered resistance and ignored the ban, especially in the rural areas where authorities were barely present. In 1928, fueled by the fact that boxing have become legal in the United States in the previous year, cockers got the Puerto Rican legislature to repeal the van. Nevertheless, then governor Horace M. Towner vetoed the bill, claiming that cockfights ended in quarrels and murder, a completely false allegation.[27] The change only came in 1933 when, in the face of the devastation and misery of Depression times, Governor Robert H. Gore, who had attended cockfights in Kentucky, legalized cockfighting in order to "make Puerto Rico's tourist economy more attractive to American visitors."

Sunday was the day of cockfighting, even if only for the men and boys. There were official pits or "galleras" in every town where men gathered under a roof to watch a fight between two of these animals, sometimes to their death. American authors described what happened there, noticing the betting system in which all bets, though verbal or by a simple gesture, have always been honored. This is why cockfighting is called "the gentlemen's sport" in Puerto Rico: "In betting the men never deposit their money. All wagers are paid at the end of the afternoon fights. A man has to call out his bet at the top of his voice, and his ears or eyes must then catch the answer" (March 1899, 452).

One of the most detailed accounts of what went on in a cockfighting pit or "gallera" was provided by an American cavalryman who was very fond of gambling himself but couldn't understand the close relationship between owner and fighting cock:

> Every town, no matter how small, boasts a cock-pit.... Starting on Saturday afternoon the natives begin to flock into the towns from the surrounding plantations, very often tramping ten, fifteen or twenty miles, just for the chance to bet and lose their paltry earnings of the week, a peso or two. A peso looks as large to them as a twenty dollar bill does to the average American citizen.
>
> Not every native owns a game cock, but those who do are looked on as "lucky devils," by their less fortunate brethren. Each and every one of them has a following of his very own, just as much as have the owners of racing stables.... If a native chances to own a chicken which has survived a dozen or more battles and has been victorious, his record as a rare sport is established, but he is at the same time obliged to give his opponent heavy odds.
>
> The tiers of seats are filled with a howling mass of perspiring Puerto Rican humanity, with a sprinkling of laughing soldiers, who pose more as disinterested spectators, though they may have a few centavos up on

the coming fight just to make it interesting. [After the first round of the fight ...] They are rubbed down, the blood is washed ... and if the skin around the eyes ... is hanging so as to obstruct the sight, the particles are trimmed off with a pair of shears. This alone is a repulsive sight. But the filthy habit the natives have of biting the chicken's neck, and running their mouths along the feathers to circulate the blood, and then resuscitating the crippled by taking a mouthful of water and forcing it down the throat by firmly holding the parted beak between the teeth, was positively sickening.

The chickens are again placed in the ring.... All this time the yelling of a hundred natives betting on their favorites, was like bedlam let loose. It was impossible to hear one's self-think, and in all probability no more than five pesos had changed hands. Take it all in all, cock fighting did not appeal to the American soldier who would rather witness a good, fair, pugilistic encounter ... (Oliver 1900, 218–21)

Only a few Americans saw no fault in the treatment of the cocks:

Surely no infant ever received such attention from fond parents as this skinny bird. (Ober 1899, 182)

Their owners take good care of them and endeavor to keep them in good condition for fighting.... They are the pets and often the most valued possessions of their owners. (George 1900, 35, 65)

In 1908, we began to find American writers who harshly criticized cockfighting as "degrading" or "brutal" and who celebrated the prohibition of this form of entertainment. A common absurd inference was that the money spent on it was what kept the Puerto Ricans deep in poverty:

Cockfighting is the national sport. This degrading amusement is quite universal in the island. Every town has connected with it a cockpit.... The money that is lost and won in this brutalizing sport would go far to keep the families of the participants in food and clothing.... It does not seem to have occurred to the people that it is either brutal or debasing. As was to be expected, one of the first things the United States did after taking possession of the island was to prohibit cockfighting. It is to be hoped that in coming years the sport will be entirely banished. (Seabury 1908, 49–50)

But the endurance of cockfighting in Puerto Rico was evident in a 1973 account of what happened in a "gallera":

Cockfighting is the Puerto Rican means of getting animals to enhance your machismo for you. There are "galleras" (cockpits) in every community, that have daily bouts from November 1 to August 31. During the whole evening, it will be the human participants, not their surrogate heroes that are most fascinating. This is Puerto Rico's national pastime.... the audience stands, shouts, points, waves. They resemble not bullfight fans but Wall Street brokers screaming for attention on the floor of the stock exchange. They are betting, with shouts to attract potential bettors and hand signals to seal the bargain ... The winner is declared. Bets are paid off as men scurry across the ring and waitresses scurry on the outside bringing drinks.... Television hasn't killed it. In fact, the fights are often televised. The Coliseo is in the high-rent district. A bar and slick restaurant are part of the operation.... you get the impact of seeing educated, affluent people enjoying what to us is a barbaric sport. (Rand, A., 1973, 131–32)

In 2008, cockfighting was declared illegal in all US states, and the Farm Bill of 2019 extended this to all US territories. Then, in December 2019, the Governor of Puerto Rico kept cockfighting legal on the Island for another five years as a domestic activity in defiance of the bill. The government stated that there were, at the time, seventy-one registered "galleras," (cockpits) generating $65 million a year and creating 7,200 jobs.[28] Court litigation is expected regarding this issue.

Even though the US government tried to ban cockfighting, Puerto Rican *galleros* have so far resisted those moves. In J. M. Davis's view, when animal protectionists opted to attack *galleros* for their "animal depravity" in a punitive, violent way, instead of creating a "culturally sensitive humane educational program" highlighting the suffering of the animals, they set the stage for a nationalistic response on their part, since they perceived the ban on cockfighting as "an intrusive way for American imperialists to control."[29] The controversy turned into another battleground for the nationalist defense of Puerto Rican culture and of Puerto Ricans' right to self-determination, a battle that Puerto Rican *galleros* still seem prepared to fight as long as needed.

"A NEW SPORT TO THE BOYS": GROUP SPORTS

Eleven years before the US invasion, a Puerto Rican physician and intellectual criticized the islanders´ lack of interest in physical sports: "It is sensitive that there is no game that exercises the muscular system of the peasant ... on the contrary, cockfighting and gambling ... dominate the jíbaro."[30] This will also be noticed and criticized by several American authors particularly because by the end of the nineteenth century, group physical sports, such as baseball, basketball, and football, had become very popular in the United States. "Until baseball was introduced by the American soldiers, there seems to have been little out-door sport" (Fowles 1910, 62).

Regarding the value given (or not) to sports, we can identify the relationship it had with the Catholic vs. Protestant theologies. As explained by Erich Golbach, in Catholic theology, scholasticism established a dichotomy between soul and body in which the soul had clear preeminence. But Protestant reformer Martin Luther changed this when he established that work, as well as any common activity, "was considered a service rendered to God and to one's neighbor."[31] Calvinists and Puritans adhered to this concept and added the predestination of those who will receive from God eternal salvation instead of eternal damnation. Those predestined to eternal salvation will show it through their hard labor, in which they anxiously engaged to prove to their community that they were predestined to salvation. But such a life based on labor, worshiping, and family life required "some refreshing moments in his life . . . a relaxation from time to time . . ."[32] For this, Puritans proposed sports activities, but as in so many Puritan practices, it was considered "a necessary duty" for males only. Regarding sports, rules applied: "He may not overexert his body, he may not spend too much time or money . . . [and were] strictly prohibited on the Sabbath . . ."[33] In this sense, modern sports emerged within the Puritan set of values and soon aligned with capitalism as the elements of competition and professionalism were added.

Since the US invasion, the sportive practices of American soldiers were a source of amusement for Puerto Ricans who were not used to any kind of group exercise: "The game of leap frog, which the men used to play evenings, or for exercise in the mornings, afforded the natives great amusement, and introduced a new sport to the boys" (Edwards 1899, 169).

The American colonial government in Puerto Rico brought group sports that were already popular in the United States, such as baseball and basketball. They were expected to promote sports ethics, personal character, team spirit, and general health, as well as to substitute all gambling. But they found it difficult to adapt seamlessly to Puerto Rican culture. American authors warned that Puerto Ricans lacked the ethics to play the group sports as they would cheat, refuse to accept defeat, and use violence to prevail if needed:

> The Porto Rican when it comes to team work is lacking in what the Anglo-Saxon considers the first element of a good sport. . . . Distrust is universal here. . . . In his sport the end is likely to justify the means. A little cheating is all right, if you are not found out. . . . The public school has been the great agency in teaching the national game. It is

now impossible to go into the remotest "barrio" and not find a baseball diamond. (James 1927, 29)

The fact that sports are thus practiced and enjoyed does not necessarily guarantee the fixity of sporting standards . . . the idealized concepts of sport and fair play in Puerto Rico are not always inviolate . . . umpires get beaten up somewhat oftener than is the custom farther north . . . games sometimes end in rioting. . . . They just can't stand defeat, it is alleged, and their fervor of protest has odd forms of expression. (White 1938, 280)

On their part, new schools began to integrate playgrounds, which enhanced the outdoor sports opportunities for children: ". . . up to the time the public-school playgrounds were established a very small percentage of the pupils enrolled participated, thereby limiting the influence and benefits of outdoor sports" (Verrill 1914, 207).

After the quick modernization of the Island in the 1940s and '50s, team sports were instituted in all communities. And as tends to happen, those that required special gear and/or special playing grounds (e.g., golf, tennis, bowling) were reserved for the elite who could afford them: "Golf, tennis, basketball, bowling, and other games familiar to North Americans are played in Puerto Rico. There are wrestling and boxing matches, too. But above all other sports, Puerto Ricans like baseball" (McGuire 1963, 84).

THIS CHAPTER

American authors easily related to the entertainment of the Puerto Rican elites. But when they observed lower-class Puerto Ricans enjoying parties, dancing, music, gambling, etc., they assumed that Puerto Ricans were enjoying their wretched living conditions and that for them, poverty was some sort of "a choice." Cultural differences prevented them from understanding the innate zest of life shared by most Caribbean peoples.

In their quest to keep the solemnity of Sundays and guided by their Puritan values against all idleness, most Protestant missionaries condemned the sensuality of dancing, the celebrations associated with Catholic saints, gambling, and both bullfights and cockfights. They could not understand the liberating effects these communal activities provided nor the hope gambling brought to hopeless people. But in the end, every intent of regulating or prohibiting Puerto Ricans' traditional entertainment was disobeyed, and keeping these became a nationalistic defiant exercise.

Chapter 13

"WE ISS ONE HAPPY PEOPLE"

On Puerto Ricans' Values and How They See Life

Throughout the analysis of the selected books, a frequent use of the plural to refer to Puerto Ricans was observed, as in "they do ..." or "they are like...." This was particularly noticeable when enumerating Puerto Ricans' character traits. This phenomenon has been identified as "the mark of the plural":

> The colonized is never characterized in an individual manner; he is entitled only to drown in an anonymous collectivity ("They are this." "They are all the same."). If a colonized servant does not come in one morning ... He will say, "You can't count on them." It is not just a grammatical expression. He refuses to consider personal, private occurrences in his maid's life ... and his maid does not exist as an individual.[1]

This "mark of the plural" is also called a "generic generalization," and it communicates that one group (Puerto Ricans/the colonized) "is essentially different from another" (Americans/the colonizers).[2] Therefore, these plurals "presuppose and reinforce a division between an in-group ("us") and an out-group ("them")." Their use diminishes the status of "the other" (in this case, the Puerto Rican) forever since the characteristics assigned to him/her are portrayed as part of his/her inherent nature, which is understood as immutable as a congenital defect. Othering the colonized homogenizes them in a collective "they" portrayed as amenable to domination and a potential labor pool.[3]

To this, Edward Said added that defining "the other" as essentially different from "us" justifies the right of the "us" "not only to manage the nonwhite world but also to own it."[4] Since the described colonized have no access to these texts that describe them, and since the American readers have no direct contact with the colonized subjects, these descriptions stand, and they become part of the stereotypes about the colonized that will define them forever.[5] In the process, the individuality of the colonized subjects is negated and they become "generic beings that can be exchanged for any other native."

Not all of the characterization lists about Puerto Ricans were completely negative; some combined positive and negative traits or sometimes followed something positive with a clarification that some of the good American qualities were absent in them:

> They are ignorant, filthy, untruthful, lazy, treacherous, murderous, brutal, and black. (Herrmann 1900, 35)

> The author found the men he met socially pleasant, generous and eager to please, gentlemanly in every aspect. They lack some of the qualities of the stalwart American type, but this is due to their civic condition. (Rector 1898, 49)

> On the whole, the Porto Rican is courteous, hospitable, industrious, peaceable, law-abiding, and intelligent. . . . The people, like those of all other countries, have the good and bad qualities commingled in fair proportion. They are readily adaptable, impulsive, excitable, talkative to a degree, demonstrative. (Grose 1910, 178–79)

In terms of their physical appearance, a few American authors ventured into the difficult task (due to the variety of physical looks) of providing all-encompassing descriptions of Puerto Ricans. As expected, they usually compared them with Americans:

> Both men and women have fine heads of hair, and the men has soft and silky mustaches and beards. The skin is otherwise smooth, and in general the complexion is free from disfigurement. Muscular types of either manhood or womanhood are extremely rare; the length of the average arm being no better than that of an American girl of fourteen, and the leg being no larger or stronger than the arm of an average New York man. In a social gathering a Porto Rican gentleman seems a slender youth alongside of his colleague from England or America. (Hamm, *Porto* 1899, 68)

"AN APPRECIATION FOR THE ABSTRACT":
POETS AND ORATORS

Several authors referred to the common use of poetry by Puerto Rican men, some in the context of romancing a woman and some in the context of politics.

The quality of the oratory of the common Puerto Rican was also acknowledged by American authors as rich in verbosity. Most American authors considered these abilities as innate in Puerto Ricans:

> The tropics is the region of emotion. Every man there is an orator or a poet. They talk little in the tropics; they declaim. (Wilson 1905, 128)

> The Porto Rican has a decided taste for purely intellectual questions. At a railroad station, in the drugstore, or wherever men are wont to congregate we are always sure of a keen discussion on any religious or philosophical question if we but take the trouble to start it. An appreciation for the abstract seems to be inherent with these islanders. (James 1927, 17–18)

> The American will discover that the Puerto Rican likes to make speeches. Oratory is loud, dramatic, strongly accentuated with gestures. When listening to an orator, one can hardly tell if he is speaking about some little local incident or something of world-shaking proportions. (Petrullo 1947, 50)

And no other theme brought the most eloquent and exuberant sentimentality in both poetry and oratory than the protective love that most Puerto Ricans feel for their homeland, as an American journalist noticed:

> ... it is refreshing to meet so widely among the people their worthy pride in the local poets, dramatists ... (etc.) ... showing the very quality always recognized in the Puerto Rican, his love of home and his devotion to his beautiful island.... These characteristic fervid phrasings ... fairly indicate the sentimentality with which the island people regard their fair land and make their superlatives of devotion a commonplace. (White 1938, 324–26)

"BLESSED WITH AN ACTIVE IMAGINATION": EDUCATED ILLITERATES

As explained before, the colonizers need to portray the colonized as inferior in every possible way; they need this in order to justify to themselves the colonized's subjugation. One of the areas in which this was easier to present was the literacy level of Puerto Ricans. Certainly, it was low in 1898, but the portrayal of the illiteracy of Puerto Ricans will reach absurd levels when the

American authors claimed that even the elite classes were illiterate, which was not generally true.

In July 1898, almost all the rural population was illiterate, and when the whole island was considered, 79.6 percent of the population was deemed illiterate.[6] This description, though, gives no value to informal education which goes beyond just reading and writing. The 1899 US Census discovered that one hundred percent of the population of the Island was capable of "answering educational questions," a statistic that points to a high level of thought despite the fact that only 16.6 percent of those censused were able to read.[7] But Americans only took into consideration the literacy level and, therefore, considered Puerto Ricans as "ignorants."

To measure the level of education of Puerto Ricans, the only consideration was their reading capability: "One never sees a book or a magazine in these houses, though in two or three of the larger cities there are many literary men. Reading is not a strong point of the island population" (Dinwiddie 1899, 153). Only one American correspondent recognized the "refinement" of the elite class: "The daughters of the well-to-do are sent to convents on the island, while the sons go abroad to be educated. Among this class there is considerable culture and refinement, and most of them speak English" (Hall 1898).

Furthermore, several authors recognized intelligence in the Puerto Rican masses as well as an astuteness that helped them overcome their lack of formal education:

> In spite of this lack of knowledge of the world above him he has one quality which is his ever ready defense, his astuteness. There is one phrase much used in describing the jibaro's acuteness of observation. Referring to a trade it is said: "Para un jibaro, otro, y para los dos, el demonio," which means, "To get the best of a jibaro, employ another, and to catch both, Satan himself must take charge of them." (Ashford and Gutierrez 1911, 14)

After the US invasion, new schools were opened, and eventually, the level of illiteracy went from eighty percent to forty-one percent by 1930, ten percent in 1980, and eight percent in 2010.[8] In 1903, the Normal School of the University of Puerto Rico was established in Río Piedras to educate future teachers. It eventually added other faculties to become the University of Puerto Rico. In 1912, funded by American Presbyterian donors, the Polytechnic Institute was founded in San Germán as the first private university, and its instruction was in English. It later became bilingual, turning into the Universidad Interamericana.

In the 1930s, the first recognition of the intelligence of Puerto Rican adults (Puerto Rican children were considered even smarter than American ones by many American authors since the end of the 1900s—see chapter 16) was recorded by an American couple: "The Porto Rican possesses a superior intelligence with the ability to grasp an idea readily. He is likewise blessed with an active imagination. An almost complete lack of self-consciousness allows him to exercise both his intelligence and imagination without stint" (Van Deusen and Van Deusen 1931, 163).

In 1984, an American journalist acknowledged the high value Puerto Ricans gave to education, but at the same time, recognized the inadequacy of educational facilities when the huge budget devoted to education by the colonial government was considered, a contradiction that is still a reality in Puerto Rico:[9]

> Puerto Ricans, however poor, and whatever their viewpoint, have a passionate desire that at least one of their children should have the advantage of a college education. In general, the public schools in Puerto Rico are of low standard. The buildings are run down; the equipment poor; and the dropout rate is high, starting even before high school is reached.... Puerto Rico spends a third of her budget in education, one of the highest percentages in the world. Yet the schools on the whole, especially in rural districts, are below standard. (Samoiloff 1984, 115)

"MAN DOES NOT LIVE BY BREAD ALONE": RESPECT, "DIGNIDAD" AND PERSONALISM

Puerto Rican peasant workers were very poor, working really hard just to survive one week at a time. Having no land and no property to leave to their offspring, the only valuable thing left was respect. Being respected by his/her peers was so important that many Puerto Ricans frequently engaged in fights after hearing words that they perceived as disrespectful. Tolerance to disrespect was short-fused, and they were even willing to fight their bosses just to keep the respect of their community: "If disrespect turned into abuse of trust, there were people who could not take it anymore, who took the machete and confronted the foreman, or the landowner himself, even if they had to go to jail later."[10]

The Puerto Rican concept of "dignidad" is usually translated as "dignity," defined by the Merriam-Webster Dictionary as "the quality or state of being worthy, honored, or esteemed." But any Puerto Rican will agree that it means much more than that: something inexplicable with words that is only understood in all its magnitude by another Puerto Rican. Ronald Fernández translated it as "consideration," but that term doesn't cover its true meaning.[11]

For Puerto Ricans, its meaning is closer to the original Latin "dignitas" meaning "intrinsic merit," since this personal respect belongs, in the same magnitude, to every human being regardless of their race, age, gender or social standing, and it's commonly alluded to in phrases like "me lo pueden quitar todo, menos mi dignidad" ("they can take away everything, but for my dignidad").[12] A poor person can expect the same respect from wealthy people than viceversa, as long as he/she behaves with dignity and pride. Also, since everyone's "dignidad" must be respected, a Puerto Rican will typically avoid humiliating someone else, and will rather be humble about his/her attributes than brag about them. Everybody should be allowed to save face.

Unsurprisingly, American authors had great difficulty trying to decipher the meaning of "dignidad" and why it was so important to the Puerto Ricans they encountered:

> [The author, who is clearly prejudiced against Puerto Ricans, speaks to a follower of the Popular Party:] ..."Did you vote for Muñoz Marín?"
> "Oh yes, Señor. I would prefer to vote for Don Luis than to beat my wife."
> "Why?"
> The old looked surprised at my ignorance... "Because he is for us—the poor people. So we are for him."
> "What has he done for you?"
> "Oh, he has given us many things."
> I looked at the man's bare, scabrous feet, his torn shirt, and frayed trousers ...
> "What has he given you?"
> "He has given me dignity, Señor." (Brown 1945, 183)

> A man, any man, despite his station in life, is thought to be worthy of respeto.... Any falta de respeto ... toward a man violates his dignity. The poor man who stoically accepts God's will does so not only because he is resigned to his fate, but also because to whimper and whine is undignified. Involved here, also, is the concept of verguenza.... One of the supreme insults to a traditional Puerto Rican is to call him a "sinverguenza".... implying that he lacks moral standards and dignity.... Two of the most pejorative terms are "ñangotado" (to be in a stooped, kneeling position) and "aplatanado" (to be flattened out), meaning the man who endures stress not with stoicism, but with docility, and, thus, lacks dignity. (Wagenheim 1970, 211–12)

American governor Rexford G. Tugwell misunderstood the pride Puerto Ricans associate with their *dignidad* with the pride he knew from American culture. To him, it was about being right all the time instead of it being about the lack of need to humiliate anybody. Even though he admitted that he didn't really understand the term, he condemned *dignidad* because it went against the "principle of fair competition" that dominated American culture:

> They possess a pride which is almost an obsession and which leads frequently to the substitution of fancy for fact. In individual relations this trait prevents the public acknowledgment of inferiority of any kind and leads to the covering up of weaknesses and incompetencies. Such protection permits the mediocre to prosper in the professions, excuses inadequate preparation for the trades and so on. The demand for recognition of individual and collective dignidad is not a trait easily understood by others; and its consequences are not easily assessed. By now, I was beginning to grasp and worry over its implications.... The danger in the prevalent Puerto Rican trait was obvious: it might lead to the avoidance of outside competition, to the establishment and protection of mediocrity and so to a general lowering of the levels of competence.
> ... It was the task of the new Puerto Ricans to purge themselves of the falseness in their pride, to accept world standards, to combat mediocrity.... Dignidad, in its Puerto Rican manifestation, was deeply rooted; and its eradication—even its modification—would not be easy.... This intense desire to be accepted at face value without examination because of the danger that an inferiority may be exposed lies behind more policies than even the most intelligent Puerto Ricans will admit. (Tugwell 1947, 487–89)

Mennonite missionary Justus G. Holsinger was the one who most closely came to understand the meaning of *dignidad*, as he associated it with personalism, which valued every person for his/her condition as a human being and valued human relations over any other. He devoted several pages to explaining the concept, providing illustrative examples:

> ... personalism—the conviction that a human being as such has intrinsic worth and integrity, and is valued for his uniqueness as an individual... found expression in personal contacts and human relationships. The Puerto Rican attached greater value to personal contacts than to impersonal and institutional relationships. To tell a Puerto Rican friend that you are too busy for a social engagement or even for a cup of coffee with him may endanger one's friendship, since this leaves the impression that one's business or work is more important than his social relationships. Socializing to the Puerto Rican is not a means to an end but an end in itself. He is inclined to resent the American businessman's friendliness

frequently used as a means to further his business success. The Puerto Rican will befriend you whether you buy from him or not, in fact, he will direct you to his competitor down the street if he does not have the merchandise which you need.

..."respeto" and "dignidad." . . . These two values combined to top all the values of the traditional Hispanic culture. To be a human being, in the mind of the Puerto Rican, was to enjoy self-respect, and no one can attain self-respect unless he is respected by others. The element of "respeto" was communicated among equals, superiors, and subordinates. One's very social existence was predicated on the bonds of respect and no matter how poor or how humble one was, he was entitled to the respect due him as an individual on his particular level of living.

. . . one was given respect in accordance to his position on the social ladder . . . but those in higher positions respected those on lower social levels as individuals living on that level. The manner in which a wealthy person gave a beggar a coin, for example was with respect and was more important to the beggar than the value of the coin itself. Even a beggar in the traditional society enjoyed a certain degree of respect as a human being. The traditional Hispanic culture, however, did not equate respect with equality. To respect someone on a lower level was not taken to mean that equality existed between the two levels of society nor that the one on the lower level was entitled to all the comforts of life as one on the higher level.

Certain men in the La Plata community had earned positions of high respect and were addressed as Don Paco, Don Plácido . . . Their wives were likewise accorded the same respect and were addressed as Doña Juana, Doña Ramona . . . To address these respected individuals without "Don" or "Doña" was considered an act of disrespect. This method of addressing persons became automatic and one does not stop to ask who was entitled to these titles of respect. . . . Nothing made me feel more a part of the community and culture than to be addressed in this manner, by adults and youth alike. It became a common practice for older men in the community to also tip their hats to me as a symbol of respect.

"Dignidad" was a value closely associated with "respeto." There is no word in the English language which conveys quite the same meaning as "dignidad" in Spanish. It can best be translated to mean "he carries himself with self-respect." The traditional Hispanic person guarded very jealously the self-respect which he had earned and felt deeply injured if he was not accorded that respect. So long as he felt respected he could carry himself with dignity and integrity. Self-respect was a part of his social existence and was among his highest values. On one occasion a young "americano" took it upon himself to correct a highly respected Puerto

Rican administrator on the way he pronounced "heifer." This caused offense to the Puerto Rican since he took it as an act of disrespect.... He commanded the respect of others and in doing so he could carry himself with dignity. (Holsinger 2013, 161–64)

Puerto Rican personalism was further explained by an English teacher at the Colegio de Mayagüez. He learned that relations were not based on your social class but on having a gregarious personality and on relating to others with affability:

Everything is on a personal basis in Puerto Rico. You think and care about yourself, your family and your friends, certainly not about strangers. You do something for a person because you know him and like him. Outside of San Juan, which is a big city, it is even difficult to rent a house unless you have connections with someone who has a house to rent. How do you know you <u>want</u> to rent a house to someone if you don't know him? Puerto Ricans are the most hospitable people in the world, and, when they say "Mi casa, su casa" ("My house, your house") they mean it, and when invited to someone's house, more food and drinks are offered, and pressed on you, than anyone could consume. But this is after it has been established that you are <u>buena gente</u>, literally "good people." (Cooper 1994, 82)

And an American journalist noticed the implications of personalism in workplace relations:

In Latin tradition, most Puerto Ricans will rather work at lower wages for an employer who takes them shopping in his car, sits down with them occasionally, and asks them about their children than for an impersonal employer who pays them a higher wage but who yells at them, watches them suspiciously to see if perhaps they are stealing, and insults their sense of "dignidad."... it is typically Puerto Rican that both workers and employers are aware that man does not live by bread alone. (Gruber 1960, 77, 80)

"THERE MUST NEVER BE SILENCE AND THEY MUST NEVER BE ALONE": NOISINESS AND UBIQUITY

The level of noise tolerance of cultures varies; Puerto Ricans complain about how noisy the Dominican Republic is, but other cultures, as is the case with the US Americans, complain about Puerto Rico for the very same reason. It is true; Puerto Rico is quite noisy. Puerto Ricans like their music loud, so houses tend to have permanent music played at high volume "even when a visitor attempts to speak with the occupants"; also, when people gather, "there is a kind of nervous anxiety about making oneself heard as often and as loudly as possible."[13] The whole body is used to express the heartfelt emotions Puerto Ricans value so much.

Several American authors commented on the loudness of Puerto Ricans and on the excited way in which they talked, several of them describing a Puerto Rican gathering with different people talking at once, a situation quite familiar to most of us in Puerto Rico:

> They are impulsive, excitable, talkative, demonstrative. On the streets, in the stores, in the homes, they talk in loud tones accompanied by many varied and suggestive gesticulations. The movement of the hands and arms, the expression of the countenance, the positions of the body, the inimitable shrug of the shoulders, enable the listener to understand much of the conversation without hearing a word. With their naturally excitable nature, it is almost impossible for them to wait until one person finishes speaking, but several, and sometimes the whole company, are talking at once. . . . In the plazas, where they gather . . . instead of a quiet friendly conversation you soon hear every group talking in high and loud tones. . . . The habit of giving immediate expression to their thoughts has become so fixed that frequently one hears persons as they walk along the streets talking aloud to themselves. (Fowles 1910, 46–47)

> "Why are you always making a noise, Fernando?" I asked him once. He arched his eyebrows in surprise. "Because I am happy man. I make music all day. All Puerto Ricans, they love the music. We iss one happy people." (Brown 1945, 15)

Puerto Rican cities were also considered too noisy for American sensibility, particularly San Juan:

> Apparently the Porto Ricans love noise, for San Juan is the noisiest spot I have ever seen, and the other towns—and even the small villages—are almost as bad. The clang of trolley cars, that rattle and roar of carts and drays, the honk of auto horns, the jangle of gongs on carriages, the roaring of open mufflers, and the screams and calls of itinerant vendors all combine to create a perfect babel of sound, which continues from dawn to midnight without cessation. (Verrill 1914, 107)

Car drivers and their use of car horns were on the list of offensive noisemakers that unnerved American authors:

> Nowhere else does one find horns of such volume of sound, such rasping note, in such discordant key.... Then comes the outstanding discovery that the automobile horns of Puerto Rico are thus and so because the Puerto Ricans like them that way. Manufacturers have learned that they must deliver such horns to be acceptable. (White 1938, 125)

And, in an absurd and pathetic effort to emphasize the big transformation that industrialization brought to the Island, an American journalist writing in 1960 claimed that Puerto Rican noisy atmosphere belonged to the past, including the ever-present crying babies:

> Babies don't seem to cry as vociferously as they used to, cars and buses are quieter. Gone are the rickety buses of a few years back—the raucous "guaguas"[14] with entrances in the rear and such picturesque names as "In God We Trust" and "La Coqueta." And there is not the noise of the loud radios of the cantinas that used to be so notorious. (Hancock 1960, 13)

Like everything else in life, the size of Puerto Rico can be considered large or small, depending on your point of reference. In general, Puerto Ricans tend to judge distances within the Island using their own peculiar scale: for example, covering a distance of thirty-five miles is considered a long trip because that represents crossing the island from North to South. This phenomenon, which is part of what is called insularity or insularism, was identified and discussed by an American missionary who considered it somewhat "contagious" after a long stay in Puerto Rico:

> Porto Rico is such a compact little island that you feel as though you could easily take it in visually and mentally. But it grows upon you as you proceed, and make some astonishing impressions. Preconceptions gained from books and travelers' tales begin to fade as soon as you catch first glimpse of the land, and figures become evasive. You fall into the native point of view, and realize that Porto Rico never seems small to a Porto Rican, any more than his little horse does or that he does to himself; and in a measure to come to sympathize with him in his insularity.... To him, therefore, San Juan, a little city of less than thirty-five thousand inhabitants—the size of a suburb of New York or Philadelphia—is a great metropolis, and "la capital" is esteemed as Cubans esteem Havana, or the French Paris, or the English London. (Grose 1910, 179, 181)

Occupying a small (8,897 kms²) and overpopulated (264 persons per square mile in 1899)[15] island, even during the first years after the US invasion, Puerto Ricans seemed to be "everywhere." A common saying in Puerto Rico is that Puerto Ricans are "like white rice" ("como el arroz blanco"), meaning that they are "everywhere," referring to white rice being present in almost every Puerto Rican meal. Even when Puerto Ricans travel outside of the Island, it is the general impression that wherever you go, you will find a Puerto Rican. Furthermore, it is also the general impression among Puerto Ricans that whenever some dramatic world event such as a terrorist attack, a tsunami, an earthquake, or an armed revolution happens, there is always a Puerto Rican living there, whether it is in Saudi Arabia, Singapore, Sweden, the Bahamas, or Uruguay.

Beyond frequently commenting that Puerto Rico is the most overpopulated island in the Caribbean, some American authors shared their experiences with the ubiquitous Puerto Ricans, and several even ventured to "explain" the phenomenon:

> Most Puerto Ricans, having been raised in small houses with large families, are frightened of being alone. Happiness is associated with people and noise, and it was inconceivable to the students that I might want to be alone.... on a tropical island, a great deal of your living could be outdoors, and the yards and sidewalks, not to mention the roads in the country, were always crowded with people. [When he tried to rent a house in the countryside to live with privacy, he confronted problems:] ... Our main problem, it turned out, was that no one understood what we wanted or why we wanted it. When we mentioned the term "privacy," it was a word they understood, but a concept they didn't understand. If you have grown up in a large family on a small, crowded island, you want noise and close neighbors, to reassure you, to make you feel safe. Being alone, away from other people, was a very frightening prospect for most Puerto Ricans.... Who would you talk to? ... Why would you want to live alone way out in the country? What were you planning to do that you didn't want the neighbors to see? (Cooper 1949, 28, 94, 121)

In 1945, American teacher Wenzell Brown, in conversation with his friend Cecilian Cofresí, presented a more reasonable explanation for the Puerto Rican fondness for noise and company:

> Then as I spoke in puzzled terms of the radios that howled through the night, Cecilian answered me with usual sharpness. "Of course our people like music, Nick." "But it's not music. It's one infernal row. Anyway

they don't listen, they're always yelling over it." Cecilian spoke solemnly this time. "Our people must have noise, Nick. They must always be a part of something else, a part of a pulsing rhythm or a fierce argument. They must quarrel or sing or drink. But there must never be silence and they must never be alone. When there is silence, you have to think; and what is there to think of but misery and despair? When you're alone, you have to look at yourself. Doesn't that frighten you? Hunger we can endure, pain, work, but not silence—not loneliness." (Brown 1945, 101)

"NEARLY EVERYONE SMILED AT EVERYONE ELSE": GOOD HUMORED PEOPLE

As mentioned before, many American writers highlighted the good character of Puerto Ricans, trying to portray them as "good acquisitions" for the United States and hinting at their disposition to become "good Americans":

> The Puertorriqueño is not an anarchist or an insurrectionist, for he knows no other life and does not starve or grow cold, while the burdens of oppression are his birthright handed down for centuries. He is, then, in spite of his wretchedness, dirt, and poverty, as we see it, a fairly-contented man—representing the majority—into a self-respecting, useful, franchised citizen of the United States, it can be done, for the reasons that he is docile, obliging, appreciative of favors, and, best of all, possesses and inbred courtesy and politeness, and an equability of temperament, which permit him to readily absorb new ideas. . . . if we do not abuse our power, Puerto Rico may be made a twentieth-century Garden of Eden . . . (Dinwiddie 1899, 166)

> As we [he and his wife] walked along the streets, I noticed that most people, including pretty young girls, would smile at me in passing. At first I thought this must be due to my magnetic personality, but I soon realized that was not so at all; nearly <u>everyone</u> smiled at everyone else. It just seemed like a simple, natural way for human beings to greet each other. (Delano 1997, 72, underlined in the original)

Praising Puerto Ricans and at the same time colonizing and exploiting them was not a contradiction, judging by the words of this journalist:

> There is an additional charm of a people foreign by nature, speaking a foreign language, yet ever smiling and courteous—a peaceful,

happy, lovable people, the mingling with which brings the right feeling into the heart. . . . Benevolent Uncle Sam is going to work out a very happy people for these long-oppressed people and incidentally develop for himself one of the most productive little territories in the world. (Du Puy 1914, 116)

"NEITHER STYLE NOR CLEANLINESS": FASHION SENSE[16]

When describing this theme, American authors frequently avoided attributing the scantiness of clothes to Puerto Ricans' abject poverty, attributing it instead to some fashion fad of the tropics. The absence of shoes is commonly discussed, too, with some authors claiming that shoes are not used because they are not needed, once again dismissing the poverty that prevented Puerto Rican *jíbaros* from buying shoes:

> Comfort and economy appear to be the chief ends to be served in the matter of wearing apparel. Neither style nor cleanliness seems to be of any consideration with the masses. Many men and women are barefooted. . . . Masculine apparel usually consists of a battered hat, a cotton shirt, cotton trousers, and shoes—sometimes. (Robinson 1899, 39)

When describing the elite fashion style, some American authors identified the absurdity of the use of woolen suits by men in their effort to imitate European fashion:

> The fashions for men and women alike are imported, especially from Paris and London. Those who are in comfortable circumstances dress just like people in European countries. The men wear woolen clothes all the year round. . . . In the small towns, men dress after the fashion of the cities, except that their clothes are made of linen. Woolen fabrics are uncomfortable, and they are considered a luxury to be donned only on Sundays and holidays. (Hall 1898)

Much later, the last American governor commented on how he discovered that Puerto Ricans did recognize a so-called "winter season" in which fashion, indeed, changed:

> It was mid-April of 1942 now and hot weather had come. What that meant in Puerto Rico was that the temperature had risen, on the average, some five degrees. . . . To the newcomer it is strange, in apparent

summer weather, to be told by the local folk that it is winter now and not suitable for bathing; also that heavier clothes are indicated. I recall being embarrassed once . . . by turning up at a Cabinet dinner in a white jacket and facing a company dressed to a man in formal black. I had forgot—or, to be honest, did not know—that winter received full social acknowledgment throughout the Antilles. (Tugwell 1947, 328)

American authors noticed a peculiarity that others have recognized, and that is commented on in many travel guides for future visitors: the importance of looking clean and well-put-together or "presentable" shared by most Puerto Rican men, women, and even children.[17] This Puerto Rican trait has been discussed by anthropologist David Landy:

The people take great pride in their bodily cleanliness and in their dress, and it is a matter of honor to have clean and, if possible, new clothes. Clothes which are the least bit torn or patched are abhorred, but of course they are worn when nothing else can be bought. . . . This pride in appearances means that a presentable façade must be maintained at all costs, making for an ill-afforded conspicuous consumption which has been noted by many observers.[18]

Americans seemed quite impressed by Puerto Rican fashion:

. . . washing day comes every day in Porto Rico, for even the hundreds of peons in the cane fields are dressed in white linen, and to appear well clothed seems to be one of the universal Porto Rican characteristics. (Douglass 1910, 17)

The Porto Rican is extremely fond of the spectacular. This is manifested in the gaudy wearing-apparel of all classes . . . (Fowles 1910, 47)

This care for personal appearance is found in all social classes, each one taking care of their looks according to their financial possibilities. When New Deal photographer Jack Delano and his wife Irene visited the "El Fanguito" slum, a poverty-stricken, smelly, and muddy place, they noticed:

When we came back early one morning, the sight that most impressed us was of people, young and old, coming out of their shacks to go to work, the girls in pretty dresses, the men in white suits or shirts. Most people smelled of rubbing alcohol and carried their shoes in their hands, as they stepped gingerly along the flimsy bridges to the dry area.

> We could not but admire the spirit of such people, who would not allow their poverty to affect their self-esteem. (Delano 1997, 82)

Oddly, this American missionary came to exactly the opposite conclusion regarding personal appearance care. It makes one wonder what his standards were, although a dislike for colorful clothing can be expected from a New England Puritan:

> Except on dress occasions, the Porto Ricans are prone to be careless in their personal appearance. Men and women of the poorer classes wear soiled clothing most of the week, but on Sunday they come out arrayed in garments starched so stiff that they could stand alone.... The women of the higher classes come to coffee in the morning with disheveled hair and garments loosely put on.... Even when dressed for the street one cannot help noticing that in many cases there are evidences which betray the lack of neatness and care.... Among the poorer classes, there is a decided lack of taste displayed in the choice of colors. Yellow, green, pink and red in all sorts of combinations are the prevailing colors. (Fowles 1910, 59)

The machete was commonly identified as an accessory to every Puerto Rican male *jíbaro*'s attire:

> ... the machete, universally carried by the peon, and which is never out of his sight or grasp.... it only attracts attention when it is absent. He acquires it early in life, and parts with it only through stern necessity, as, for example, when funds are needed for gambling, or for betting on a favorite fighting cock.... With the machete the peon hews down the trees for corner posts to his hut, lops off the leaves of palm for thatch and bedding, digs holes for setting out tubers and plants, and sometimes, though rarely, removes the weeds from his garden. (Ober 1904, 233)

It is in 1984 that we get the first description of the attire of the modern working-class Puerto Rican. But the journalist seemed to refer to an earlier fashion because by 1984, the use of hats had already disappeared from Puerto Rican streets:

> For the working man, a large straw hat, old dark-colored pants and an open shirt are customary. For best occasions a "guayabera," a loose short-sleeved, open-necked, highly embroidered shirt is worn over long

pants. Unlike tourists or American residents, however hot the weather, Puerto Rican men do not wear "shorts." (Samoiloff 1984, 173)

THIS CHAPTER

In a colonial relationship, both colonizers and colonized create stereotypes of each other based on their particular experiences and readings, in a process of otherization. American authors perceived Puerto Ricans as prone to express their ideas and feelings with poetic language, intelligent and astute, happy-go-lucky people who they will find anywhere and everywhere and that loved noise. Yet they could not quite understand the need of Puerto Ricans for the respect they deserved as humans, their lack of tolerance for humiliation, and the paramount importance they gave to social relationships. This discrepancy in the approach to social interactions will only make contacts difficult for both since their relationship was intrinsically unequal and based on domination of one and the submission of the other. There can be no respect in a colonial relationship.

Chapter 14

"PEOPLE WHO WILL ALWAYS 'BE THERE'"

On Puerto Ricans' Relationships with Family, Friends, and Strangers

"MI CASA ES TU CASA": ON PUERTO RICAN GENEROSITY

Eleven years before the US invasion, Puerto Rican intellectual Francisco del Valle Atiles wrote about the generosity of Puerto Ricans:

> ... the jíbaro has nothing of its own when it comes to exercising charity. The stranger will find the most ample hospitality in the humble bohío [hut], even when he is a stranger ... the family of the Puerto Rican peasant will give everything they have to the guest who knocks at their door, without any interest; when it is a question of remedying a need, of saving someone from danger, of serving someone in cases of illness, no consideration stops our jíbaros, not even the damages that may result from it.[1]

Indeed, this generosity was shown to the American soldiers as they arrived at the different towns (see chapter 5). The entrance of these cavalry troops into the western town of Mayaguez illustrates this point:

> ... we stuffed ourselves with the mangoes, bananas and cocoa nuts which the natives had piled along the road for our benefit, and which they distributed among us promiscuously.... For a half-mile leading into the city the natives, who had flocked from every quarter, shouted and capered around us. They seemed to have gone mad for joy.... Cakes, candies, cigars and cigarettes were showered on us by the storekeepers, and some of the spectators even threw small silver coins amongst us, which the spry natives fought for in many lively scrambles, the lucky

finders shouting more lustily than the others that the "Americano was mucha Bueno." (Oliver 1901, 121)

In 1966, Puerto Rican hospitality and generosity towards Americans were analyzed by René Marqués. To him, they result from the colonial inferiority complex that the Puerto Rican feels when dealing with Americans: "In order to tolerate his humiliating condition he has to find an excuse for it and admit that he is <u>inferior</u> to the North American. This motivates his obsequiousness ... expressed in ways which closely approach servility. He hopes in this way to acquire or to incorporate the 'superiority' of that feared and envied being, but, of course, he never can."[2]

To understand Puerto Rican generosity, we have to keep in mind that the Puerto Rican of 1898 did not yet have a capitalist economic perspective regarding everyday life. He was not used to giving everything a monetary value, as in "Time is money," like the Americans. Many anecdotes illustrate the bafflement of Americans dealing with Puerto Ricans' selfless attitude:

> As a little instance illustrating the kindness of their hearts when properly treated: An old lady, living in a little hut near one of our outposts, pounded our coffee in her old wooden mortar, boiled it over the little charcoal fire, and did everything possible for us for several days, and poor as she and her daughters, Manuella and Eulalia, were, she refused any payment, although we finally insisted on leaving part of our coffee, etc., with her. The boys on that outpost will all bear glad testimony to this simple, kindly, hospitality. (Rossiter [1900?])
>
> There is a genuine neighborliness, especially among the poor. In the slum areas of the big cities in the States ... it is like a jungle.... But in Puerto Rico, neighbors take care of each other. If one man is out of work, or if a family is in trouble, friends and relatives help out.... Invariably, if a stranger shows good will, this type of responsiveness and generosity will be shown to him or her. There is an everyday saying, "Mi casa es tu casa." ... At Christmas time ... hospitality is widespread. All houses are open to friends for food and drinks and music and gaiety. (Samoiloff 1984, 160–61)

According to Albert Memmi, the colonizers tended to interpret all the colonized's traits as negative, including his hospitality and generosity.

> This hospitality is a result of the colonized's irresponsibility and extravagance, since he has no notion of foresight or economy. . . . the

festivities are wonderful and bountiful: but what happens afterward? The colonized ruins himself, borrows and finally pays with someone else's money! Does one speak, on the other hand of the modesty of the colonized's life? Of his not less well known lack of needs? It is no longer a proof of wisdom but of stupidity[3]...

As evidence of what Memmi explained, examples illustrate how a good character trait, such as generosity, can end up being associated by Americans with negative adjectives such as "oppressive" or "pathetic":

> ... the Spanish [meaning "Puerto Rican"] private citizen has but one fault as a host. He overdoes things in the matter of hospitality. His guest must eat more than he ought, drink more than he wants, and accept courtesies until they become little short of oppressive. (Robinson 1899, 83)

> Their patience is infinite and their good nature boundless, while their inborn courtesy never permits them by word or sign to say or do anything that might wound the sensibilities of a stranger. Their politeness is so gentle and natural as to be almost pathetic, and is appreciated by all who come within the radius of its influence. (Olivares, *Vol. 1* 1899, 368)

An American missionary completely misunderstood the figurative expressions of Puerto Rican's diplomacy and good manners and interpreted them as "extreme":

> The courtesy of the Porto Rican often runs to the extremity—and outcome of exaggeration. We must not take him too literally. On the announcement of his new-born babe will appear the startling statement, "He is yours." Express the slightest interest in a thing and the proprietor will tell you that you are welcome to it, even though it be the house which has lodged him and his family for generations. One of the favorite stories both among the Porto Rican and the resident Americans is that during the visit to the home of a cultured Porto Rican, a northern tourist expressed his admiration on a beautiful picture—an heirloom of the family. With his customary courtesy, the host made the formal reply that the picture was the property of his guest. The literal American, however, took his friend at his word and next morning sent a man to bring away his newly acquired work of art. Needless to say the man returned empty-handed, but with a positive opinion as to the prosaic nature of the northerner's make up. (James 1927, 15)

But this American teacher saw virtue instead of fault, even in Puerto Rican gossip. In her analysis, Latin American gossip, compared to American gossip, was not sneaky and was actually helpful. Corinne Dean unveiled the intrinsic relationship between gossip and the hospitality and generosity she found in Puerto Rico:

> Edna St. Vincent Millay once said of the French people: "Their rudeness is more gracious than other people's courtesy." I think this can be applied to Latin people in general. Take gossip, for example. In America it's a vicious, destructive force that warps the mind and constrains the body of both gossiper and "gosipee." But gossip among the Latins has a graciousness and constructiveness about it that makes it more of a virtue than a fault—or, at most, a seductive fault. The Latins are full of these seductive faults, which if I may paraphrase, "are more charming than other people's virtues."
>
> First of all, Latin gossip is frank and open; secondly, genuinely helpful. The Latins don't snoop; they ring the bell and come in the front door to find out what you are doing and why. They don't peek to find out where you are going, they meet you ahead on and ask you point blank—then go out of their way to take you there. The fact that even a person with impaired vision could find the one bank in the one plaza does not prevent them from escorting you to the bank and right up to the man you said you wanted to see. Of course they have already asked you and you have already told them all the details. Annoyed as you may have been for having to tell a comparative stranger (no one is a complete stranger among the amiable Latins) about your personal errand, you find yourself grateful for their polite meddling with its view to helping.
>
> Compare this to New York, where all of us have seen people wander around subway stations obviously lost or confused while everyone stared and nobody meddled to see if he or she could be of any assistance. What a difference between the way a stranger is treated in New York and the way I was treated upon my arrival in Puerto Rico.
>
> [During her ride in public transportation from San Juan to Humacao, Corrine Dean forgot the information regarding her destiny, and became quite nervous. It got darker and, not knowing Spanish, she surrendered and fell asleep. Then, to her surprise:] . . . the driver awakened me and said in his ninety per cent English: "Señorita Dean . . . zees ees where you supposed to leeve. La Señora is expecteeng you. . . . I hope you like to teach een Puerto Rico." . . . The driver not only knew my name but where I was going, what and how many people I was to see, where I was to live, and where I was to teach. (Dean 1944, 15–16, 18)

Most American authors were impressed by the level of generosity of Puerto Ricans of all social classes, sharing whatever they had, not only with friends and relatives but with neighbors and foreigners, too. As William Dinwiddie put it: "The man who learns to appreciate the simple, open hearted hospitality of the Puertorriqueños secures much that is pleasurable in life" (Dinwiddie 1899, 48). Such is the case of the heartfelt praise of Puerto Rican generosity by this American:

> I left Puerto Rico . . . the promise of adventure that I had been enjoying for more than five years . . . and my emotion was that of one departing from home rather that of a man homebound. . . . Nowhere can one find people more honest and diligent, more warm-hearted and generous, more loyal and friendly. From the judge on the bench to the "cocinera" in the kitchen. . . . Generosity, especially to their kin, was so natural as hardly to be counted a virtue. . . . When you enter the Spanish or Puerto Rican home, you are welcomed to "this, your house." (Lord 2004, 55–57)

The generosity of Puerto Ricans is sometimes mixed with pity towards those less fortunate. This is compounded in a common Puerto Rican phrase: "¡Ay, bendito!," which might be translated as "The poor thing!" when referring to a particular person in a tough situation. The phrase, though, is also used as an exclamation when bad news is received, in the same way an American might say "Good gracious!" or "Gee!". An American governor tried to explain it:

> An exclamation—literally, "Oh, blessed"—with many uses ranging from expressing mild interest to great indignation. To illustrate the sense in which it is usually used: should you complain that, for instance, a certain government employee is lazy, illiterate, incompetent, dishonest and a little weak in the head, it is not unlikely that the person to whom you complain (if he is a Puerto Rican) will agree entirely with your estimate and then say, "But ay bendito! he has ten children! He must have a job!" (Tugwell 1947, 74)

Puerto Rican hospitality sometimes proved to be disruptive of American administrative procedures, as happened when it made it impossible for the Commissioner of Education to supervise schools:

> In the smaller towns the arrival of the "Comisionado" was a great event. We were met by delegations of school children, gaily dressed and carrying banners with eloquent speeches of welcome fairly bursting from their lips. There might be an open-air banquet with a pig roasting on

a spit . . . with a bountiful supply of yams, yautía, plantains, and many fruits and vegetables unknown to northern appetites. It was almost impossible to make the Puerto Rican teachers understand that we really wanted to see the schools in everyday dress and operation: to them that seemed wholly lacking in hospitality and in respect for the official from the Capital. (Lord 2004, 39)

And the cultural gap became evident as a young couple of American missionaries ended up at the dinner table of a plantation family. Between the different tastes in food and the different sets of table manners, the generosity of the Puerto Rican hosts was noted:

We started on horseback . . . stopped at an old plantation and asked for some water and permission to eat our lunch under some large shade trees near their house. . . . They would not hear to our eating a cold lunch, but urged us to honor them with our presence at dinner. The house of the good señora was "a sus ordenes" (at your orders), as were also her sons and anything else she had. A peon was sent to drive up a cow which they milked and then presented me with a glass of milk. We were then escorted about the plantation . . .

The table was laid with a once white oilcloth . . . Everybody was extremely solicitous for our welfare and seemed a little bit hurt that I should hesitate to pitch right in to any or all of the various dishes set within my reach. . . . Finally, one of the men . . . with his own fork and knife, helped me most generously, and said, "Now eat." He then served Harry in the same fashion . . . we . . . ate for dear life. . . . another brother . . . offered me the pork, but I thanked him . . . he seemed to think that I was bashful, so he arose in his chair just across the table from me, licked his knife all clean and cut me another chunk of pork . . . I almost balked at this, but I have learned . . . that we must never offend people, so I ate on in grim silence, and was glad when the dessert came. . . . We had been allowed to share freely the best they had to offer and we would have been worse than Hottentots[4] had we failed to recognize the honor they were paying us.

The Porto Rican is ever agreeable and courteous, whatever his station in life or the condition of his home. The people are generous almost to a fault, and even the humblest mountain dweller who has never known anything beyond his rickety hut and his machete who cannot write his own name or tell you what a shoe feels like, will doff his sombrero with as much dignity and offer you such hospitality as his humble roof affords with as much ease and grace as the most finished gentleman of the land, only he shows more native grace and less of studied mannerisms. He never thinks of apologizing for what he has to offer, but he and his wife and his family are all so graciously "at your service" that you forget everything except that you are the guest of honor, and it is not always easy to do justice to the situation. (Blythe 1911, 131–32, 134–37)

Charles H. Rector reported how, in 1898, a rich man from Mayagüez "with the pride of a knight and the manners of a perfect gentleman" sheltered seven unexpected Americans during a copious rain, offering them "a splendid dinner . . . and . . . pleasant conversation." When one of the Americans attempted to pay the host with a ten-dollar bill, he refused to accept the money because "he was entertaining gentlemen and friends" and because "he was not an innkeeper" (Rector 1898, 166, 169). Many testimonies accounted for Puerto Ricans' generosity:

> The Porto Rican excels in social life. He has the fine manners and dignity of his Spanish ancestors, and adds to them the lighter spirit and congeniality of the New World. He is very hospitable, and treats like the proverbial returned prodigal. It is not true that this courtesy and hospitality are mere affectations, or a series of social shams. They are not now and never have been. The manners have developed through the centuries, and represent strong mental and social tendencies. The Spanish gentleman who lives upon a few cups of coffee to-day in order that he may serve you a partridge to-morrow, takes as much pleasure in the self-sacrifice, and in the delight which he confers as the guest himself in the excellence of the entertainment. It is not uncommon for the head of a family to pawn jewels and heirlooms in order to obtain the means for a lavish entertainment of relatives and friends. The custom is unthrifty, extravagant, wasteful, and at times ruinous; but it expresses an altruistic tendency which has been developed through generations. . . . When you are entertained by a comparative stranger or a chance acquaintance, you incur the obligation of returning the compliment in some way or other. It may be in the form of a dinner, a handsome present to the children of the house, a piece of jewelry for one of the members of the family, or even in a horse and harness. You should also present substantial douceur to the servant. (Hamm, *Porto* 1899, 94–95)

Three to seven decades after the US invasion of Puerto Rico, the society had changed a lot, as expected, but the generosity of the people still astonished American authors when received:

Another experience ... took place on the far side of Barrio Certenejas of Cidra. I was helping a very poor family build a latrine.... Around 9:15 the lady of the house came to me with a cup of coffee and two hard-boiled eggs. I was at a loss for words. Really, I was not hungry because I had already eaten. Secondly, I could not imagine where this lady got the eggs because they were so poor.... I ate it, and the lady watched me with a glow in her eyes. I came to the conclusion that the lady wanted to share something with me for the work I was doing for them. It was a moving experience I will always remember. (L. Birky in Falcón and Lehman 2014, 67)

New Deal photographer Jack Delano and his wife, graphic designer Irene, arrived in Puerto Rico in 1941, not knowing that they would spend most of the rest of their lives there. They soon came in contact with the generosity of Puerto Ricans: "Irene was fond of the folk art we found in many houses, especially the little carvings of saints, but she soon learned not to admire them too much, for when she did, they would always be presented to her as gifts" (Delano 1997, 82). Yet the following experience they had is the most heart-touching of all:

One day in the mountains ... it began to pour, we heard a woman's voice cry out, "Por acá, Señora. Don't get yourself wet!" The voice came from a wooden shack on the roadside, and there we ran for cover.... the house ... was made from a haphazard collection of old planks and scrap lumber. Rain poured through holes in the rusty tin roof. The furniture consisted of a small table covered with oilcloth and one rustic bench, on which we sat at the insistence of a pale, barefoot, smiling little woman. A tall, gaunt man stood in a corner with arms folded. From behind his legs, two small children peeked at us timidly. Another child, bundled in rags and obviously ill, lay on the floor.

Through the doorway in the back, we could make out several glistening eyes and hear the murmurs of more children. Above us, the rain clattered on the tin roof, and below, a white hen pecked desperately at a few grains of rice in the cracks of the wooden floor. It was growing very dark and the woman lit the wick of an old beer bottle filled with oil. She ordered one of the girls to prepare coffee. "I hope you like it black," she apologized. We have no milk or sugar." ... Irene had a few chocolates in her purse and she offered them to the woman, who passed them to the eldest girl, who in turn distributed them among the children. From the back room we could hear excited whispers, "¡Cocholate!, ¡Cocholate! [sic] We learned from the man that he had injured his back in an accident in the cane fields and had not been able to work.... "Then what do you live on?" Irene asked.

"Well," the woman replied, "people in town sometimes give me laundry to do; the neighbors help out. There are wild fruit trees around and when this old hen decides to give us a couple of eggs, I make an omelette and we share it." Then she added, with a touch of pride, "Nos defendemos, Señora, no se preocupe" (Don't worry, Señora, we take care of ourselves).

By the time the rain stopped, night had fallen. We said our goodbyes and got into the car. I turned on the motor and was about to leave when a little boy came running out of the house, calling, "Wait! Wait a minute!" He reached in through the open window and dropped a little paper bag into Irene's lap, saying, "For you, Señora." Deeply moved by the experience, I drove in silence.... Then I remembered the little paper bag. "What's in it?" I asked. She looked inside and said, "Two eggs." (Delano 1997, 82–83)

In the 1950s, an American college teacher at CAAM, Mayagüez, discovered an awkward situation ensued whenever he tried to invite his students or others for drinks at local bars:

At first I tried to buy drinks for the students or others in a bar, to try to return their hospitality. But this was not acceptable. It was their island; they were the hosts and I was the guest.... They thought all continentals were rich, that we thought all Puerto Ricans poor, and they had to prove that they could afford to buy me drinks and food. If I turned down a drink it meant either that I didn't like them or I didn't think they could afford to buy it, either reason a personal insult. It was pointed out to me finally by the other continental teachers that I didn't have to drink the beer or eat the food, all I had to do was accept it. But that ran counter to my northern Puritan upbringing. If I didn't eat the food, that would be wasting it and wasting things was sinful . . . (Cooper 1994, 29)

This same teacher recorded his experience with the Puerto Rican tradition of gifting well-liked teachers and the competition it generated between teachers:

It shouldn't have surprised me, of course that on the last day of class there was a large package on my desk, beautifully gift-wrapped. That first semester, I noted in my diary, they gave me "two lovely sport shirts." The presents were not, of course, given because you gave them passing grades, but to thank you for teaching them something. The only slightly mercenary note in all this I discovered, was that there was a great deal of rivalry among the teachers about who had been given the nicest or most expensive present. As the teachers met in the hall, I overheard a lot of, "What did you get?" "Wait till you see what I have"... (Cooper 1994, 86)

While on a return visit to Puerto Rico in 1969, this Mennonite missionary wanted to go by bus from Old San Juan to Summit Hills and got frustrated trying to understand the bus system. Nevertheless, he got immediate help from Puerto Rican bus travelers:

> I had become exhausted and exasperated... One lady who has spent her childhood in New York City told me that she was taking Bus 19 and would see that I got to Summit Hills. She was most consoling to me when she said to me, "You can't get lost in Puerto Rico; we won't let you." Those words speak better than anything I could say about the Puerto Rican spirit of helpfulness. In the midst of all the confusion and frustration I found a kind heart that could empathize with me in my frustration.... The next morning I took the same route back to Old San Juan, the trip was uneventful except that I stood in the packed aisle with an armful of books. I again experienced the kindness of the Puerto Ricans when a girl who was seated offered to hold my books that were sliding apart as I tried to keep my balance as the bus made turns and sudden stops in the congested traffic. (Holsinger 2013, 119)

Indeed, helping others has always been a source of satisfaction for Puerto Ricans. This was finally corroborated in 2016 when a collaborative study concluded that, even though going through a major financial crisis, 74.9 percent of Puerto Rican homes made informal donations, thus surpassing the generosity rate of the United States and other countries.[5] In the 1970s, an American travel writer recommended the Island to future tourists: "Chances are your smiles will be answered by more smiles, not because tourist money is important, but because to the Puerto Rican waiting at a bus stop you are not 'Washington' but a stranger looking for Calle Cruz. Puerto Rican people are great smilers" (Rand, A. 1973, 31).

"IT IS THE FEELING THAT COUNTS": EXTENDED FAMILIES

Margherita A. Hamm paid particular attention to family affairs, discovering a respectful and dignified treatment of the elderly that is still uncommon in capitalist Protestant societies like the United States, where people's value depends on their productivity: "if you're no longer working, you've lost the main value that society places on you."⁶ Indeed, many American poor are "senior citizens" who are estranged from their family members. Most Americans do not express "any particular respect for the old, or a feeling that their experience might enrich family life."⁷ In contrast, Hamm described an elite family scene in Puerto Rico:

> The father may be a millionaire, the son the honor man of a university, and the grandfather old, poor and but half-educated, but in every case it will be the grandfather who is the head of the family and in every case he will receive the respect, the obedience and the filial affection found in colder climates only among the little children. It is the same on the mother's side. The grandmother is the head of the family. She dresses in bright-colored silks and laces. She uses a little rouge, she sings, plays some musical instrument, dances, tells stories, engages in cards, and is the youngest among the young. When the family breaks up in the evening everybody kisses everybody else good-night, and an atmosphere of love and kindness seems to pervade every home. (Hamm, *America's* 1899, 84–85)

According to an American priest, every member in the Puerto Rican family had a well-defined role, and even though the hierarchy was patriarchal, it still provided stability because everybody knew how to behave according to their role, which made them feel fulfilled:

> Parents play an important part in the selection of the marriage partner of the son or daughter, the husband has a dominant role in the family; the wife's role is subordinate, oriented to home and children. Children are loved—sometimes give the impression to Americans of being pampered—elders are respected, and the old folks have a position of influence and respect that is common in traditional rather than modern families. The husband expects to be the provider, to make the important decisions, often without consulting the wife; commonly he has controlled the money and has often done the shopping; he disciplines the children, and sometimes disciplines the wife.
>   ... stability does not depend on "togetherness" in the American sense, but on a clear understanding of roles, of expectations. By doing that which is expected of a man, a woman, a son, a daughter, the Puerto Rican enjoys the satisfaction of being a good man, a good wife, a good child. He has a sense of personal dignity and pride, and enjoys the respect and esteem of his family and friends. (Fitzpatrick 1996, 143)

Puerto Rican children are typically dotted on, as an American journalist noticed: "Their kindness to children is often mentioned . . . children are allowed to do almost anything in Puerto Rico, one feels after being there awhile" (Rand, C. 1958, 50). Regarding the treatment of children within the family, particularly elite families, Hamm compared it with the United States, where typically, children were never allowed to participate in "adult gatherings." She also evaluated family feelings, praising them:

> The discrimination against children which prevails in many American and English families is seldom seen. They appear at the table, and even in the case of little tots, are as polite and decorous as their parents and grandparents. There is a strong family feeling among the people, and filial love and respect are more noticeable if not stronger than among the colder-blooded races. (Hamm, *Porto* 1899, 107)

Poverty and malnourishment did not prevent mothers from feeling proud of their offspring, as happens elsewhere. The humble mothers' pride in their babies was noted: "Little brown children played about, and, if we stopped to admire the scene, mothers brought their babes to the door, that we might admire them" (Howe 1910, 86–87).

But from his foreign perspective, an American missionary saw the Puerto Rican family as an overbearing force that operated against its youngest members, limiting their job opportunities and their development of individual personalities:

> For the honor of the family the Porto Rican will make any sacrifice. There are dozens of young men in Porto Rico today who are trained in the States and had started in some promising professional career; yet they quit their profession to return to the land of their birth in order to satisfy one or both parents who could not be separated from their "niños." If one is a member of a "buena familia"—a good family—he is likely to be forgiven a multitude of sins and weaknesses. What the family wealth will do for the prodigal in the States, the family name will do for the Porto Rican scapegoat. (James 1927, 24–25)

In the early 1950s, an American English teacher commented on his understanding of the loose definitions of who are "members of the family":

> The real problem in trying to understand Puerto Rican family relationships is their very flexible and imprecise view of these relationships. To begin with, the words "father," "brother" and even "cousin" are not in any

way used as we would use them in English. Part of this is a matter of translation, but it is much more than that. The students thought we were all very hung up on words, names and exact relationships. If a person acts toward you in the capacity of a father, then he is your father. It is the <u>feeling</u> that counts. "Brothers," of course, includes both males and females, as the Spanish word hermanos does, and the word "cousin" refers to any close friend, who may or may not be a blood relation. While it was true that many of our students were related, I soon learned that if a student introduced you to someone as a cousin, all this meant was that he was a close friend. When, at a dance, a student introduced you to a girl as his cousin, it meant he was seriously interested in her. If an older man introduced you to a woman as his cousin, it meant she was his mistress.... There has never been any strong feeling, as is common in the United States, that a child should live with his blood father or mother. Since most Puerto Ricans have large families, probably most children would live with and be brought up by a blood relative, but it is the psychological relationship that is important. There were many practical reasons for this looser system of relationships. One was the constant back and forth migration between the island and the mainland. (Cooper 1994, 89, 91–92)

In Puerto Rican families of the past, it was common to raise as their own the orphaned children of other family members or close friends. These children were known as "hijos de crianza" (or reared offspring) and were defined by anthropologist David Landy, who did research in Puerto Rico in the 1950s, as "children of rearing" including "stepchildren and offspring of former matings, legal and nonlegal," "grandchildren" and "a miscellany of nephews, nieces, children of distant relatives, and 'foster' children (legal and nonlegal)."[8] This practice was considered "peculiar" by the scientists in charge of a Brookings Institution study made in 1930: "With the death of the mother, the neighbors divide the children among themselves. In conversation one will be told that 'This child came to me at birth, this one when he was 6 months old, and that one when he was 2 years of age.' Children in school will speak of a brother or sister "de crianza" (by rearing)."[9] This practice was also commented on by American authors:

In Puerto Rico, then, the family, usually a big one, is important.... To a child, especially, this must give a sense of security.... If anything should happen to the immediate parents.... A child can always be sure of affection. The relatives will always arrange for one or another of them to look after the children in their own households with their own children. For adults, too, this sense of belonging must be of importance. Here on the island a person knows that whatever happens, there are people close to him or her—family, relatives, friends—who will share in sorrows, pleasures, and successes. (Samoiloff 1984, 164)

Indeed, in Puerto Rico, close friends can also be considered family and are counted on as such. This means that they are expected to share both in times of happiness and in times of sadness or need. All are together in good or bad:

> In the presence of troubles, the Puerto Rican is keenly conscious of one all-pervading resource: his family. The brother, the cousin, the "compadre," the good neighbor, the parish priest, the store-keeper, are the traditional human institutions that make the difference between sorrow or joy . . . In the recurrent crisis of human life, "troubles" have led the Puerto Rican to weave around himself the protecting net of human loyalties, of people he can count on, of people who will always "be there." Likewise, in the facing of troubles, in knowing what to do and on whom to count on, a man enjoys prestige and respect. He is one on whom other people can depend. And the credit of the store-keeper, the loaf of bread from the friend next door, the bag of vegetables from the cousin in the country, are still familiar weapons in the struggle with poverty . . . (Fitzpatrick 1996, 142–43)

Unfortunately, modernity has had its effects and has eroded, to an extent, the traditional respect and veneration for the aged as the importance of acquiring goods and/or the growing financial insecurity have turned many elders into victims of the opportunism of their adult offspring.[10] Nowadays, it is not uncommon to find Puerto Rican grandparents in charge of their grandkids or providing food and shelter for their adult offspring.

"FOR GUIDANCE AND FOR ADVICE": *COMPADRAZGO*

"Compadrazgo" is a Spanish term to describe the relationship between a godfather and the parents of his godchild. The term has been translated to English as "coparenthood," which is more accurate than "god-parenthood" since, quite frequently, the relationship was not based on the Catholic baptism of a child, and it comes from the Latin *compater* and *commater* (in Spanish, "compadre" and "comadre").[11]

These relationships were extremely strong, at least until the 1950s, when Puerto Rican society became more urban and industrialized and, therefore, more "modern." Frequently a poor family asked their *hacendado* to become one of their children's godfathers, an honor that the *hacendado* could not reject without offending the parents. The bond thus created secured the family a piece of land to farm and work with the *hacendado*, while the latter secured the loyalty of the "compadre."[12] But the relationship represented a lot more than an exchange of gifts or privileges, and frequently fostered lifetime friendships between parents and godparents based on deep respect. An American rural sociologist explained it:

> They [the planters] exercise a sort of patronage over the country people who work for them, many of whom live in houses on land provided by the landlord. The laborers look to the landlord for guidance and for advice in practically all matters pertaining to their economic life, and the planter usually reciprocates by caring for the welfare of the countryman to the best of his ability. (Fleagle 1917, 6)

For some social analysts, in the case of Puerto Rican peasants, the relationship was another form of solidarity and mutual protection system developed by the poor to survive under dire circumstances.[13] Once a *compadrazgo* relationship was established, the involved adults became mutual sources of emotional and economic support, and in case of the death of the parents, which happened quite frequently,[14] they typically took charge of the orphans. This is described in detail by an American-Puerto Rican physicians' team:

> ... there is no masonry so strong as that existing among the jibaros of Porto Rico. Bound to each other by the most intricate ties of relationship and by a still more potent one, the eternal bond conferred by the title "compadre" or godfather, they share their troubles and shield each other as though they belonged to one great family. It is really wonderful to see how quickly and with what complete self-abnegation and orphaned child or widowed mother is gathered into some poor neighbor's hut and there cared for. (Ashford and Gutierrez 1911, 13–14)

THIS CHAPTER

Even though some analysts ascribe Puerto Ricans' generosity and hospitality to a sense of inferiority when dealing with a "superior" American, these attributes are much more central in Puerto Rican culture and are expressed as well towards other foreigners and other Puerto Ricans. Puerto Ricans, particularly those from the lower classes, still count on the close-knit network of care and affection provided by friends and family in the rough times that they so frequently confront. Interestingly, most American authors, even those that complained about Puerto Rican nosiness, ended up enchanted by the kindness and generosity of the islanders.

Chapter 15

"THOSE INDESCRIBABLE EYES"

Puerto Rican Women

As said, at the time of the US invasion, Puerto Rico was still unindustrialized, while the United States was the epitome of industrialization and modernity. The American economy was already based on industries and industrialized farms, and earning a wage and being a consumer were part of the accepted lifestyle there, at least for the men.[1] American elite and middle-class women remained in the "home sphere" and devoted their time and energy to "creating a serene, loving, virtuous home environment."[2] Those who could afford it hired working-class women to take care of the domestic tasks, which they then supervised.

In Puerto Rico, at the time, many lower-class women were part of the working class, especially in tobacco and coffee production, but also in needlework and as domestic servants in elite homes. Only Puerto Rican elite women were able to hire house help whenever it was affordable: nannies, cooks, cleaning ladies, washers and ironers, gardeners, and chauffeurs. The absence of a middle class generated a gap between the lifestyles of women of both classes, that American authors noted.

Surprisingly, a few American authors writing in the 1940s and 1950s came to the conclusion that Puerto Rican society was matriarchal. They wrongly interpreted the control women had over domestic issues as "a great deal of power":

> Puerto Rico is a matriarchal society. . . . men never discussed sexual problems between husband and wife. The wife in Puerto Rico ruled (and still does) the house, the husband, the children and makes all the important decisions. (Flax 1995, 19)

> As an outsider, it was very difficult to learn much about the status of women in Puerto Rico . . . As the stable psychological and physical

center for an often chaotic extended family, they wielded a great deal of power. (Cooper 1994, 101)

English teacher Jim Cooper understood that since Puerto Rican women controlled their husbands' and sons' incomes, they were very powerful. But in reality, the control of the home economics was not paralleled with control of any other aspect of the women's lives:

> The men earned the money, but the women decided how it was to be spent. Many Puerto Ricans simply flatly refused to believe you if you tried to explain to them that in many American households, particularly those from northern European ethnic backgrounds, the men manage the money and women must run the house on an allowance and <u>ask</u> their husbands for spending money. The American idea that women are spendthrifts and genetically incapable of dealing with money (or mathematics) they <u>know</u> is a lie. It is men who can't be trusted with money. They'll spend it all on rum and other women. Now, <u>that</u> is a genetic fact. They can't help it. It's just the way they are.
>
> When the man came home with his salary, he gave it to his wife to run the house and raise the children. She then gave him whatever allowance she felt she could spare, and she tried to spare him as much as possible, but the home and children came first, and he knew it. If she was a good wife, a good manager, he'd have that much more for himself, but he wanted his children, particularly his sons, spoiled, just as he was.
>
> "But who makes the decisions in your family? . . ."
> "My father. My mother would never go against what he wants to do."
> "Now seriously. Who really makes these decisions? . . ."
> Finally, "First he goes and talks it over with grandma."
> "You mean your grandmother really makes the decisions?"
> "In a way. I mean, my father would never do anything his mother didn't want him to." (Cooper 1994, 108–9)

Margherita A. Hamm, a war correspondent, paid a lot of attention to Puerto Rican elite women's lives during her two trips to the Island and got a more accurate impression of their lack of power over their everyday lives. Coming from New York, where marital relationships were beginning to change by the end of the nineteenth century, she expressed her pity for what she interpreted as the lives of Puerto Rican elite women being constantly watched and controlled:

> The condition of woman is very inferior, and as a result, or a concomitant, morals are none of the best. The men treat women with exquisite

courtesy, both in speech and action. They foresee every want, and they bestow attention with tact and delicacy, but it is the master pleasing the slave, and not one human being treating his equal. The woman cannot go out alone without losing caste and being insulted. She cannot receive a visitor alone, not even when that visitor is her "fiancé." She cannot go to an opera, concert, theatre or reception alone. Even in going to church she must be accompanied by a servant or a duenna. The husband is always jealous of the wife, though not in the same way as men are of our own race. He does not seemingly object to her smiling, winking, or waving a fan from her veranda at a strange passer-by, neither does he object particularly to her demure and disguised flirtations in church, but if she receives an octogenarian caller in his absence there is bound to be trouble in the camp. On the other hand, he himself looks very lightly upon his obligations to his spouse. (Hamm, *Porto* 1899, 99–100)

"THIS DUSKY TROPICAL BELLE": ATTRACTIVENESS

Countless poets, singers, and writers, both from Puerto Rico and foreigners, have praised the allure of Puerto Rican women. The studied American authors joined them in their praise, some with a lot of detail, especially regarding elite women, hereby called "ladies":

That the ladies are charming, goes without saying. . . . They are insular, even provincial perhaps, but they possess charming traits of character, gentle manners and speech, goodness of heart, and unaffected frankness with their friends. Their glances are swift and meaning . . . their features are not always classically regular, but usually attractive. They are petite of form and have small hands and feet, dress in the same style from Paris . . . and, in a word, are thoroughly feminine. It is this charm of femininity that makes the creole, whether French or Spanish, so potent with man. Brunettes prevail and blondes are a rarity. The large eyes, black as night; the peachblow complexion; hair abundant, dark and glossy as a raven's wing; gracefully moulded, voluptuous form . . . (Ober 1899, 169–70, 173)

Others were able to overcome their biases and also praised the enchantment of lower-class Puerto Ricans. Some were really mesmerized by the sight of women of different skin colors:

... the Porto Rican women, especially the young women, all have beautiful eyes, and masses of beautiful black, black hair.... The Corporal [referring to himself] did see a girl in Aibonito with eyes so deep and true, such a wonderful combination of hazel and gold and black, that he simply stood speechless and gazed spellbound, like a hypnotized being whose very soul was being drawn into those lovely, fathomless, liquid eyes, and she, as innocently as a fawn, gazed back, wondering, no doubt, what new species of lunatic "Americano" it was. The Corporal doesn't know what color her hair was, or the shape of her mouth or nose, but those indescribable eyes are photographed on his memory forever. She was the only one he met that at all compared with our girls at home ... (Rossiter [1900?])

[As they encountered a woman singing out loud:] A wild, picturesque figure she presents, too, such as is met with seldom save in the islands of the tropics ... Her ancestors, not very far removed, may have roamed in their primitive life amid the jungles of the Congo or the Niger, but she has unmistakably the strain of another race, which blends happily with that of her own people, and gives shapeliness to feature and limb.... this dusky tropical belle.... Casting a half defiant, half frightened glance at us, the "sable[3] Aphrodite" gives her dusky head a toss ... and resuming her song, follows her way down the valley, leaving behind only the dream of the picture we have seen. (Browne and Dole 1907, 1418)

Still, others were harsh when commenting on the looks of common Puerto Ricans and, when acknowledging some beauty, referred to it as ephemeral:

... young girls from twelve to sixteen, and ... middle-aged women from thirty to forty ... even these plump specimens are not stalwart or well built. They are fat and generally flabby. (Hamm, *Porto* 1899, 68)

The beauty and charm of these tropical girls are as evanescent as irresistible while they last. Like the lovely flowers of their island, they mature very early, but fade as rapidly. The prettiest girl will be plain before she is thirty, and a handsome middle-aged woman is rarely seen. (Olivares, *Vol. 1* 1899, 353)

In her research about sexuality and race, Suárez Findlay recognized that "Puerto Rican women as well as men found great pleasure and excitement in flirtation and sex."[4] Flirting has been studied in depth in the United Kingdom, and their research concluded that "flirting is a basic instinct, part of human nature," genetically programmed in us to secure reproduction and, therefore, the survival of our species.[5] But the study also acknowledged that American Puritanism gives "a bad name" to flirting; it forbade and punished *all* nonreproductive sexual activities.[6] So, although most male authors enjoyed it, this female author criticized the natural practice of flirtations she observed among elite Puerto Rican women:

> The women are gentle, polite, affectionate and hospitable. They are inquisitive, talkative, nervous and excitable. They love social diversions and all amusements which they are permitted to attend, and they dote on flirting. They cannot imagine how the men and women of the northern races refuse to indulge in the harmless pastime, and much less how they look down upon it. They themselves believe that a woman who will not flirt is either eccentric, or is about to take the veil, and as for a man who refuses to respond to the advances of a woman they regard him as "an animal of a low order of intelligence." (Hamm, *Porto* 1899, 133)

Contrasting all other studied descriptions of Puerto Rican women, an American soldier wrote an offensive and mocking description of a kind-hearted Puerto Rican woman who worked at the hospital where he spent a short time. The soldier dedicated two full pages to sarcastically insulting this poor woman, of which this is an excerpt:

> No description of the hospital would be complete without some mention of its bogie or familiar imp. About twenty-five years old, of a light chocolate brown, tall, spare, and indescribably unneat in her negligée native costume, Saturnina was as uncanny a presiding genius as ever seconded the God of healing. Like many women of her race on the island, she had lost her two upper front teeth; the aperture thus formed she alternately used as the socket for her cigar or as a cleverly managed channel for expectoration. A dark skirt, a loose white shirt open at the throat, and a shawl of various colors around her shoulders, constituted her usual apparel. Her woolly hair was arranged in two stiff, hornlike excrescences over either ear, and covered with a cloth or handkerchief secured by fancy pins, in guise of mantilla. This nightmare, bending over our cots with a steaming bowl of rice, gruel or milk, will follow us for many a day through uneasy dreams. Yet Saturnina was kind of heart. . . . Her sense of the proprieties was entirely minus. Often did I curse my scanty knowledge of Spanish when Saturnina would come

into our room and irrepressibly entertain us with remarks that would have made a Comanche blush. Not that there was any guile in her; her conversation was perpetrated with the ignorant carelessness of a two-year-old child; and all the lectures the ladies [American nurses] gave her on this head produced only blank non-understanding. Poor black, heinous, kind-hearted Saturnina! (Cammann 1899, 220–21)

Not even modernity changed the interest of Puerto Rican women in their physical appearance and fashion, according to this 1984 comment: "Women "libbers" are a minority. Most Puerto Rican women want to look pretty, feminine, and pleasing to their men" (Samoiloff 1984, 167).

"THIS MASK OF BEAUTY": USE OF MAKEUP

Several male authors made detailed observations regarding the use of makeup by Puerto Rican women, giving the impression that American women did not use it. Indeed, the Puritan tradition so powerful in New England, where most of the studied American authors came from, condemned the use of makeup by Puritan women, as was clearly espoused by Cotton Mather, the minister of Boston's First Church in 1692.[7] On their part, and to this day, Puerto Rican women are recognized for their general good looks, partially due to their masterful use of makeup in everyday life (as opposed to using it only for special occasions or parties). Discussing elite women, Ober used a detailed description to discuss the common practice:

> The ladies do not veil their faces . . . though they protect them with powder, unsparingly and unblushingly applied. Visit any school in the island and you will find teacher and scholar alike wearing this mask of beauty. Even the pupils of the art schools, as well as the workwomen in the cigar shops, use the powdery protection against the sun's rays. . . . by the side of every woman . . . lies a little box of powder and a rabbit's foot. There is nothing unusual in this public use of the article, since its application is so universal, through long custom, and all ladies regard it as an indispensable adjunct of the toilet, and absolutely necessary to make them attractive; which is, or should be, their highest ambition. (Ober 1899, 174–75)

This female author noticed the use of makeup differently, insisting that it somehow responded to the hot climate and that it was used to conceal greasy faces:

> There is a liberal use of cosmetics by the sex, although this is, so far as my experience is concerned, a characteristic of social life in all warm countries. [After stating that soap is barely used on the faces:] . . . the women . . . of the middle class bathe every day, and of the wealthier two and three times a day. The effect of their prejudice [against soap] is seen in the faces of the women, which are nearly always shiny, or else well powdered to conceal the shine. . . . Every woman is powdered. Nineteenths enhance their charms with rouge, and more than a few make use of coloring for the lips. In full toilet the Porto Rican women make a very engaging and delightful picture. (Hamm, *Porto* 1899, 122, 131)

Two American missionaries commented on the use of makeup by Puerto Rican women in a negative way or plainly ridiculed the darker ones for using makeup to "lighten their color":

> An abundant use of cheap perfumery and face powder is also noticeable among the Porto Rican women. Even the blacks lighten their color by a generous application of powder. (Fowles 1910, 59)

> How those brides do adorn themselves for their husbands! On the hottest days they plaster their faces with powder and the perspiration runs down in little rivers through it, but they never touch it for fear of losing some powder. What makes me laugh is the sight of the dusky belles with white smudges on their cheeks and across their foreheads, while the spaces between are left quite natural. (Blythe 1911, 98)

"THE ENSEMBLE IS STARTLING": FASHION SENSE

Most Puerto Rican women will probably agree that looking well-put-together or "emperifollarse" is a cultural trait in Puerto Rico, even for many men.[8] Regardless of their social class, Puerto Rican women are taught to be clean, with well-styled hair and color-coordinated attire, within their financial means whenever away from home. It is a part of their identity that tends to be taken for granted and is only noticed when living away from the Island in countries like the United States or Great Britain, with totally different everyday fashion cultures. This particular care for personal appearance puzzled US Secretary of the Interior Harold L. Ickes during his 1938 visit to a slum:

> We inspected two or three slum areas [in San Juan], and they are the worst slums that I have ever seen. . . . there are no sanitary facilities at

all.... The houses appear to be dirty and unkempt.... Notwithstanding these terrible conditions, generally speaking, the people in the slums, and especially the younger women, had the appearance of being neat and clean, although I cannot see how they can possibly be clean, considering the surroundings in which they live. (Ickes 1953, 504)

Several American authors commented on female apparel. Of course, distinctions were made according to the social class of the wearer. Authors typically avoided attributing any lack of elegance to poverty. Indeed, some marveled at the good taste in the fashion of even people who lived in poor shacks:

Bright colors are affected by the Porto Rican women, and where there is a crowd of them together on the move, the ensemble is startling. (Moore 1907, 38)

... if the Porto Ricans can be said to have any artistic bent at all, it seems to express itself in the question of clothes. They have a perfect genius for making the most of things in any line, but especially in regard to their clothes. There is a breezy fluffiness and a style about the cheapest bit of pink lawn and lace and ribbon, when it has once been through the hands of a seamstress, that truly does them credit.... To see people on the plaza or at the church in the evening you might reasonably conclude that they were at least in comfortable circumstances, and you would, if you were at all new here, take it for granted that their homes were clean and orderly. But follow them home, and you will find that the great majority of them live in huts or little shacks with smoky walls ... The mystery is how they keep so presentable, and the ease with which they carry the burden of their poverty is nothing short of incredible. (Blythe 1911, 98–99)

The Puritans were very conservative and very intolerant of any deviance from their strict codes of conduct and appearance.[9] They dressed accordingly and considered any showing of skin "a distraction"; so, for them, clothing's only purpose was to cover the body, particularly the female body. Some American authors were appalled at the relaxed and revealing attires of Puerto Rican women of all social backgrounds:

Jibaras lounge in their doorways with a single thin garment about them, so unfastened and opened as to disclose a large part of the anatomy within, the remainder being half-visible through the flimsy fabric of the dress. Well-to-do and well-bred women go about their houses in the morning with a light wrapper and a pair of slippers, a costume well calculated to reveal every physical peculiarity. (Hamm, *America's* 1899, 84)

Due to the difference in climate, headwear had to be different. Margherita A. Hamm described the romantic looks of the "mantillas" and commented on how they could be used for flirting:

The headwear is simple and romantic. The universal style is the mantilla, which may be anything from a piece of crocheting or knitting to a priceless bit of old Gothic lace. The mantilla is usually worn with the point falling down to the level of the eyebrows. Coquettish wearers carry the point down till it brushes the tip of the nose, which throws the great brown eyes out into beautiful relief, and often increase the artistic effect by bringing the lower end around the cheek and lips, so as to imitate the veiled beauties of the old Saracen seraglios. The color of the mantilla is usually black. The next favorite is old gold, orange gray, or Spanish yellow, which is known as "la blonda." (Hamm, *Porto* 1899, 123–24)

Hamm also praised the creative use of headscarves by Puerto Rican women of the lower classes:

The workingwomen and the peasantry wear the most gorgeous headwear imaginable. It consists of a huge handkerchief printed in glaring colors, ranging from the familiar red and yellow bandana, so popular with darkies of the Southern States, to fantastic designs in stripes, circles, stars and leaves. Blue is rarely employed, the colors of the Spanish flag, blood and gold, being universal favorites. The bandana may be worn like a mantilla, like a cook's cap, a socialist's bonnet or a Sikh turban. Long practice enables the women to weave it into all sorts of odd shapes and effects. The contrast with the blue-black hair and the olive skin is always striking, and generally very artistic. (Hamm, *Porto* 1899, 124–25)

Hamm showed an inordinate interest in shoe wear and widely commented on those she saw while in Puerto Rico. Regarding the lower classes, she seemed to describe what we call today "chancletas" (flip-flops she called "sandals") and "alpargatas" (espadrilles she called "slippers"):

The influence of the climate can be noticed in the footwear of the women. Many of the field hands wear a sandal made of pleated or stitched rope, with a single band across the instep. . . . A grade higher than this is a slipper made with the same kind of rope sole, but with uppers of strong drill or cotton cloth in checks, stripes, bars or plaids. These are worn by women and men alike . . . Next in cost comes a long series of Moorish, Turkish and Spanish slippers, made of enameled cloth, leatheret, leather, kid, patent leather, morocco, cordovan, alpaca, silk, satin, and even velvet. They range from natural colors to every stripe of the rainbow . . . (Hamm, *Porto* 1899, 125)

Regarding hosiery, Hamm was able to understand that a hot climate had to influence its use or lack thereof. She also enjoyed the variety of colors in them:

Hosiery is regarded as much a luxury as a necessity. It is a little surprising the first day or two to see well dressed, bejeweled women in handsome homes going about their rooms in slippers and bare ankles, but when the novelty wears away the practice receives approval. It keeps the body much cooler, and the feet and ankles in far better condition than the northern habit of putting on strong, well-woven stockings at the beginning of the day. The difference is that while only one American woman in three has a pretty and undisfigured foot, nine out of ten in Porto Rico enjoy this satisfying privilege. . . . Stockings are required in going to church, and at all formal and informal social functions. They are not a necessity when riding mules and horses. An amusing sight may be seen on the roads leading to the churches on Sunday morning. When the rider gets within a half-mile of the sacred edifice she produces in the panier a pair of handsome stockings and puts them on with the same calm indifference as a woman of northern countries puts on her gloves. The hosiery runs more to bright colors and contrasts than to plain black and other solid colors. (Hamm, *Porto* 1899, 126–27)

The then ubiquitous, and somewhat still used, fan was discussed by Hamm. The mentioned "fan-dagger" seemed to refer to a defense weapon then used by Puerto Rican women.:

No Porto Rican woman is ever without a fan, and nearly all have a good collection of those cooling instruments. The prevailing type is made with sticks of native wood. . . . The parasol fan is a novel sight to a northern visitor . . . A very ugly contrivance is the fan-dagger, in which the outer stick is a sheath containing a sharp-pointed keen-edged blade of steel. It can be easily released, and makes a very deadly weapon. Now and then the visitor runs across feather fans of various kinds. A popular type is the urraca or magpie plume. (Hamm, *Porto* 1899, 133, 136–37)

With her usual level of detail, Hamm praised the fashion donned by Puerto Rican older women, which she compared favorably to that in the United States:

Noteworthy is the habit which the old ladies have of dressing in bright colors and pretty frocks. Americans with grim humor, but deplorable taste, insist upon their old people wearing black clothes of formal cut, as if to indicate that the mourning they wore was in honor of their approaching dissolution. . . . It is therefore a novel pleasure to see pretty, graceful old ladies gleaming in lilacs, sulphur rose, and sky blue, rustling in satin and fluttering in lace. It is in keeping with the light-heartedness and affectionate activity which characterizes the aged ladies of this land. (Hamm, *Porto* 1899, 107)

But in the 1960s, as the miniskirts flourished, the clash between American and Puerto Rican fashion trends cost an English teacher her job:

But San Juan was a problem for one of the other young newly hired teachers. Mini-skirts were in fashion at the time, many of them two or more inches above the knee, and Joann was very fashion conscious. There were no clothes in her wardrobe that were not up-to-the-minute chic. She had a good figure and was soon wildly popular with the male students. Early in the school year, Joann was called in by the administration and told that she would have to wear longer skirts. She refused . . . saying that miniskirts were stylish, everyone in the States was wearing them, and for her to wear longer skirts would be taking away her freedom and her personality. . . . she was fired. (Cooper 1992, 151)

In 1984, an American journalist confirmed the effect of consumerism in an already fashion-oriented feminine population in Puerto Rico:

Among the women, there is great interest in dress. School children wear uniforms . . . The uniforms colors are different for different schools. Once beyond school age, the young dress in the brightest mixture of colors. . . . They love clothes and a great deal of money, when available, goes into buying clothes. When married, the women still wear bright dresses, but their clothes are more sedate than those of young girls. Most Puerto Rican women wear earrings. Nearly all baby girls have their ears pierced early. (Samoiloff 1984, 173)

"A FLOCK OF CAGED SINGING BIRDS": ELITE WOMEN

The life of Puerto Rico's elite women in the early twentieth century is generally described as a secluded one since they spent most of their time at home, at family members' and friends' homes, or at church. They rarely went to the market, letting their servants deal with the household shopping. Women in the upper classes, if married, typically supervised the work of the house's servants, who might include a cook, a cleaning lady, a cloth washer and ironer, a chauffeur, and a nanny. Besides supervising all these servants, these women spent their time visiting each other and doing embroidery and needlework. Americans described different aspects of the Puerto Rican elite women's lifestyle as they interpreted them, mostly as ignorant beauties:

> The girls of the better class are brought up from babyhood under a constant surveillance. . . . The growing bud is taught to play the piano or guitar, to embroider, to sing a little, to dance a little less, to speak and read French, to powder her face with art, and to walk like a very queen. She is usually married before she is seventeen, especially if her father has money; and, until the day of her death, she never sees a modern newspaper, never goes slumming, and never soils her gentle hands with work of any degree. She is apt to love her husband devotedly, and does not think her career fitly rounded until she is a mother. (Herrmann 1900, 36–37)

Elite women were a rare sight downtown except for the Sunday mass and the promenades at the plazas, and especially young elite women did so in the company of their chaperones or duennas, already discussed in chapter 8.

> There is a genuine aristocracy in Porto Rico. . . . The women of this class are rarely seen upon the streets, they do not hang out the windows nor lean dreamily over the balconies, and only a few of them go out to walk in the plaza when the military band plays. There are any number of bewilderingly beautiful girls in Porto Rico, but the visitor will hardly become aware of their presence until he visits some aristocratic ball or exclusive social entertainment. . . . Heretofore it has been the custom of the Porto Rican belles to take their outings in Europe, where many of them found titled husbands and aristocratic homes; but now their dark eyes are turned languishingly toward the United States. . . . Shut within the walls of their beautiful gardens, screened from all gaze of strangers, they have no more concern with the world than a flock of caged singing birds. (Olivares, *Vol. 1* 1899, 353, 383)

A telling incident regarding the importance of having a good reputation in the higher classes arose when a group of Puerto Rican teachers was sent to the United States in the summer of 1904 for a special four-week course at Harvard and Cornell Universities. There, they were expected to meet and mingle with six hundred American teachers:

> It was no small task to persuade the conservative Puerto Ricans that it would be proper for their young women teachers to take such a trip: but when we invited several ladies of recognized social standing to accompany us as chaperons, engaged a priest as spiritual adviser, and promised to maintain scholastic discipline at all times under the strict eyes of superintendents and principals . . . our quota was at length filled. (Lord 2004, 48)

Some authors noticed that the elite women of Puerto Rico lacked interest in sports, including bicycling, which, by the 1890s, was raving in the United States, with American women "riding in large numbers" the Rover bicycles created for them.[10] Bicycling, as well as any strenuous exercise, was seen as unfeminine in Puerto Rico, but in the United States, it was seen as a symbol of the emancipation of women since it provided them with transportation independence:

> The life of the women of the middle and upper classes is essentially indoor. Of walking as an amusement, of long constitutionals, of light sports and exercises, they are completely ignorant. Owing partly to their education and habits and partly to the lethargy produced by the tropical climate, they look down upon all physical activity, excepting dancing. I spoke to many Porto Rican ladies about gymnastics and calisthenics, and in every instance but one of my listeners seemed to regard these things as evidences of eccentricity. The one in question said that exercise might make a woman healthier, but certainly it would make her harder, and therefore less handsome. (Hamm, *Porto* 1899, 121)

But all this began to change under the American influence, and by the 1930s, an American journalist commented on the new ways:

> Formerly a girl of this class was rarely seen in public, and never alone with a young man. Since the coming of the Americans, these conventions have been largely discarded, and the fair Porto Ricans now enjoy much the same freedom as their sisters in the States. I see them motoring about the city and the suburbs, attending the horse races and carnivals, and, in short, patronizing sports of all kinds. (Carpenter 1930, 267)

Modernity surely changed the subjects discussed by American authors. By the early 1950s, an English teacher had commented on the lack of acceptance of contraceptive methods in Mayagüez's society. As usual, the burden of preventing premarital sex was exclusively on the young women, as young men were widely understood as "insatiable":

> In those days before the pill, what really mattered was keeping your daughter from getting pregnant.... When continentals tried to explain that American girls were taught to protect themselves, people simply shook their heads. It was not a possibility. If a young man and woman were alone together ... This was why women could not wear slacks or shorts or bathing suits at the beach. Much too provocative. Condoms take all the pleasure from the man, and, anyway, can only be used with prostitutes to try to prevent disease. Even among the educated, the diaphragm was not known ... (Cooper 1994, 127)

This same English teacher attempted to incorporate his American wife Gretchen, also an English teacher, into the Mayagüez elite, where he and other Americans had already been accepted, but his efforts failed. According to his interpretation of the events, the elite mothers rejected the liberal behavior of Gretchen as a bad example and rejected him for not marrying a Puerto Rican. His story highlights a time in which the Puerto Rican elite was still trying to preserve its old ways and rejecting American modernity values:

> On that Saturday evening, after leaving a student dance in the cafeteria, we thought we would stop in at a fraternity dance downtown, at a fraternity house we'd been to several times before. We were just barely inside the door and were about to go out onto the dance floor when a group of students told us, none too politely, that we were not welcome at their dance.... we could see the girlfriends and their mothers seated across the dance floor who stopped talking to one another to stare at us and then smiled and nodded their approval as we turned to leave.
>
> This was embarrassing at the time, of course, and for the next few days we were more than just indignant, but it really just confirmed what we already knew and what had been told us by the students and teachers. The people who were spreading stories about us, the people it turned out we were fighting were the matrons of Mayaguez society, not, of course, their husbands, who were living their own lives. These were the women who were trying to find husbands for their daughters, who arranged the dances, who were fighting to keep the old chaperone system, who

looked at every unmarried continental male as a possible husband, and they had been remarkably successful. But not only did I bring a bride from the States, she was a teacher, with some of their sons in her classes, and she did all the things that no decent girl or woman would do. They had heard horror stories of the behavior of women in the States, going on dates unchaperoned, living alone, but here was an example in their very midst.

While what was going on could not exactly be called class warfare, the lines were perfectly clear. It was the old families, what Beckwith when I first arrived had called, with a sneer, "the so-called upper crust," who were scandalized and infuriated by us. . . . We were a threat to the system, the threat of change, and with it their very precarious feelings of superiority. (Cooper 1994, 145–46)

"WE CANNOT IMAGINE A SADDER, MORE HOPELESS LOT": WORKING WOMEN

At the beginning of the twentieth century, besides taking care of the housework, lower-class women in Puerto Rico frequently worked with their partners in the little plots they might have had. Housework at the time in the countryside meant that women had to cook for the family, bath the children, wash all clothes in a stream, clean the hut, cut and bring wood for cooking, fetch water from long distances, and care for any animals they might have.

Many women also worked with their partners in the coffee *haciendas*, either picking the grains or separating them according to their size.[11] Other women worked in the tobacco haciendas, mostly separating the tobacco leaves from their stems using their frontal teeth, a practice that caused mouth cancer to many. And still, many other women worked as cooks, laundresses, maids and/ or nannies for elite families. Unfortunately, all this effort did little to enhance the quality of their lives:

[A missionary's testimony:] "What of the poor, degrade shack women, who far outnumber their more fortunate sisters? We cannot imagine a sadder, more hopeless lot than theirs. They live crowded into little one-roomed shacks which often have no floor but the earth, and no furniture save perhaps a hammock and a heap of old rags for sleeping. Except in harvest-time, when work is plenty, many a family has but one meal a day, and often the woman has to earn that. In nearly every household there is a feeble old mother, or grandmother, and there is scarcely a day that someone is not sick—and there is no money for doctors or medicine.

And so the long days and years stretch themselves on to the end, with no brightness, no hope." Jennie L. Blowers (Guernsey 1907, 61–62)

Several authors described the working conditions of girls and women picking or classifying coffee, at which they earned some twenty-five cents per day (around seventy-five percent of what men earned), almost in a blissful way that was totally unrealistic. The impression was that Puerto Rican coffee workers were happily clad in rags and gladly underfed with bananas:

> ... the ragged, tattered pickers, large and small, father, mother, and a brood of partially clothed children, make one of the most picturesque sights in this island of loveliness. In the early morning they trudge out from their little thatch-roofed huts, with home-made baskets slung on bands from their shoulders or balanced carelessly on their heads. . . . Later, from the depths of every thicket, comes the chant of singing voices, and the chorus is feminine, the woman of poverty, somehow, knowing how to be happier than the man. (Dinwiddie 1899, 91)

On the other hand, Olivares was able to recognize the limited opportunities for women to actually become financially independent:

> Among the women of the poor there is little chance for a girl of humble parentage to make her own living. Outside of school teaching or acting as governesses, there are no openings whatever. Women are not employed in the stores.... There are women, of course, in the dressmakers' shops, but these are poorly paid.... it is said that they sew beautifully with the needle.... The wages of servants of all kinds are very low, especially women servants. Maids get from $3 to $3.60 a month, and for this sum they will do anything. (Olivares, Vol. 1 1899, 303–4, 307)

With the US invasion, a new industry began: the needlework industry. Many Puerto Rican women already had dexterity in delicate sewing, knitting, fretwork and embroidery, all arts taught over generations. Now American businessmen, representing Philadelphia's needlework industry, roamed Puerto Rican towns offering textile piecework to women who then worked from their own homes, and who were paid negligible amounts of money for high-quality pieces (gloves, slippers, etc.) that were then sold in select American stores with high profit margins. This industry began to open sewing workshops in Puerto Rico around 1918, and by the 1950s this was the second export industry and the first source of employment for Puerto Rican women.[12] Some American missionaries commented on the quality of their work: "Woman's work is clearly defined in this island. It is needlework, and the beautiful embroideries and fine drawn-work that are shown to the admiring guest, speak of many hours passed with the needle and scissors" (Johnston 1905, 152).

Another common source of employment for lower-class women was as housekeepers at Puerto Rican elite houses. They received extremely low wages for their hard work, as was documented in 1931:

> Domestic service is one of the most widespread means of earning a living. As this type of labor is very cheap, homes in Porto Rico, which in the States would be deemed far too modest to employ a servant, have in them one or even two domestics. Only at the lowest level, when the family occupies a cabin of but one or two rooms, do we find the woman of the house doing all the family work. (Van Deusen and Van Deusen 1931, 166)

From very early on, the conflict of mothers who worked outside their homes so that their families could survive ensued. In order to earn at least a little bit of money, they had to leave their older children or neighbors in the care of their younger children, thus being unable to adequately supervise their care and raising. Their dilemma was presented by an urban sociologist:

> Among the indirectly harmful results . . . is the separation of the mothers from the children of the family. . . . The mother . . . either leaves the children in the care of a neighbor, or leaves them at home where the older children take care of the younger. This deprives the children of the mother's influence and allows them liberty to associate with children who may be undesirable companions . . . (Fleagle 1917, 52)

Once again is Margherita A. Hamm, the author who, in the greatest detail, described the multiple jobs performed by Puerto Rican working women, recognizing their hard work:

> Among the Jibaras the women do as much of the hard work as the men. They cut the cane, stack and load it into the carts or carry it on the head to the mill. They cultivate the vines and fruit trees and kitchen gardens. They bring the produce to the markets and sell it there. Fish women aid their husbands on the water, carry their capture to the market, and there dispose of it. . . . They work in the coffee plantations and the tobacco fields, and a few of them in the manufacture of tobacco. They are also engaged in book binding, dyeing, upholstering, dressmaking

and tailoring. They act as teachers, domestic servants, governesses and duennas. Large estates usually have a caballeriza, or woman outrider, who precedes the ladies of the family when they go visiting.... Another woman is the floor scrubber and polisher, who carries with her an armament of brushes, and half-cocoanuts, and who after cleaning the floor thoroughly, will oil, or paraffine it, and then rub it until it gleams like a mirror. (Hamm, *Porto* 1899, 137–38)

Hamm also noticed the wide presence of working women in commercial settings:

Many widows and married women are successful cafeteras, or coffeehouse keepers, and fondistas or restauranteurs. Women are successful as peddlers and agents for the sale of all sorts of goods. They are street musicians of about the same class there as the Italian organ grinders are here. They may be found keeping a hotel or in charge of one, and they have one business that seems peculiar to the island. It consists of going to the stores in the early morning, selecting a stock of goods, carrying it to a list of customers, and there selling what is brought, and taking orders for similar or other goods.

The saleswoman is accompanied by a clerk from the store, who carries with him a purse full of small change, and who receives the payment for all goods sold. The woman receives a commission upon her sales, and often makes a very good living. Many positions held by women in this country are occupied by members of the religious sisterhoods. Thus they serve as trained nurses, as invalid's companions, as readers, preceptors, book agents, art critics, garden directors and advisers in household economics. (Hamm, *Porto* 1899, 138)

With a completely opposite opinion, and claiming that Puerto Rican peasant women spent their days in laziness, an American political science professor showed a lack of understanding of poverty and of housework:

The relatively small amount of productive and remunerative labor performed by women is an interesting and peculiar fact ... Even under the more primitive conditions of the interior of the island, where it might be supposed that the burden of work would be shifted to the women, we find them leading lives of comparative idleness. In spite of the large families, the amount of housework is small, owing to the simple arrangement of the dwelling. A small hut with two or three rooms does not offer a complex problem of household management. The large amount of leisure, instead of being used in adding to the income of the family, is spent in idleness. (Rowe 1904, 105)

The American colonial government brought important changes in Puerto Rican women's lives. Beyond being able to divorce, and becoming further exploited by the needle industry, new job opportunities opened for some women. More educated women became teachers in the new schools, and nurses' aides in the new hospitals that opened. Some were even able to access other government jobs, like census enumerators in 1899, as sixty-two of the 911 enumerators hired were women: "... this was the first time that women were given public employment, other than teaching, in Porto Rico" (Seabury 1908, 164).

By the 1950s, an English teacher in Mayagüez's CAAM commented on the new careers created by modernity and also shared his understanding of what he considered a contradiction between the desirability of education and employment and the "necessity" of a husband:

> ... in the schools there were proportionately many more women on the island in supervisory positions, such as principals and superintendents, than there were on the mainland.... There were also a large number of women, all married, teaching on the university level.... Puerto Rican women had been running things in their homes for a long time, and when they went into the schools they ran them too. [This] ... did not, however, solve the problems of raising daughters on the island. An education, a degree, was very nice, but in order to get a decent job you still had to be married. Society, the economy and the world might be changing, but in Mayaguez a major concern for a mother was still to find her daughter a husband. (Cooper 1994, 106)

"AT EVERY WAYSIDE BROOK, RIVER, AND STREAM": THE WASHERWOMEN

Of all the women who captured the attention of American male authors, the washerwoman is certainly the most commented on. Americans seemed to be captivated by the sturdy way in which they conducted their activity and described it in great detail:

> The laundresses carry on their vocation daily at every wayside brook, river, and stream. Barefooted and barelegged with skirts tucked up well out of reach of the water in which they stand, or by which they kneel ...

The American housewife, upon viewing the dazzling whiteness of the linen returned to her by the Porto Rican laundress, is unable to comprehend how such results can be attained with no better appliances than cold water and soap. The explanation lies in the fact that the linen is washed on three or four successive days, receiving each time a vigorous beating with a small wooden paddle.... After each cleansing the clothes are spread upon the ground to bleach for hours under a tropical sun. After the third or fourth washing the linen is starched and then dried again. (Seabury 1908, 31–32)

American soldier Charles Creager seemed so enthralled with the work done by Puerto Rican washerwomen that he explained it in all its facets, including the ironing and delivering of clean clothes. His description of the laboriousness of these humble women contrasts the allegations of "laziness" attributed to them:

The washerwomen of the city [Guayama] reaped a harvest of which they had never so much as dreamed. They had all they could do and more, but they kept at it night and day, determined to do all in their power for the comfort and convenience of the soldiers, and at the same time to earn a livelihood for themselves.... Their work, however, was entirely satisfactory, but their manner of selecting clothing and their persistency in getting it mixed up as to owners was the source of no little annoyance to their patrons.

There was no regular laundry in the city. All this work was done by women who took the clothing to the creek and there removed dirt and filth with the aid of soap, cold water, and hard work. The garments were each given a good coat of cocoa soap and then they were squeezed and beaten on rocks. There were no washboards used, such as American women use for that purpose, but these women squatted down in the middle of the stream and rubbed the clothing on the rocks with their hands or with corn cobs and smooth board paddles.

After they had been thoroughly cleansed in this way they were carefully rinsed and spread upon the clean pebbles to dry. During the process of drying, the women could take cocoanut shells of water and sprinkle them. This, with the aid of the bright sun, rendered every piece as immaculately spotless as when it left the store. Rio Guayama was literally lined with washerwomen during the entire stay of the soldiers at Guayama.

The process of ironing was much the same as that used in the states except that the irons were rude instruments to say the least, and that they were heated on charcoal burners. After the clothing had all been ironed and carefully folded, it was piled in a heap and delivered according to the memory of the one who had collected it.... The compromising feature of it all, was, that ten cents paid for the largest washing that could be delivered. Prices advanced later on, however, and it was an every-day occurrence for a soldier to pay fifty cents to get a shirt washed or go to the creek and do it yourself. (Creager 1899, 184–86)

William Dinwiddie described the return home of a washerwoman as if she had a stressless life of leisure and contentment:

After a long day's toil (it might as well be, perhaps, after a day of lazy dozing, but the Puertorriqueños work when they can), the women plod home in the dying sunlight, with swaying hips and stiff necks, carrying balanced on their heads, huge bundles of damp clothes, washed in the near-by river, which they throw in an empty corner of the hut for tomorrow's ironing.... and prepare the frugal meal for the family ... and welcomes the home-coming of a bare-footed, ragged, cotton-appareled husband, who wearily climbs the narrow, winding pathway.... The little children are already creeping into the house, to lie down in off corners for a night of dreamless slumber, clasping some morsel of food. (Dinwiddie 1899, 163)

THIS CHAPTER

Puerto Rican women mesmerized many American authors because of their attractive appearance. They were commonly sensualized and described as flirtatious. Moved by their Puritan background, with its strict codes of female behavior, they were quick to criticize Puerto Ricans for the use of makeup and other accessories. Still, some were happily surprised by the general fashion sense of even lower-class and elder women. Regarding working women, many accused them of a laziness that their own descriptions contradicted. They were also used as examples of the colonizers' "happy within poverty" theories even though they frequently recognized them as hard-working.

"BRIGHT-EYED LITTLE FELLOWS"

Puerto Rican Children

The selected books widely comment on Puerto Rican children's appearance and expressions. But the description of Puerto Rican children's lives made by William Dinwiddie in 1899 stands out because of its offensive tone and sarcasm and because it implied that children were cost-effective commodities for their families:

> Children are an ever present and abundant factor in the domestic economy of the peasant's life. . . . it costs nothing for their clothes, for they run about in the sunshine and the rain just as God made them, and sleep in odd corners without cover, for the first half-dozen years of their baby lives, while, when older, a single discarded, tattered garment adds to their natural grace the shield of decency. So they live, without expense and with little tenderness bestowed on them in the shape of material comforts, though the mother's kiss is often given, and the father taps the little head. They soon toddle, at the command of the mother, to do small errands, to help weed the garden, to bring in a handful of wood for the fire, to dig the tubers for a meager meal, and lastly to hold up their tiny hands and, with pleading eyes, gain a copper from the passer-by on the roadside. They are a good investment in the family; the majority of them die at an early age, and it costs but a few strained hours to the mother's heart, a bit of cloth for a shroud, and the energy needed to carry the tiny form to the potter's field. . . . at a varying age, they rebel against the paternal banker, and live for themselves, in poverty and in bondage to the landed kings, just as the generations who came before them. (Dinwiddie 1899, 159)

Following Dinwiddie's line of thought, a children's book author described Puerto Rican children as "happy" within their wretchedness. Her description raises the question: how did she know that they "want little"?

Children in Puerto Rico sleep on the floor or in a hammock, and they eat whenever or wherever they can find fruit or vegetables within their reach. Sometimes they smoke too. . . . They have no toys, no books, no pictures, no fine clothes or homes; yet, for all that, they are cheerful and contented. They have little, but they seem to want little. (George 1900, 32)

Several American soldiers developed more personal relations with the children, who tended to follow them around and offered to provide them with all kinds of services in exchange for some coins or ration food. As becomes evident from their stories, the soldiers enjoyed the submission of these poor children and referred to them as if the children were sorts of pets they kept for their own amusement. Some American soldiers enjoyed humiliating them by making them do "acrobatics" and "tricks" in exchange for the hardtacks they found repulsive, just as if these poor kids were dogs:

[In Aguadilla:] They overran the camp like a lot of flies on a piece of fly-paper as soon as we commenced to eat. We hugely enjoyed the stunts we made them go through with before we gave them a single morsel, by making them turn "back flips," hand-springs and all sort of antics. It was a sight such as would have pleased the professional taste of a circus man. . . . Fancy half a hundred brown or black urchins tumbling around on the ground, the troopers shouting around their approval to some youngster who was fairly turning himself inside out, to please the fastidious taste of the man who held a hardtack temptingly in mid air. The audience of approving natives, the majority of whom were the parents of these juvenile acrobats, were waiting to grab their offspring as soon as their arms or tin pails were filled with provender. (Oliver 1900, 200)

The 1899 Census confirmed to the American colonial authorities that Puerto Rico had a generally young population, which soon became the target of the Americanization campaign discussed in chapter 5: "The median age of Porto Rico is 18.1 years. [USA: 21.9; Cuba: 20.7] . . . the number of children under ten years of age is larger, in proportion to the population than in Cuba or the United States, or than any European country except Belgium" (Seabury 1908, 165–66).

Once modernity came into play and the colonial government began to enhance the quality of life of Puerto Ricans, the lives of children began to change, as well as the perception Americans had of them. In 1984, an American journalist described Puerto Rican children in a much favorable light:

> Perhaps because of the large family unit, the children all seem happy and have a great deal of security. Puerto Ricans show great affection for their children. They are pleasant, gay, young people. A group of children coming out of school at the end of a lesson period are all laughing and playing.... On a school bus a group of children, boys and girls, will chatter noisily. On a bus, a small girl or boy will give up his seat for an older person. Most of the children have this natural and pleasing politeness toward older people. (Samoiloff 1984, 164)

"A PIECE OF STICK FOR A HORSE": CHILDREN'S PLAY

Several American authors mentioned children's play. When the mentioned games require buying a ball, marbles, or a hoop, we can interpret that these games were played by elite children:

> Children do not have as good a time in that warm climate as in the States. They play pelota or ball, los trucos or marbles, they roll the aro or hoop. They are skillful with the cuerda, or skipping rope, and indulge in escondite and paso, the former of which is like our hide and seek, and the latter is the old game of parr. (Hamm, *Porto* 1899, 133)

Others may have been played by both elite and poor kids. In the case of poor kids, American observers generally used their own childhood games as parameter:

> The children have trinkets and playthings of the crudest character, and a naked baby boy is a happy youngster when riding a piece of stick for a horse, while his nude sister sits and fans herself, with haughty mien swaying a bit of palm-leaf. (Dinwiddie 1899, 160)

> ... nude children play and romp in the streets. The children are of all colors, from jet black to a creamy yellow, and all appear to be on a level of perfect equality. They are bright-eyed little fellows, but much more quiet than American children. They do not shout and laugh in their play, and as we drive by, they watch us demurely, often accosting us respectfully with "Buenos días, señor" (Good day, sir). Many of them

gave a lean and hungry look, with protruding stomachs . . . (Olivares, *Vol. 1* 1899, 371)

This anonymous book, obviously considering American country life as the best possible, suggested that Puerto Rican children were missing a lot of fun because they had no barns. All the rivers, mountains, and beaches were useless; they needed barns.

Porto Rico has no barns, we are told by an American visitor, and the vision of a barnless region, so far as sentiment is concerned, is not welcome. How much the children of that island had lost! No haymow sports; no hiding in fragrant recesses; no leaps into friendly depths of the harvest of the meadows; no rainy-day delights, shared with swallows darting in and out; no memories of such hours to give their pleasant sadness to later years. . . . A typical barn, duly stored with hay, with children to illustrate its capacity for giving space and suggestion of fun, would be an importation which boys and girls of the island would appreciate, especially in the rainy season. (*Greater America* 1900, 18)

"CLAD SIMPLY IN 'SUNSHINE AND A SMILE'": CHILDREN'S NUDITY

One of the constants in the descriptions of Puerto Rican small children is their nakedness. Almost every American commented on this, at least up to the 1960s. This is understandable if we consider the Puritan origins of the American system of values which considers nudity a source of "evil" conduct and thoughts, and clearly sinful in public.[1] In that society, shaming was a common source of punishment and determent, and American morality became forever interested in regulating total or partial nudity.

The nudity of Puerto Rican children was a sign of poverty. It is hard to imagine that Puerto Rican parents would not have preferred to have clothes and diapers for their babies and toddlers. But mothers of all times can attest to how costly these two are. Since infants and children grow fast, clothes only fit them briefly. And cloth diapers were very expensive, as well as extra work for the overburdened mothers. Peculiarly, this relationship between children's nudity and poverty is overlooked by most authors.

Frederick A. Ober saw Puerto Rican children's nudity in a benign way, part of the "happy within poverty" image that many writers portrayed: "The children . . . in their innocence, they see no harm in going naked; they are certainly free from the pruriency which attends the wearing of clothes; their forms are symmetrical, their health is generally good. . . . child life in the tropics . . . without any alloy of unhappiness" (Ober 1899, 167–68).

Other authors also took children's nakedness lightly and avoided mentioning poverty as its cause:

> In by-streets and open houses it is common to see children, ranging in age from mere infants to five and six years, wearing nothing but a birthday dress. . . . [With sarcasm:] The streets are full of future presidents and ladies of the White House—black, some of them, to be sure . . . Many of them wear little more than the garb with which nature endowed them . . . (Blythe 1911, 26, 160)

> The Indians went naked the year around, and today thousands of children do the same. They are clad simply in "sunshine and a smile" with occasionally a straw on the head. (Grose 1910, 173)

A few still commented on the children's partial nudity in the 1950s:

> The kids liked to come out and stare at us. . . . The little boys, staring wide-eyed and dressed only in white cotton underwear tops . . . and the little girls, all wearing white cotton underwear bottoms. . . . This was the normal dress for children in rural areas. This way they only had to wear one pair of underwear for two children, and decided that the reason the boys always wore the tops and the girls the bottoms was so they could show off the boys and hide the girls. (Cooper 1994, 42)

As explained before, American culture "was heavily influenced by Protestant values, which included chastity, modesty, and the link between sexuality and original sin."[2] Therefore, as expected, some other authors despised the practice of letting little children wander around naked from a moral point of view, even suggesting an alleged lewdness on the part of the older children that speaks more about their Puritan obsession with sex than about what was in the minds of Puerto Rican children:

> Owing no doubt to the low morality, as well as to the warm and enervating climate there is a certain immodesty throughout Porto Rico which makes a Northerner somewhat ill at ease for a week or so. Children play around absolutely nude. Lusty boys of seven and eight, pretty little girls of six and seven, wander about as did Adam and Eve in Eden. . . . The American officers . . . have succeeded in inducing a few thousand parents to put some raiment upon children between three and nine years

of age. How far the experiment will prevail is a nice question. (Hamm, *America's* 1899, 84)

"WITH THEIR PROTRUDING STOMACHS": MALNOURISHED CHILDREN

Despite their parents' best efforts, many children who lived in extreme poverty grew up with the telling symptoms of malnutrition. They shared the lack of a proper diet with their parents, but in their case, it became evident in their bloated stomachs, also called "banana stomachs," in all probability *Kwashiorkor*, a severe malnutrition symptom observed in children who lack protein in their diet.[3] An emotionally detached American soldier described a ghastly scene of malnourished children begging for food, just to end it with a comment on how much merry they got from these poor children:

> The children just swarmed over town like a lot of flies alighting on anything that was anyway edible.... with their protruding stomachs, large heads and thin legs and arms.... Just as soon as mess call sounded, they would be on hand to aid us in clearing away the grub. They resembled a troop of monkeys, as they squatted on the ground with the most solemn expression, and so totally unchild like that they were a pitiful sight. Their big brown eyes bulged out of their little, pinched, starved faces, as they watched our every mouthful. One puny arm encircled a tin can and the other hand busily scratching, while they waited for some morsels of food to be tossed at them.... These children were the source of so much merriment amongst us... (Oliver 1900, 159–60)

In the 1920s, as poverty became even worse than it had ever been under Spain, the existence of malnourished and "banana-bellied" children became unavoidable. At the time, Puerto Rican intellectual Nemesio R. Canales wrote: "Everywhere children with swollen bellies, without color or joy, will give you the horrendous sensation of a deformed childhood, of a decrepit childhood, in whose tender flesh anemia, malaria, tuberculosis are relentlessly fed..."[4] Still, a Baptist missionary took notice of their level of desperation:

> [In Adjuntas:] A woman has just left who wants to give me one of her little girls. Many offer me children, and one cannot wonder, when they are so plentiful, and food and clothing so scarce.
> [In Yauco:] ... There are famine sufferers even here. This afternoon in my stroll about town, I found a homeless, starving, sick boy gasping

in the deep, cobwebby doorway of a closed warehouse. I got milk and bread and fed him a little, and then hurried to the small hospital on the town's edge. (Duggan 1920, 45, 53)

In the 1930s, poverty became even more rampant after the capitalist exploitation of the workers kept its course during the Great Depression and after the terrible 1928 San Felipe hurricane. Once again, children faced malnutrition every day: "Incidentally, in the back country in Puerto Rico they use a very expressive phrase. If you ask a man how many there are in his family, instead of answering, for example, twelve people, he will reply, "Sir, I have twelve mouths." To him the feeding of his children is a constant problem" (Roosevelt Jr. 1937, 123).

Some American authors writing through the 1940s denounced the poor conditions in which Puerto Rican poor children were raised: "I saw children beaten by disease and on the verge of starvation, in slum dwellings—if you can call them dwellings—that make the hovels of Calcutta look healthy in comparison.... I found that infant mortality in Puerto Rico is the highest in the world, four times that of the United States" (Gunther 1940, 423–24).

In 1942, as a result of the war rationing and the U-boat blockade of the Caribbean, food became scarcer than ever before. In a humanitarian effort, the wife of then-American governor Rexford G. Tugwell, Grace F. Tugwell, organized four hundred stations where all children were welcomed to get one simple meal a day, all based on what was available: milk, oatmeal, and dried eggs. In his memoirs, Tugwell described the disturbing scene of the malnourished children who went to the stations:

> The children came at the appointed hour, sometimes alone, sometimes with older brothers or sisters, and stood in line with the heartbreaking obedience of malnourishment. Sometimes there were two or three hundred. When they were admitted they sat in expectant rows waiting for their glass or their bowl. The hunger of children is not a thing men like to see; it brings home too crudely our social failures. (Tugwell 1947, 430)

"NATURALLY BRIGHT AND ANXIOUS TO LEARN": PUERTO RICAN STUDENTS

According to the US Census of 1899, at the time, the Island had a total of 25,798 students who represented a low eighty percent of the population between five and seventeen years old.[5] Of these, 59.2 percent were boys and 40.8 percent were girls. Those classified as "white" were 67.9 percent, and those classified as "Black" were 32.1 percent.

In July 1898, Puerto Rico had 554 schools, and seven out of every eight were public. Of these, 380 were boys' schools, 138 were girls' schools, and twenty-six were high schools ("colegios de segunda enseñanza").[6] Although the schools were few and mostly urban, the 1899 US Census revealed that each school was in its own school building and "the reported seating capacity (29,164) was about 8% greater than the entire number of pupils (27,118)."[7] This meant that there was enough room and seats for all students. Also, the census identified 623 teachers (243 female and 375 male), which implies a ratio of 43.5 students per teacher, a ratio smaller than that recorded for schools of the Island in 1952–53 (49.5 students per teacher).[8]

The American colonial government began to transform the educational system following the American model of "secular, co-educational, graded school" in every town.[9] The teaching methods used during the Spanish colonial government were frequently criticized by American authors for not being modern or progressive:

> Formerly lessons never bothered the small Puerto Rican, or indeed any other Puerto Rican child. He played "hookey" all day long, and no truant officer disturbed him, or dragged him off to school. . . . He never saw a schoolhouse or the inside of a schoolroom. He never saw a book. But, for that matter, neither did his father or mother. They can neither read or write; nor can many of their neighbors. The buildings used for school purposes are seldom anything more than thatched huts. Sometimes two or three rooms are given to the school in the house where the teacher lives. . . . Arithmetic problems are often worked put on the floor with bits of clay.
>
> The pupils are bright and quick to learn, but there is no discipline in the classroom. They come and go as they please. They stay at home if they wish. . . . Their parents are careless and indifferent to the advantages of an education and make no efforts to induce their children to attend school, or to study. (George 1900, 31, 33–34)

At the time of the US invasion, Puerto Rican schools were gender-segregated. This was noted by a few American authors as a backward practice since it departed from the coed practice acquired[10] in the United States during the first half of the nineteenth century as a resurgence of evangelical Protestantism proposed that the new republic required educated women for their roles as mothers and missionaries of virtue. The practice began in the countryside, where the dispersion of population made the average class small; to ensure schools within reasonable walking distance for boys and girls, it was cheaper to have them share the scarce classrooms.

[Under Spain:] It was expected that when a boy reached the age of eight years he should go to a boys' school, and every girl to a girls' school. But this was not a law carried out and enforced. It is an index of many other conditions of the island to know that in the schools there is no association of the sexes, girls and boys being taught in different places altogether. Not only are there no mixed schools, but boys are always taught by men and girls by women teachers. The only exception to this is that children under five years go to mixed schools, and the teachers of those schools are women. (White 1898, 445–46)

Sometimes, Puerto Rican children were described as primitive and ignorant but as curious and willing to learn. Several authors recognized in them a sort of "natural smarts," a precondition for their future assimilation as Americans once they absorbed the fundamentals of "American civilization." Many American authors expressed a variety of accolades for Puerto Rican children:

If there is one thing more than another that strikes the visitor with surprise, it is the wonderful advance the native pupils of the average schools have made in the acquisition of English.... it is an admitted fact that the Puerto Rican children are remarkably bright and acquisitive. This is shown by the fact that they mastered in six months all the studies usually allotted for a year in the schools of their grade in the States. This precocity does not necessarily indicate a high degree of intelligence, but rather an aptitude for elementary learning. (Ober 1904, 251)

Teachers assert that the Porto Rican child is bright and intelligent, quick to understand and with great facility in memorizing. His imagination is surprisingly active, and he is naturally artistic. On the other hand, he lacks energy, both mental and physical. It could hardly be otherwise, in view of the unhygienic conditions, and the absence of proper food and clothing under which not only the child but his ancestors for several generations, have existed. (Guernsey 1907, 63)

Some American authors even considered Puerto Rican students as better and/or smarter than American ones:

One will be surprised to see what clean, bright-faced children come out of the dreary, filthy homes. And then, there are no more alert learners in the world than the Porto Rican children. They are quicker in perception and appreciation than the children in the States, though possibly more superficial and showy... (Wilson 1905, 135)

Here is something that will surprise the boy and girl readers of this book: Every teacher who has had experience both in the United States and Porto Rico said that he preferred to teach the Porto Rican children. The teachers explained that the children of Porto Rico seemed more eager to learn than children of the United States, and that they are even brighter. (Boyce 1914, 440)

Sadly, the reality of poverty dictated that many Puerto Rican students could not complete more than a couple of years of education since their parents needed them to work in the fields driving oxen or planting crops, or in workshops for a wage in order to increase the family income or to stay at home to take care of the smaller children of the family while the mothers worked for a wage. Indeed, the 1899 US Census revealed that "the average attendance was only about four sevenths [4/7] of the pupils enrolled."[11] This was mentioned by several American authors, although a journalist represented this situation, clearly fueled by poverty, as allegedly the result of parental abuse:

> ... the attendance is constantly broken by the necessity, or pretext, that the little ones must assist the parents to earn a living.... under tropical suns, it is much easier for indolent parents to command the children to bear the brunt of the daily work to do it themselves, that it is only by the persevering effort of the children themselves, who look upon school as a happy recreation, that they ever get within the doors of the educational edifices. Under these harrowing conditions ... the great majority of them never acquire more than the merest smattering. (Dinwiddie 1899, 201)

On the other hand, an American missionary recognized the incredible sacrifices that many parents made in order to send their children to school. The following anecdotes touch the heart, as they are shared with the particular sensibility of female missionaries:

> The poor people of Porto Rico are making unusual sacrifices to educate their children. No compulsory law is necessary. Attendance is higher in percentage that in any State of the Union except Massachusetts, which State exceeds Porto Rico only by one per cent. Hundreds of children carry their shoes and stockings to and from school in their arms. It is a common experience to see the pupils at dismissal leave the school, sit down by the roadside, remove shoes and stockings and climb rugged and jagged mountain trails barefooted to save the shoes and thus prolong

their use. I know women who sit on the river rocks all day and every day washing clothes to keep their children in school.

In a mountain district above Corozal a boy was found in school wearing a peculiar shirt—at least four times his size. Upon inquiry it was learned that the boy had only one shirt and that one was being washed. That the boy might not miss a day in school his father gave the son his only shirt. The father that day, naked to the waist, carried a case of merchandise on his head over the mountains, under the palms, in a fierce tropic sun, a distance of twenty miles and return, that his son might learn.

At Juncos I saw a boy in school who was unusually self-conscious and who, in moving about from class to seat, never turned his back to me. Inquiry of the teacher told the story.... my teacher-friend's explanation led me to watch. As the boy passed out I saw that all the shirt he had in this world was on the front of his body! Hiding the shame of his poverty, there he was in school, dressed only in a pair of tattered trousers and half a shirt. He was to me a genuine little patriot... (Guernsey 1903, 127–28)

A few other American writers also recognized the enormous sacrifices that the children, and sometimes their parents, made in order to get an education:

The eagerness of the children to learn is shown by the fact that some of them walk between two and three miles to school every day. Many of them bring chairs, benches, boxes, anything that will serve as a seat.... Hundreds of boys and girls carry their shoes and stockings to and from school in their hands. (Seabury 1908, 173, 175)

A number of the children even take their lessons home with them at night, and by the light of a flickering, crazy little torch lamp they teach their parents what they have learned through the day.... and you should just hear them review their Bible lessons! (Blythe 1911, 168)

Without proper nutrition, students could not perform at their best in school, even though they had the intelligence and the curiosity to excel academically. Some American authors realized it:

The state of the children is pathetic in the extreme.... The children are naturally bright and anxious to learn. As soon as our Government made opportunities for them to attend school they accepted them eagerly. But the great majority showed plainly that they were suffering from lack of food and hygienic neglect. They did not go to school with a hop, skip and jump, laughing and shouting in their glee, as our little ones do.

They were unnaturally quiet and demure in their manner, with an ever-present look of hunger in their little eyes . . . (Olivares, *Vol. 1* 1899, 333)

Under the American colonial government, school hours increased, and school supplies became available:

School hours are from eight to eleven in the forenoon, and from one to four in the afternoon. There is no weekly holiday; school is in session every day except Sunday. Twice a year there are fifteen days' vacation. . . . The children are eager to learn, and supplies of all kinds are provided, including blackboards, charts, books, paper, pencils, and maps. Each teacher has about fifty pupils under his care. . . . The American flag now floats over every schoolhouse and is found in every schoolroom. (Seabury 1908, 168, 170–71)

Puerto Rican children of newly converted Protestant families attended Sunday school. There, the missionaries tried to teach them new cultural values that sometimes contradicted those they had learned at home. Due to the cultural differences, misunderstandings were common, as shown in the anecdote of a young missionary who offered a party for her Sunday school students at her home, only to face the innocent and candid comments of the students regarding her lemonade; evidently, she was not prepared for their honesty:

I invited about 75 small children of the Sunday school . . . making cookies for them . . . making lemonade . . . If you want to hear at the exact truth concerning what they think of a thing, trust children to give it to you. . . . These children certainly did give me their unvarnished opinions of my refreshments. . . . they said the lemonade was nasty—which it certainly was for I had put pounds and pounds of sugar into it; but I didn't like to be told so by 75 uppish little noses. (Blythe 1911, 90–91)

School children were frequently represented as the promise of a future Americanized Puerto Rican: ". . . the promise is safe, that out of the childhood of the island, if intelligently directed, will arise a citizenship imbued with the impulse and aspirations of a new and fairer civilization" (Wilson 1905, 135). But in 1908, a young American missionary questioned if the Americanization campaign was fair to Puerto Rican children or if it even had any chances of success: "I have always had my doubts as to the justice and the success of the prevailing method of teaching here, for neither Porto Rican nor American teachers are supposed to use anything but English in the classes above the second grade" (Blythe 1911, 189).

In 1914, an American travel writer blamed the Spanish culture acquired at home for the slowing of the Americanization process, which in his estimation was going to last "at least two generations" since Puerto Rican students reverted to their culture whenever at home, as had happened with Native Americans students forced to attend assimilating schools in the United States:

> The greatest tumbling block is the home life. Just as many Carlisle Indian students[12] revert to their blankets and ancestral ways on returning to the reservation, the schoolchildren of Porto Rico drop back to their Spanish civilization at home. How we are to graft what is best in American life to this Spanish stock and make it grow is going to be a difficult question to answer.... It will take at least two generations, in my opinion, to accustom these people to the things in our American civilization which make for comfort and broad culture. Of course, I am referring to the masses. (Boyce 1914, 443)

Although the American colonial government spent millions of dollars in enhancing the education system, by the 1940s, the lack of classroom materials was documented by an American teacher apparently unaware that he was criticizing his own American government:

> [At Juan Morel Campos School in Ponce:] There were sixty-odd children in the room, ranging in age from eleven to twenty-three. There were about forty-five seats; so many of the children had to double up. Most of the seats and desks were broken and only a few were attached securely to the floor. Fully grown boys straddled desks meant for five-year-olds. I scrabbled through the drawers of my desk, looking for chalk, pencils, papers, books—anything I could use. Save for odds and ends of paper, a set of the previous year's report cards, two rusted razor blades, the drawers were empty.... Suddenly ... I broke into laughter. [After asking the principal for chalk, he answered,] ..."The Puerto Rican teachers can get along with nothing. Why shouldn't you?" (Brown 1945, 31–32)

Only one American author, Jim Cooper, taught English at the college level, specifically at the then-called College of Agriculture and Mechanic Arts (the Colegio, or CAAM), from 1951 to 1954. His comments regarding his students' behavior in the classroom can give us an idea of the way they learned to behave at school. One of the complaints of Mister Cooper, as he was called to his displeasure, was the lack of discipline of the students, at least from his American point of view:

It must be kept in mind that, in all the classes, there were only about two thirds of the students in the classroom at one time. The other walked in and out of the room at will . . . chattered with their friends in the hall and went to the water fountain or the toilets. The commonest excuses for missing classes or tests were, of course, the deaths of relatives, or the coming and going of relatives to New York. One of the teachers announced during the first class every semester that only two grandmothers were allowed to die each semester. (Cooper 1994, 21, 87)

The constant talking in the classrooms, as well as the frequent absences of children between the fifth and ninth grades due to a variety of causes ("rain, illness, keeping children home to work, and lack of shoes and clothes") were reported in David Landy's research.[13] Lanny Thompson argued that the requirement of absolute obedience aimed at producing "subjects domesticated in body and mind" who "would police themselves."[14]

The most fascinating experience narrated by Cooper was his original frustration when he noticed how Puerto Rican college students "cheated" in his exams and his personal process of analyzing and finally understanding that the so-called "cheating" was actually a collaboration among students traditionally fostered by their Puerto Rican teachers. He then realized another fundamental cultural difference: the emphasis on collaboration instead of on competition:

> Cheating goes on in all schools everywhere, of course, but I had never seen it done as openly and outrageously as it was in Puerto Rico. Also, as with so many things at the Colegio, one's definition and understanding of what was and was not cheating depended in great part on one's cultural background. When I started asking students why they were looking at another student's paper during an exam, they replied with no embarrassment, "Because I don't know the answer, and maybe he does." If I asked the other student why he let him look at his paper, I got some such answer as, "But I'm just trying to help him. He's my friend." "But this is an examination." "I know. That's why I'm helping him, so he'll get a better grade. Don't you think you should help your friends?"
>
> It was during the second year . . . that I began to understand the student's attitudes. Starting in the first grade in Puerto Rican schools, teachers tell students to look at their neighbor's paper if they don't know the answer. They are encouraged to help and get help from their friends and neighbors. This attitude infuriated one or two of the new continental English teachers.
>
> The problem was, of course, much more complicated than that, and it was tied up with a very basic fact of Puerto Rican life. From earliest

childhood, they were taught to be cooperative, not competitive. This was in great contrast to the attitudes taught in a great many if not most American families and schools. Often classrooms are run like athletic teams. You are in competition not only with your classmates but with the students in other classes and the students in other schools. The way to win, to get ahead is to beat out the others, your competition, so you get the prize, the gold star, your name on the honors list. It's the attitude summed up by the old army expression, "I've got mine."

A Puerto Rican student will let his neighbor look at his test paper because he wants to help him get a good grade. An American student will hide his paper from his neighbor because he is only interested in getting a good grade himself and certainly is not out to help what he thinks of as a competitor, a rival.... In the schools on the island, with over forty students in a classroom, no substitute teachers, and where all the students would be passed on, no matter what, simply to make room for the masses of children coming up from the lower grades, this "helping" certainly makes sense. To suddenly change the system and all the signals the first few months at a college or university is an almost impossible thing to do.

The real problem I discovered was in trying to explain to the students that, yes it was a good thing to help your friends, but that you should not help them on an exam. But when the students learned that the exams really counted and that they would not automatically pass a course, my logic was incomprehensible. Shouldn't you help your friend when he really needs help? (Cooper 1994, 79–81)

Jim Cooper also realized that Puerto Rican personalism, in which relationships are more important than any other consideration, likewise applied to teacher-student relationships. This realization complicated his grading practices when his Puerto Rican students interpreted a bad grade as a personal rejection:

"Teacher, what grade did you give me?"
"I didn't <u>give</u> you a grade. You <u>earned</u> one.... I'm sorry but you're only getting a D."
"Why don't you like me?"
"I do like you."
"Then why didn't you give me a good grade?"
"Because you didn't earn a good grade."
"Yes, but my English is very poor. I can't write English."
"I know you can't. That's why you're getting a D."

> ...What these conversations always came down to in the final analysis was the inability to understand how you could give a bad grade, not to mention, a failing grade to someone you liked. (Cooper 1994, 83–84)

"IN BOXES OR ON DOOR-STEPS": STREET CHILDREN

Wayward children were assumed to be the result of inappropriate parental supervision and/or illegitimacy.[15] Even before the US invasion, "street children" ("niños de la calle") became an obstacle to the modernization of Puerto Rico and were characterized with epithets such as "tramps, ragamuffins, abandoned and delinquent" that the government must intervene with.[16] Some American missionaries commented about their prevalence in the 1900s: "And there are thousands of little ones ... orphaned waifs, picking up food and shelter as best they may. Sometimes they become servants in families of the well-to-do, but this is often a pitiable lot, for they are treated as slaves. Their food is a pan or cocoanut shell of rice or beans, which they sit upon the kitchen floor to eat" (Guernsey 1907, 60–61).

The wayward children jeopardized the future of prosperity and progress planned for the Island as they were expected to turn into the criminals and unproductive people of the future. To prevent that, in 1908, the US colonial government inaugurated Puerto Rico's first youth correctional institution for minors under sixteen: the Industrial School or Reformatory School of Mayaguez.[17] And in 1915, the first special court for the prosecution of minors was created in Puerto Rico.[18] It ended up caring for orphaned or mistreated children, undisciplined children, and young criminals.

Many street children were lower-class children who worked as street peddlers or in other capacities in order to supplement their families' income, although a few could have been homeless kids. Since under the US colonial government, their education became a priority, new regulations were passed to secure their attendance to school, at least up to the third grade, whenever possible. It is significant that orphans' education was not protected by the law. An American explorer explained in 1914:

> A law was passed ... no child under 14 ... who has not received a certificate of the department of education to the effect that he has finished ... third grade of the rural or the eighth grade of the graded schools ... can be employed in any lucrative occupation during the hours public schools are in session. Exception is made ... children who reside in a community in which there is no school within a reasonable distance ... and of any orphan child ... as well as any child whose parents are

invalids and dependent exclusively on the work of the child . . . These children are, nevertheless, required to attend a night school [if available within one kilometer of their residence]. (Verrill 1914, 195)

In 1917, an American rural sociologist discussed the homeless children's situation as a public security issue as he associated them with criminal activity, although without evidencing his assertion. Fred K. Fleagle identified its causes as being born in consensual marriages, poverty, and homelessness, which, in his view, besides causing criminal behavior, also generated weak-mindedness and insanity. These children were "a danger to the security of the community" as they were propagators of more generations mirroring their homelessness, poverty, and degeneration. But Fleagle seemed relieved by the "fact" that these street children had a high death rate:

According to the last report of the Insular Chief of Police, it is estimated . . . at the present time about 10,000 homeless children under 12 . . . who live by whatever means they are able, many of them begging or stealing . . . sleeping at night in boxes or on doorsteps . . . These children are, for the most part, deserted and abandoned children of illegitimate parentage, or orphan children . . . and they constitute a fertile soil for the implanting of criminal tendencies . . . They constitute a danger to the security of the community, and if it were not for the relatively high death rate that is found among people of this class, the Island would soon be overrun by citizens brought up under these criminal-forming conditions. (Fleagle 1917, 32–33)

Children's work remained legal until 1921, when a working permit was required to restrict the places of work and working hours since they had to go to school, too.[19] By 1930, 27.5 percent of Puerto Rican children between ten and fifteen were employed. Several American authors described with interest their encounters with children who worked as peddlers in the streets of the Island. In 1938, an American journalist claimed that these children committed petite crimes in order to be housed at the Correctional School of Mayaguez, knowing that there they would be fed and housed:

. . . not only does residence in the school carry no odium to the boys thereafter, but that youngsters seek the privilege of confinement, as an opportunity to be well housed and fed, and well taught in something that will be of value. Indeed, boys are commonly known to seek admission by the committing of some small offense which will gain that reward for them, and to falsify their age so as to confront no barrier to their aspirations. (White 1938, 129)

Earl Parker Hanson commented on Puerto Rican children's "gangs" during the Depression: "... starvation was found everywhere.... Most of the cities were infested by "wolf gangs" of children ranging in ages from six to sixteen, many of whom had no idea of who their parents were. They pilfered and robbed ... They slept where they could ... The authorities could not cope with them ..." (Hanson 1960, 77).

Hanson also made an outrageous and unverifiable (after in-depth research on the mentioned Chillicothe Reform School in Ohio) allegation regarding these children, a comment that seemed to be an "urban legend" imported from the United States:

> Teenagers were for a time successful in a special racket. They entered post offices and smashed boxes—always before witnesses. As mailboxes were federal property, they were then tried in the federal court and sentenced to the federal reform school in Chillicothe, Ohio. When one of them was sentenced, his family called in all the neighbors for a celebration that could not have been more joyful if he had won an appointment to West Point. He was going to a place where, for a number of years, he would get an education, learn English, learn a trade, and enjoy free food, clothing and housing. The crime wave stopped when the federal judge caught on to what was happening and stopped sending Puerto Rican boys to Chillicothe. (Hanson 1960, 77–78)

THIS CHAPTER

Since the very beginning of the American colonization of Puerto Rico, its children became targets for Americanization. Two aspects surprised Americans the most: the nudity of the youngest, and their hunger. Their nude bodies were seen as evil or lewd; their hunger was frequently faced with abuse and laughter, especially their bloated stomachs.

In schools, where they were to be Americanized, these malnourished children earned the respect of their American teachers who were surprised by their brightness and curiosity. And when they abandoned school after a few years due to their poverty, their parents were blamed as "bad parents." These children were meant to symbolize the prosperous future of this American paradise, and when they did not fit this profile, they were considered "dangerous," criminalized and put away from sight.

Chapter 17

"THEY WANT RICE AND BEANS FIRST"

Food, Drinks, and Smokes

The consumption of food, drinks, and smokes have served as a point of encounter for different cultures since immemorial times. It has integrated economies and have piqued curiosities. During the second half of the nineteenth century, the United States was the scenario for a phenomenal economic transformation of life through fast industrialization, an outstanding development that changed how Americans related to their food. As faster transportation was made possible through the invention of railroads and steamships, Americans who used to eat locally raised foodstuffs, now were able to eat food from other parts of the country or of the world, as long as they could afford them.[1] Interest in tasting new foods from other cultures began to develop but, sadly, the interest in and acceptance of the new food did not translate into respect for those who harvested or cooked it.

American authors' attitudes about Puerto Rican food were very diverse. Some embraced and celebrated it; others suffered it. The authors seemed to consider it either too flavorful, too heavy on the stomach, or too bland:

> Puerto Rican cookery is at first a disappointment to an American visitor. The use of olive oil instead of butter, the liberality displayed toward onions, shallots, garlic and chilies, the prodigality of spices and condiments, the perpetual cooking of fruit instead of their service raw, are in the beginning novel and oftentimes unpleasant. (Hamm, *Porto* 1899, 139)

> The food is rarely "hot," but it is spicy, relying on oregano, coriander, sweet pepper, onion, and garlic. If these do not dominate, then sugar will be in quantities that are hard to comprehend until you . . . watch the customers open three, four, even five envelopes of sugar for one expresso-sized coffee cup. . . . There are so few good restaurants out on the island

that you are usually better off going to any hotel's dining room instead of wandering in search of better fare. (Rand, A. 1973, 110, 120)

But those Americans who stayed on the Island for longer periods, such as Kal Wagenheim, provided a much more appreciative description of Puerto Rican dishes:

> ... the typical meal.... For breakfast, eggs (usually boiled or fried), American cereals, coffee, and toast are common. But for lunch and dinner, rice and beans comprise the nucleus of the meal, in combination with meat or poultry. The plátano [plantain] ... and the guineo [banana] ... are also mainstays in Puerto Rican cuisine.... Typical country staples are starchy roots, such as the batata [sweet potato] ... the yautia [yauthia] ... the ñame [yam] ... the calabash, and the eggplant. Another traditional favorite is bacalao ... who is served stewed with vegetables, in an omelet, or in a vegetable salad platter known as the serenata. Fresh fish is not too common.... Lechón asado [roasted pig][2] ... is indispensable at Christmas or for other special occasions.... The pig ... is popular on island cuisine. In addition to pork chops and pig's feet, there are: cuchifrito, a mixed stew of pig innards; mondongo, pork tripe cut into tiny pieces and stewed in a sofrito; gandinga, chopped pork liver, heart, and kidney, cooked with various condiments.... Other favorites are arroz con pollo ... asopao ... pastel ... Sancocho ... mofongo ... alcapurria ... carne mechada ... biftec ... is thinner and tougher than American cuts, but tasty.... The most popular snacks are fritters: bacalaito ... pastellillos ... rellenos de papa.... Puerto Rico's more ubiquitous dessert is flan ... (Wagenheim 1970, 181–82)

Different kinds of food were described in comparison with American food and cooking practices, with each author discussing those they considered more interesting:

> ... The fish market is very rich ... The natives, nevertheless, prefer salted or smoked codfish or codfish cured with rock salt ... This is known as bacalao, and is found in every table from the captain general's, to the poorest Jibaro.... Various kinds of pies, called empanadas, are another feature. They correspond to the vol-au-vents of the French cuisine, and the noble meat pies of England. These empanadas are excellent when served hot from the kitchen, and also make capital cold dishes the next day. (Hamm, *Porto* 1899, 141, 143, 146–49)

As a general rule, the Puerto Rican does not eat green vegetables. To him such foods as lettuce and carrots are "yerba (grass)," and unfit for human beings. He much prefers rice and beans and bread and coffee. (Morton 1949, 91)

The standards of cleanliness in the kitchen were also different and a frequent source of worry and distrust. For a newlywed missionary, dealing with a Puerto Rican cook was a big challenge since she didn't trust the cleanliness of her cook's kitchen habits, as she complained in her letters:

I'm starving by inches, for I just cannot eat Carmela's soup when I am perfectly certain that she cooked it in the dish-pan or something of equal rank and dignity, and that she didn't wash the meat, and that she has sampled it over and over to make sure that it is perfectly palatable. Poor faithful Carmela! She religiously serves me this stuff three times a day, which I do thrice refuse, and each time she returns looking just a little bit more injured. (Blythe 1911, 43)

During the nineteenth century, Americans became habituated to the consumption of white bread made of white flour produced in new automated mills; by 1900, they were consuming two hundred pounds of wheat per person per year.[3] Because of this they soon noticed the Puerto Rican bread and seemed to enjoy it. In Puerto Rico, still to this day, there are bakeries ("panaderías") in every neighborhood and they all offer "pan de agua" (water bread) and "pan sobao" or "pan de manteca" (lard bread).

Great attention is paid to bread and pastry. The common form is the so-called Spanish bread, which is a load or stick from a quarter and an inch to an inch in diameter, and three or four feet long. A feature of this style of loaf is that it is all crust, and no crumbs, and that when eaten by invalids or dyspeptics it never sours or ferments in the stomach. (Hamm, *Porto* 1899, 143)

In the United States, up to the 1920s, Italian immigrants were criticized for their "fondness for garlic, which was deemed too pungent by those used to blander cooking styles."[4] Similarly, complaints about the generous use of garlic in Puerto Rican cooking were quite common: "As to food ... everything floats in lard, garlic abounds in the most innocent-looking dishes, and the menu is like the laws of the Medes and the Persians. I am afraid my missionary zeal will not survive many weeks of this" (Blythe 1911, 51).

Plantains are starchy banana-like fruits that must be cooked before being eaten. Like bananas, they belong to the species *Musa X paradisiaca*, are native to Asia, and arrived in Puerto Rico from Africa, along with enslaved Africans.[5] Puerto Ricans eat it fried, boiled, or roasted in a variety of plates. They baffled many American authors since they couldn't understand these "strange bananas" which were cooked while green-colored as a staple for the poor:

> The banana and its twin brother, the plantain, are favorite subjects of culinary science. Banana fritas are the Porto Rican equivalent of the familiar fritters of our country, but they are usually cooked in much hotter grease or oil, and so are very crisp on the outside.... huevos con bananas, in which the bananas are fried, the eggs hard-boiled and cut into long, thin slices, and placed between the slices of the fruit. (Hamm, *Porto* 1899, 144)

Regarding meat, pork, poultry, and fish, authors commented on the difference in their use and quality as follows:

> The first thing that will strike you is the absence of mutton and lamb. About the only meat that you will see offered for sale is beef and pork... The Porto Ricans eat but little meat, and the little that they do eat is principally beef.... cut and sold in chunks ... There are only two kinds of meat—meat with bones and meat without bones... They have no cold storage plants, and the meat has to be eaten the same day it is killed. Naturally it is tough and unpalatable to Americans ... The people consume a great deal of dried beef which is brought from Venezuela and other South and Central American markets. It is as salty as brine and is cooked and served in various kinds of stews with rice.... No hog is allowed to run loose in the island. They are tethered with ropes around the neck ... Hog-killing time is a festive season in the country, just as it used to be with us. When one is to be killed the neighbors come in and help, and all have a grand feast.... Turkeys are not as popular with the Porto Ricans as they are with us, and they sell for much less, in proportion, than chickens do. (Olivares, *Vol. 1* 1899, 3363–65)

The fact that white short-grain rice and stewed beans were staple food, even in elite households, became evident when, in the summer of 1902, a group of Puerto Rican teachers spent four weeks in the United States taking courses at Harvard and Cornell Universities: "Then there was the near mutiny in Boston because the food was not satisfactory—there was a lack of beans! Only by introducing a chef who cooked beans in Puerto Rican style was this revolt quelled" (Lord 2004, 50).

Governor Rexford G. Tugwell recorded in his diary the dangerous situation in 1942 when, as part of their World War II operations, German submarines blockaded the Caribbean Sea entrances,[6] making it impossible to import rice, beans, and cod:

> . . . by fall we should have a betraying exhaustion of rice and of beans, the foods all islanders eat every day—poor and rich, they want rice and beans first, and only afterward whatever else is available! Next, of course, bacalao (dried fish) which is the poor man's substitute for meat and is used for flavoring the rice. These three are the favored ingredients of the daily dish eaten by nine-tenths of the workers in Puerto Rico as many times a day as they can be afforded. (Tugwell 1947, 242)

Modernity arrived over time, and by the 1960s, food preferences had changed to incorporate many American foods. Still, rice and beans and roasted pork remained the favorite:

> The Puerto Ricans enjoy many native foods, but they also like the food introduced from the States. . . . Hamburgers and steaks, served with French-fried potatoes, are now favorite foods in Puerto Rico. (McGuire 1963, 84)

> Rice is a staple in Puerto Rican diet. Rice and beans are a traditional dish. . . . A pig roasted outdoors on a spit is essential for any party. (Samoiloff 1984, 173–75)

"SERVED IN COURSES": THE ELITE TABLE

Most Americans described the food they consumed at hotels or elite residences where they were guests. We can easily see how food habits differed. Breakfast was considered too simple for American taste:

> . . . the early morning meal as offered to guests of the hotel [Hotel France in Ponce], was not a real breakfast, but merely coffee. Now, that doesn't mean, as it does in other countries, coffee and rolls, or coffee and boiled eggs, or coffee and toast and bacon, but actually only a cup of black coffee or coffee and hot milk. It is true that the American visitors, after an effort, established the precedent that they could have boiled eggs

and bread and even sometimes a banana, but the innovation was not approved by the people of Puerto Rico, who looked on and marveled that one could eat so heartily at such a time of day. (White 1898, 409)

An early visitor wrote that dinner "is the meal of the day, and is eaten between six and seven o'clock. This is the native's only full, heavy meal, and this fact may account for his ability to eat a quantity of food which leaves the average American a victim to indigestion and remorse" (Dinwiddie 1899, 153). But an American missionary seemed to consider the Puerto Rican dinner menu quite boring:

> The different meals are about the same as on the continent of Europe. Bread and coffee in the morning, meat breakfast between eleven and twelve, and dinner about six or seven in the evening. Dinner is the one full meal of the day . . . is served in courses. Soup, fritters, two or three kinds of meat, rice, red beans, salads, dessert, fruit, coffee and wine is an average dinner. There is no fixed order in the serving of the courses so that one is not sure what article of food comes next. . . . There is a marked sameness in the bill of fare week after week. (Fowles 1910, 36)

War correspondent Margherita A. Hamm offered the most detailed description of the lavish eating habits of the Puerto Ricans of the higher classes. It is noticeable that she called plantains "bananas" and that she made distinctions between "working people" and "wealthy people." The unending list of options makes one wonder how many cooks were needed for such feasts:

> In social life the first meal is an early breakfast, known as the desayuno. In its simplest form it consists of a large bowl of coffee, sugar and condensed milk. With working people a piece of bread and cheese, a raw onion, and a fruit are added to the coffee. Among the well-to-do the coffee is reinforced with biscuits, rolls, fruit, and sometimes a little cold fish or meat. It is served between 6 and 8 o'clock in the morning, the working people taking it at the former hour, the wealthy people at the later hour, and usually in bed.
> The next regular meal is a second breakfast, known as the almuerzo.[7] This meal is unlike anything in American social life, and ranges from the French "dejeuner a la fourchette" to the tiffin of the far East. It is a generous, substantial meal, with several or many courses, and cooked and served with the same care and skill as dinner. At one house the bill of fare consisted of an omelet for the first course, some delicious fried fish

for the second, and some broiled chicken for the third. There was fruit in epergnes from which the guests helped themselves as they pleased. There were also three dolces or sweetmeats, one being a guava paste, which is brown, and about as hard as cream bonbons, a second being a pineapple jam of about the same consistency of Scotch orange marmalade, and the third being a compote or macedoine of stewed fruits in honey.

Another almuerzo began with the waiter bringing a large tray on which were dishes containing sliced Vic sausage, sardines, tuna fish in oil, radishes, olives and cold sliced meat, spiced or seasoned. Each guest helped herself to as many of these appetizers as she desired, and ate them with some excellent bread. There was canned butter on the table, but no one excepting one American used it. It must have been too rich for the Yankee palate, because he did not try it a second time, nor finish the piece put upon his plate. Then came several hot dishes, including a Spanish omelet, a very nice hash made of mutton, green chilies, onion and tomato, and some chops which were not broiled but fried. These were cooked with bananas, making a very agreeable combination. The next part of the meal consisted of cold dishes, and included a Spanish salad, in which there was very little meat, and a bewildering variety of vegetables. I noticed lettuce, chicory, onion, shallot, green and red chilies, parsley, and queerest of all, spearmint. The dressing was a French dressing, but the pepper was reinforced by cayenne, and, I think, a little mustard. It was a novel mixture, but it can be commended both for palatability and health.

In some homes a light luncheon, known as merienda, is served, but more frequently coffee and biscuits, and a piece of fruit take the place of a regular meal.... Another off tropical beverage is tea, in which has been steeped a spray of lemon verbena. The intense perfume of that popular flower communicates itself to the hot fluid, and makes it about the most odorous drink imaginable.

Comida or dinner is the big meal of the day, and is served anywhere from 5 to 8 o'clock. It is a course dinner, but not so elaborate and many-numbered as the French "table d'hote," nor so heavy and simple as the English meal. There is a soup which is always rich and appetizing.... Of these the more prominent are the black bean soup, the shrimp soup, and the dish known as "old clothes," rojo viejo. The next course of the dinner is an "entrée" or made dish, of which the favorite specimen is chicken and rice prepared very much like the pilau of the Mediterranean. The third course is a highly flavored stew of veal or pork cutlet, and as if to show the pressure of the Anglo Saxon, a biftek, in which mutilated word it is still easy to see the wholesome English word beefsteak. Then follows a dessert, both hot and cold fruits, cheese and coffee. Dinner and second breakfast are washed down with Spanish wine, or, when the homes are well-to-do, with the vintages of France.

... Late in the evening a cena or supper is served, which is sometimes replaced by a tea, consisting of a cup of tea, a piece of toast, a biscuit, or a sweet cake. Some Spanish "bon vivants" add a wineglass of arrack or other liqueur to their tea as a sort of nightcap. (Hamm, *Porto* 1899, 102–5, 107)

As if all these details were not enough, Hamm proceeded to describe the table decoration and etiquette in Puerto Rico:

The dining room is always decorated with good taste, the table linen is usually embroidered, the glass and china are of the best quality. The knives are shaped more like a dagger than the silver-plated ware of the United States. They have good strong steel blades, and ivory or mother-of-pearl handles. An odd feature is in serving the various foods hot and cold. They are placed, no matter whether animal or vegetable, in one dish of china, porcelain, earthenware or metal, and this in turn is placed in a larger second one. Whether this is done to prevent the dripping or overflow of contents upon the tablecloth, or to keep the heat in the hot dishes, is impossible to ascertain. There is a more lavish use of plates than in other countries. The dinner plate is small. . . . The rule is to put only one thing, and comparatively little of that, upon one plate. This is carried so far that where lamb chops, fried potatoes, and small stuffed tomatoes are served, the guest will put a tiny chop upon one plate, three potatoes, or rather three slices of potatoes, upon a second, and a tomato smaller than an egg upon a third. (Hamm, *Porto* 1899, 105–6)

Finally, Hamm described what can be called "the finger cleaning ceremony":

Most extraordinary of all is the finger-bowl service. This is a ceremony which is almost as good as a play. When done in proper style in the best houses, the silver man brings a silver salver on which is a beautiful linen doily. Upon this rests a dark-colored finger bowl, one-third filled with cold water. In the finger bowl stands a tall wineglass filled with perfumed water, the perfume being orange-flower water, rose water, tincture of benzoin, or a few drops of myrrh. Alongside of the bowl are three wooden toothpicks, a slice of lemon, and two medium-sized napkins.

The guest removes the wineglass from the bowl, and puts it on one of the napkins on the table alongside of the salver. He then, using the lemon as a piece of soap, washes both hands in the finger bowl, and dries them with the second napkin, which is placed to the left of the salver. He then moves the wineglass nearer, covers his mouth with the first napkin, uses one or all of the toothpicks, rinses his mouth with the perfumed water, ejects into the bowl under cover of the napkin, then wipes the mustache and lower face with the linen, and lays it over the bowl and wineglass. (Hamm, *Porto* 1899, 106)

Regarding table settings, William Dinwiddie commented, not without highlighting some bad table manners:

The positions of honor at a dinner-table are, among the older and non-traveled residents, in the following order: the head of the table to the most distinguished guest; the rest, in the order of their rank and importance, ranged around to the right, the host occupying the last seat after his guests. The women sit at the left of the table, all together. Among the more cultured classes, the host occupies the head, the hostess the foot, the places of honor being the seats to the right and left of the host.... Dinner is served, one article of food at a time, and the plates, knives, and forks are changed with each. At least a dozen such changes take place during a single meal.... Napkins, where used, are generally as large as towels... and it is slightly shocking to catch a pretty, black-eyed señorita slyly wiping her rosebud mouth on the edge of the tablecloth. (Dinwiddie 1899, 152–53)

The imported Danish butter, afforded only by Puerto Rican elites at the end of the nineteenth century, was the subject of frequent complaints. It seems that it deteriorated in the hot climate: "The climate is so warm and humid that butter in tubs will not keep at all, and that in cans develops a semirancid taste within forty-eight hours; in fact, many tins of the best Danish butter undergo a slight chemical change from the heat even before they are opened, and thus give a stranger a false idea of the original quality of the goods" (Hamm, *Porto* 1899, 139).

And the "after-dinner" of the evening, left some American authors dissatisfied because it was not as entertaining as they expected: "The evenings in the home.... The men smoke their cigarettes—the women never smoke—and a flow of small talk, filled with simple jokes and sallies, constitutes the entire evening's amusement. Where they have pianos, the daughters exhibit their limited skill on instruments, which are jangled and out of tune" (Dinwiddie 1899, 153).

"HE CAN GET NO BETTER": THE *JÍBARO* TABLE

Only a few American authors discussed the poor peasants' food habits for obvious reasons: they did not frequent lower-class homes at dinnertime, and even if they did, there was little to comment on. In 1911, a team of physicians described in detail the food consumption of a relatively prosperous peon. Their description leaves to the imagination of the reader how much less was the amount and quality of food for the poor:

> The food of the jibaros is poor in fats and the proteids are of difficult assimilation, being of vegetable origin, as a rule. . . . He arises at dawn and takes a cocoanut dipperful of "café puya" (coffee without sugar). Naturally, he never uses milk. With this black coffee he works till about 12, when his wife brings him his breakfast, corresponding to our lunch. This is composed of boiled salt codfish, with oil, and has one of the following vegetables of the island to furnish the carbohydrate element: Banana, platano, ñame, batata, yautia. . . . At 3 in the afternoon he takes another dipperful of coffee, as he began the day. At dusk he returns to his house and has one single dish, a sort of stew, made of the current vegetables of the island with rice and codfish. At rare intervals he treats himself to pork, of which he is inordinately fond, and on still rarer occasions he visits the town and eats quantities of bread, without butter, of course. . . . Of all this list of country food, there are only three elements that are bought—rice, codfish, and condiments. Rice is imported from the United States, and codfish from Nova Scotia. The bread . . . is made of American flour. . . . This is a normal jibaro diet. With the wage paid him he can get no better. . . . . . the fact is he does not get the menu detailed above save when he can be said to be prosperous. (Ashford and Gutierrez 1911, 12)

As mentioned, to send hot lunch to their husbands and/or sons working in the sugarcane or coffee plantations, women needed to carry it in a special set of usually three separate tin containers, one over the other, with a handle, called "fiambreras." American anthropologist Sydney W. Mintz described its use:

> As the sun climbs, each woman begins to prepare the hot lunch which must be carried out to her man in the fields, no matter how far away he may be working. No Puerto Rican cane worker will settle for a cold midday meal. . . . Nests of pots hung on wire frames are the lunchboxes of the Puerto Rican countryside. . . . But no matter what else, one tin

container is always full of rice, another of red or white beans in a mild sauce. Rice and beans are the staple of the lower-class Puerto Rican.[8]

In the 1930s and 1940s, the peasants' diet showed little improvement due to the fact that their wages, although higher, were not adjusted to inflation, so their buying capacity remained extremely limited:

> A common idea is that the "jíbaro" eats only rice and beans and dried codfish, but this is not altogether correct. The "jíbaro's" diet, like any man's the world over, is limited only by his pocketbook and the variety of procurable edibles. Naturally in an agricultural land he is forced to be for the most part a vegetarian. In addition, then, to the imported staples of rice, brown beans, and codfish, he eats plantains, bananas, breadfruit, tropical yams, cassava, potatoes, avocados, corn, "yautia," chayotes, okra, taros, and numerous other vegetables, tubers, and fruits, some of which he grows himself if fortunate enough to have a garden-patch. And always there is coffee, usually taken black, for seldom does the "jíbaro" possess a goat, much less a cow. The pig or the few fowls occasionally seen near his "bohío" he may hold in reserve or sell at market. The "jíbaro" trades at the small rural grocery or at the store of his employer, where, in addition to purchase necessities, he may now and then regale himself with some canned or preserved product. But it must be remembered that his buying capacity is extremely restricted owing to his low wages and uncertain seasonal employment. (Van Deusen and Van Deusen 1931, 172)

"THE EVER-PRESENT GUAVA PASTE WITH CHEESE": SWEETS AND FRUITS

Since there were no sugar refineries on the Island at the end of the nineteenth century, Puerto Rico produced only brown sugar. Some early American visitors noticed the absence of white sugar in Puerto Rican tables: "I do not remember of seeing any refined sugar used in the hotels and homes in Porto Rico. . . . That which is employed mostly in Porto Rico is a coarse, yellowish sugar with a pleasant taste" (Hamm, *Porto* 1899, 169).

War correspondent Albert G. Robinson claimed to have experimented with every "fruit, paste, confection, and compound, solid or liquid" sold in the streets of Ponce, and he particularly favored what he called "hoky-poky" and is known in Puerto Rico as a "piragua" consisting of shaved ice covered with flavored syrup and served in a paper cup. In his description, he emphasized the dirtiness of the seller and implied her submissiveness towards him:

> I think that the most generally satisfactory experiment which I tried was the local ice-cream served after the manner of that variety known in America as the "hoky-poky." A dusky damsel, clad in none too abundant, and not over-immaculate raiment, intimated in sign language, backed by a pleasant smile and the word "dos" . . . that it would be her pleasure to serve the "Americano." . . . The compound appeared to be nothing more than frozen cocoa-nut milk slightly sweetened. I recommend it. (Robinson 1899, 40)

An American journalist discovered the "Porto Rican style" to eat an orange: ". . . oranges. . . . We buy some and, as we go on, eat it in native Porto Rican style. This means removing the peel, cutting a piece from the top, and then sucking out the juice. Oranges are much liked by these people, and at the railway stations and street corners are often sold already peeled" (Carpenter 1930, 262).

What Americans called "tiny strawberries" were actually a form of raspberry (*Rubus rosifolius*) that Puerto Ricans know as "fresa de montaña" or "mountain strawberry." It was introduced from Asia and grows in the central mountains.[9] The largest ones reach one inch and they were described in detail by the Van Deusens, who encountered its young sellers while crossing through the Carretera Central at the Aibonito pass:

> Here and there in this vicinity little boys and girls run out into the highway holding towards us small boxes or baskets filled with bright red berries, while they cry, "¡Fresas! ¡Fresas!" . . . the so-called mountain "strawberry" of Porto Rico . . . these berries glow more dazzling crimson than strawberries, while in appearance they somewhat resemble raspberries. We eat a few. They are sweet and delicious. These are the mysterious "fresas," which are found in one other part of the globe—the Himalaya Mountains! How, when, and by whom they were brought to Porto Rico is an intriguing botanical mystery. (Van Deusen and Van Deusen 1931, 304)

The practice of "cooking fruits" is not quite clear. But it can be surmised that it refers to making fruit pastes or "dulces." These are still made with a variety of fruits: orange, mango, guava, coconut, papaya, etc., and even with some roots like sweet potatoes:

> Nearly all the fruits, and more especially the guava, pineapple, quince, plum and orange, are converted into all sorts of jams, jellies, marmalades, pastas and conservas. (Hamm, *Porto* 1899, 140, 180)

> ... urchins offered us "cocoa dulce," [must mean "dulce de coco" = "coconut's sweet"] a mixture of sugar and cocoanut in all shades of yellow and brown, for one centavo. It was sweet and we bought it learning later that the color was determined by the cleanliness of the native confectioner. (Fiala 1899, 60)

Other desserts were mentioned, including the most commonly cited by American authors: guava paste with cheese, still a favorite in Puerto Rican tables: "For desserts there came no sweetmeats or pudding or custards of any traditionally dainty French sort, nor even fruit except rarely, but always and regularly, twice or even three times a day, the ever-present guava paste with cheese of goat's milk" (White 1898, 408).

The food and drinks shared at dances and other fiestas, especially Christmastime ones, were described in delicious detail by the Van Deusens:

> The refreshments at dances and other "fiestas" were mainly concocted from native-grown ingredients. Sweetening consisted of the crude brown sugar.... Among the beverages were "horchata," almond-flavored rice water; "sangria," five parts brown-sugar water and one part red wine; "guarapo," cane juice, and always strong black coffee. The more substantial part of the collation was made up of various puddings such as "majarete," a mixture of cornmeal and coconut milk; "manjar blanco," or "nuevo mundo," a combination of sugar, coconut milk, and rice flour; "bienmesabe,"("it tastes good to me") a thick syrup of coconut milk, sugar, and eggs, often poured over cake; "budín," a kind of bread pudding, and, without fail, "arroz con perico," sometimes made of rice and grated coconut, but usually of rice cooked with brown sugar and flavored with ginger. It is said that he who eats too much "arroz con perico" cannot stop talking, and since "perico" means parrot there may be some truth in the saying! The feast was enhanced with "dulces"—sweet pastes made of brown sugar and the pulp of native fruits, such as "guayaba," "mamey," pineapple, orange, and coconut, and also of the "yucca" and sweet potato. Most of these dishes and many other similar ones are still popular. Especially delicious are the "pasta de mango," and the "pasta de guayaba"—guava paste.... a feast which consists of an array of dainties, its substantial factors being "pasteles," (cakes of plantain,

with an intricate mixture of meat, raisins, olives, and so on, wrapped and steamed in green banana leaves, always associated with Christmastide) "arroz con pollo," and if at all possible "lechón asado"—roast pig. (Van Deusen and Van Deusen 1931, 177, 179)

"A RICHNESS OF FLAVOR AND PERFUME": PUERTO RICAN COFFEE

Coffee was the number one export of Puerto Rico at the time of the US invasion, and its best markets were in Europe, where it was considered by connoisseurs as "the best coffee in the world," a favorite in France, Germany, and Spain.[10] Its use is so universal in Puerto Rico that even infants and children drink it, even if diluted with milk.[11] American authors loved it:

> The Porto Ricans regard it as the best coffee of the world. They prepare it in a way very different from that familiar to most American households. The first difference is in the roasting. They go far beyond the medium or dark brown which we prefer, and almost reach a brown black. The result of this over-roasting is to produce a beverage that is so dark as to be of the same hue as the black after-dinner coffee of the French. Instead of grinding it in a mill, they crush it between two stones, or pound it with a pestle in a mortar. They put the crushed fragments in a pot with boiling water, which they bring to a quick boil over a hot fire. Then they strain it through a fine cotton bag, an old bandana handkerchief, or a filtering cone made of cloth or felt prepared for the purpose. The resulting fluid is perfectly clear and transparent, despite its very dark color, and has a richness of flavor and perfume which cannot be too highly extolled. . . . The people, both natives and foreigners, drink it in very large quantities, and apparently are not injured thereby in their digestion. (Hamm, *Porto* 1899, 162–63)

Apparently unaware that what he was describing was the result of poverty instead of choice, this American soldier explained how poor Puerto Ricans roasted and ground their coffee beans together with the seeds of the plant known as "hedionda"[12] in order to make it last longer while still keeping some coffee smell: "The bean of the gedianda, a small bushy weed, is largely used as a substitute for coffee, and makes a pleasant drink reputed to possess value in aiding digestion and promoting health" (Hannaford 1899, 250).

And a Disciples of Christ missionary remarked on how much coffee he had to accept and drink while visiting his Puerto Rican potential brethren:

Since Puerto Rico produces the finest coffee in the world, the people are naturally great coffee drinkers. Being most hospitable, they always want to serve visitors with refreshments. In the rural sections, coffee is the one thing they always have. Therefore, if one makes a dozen visits in an afternoon, he must have capacity for at least a dozen cups of coffee. After one is on friendly terms with a family, a cup ceases to be a cup and becomes a large cocoanut shell. (Morton 1949, 48)

"THEY KNOW WHEN TO STOP": PUERTO RICAN ALCOHOLIC BEVERAGES

The Puerto Rican and American traditions regarding the use of alcohol were different at the time of the US invasion. Many Puerto Ricans followed the Spanish cultural habit of drinking daily and, like them, "valued the ability to 'hold one's liquor'. . . . They did not have the habit of complete drunkenness. . . . In fact, the Spanish believed that to call someone a drunkard was considered the worst possible insult one could level against another person."[13] In the Spanish colonies in America, laborers used alcohol to passively resist their exploitation but, again, drunkenness was infrequent.

In colonial North America, partly because of the lack of potable water," beer and wine were considered essential for daily life as it served "for food, medicine and medium of socializing" even for the Puritans.[14] But by 1677, alcohol was already understood as a problem, and Catholic and Protestant missionaries, as well as colonists in general, wanted to control drinking as another way of controlling people's behavior. During the nineteenth century, alcohol consumption "rose tremendously" (The average per capita consumption of alcohol went from 1.7 gallons of beer in 1863 to twenty-one gallons in the 1910s) as workers turned to alcohol "to cope with the social upheaval of industrialization" and drinking at saloons, segregated by class, became "the predominant form of leisure for men."[15] In response, Protestant middle-class women organized temperance groups across the United States pushing for a "betterment" of the working classes.

Rum was invented in the Caribbean islands in the sixteenth century.[16] The consumption of rum was (and still is) ubiquitous in social spaces for all kinds of Puerto Rican celebrations: birthdays, weddings, baptisms, etc. In Puerto Rican elite homes at the end of the nineteenth century, alcohol was often the first offering to visitors: "Immediately after the introduction and before being taken away by his host to remove the dust from his garments, the newly arrived is invited to wash the dust from his throat" (Ober 1899, 186).

Puerto Rican rum was qualified as very strong and as the cause of murderous mindsets, but an American soldier also ascribed its curative effects against poisons:

> I had my first and last taste of Puerto Rico rum while on this scout. [After meeting a peon:] . . . as we knew the Spanish word for water, we said "Dos agua," meaning two drinks of water; signifying that we were very thirsty by pointing to our mouths. . . . diving into the underbrush he appeared a few moments later with two gourds filled with liquid. Our Spanish must have been very poor, or the native misunderstood our meaning, for before we had swallowed two mouthfuls we sputtered, coughed and choked, and dropped the gourds as if the contents has been red-hot. The native looked at us in amazement and disgust. Without a doubt he could have drank both of our shares and would hardly have felt it. Many times afterwards I saw this stuff used by the natives almost as plentifully as water, that is internally. "Agua, wretch!," we both exclaimed in a threatening tone. The native, with a "Si, signor," rushed away and soon came back with a tin pail of agua, with which we refreshed ourselves . . . The native disappeared with his empty pail, and probably spread the report that the American soldier was strictly temperate, as we surely were when it came to drinking sugar-cane rum. . . . the sugar-cane or cocoa-nut rum. Both of these drinks require but a very small quantity to make a man insanely murderous and ready to kill on the slightest provocation. . . . the tarantula . . . The bite is not considered deadly poisonous by the natives who counteract it by drinking quantities of rum as an antidote. (Oliver 1901, 124–25, 175, 210)

For many Puerto Ricans, alcohol (mostly rum) was (and still is) a source of relaxation for people who work very hard and still struggle economically. For poor workers, it was a source of "physical strength," as a rural sociologist noted:

> There is a constant sale for goods of this sort [alcohol], usually to the workingmen and poorer class of people, who purchase in small quantities, a drink at a time, for three or five cents; many of them, no doubt, attempting to keep up their physical strength by the use of such a stimulant, since a more noticeable stimulating effect is produced by five cents' worth of rum than could be obtained through the consumption of five cents' worth of food. When this custom becomes as prevalent as it is in Porto Rico, it involves serious evil effects. (Fleagle 1917, 94)

American soldiers were constantly surprised by how well Puerto Ricans "held their liquor" without getting drunk. These young men were used to "heavy drinking," but the concept was not commonly seen in Puerto Rico. As A. F. Beard, secretary of the American Mission Association, commented in 1900: "Drunkenness was virtually introduced to the island by North Americans, who were the only people he saw drinking to excess ..."[17] The US military tried to control the excessive alcohol consumption of its men: "The orders that men were to go in no store or building of any kind were given, and a guard stationed at all liquor stores (which in Porto Rico means all stores) saw that this rule was strictly enforced. In spite of this certain men managed to "fall off the water wagon" with a bang" (Edwards 1899, 88).

Even though there were exceptions to this, most Puerto Ricans then (and still nowadays) did not regularly binge on alcohol to the point of blackout as American drinkers so frequently did (and still do). Many American authors emphasized this difference:

Drunkenness is practically unknown among them, in spite of the fact that they consume annually an average of nearly two gallons of rum for each man, woman and child. . . . A dram three times a day is about their limit. . . . It is a very rare thing to see one of them intoxicated. . . . Previous to the advent of the Americans there was not a saloon on the island, but in nearly every store there was a small bar where beer, cognac, wine, aqua ardentia, etc., were freely dispensed. These liquors, however, were drunk sparingly, for the Porto Ricans, like nearly all natives of tropical regions, are a temperate people. (Olivares, *Vol. 1* 1899, 332, 371)

On the streets one is greeted by drunken men—Americans, too, for when a Porto Rican wants to get drunk he usually stays at home to do it. The only closed salons here are American. . . . our teachers found a man lying in their yard, intoxicated . . . "Es Americano," he [the policeman] said, "Un paisano suyo". . . . And we said "Yes" and felt mighty proud of him! . . . In the time we have lived here we have seen but one intoxicated Porto Rican and he was still in possession of his legs. This is not to say, however, that the people here do not drink, though they do not drink as we do. They sip a great deal, and to refuse the social glass is to make oneself noticeable and "queer," but they know when to stop. (Blythe 1911, 158)

The omnipresence of alcohol in Puerto Rican business establishments of all sorts was noticed: "From all appearances the majority of them either carry a stock of liquor as an adjunct to a stock of miscellaneous merchandise . . . or a stock of miscellaneous merchandise as an adjunct to a bar-room. I was told that there were no restrictions there upon the sale of liquor, and I could see no evidence of any. Yet I saw no intoxication" (Robinson 1899, 76–77).

But after over a decade of colonizing Puerto Rico, and largely due to the influence of American Protestant missionaries there, by 1916, temperance movements were already organized around Protestant churches. As the US Congress discussed what would become the Jones Act of 1917, American missionaries claiming to represent Puerto Ricans' interests lobbied to include in the act a Prohibition Clause to be confirmed in a referendum.[18] This referendum, the first ever in Puerto Rico, was to be celebrated on July 16, 1917. During the prereferendum campaign, the opposition against temperance, which included the American governor of Puerto Rico, Arthur Yager, as well as the Catholic Church, correctly argued that drunkenness was not a general problem among Puerto Ricans because alcohol was part of the general workers' diet, it alleviated their tough lives, and intoxication was not its purpose.[19]

Yet the Protestant missionaries in Puerto Rico developed a successful campaign through sermons, poems, meetings, articles in *La Voz Evangélica*, and the organization of Temperance Leagues in almost all towns with the participation of Puerto Rican elite women, union leaders, and other professionals.[20] They obtained 61.5 percent of the votes, and, as a result, the until-then prosperous alcohol industry stagnated for over a decade. The referendum and temperance themes were discussed by a few American authors:

> Porto Rico voted herself dry in 1917. The majority make the more likely assertion that the result was largely due to a mistake on the part of the ignorant peons. The "dries" chose as their party emblem the green coconut, a favorite rural beverage. Their opponents [the wets] decorated the head of their ballot with a bottle. Now, the bottle suggests to the jíbaros of the hills the Spaniards who keep the liquor shops, and they hate the Spaniards.... (Franck 1920, 285–86)

The temperance movement ended up being a disaster both in the United States, where it engendered new and powerful mafias based in the sale of illegal alcohol, gambling and prostitution, and in Puerto Rico, where home-made illegal alcohol became generalized (see chapter 9). Other problems arose as well: adulterated alcohol became a health hazard, and the combination of administrative corruption and collective disobedience made its control impossible at a time when the Depression made the revitalization of the lucrative rum industry necessary.[21] Finally, to the dismay of the Protestants, the Prohibition of alcohol ended on March 13, 1934.

Only one author commented about beer as a preferred alcoholic drink. Oddly, this comment was written in 1899, which should be interpreted as applying only to the elite class, since other classes would not have been able to keep beer cold without some cooling system. Another possibility is that this author might have been confused with another mild alcoholic drinking popular in Puerto Rico: "maví," a beverage based on the boiled and fermented bark of the maví tree (*Colubrina arboresens*)[22] native of Central America, the Caribbean, and south Florida: ". . . something must be said about their fondness for beer, which they prefer to any other drink. Beer, despite its very high price, is used daily in the house as a tonic before meals; and it is also used at parties and festivals, at the theatres, balls, etc., no other drink being so much in demand" (Morris, *Our Island* 1899, 206).

A more recent "cultural institution" was born after industrialization and modernity had an effect on Puerto Rican customs. It was the "Social Friday," which consisted of meeting with friends and coworkers every Friday after working hours to enjoy beer and/or drinks at a bar. Originally, only men enjoyed this Friday ritual, but eventually, modern women joined them:

> I first learned of "sociales Viernes," "social Friday" while living there. This is a cultural practice exercised by men—at least back then it was. . . . Too many of the husbands, after excessive drinking, returned home to beat their wives, if they felt so inclined. . . . Today, the weekly ritual of "sociales Viernes" has morphed. In these times it is more likely to see the women included in the Friday social. . . . Back in the 1980's, one need only drive past the bars on a Friday evening to see large gatherings of men outside on the corner socializing and blowing a goodly share of their weekly paychecks. (Tavenner 2010, 184–85)

"THE CHEAPEST LUXURY THAT THE PORTO RICAN CAN INDULGE IN": SMOKES

Since the seventeenth century, New England Puritans banned tobacco smoking in public. To them, tobacco was "a God-given medicine" that should not be abused.[23] Its leisure use was associated with alehouses and theatric plays, with whores and irreligiousness. Over time, as modernity began in New England, tolerance developed towards men's habit of smoking . . . but only men's. The fact that Puerto Rican women smoked was remarked by several American authors during the first years of American colonization. Of course, they were almost always referring to lower-class women:

> The peasant woman dearly loves her black cigar, and a sight which arouses risibility is the common one of a huge, black aunty rolling

down the center of a street, burdened with head-balanced load heavy enough for a horse, placidly smoking an inky cigar of able proportions, whose clouds of smoke enshroud her head.... Envy her; she has only half enough to eat, but is rich in the soothing of nectar nicotine. (Dinwiddie 1899, 126)

But by the early 1950s, the situation turned upside down as, by then, American women smoked cigarettes while Puerto Rican elite women, especially those married, did not, at least in public. An English teacher brought his new wife to live in Mayagüez, and the differences became evident:

But one problem which had never crossed my mind was that Puerto Rican women did not smoke, certainly not out of the privacy of their own homes. When advised by teachers at the Colegio that she [his American wife] really should not be seen smoking on the street, we decided there was really no problem. If, when driving ... we stopped ... Gretchen simply handed her lit cigarette to me.... This hardly fooled anyone. Besides, the word was out. Gretchen not only went into restaurants and had drinks with her husband, but after the drink was served she lit up a cigarette. (Cooper 1994, 133)

A disturbing scene regarding the habit of smoking among Puerto Rican infants was narrated by a soldier: "[In Salinas:] The natives here were numerous and dirty, and manifested a great deal of interest in all we did. I remember my amazement at seeing a baby girl, not more than three years old, pick up the butt of a cigar I had thrown away and calmly smoke it like a connoisseur, her mother sitting by with never a word of protest" (Cammann 1899, 186–87).

General smoking comments were found here and there, as well as a few notations on the use of chewing tobacco:

Smoking is very nearly a universal habit, even among the women. Cigars and cigarettes are everywhere—on the streets, in public conveyances, in the restaurants and cafes, and in all the private houses. You cannot escape from the odor of burning tobacco.... Smoking is about the cheapest luxury that the Porto Rican can indulge in.... The cigars as a rule are roughly made and smoke unevenly. (Olivares, *Vol. 1* 1899, 336)

The chewing tobacco used by the natives was sold by the yard. It was cured with rum and molasses and twisted into ropes about one hundred feet long and as thick as my finger. (Carpenter 1930, 258)

THIS CHAPTER

Food has been an essential tool in the process of colonization. The food of the colonized is interpreted to be as savage and uncivilized as them. Americans complained that it was too spicy, too bland, too garlicky, etc. They were happy to see that the peons "were content" with a diet of rice and beans, plantains, bread, and seasonal roots and fruits, so they concluded that, since they liked them so much, that´s all they needed. Like with poverty, they conveniently interpreted that the meatless diet was "a preference" they should "respect." Regarding the use of alcohol and both cigars and cigarettes, it was criticized as a waste of money that should be used for food, thus disregarding the universal need of hard-working peons for some relief from their tough and hopeless lives.

Chapter 18

"DEAR ME! WHAT A BUSY, NOISY PLACE!"

On Commerce and Animal Treatment

"THEIR YANKEE BRETHREN WERE NOT TO BE TRIFLED WITH": PUERTO RICAN STORES

Trying to explain why Africans lacked capitalistic entrepreneurs, Ali A. Mazrui had an interesting theory.[1] He explained, regarding Africans, that their lack of a winter season results in simpler forms of shelter and body-covering but that, furthermore, it also impinges on their ability to foster a culture of planning and the will to anticipate. Therefore, capitalism was more immature in Africa because capitalism involved accumulation and investment, and investment involved calculation and anticipation, which were unnatural in tropical weather. In this regard, in the 1960s, a Mennonite missionary analyzed the dichotomy between American middle-class capitalist values and Puerto Rican peasantry's life values:

> In this process of Americanization of the island there has been a conflict of two value systems at work—the traditional Hispanic value system on the one hand, and the American middle-class functional value system on the other. The predominant value of the latter system is what [Henry] Wells terms the "welfare value," which includes the desire for material abundance, good health, education, and other attributes of high standards of living. This welfare value is counter to the traditional Hispanic values where the upper levels of society disdained physical labor, technical skills, and non-humanistic learning.
>
> Well into the twentieth century Puerto Ricans in general did not perceive the accumulation of money as an end in itself. Professional acquaintances of mine in the 1940s did not invest their salaries in savings and bank accounts. They were more inclined to spend their monthly salaries for those things that brought present value and pleasure. The survey of the Aibonito and La Plata communities showed even today

Puerto Rican families are more inclined to invest their savings in homes than in savings accounts. (Holsinger 2013, 167–68)

At the time of the US invasion, capitalism was still beginning to develop in Puerto Rico since Spanish colonialism was mercantilist. A few authors recognized that Puerto Rican tradesmen were not as eager to sell as capitalist American ones, and many struggled to understand the shopping practices of the Puerto Rican poor, which made no sense to a capitalist mind:

> Usually only a penny's worth of anything is bought at a time, the most expensive method of buying. When she goes to the store the peasant woman will buy one cent's worth of sugar or one cent's worth of rice. In the course of a day should she need five cents' worth of rice, she would send a child five times or go herself. . . . No one in Porto Rico is ever in a hurry. (Boyce 1914, 422)

> When he [the American visitor] goes into shops little attempt will be made to show him or sell him anything; in fact he may be totally ignored as a customer. . . . He will conclude, of course, that the Puerto Ricans lack business drive and ambition. (Petrullo 1947, 136)

But, many Puerto Ricans were fast in adapting to the new circumstances and soon learned how to increase their profits. Because of this, during the US invasion, American soldiers distrusted the local store owners, complaining that they were charging them outrageous prices. Once again, the authoritative tone of the soldier-writers is noticeable as they brand Puerto Rican businessmen as dishonest. Curiously, they saw themselves as victims of even the poor local washerwomen:

> . . . as the acquaintance with the soldiers increased, the people began to feel sorry that they had been so liberal and it seemed that they were determined to "make up" for the mistakes they had made in the past and prices began to rise. An American dollar began to depreciate in the native markets . . . Merchants doubled the price in everything they offered for sale and women who did laundry work advanced their rates to many times the original figures. . . . This led to more or less ill feeling against the natives, and determined to "break even" with them, all sorts of Yankee tricks were played by the soldiers. There was very little serious trouble between the soldiers and the natives, but there were several small fights and the privilege of the camp was denied a certain class of merchants. (Creager 1899, 210–11)

This self-image of victims contrasts with the remorseless confessions of these American soldiers: one of them narrated how they paid in stores with Confederate money[2] that had no value but that Puerto Ricans accepted due to their ignorance regarding American currency; another narrated how, in exchange for Puerto Rican food, they gave the natives inedible canned meat; and the last one stole from Puerto Rican stores whatever he wanted:

> The Corporal . . . never expected to see . . . the Porto Ricans . . . accepting a lot of Confederate money, brought down from Charleston by a number of our boys, who seemed to have bid good-bye to conscience as they left the shores of the United States. (Rossiter [1900?])

> . . . by the use of troop money at the command of the commissary we were able to procure native food—cornmeal and plantains: and as delicacies, bananas and guava jelly. . . . A quantity of canned meat unfit for use was exchanged for native food products, the Porto Ricans being eager to procure the meat we threw away. (Fiala 1899, 102)

> I saw many other instances . . . where the thieving Puerto Ricans overcharged the soldiers unmercifully. But . . . if they were obstinate and did not come down to a fair price the soldier would jump over the counter and help himself, always paying for whatever he took. Nine times out of ten it was not the price asked, but it was more than they could get from the townspeople. This may sound a trifle high-handed and domineering, but what were we to do? We surely took the most direct course to teach our future colonists that their Yankee brethren were not to be trifled with. (Oliver 1900, 168)

But a few Americans praised the honesty of Puerto Ricans and the lack of greed on the part of store employees, who never harassed potential clients:

> Nowhere can one find people more honest and diligent, more warmhearted and generous, more loyal and friendly. . . . in the ordinary affairs of life scrupulous honesty is the almost invariable rule. You will not be gypped in a Puerto Rican shop. . . . Your cook will not add a penny to the price of the supplies she buys for you in the market: even your coach driver will ask you to pay only the recognized charge for his services. On the contrary, those whom you employ will guard your interests as if they were their own. (Lord 2004, 55)

In so ordinary an act as shopping one at once senses some of the island quality. Shopkeepers and their dark-eyed girl assistants are uninsistent, almost shy. No one is brusque, there is no clamor. Responsively one lowers one's own voice. It is the first symptom of that deep relaxation that Puerto Rico is to bring, a rest of the spirit which is never touched with dullness, that leaves the mind refreshed. (Vandercook 1939, 11)

Several commercial practices of Puerto Ricans were routinely mocked by American authors. One of them, soon after the invasion, was the practice of claiming to speak English just to attract American customers without actually commanding the language.

I wanted a rubber blanket. Rubber blankets do not seem to be a common article in Ponce. I visited some twenty or thirty stores. Half of them displayed the sign of "English Spoken." I found no difference between those and the others.... I tried words and then gymnastics.... I got everything but the thing I wanted.... from a mackintosh to a box of sardines." (Robinson 1899, 41–42)

The differing ways of "doing business" were highlighted. And the subtle ways of Puerto Rican storekeepers ended up being favored by some Americans:

This courtesy is not confined to the social life. It permeates and influences every phase of living. In the business world, for example, although the Porto Rican has few equals when it comes to shrewdness, he does not depend upon the complicated efficiency system of his northern brother. He has a way of ingratiating himself into the confidence of his customer and establishing a personal friendship. Instead of a monthly statement, when he is in need of money, he will hand you a signed receipt. A more subtle method could hardly be devised to raise the necessary cash. By way of contrast an American grocery store on the island prints some such legend as this at the bottom of its bills and statements: "This is not a bank. Bills are payable promptly the first of every month. Interest will be charged on all overdue accounts at legal rate." This method no doubt works well with the American clientele which the store serves, but it will not work with the Latin element. (James 1927, 14)

American authors also found the multifunctional arrangement in which stores were set up, as well as the nature of their names, confusing. They tended to describe them as a senseless mismatch of merchandise:

Dry goods stores are numerous and the stocks seem fairly good, though often they appear incongruous by their variety. One buys a yard of calico or a saddle, a mantilla or a machete, in the same store.... The tailor may or may not carry a line of shirts and hats. A "zapateria" may sell only shoes, but many of those combinations of dry-goods, hardware, crockery, and saddlery, carry also a line of shoes and slippers. The bakery ("panaderia") may also sell cigars, cigarettes, and liquors, as may the purveyor of canned goods and delicatessen.... There may be a system to it all, but the stranger cannot tell where he may find the thing he wants.... In Yauco I purchased cigars at a store where I might have purchased pencils, ink, and schoolbooks. In a store in Mayaguez I was offered fountain-pens, slippers, straw hats, children's toys, and furniture in the same establishment. (Robinson 1899, 174–75)

The stores are the only deceptive features of business life in a Porto Rican town. Everything else is open to the public, but the shops are not what they seem. In front of each there is a little cave-like reception room surrounded by shelves and usually filled with customers.... The entire space will not contain more than a few hundred dollars' worth of goods and the stranger gets the impression that the shops are very insignificant affairs; but back of these little rooms there are immense warehouses filled with bales and boxes of merchandise.... All the signs are in Spanish, and many of them afford no idea of the nature of the business. For instance ... La Nina ("The Maiden") has gentlemen's shirts and hats for sale, while La Hijah de Borinquen ("The Daughter of Borinquen") is a barber shop. (Olivares, *Vol. 1* 1899, 367)

Imperialism is about satisfying the needs of the metropolis and not those of the colony. The colonized were expected to become captive consumers of the imported goods that the American empire needed markets for. This American journalist candidly revealed that "a new order" had arrived on the Island in 1898 and that any merchants who did not adapt to it would "have to go soon":

An American grocery store or dry-goods store would be out of place today in all but three or four of the cities. But as the American population begins to enter the island it will demand the same comfort and supplies with which it was familiar at home, and by contact will teach the people of Puerto Rico to want things of the same sort. Then the retail store ... will find business waiting for him.... if the local merchants cannot adapt themselves to the changing conditions they no doubt will have to go soon. (White 1898, 438–39)

Sure enough, in order to stay in business, Puerto Rican merchants abandoned practices such as haggling and adapted to the new American ways, as recorded in 1914:

> In costume, business and other matters, the Porto Ricans have adopted American ideas and customs with wonderful facility; the large stores are up-to-date, stocked with American and European goods, and there is no longer the "last price," as in Cuba and other Spanish-American lands. Cash registers, pneumatic money-carriers, elevators, bargain sales, and auto deliveries are now a necessary part of Porto Rican business . . . (Verrill 1914, 17)

But some American popular business practices took a long time to take hold in Puerto Rico. Such is the case of the pawnbroking business. Puerto Ricans had already developed a close-knit support system: In times of economic hardship, compadres and other family members generally shared whatever they had with those in need. Money loans were frequent when medicines were needed. The practice of pawnbroking was finally recognized and regulated in Puerto Rico in 1975 with the "Ley de Préstamo de Prendas" (Pawnbroking Act).[3] In the United States, the situation was quite different: first recorded in the Dutch New Amsterdam colony (today New York) in 1657, the practice of loaning money with material goods as collateral became a necessity during the US Independence War (1775–1873) as cash became scarce.[4] Since then, the practice became part of the informal economy of the new republic and became a formally recognized occupation in the early nineteenth century. The absence of pawnbrokers in Puerto Rico was noticed by an American explorer: "It is possible that there are pawnshops in Porto Rico, but the author never saw one . . . ; possible Porto Ricans never have anything worth pawning or perhaps they are never sufficiently in want to require the services of an 'uncle'" (Verrill 1914, 106).

A "colmado" in Puerto Rico is a small market that might encompass a small grocery store, a bar, and even a dancing place, all in one. In 1945, an American teacher with the propensity to describe everything Puerto Rican in the worst possible light commented on his experience at small *colmados*, emphasizing their lack of hygiene:

> The proprietor spit on the floor as we entered, then rubbed his wet mouth with his hand. He was barefoot and a great sore spread across his ankle and up his leg till the trouser leg hid it. . . . His wet fingers clutched the inside of the cups as he poured the rum into them. The driver handed me one of the paper containers which I accepted gingerly, noting the flyspecks on its surface and the yellow tint of the paper. . . .

Men played dominoes, poker, or dice . . . usually the Puerto Rican. . . . is content to drink and talk. Each one of these colmados has a stepped-up juke box that can be heard for three or four blocks, and a radio usually plays simultaneously. (Brown 1945, 24, 102)

"A CONSTANT KALEIDOSCOPIC ENTERTAINMENT": STREET PEDDLERS

American writers dedicated a good part of their writings to discussing Puerto Rican street peddlers and how clever they were. Of all of them, American authors considered most peculiar the milk peddler, whose ultranatural way of dispensing his goods was, as some acknowledged, the best evidence of the purity of his product:

> A curious feature of the streets is the milk delivery. . . . This takes place before and during the noon. . . . The milkman drives from door to door from one to four or five cows, each branded with a number and usually one or more of them accompanied by a calf. The driver cries his approach, and the customer . . . sends out a pan, pail, bottle, or cup, which he hands to the milkman. The milkman puts into the receptacle the quantity of milk paid for, which he induces the cow to yield after the usual manner. (Hall 1898)

Some enjoyed the way in which peddlers advertised their goods for the benefit of potential customers, while others complained of it considering it a "noise":

> In its towns a succession of strange sights and sounds present a constant kaleidoscopic entertainment. Street venders, carrying their goods on their heads, or in huge panniers on diminutive ponies, cry their wares in quaint and pleasant-sounding tones. (Hannaford 1899, 240)

> . . . the barking of the confectionery venders causing a discordant noise all day long. (Oliver 1900, 209)

Haggling was noticed by some American authors who commended it: "To a bystander, haggling over prices is most amusing. Buyer and seller regard each other for the time as enemies, and prices are fixed and discussed accordingly. To the Anglo Saxon visitor the curious part of it all is, that no matter how close the bargaining, the business is conducted with unfailing politeness" (Seabury 1908, 30).

The coconut peddler, frequently a poor kid with a dexterity for climbing palm trees, and for opening the coconuts with his machete, amazed American authors and was frequently photographed:

> ... a "cocoa-de-agua" is composed of a green cocoanut, a small black boy with no more clothes on that the law demands, and a savage-looking knife about two feet long. The railway station is his favorite haunt, and when you toss him a penny, he will flop himself down upon his knees and cut a hole in the top of the cocoanut so quickly that it will make your head swim. (Blythe 1911, 58)

Not yet conceding that Puerto Ricans were not lazy as the myth claimed, some authors commented, quite contradictorily, on the pervasiveness of street peddlers, at least in San Juan and Ponce:

> Men and women walk long distances through the country bearing heavy burdens upon their heads, shoulders or backs.... The banana and plantain men carry their fruit fastened to poles.... the vegetable man ... carries on his head on an immense board, sometimes five feet long.... The dulce seller, too, carries his tray of cocoanut dulces, guava jelly and other sweets on his woolly pate; as do also the sellers of fruits, bread, cakes, bottled coconut milk and trinkets.... The hat weaver and the broom maker carry their wares on a shoulder pole, with a load fastened to each end so as to balance it.... always comes very early in the morning ... the baker.... bread is not baked in the house. It is always bought.... The butcher, on horseback, brings meat hanging from hooks in frames. Much of the poultry is brought to town in great odd wicker coops stung across the backs of ponies. (George 1900, 37, 39)

One of the last comments regarding street peddlers was in a book that purported to celebrate the "successful" transformation of Puerto Rico through its fast industrialization in the 1950s. This author, writing in 1960, compared it with previous years:

> The morning street noises that added a picturesque touch ... are rarely heard today: the musical lilt of the vegetable peddler pushing his cart along the shady side of the street has been replaced by the supermarket. The song of the egg man who used to deposit eggs (a little larger than those of the robin) in baskets let down from the second-story balcony is not heard any more either. Bigger eggs and fresher are also bought in the supermarket. And hardly any of the new bungalows have second-story

balconies. The "chicharrón" peddler still shouts his wares ("cracklings" or roast pig skin, golden brown and delicious) and still, for a few cents, a sidewalk vender will peel an orange for you with a knife so sharp that the peeling reaches in one long strip unbroken to the ground. But their stands are movable carts in front of modern air-conditioned department stores. (Hancock 1960, 13)

"PANDEMONIUM REIGNS": THE PLAZA DEL MERCADO

As is still the custom in many European countries, for many years, Puerto Ricans bought their food every day at the open markets held in every town during the morning hours:

> The daily supply of food is always procured at the market, where from 6 o'clock to 10 A.M. each day, Sunday included, the servants of all the wealthy families and the mistresses and children of the poor, prepare for the purchase of their daily supplies. . . . From 6 o'clock to 10 pandemonium reigns; after that the crowd of purchasers dwindles away one by one, and the place is silent . . . (Rector 1898, 137, 142)

These markets were even more crowded on Sunday mornings and, as expected, were interpreted as chaotic and noisy places by most American authors:

> Dear me! What a busy, noisy place! People from every race and nation seem to be gathered here. Big people, little people, babies, roosters, dogs, donkeys, horses! What talking, shouting, laughing, crying, crowing, barking, and braying! . . . Men are smoking, lounging about, and bragging about their game-cocks; women are making small purchases and gossiping with neighbors; babies are tumbling about on the ground, devouring bits of fruit that come in their way: but all are good-natured. (George 1900, 21)

But the most detailed description of the morning markets is provided by Margherita A. Hamm, who described, beyond social class differences, all kinds of exchanges in a chaotic atmosphere that she found comedic:

> As the buyers increase conversation rolls out, until it finally becomes a perfect tumult. Everybody seems to be talking to everybody else, and for the moment the visitor's mind leaps from the plaza to the Stock Exchange in Wall Street on a busy morning. The same spirit underlies both. . . .

The funniest part of it all is when the buyer and the seller begin to quarrel over the amount necessary for a family. They have agreed upon the unitary price, but the buyer insists that his or her family can live upon one pound, while the seller declares that one pound means starvation, and that the family must take two pounds or die; or else when the opposite kind of a bargain is struck, the peasant is certain that "una libra" will be enough for a family of three, and will in fact support five, while the housewife or servant vows with tears that each member of the family can eat "dos libras," and then feel hungry and want more. This style of bargaining based upon the size of families and the dimension of appetites is a royal novelty to sightseers from America. The market closes at 11, and toward the end the character of the customers change greatly. In the early morning and up to 9 o'clock the buyers were evidently people who had money and were willing to pay fair prices for what they bought. They were followed by a second class who had but little money, and wanted to buy the inferior and cheaper articles left by the first. These, in turn, are replaced by the very poor, and by beggars who expect to get something for a few cents, or to receive as a charity from the good-natured farmers enough of the unsold produce to keep them alive for another day. (Hamm, *Porto*, 1899, 117–18)

As time went on, the US colonial government in Puerto Rico began to change the way in which business was done, and being heavily influenced by American Protestant missionaries, they moved to suppress all business transactions on Sundays as this was considered the "day of the Lord." Such a poorly thought decision had terrible consequences for the peasants who, by losing their Sunday markets, also lost an important part of their livelihoods:

One cannot blame the Porto Ricans if they chafe more or less under American rule; we have taken much from their lives, and while we have given a great deal in some ways, yet we leave much to be desired in others. Our sanitation, road building, schools and other institutions are beyond all praise, but why should we insist on closing every shop and store on Sundays, thus depriving innumerable poor country people of their only means of revenue and recreation, when we allow moving picture shows, amusement resorts, and similar things to remain wide open for the amusement of the better classes? (Verrill 1914, 19)

For good or bad, the new "American way," based on the philosophy of "time is money," eventually became the norm in the business world, a world in which Puerto Ricans were expected to disregard family and friendship as they pursued their economic goals. This was explained by American anthropologist Sydney W. Mintz after studying Santa Isabel's sugarcane community in the early 1950s:

> The new emphasis on cash income, the elimination of noncash services, the introduction of new consumers' goods, and the opportunity to earn money by intensified effort began to push aside older standards. Workers could begin to think of getting security more through material possessions or money-making skill, and less through the fulfillment of customary noneconomic obligations and the extension of personal friendships.[5]

"WITH NO LOVE OF GOD IN THEIR HANDS": THE TREATMENT OF ANIMALS

The theme of cruelty towards animals was of great importance for American authors. Many of them alleged that Puerto Ricans were cruel in their treatment of their horses as they over-packed them and/or prodded them to move faster. They also considered the kind of yoke used in oxen, as well as the use of stingy objects or whips to urge them to move. In 1918, an American missionary portrayed Puerto Ricans as extremely cruel regarding all animals:

> Again and again, as we journey along, we are brought face to face with the utter indifference of the people to the suffering of animals; with no love of God in their hands, only fear of eternal punishment they manifest no love toward the animals He created and no S. P. C. A. [the American Society for the Prevention of Cruelty to Animals] brings the law to bear to save the poor creatures from neglect and the uncertain tempers of their owners. (Wilcox [1918?])

As early as 1905, the Insular Police already reported that they had processed 6,500 offenses of animal cruelty (including cockfighting, among others).[6] American views on this matter can better be understood if we revise the history of Americans' sensitivity towards animals as it emerged around the turn of the nineteenth century. The interest in the protection of animals was first voiced in the United States in 1786 by Philadelphian physician Benjamin Rush, a signer of the US Declaration of Independence who advocated the idea that "In order for the American Revolution and the great experiment in republicanism to succeed ... [their new nation needed to] instill republican and Christian values in Americans" such as "temperance, education reform, abolitionism, and the humane treatment of animals."[7] His ideas were inspired by those of John Locke, Thomas Tyron, and Alexander Pope, and by Quaker philosophy, among others.

Nonetheless his ideas "did not fit into the individualistic, liberal world that the United States was quickly becoming," and the movement remained one of the urban upper—and middle classes.[8]

It was eighty years later, in 1866, when the New York Legislature passed the first effective law against cruelty in the United States and when the American Society for the Prevention of Cruelty to Animals was created. These two events happened only some thirty years before the US invasion of Puerto Rico, and the idea of animal protection had already spread with proper legislation approved in most of New England.[9] Therefore, it is logical to surmise that this concept was in the minds of many New Englanders who visited Puerto Rico in the years following the invasion, some of whom evidently perceived that Puerto Ricans, as "Latins," were barbarous and needlessly cruel towards animals and, according to several American authors, towards any living being:

> ... bird and animal life has been well-nigh exterminated from the Island by the density and cruelty of the population.... It is quite possible that the poor Porto Rican who kills the beautiful song-birds for food is more excusable than the American lady who has them killed for decoration. Yet the universal callousness of the Porto Rican to the suffering of animals is one of the impressions most strongly and frequently forced upon the American visitor, and, sad to say, the same callousness, born partly of misery and partly perchance of the seemingly innate cruelty of the Latin temper, extends to little children, to the poor, to the aged and to women. One who has seen even a glimpse of it is at once clear that the primary business of the missionary in Porto Rico is not theological. It is ... to try to substitute a new tenderness toward all living creatures, a new sympathy for suffering and a new reverence for humanity. (Douglass 1910, 12–13)

In reality, different perceptions of the value of animal life were operating. Because of their lower level of education and income, Puerto Rican peasants were not as predisposed to recognize human characteristics in animals, a phenomenon known as "anthropomorphism," as their American critics, a 2018 study suggests.[10] Their society was still focused "on subsistence and safety," and they still valued horses, oxen, and fighting cocks for their "utilitarian purposes." This important cultural difference became obvious in the 1950s narration made by an American Catholic priest who held in Puerto Rico summer institutes to train others in preparation to work with Puerto Ricans in New York:

> During the second year of the Institute religious sisters came for the first time. When they were departing ... an interesting conflict of culture

took place. The Puerto Rican chef named "Eddie"... told the sisters he will prepare a "despedida" (a farewell) in truly Puerto Rican style. They would have "lechón asado" (suckling pig) for their farewell dinner.... Eddie bought the pigs on the hoof and had them tied on the lawn outside the dining area. Over the two last days, the sisters took a real liking of the pigs, even saw them as their little friends.... The sisters could not eat the suckling pigs, they were so sorry that these little creatures, to whom they had taken a liking, had been killed. Eddie was disappointed, but his only remark to me was: "Padre, you did not teach them enough about our culture." (Fitzpatrick 1996, 26)

"MARVELS OF STRENGTH AND ENDURANCE": PUERTO RICAN HORSES

At the end of the nineteenth century, the most common mode of transportation in Puerto Rico, beyond walking, was the horse. For American soldiers, Puerto Rican horses became a commonly discussed theme. These animals were the descendants of the Arab, Berber, and Andalusian horses brought by the Spanish colonizers. Americans were impressed by their small size and by their strength, but they insisted on calling them "ponies." A war correspondent felt pity for the "ponies": "Personally, I can find no pleasure on board of a Porto Rican pony. The beasts are so small that it seems a cruelty to put even ten stone weight on their bony backs" (Robinson 1899, 125). He also commented on the riders' postures with sarcasm:

> ... about the streets ... one sees scores and scores of the little, scrawny, island ponies, hardly larger than good-sized rocking-horses, gaunt, bony, and pitiful, with their fruit-filled basket-work panniers surmounted by the proprietor of the outfit, who rides in much the attitude of one sitting on a chair, with his bare feet hanging in front of the horse's chest, and flapping about with every step which the animal takes. (Robinson 1899, 41)

Other American authors praised the Puerto Rican horses for their sturdiness:

The small native horses, looking like broken-down ponies, are marvels of strength and endurance. Used as pack horses they carry all merchandise into the interior, over roads that are not more than trails, through swollen streams, up and down mountain paths, living on nothing but grass, for grain as feed for horses they do not know. Yet the American officer was always glad to leave his big army horse for one of these easy-gaited, sure-footed ponies if he had a journey to make into the interior. One may go in any direction, and find his way leading over roads ... along the edge of precipices, or creeping snake-like about the base or side of a mountain ... (Edwards 1899, 255)

The packs these little creatures bring in from the country to the town markets astonish the new-comer. Oranges in immense round panniers, three hundred pounds weight, and the vender on top; a pair of hogs weighing one hundred and fifty pounds apiece in two great baskets, one on each side; and a mountain almost of baled grass—these, with others equally grotesque and to the pony oppressive, are common sights. Entire families may be seen coming to town on a single pony, the man astraddle, the wife seated behind him, and four or five children carried in baskets slung at the two sides. Trunks, furniture and just about everything else are transported along and over the mountain steeps, with comparative celerity and no accidents, upon the backs of these patient and intelligent little animals. (Hannaford 1899, 254)

As expected, Puerto Rican horses were used in carriages, too. American authors frequently described what they understood as animal abuse. Most concerns were about overburdened or overworked animals and the use of whips or sharp objects to prod them to move:

The old fashioned coaches are drawn by small ponies, and these brave animals carry us up hill and down hill, through deep mud holes, over rocks, into and out of ruts, a terrific pace.... The driver lashes the poor beasts until it seems as if his arms must be lame, but our protests have no effect on him. (George 1900, 40)

Oddly, in a clear case of anthropomorphism, Olivares complained about owners causing embarrassment to their horses:

The pony is also subjected to numerous indignities, some of which must be very humiliating ... for he sprang from the pure-blooded Arabian stock. For instance, when the roads are bad and the yellow mud sticks like glue, the Porto Rican braids the tail of his pony and ties it up over his back to the saddle or the harness, giving him a ludicrous appearance that is calculate to excite the mirth of all light-minded spectators.... but these even-tempered ponies take it all in good part and cheerfully acquiesce in every indignity that is imposed upon them. (Olivares, *Vol. 1* 1899, 377, 379)

The fast leap into modernity that Puerto Ricans experienced in the 1940s and 50s turned obsolete the horse as a mode of transportation. The new middle class opted for cars bought through bank loans. From them on, horses became a source of entertainment for those who could afford them besides their cars.

"YELLING 'OW—AMO—CARAJO'": PUERTO RICAN OXEN

For farmers, the most common way to take care of their land was the oxen cart or bullock. Oxen were also used to carry heavy burdens. Some American authors considered Puerto Rican oxen of great quality:

The oxen of the island are perhaps superior to our own." (Rector 1898, 73)

The principal draft animals are oxen. . . . . . . it must be said that the indigenous ox has been highly bred to a quicker draft animals than is ever seen elsewhere. (Dinwiddie 1899, 172)

The style of the oxen's yoke used in Puerto Rico, being different from the style used in the northern United States, was commonly questioned by American authors who considered them either inappropriate, primitive, or plain cruel. But opinions were divided among American authors: some emphasized what they considered animal cruelty as if it was common in Puerto Rico; others saw the local yoke as superior:

In the island, oxen are firmly yoked from the horns, in place of the lose yoke on the shoulders known to us in America. Considerable criticism has been indulged in, by the late invaders, regarding this cruel manner of handling the beasts; but, as a matter of fact, a yoke firmly lashed at the base of the horns . . . is far preferable to an open yoke which wears the shoulders into blisters at every step. They move more easily in the stiff yoke, and back admirably, which is a movement not executed with the open yoke. (Dinwiddie 1899, 172)

An American soldier hinted that one of them would have killed an owner of oxen in response to what he perceived as "cruelty" towards the animals:

. . . the characteristic cruelty and thoughtlessness of the natives . . . perhaps, engendered by the reception of a similar treatment inflicted upon themselves by their oppressors, as inherent in a low caste type. It consisted in the abandonment upon the blazing hot, sunbaked road of an ox, whose head was twisted two-thirds of the way around by the weight of the ponderous wooden collar used to yoke them in pairs, from the thrall of which his happier fellow had been released. Had the man guilty of this wanton barbarity been at hand Blake would have killed him—he even admitted as much to me. (Cammann 1899, 248)

The treatment of the oxen by their owners was also questioned and described as harsh because, according to some American observers, Puerto Rican peasants urged the animals to move forward by hitting them with sharp objects, sticks, or punches, even after US colonial military governor General Guy V. Henry banned the practice:

The drivers . . . use an ox-goad dialect, and profanity—all in profusion. They seem never happy unless they are jabbing the flank of a bull and yelling "ow-amo-carajo" at the top of their lungs. (King 1929, 67)

[Yoked oxen] are driven, not with words or whip, but with a goad. . . . If they do not follow fast enough to please him, he urges them along by prodding them. The end of the goad is shod with a sharp spike of steel, three inches or more long. Often we see these oxen dripping with blood, and seamed and scarred with wounds. . . . All day they stand or travel in the hot sun without water or food. . . . Even when they stop to rest, no one thinks of putting them in the shade. . . . Almost all people are cruel to their animals, yet they seem not to realize that they are doing wrong. It is a custom, that is all. (George 1900, 41)

The first following author, a journalist, after pointing what he considered the general cruelty of Puerto Ricans towards their animals, hinted that some American soldiers physically attacked those "abusers," implying that violence against humans was an appropriate way to stop violence against animals. The second author is a female poet who ascribed violence to "Latin blood" but then did not hesitate to violently attack a Puerto Rican man with a slap in the face in an effort to protect horses. Both of them are examples of imperialistic righteousness, and both showed more empathy for the animals than for human beings of a different ethnicity:

The inhabitants are the most cruel in their handling of beasts of burden and, in fact, of all living creatures below the grade of mankind that could be imagined. . . . Many an American soldier has knocked down these cruel drivers for their abuse of the patient beasts, but the drivers do not improve with the thrashing. (Hall 1898)

> Wherever the Latin blood is found, there too is found appalling indifference to the suffering of animals and fowls. . . . I repeatedly begged one driver I had engaged to put up his whip, and let his willing horse trot along unmolested. I had engaged him by the hour, and I was in no haste. After the third sullen defiance of my request, I reached over and administered a sharp slap on the fellow's cheek. For the remainder of the drive his horse was free from the lashing of the whip. Sometimes it requires an object lesson to teach certain types of mind that you are in earnest in your determination to protect animals against more brutal animals. (Wilcox 1909, 188–89)

Finally, an American soldier from Wisconsin shared this story that contradicts the accusations of brutality made by other Americans:

> While on outpost near Ponce, the sound of boys singing, or chanting, a sort of hymn was borne to our ears for several days. It came up from the valley and reminded them one just a little of St. Michael's chimes in Charleston. Becoming curious, some of our boys followed the sounds one day and found a native ploughing with eight fine oxen, and perched on the ox bows were three little boys, industriously singing to the oxen. It seems the music had a quieting effect. One little fellow will begin; the second will take it up where the first left off, and then the third carried it along. It was all very unique. (Rossiter [1900?])

"HARMLESS, USEFUL LITTLE FELLOWS": DOGS AND OTHER LOCAL ANIMALS

Few American authors made observations regarding dogs, cats, or any other pets they might have seen while in Puerto Rico. The few who did evidence the particular view that American culture still has regarding these animals: an inclination to anthropomorphize their pets, who are treated as if they were their kids, showing all kinds of affection, such as kisses and hugs, to them. American authors also pointed to a problem still prevalent in Puerto Rico: an abundance of stray dogs, sometimes sick:

> The dog, so loved in cold countries, seems to lose his honored standing with man in the tropics. In every city there are pariah or street dogs and they form about as melancholy and pitiable a class of quadrupeds as can be found. They earn their living as street scavengers, and judging from appearances, their remuneration is small and irregular. When dogs are

cultivated it is apparently without any reference to breed, quality or character. All that the average señora desires is a round, fat little creature that will bark at every guest, and wag his tail at every member of the family. Under such auspices, valuable animals are not to be expected. Two-thirds of all I have seen in the island were "mongrels and curs of high and low degree." What exceptions there are belong usually to Englishmen, Americans, and Germans. When you see a well-bred dog in any city or town you may be certain that there is a foreign family, if not a foreign colony, in the immediate neighborhood. (Hamm, *Porto* 1899, 40–41)

Besides the pests discussed in chapter 11, several other animals are referred to in the studied books. Three frequently mentioned during the US invasion are the agouti, the armadillo, and the iguana, of which only the iguana survives. Both agoutis and armadillos are extinct nowadays in Puerto Rico, but apparently, they were commonly seen by the turn of the twentieth century.[11] Agoutis are rainforest rodents that live in burrows.[12] The three were consumed regularly around the time of the US invasion:

The meat for our dinner consists of fish, and the flesh of the armadillo, the agouti and the iguana.... The agouti is a little animal resembling a rabbit. It lives on vegetable food, and finds a home in the rocky hillsides and on the borders of the woods. As game is not plentiful, it is sometimes used for food.... The armadillo and iguana are preferred for food, however. It is not an easy matter to catch an armadillo.... It can dig a hole in the ground almost as fast as a man can dig with a pick and spade ... It lives chiefly upon beetles, grubs and worms, which it hunts by night.... The iguana[13] ... grows to three or four feet in length.... The flesh, when cooked, resembles chicken or veal, and is a popular dish with the natives. (George 1900, 66)

Little crabs ("cocolías") and the Puerto Rican "house lizards"[14] were also mentioned: "Little crabs rattle gaily over the floor and sometimes crawl into our shoes, where we find them in the morning; friendly but ugly lizards croak from the walls and roof, where they pass the night hours in catching insects.... These lizards are found in and about most of the houses and are harmless, useful little fellows" (George 1900, 62).

Even though they were found everywhere in Puerto Rico for a long time and can still be heard in many places, the national animal, a minuscule frog we call "coquí,"[15] was only mentioned by three American authors. This is particularly notorious since the males make pervasive sounds throughout the night that are difficult to ignore:

I became conscious, as my thoughts wandered, that I was hearing a lovely sound for the first time.... a sweet, clear pure note, exotic, strangely enchanting—a chorus of them, perfectly in tune—filled the still night. Was it a bird, some stranger I had never heard of in this land of surprises? It was a first experience with the coquí (Eleutherodactylus portoricensis), that modest sweet singer of the Puerto Rican countryside in the darkness. (Tugwell 1947, 53–54)

Only one type of insect was relished by some American authors: the Puerto Rican firefly or "cucubano."[16] They are described as children's pets and women's adornments, as well as some sort of lantern:

[In a children's book:] It is a net filled with the fireflies.... Manuel is going to make pets of them. He will put them in a little wicker cage, feed them with sugar, and they will grow quite tame.... The fireflies of Porto Rico are the largest and most brilliant in the whole world.... Some of the poor people in Porto Rico use no other light at night, except these little creatures. Manuel carries the net very carefully.... He does not wish a single beetle to be injured or frightened.... he sees his mother on the veranda, "you shall wear the most beautiful one I have in your lace dress tonight." What a strange idea this seems to us! but the smiling lady... does not seem at all surprised. She often fastens the living gems under the thin net of her evening gown; perhaps they will glisten in her shoulder, perhaps at her throat, or in her hair. (Wade 1902, 18–20)

THIS CHAPTER

During the first years of colonization, Americans struggled to understand the nonexistence in Puerto Rico of the aggressive capitalism they were used to. For Puerto Ricans, personal relationships were far more valuable than the accumulation of goods or competition. With their usual fatalism, Puerto Ricans who lived rough and short lives saw money as something they should spend and enjoy with their friends and family while they were still alive, instead of something to be accumulated in order to obtain goods in a future that might never come. However, over time, especially after the fast modernization of the 1950s, Puerto Ricans became captive and eager consumers of imported goods from the United States.

American writers frequently criticized the way Puerto Ricans treated their animals. These accusations are indicative of a class gap: the accusers belonged to the upper and middle classes in the United States that had developed a particular sensibility towards animal suffering. But American farmers shared the utilitarian perception that Puerto Rican peasants had of their animals. These class differences were not acknowledged by American authors who instead used the theme to bolster their view of Puerto Ricans as backward and uncivilized people. As they expressed their imperialistic righteousness, they frequently showed more empathy for animals than for the Puerto Rican poor.

"TO BE BORN IN PORTO RICO IS, FOR ME, A PRIVILEGE": CONCLUSION

Colonialism produces deprecation of locals by the colonizers and, at the same time the colonized assimilate these negative representations of themselves. This undermines the colonized resistance if the colonized are not aware or do not understand where these representations of themselves originated. This book highlighted their origin, hopefully provoking an introspection on who defined the so-called "Puerto Rican character" in the first place.

Informal colonizers created in their writings the stereotypes that later guided the empire´s colonial policies. Their biased understandings of Puerto Ricans became the standard for the interpretation of everything Puerto Rican in the United States: from our political positions to our responses to hurricanes. So, even though they were biased, they later became reinforced by repetition and by the "self-fulfilling prophecy," as the colonized tend to accept the definitions made by the colonizers as true because they perceive the colonizers as superior. The only solution to this is the end of colonialism.

Puerto Ricans have been told for over a century that we owe progress and modern society to United States' imperialism. We have been labeled "the happy colony." Implicit in this conception is that, without the US invasion and colonization of Puerto Rico, we would be poorer and we would not have nice highways, airports, shopping centers, hospitals, schools, or universities. But such an idea is ridiculous. As Albert Memmi explained, each country in the world moves forward to its own pace and follows its own path. Puerto Rico was not a poor country in 1898, and if the fruit of the labor of so many Puerto Ricans throughout the last 124 years had been reinvested there, it would be much richer than it is nowadays as a colony:[1] "Why must we suppose that the colonized would have remained frozen in the state in which the colonizer found him? . . . Other small countries have transformed themselves greatly without being colonized."[2]

Have Puerto Ricans been assimilated? I don't think so. Some of the studied American authors agree: "Puerto Rico will never be "spoiled." Its character is too fixed, too definite, its charm is too substantial" (Vandercook 1939, 4). Puerto Ricans used a common tactic of the colonized that is called "accommodation," and that has been defined as an adjustment "to the circumstances of colonial rule and interference without entirely accepting subordination."[3] This strategy does not require action, and is almost invisible because it has to do with how we think rather than with how we act. I will venture to say that deep inside, all of us Puerto Ricans know that psychologically, spiritually, and culturally we are independent from the United States, and all of us cherish that. As an American explorer realized in 1914: "American though Porto Rico may be, yet it is merely on the surface; at heart the Porto Rican is a Porto Rican first, last, and all the time, and to his credit be it said, for our colonial policies are far from perfection, and we have much to learn" (Verrill 1914, 18).

Resistance is not always armed or violent (although many Puerto Ricans have resisted that way and paid with their youths and lives for it). Resistance can also be spiritual, like the resistance of so many slaves kidnapped and brought to be sold in the Americas. Is that resistance less powerful? Not at all. I believe that it is the hardest for the empire to destroy, because the empire cannot control it.

This accommodating resistance becomes obvious in the way Puerto Ricans call the Island: "país," or "country," even though it is not one, at least technically. We complain about the things that happen "en este país" ("in this country") and we prefer eggs, meat, and fruits "del país," meaning "from Puerto Rico" in opposition to those "americanos." We refuse to call dollars by their name and insist in calling them "pesos" as well as calling quarters "pesetas." "Even he [referring to then Governor Luis A. Ferré], as does every other Puerto Rican, refers to the island as "el país" ("country" or "nation"), which only proves that semantics is a lively sport on this Caribbean island" (Wagenheim 1970, 155).

Any Puerto Rican, on the Island or in the diaspora, will rapidly convey to any person he/she meets, the pride he/she feels about being Puerto Rican. Even a pair of American writers noticed: "The Porto Ricans, as a rule, have distinguished themselves for their love of homeland . . ." (Browne and Dole 1907, 1441). Any Puerto Rican will also show the strong emotions that our flag and our national anthem inspire in us. Our Spanish language, our food, our music, have become our weapons against the empire's domination. The fact that after 124 years we still speak Spanish every day and identify ourselves as Puerto Ricans, calling our Island "our country," tells by itself a story of resistance. We are still resisting and will continue to do so.

In 2010, an English teacher wrote about her experiences visiting the Island in the company of a Puerto Rican author who taught her about the "fierce pride" and love we Puerto Ricans feel for our Island: "Lourdes genuinely loves her island and her Spanish/Puerto Rican heritage. She's eager to share her mixed culture with a fierce pride and I admire that.... Lourdes said, 'To be born in Puerto Rico is, for me, a privilege'" (Tavenner 2010, 193, 198).

Colonialism is designed to take away from us, the colonized, our culture and identity, our confidence, our voice, our power. This is attained over years and years of physical and emotional aggressions, both collective and individual, and this happens with impunity. All efforts of resistance are crushed, some forcefully and some more subtly. Little by little, the empire takes away control from our lives, leaving us with a feeling of impotence. Through systematic humiliation and devaluation of our people and our culture, the empire extinguishes our hope and energy.

Memmi discussed how the colonized ends up responding to the constant and systematic degraded portrait of themselves created by the colonizer: "He ends up recognizing it as one would a detested nickname which has become a familiar description."[4] As these pages showed, colonialism has questioned our humanity and our identity. Injuries inflicted by colonialism have hindered us and have become evident in a variety of mental pathologies which, as Frantz Fanon postulated, are the direct product of oppression.[5] But, also according to Fanon, the colonizer only succeeds in breaking the identity of the colonized "if the latter admits loudly and intelligibly the supremacy of the white man's values." Even though Puerto Rico is still a colony, I believe that most Puerto Ricans reject the colonizers' values every day.

I find interesting the fact that in Puerto Rico, the few Puerto Ricans who at least vocally claim to feel "American," meaning US American, are commonly scorned as "pitiyanquis." In a column by poet and journalist Luis Lloréns Torres and published in *La Democracia* in March 30, 1915, he used the term and explained that it referred to "snobbish 'boricuas'... imitating American 'gentlemen.'"[6] Kal and Olga Jiménez de Wagenheim described a "pitiyanqui" with derision as "the individual who casts aside his own culture, and becomes a 200 per cent American."[7]

Moreover, as has happened to every empire in history, at the present time, the US empire is facing its internal contradictions, and its society is struggling with powerful divisive forces that can no longer be ignored and predict its decadence as an omnipotent nation. This evokes, though in the American case, Aimé Césaire's prediction about the effects of colonialism in Europe: "... colonization works to decivilize the colonizer, to brutalize him ... to degrade him ... at the end of all these lies that have been propagated, all these punitive expeditions that have been tolerated ... all the boastfulness that has been displayed, a poison has been distilled in the veins of Europe and, slowly but surely, the continent proceeds towards savagery."[8]

Not even the most powerful empires can evade forever the internal effects of the destruction and violence they bestow on other nations. What sense does it make, then, to stay attached to a falling empire? As Frantz Fanon suggested in reference to the decadent French empire: "Europe now lives at such a mad, reckless pace that she has shaken off all guidance and all reason, and she is running headlong into the abyss; we would do well to avoid it with all possible speed."[9]

I hope this book increases the resilience of all Puerto Ricans, because here you have been confronted with what we are to them, and it is evident to me that we can never attain an equality-based relationship with Americans, even those who like and respect us, until we put an end to colonialism. Inequality is intrinsic to colonialism; it is what defines the whole relationship, and there is no respect while inequality and subordination reign. As Memmi wrote, it is time for us to cease defining ourselves through the categories imposed by our colonizers: "... the colonizer's rejection is the indispensable prelude to self-discovery.... After having been rejected for so long by the colonizer, the day has come when it is the colonized who must refuse the colonizer."[10]

APPENDIX 1

GENERAL NELSON A. MILES PROCLAMATION

July 28, 1898

To the Inhabitants of Puerto Rico:

In the prosecution of the war against the kingdom of Spain by the people of the United States, in the cause of liberty, justice, and humanity, its military forces have come to occupy the island of Puerto Rico. They come bearing the banner of freedom, inspired by a noble purpose to seek the enemies of our country and yours, and to destroy or capture all who are in armed resistance.

They bring you the fostering arm of a free people, whose greatest power is in its justice and humanity to all those living within its fold. Hence the first effect of this occupation will be the immediate release from your former relations, and it is hoped a cheerful acceptance of the government of the United States.

The chief object of the American military forces will be to overthrow the armed authority of Spain, and to give the people of your beautiful island the largest measure of liberty consistent with this occupation. We have not come to make war upon the people of a country that for centuries has been oppressed, but, on the contrary, to bring you protection, not only to yourselves, but to your property; to promote your prosperity, and bestow upon you the immunities and blessings of the liberal institutions of our government.

It is not our purpose to interfere with any existing laws and customs that are wholesome and beneficial to your people so long as they conform to the rules of military administration of order and justice. This is not a war of devastation, but one to give all within the control of its military and naval forces the advantages and blessings of enlightened civilization.

Nelson A. Miles,
Major-General, Commanding United States Army.

APPENDIX 2

BIBLIOGRAPHY OF ANALYZED AMERICAN AUTHORS

Ashford, Bailey K. *A Soldier in Science. The Autobiography of Bailey K. Ashford*. New York: William Morrow and Co., 1934.

Ashford, Bailey K., and Pedro Gutierrez-Ingaravidez. *Uncinariasis (Hookworm Disease) in Porto Rico. A Medical and Economic Problem*. Washington, DC: Government Pinting Office, 1911.

Baldwin, James. *Our New Possessions. Cuba, Puerto Rico, Hawaii, Philippines*. New York: American Book Co., 1899.

Blythe, Marion. *An American Bride in Porto Rico*. New York: Fleming H. Revell Co., 1911.

Boyce, William D. *United States Colonies and Dependencies*. Chicago: Rand McNally & Co., 1914.

Brameld, Theodore. *The Remaking of a Culture. Life and Education in Puerto Rico*. New York: John Wiley & Sons, Inc., 1959.

Brown, Wenzell. *Dynamite on Our Doorstep, Puerto Rican Paradox*. New York: Greenberg Publisher, 1945.

Browne, Waldo G., and Nathan Haskell Dole. *The New America and the Far East. Vol. VIII*. Boston: Marshall Jones Co., 1907.

Cammann, William C. *The History of Troop "A," New York Cavalry U.S.V., From May 2 to November 28, 1898 in the Spanish-American War*. New York: R. H. Russell, 1899.

Carpenter, Frank G. *Lands of the Caribbean*. New York: Doubleday, Doran & Co., 1930.

Carpenter, Vere C. *Puerto Rican Disciples: A Personal Narrative of Fifty Years with Christ in the Island of Enchantment*. Florida: The Christian Press, 1960.

Church, A. M. *Picturesque Cuba, Porto Rico, Hawaii and the Philippines. A Photographic Panorama of Our New Possessions*. Springfield, OH: Mast, Crowell & Kirkpatrick, 1898.

Cooper, Jim. *Down on the Island: Mayaguez, Puerto Rico, 1951–1954*. Wisconsin: no publisher, 1994.

Creager, Charles. *The Fourteenth Ohio National Guard—the Fourth Ohio Volunteer Infantry. A Complete Record of this Organization From its Foundation to the Present Day*. Ohio: The Landon Printing & Publishing Co., 1899.

Crowell, Katharine R. *Sea Breezes: A Sketch of the Presbyterian Hospital at San Juan*. New York: Woman's Board of Home Missions of the Presbyterian Church, 1907.

Dana, Arnold G. *Porto Rico's Case, Outcome of American Sovereignty, 1898–1924, 1925–1928.* New Haven, Conn.: The Turtle, Morehouse & Taylor Co., 1928.

Davis, Richard H. *The Cuban and Porto Rican Campaigns.* New York: Charles Scribner's Sons, 1898.

Dean, Corinne. *Cocoanut Suite, Stories of the West Indies.* Boston: Meador Publishing Co., 1944.

Delano, Jack. *Photographic Memories.* Washington, DC: Smithsonian Institution Press, 1997.

Detweiler, Charles S. *The Waiting Isles. Baptist Missions in the Caribbean.* New York: Fleming H. Revell Co., 1930.

Dewell, James D. *Down in Porto Rico with a Kodak.* New Haven, Conn.: The Record Publishing Co., 1898.

Dinwiddie, William. *Puerto Rico, Its Conditions and Possibilities (1899).* San Juan: Fundación Puertorriqueña de las Humanidades, 2005. Facsimile reprint of the New York: Harper & Bros, 1899 edition.

Dorvillier, William J. *Workshop, U.S.A. The Challenge of Puerto Rico.* New York: Coward-McCann, Inc., 1962.

Douglass, Paul H. *Congregational Missionary Work in Puerto Rico: Conducted by the American Missionary Association.* New York: American Missionary Association, 1910.

Drury, Marion R. *Mission Triumphs in Porto Rico and Santo Domingo: A Story of Progress and Achievement in the West Indies.* Ponce, PR: Puerto Rico Evangélico Press, 1924.

Du Puy, William A. *Uncle Sam's Modern Miracles.* New York: Frederick A. Stokes Co., 1914.

Duggan, Janie P. *Child of the Sea, A Chronicle of Porto Rico.* Philadelphia: The Judson Press, 1920.

Dunne, Finlay P. *Mr. Dooley in Peace and in War.* Boston: Small, Maynard & Co., 1905.

Edwards, F. *The '98 Campaign of the 6th Massachusetts, U.S.V.* Boston: Little, Brown and Co., 1899.

Ezratty, Barbara T. *Puerto Rico: Changing Flags, An Oral History 1898–1950.* Maryland: Omni Arts, Inc., 1986.

Falcon, Rafael, and Tom Lehman, editors. *Mennonite Memories of Puerto Rico.* no place: no publisher, 2014.

Fiala, Anthony. *Troop "C" in Service; An Account of the Part Played by Troop "C" of the New York Volunteer Cavalry in the Spanish-American War of 1898.* New York: Eagle Press, 1899.

Fitzpatrick, Joseph P. *The Stranger Is Our Own: Reflections on the Journey of Puerto Rican Migrants.* Kansas City: Sheed & Ward, 1996.

Flax, Herman J. *Life to Years.* Rockville, Maryland: no publisher, 1995.

Fleagle, Fred K. *Social Problems in Porto Rico.* Boston: D. C. Heath & Co., 1917.

Forbes-Lindsay, Charles H. *America's Insular Possessions, Vol. I.* Philadelphia: The John Winston Co., 1906.

Fowles, George M. *Down in Porto Rico.* New York: Young People's Missionary Movement of the US and Canada, 1910.

Franck, Harry A. *Roaming Through the West Indies.* New York: The Century Co., 1920.

George, Marian M. *A Little Journey to Puerto Rico for Intermediate and Upper Grades.* Chicago: A. Flanagan Co., 1900.

Graham, Stephen. *In Quest of El Dorado.* New York: D. Appleton & Co., 1923.

Gray, Arthur R. *The New World.* New York: The Domestic and Foreign Missionary Society, 1920.

Greater America: The Latest Acquired Insular Possessions. Boston: Perry Mason Co., 1900.

Grose, Howard B. *Advance in the Antilles. The New Era in Cuba and Porto Rico*. New York: Young People's Missionary Movement of the United States and Canada, 1910.
Gruber, Ruth. *Puerto Rico, Island of Promise*. New York: Hill and Wang, 1960.
Guernsey, Alice M. *Citizens of Tomorrow. A Study of Childhood and Youth from the Standpoint of Home Mission Work*. New York: Fleming H. Revell Co., 1907.
Guernsey, Alice M. *Under Our Flag A Study of National Conditions from the Standpoint of Woman's Home Missionary Work*. New York: Fleming H. Revell Co., 1903.
Gunther, John. *Inside Latin America*. New York: Harper & Brothers Publisher, 1940.
Hall, Arthur D. *Porto Rico: Its History, Products and Possibilities*. New York: Street & Smith, 1898.
Halstead, Murat. *Pictorial History of America's New Possessions. The Isthmian Canals and the Problem of Expansion*. Chicago: W. S. Reeve Publishing Co., 1899.
Halstead, Murat. *Triumphant America and Her New Possessions*. Chicago: Colonial Publishing Co., 1899.
Hamm, Margherita A. *America's New Possessions and Spheres of Influence*. New York: F. Tennyson Neely, 1899.
Hamm, Margherita A. *Porto Rico and the West Indies*. New York: F. Tennyson Neely, 1899.
Hancock, Ralph. *Puerto Rico, A Success Story*. New Jersey: D. Van Nostrand Co., 1960.
Hannaford, Ebenezer. *History and Description of Our Philippine Wonderland and Photographic Panorama of Hawaii, Cuba, Porto Rico, Samoa, Guam, and Wake Island*. Ohio: The Crowell & Kirkpatrick Co., 1899.
Hanson, Earl P. *Puerto Rico, Land of Wonders*. New York: Alfred A. Knopf, 1960.
Harris, Alice. *Puerto Rico Fact and Fable*. New York: Golden Galleon Press, 1932.
Harris, J. Will. *Riding & Roping. The Memoirs of J. Will Harris*. San Juan: Interamerican University of Puerto Rico, 1977.
Herrmann, Karl S. *From Yauco to Las Marias. Being a Story of the Recent Campaign in Western Puerto Rico by the Independent Regular Brigade, Under Command of Brigadier-General Schwan*. Boston: Richard G. Badger & Co., 1900.
Hill, Robert T. *Cuba and Porto Rico with the Other Islands of the West Indies*. New York: The Century Co., 1898.
Holsinger, Justus G. *Puerto Rico, Island of Progress*. no place: Tom Lehman, 2013.
Holsinger, Justus G. *Serving Rural Puerto Rico. A History of Eight Years of Service by the Mennonite Church*. Pennsylvania: Mennonite Publishing House, 1952.
Hough, Samuel S. *Our Church Abroad*. Ohio: Otterbein Press, 1916.
Howe, Edgar W. *The Trip to the West Indies*. Topeka, KS: Crane Company, 1910.
Ickes, Harold L. *The Secret Diary of Harold L. Ickes. The First Thousand Days, 1933-1936*. New York: Simon & Schuster, 1953.
James, Arthur. *Thirty Years in Porto Rico. A Record of the Progress since American Occupation*. San Juan: Porto Rico Progress, 1927.
Johnston, Julia H. *Indian and Spanish Neighbors*. New York: Fleming H. Revell Co., 1905.
Jones, Chester L. *Caribbean Interests of the United States*. New York: Appleton & Co., 1916.
Jordan, William F. *Crusading in the West Indies*. New York: Fleming H. Revell Co., 1922.
Kellogg, Eva M. C. *Cuba and Islands of the Sea*. Boston: Silver, Burdett & Co., 1898.
King, George G. *Letters of a Volunteer in the Spanish-American War*. Chicago: Hawkins & Loomis, 1929.

Lord, Everett W. *Under the Tropic Sun: An Account of the Origins of the Department of Education of Puerto Rico, in the Early Days of the 20th Century*. Caguas, PR: Editorial Marqués de Cundiamor, 2004.

Mabie, Hamilton W. *Our Country in Peace and in War*. Philadelphia: W. E. Scull, 1899.

March, Alden. *The History and Conquest of the Philippines and Our Other Island Possessions*. Philadelphia: WM. E. Scull, 1899.

Marden, Philip S. *Sailing South*. Boston: Houghton Mifflin Co., 1921.

Mathews, George M. *Report of an Episcopal Visit to Porto Rico*. Ohio: Foreign Missionary Society, 1912.

Maus, Cynthia P. *Puerto Rico in Pictures and Poetry*. Idaho: The Caldwell Printers, 1941.

McGuire, Edna. *Puerto Rico, Bridge to Freedom*. New York: The Macmillan Company, 1963.

McLean, Robert, and Grace P. Williams. *Old Spain in New America*. New York: Association Press, 1916.

Miles, Nelson A. *Serving the Republic. Memoirs of the Civil and Military Life of Nelson A. Miles*. New York: Harper & Brothers Publishers, 1911.

Mills, Job S., William R. Funk, and Samuel S. Hough. *Our Foreign Missionary Enterprise*. Ohio: United Brethren Publishing House, 1908.

Mixer, Knowlton. *Porto Rico, History and Conditions (1926)*. San Juan: Fundación Puertorriqueña de las Humanidades, 2005. Facsimile Reprint of New York: The MacMillan Co., 1926 edition.

Moore, J. Hampton. *With Speaker Cannon through the Tropics. A Descriptive Story of a Voyage to the West Indies, Venezuela and Panama*. Philadelphia: The Book Print, 1907.

Morehouse, Henry L. *Porto Rico: A Narrative Sketch of Baptist Missions in the Island*. New York: The American Baptist Home Mission Society, 1904.

Morris, Charles. *Our Island Empire. A Hand-book of Cuba, Porto Rico, Hawaii, and the Philippine Islands*. Philadelphia: J. B. Lippincott Co., 1899.

Morris, Charles. *The War with Spain; A Complete History of the War of 1898 between the United States and Spain*. Philadelphia: J. B. Lippincott Co., 1899.

Morton, C. Manley. *Kingdom Building in Puerto Rico*. Indianapolis: The United Christian Missionary Society, 1949.

Neely, Frank T. *Neely's Panorama of Our New Possessions. Filipiana*. New York: F. Tennyson Neely, 1898.

Ober, Frederick A. *A Guide to the West Indies and Bermudas*. New York: Dodd, Mead & Co., 1908.

Ober, Frederick A. *Our West Indian Neighbors: The Islands of the Caribbean Sea*. New York: James Pott & Co., 1904.

Ober, Frederick A. *Puerto Rico and Its Resources (1899)*. San Juan: Fundación Puertorriqueña de las Humanidades, 2005. Facsimile Reprint of New York: Appleton and Co., 1899 edition.

Odell, Edward A. *It Came to Pass*. New York: Board of National Missions, Presbyterian Church in the U.S.A., 1952.

Olivares, José de. *Our Islands and Their People as seen with Camera and Pencil, Vol. I*. St. Louis: N. D. Thompson Publishing Co., 1899.

Olivares, José de. *Our Islands and Their People as seen with Camera and Pencil, Vol. II*. St. Louis: N. D. Thompson Publishing Co., 1899.

Oliver, William H. *Roughing It with the Regulars*. New York: William F. Parr Printer, 1901.
Petrullo, Vincenzo. *Puerto Rican Paradox*. Philadelphia: University of Pennsylvania Press, 1947.
Phillips, Henry Albert. *White Elephants in the Caribbean. A Magic Journey through all the West Indies*. New York: Robert M. McBride & Co., 1936.
Photo-Gravures of Picturesque Porto Rico. San Juan: Hardie Bros., 1899.
Pierce, Frederick E. *Reminiscences of the Experience of Company L, Second Regiment Massachusetts Infantry, U.S.V., in the Spanish-American War*. Massachusetts: E. A. Hall & Co., 1900.
Rand, Abby. *Abby Rand's Guide to Puerto Rico and the U.S. Virgin Islands*. New York: Charles Scribner's Sons, 1973.
Rand, Christopher. *The Puerto Ricans*. New York: Oxford University Press, 1958.
Rector, Charles H. *The Story of Beautiful Porto Rico. A Graphic Description of the Garden Spot of the World by Pen and Camera*. Chicago: Laird & Lee Publishers, 1898.
Richardson, Lewis C. *Puerto Rico, Caribbean Crossroads*. New York: U.S. Camera Publishing Corp., 1947.
Robinson, Albert G. *The Porto Rico of To-day: Pen Pictures of the People and the Country*. New York: Charles Scribner's Sons, 1899.
Rollins, Frances. *Getting to Know Puerto Rico*. New York: Coward-McCann, Inc., 1967.
Roosevelt Jr., Theodore. *Colonial Policies of the United States, 1937*. New Hampshire: Ayer Company Publishers, Inc., 2000.
Rossiter, Emanuel. *Right, Forward, Fours Right, March! A Little Story of "Company I"*. No place: No publisher, ca. 1900.
Rowe, L. S. *The United States and Porto Rico, with Special Reference to the Problems Arising Out of Our Contact with the Spanish-American Civilization*. London: Longman's, Green & Co., 1904.
Samoiloff, Louise C. *Portrait of Puerto Rico*. New York: Cornwall Books, 1984.
Schloat, G. Warren. *María & Ramón. A Girl and Boy of Puerto Rico*. New York: Alfred A. Knopf, 1966.
Seabury, Joseph B. *Porto Rico: The Land of the Rich Port. The World and Its People. Box XII*. New York: Silver, Burdett & Co., 1908.
Stevens, Walter B. *A Trip to Panama. The Narrative of a Tour of Observation through The Canal Zone, with Some Accounts of Visits to Saint Thomas, Porto Rico, Jamaica and Cuba, by the Commercial Clubs of Boston, Chicago, Cincinnati and St. Louis, February 18th-March 14th, 19*. St. Louis: Lesan-Gould Co., 1907.
Stoddard, Charles A. *Cruising Among the Caribbees. Summer Days in Winter Months*. New York: Charles Scribner's Sons, 1903.
Taft, Marcus L. *Three Trips to the Tropics or The West Indies in Winter, 1903, 1904, 1905*. New York: unknown, 1905.
Tavenner, Mary Hilaire. *Puerto Rico, 2006: Memoirs of a Writer in Puerto Rico*. Ohio: Dutch Ink Publishing, 2010.
Tugwell, Rexford G. *The Stricken Land. The Story of Puerto Rico*. New York: Doubleday & Co. Inc., 1947.
Van Deusen, Richard J., and Elizabeth Kneipple Van Deusen. *Porto Rico, A Caribbean Isle, 1931*. San Juan: Instituto de Cultura Puertorriqueña, 2012.

Van Middeldyk, Rudolph A. *The History of Puerto Rico From the Spanish Discovery to the American Occupation (1903)*. San Juan: Fundación Puertorriqueña de las Humanidades, 2005. Facsimile Reprint of New York: D. Appleton and Co., 1903 edition.

Vandercook, John W. *Discover Puerto Rico*. New York: Harper & Brothers Publishers, 1939.

Verrill, A. Hyatt. *Porto Rico Past and Present and San Domingo of Today*. New York: Dodd, Mead & Co., 1914.

Verrill, A. Hyatt. *The Book of the West Indies*. New York: E.P. Dutton & Co., 1917.

Vivian, Thomas J., and Smith, Ruel P. *Everything About Our New Possessions*. New York: R. F. Fenno & Co., 1899.

Wade, Mary H. *Our Little Porto Rican Cousin*. Boston: L. C. Page & Co., 1902.

Wagenheim, Kal. *Puerto Rico, A Profile*. New York: Praeger Publishers, 1970.

Waid, Eva C. *From Plaza, Patio and Palm. A Book of Borrowings*. New York: Council of Women for Home Missions, 1916.

White, Trumbull. *Our New Possessions. Four Books in One. A Graphic Account, Descriptive and Historical, of the Tropical Islands of the Sea Which Have Fallen Under Our Sway . . . Book II*. Chicago: National Educational Union, 1898.

White, Trumbull. *Puerto Rico and Its People, 1938*. New York: Arno Press, 1975.

Wilcox, Ella W. *Sailing Sunny Seas*. Chicago: W. B. Conkey Co., 1909.

Wilcox, F. W. *Seeing Porto Rico*. New York: American Missionary Association, ca. 1918.

Willets, Gilson. *Photographic Views of Our New Possessions, The Philippines, Puerto Rico, Cuba*. Chicago: Waverly Publishing Co., 1898.

Wilson, Edward S. *Political Development of Porto Rico (1905)*. San Juan: Fundación Puertorriqueña de las Humanidades, 2005. Facsimile Reprint of Columbus, OH: F. J. Heer, 1905 edition.

Winslow, Isaac O. *Geography Readers—III. Our American Neighbors*. Boston: D. C. Heath & Co., 1910.

Wright, Hamilton M., C. H. Forbes-Lindsay, John F. Wallace, Willard French, Wallace W. Atwood, and Elizabeth Fairbanks. *America across the Seas. Our Colonial Empire*. New York: C. S. Hammond & Co., 1909.

Wood, Leonard, William H. Taft, Charles H. Allen, Perfecto Lacoste, and Marion E. Beall. *Opportunities in the Colonies and Cuba*. New York: Lewis, Scribner & Co., 1902.

APPENDIX 3

AMERICAN AUTHORS' INFORMATIVE TABLE

General information regarding the selected American authors, in their surnames' alphabetical order, whenever available. Notice that the number of authors does not correspond to the number of studied books since some books had multiple authors, a few were anonymous, and sometimes we studied more than one book from the same author. The asterisks (****) indicate when the information was not found after researching.

Complete name	Dates of birth/death	Pertinent personal data	Time in Puerto Rico
Ashford, Bailey K(elly)	1873–1934	MD, Major, Medical Corps, US Army. Afterward taught full-time at the School of Tropical Medicine, which he helped establish in San Juan. Physician and coresearcher with Dr. Pedro Gutiérrez Ingaravidez.	Came with the US invasion. Afterward, member of the Porto Rico Anemia Commission that treated uncinariasis, and instructor at the School of Tropical Medicine.
Baldwin, James	1841–1925	Educator and school superintendent/ textbooks' editor and children book's author	****
Blythe, Marion	****	Presbyterian missionary	Came as a newlywed with her Presbyterian missionary husband in 1905. Lived in Aguadilla, San Sebastián and Lares

(*continues*)

(continued)

Complete name	Dates of birth/death	Pertinent personal data	Time in Puerto Rico
Boyce, William D(ickinson)	1848–1929	Travel writer and newspaper publisher	****
Brameld Theodore	1904–1987	Leading philosopher and educator with a PhD	Had a faculty post at the University of Puerto Rico for three years
Brown, Wenzell	1911–1981	English teacher	Taught at Ponce and San Sebastián in 1936–38. Returned in 1945 for several months
Browne, George W(aldo)	1851–1930	Novelist, poet, historian, lecturer	****
Cammann, William C.	****	US cavalry soldier	Came with the US invasion forces
Carpenter, Frank G(eorge)	1855–1924	Journalist, travel writer, photographer, lecturer on geography	Came right after the Spanish-American War
Carpenter, Vere C(lifton)	1878–1966	Disciples of Christ Church's missionary	Stayed as a missionary for forty years (1906–1944) in Ciales
Church, A. M.	****	Probably a war correspondent/ photographer	Probably reported during the Spanish-American War
Cooper, Jim	****	English teacher	Taught at the University of Puerto Rico's Mayagüez Campus in 1951–1954. Returned with his wife in 1966 as director of the Interamerican University in Barranquitas. In the early 1970s, lived in Aguadilla and San Germán.
Creager, Charles E(dward)	****	US infantry volunteer, sergeant major of the Ohio National Guard	Came with the US invasion forces
Crowell, Katherine R(oney)	1854–1926	Presbyterian missionary	Served at the Presbyterian Hospital of San Juan

(continues)

(continued)

Complete name	Dates of birth/death	Pertinent personal data	Time in Puerto Rico
Dale, Haskell Nathan—coauthor	1852–1935	Journalist, editor, translator, and author	****
Dana, Arnold G(uyot)	1862–1947	Newspaper editor, statistician, and author	After retiring, visited for six weeks in 1927 and studied economic conditions
Davis, Richard Harding	1864–1916	War correspondent, journalist, magazine editor, and fiction writer	Came with the US invasion
Dean, Corinne	****	English teacher. The only African-American author in this study	Taught at Ponce de León School in Humacao during the 1930s
Delano, Jack	1914–1997	Photographer for the Farm Security Administration (FSA) and freelancer	Arrived with his wife (Irene) on a three-months assignment in 1941. Returned in 1945 under a Guggenheim Foundation one-year grant. Later settled for fifty years working for the Community Education Division of the Public Instruction Department
Detweiler, Charles S(amuel)	1878–1962	Baptist missionary	Served in 1909–1919
Dewell, James D(udley)	1837–1906	Governor of Connecticut (1897–99) and businessman	Came on a business trip for ten days in January 1898, before the US invasion
Dinwiddie, William	1867–1934	Journalist and war photographer	During the US invasion, spent two months traveling the Island sponsored by the editors Harper & Brothers to gather information for his book

(continues)

(continued)

Complete name	Dates of birth/death	Pertinent personal data	Time in Puerto Rico
Dole, Nathan H(askell), coauthor	1852–1935	Editor, journalist, translator, and author	****
Dorvillier, William J.	1959–2008	Journalist. Founder, publisher, and editor of Puerto Rico's the *San Juan Star*	Came first in 1939 for his honeymoon and stayed to found the *World Journal* (1940–45). Was correspondent for *El Mundo* in Washington (1946–53) and worked in the *San Juan Star* (1953–67)
Douglass, H(arlan) Paul	1871–1953	Congregational missionary, Correspondent Secretary for the American Missionary Association (AMA), pastor, and urban sociologist	Probably served in Puerto Rico
Drury, Marion R(ichardson)	1849–1939	United Brethren minister and missionary, college president, editor, and compiler of several books	Came to serve in Ponce in 1922
Du Puy, William A(therton)	1876–1941	Author and journalist	****
Duggan, Janie Prichard	1861–1938	Baptist missionary	Served in Puerto Rico in 1899–1911
Dunne, Finlay Peter	1867–1936	Humorist and writer of Irish origin	****
Edwards, Frank E.	****	Private from Massachusetts, later promoted to Second Lieutenant	Came with the US invasion forces and stayed until Oct. 21, 1898
Ezratty, Barbara Tasch	****	Journalist, teacher, and writer of cooking books and others	Moved in 1969 and taught at a private school. Conducted interviews for twenty-five years for the studied book.

(continues)

(continued)

Complete name	Dates of birth/death	Pertinent personal data	Time in Puerto Rico
Falcón, Rafael	****	Born in Aibonito; coeditor of a book written by several Mennonite volunteers for the Civilian Public Service (CPS) in Puerto Rico during the 1940s to 1970s. Professor of Spanish at Goshen College, IND, with a PhD.	Coauthor/born in Puerto Rico
Fiala, Anthony	1869–1950	Volunteer cavalryman from New York, a private, and war correspondent for the *Brooklyn Daily Eagle*	Came with the US invasion forces
Fitzpatrick, S. J. Joseph P.	1913–1995	Jesuit priest who ministered to Puerto Ricans in New York. Had a PhD in Industrial Sociology. Developed the Institute of Intercultural Communication at the Catholic University in Ponce, where mainland priests and nurses learned Spanish and Puerto Rican culture, and then spent one month serving at a Puerto Rican parish.	Visited in 1952 for a month. Then came every summer between 1957 and 1972 to administer his six-weeks institute
Flax, Herman J(acob)	1917–2012	An Orthodox Jew and a physiatrist	Came in 1941 after marrying Puerto Rican Josefina Guarch. Practiced medicine in Bayamón, Arecibo and Morovis. Became a widow in 1973 and left the Island in 1991. His son Hjalmar is a Puerto Rican poet

(continues)

(continued)

Complete name	Dates of birth/death	Pertinent personal data	Time in Puerto Rico
Fleagle, Fred K.	1903–1966	US rural sociologist and college professor	Stayed for ten years as a University of Puerto Rico instructor and dean
Forbes-Lindsay, C(harles) H(arcourt)	1860-****	Travel writer	****
Fowles, George Milton	****	Missionary	Probably served in Puerto Rico
Franck, Harry A(lverson)	1881–1962	Travel writer	Came as a newlywed for an eight-months tour of the Antilles
Funk, W(illiam) R(oss)— coauthor	1861–1935	Agent for the United Brethren Publishing House	Part of a 1900–1908 delegation sent by the Foreign Mission Board of the United Brethren Church to investigate their missions
George, Marian M(innie)	1865-****	Author of children's books	****
Gray, Arthur R(omeyn)	1875–1933	Episcopal missionary	Probably served in Puerto Rico
Grose, Howard B(enjamin)	1851–1939	Baptist minister, President of the University of North Dakota (1890–92), history professor, assistant editor of the *Watchman* in Boston, and Editorial Secretary of the American Baptist Home Mission Society (1904–10)	Probably served in Puerto Rico
Gruber, Ruth	1911–2016	Photojournalist and author	Came in 1958 to write a series of articles for the *New York Herald Tribune*

(continues)

(continued)

Complete name	Dates of birth/death	Pertinent personal data	Time in Puerto Rico
Guernsey, Alice M(argaret)	1850–1924	Missionary and author of books of stories by missionaries serving in Puerto Rico that were published in the *Congregationalist*	****
Gunther, John	1901–1970	Journalist and author	Spent a few days in San Juan and visited the countryside
Gutierrez Ingaravidez, Pedro—coauthor	1871–1935	Physician and co-researcher with Dr. Bailey K. Ashford. Member of the Porto Rico Anemia Commission that treated uncinariasis and Director of the Tropical and Transmissible Diseases Service of Puerto Rico	Coauthor/born in Puerto Rico
Hall, Arthur D.	****	War correspondent	****
Halstead, Murat	1829–1908	Newspaper editor, magazine writer, and war correspondent	Came during the US invasion
Hamm, Margherita A(rlina)	1871–1907	Canadian-born war correspondent, journalist, and poet. First woman covering a war from the front lines	Came before and during the US invasion. As Inspector of Supplies in Puerto Rico (1896–1899), was active in the aid of the sick and injured American soldiers
Hancock, Ralph	1903–1987	Journalist and foreign correspondent from Latin America for various press services	****
Hannaford, E(benezer)	1840–1905	A Union Civil War officer native of England and author	****

(continues)

(continued)

Complete name	Dates of birth/death	Pertinent personal data	Time in Puerto Rico
Hanson, Earl Parker	1899–1978	Engineer and geographer	In 1935–36 was a consultant for the Puerto Rico Reconstruction Administration (PRRA) and became Executive Secretary of its Planning Division. In 1955 moved to the Island. In the 1960's was consultant for the Department of State of Puerto Rico and a columnist for the *Island Times* newspaper
Harris, Alice	1870–1970	Missionary and documentary photographer	Served several months in Puerto Rico
Harris, J(ohn) Will	1876–1956	Presbyterian missionary and Freemason. In 1912, founded the Polytechnic Institute of Puerto Rico (today Interamerican University)	Served in San Germán since 1906 and left the Island when he retired in 1937
Herrmann, Karl Stephen	****	Army artillery private	Came with the US invasion and stayed for a period afterward as an interpreter
Hill, Robert T(homas)	1858–1941	Worked for the US Geological Survey in 1886–1903	Came in 1898 to explore possible gold and copper mining in Puerto Rico. Made two exploration visits

(continues)

(continued)

Complete name	Dates of birth/death	Pertinent personal data	Time in Puerto Rico
Holsinger, Justus G(eil)	1911–2007	As a Mennonite conscientious objector to World War II, was consigned by the Civilian Public Service (CPS) to the Brethren Service Commission to serve in the rural PRRA community of La Plata	Served as Community Service Director in La Plata in 1942–44 and returned in 1948 to direct the La Plata Mennonite Project. He left in 1952 but returned in 1969 for six months to observe and study the effects of industrialization in Puerto Rico.
Hough, Samuel S(trickler)	1864–1944	Secretary of the Foreign Missionary Society, United Brethren in Christ	Part of a 1900–1908 delegation sent by the Foreign Mission Board of the United Brethren Church to investigate their missions
Howe, E(dgar) W(atson)	1853–1937	Newspaper and magazine editor, novelist	Traveling with a group of friends, spent a night and a day in San Juan
Ickes, Harold L(e Clair)	1874–1952	Secretary of the Interior between 1933 and 1946	Toured Puerto Rico in 1938 as part of an inspection visit
James, Arthur	****	Missionary	Spent thirty years in Puerto Rico
Johnston, Julia H(arriette)	1849–1919	Presbyterian teacher, author and musician	****
Jones, Chester Lloyd	1881–1941	Professor of political science and commercial attaché in Madrid, Havana, and Paris	****
Jordan, William F.	****	Canadian naturalized citizen in the US. Worked for the Foreign Agencies Committee of the American Bible Society	Came in June 1910 to study the field and advise on the Bible distribution in Puerto Rico. Traveled through San Juan, Ponce and Mayagüez, and some smaller towns, and lived in Puerto Rico in 1910–13

(continues)

(continued)

Complete name	Dates of birth/death	Pertinent personal data	Time in Puerto Rico
Kellogg, Eva M(ary) C(rosby)	1860–1947	Travel books writer	****
King, George G(lenn)	****	Volunteer infantry soldier from Massachusetts	Came with the US invasion forces
Lehman, Tom—coauthor	****	Missionary and librarian. Coeditor of a book written by several Mennonite volunteers for the Civilian Public Service (CPS) in Puerto Rico during the 1940s to 1970s.	****
Lord, Everett W(illiam)	1871–1965	Educator and reverend of the Methodist Church	Came in 1902 with his wife to be Assistant to the Commissioner of Education and stayed for five years. Returned in 1924 to establish the College of Business Administration of the University of Puerto Rico and be its dean from 1926 to 1929
Mabie, Hamilton W(right)	1846–1916	Essayist, critic, and lecturer, as well as editor for the *Outlook* (then known as the *Christian Union*)	****
March, Alden	1869–1942	Correspondent for the *New York Times*	Probably came during the US invasion
Marden, Phillip Sanford	1874–1963	Editor-in-chief and president of *Courier - Citizen Co.* Traveled around the world and wrote travelogues	Spent a brief winter holiday cruising in Puerto Rico
Mathews, G(eorge) M(ichael)	1848–1921	Episcopal bishop of the United Brethren Church	Visited the mission in the southern part of Puerto Rico between January and part of February of 1911.

(continues)

(*continued*)

Complete name	Dates of birth/death	Pertinent personal data	Time in Puerto Rico
Maus, Cynthia Pearl	1878–1970	Pioneer leader in youth work and author	Spent the winter of 1939–1940
McGuire, Edna	1888–1980	Educator	The Foreword of her 1963 book on Puerto Rico was written by then Governor Luis Muñoz Marín
McLean, Robert	1882–1964	Superintendent of Mexican Work in the South West Home Mission Board of the Presbyterian Church	****
Miles, Nelson A(ppleton)	1839–1925	Lieutenant General of the US Army in charge of the US invasion of Puerto Rico in the Spanish-American War	First Military Governor of Puerto Rico from August to October of 1898
Mills, J(ob) S(mith)	1848–1909	Bishop of East District for the Foreign Missionary Society of the United Brethren Church	Part of a 1900–1908 delegation sent by the Foreign Mission Board of the United Brethren Church to investigate their missions
Mixer, Knowlton	1869–1939	Social worker and writer, worked for the Red Cross during World War I (1917–1920) and later in Puerto Rico, the Philippines, and Japan	Was Executive Secretary of the Puerto Rican Chapter of the American Red Cross from 1921 to 1922
Moore, J(oseph) Hampton	1864–1950	Republican member of the US House of Representatives for Pennsylvania	Traveled in November 1906 with a group of representatives and US President Teddy Roosevelt
Morehouse, Henry L(yman)	1834–1917	Had a PhD in Divinity/ Corresponding Secretary of the American Baptist Home Mission Society	Traveled through the West Indies for two months
Morris, Charles	1833–1922	Journalist, novelist, and author	****

(*continues*)

(continued)

Complete name	Dates of birth/death	Pertinent personal data	Time in Puerto Rico
Morton, C(lement) Manley	1884–1922	Missionary for the Disciples of Christ Church	Served in Puerto Rico for at least twenty-five years (1924–49)
Neely, F(rank) Tennyson	1863–1941	Publisher and compiler	****
Ober, Frederick A(lbion)	1849–1913	Naturalist, writer, and lecturer	Visited first in the winter of 1879–80. In 1893 visited as West Indian Commissioner for the Columbian Exposition, and in 1899, was sent by a magazine to write on opportunities for potential investors
Odell, Edward A(lbert)	1879–1965	Presbyterian missionary	Served in Lares (1906–1908) and then in San Juan as superintendent of the Presbyterian Mission
Olivares, José de	1867–1942	Mexican-American from California, war correspondent, US soldier, writer	Came with the US invasion forces
Oliver Jr., William H.	****	Cavalry regular soldier	Came with the US invasion forces
Petrullo, Vincenzo	1906–1991	Italian naturalized citizen of the USA. Had a PhD in Anthropology and worked for the Office of Strategic Services (now CIA) in 1941–44 as an intelligence analyst assigned to Latin America.	After World War II, worked for a year on a research project for the Governor of Puerto Rico
Phillips, Henry Albert	1880–1951	Author, editor, and lecturer	Spent two years traveling through the West Indies and ten days in Puerto Rico as a house guest of American governor Blanton Winship in La Fortaleza

(continues)

(continued)

Complete name	Dates of birth/death	Pertinent personal data	Time in Puerto Rico
Pierce, Frederick E(verett)	1862–1953	A Captain during the Spanish-American War, and also a Mason	Came with the US invasion forces
Rand, Abby	****	Travel writer and editor of *Ski* magazine	****
Rand, Christopher	1912–1968	Journalist for the *New Yorker* from 1947 until his death, travel writer	****
Rector, Charles H.	****	Author	Visited on a sailing trip around the coast twice and then traveled inland by railroad, coach, and pony, crossing fourteen towns.
Richardson, Lewis C(utter)	1902–1967	English teacher	Came in 1924 to teach in Utuado High School. Married a Puerto Rican and stayed. Taught at the University of Puerto Rico since 1928
Robinson, Albert Gardner	1855–1932	War correspondent for the *Evening Post* of New York	Came with the US invasion forces and stayed until October 1898
Rollins, Frances	1928–2016	Children's book writer	****
Roosevelt Jr., Theodore	1910–1944	Son of President Theodore Roosevelt, politician and soldier	Governor of Puerto Rico from October 1929 to January 1932
Rossiter, Emanuel	****	First Lieutenant of Wisconsin's National Guard	Came with the US invasion forces
Rowe, L(eo) S(tanton)	1871–1946	Professor of political science, had a PhD in Finance, and was a lawyer	Member of a commission to revise and compile the laws of Puerto Rico (1900–01) and Chairman of the Porto Rican Code Commission (1901–02)

(continues)

(continued)

Complete name	Dates of birth/death	Pertinent personal data	Time in Puerto Rico
Samoiloff, Louise Cripps	1904–2001	Journalist, editor, writer, and advocator for Puerto Rican independence	First visited Puerto Rico in 1959 and kept doing so until the early 1970s, when she moved to Dorado with her Russian husband.
Schloat, G(abriel) Warren	1914–2000	Animator and children's books author. Traveled widely to gather material for his books	****
Seabury, Joseph Bartlett	1846–1923	A reverend from Massachusetts	****
Smith, Ruel P(erley)	1869–1937	Novelist and newspaper editor	****
Stevens, Walter B(arlow)	1848–1939	Journalist and writer. Press Representative for the St. Louis Commercial Club	Visited the area with other club members to examine the work of the construction of the Panama Canal and business opportunities
Stoddard, Charles Augustus	1833–1920	Presbyterian clergyman, editor of the *New York Observer* and travel writer	Spent part of the winters of 1902 and 1903 in the West Indies
Taft, Marcus L.	****	****	Traveled to Puerto Rico with his brother as tourists in January 1903, and returned for the winters of 1904 and 1905
Tavenner, Mary Hilaire (Sally Lynne)	1948–	Author, educator, and public speaker. Was a Syracuse Franciscan nun for almost twenty years	Came as a Catholic nun to teach English in 1984 but lasted only three months. Returned for three weeks in December 2006, and for ten days in December 2007
Tugwell, Rexford G(uy)	1891–1979	An economist with a PhD and a writer. Last American Governor of Puerto Rico	Governor of Puerto Rico in 1941–1946

(continues)

(continued)

Complete name	Dates of birth/death	Pertinent personal data	Time in Puerto Rico
Van Deusen, Richard J(ames)	1879–1972	A lawyer who had worked as a stenographer for US companies in Perú and Argentina	Came in 1908 as Secretary to the Auditor of Puerto Rico and, after holding other offices, became Military Aide of Gov. Arthur Yeager during World War I and Secretary of Gov. Horace M. Towner in 1928–29. Lived in Puerto Rico for twenty-nine years until 1937
Van Deusen, (Edith) Elizabeth Kneipple— coauthor	1902–1966	Married Richard J. Van Deusen in 1926. An English teacher, writer, and correspondent for the *New York Tribune*. Writer of English books for Puerto Rican children	Taught English at Escuela Superior Central in Santurce and became English Supervisor for the Department of Education. Lived in Puerto Rico for eleven years until 1937.
Van Middeldyk, R(udolph) A(dams)	1832–****	His book is considered the first history of Puerto Rico written by an American	Was the Librarian of the Free Public Library of San Juan
Vandercook, John W(omack)	1902–1963	Foreign correspondent and writer of novels and non-fiction books	****
Verrill, A(lpheus) Hyatt	1871–1954	Zoologist, explorer, illustrator and author	Traveled extensively through the West Indies on archaeological expeditions
Vivian, Thomas J(ondrie)	1858–1925	British coauthor and editor living in New York	****
Wade, Mary Hazelton (Blanchard)	1860–1936	Boston teacher and children's books writer	****

(continues)

(continued)

Complete name	Dates of birth/death	Pertinent personal data	Time in Puerto Rico
Wahengeim, Kal(man)	1935-	Editor/publisher of the newsletter *Caribbean Update*. A former correspondent for the *New York Times*. Author/translator of several books on Puerto Rico	Married Puerto Rican Dr. Olga Jiménez and visited frequently afterward
Waid, Eva Clark	1869–1929	Missionary, author, poet	****
White, Trumbull	1868–1941	Author, historian, war correspondent, traveler	Came in 1898 with his wife and stayed for a while. Returned in 1937
Wilcox, Ella Wheeler	1850–1919	Author and poet	****
Wilcox, Mrs. F. W.	****	Congregationalist missionary	Probably served in Puerto Rico
Willets, Gilson	1869–1922	War correspondent	Probably came with the US invasion forces
Williams, Grace Petrie—coauthor	****	Presbyterian Home Mission Board member and coauthor with Robert McLean	****
Wilson, Edward S(tansbury)	1841–1919	Appointed Marshall of the Federal Court in 1900 and again in 1904	Worked in Puerto Rico in 1900–1908
Winslow, I(saac) O(scar)	1856-****	Children's book author	****
Wood, Leonard	1860–1927	Brigadier general and former Governor-General of Cuba, a coauthor	****
Wright, Hamilton M(ercer)	1875–1954	Writer and coauthor	****

Source: General research conducted via Google and/or data provided by the authors in their respective books.

NOTES

INTRODUCTION

1. When we use the term "Puerto Rico," we refer to its whole archipelago, including Vieques, Culebra, Mona, Desecheo, Caja de Muertos, and other smaller islets.

2. From this point on, I will use the term "American" to refer to people who came to Puerto Rico from the United States. The term is incorrect, since "American" should refer to the natives of all the Americas: North, South, and Central America, as well as the Caribbean islands. But even though in Spanish we can call them "estadounidenses," in the English language there is no other reasonable way to refer to the people from the United States of America.

3. Marcus J. Wright, *Wright's Official History of the Spanish-American War* (Washington, DC: War Records Office, 1900), 492.

4. Héctor A. Negroni, *Historia Militar de Puerto Rico* (Madrid: Ediciones Siruela, S. A., 1992), 326–27.

5. As quoted in Ronald Fernández, *The Disenchanted Island. Puerto Rico and the United States in the Twentieth Century* (Westport, CT: Praeger Publishers, 1996), 10.

6. Negroni, *Historia*, 340.

7. As quoted from an undated letter that Betances sent from Paris to Julio Henna, then President of the Puerto Rico Section of the Cuban Revolutionary Party in Ángel Rivero, *Crónica de la Guerra Hispanoamericana en Puerto Rico* (Río Piedras: Editorial Edil, 1998), 19.

8. René Marqués, *The Docile Puerto Rican* (Philadelphia: Temple University Press, 1976), 33.

9. From this quote on, I respect the original orthograph in which the documents were written. A separate bibliography of the American authors under study in this book is provided in appendix 2 along with a table with basic data on each author provided in appendix 3.

10. Of the books published in the 1898–1899 period, two were children's books. Three were authored by women: one by Eva M. Kellogg, and two by war correspondent Margherita A. Hamm.

11. Stuart B. Schwartz, "Introduction" in *Implicit Understandings. Observing, Reporting and Reflecting on the Encounters between Europeans and Other Peoples in the Early Modern Era* (Cambridge: Cambridge University Press, 1994), 2.

12. Shelley Baranowski et al., "Tourism and Empire," *Journal of Tourism History* (August, 2015): 1–29.

13. Ivona Grgurinović, "Anthropology and Travel: Practice and Text," *Studia Ethnologica Croatica* 24: 48–49.

14. Peter Hulme and Tim Youngs, "Introduction" in *The Cambridge Companion to Travel Writing* (Cambridge: Cambridge University Press, 2002), 4.

15. David Leviatin, "Introduction" in Jacob A. Riis, *How the Other Half Lives: Studies among the Tenements of New York*, (Boston: Bedford/St. Martin's, 2011), 29.

16. Leviatin, *Introduction*, 29.

17. Leviatin, *Introduction*, 30.

18. The exceptions are sociologists Joseph P. Fitzpatrick and Fred K. Fleagle, and anthropologist Vincenzo Petrullo. They were included in the selection because their books were not the result of their formal research of Puerto Rican culture.

19. Some important American anthropologists who studied Puerto Ricans and/or their culture were Jesse Walter Fewkes, Franz Boas, John Alden Mason, Julian Steward, Sydney W. Mintz, Helen Safa, and Oscar Lewis. See Duany, Jorge. "Imperialistas reacios: Los antropólogos norteamericanos en Puerto Rico, 1898–1950," *Revista del Instituto de Cultura Puertorriqueña*, no. 97 (1987).

20. As referred to in Hussein Fahim and Katherine Helmer, "Themes and Counterthemes: The Burg Wartenstein Symposium," in *Indigenous Anthropology in Non-Western Countries*, ed., Fahim, Hussein, (Durham: Carolina Academic Press, 1982), xi–xx.

21. Duany, *Imperialistas reacios*, 3.

22. Clifford Geertz, *The Interpretation of Cultures* (New York: Basic Books, 1973), 13.

23. Albert Memmi, *The Colonizer and the Colonized* (Boston: Beacon Press, 1965), ix.

24. Frantz Fanon, "National Culture," in Bill Ashcroft, et al. eds., *The Post-Colonial Studies Reader* (London: Routledge, 2002), 154.

25. Tzvetan Todorov, *Nosotros y los otros* (México: Siglo XXI, 2013) 115–19, 308.

26. Robert Wokler, "From *l'homme physique* to *l'homme moral* and Back: Towards a History of Enlightnment Anthropology." *History of the Human Science* 6, no. 1, (1993):127.

27. A. Greenfell Price, *White Settlers in the Tropics* (New York: American Geographical Society, 1939), 2.

28. Price, *White Settlers*, 37.

29. Antonio S. Pedreira, *Insularismo* (San Juan: Editorial Venezuela, 1942), 33.

30. Pedreira, *Insularismo*, 38–39.

31. The "myth of the noble savage" is associated to Jean Jacques Rousseau's philosophy as exposed in his *Discourse on the Origins of Inequality among Men* (1754), but he never used the term itself. The term became popular after British novelist Charles Dickens published a satirical essay: *The Noble Savage* (1851).

32. Todorov (2013), *Nosotros y los otros*, 308, 315.

33. Tracey Rizzo and Steven Gerontakis, *Intimate Empires. Body, Race, and Gender in the Modern World* (New York: Oxford University Press, 2017), 5, 208–9.

34. Samuel Silva Gotay, *Protestantismo y política en Puerto Rico: 1898–1930* (San Juan: Editorial de la Universidad de Puerto Rico, 1997), 64.

35. *New Testament*, Matthew 5:15.

36. David Spurr, *The Rhetoric of Empire. Colonial Discourse in Journalism, Travel Writing, and Imperial Administration* (Durham, NC: Duke University Press, 1993), 76.

37. Rizzo and Gerontakis, *Intimate Empires*, 211-12.

38. Heather Streets-Salter and Trevor R. Getz, *Empires and Colonies in the Modern World. A Global -Perspective* (New York: Oxford University Press, 2016), 287.

39. Josiah Strong, *Our Country: Its Possible Future and Its Present Crisis* (New York: The Baker & Taylor Co., 1891), 28, 222.

40. Rizzo and Gerontakis, *Intimate Empires*, 45-46.

41. British writer Rudyard Kipling published this poem for the first time in 1899 in the *McClure's* magazine under the title: "The White Man's Burden: The United States and the Philippine Islands." The poem promotes the imperialist expansion of the Western white man as an act of moral responsibility.

42. Memmi, *The Colonizer and the Colonized*, 57.

43. Memmi, *The Colonizer and the Colonized*, 57, 61.

44. Abdul R. JanMohamed, "The Economy of Manichean Allegory," in *The Post-Colonial Studies Reader*, ed. Bill Ashcroft, Gareth Griffiths, and Helen Tiffin (London: Routledge, 2002), 18–23, 19.

45. Memmi, *The Colonizer and the Colonized*, 71-72.

46. Memmi, *The Colonizer and the Colonized*, 83.

47. Memmi, *The Colonizer and the Colonized*, 66–67.

48. The center of Puerto Rico consists of a high mountain range that runs from East to West, called "la Cordillera Central."

49. Todorov (2013), *Nosotros y los otros*, 21–30.

50. Edward Said, *Orientalism* (London: Routledge & Kegan Paul, 1978), 48-49.

51. Memmi, *The Colonizer and the Colonized*, xii, 11–13.

52. Franz Fanon, *The Wretched of the Earth* (New York: Grove Press, 1963), 210.

CHAPTER 1: "OH, DEAR LORD, WHY DIDST THOU EVER INSPIRE ME TO GO TO PUERTO RICO TO TEACH?": ABOUT THE SELECTED AMERICAN AUTHORS

1. W. B. F., *In the West Indies* (London: Arnold Fairbairns, 1905), 32.

2. Álvaro Fernández Bravo, "Los relatos de viaje en América Latina," *Explora* (MEC: Argentina, 2007), 2.

3. Marqués, *The Docile Puerto Rican*, 52–53.

4. Aida L. Morales Tejeda, "Santiago de Cuba: Miradas e imágenes urbanas en los relatos de viajeros," *Anales del IAA*, 46, no. 1 (2016), 94.

5. Eugene V. Mohr, "Language, Literature & Journalism" in *The American Presence in Puerto Rico*, ed. Lynn-Darrell Bender (San Juan: Publicaciones Puertorriqueñas, 1998), 169.

6. Mohr, "Language, Literature, & Journalism," 170.

7. Female independent authors in this study's sample are Kellogg (1898), Hamm (2 X 1899), George (1900), Wade (1902), Guernsey (1903 + 1907), Johnston (1905), Crowell (1907), E. W. Wilcox (1909), Blythe (1911), Waid (1916), F. W. Wilcox (1918), Duggan (1920), Harris (1932), Ezratty (1986), Maus (1941), Dean (1944), Gruber (1960), McGuire (1963), Rollins (1967), Rand (1973), Samoiloff (1984) and Tavenner (2010). Coauthors are Williams (1916) and Van Deusen (1931).

8. Susan Bassnett, "Travel Writing and Gender" in *The Cambridge Companion to Travel Writing*, ed. Peter Hulme and Tim Youngs (Cambridge: Cambridge University Press, 2002) 242–45.

9. Negroni, *Historia*, 327–28.

10. See Frank C. Carpenter, "Plans of Government Suited to Porto Ricans," *The Brooklyn Daily Eagle*, October 8, 1899, 19.

11. Joseph A. Fry, "Imperialism, American style, 1890–1916" in *American Foreign Relations Reconsidered, 1890-1993*, ed. Gordon Martel (London: Routledge, 1994), 64.

12. Paul H. Douglass, *Congregational Missionary Work in Puerto Rico: Conducted by the American Missionary Association.* (New York: American Missionary Association, 1910), 6.

13. Ellen Walsh, "Advancing the Kingdom: Missionaries and Americanization in Puerto Rico, 1898–1930s" (Doctorate thesis, University of Pittsburgh, 2008), 190.

14. Patrick Brantlinger, "Victorians and Africans: The Genealogy of the Myth of the Dark Continent" in *"Race," Writing, and Difference*, ed. Henry Louis Gates Jr. (Chicago: The University of Chicago Press, 1986), 197.

15. Elizabeth Colson, "Culture and Progress," *American Anthropologist* no. 78 (1976): 103.

16. Everett W. Lord *Under the Tropic Sun: An Account of the Origins of the Department of Education of Puerto Rico, in the Early Days of the 20th Century.* (Caguas, PR: Editorial Marqués de Cundiamor, 2004), 25.

17. Tanfer Emin Tunc, "Manifest Destiny's Child: Mary Hazelton Blanchard Wade and the Literature of American Empire," *Children's Literature in Education* 48, no. 3 (2017): 246. This article made a thorough analysis of Wade's children's books which I used to write this section.

18. Term used in Karen Sands-O'Connnor, "The Stratemeyer Chums Have Fun in the Caribbean: America and Empire in Children's Series," quoted in Tunc, "Manifest Destiny's Child," (2017), 249.

19. Tunc, "Manifest Destiny's Child," 255.

20. Tunc, "Manifest Destiny's Child," 260.

21. Even though Puerto Rican cuisine is very flavorful due to the use of abundant spices, it is typically not "hot" or "spicy."

CHAPTER 2: "THEY CONSIDERED THEM CONQUERED ANIMALS":
ON HOW COLONIALISM PERMEATES ALL

1. Salvador Brau, *Historia de Puerto Rico* (New York: D. Appleton & Co., 1904), 181.

2. Edmundo E. Valera Jr., "Imperialism of Righteousness: The Influence of the American Protestant Social Gospel on Foreign Missions and Expansionism, 1890–1910" (Doctorate Thesis, Department of Theology, Fordham University, 1998), 167.

3. Abdul R. JanMohamed, "The Economy of Manichean Allegory: The Function of Racial Difference in Colonialist Literature" in *"Race," Writing, and Difference*, ed. Henry Louis Gates Jr. (Chicago: The University of Chicago Press, 1986), 87.

4. See Jennifer J. Wallach, *How America Eats: A Social History of U.S. Food and Culture* (Lanham: Rowman & Littlefield Publishers, Inc., 2013), 102.

5. A reference to a technique of applying anthropometry to the identification of suspects and criminals through their physical characteristics that was developed in France in 1879 by Alphonse Bertillon.

6. Memmi, *The Colonizer and the Colonized*, xxvi.

7. Fanon, *The Wretched of the Earth*, 41.

8. Aimé Césaire, *Discourse on Colonialism* (New York: Monthly Review Press 2000), 41.

9. Memmi, *The Colonizer and the Colonized*, 86.

10. JanMohamed, "The Economy of Manichean Allegory," 87.

11. Barnacles are arthropods that attach themselves to animals like crabs and lobsters, among others.

12. Guillermo González, *The Governor's Suits. A Psychiatric Perspective of Puerto Rico*, (USA: XLibris Corp., 2007), 28, 37.

13. Césaire, *Discourse on Colonialism*, 43.

14. Marqués, *The Docile Puerto Rican*, 30.

15. See Francisco Moscoso "La conquista española y la gran rebelión de los Taínos," *Pensamiento Crítico* 12, no. 62 (February-April 1989), 2–16.

16. These slave revolts were widely documented in Guillermo A. Baralt, *Esclavos rebeldes: conspiraciones y sublevaciones de esclavos en Puerto Rico (1795–1873)*, (Río Piedras: Ediciones Huracán, 1982).

17. See Francisco Moscoso, *La revolución puertorriqueña de 1868: el Grito de Lares*, (San Juan: Instituto de Cultura Puertorriqueña, 2003).

18. In the 1930s the political militancy of the Nationalist Party was countered through a 1927 massacre of militants and the incarceration and torture of its leader, Pedro Albizu Campos; in the 1960s the FBI subdued nationalist movements through its counterintelligence program COINTELPRO; and in the 1980s the nationalist movements were virtually eradicated as Macheteros leaders were given disproportionately large prison sentences for minor charges. See Laura Briggs, *Reproducing Empire: Race, Sex, Science, and U.S. Imperialism in Puerto Rico* (Berkeley: University of California Press, 2002), 10–11.

19. See Patricia Levy and Nazry Bahrawi, *Cultures of the World—Puerto Rico*, (New York: Marshall Cavendish Benchmark, 1995), 69.

20. See Victor S. Clark, *Porto Rico and Its Problems* (Washington, DC: The Brookings Institution, 1930), 37.

21. Clark, *Porto Rico and Its Problems*.

22. Loida Figueroa Mercado, "Puerto Rico—Cultura y Personalidad," *Revista de Ciencias Sociales* 7, no. 1–2 (March–June 1963): 96.

23. Julia M. Ramos-McKay, "Locus of Control, Social Activism, and Sex Roles in Puerto Rican College and Non-College Individuals" (Master's thesis, Department of Psychology, University of Massachusetts-Amherst, 1976), 7.

24. Fanon, *The Wretched of the Earth*, 54–55.

25. Miriam Biascoechea-Pereda, Understanding the Pendejo Phenomenon in Puerto Rico: An Example of Culture-Specific Therapy, doctoral dissertation, Minneapolis: Walden University, 247–48, 263.

26. Biascoechea-Pereda, *Understanding*, 278.

27. Tana E. Wood et al., "On the Shoulders of Giants: Continuing the Legacy of Large-Scale Ecosystem Manipulation Experiments in Puerto Rico," *Forests* 10, (2019): 210.

28. Michael Lapp, "The Rise and Fall of Puerto Rico as a Social Laboratory, 1945–1965," *Social Science History* 19, no. 2 (1995): 182.

CHAPTER 3: "LIVING FROM HAND TO MOUTH":
ON THE POVERTY OF PUERTO RICANS

1. For most of the data included regarding the coffee industry before the US invasion, we used Mabel M. Rodríguez Centeno, "Tiempos de crisis: Los campesinos y el café en Puerto Rico durante el cambio de siglo y la Gran Depresión," *Agroalimentaria* no.11 (2000): 1–23.

2. Santiago-Valles, "La concentración," 38–39.

3. Luis Pumarada O'Neill and Rafael Pumarada, *Contexto Histórico: Industria cafetalera en Puerto Rico, 1736–1969* (San Juan: Oficina Estatal de Preservación Histórica de Puerto Rico, 1989), 35.

4. María Dolores Luque, "Los conflictos de la modernidad: La elite política en Puerto Rico, 1898–1904," *Revista de Indias* 57, no. 211 (1997): 716–17, 719.

5. Luque, "Los conflictos," 720.

6. Fanon, *The Wretched of the Earth*, 44.

7. This was reported in detail in Fernando Picó, "La revolución puertorriqueña de 1898: La necesidad de un nuevo paradigma para entender el '98 puertorriqueño," *Historia y Sociedad*, no. 10 (1998): 7–22.

8. Andrés A. Ramos Mattei, "The Growth of the Puerto Rican Sugar Industry under North American Domination: 1899–1910" in *Crisis and Change in the International Economy, 1860–1940*, ed. Bill Albert and Adrian Graves (Norwich: ISC Press, 1984), 124.

9. See Kelvin A. Santiago-Valles, "La concentración y la centralización de la propiedad en Puerto Rico (1898–1929)," *Hómines* 8, no. 1 (1984): 129–56. The *South Porto Rico Sugar* from New Jersey owned *Central Guánica*, the second largest sugarmill of the world. (Fernández, *The Disenchanted Island*, 1996), 74.

10. See Humberto García Muñiz, "La plantación que no se repite: Las historias azucareras de la República Dominicana y Puerto Rico, 1870–1930," *Revista de Indias* 65, no. 233 (2005): 183–84.

11. Fernández, 99.

12. James L. Dietz, *Historia de la economía de Puerto Rico* (Río Piedras: Ediciones Huracán, 1989), 158.

13. As quoted in Fernández, 115.

14. This theme is widely discussed in Gervasio L. García and A. G. Quintero Rivera, *Desafío y Solidaridad*, (Río Piedras: Ediciones Huracán, 1986), 90–91. Also see Fernández, 116–17.

15. Fernández, 121.

16. For details on what Puerto Ricans and other Caribbean peoples faced in 1942 see Ligia T. Domenech, *Imprisoned in the Caribbean: The 1942 German U-Boat Blockade* (iuniverse, 2014).

17. Santiago-Valles, 204–5.

18. Fernández, 66.

19. For more on massive sterilization in Puerto Rico, see Harriet P. Presser, "The Role of Sterilization in Controlling Puerto Rican Fertility," *Population Studies* 23, no. 3 (1969):

343–61. For more on the testing of oral contraceptives on Puerto Rican women see Drew C. Pendergrass and Michelle Y. Raji, "The Bitter Pill: Harvard and the Dark History of Birth Control," *The Harvard Crimson*, September 28, 2017.

20. Pedro A. Malavet, "Puerto Rico: Cultural Nation, American Colony," *Michigan Journal of Race and Law* 6, no. 1 (2000): 53.

21. Naomi Klein, "Puerto Ricans and Ultrarich 'Puertopians' Are Locked in a Pitched Struggle Over How to Remake the Island," *The Intercept*, March 20, 2018.

22. Santiago-Valles, 184.

23. See J. K. Galbraith, *The Affluent Society* (1958) in Dwight Macdonald, "Our Invisible Poor," *The New Yorker*, January 19, 1963, 1.

24. Michael Harrington, *The Other America: Poverty in the United States* (1962) in Macdonald, "Our Invisible Poor," 9.

25. Jennifer J. Wallach, *How America Eats: A Social History of U.S. Food and Culture*, (Lanham: Rowman & Littlefield Publishers, Inc., 2013), 192.

26. Metro Puerto Rico, April 26 2021, "CENSO estima población de Puerto Rico es de 3.3 millones."

27. Patricia K. Smith, "The Economics of Anti-Begging Regulations," *The American Journal of Economics and Sociology* 64, no. 2 (April 2005): 549–50.

28. Lorraine Boissoneault, "The Myth of Professional Beggars Spawned Today's Enduring Stereotypes," *Smithsonian Magazine*, March 30, 2017.

29. As quoted from Stephen Pimpare's *A People's History of Poverty in America* in Boissoneault (2017).

30. *Código Penal* (1902), San Juan: Asamblea Legislativa de Puerto Rico, Título I, Art. 265, 585.

CHAPTER 4: "NEITHER ALIENS NOR AMERICANS": THE CONVOLUTED POLITICS OF THE COLONY

1. Figueroa, "Puerto Rico—Cultura y Personalidad," 96
2. Quoted in Fernández, *The Disenchanted Island*, 14.
3. Luque, "Los conflictos," 709.
4. Santiago-Valles, "La concentración," 156.
5. Ellen Walsh "The Not-So-Docile Puerto Rican: Students Resist Americanization, 1930," *Centro Journal* 26, no. 1 (Spring 2014): 163.
6. José A. Cabranes, "Citizenship and the American Empire," *University of Pennsylvania Law Review* 127 (1978): 408.
7. Fernández, 71; Harry Franqui-Rivera, "Why Puerto Ricans Did Not Receive U.S. Citizenship So They Could Fight in WWI," *Centro Voices E-Magazine*, Accessed November 9, 2020. Another reason for imposing an unwanted US citizenship was the growing desire for independence in Puerto Rico at the time (Fernández, 33.)
8. Quoted in Fernández, 65.
9. Quoted in Fernández, 66.
10. Santiago-Valles, 156.
11. Víctor García San Inocencio and Víctor Rivera Hernández, *Derechos Humanos y Corrupción* (San Juan: Comisión de Derechos Civiles de Puerto Rico, 2015), 22, 25.

12. David Landy, *Tropical Childhood, Cultural Transmission and Learning in a Rural Puerto Rican Village* (Chapel Hill: The University of North Carolina Press, 1959), 56.

13. Bolívar Pagán, *Historia de los partidos políticos puertorriqueños (1898–1956). Tomo I* (San Juan: Librería Campos, 1959), 201.

14. Fernández, 111.

15. Fernández, 153–56.

16. Fernández, 186.

CHAPTER 5: "WE THINK WE ARE BETTER THAN OTHER PEOPLE": ON THE ONSET OF THE RELATIONSHIPS BETWEEN COLONIZERS AND COLONIZED

1. Negroni, *Historia*, 312–13.

2. (July 21, 1898), "Porto Rico to Be Held Permanently," *Oakland Tribune*, 1.

3. Figueroa, "Puerto Rico—Cultura y Personalidad," 98.

4. Fanon (1963), *The Wretched of the Earth*, 53–54.

5. For full content, see appendix 1.

6. Klein, "Puerto Ricans and Ultrarich 'Puertopians,'" n. p.

7. Fernández, *The Disenchanted Island*, 15.

8. As defined in the Merriam-Webster.Com Dictionary. The term was popularized after the publishing in 1958 of a collection of stories titled *The Ugly American* by Eugene Burdick and William J. Lederer. In 1963 the book turned into a film with the same name directed by George England and starred by Marlon Brando.

9. Solsiree del Moral, "Colonial Lessons: The Politics of Education in Puerto Rico, 1898–1930," *The American Historian*, May 2018, 41.

10. English was the classroom language in Puerto Rico's public schools as follows: 1900–05: Grades 9–12/1905–16: all grades/1916–34: Grades 6–12/1934–37: Grades 9–12/1937–42: Grades 3–12/1942–45: Grades 7–12/1945–49: gradual transition to Spanish in all grades/1949–today: Spanish as classroom language in all grades. See Joshua Angrist, et al., "Is Spanish-Only Schooling Responsible for the Puerto Rican Language Gap?" (Cambridge, MA: National Bureau of Economic Research, January 2006), Working Paper 12005, Table I.

11. Fernández, 55.

12. This 54 percent was according to the results of the Pruebas Puertorriqueñas de Aprovechamiento Académico (PPAA). See Mylord Reyes Tosta, "El aprendizaje del español y del inglés en Puerto Rico y sus influencias extranjeras," *Scientific International Journal* 10, no. 3 (September-December 2013): 44–53.

13. Malavet, "Puerto Rico: Cultural Nation," 44.

CHAPTER 6: "FROM THE YELLOW PINE OF CASTILE TO THE MAHOGANY OF AFRICA": ON THE RACIAL TYPES AND SOCIAL CLASSES

1. See Alan Goodman and Joseph L. Graves, Jr., *Racism Not Race: Answers to Frequently Asked Questions* (New York: Columbia University Press, 2022).

2. Henry Louis Gates Jr., "Introduction: Writing "Race" and the Difference it Makes," in *"Race," Writing, and Difference*, ed. Henry Louis Gates Jr. (Chicago: The University of Chicago Press, 1986), 1–20.

3. F. James Davis, *Who is Black? One Nation's Definition* (Pennsylvania: The Pennsylvania State University Press, 2001), 5.

4. Davis, *Who is Black?*, 15.

5. Comisión de Derechos Civiles de Puerto Rico, *¿Somos Racistas? Cómo podemos combatir el racismo* (1998), 19.

6. Jorge Duany, *Neither White nor Black: The Politics of Race and Ethnicity among Puerto Ricans on the Island and in the Mainland*, paper presented at the conference "The Meaning of Race and Blackness in the Americas: Contemporary Perspectives," Brown University, Providence, February 10–12, 2000, 2.

7. Idsa E. Alegría Ortega, "Ejes temáticos del pensamiento racial en Puerto Rico: una aproximación," *Revista de Ciencias Sociales* 17 (2007): 164.

8. Landy, *Tropical Childhood*, 32.

9. War Department's Office Director Census of Porto Rico, *Report on the Census of Porto Rico, 1899* (Washington: Government Printing Office, 1900), 58.

10. Nélida Agosto Cintrón, *Religión y cambio social en Puerto Rico (1898–1940)* (San Juan: Ediciones Huracán, 1996), 59.

11. Landy, 32.

12. As quoted in Fernández, *The Disenchanted Island*, 56.

13. As discussed in Robinson [(1899), 194, the 1887 Census reported 480,267 white people; 248,690 pardos (he calls them gray); and 77,751 morenos (he calls them brown or swarthy). According to these numbers, only 9.6 percent of Puerto Ricans were Black vs. 59.5 percent of white people.

14. Eileen J. Suárez Findlay, *Imposing Decency. The Politics of Sexuality and Race in Puerto Rico, 1870–1920* (Durham: Duke University Press, 1999), 23–24.

15. Fanon (1963), 39.

16. Clark (1930), 8

17. Comisión de Derechos Civiles de Puerto Rico, 19–20.

18. Luis Rafael Sánchez, *No llores por nosotros, Puerto Rico* (Hanover, NJ: Ediciones del Norte, 1998), 21.

19. Suárez Findlay, *Imposing Decency*, 37.

20. Duany (2000), *Neither White nor Black*, 6.

21. Duany.

22. Fernando Picó, "Cafetal Adentro: Una historia de los trabajadores agrícolas en el Puerto Rico del Siglo XX," *Revista El Sol*, XXX, no. 1 (1986): 5.

23. Gervasio L. García, "El otro es uno: Puerto Rico en la mirada norteamericana de 1898," *Los Americanos. Revista de la Universidad de Puerto Rico La Torre* XIV, no. 53–54 (July-December, 2009): 203.

24. Picó (1986), "Cafetal Adentro," 5–6

25. Picó, 34.

26. Kelvin A. Santiago-Valles, *"Subject People" and Colonial Discoursed. Economic Transformation and Social Disorder in Puerto Rico, 1898–1947* (New York: State University of New York Press, 1994), 46–47.

27. Idsa E. Alegría Ortega, "Ejes temáticos del pensamiento racial en Puerto Rico: una aproximación," *Revista de Ciencias Sociales* 17 (2007): 175.

CHAPTER 7: "SONG, LAUGHTER AND MAÑANA": ON THE MYTH OF THE LAZY PUERTO RICANS

1. Memmi, *The Colonizer and the Colonized*, 79.
2. González, *The Governor's Suits*, 41–42.
3. Ángel López Cantos, "La mujer puertorriqueña y el trabajo, siglo XVIII," *Anuario de Estudios Americanos* 57, no. 1 (2000): 199.
4. García (2009), "El otro es uno," 220, 222.
5. Erich Golbach, "Protestantism-Capitalism-Sports," *Journal of Sport History* 4, no. 3 (Fall 1977): 291.
6. This section is based on Picó (1986), "Cafetal Adentro," 4–36.
7. Picó (1986), 19.
8. José A. Mari Mut, *Insectos de Puerto Rico* (n. p.: Ediciones Digitales, 2015), 98, 105.
9. Mari M.
10. G. Robert Blackey, "Gaming, Lotteries, and Wagering: The Pre-Revolutionary Roots of the Law of Gambling," *Rutgers Law Journal* 16, no. 2 (1985): 237.
11. Wokler, "From *l'homme physique*," 127.
12. Gervasio L. García, "Economía y trabajo en el Puerto Rico del Siglo XIX," *Historia Mexicana* 38, no. 4 (1989): 855.
13. García, "Economía y trabajo," 864.
14. García, 865.
15. In 2021 Puerto Ricans celebrated a total of nineteen holidays in contrast with only ten celebrated in the United States.
16. This phrase refers to German composer Richard Wagner (1813–1883) who spent over twenty-five years composing the cycle of four epic music dramas "Der Ring des Nibelungen."

CHAPTER 8: "LUST WAS WRITTEN IN THE VERY FACES OF THE PEOPLE": ON THE MORALITY OF PUERTO RICANS

1. Fanon (1963), *The Wretched of the Earth*, 39–41.
2. Suárez Findlay, *Imposing Decency*, 48–49.
3. Suárez Findlay, 20, 22–23.
4. Suárez Findlay, 25, 43.
5. Suárez Findlay, 28–29.
6. Chancletero" refers to a producer of "chancletas" or sandals, which, although commonly used by Puerto Rican women while at home, are considered less elegant than shoes.
7. Ellsworth Huntington, "The Adaptability of the White Man to Tropical America," *The Journal of Race Development* 5, no. 2 (1914): 202..
8. Sydney W. Mintz, *Worker in the Cane, A Puerto Rican Life History* (New York: W.W. Norton & Co., Inc., 1974), 89.

9. Miguel Á. Urrego Ardila, *Familia, biopolítica y cambio de orden colonial. San Juan de Puerto Rico, 1898–1930* (Morelia, México: Instituto de Investigaciones Históricas de la Universidad Michoacana de San Nicolás de Hidalgo, 2016),118, 123.

10. Mintz, *Worker in the Cane*, 275.

11. Suárez Findlay, 45–48.

12. Suárez Findlay, 129.

13. Richard Solomon, "Sexual Practice and Fantasy in Colonial America and the Early Republic," *Indiana University Journal of Undergraduate Research* 3 (2017): 25.

14. Urrego Ardila, *Familia*, 129–31.

15. *Diario de Sesiones, Procedimientos y Debates de la Asamblea Legislativa de Puerto Rico*, Vol. I, no.10, San Juan, August 8, 1952, 90.

16. Dr. José M. Stycos, in his study on Puerto Ricans' fertility, identified as manifestations of "machismo" the need men have to prove their fertility by having a child as soon as possible, the anxiety regarding having a male child (if girls are born, the search for the baby boy continues as long as needed), and the frequent extramarital relationships. See Angelina S. de Roca, "Algunos valores prevalecientes en la sociedad puertorriqueña," *Revista de Ciencias Sociales* no. 1–2 (1963), 133–34.

17. Levy and Bahawi, *Cultures of the World*, 68.

18. Eunice Mendoza, "Machismo Literature Review" draft submitted to the Center for Public Safety Initiatives of the Rochester Institute of Technology, New York, 2009, 6.

19. Laura Briggs, *Reproducing Empire: Race, Sex, Science, and U.S. Imperialism in Puerto Rico* (Berkeley: University of California Press, 2002),19.

20. Ronald W. Pies, "Masks, Machismo, and the American Man-Child," *Psychiatric Times*, June 29, 2020.

21. Elizabeth A. McClintock, "Should Marriage Still Involve Changing a Woman's Name?," *Psychology Today*, September 6, 2018.

22. Landy, *Tropical Childhood*, 52.

23. This is incorrect: she keeps her father's last name.

24. Carol Faulkner, *Unfaithful: Love, Adultery, and Marriage Reform in Nineteenth-Century America* (Philadelphia: University of Pennsylvania Press, 2019), 5.

25. Suárez Findlay, 32–33.

26. The concept of "dignidad," as seen in Puerto Rico, is discussed in detail in chapter 13.

27. Miguel Ángel Urrego, "Cambio de soberanía y confrontación moral en Puerto Rico, 1898–1920," *Revista Mexicana del Caribe* 7, no. 13 (2002): 143.

28. Urrego, "Cambio," 144.

29. As explained in a police report in Urrego (2002), 146.

30. Sander L. Gilman, "Black Bodies, White Bodies: Toward an Iconography of Female Sexuality in Late Nineteenth-Century Art, Medicine, and Literature" in *"Race," Writing, and Difference*, ed. Henry Louis Gates Jr. (Chicago: The University of Chicago Press, 1986), 240.

CHAPTER 9: "KNOWN BY THEIR FRUITS": ON VIOLENCE, ILLEGALITY, AND POLICING

1. Fernando Picó, "Las construcciones de lo español entre los militares norteamericanos en Puerto Rico, 1898–99," *Revista de Indias* 57, no. 211 (1997): 625–27.

2. For more details about these groups and their actions, see Fernando Picó, *Puerto Rico 1898: The War after the War* (Princeton: Marcus Wiener Publishers, 2004).

3. Picó (1997), "Las construcciones," 627.

4. Santiago-Valles, "La concentración," 172–73.

5. Fanon (1963), *The Wretched of the Earth*, 51.

6. Fanon, 54.

7. Landy, *Tropical Childhood*, 114, 116.

8. See David J. Silbey, *A War of Frontier and Empire: The Philippine-American War, 1899-1902* (New York: Hill and Wang, 2007).

9. Landy, 57.

10. The Jones Act of June 1917 included a referendum where Puerto Rican voters (only literate and landowner men, at the time) voted to establish the Prohibition in July of 1917. After a campaign of meetings and marches in its favor by the Protestant missionaries, and against it by the liquor industry, the Prohibition won and was put in effect on March 2, 1918. José M. González Cruz, "Destilando caña: Resistencia y ron clandestino en la Isla de Puerto Rico," (master's thesis, Universidad de Brasilia, 2014), 32–35.

11. When it is white and pure, it is called "ron caña"; when it is "cured" with fruits, nuts, meat or seafood, it is called "pitorro." See González Cruz, "Destilando caña," 10.

12. Santiago-Valles, 163–77.

13. *Junta de Planificación de Puerto Rico, Criminalidad en Puerto Rico: Serie Histórica 1900-2009* (San Juan, 2010),11.

14. Mintz, *Worker in the Cane*, 18.

15. Junta de Planificación, *Criminalidad*, 11.

16. The creation of the Insular Police was enacted by General Order #15 of February 9, 1899. See Junta de Planificación, 3.

17. Only Ponce, Mayagüez, Arecibo, Aguadilla and Yauco retained their Municipal Police forces after 1902.

18. Junta de Planificación, 4, 6.

19. Junta de Planificación, 7, 9.

20. Lanny Thompson "Colonial Governmentality in Puerto Rico and the Philippines: Sovereign Force, Governmental Rationality, and Disciplinary Institutions Under US Rule," in Søren Rud and Ivarsson, Søren, eds., *Rethinking the Colonial State: Political Power and Social Theory*, vol. 33, (Bingley, UK: Emerald Publishing, 2017), 31.

21. Thompson, "Colonial Governmentality."

CHAPTER 10: "THE BODY WAS THERE BUT NOT THE SOUL": ON THE PUERTO RICANS' RELIGIOUS PRACTICES

1. Fanon (1963), *The Wretched of the Earth*, 67.

2. Edward L. Cleary, OP, "Puerto Rico: Lay Preachers Who Preserved Catholicism" in Edward E. Cleary, ed., *The Challenge of Priestless Parishes: Learning from Latin America* (New Jersey: Paulist Press, 2014).

3. Fernando Picó, "Iglesia y trabajadores en Puerto Rico, siglos XVII y XIX," *Boletín Oficial de la Diócesis de San Juan* no. 10–11 (1986): 36–63, as quoted in Samuel Silva Gotay,

Catolicismo y política en Puerto Rico bajo España y Estados Unidos: Siglos XIX y XX (San Juan: Editorial de la Universidad de Puerto Rico, 2005), 81.

4. Silva Gotay (2005), *Catolicismo y política*, 37.

5. See Reinaldo L. Román, *Governing Spirits: Religion, Miracles and Spectacles in Cuba and Puerto Rico, 1878–1956* (Chapel Hill: The University of North Carolina Press, 2007), Edil Torres Rivera, "Espiritismo: The Flywheel of the Puerto Rican Spiritual Traditions," *Revista Interamericana de Psicología* 39, no. 2 (2005): 295–300; and Andrés I. Pérez y Mena, "Cuban Santería, Haitian Vodun, Puerto Rican Spiritualism: A Multicultural Inquiry into Syncretism," *Journal for the Scientific Study of Religion* 37, no. 1 (1998): 15–27.

6. Francisco Del Valle Atiles, *El campesino puertorriqueño: sus condiciones físicas, intelectuales y morales* (San Juan: Tipografía de José González Font, 1889), 128.

7. See Julian H. Steward et al., *The People of Puerto Rico* (Board of Trustees of the University of Illinois, 1956), 86.

8. Here Sabbath refers to Sunday, the day of rest and devotion in Christianity.

9. *Catechism of the Catholic Church* (Citta del Vaticano: Librería Editrice Vaticana, 1993), 2428.

10. Max Weber, *The Protestant Ethic and the Spirit of Capitalism* (London: Routledge, 2001).

11. A doctoral dissertation argued that the missionaries "were aware that their work would lead to an expansion of trade" or, in words of war correspondent Margherita A. Hamm: "every missionary is a salesman for the manufactures of Christdom!" See Valera Jr., "Imperialism of Righteousness," 165.

12. Walsh, Ellen, "Advancing the Kingdom," 20.

13. Urrego Ardila, *Familia*, 70.

14. Cleary, "Puerto Rico: Lay Preachers," no page numbers.

15. Cleary.

16. See Ana Lourdes Suárez, "Devociones, promesas y milagros. Aproximación a dimensiones de la espiritualidad en sectores populares," *Ciencias Sociales y Religión/Ciências Sociais e Religião* 18, no. 24 (January-July 2016): 56.

17. Since the religious habit did not correspond to the fashion of the time in which it was used, dressing with it implied the sacrifice of disregarding luxury and fashion, something particularly tough to do in festive occasions where others were showing their best. See José Antonio Melgares Guerrero, "'Romper un hábito'. Costumbre penitencial que languidece en nuestros días," *Revista Cangilón* no. 17 (December 1988): 5–7.

18. Cleary, no page numbers.

19. Agosto Cintrón, *Religión y cambio*, 59.

20. Jean Pierre Bastian, "Emancipación política de 1898 e influencia del protestantismo en Cuba y Puerto Rico," *Anuario de Historia de la Iglesia* no. 7 (1998): 155.

21. Silva Gotay, Samuel (1997), 64.

22. The use of "Jesus" as a proper name is more common in Latin America than in Spain, as it became popularized from the 1700s on as a way to get the special favor of Jesus for the newborn. See Lidia Becker, *Nombres de persona en español: Historia, situación actual y onomástica popular* (Berlin: Peter Lang, 2018), 20.

23. Each US state has different regulations regarding which names are allowed for babies born in them. As such, in 2012, over eight hundred children were named "Messiah," 3,758 were named "Jesus," about five hundred were named Mohammed, and twenty-nine were

named Christ in the United States. The use of these religious names in the United States is most common among Latinos, both Catholic and Pentecostals. See Katy Steinmetz, "From Messiah to Hitler, What You Can and Cannot Name Your Child," *Time*, August 12, 2013; and Mark Oppenheimer, "In God's Name, or Baby 'Messiah', Competing Claims of Religious Freedom," *The New York Times*, August 16, 2013.

24. Edward E. Evans-Pritchard, "Sorcery and Native Opinion," *Africa* (University of Cambridge Press) 4, no. 1(1931): 45.

25. The *Corridas de Júas* is a popular festival celebrated in the early hours of Holy Saturday, right after the Meeting Procession in which the effigies of Virgin Mary and Jesus meet. At that moment, certain (usually elite) young men in the town let loose a series of effigies of Judas riding over horses who are vilified by the attendants as they run around downtown. Later, the Judas effigies are hung from trees and left there or, in some towns, set on fire. This is celebrated in Spain and several Latin American countries

26. Camille Rodríguez, "Tradición de las Fiestas de Cruz," *El Visitante*, April 29, 2018.

27. Urrego, "Cambio," 129.

28. The most recent statistics found are from a 2014 Pew Research Center report that established that fifty-six percent of the inhabitants of Puerto Rico defined themselves as Catholic and thirty-three percent identified as Protestant. Although the number of Pentecostals in Puerto Rico was not provided, the study hints to the prevalence of Pentecostals among Puerto Rican Protestants. It revealed that, in Puerto Rico, ninety percent of all Protestants and thirty-five percent of all Catholics have witnessed glossolalia (speaking in tongues), praying for the miraculous healing of someone and some uttering prophesies, which are all closely associated to Pentecostal rituals. See Pew Research Center, "Religión en América Latina," 12, 14.

29. Anthony L. LaRuffa, "Culture Change and Pentecostalism in Puerto Rico," *Social and Economic Studies* 18, no. 3 (September 1969): 273–81.

30. Héctor M. Martínez-Ramírez, "Pentecostal Expansion and Political Activism in Puerto Rico," *Caribbean Studies* 33, no. 1 (January-June 2005): 116–17.

CHAPTER 11: "A POOR SPECIMEN OF MANHOOD": ON MATTERS OF HEALTH AND DEATH

1. Spurr, *The Rhetoric of Empire*, 76.,

2. José G. Rigau Pérez, "El servicio de salud pública de los Estados Unidos en Puerto Rico, 1898–1918," no. 19: 167–68.

3. This is well-documented in Santiago-Valles, "La concentración," 53–61.

4. As quoted from *New York Herald Tribune Magazine* of December 8, 1929 by Santiago-Valles, 149.

5. Both studies are briefly quoted in Angelina S. de Roca, "Algunos valores prevalecientes en la Sociedad puertorriqueña," *Revista de Ciencias Sociales* no. 1–2 (1963), 136, quoting José M. Stycos, *Familia y Fecundidad* (Fondo de Cultura Económica, 1955), 214 and David Landy, *Tropical Childhood*, 117.

6. Rigau Pérez, 145–46.

7. Suárez Findlay, *Imposing Decency*, 117.

8. Rigau Pérez, 152.

9. *Ibid.*, 156–57, 160.

10. *Ibid.*, 165.

11. War Department's Office Director Census of Porto Rico, *Report on the Census of Porto Rico, 1899* (Washington: Government Printing Office, 1900), 114.

12. Norman Maldonado, "El Dr. Pedro Gutiérrez Ingaravídez (1871–1935) y el Instituto de Medicina Tropical," *Galenus* 43, no. 7 (December 2013–January 2014): 50.

13. See Nicole E. Trujillo-Pagán, "Worms as a Hook for Colonising Puerto Rico," *Social History of Medicine* 26, no. 4 (2013).

14. Trujillo-Pagán, "Worms," 612–13, 619.

15. Trujillo-Pagán, 629

16. Trujillo-Pagán, 615–16.

17. Information on leprosy is from Julie H. Levinson, "Beyond Quarantine: A History of Leprosy in Puerto Rico, 1898–1930s," *História, Ciências, Saúde-Manguinhos* 10, Suppl. 1 (Río de Janeiro, 2003): 225–45.

18. Levinson, "Beyond Quarantine," 227–23, 235.

19. Fanon (1963), 249.

20. These were of one of two species. The *Aedes aegypti* are found around houses and they bite during day or night, lay their eggs in clear water, are native from Africa, and are the vector of yellow fever and dengue. The *Culex quinquefasciatus* bite during dawn and twilight, lay their eggs in dirty water, are native of Asia, and are the vectors for the nematodes of elephantiasis and the Nile fever. See Mari Mut (2015), *Insectos*, 68–69.

21. Esteban Gutierrez and Frank W. Fisk, "Annotated Checklist of Puerto Rican Cockroaches," *Transactions of the American Entomological Society* 124, no. 3-4 (1998): 336.

22. José A. Mari Mut, *Fauna Casera de Puerto Rico* (edicionesdigitales.info, 2015), 37–38.

23. There are no tarantulas in Puerto Rico. Baldwin might have seen the hairy spider *Cyrtopholis portoricae* that is abundant in Puerto Rico. Many people are scared of them but they only bite if the person makes accidental contact with them, and their bite is not mortal. This spider can be found only in Puerto Rico. See Mari Mut (2015) *Fauna*, 10–11.

24. The chigoe flea or jigger is believed to be originally from the Antilles. Its scientific name is *Tunga penetrans* but the Taínos called it "nigua." It is a parasitic insect that lives in sandy soil, and it is the smallest flea, measuring one mm in length. The adult female jumps into the legs of animals or humans to burrow itself in their skin and deposit her eggs. Its infection causes itching and pain. See Mari Mut (2015), *Insectos*, 31–32.

25. Walsh (2008), "Advancing the Kingdom," 156.

26. Walsh, 157.

27. Walsh, 159.

28. See Sandra Torres Guzmán, "Doña Chencha cura con sus manos santas," *Primera Hora*, January 4, 2019; Femmy Irizarry Álvarez, "Las manos santas de Doña Mary," *Primera Hora*, April 11 2015; Jessica Ríos Viner, "Las curanderas: sanadoras en peligro de extinción," *El Nuevo Día*, April 2, 2017; Raquel Romberg, *Witchcraft and Welfare: Spiritual Capital and the Business of Magic in Modern Puerto Rico* (Austin: University of Texas Press, 2003).

29. The believe in the "evil eye" is considered the most spread magical belief in the world, and it is believed to have been born in the Near East, since it was common in Ancient Mesopotamia and Ancient Egypt. See Anton Erkoreka, "Mal de ojo: una creencia supersticiosa remota, compleja y aún viva," *Munibe* no. 57 (San Sebastián, España, 2005):

391–94; Frederick Thomas Elworthy, *The Evil Eye* (Global Grey ebooks, 1895), 6, 117. A 2014 Pew Research Center report confirmed that at least one-third (thirty-three percent) of the polled adults in Latin America still believed in the "evil eye." See Pew Research Center, "Religión en América Latina: Cambio generalizado en una región históricamente católica," November 13, 2014, 7.

30. The *Memoria de Melgarejo*, also known as, *Memoria y Descripción de la Isla de Puerto Rico* can be read at Edicionesdigitales.info.

31. Jesse Roman, "The Puerto Rico Healthcare Crisis," *Annals of the American Thoracic Society*12, no. 12 (December 2015): 1760.

32. Luis A. López Rojas, *Historiar la Muerte (1508–1920)* (San Juan: Isla Negra Editores, 2006), 20–22.

33. César Cantú, *Historia Universal, Tomo XXII* (Madrid: Biblioteca Popular Económica, 1849), 188.

34. Soledad Gómez Navarro, "La diferencia entre el desamparo y el consuelo: una reflexión sobre la muerte en el protestantismo y en el catolicismo," en *El mundo de los difuntos; culto, cofradías y tradiciones* (San Lorenzo del Escorial, 2014), 12.

35. George J. Annas, *Worst Case Bioethics: Death, Disaster, and Public Health* (New York: Oxford University Press, 2010), 12.

36. The volunteers are American soldiers.

37. Gómez Navarro, "La diferencia," 20.

38. Pedro J. Lorite Cruz, "Las exequias de niños en el catolicismo, fiesta 'alegre' a nivel iconográfico dentro de la muerte," in *El mundo de los difuntos: culto, cofradías y tradiciones* (San Lorenzo del Escorial, 2014), 230.

39. Reporting their research, Jo-Anne Grabowsky and Thomas T. Frantz, "Latinos and Anglos: Cultural Experience of Grief Intensity," *Omega: Journal of Death and Dying* 26, no. 4 (1992–93): 273–85 had recognized that Puerto Ricans experienced death with a "significantly higher grief intensity" than Anglos.

40. War Department, 117.

41. Comisión Teológica Internacional, "La esperanza de salvación para los niños que mueren sin bautismo," *Congregación para la Doctrina de la Fe*, El Vaticano, http://www.vatican.va/roman_curia/congregations/cfaith/cti_documents/rc_con_cfaith_doc_20070419_un-baptised-infants_sp.html.

42. López Rojas, *Historiar*, 33–34.

43. Grace H. Christ et al., "Appendix E: Bereavement Experiences After the Death of a Child" in M. J. Field and R. E. Behrman, eds., *When Children Die: Improving Palliative and End-of-Life Care for Children and Their Families* (Washington, DC: National Academies Press, 2003).

44. Landy, 99.

45. See Malena Kuss, "Puerto Rico" in *Music in Latin American and the Caribbean: An Encyclopedic History, Vol.2*, ed. Malena Kuss (Austin: University of Texas Press, 2007), 163.

46. The rosary involves fifteen decades of Hail Marys and the prayer is conducted and followed through the use of a circular string of fifty-nine beads which correspond to a third of the entire rosary.

47. Cleary, "Puerto Rico: Lay Preachers."

48. Frances Munet, "Grieving and Death Rituals of Latinos," *Oncology Nursing Forum* 25, no. 10 (1998): 1762.

49. María D. Muñoz Jiménez, "El Rosario de Difuntos. El 'diálogo' con las almas del purgatorio a partir del caso de Quéntar (Granada)," *Gazeta de Antropología* 31, no. 2, http://hdl.handle.net/10481/36830.

50. Urrego, "Cambio," 139.

51. Urrego, 137–38.

52. Urrego, 142.

53. As quoted in Edwards, *op. cit.*, 248–49.

CHAPTER 12: "SATAN HIMSELF WOULD DANCE IF HE COULD HEAR THEM": ON PUERTO RICAN ENTERTAINMENTS

1. Haroldo Dilla Alfonso, *Ciudades en el Caribe: Un estudio comparado de La Habana, San Juan, Santo Domingo y Miami* (México: FLACSO, 2014), 86.

2. The "Aguinaldo" is almost always a hexasyllabic or octosyllabic verse, and its melody is written in a two by four rhythm. The word "Aguinaldo" is of Celtic origin. It comes from "Iguinand," which means: "New Year's present"; in Spanish, it means "a gift given in Christmas or The Three Kings." See Cesáreo Rosa Nieves, "El aguinaldo navideño en Puerto Rico," *Pedagogía* 3, no. 1 (1955): 98.

3. Fanon, *The Wretched of the Earth*, 57.

4. Kuss, "Puerto Rico," 158.

5. Kuss, 159–60; Ángel G. Quintero Rivera, *Salsa, sabor y control: Sociología de la música tropical* (México, DF: Siglo XXI Editores, 1998), 202–5.

6. Cotton Mather, *Ornaments for the daughters of Zion* (Cambridge, Mass.: Samuel & Bartholomew Green, 1692), 17.

7. Gisela Molina Fumero and Otilia Barros Díaz, "La puertorriqueñidad. Nacimiento y desarrollo de una cultura de resistencia." *Estudios del Desarrollo Social* 7, no. 3 (July-September, 2019), online.

8. Kathiana Mejías Martínez, "A Christmas in Puerto Rico," *Cayey Students Write*, December 2019, 12.

9. Mejías Martínez, "A Christmas," 12. Today, Christmastime in Puerto Rico lasts about forty-five days: from Thanksgiving to mid-January's San Sebastian Fiestas.

10. The trauma of this new Christmas figure, so white, so fat, so associated to an unknown wintertime, was brilliantly depicted in a classic story titled "Santa Cló va a La Cuchilla" by Puerto Rican writer Abelardo Díaz Alfaro in his 1947 book *Terrazo*.

11. "Trullas a caballo" or on-horse, were enjoyed by the elite class. These *trullas* are still celebrated, but with cars instead of horses, and over time they had mostly been called "parrandas" or "asaltos."

12. This term refers to the mentioned "guiro," also known as "güícharo" in the musical instruments section.

13. The term "asalto" means "assault." Anthropological research considered that it "may help convey the element of social aggression, ritualized and accepted, to be sure, which is implicit in this kind of foray against the hospitality of one's friends. See Landy, *Tropical Childhood*, 78, footnote #3.

14. Urrego, "Cambio," 132.

15. Víctor O. Dabbagh Rollan, "La simbología de las fiestas patronales: ejemplo de Pradoluengo," *Revista de Folklore* no. 373 (2013): section 3.1.

16. Antonio Sotomayor-Carlo, Antonio, "Celebrating the Colonial Nation in San Germán's Patron Saint Festivities, 1950's," *CENTRO Journal* 20 no. 2 (Fall 2008): 106–7.

17. St. John the Baptist's Day is celebrated by Catholics on June 24.

18. Blackey, "Gaming," 236–37.

19. Blackey, 237.

20. Blackey, 266.

21. Urrego, 130–31,

22. See Alfonso Rodríguez, Alfonso, "Puerto Rico, tierra de toreo que resistió el cambio de soberanía," *La Vanguardia*, June 3, 2019; and Fernando Pereira, "Tras el rastro de las corridas de toros. El español Rafael Gómez Aguilar recopiló la historia del desarrollo de esta disciplina en la Isla, la que contó con un respaldo del público," *El Vocero*, June 27, 2019.

23. David Favre and Vivien Tsang (1993), "The Development of the Anti-Cruelty Laws During the 1800's," *Detroit College of Law Review* 1 (1993): 17.

24. Janet M. Davis, "Cockfighting Nationalism: Blood Sport and the Moral Politics of American Empire and Nation Building," *American Quarterly* 65, no. 3 (September 2013): 551.

25. Davis, "Cockfighting Nationalism," 555.

26. Davis, 566.

27. Davis, 567.

28. Jim Wyss, "Puerto Rico Tries to Save Cockfighting Industry, Defying Federal Government," *The Miami Herald*, December 18, 2019.

29. Davis, 570.

30. Del Valle Atiles, *El campesino*, 113.

31. Golbach, "Protestantism-Capitalism-Sports," 285–86.

32. Golbach, 286, 289.

33. Golbach, 289.

CHAPTER 13: "WE ISS ONE HAPPY PEOPLE": ON PUERTO RICANS' VALUES AND HOW THEY SEE LIFE

1. Memmi, *The Colonizer and the Colonized*, 85.

2. Daniel Wodak and Sarah-Jane Leslie, "The Mark of the Plural. Generic Generalizations and Race," in P. C. Taylor et al., eds., *The Routledge Companion to the Philosophy of Race*, (Routledge, 2017), 277–78.

3. Mary Louise Pratt, "Scratches on the Face of the Country; or, What Mr. Barrow Saw in the Land of the Bushmen" in Henry Louis Gates Jr., ed., *"Race," Writing, and Difference* (Chicago: The University of Chicago Press, 2986), 139.

4. Said, *Orientalism*, 194.

5. JanMohamed, "The Economy," 82–83.

6. Manuel Feraz Lorenzo and Ana Cristina Calero Rodríguez, "La política educativa española en Puerto Rico a finales del siglo XIX: un factor más de contención en las aspiraciones independentistas," *Revista Interamericana de Educación* no. 43 (January-April 2007).

7. War Department, *Report on the Census of Porto Rico, 1899*, 73.

8. Informe sobre Desarrollo Humano en Puerto Rico, 2016, "Cap. VI: Una mirada al sistema educativo puertorriqueño, Introducción" (San Juan: Instituto de Estadísticas de Puerto Rico, 2016), 160.

9. In 2019–2020, the Budget of the Department of Education was the largest of any colonial agency: $3,689 million. ["Educación presenta su presupuesto para el año fiscal 2019–2020," *Metro Puerto Rico*, June 13, 2019]. Nevertheless, a comprehensive study made in 2016 confirmed that, although the department's budget has been fluctuating around $3,500 million since 2006, the Department of Education keeps facing the same challenges: economic inequality, high school dropouts, low academic achievement rates, poor graduation rates at the university level, low male participation and exodus to the informal economy, and lack of short- and long-term planning due to excessive political partisanship. See "Cap. VI: Una mirada . . . (2016), 168, 175, 183.

10. Picó, "Cafetal Adentro," 32.

11. Fernández, *The Disenchanted Island*, 9.

12. "Dignidad" is so important in Puerto Rican culture that the first sentence in the Puerto Rican 1952 Bill of Rights reads: "The dignity of the human being is inviolable," a phrase absent from the US Bill of Rights. See Carlos E. Ramos González, "La inviolabilidad de la dignidad humana: lo indigno de la búsqueda de expectativas razonables de intimidad en el derecho constitucional puertorriqueño," *Revista de la Academia Puertorriqueña de Jurisprudencia y Legislación* 10, no. 1–2 (2010): 9.

13. Landy, *Tropical Childhood*, 119.

14. The term refers to collective transportation vehicles.

15. War Department (1900), 42. In 2019, the population density of Puerto Rico was of 835 persons per square mile, but in 2022, it went down to 366.67 per square mile.

16. This section refers mostly to male or general fashion. A description of women's apparel in particular can be found in chapter 15.

17. Laia García-Furtado, "The Joy of Always Being Emperifollá," *Elle*, July 30, 2018.

18. See Landy, 31.

CHAPTER 14: "PEOPLE WHO WILL ALWAYS 'BE THERE'": ON PUERTO RICANS' RELATIONSHIPS WITH FAMILY, FRIENDS, AND STRANGERS

1. Del Valle Atiles, *El campesino*, 132.

2. Marqués, *The Docile Puerto Rican*, 54.

3. Memmi, *The Colonizer and the Colonized*, 84.

4. This is a reference to the Hottentot (meaning "stutterer" in Dutch) or Khoikhoi tribe in South Africa. The author is trying to convey that only "savages" will not recognize that they were being honored by their hosts because the term "Hottentot" was then used for "a person of inferior intellect or culture." It is still a term of insult in South Africa. See Geoffrey Hughes, *An Encyclopedia of Swearing: The Social History of Oaths, Profanity, Foul Language, and Ethnic Slurs in the English-Speaking World* (New York: Routledge, 2015), 241–43.

5. The study, titled *Giving in Puerto Rico*, and published in September 2016, was performed through a collaboration of the *Flamboyan Foundation*, *The Indiana University Lilly Family School of Philanthropy*, and the *Kinesis Foundation*.

6. Judy Lin, Judy, "Scholar Intrigued by How Societies Treat Their Elderly," *UCLA Today*, January 7, 2010.

7. Macdonald, "Our Invisible Poor," 8–9.

8. Landy, *Tropical Childhood*, 25.

9. Clark, *Porto Rico and Its Problems*, 38.

10. Landy, 94.

11. Sydney W. Mintz and Eric R. Wolf, "An Analysis of Ritual Co-Parenthood (Compadrazgo)," *Southwestern Journal of Anthropology* 6, no. 4 (Winter 1950), 341.

12. Levy and Bahrawi, *Cultures of the World*, 67.

13. Molina Fumero and Barros Díaz, "La puertorriqueñidad," online.

14. Picó, "Cafetal Adentro," 5.

CHAPTER 15: "THOSE INDESCRIBABLE EYES": PUERTO RICAN WOMEN

1. Wallach, *How America Eats*, 112.

2. Wallach, 113.

3. In heraldry, sable is a black tincture.

4. Suárez Findlay, *Imposing Decency*, 51.

5. The Social Issues Research Center, *The Flirting Report* (Oxford, UK, 2004), 4, 15.

6. Lisa Wade, "Before Love: Puritan Beliefs About Sex and Marriage," *The Society Pages*, February 15, 2013.

7. Mather, *Ornaments*, 69.

8. García-Furtado, "The Joy of Always Being Emperifollá," no page.

9. Rachel Fleming, "Those Loose Ladies: An Examination of Scandalous Puritan Women in Massachusetts from 1635 to 1700," *Honor Theses*, Digital Commons at Salem State University, 2015, 18.

10. Glen Norcliffe, "Women and Cycling: A Revisionist Interpretation," presentation at the 28th International Cycling History Conference, Mannheim, Germany, 2017.

11. Picó, "Cafetal Adentro," 11.

12. Gabriela Quijano Seda, "'Viven del sudor de la gente': producción y resistencia en la industria de la aguja en Puerto Rico," *Iluminuras* 14, no. 33 (2013): 262–73.

CHAPTER 16: "BRIGHT-EYED LITTLE FELLOWS": PUERTO RICAN CHILDREN

1. Fleming, "Those Loose Ladies," 17.

2. Shellie Clark, "The Sexual Revolution of the 'Roaring Twenties': Practice or Perception?," *#History: A Journal of Student Research* 1 (2016): 92.

3. *Encyclopedia Britannica Online*.

4. Servando Montaña, ed., *Antología de Nemesio R. Canales* (Río Piedras: Editorial de la Universidad de Puerto Rico, 2000), 236.

5. All the data of this section is from War Department, *Report on the Census of Porto Rico, 1899*, 75–85.

6. Feraz and Calero Rodríguez, "La política educativa."

7. War Department, 84.

8. Helen F. Ladd and Francisco L. Rivera-Batiz, "Education and Economic Development," in Susan M. Collins, Barry Bosworth, and Miguel Soto-Class, *The Puerto Rico Economy: Restoring Growth* (Washington, DC: Brookings Institution Press, 2006), 211–12.

9. Thompson, "Colonial Governmentality," 32.

10. David Tyack and Elisabeth Hansol, *Learning Together: A History of Coeducation in American Public Schools* (New York: Russell Sage Foundation, 1992), 5, 28, 48.

11. War Department, 84.

12. The Carlisle Indian Industrial School was a boarding school designed to assimilate Native American children to American culture. Between 1898 and 1918, sixty Puerto Rican families were lured to send their children to study in this Pennsylvanian institution where they suffered a frontal attack to their cultural identity, which was seen as inferior to mainstream American. See Pablo Navarro-Rivera, "Acculturation Under Duress: The Puerto Rican Experience at the Carlisle Indian Industrial School, 1898–1918," *Centro Journal* 18, no. 1 (Spring 2006): 222–59.

13. Landy, *Tropical Childhood*, 59–60.

14. Thompson, 34–35.

15. Santiago-Valles, "La concentración," 163.

16. Maritza Maymí Hernández, "De títeres a ciudadanos: Las representaciones de 'los niños de la calle' y el deseo de gobernar (Puerto Rico, 1860–1920)," *Op. Cit.*, no. 17 (2006–2007): 63.

17. The school was created by Law No. 7 of March 9, 1905. (Junta de Planificación, *Criminalidad*, 24)

18. This Minors' Court was created by Law No. 37 of March 11, 1915. (Junta de Planificación, 24)

19. Urrego Ardila, *Familia*, 205.

CHAPTER 17: "THEY WANT RICE AND BEANS FIRST": FOOD, DRINKS, AND SMOKES

1. Wallach, *How America Eats*, 89–90, 192–93.

2. Its importance was highlighted by anthropologist David Landy in his research: "A family will often sacrifice during the year to keep a lean, razorback hog alive, so that at Navidades and Tres Reyes they may have relatives and friends over to share the festive boar.... Pork skins are fried (chicharrones) and nearly every other part of the animal is eaten, the intestines being stuffed with blood, liver, etc. to make blood sausage." See Landy, *Tropical Childhood*, 30.

3. Landy, 90–92.

4. At the time, Americans began to experiment with Italian food at their homes. See Wallach, *How America Eats*, 169.

5. José A. Mari Mut, *Frutas y vegetales en los mercados de Puerto Rico* (edicionesdigitales.info, 2014), 44, 181.

6. Regarding this important event in the Caribbean and World War II history, see Domenech (2014).

7. This "second breakfast" or almuerzo was explained by Dr. Cruz Miguel Ortiz Cuadra: "During the period of Spanish rule, the almuerzo was a morning snack, taken before ten o'clock. It preceded the 'comida,' the workday's principal meal . . . generally consumed after the noontime hour." Cruz Miguel Ortiz Cuadra, *Eating Puerto Rico: A History of Food, Culture, and Identity* (Chapel Hill: The University of North Carolina Press, 2013), 263.

8. Mintz, *Worker in the Cane*, 17.

9. José A. Mari Mut, *Frutas olvidadas de Puerto Rico* (Puerto Rico: edicionesdigitales.info, 2014), 17.

10. Emma A. Dávila Cox, *Este Inmenso Comercio. Las relaciones mercantiles entre Puerto Rico y Gran Bretaña, 1844–1898* (San Juan: Editorial de la Universidad de Puerto Rico, 1996), 77; Fernández (1996), 5.

11. Landy, 179.

12. This plant's name is *Cassia occidentalis L*. See Esteban Nuñez Meléndez, *Plantas medicinales de Puerto Rico: folklore y fundamentos científicos* (San Juan: Editorial de la Universidad de Puerto Rico, 1982), 349.

13. Gina Hames, *Alcohol in World History* (London: Routledge, 20120), 54, 57.

14. Hames, *Alcohol*, 50–51.

15. Hames, 72–73.

16. Hames, 55.

17. Quoted in González Cruz, "Destilando caña," 33.

18. Mayra Rosario Urrutia, "Cultura, poder y protestantismo: el desplazamiento de la industria del alcohol en Puerto Rico, 1898–1917" in Eda M. Burgos, ed., *El Conflicto de 1898. Antecedentes y Consecuencias Inmediatas* (San Juan: Editorial de la Universidad de Puerto Rico, 2000), 345.

19. Rosario Urrutia, "Cultura, poder y protestantismo," 351.

20. Rosario Urrutia, 352, 355.

21. Rosario Urrutia, 356.

22. José A. Mari Mut, *Maderas de Puerto Rico* (edicionesdigitales.info, 2013), 258.

23. David Harley, "The Beginnings of the Tobacco Controversy: Puritanism, James I, and the Royal Physicians," *Bulletin of the History of Medicine* 67, no. 1 (Spring 1993): 48.

CHAPTER 18: "DEAR ME! WHAT A BUSY, NOISY PLACE!": ON COMMERCE AND ANIMAL TREATMENT

1. Ali A. Mazrui, *The Africans. A Triple Heritage* (Boston: Little, Brown & Co., 1986), 213, 217, 222.

2. Confederate money (Confederate States Dollar) was the currency issued by the short-lived Confederate States of America that governed eleven Southern states during the American Civil War (1861–1865). Once the war ended, the Confederate money became worthless.

3. The Ley Núm. 130 of June 30, 1975 regulated the requisites for the licenses of these commercial establishments. Senado de Puerto Rico, February 8, 2007, *Quinta Sesión Ordinaria, Vol. LV, Núm. 8*, Diario de sesiones, procedimientos y debates de la decimoquinta Asamblea Legislativa (San Juan, PR, 2007), 26555.

4. Wendy A. Woloson, "In Hock: Pawning in Early America," *Journal of the Early Republic* 27, no. 1 (Spring 2007): 35, 37.

5. Mintz, *Worker in the Cane*, 267.

6. Junta de Planificación, *Criminalidad*, 12.

7. Bill Leon Smith, "Animals Made Americans Human: Sentient Creatures and the Creation of Early America's Moral Sensibility," *Journal of Animal Ethics* 2, no. 2 (Fall 2012): 132.

8. Smith, "Animals," 135.

9. Favre and Tsang, "The Development," 11. By 1890, Massachusetts, Pennsylvania, Illinois, New Hampshire, New Jersey, and Maryland had adopted similar legislation to that of New York.

10. Joshua Rapp Learn, "Survey shows U.S. citizens increasingly humanize animals," *The Wildlife Society*, January 15, 2020, accessed on July 31, 2021.

11. Robert G. Bailey, *Description of the Ecoregions of the United States*, US Forest Service, www.fs.fed.us/land/ecosysmgmt/.

12. They belong to the family Daysproctidae. Nicholas J. Saunders, *The Peoples of the Caribbean: An Encyclopedia of Archaeology and Traditional Culture* (Santa Barbara, CA: ABC-CLIO, 2005), 3.

13. The described iguana resembles the rhinoceros iguana (*Cyclura cornuta*), a species abundant in Puerto Rico and in Hispaniola in Pre-Columbian times. Nowadays, it is only found as the subspecies *Cyclura cornuta stejnegeri* on Mona Island, a part of the Puerto Rican archipelago. The word "iguana" is a Taíno Indian word. See Mari Mut, *Fauna*, 75.

14. Although Puerto Rico is home to ten species of lizards, based on the descriptions, these must have been the most well-known: the common lizards (*Anolis cristatellus*) or Puerto Rican anole. The species is native of Puerto Rico and the Virgin Islands. See Mari Mut, *Fauna*, 66.

15. Although there are seventeen species of coquíes in Puerto Rico, only two of them actually make the notorious sound of "coquí." The *Eleutherodactylus coqui* (found all over the Island) and the *Eleutherodactylus portoricensis* (found only in the mountains) are small arboreal frogs native of Puerto Rico. Unlike other frogs, they do not have webbed feet nor go through a tadpole phase. Their toe pads allow them to climb up vertical structures and cling to trees and leaves. They are one to two inches long and weigh two to four ounces. The term "coquí" refers to the sound of the call produced by the males to attract females and repel other males throughout the nights. See Mari Mut, *Fauna*, 62–63.

16. The Puerto Rican *Pyrophorous lunimosus* is a "click beetle" that is endemic of the Island. The original Taíno Indians called it "cucubano" or "cocuyo." In the countryside people used to put them in jars to use them as lanterns. Mari Mut, *Insectos*, 52.

"TO BE BORN IN PORTO RICO IS, FOR ME, A PRIVILEGE": CONCLUSION

1. As a colony, Puerto Rico is poorer than the poorest state of the United States (Mississippi), with a poverty rate of fifty percent (against Mississippi's twenty-two percent) and about one-half of the per capita income of Mississippi. See "How Mississippi Is Catching Up—and Puerto Rico Is Not" (2017), *Puerto Rico Report*, www.puertoricoreport.com, August 2.

2. Memmi, *The Colonizer and the Colonized*, 113.

3. Streets-Salter, *Empires and Colonies*, 407–8.

4. Memmi, 87.

5. Fanon, *The Wretched of the Earth*, 250. See also, in our works cited, the works on the mental pathology of Puerto Ricans by doctors Guillermo González (2007) and Miriam Biascoechea-Pereda (2008).

6. As translated in Kal Wagenheim and Olga Jiménez de Wagenheim, eds., *The Puerto Ricans. A Documentary History* (Princeton: Markus Wiener Publishers, 2008), 122.

7. Wagenheim, *The Puerto Ricans*.

8. Césaire, *Discourse*, 35–36.

9. Fanon, 312.

10. Memmi, 128.

WORKS CITED

Agosto Cintrón, Nélida. *Religión y cambio social en Puerto Rico (1898–1940)*. San Juan: Ediciones Huracán, 1996.

Alegría Ortega, Idsa E. "Ejes temáticos del pensamiento racial en Puerto Rico: una aproximación." *Revista de Ciencias Sociales* 17 (2007): 154–87.

Annas, George J. *Worst Case Bioethics: Death, Disaster, and Public Health*. New York: Oxford University Press, 2010.

Bailey, Robert G. "U.S. Forest Service." *Ecosystems Management*. March 1995. Accessed August 8, 2020. https://www.fs.fed.us/land/ecosysmgmt/.

Baralt, Guillermo A. *Esclavos rebeldes: conspiraciones y sublevaciones de esclavos en Puerto Rico (1795–1873)*. Río Piedras: Ediciones Huracán, 1981.

Baranowski, Shelley, Christopher Endy, Waleed Hazbun, Stephanie Malia Hom, Gordon Pirie, Trevor Simmons, and Eric G.E. Zuelow. "Tourism and Empire." *Journal of Tourism History* 7, no. 1–2 (2015): 100–130.

Bassnett, Susan. "Travel Writing and Gender." In *The Cambridge Companion to Travel Writing*, edited by Peter Hulme and Tim Youngs, 225–40. Cambridge: Cambridge University Press, 2002.

Bastian, Jean Pierre. "Emancipación política de 1898 e influencia del protestantismo en Cuba y Puerto Rico." *Anuario de Historia de la Iglesia*, no. 7 (1998): 145–58.

Becker, Lidia. *Nombres de persona en español: Historia, situación actual y onomástica popular*. Berlin: Peter Lang, 2018.

Biascoechea-Pereda, Miriam. *Understanding the Pendejo Phenomenon in Puerto Rico: An Example of Culture-Specific Therapy*. PhD thesis, Walden University, 2008.

Blackey, G. Robert. "Gaming, Lotteries, and Wagering: The Pre-Revolutionary Roots of the Law of Gambling." *Rutgers Law Journal* 16, no. 2 (1985): 211–67.

Boissoneault, Lorraine. "The Myth of Professional Beggars Spawned Today's Enduring Stereotypes." *Smithsonian Magazine*, March 30, 2017.

Brantlinger, Patrick. "Victorians and Africans: The Genealogy of the Myth of the Dark Continent." In *"Race," Writing, and Difference*, edited by Henry Louis Gates Jr., 185–222. Chicago: The University of Chicago Press, 1986.

Brau, Salvador. *Historia de Puerto Rico*. New York: D. Appleton & Co., 1904.

Briggs, Laura. *Reproducing Empire: Race, Sex, Science, and U.S. Imperialism in Puerto Rico*. Berkeley: University of California Press, 2002.

Cabranes, José A. "Citizenship and the American Empire." *University of Pennsylvania Law Review* 127 (1975): 391–492.

Cantú, César. *Historia Universal, Tomo XXII*. Madrid: Biblioteca Popular Económica, 1849.

"Cap. VI: Una mirada al sistema educativo puertorriqueño, Introducción." In *Informe sobre Desarrollo Humano en Puerto Rico*, 157–84. San Juan: Instituto de Estadísticas de Puerto Rico, 2016.

Carpenter, Frank C. "Plans of Government Suited to Porto Ricans." *The Brooklyn Daily Eagle*, October 8, 1899.

Catechism of the Catholic Church. Citta del Vaticano: Librería Editrice Vaticana, 1993.

Césaire, Aimé. *Discourse on Colonialism*. New York: Monthly Review Press, 2000.

Christ, Grace H., George Bonnano, Ruth Malkinson, and Simon Rubin. "Appendix E: Bereavement Experiences After the Death of a Child." In *When Children Die: Improving Palliative and End-of-Life Care for Children and Their Families*, edited by M. J. Field and R. E. Behrman. Washington, DC: National Academies Press, 2003.

Clark, Shellie. "The Sexual Revolution of the 'Roaring Twenties': Practice or Perception?" *History: A Journal of Student Research* 1 (2016): 92–101.

Clark, Victor S. *Porto Rico and Its Problems*. Washington, DC: The Brookings Institution, 1930.

Cleary, Edward L. "Puerto Rico: Lay Preachers Who Preserved Catholicism." In *The Challenge of Priestless Parishes: Learning from Latin America*, edited by Edward E. Cleary. New Jersey: Paulist Press, 2014.

Código Penal. Título I, Artículo 265, 585, San Juan: Asamblea Legislativa de Puerto Rico, 1902.

Colson, Elizabeth. "Culture and Progress." *American Anthropologist* 78 (1976): 261–71.

Comisión de Derechos Civiles de Puerto Rico. "¿Somos Racistas? Cómo podemos combatir el racismo." San Juan, 1998.

Comisión Teológica Internacional. "Congregación para la Doctrina de la Fe, El Vaticano,." *La esperanza de salvación para los niños que mueren sin bautismo*. 2007. http://www.vatican.va/roman_curia/congregations/cfaith/cti_documents/rc_con_cfaith_doc_20070419_un-baptised-infants_sp.html.

Dabbagh Rollan, Víctor O. "La simbología de las fiestas patronales: ejemplo de Pradoluengo." *Revista de Folklore*, 2013.

Dávila Cox, Emma A. *Este Inmenso Comercio. Las relaciones mercantiles entre Puerto Rico y Gran Bretaña, 1844–1898*. San Juan: Editorial de la Universidad de Puerto Rico, 1996.

Davis, F. James. *Who is Black? One Nation's Definition*. Pennsylvania: The Pennsylvania State University Press, 2001.

Davis, Janet M. September. "Cockfighting Nationalism: Blood Sport and the Moral Politics of American Empire and Nation Building." *American Quarterly* 65, no. 3 (2013): 549–74.

Del Valle Atiles, Francisco. *El campesino puertorriqueño: sus condiciones físicas, intelectuales y morales*. San Juan: Tipografía de José González Font, 1889.

Diario de Sesiones, Procedimientos y Debates de la Asamblea Legislativa de Puerto Rico. Vol. I, no. 10 (August 8, 195). San Juan.

Díaz Vélez, Jorge. *Una mirada dialéctica a las representaciones discursivas de la invasión estadounidense a Puerto Rico en 1898*. PhD thesis, University of California, Berkeley, 2017.

Dietz, James L. *Historia de la economía de Puerto Rico*. Río Piedras: Ediciones Huracán, 1989.

Dilla Alfonso, Haroldo. *Ciudades en el Caribe: Un estudio comparado de La Habana, San Juan, Santo Domingo y Miami*. México: FLACSO, 2014.

Domenech-Abreu, Ligia. *Las corridas de Júas en Isabela*. Master's thesis, Centro de Estudios Avanzados de Puerto Rico y el Caribe, 1999.

Domenech, Ligia T. *Imprisoned in the Caribbean: The 1942 German U-Boat Blockade*. Iuniverse, 2014.

Duany, Jorge. "Imperialistas reacios: Los antropólogos norteamericanos en Puerto Rico, 1898–1950." *Revista del Instituto de Cultura Puertorriqueña* 97 (1987): 3–11.

Duany, Jorge. "Neither White Nor Black: The Politics of Race and Ethnicity among Puerto Ricans on the Island and in the Mainland." Paper presented at *The Meaning of Race and Blackness in the Americas: Contemporary Perspectives*. Providence, RI, February 10–12, 2000.

Elworthy, Frederick Thomas. *The Evil Eye, 1895*. Global Grey ebooks, 2019.

Erkoreka, Anton. "Mal de ojo: una creencia supersticiosa remota, compleja y aún viva." *Munibe* 57 (2005): 391–400.

Evans-Pritchard, Edward E. "Sorcery and Native Opinion." *Africa* 4, no. 1(1931): 22–55.

Fahim, Hussein and Katherine Helmer. "Themes and Counterthemes: The Burg Wartenstein Symposium." In *Indigenous Anthropology in Non-Western Countries*, edited by Hussein Fahim, xi-xx. Durham: Carolina Academic Press, 1982.

Fanon, Frantz. "National Culture." In *The Post-Colonial Studies Reader*, edited by Bill Ashcroft, Gareth Griffiths, and Helen Tiffin, 153–57. London: Routledge, 1995.

Fanon, Frantz. *The Wretched of the Earth*. New York: Grove Press, 1963.

Faulkner, Carol. *Unfaithful: Love, Adultery, and Marriage Reform in Nineteenth-Century America*. Philadelphia: University of Pennsylvania Press, 2019.

Favre, David, and Vivien Tsang. "The Development of the Anti-Cruelty Laws During the 1800's." *Detroit College of Law Review* 1 (1993): 1–35.

Feraz Lorenzo, Manuel and Ana Cristina Calero Rodríguez. "La política educativa española en Puerto Rico a finales del siglo XIX: un factor más de contención en las aspiraciones independentistas." *Revista Interamericana de Educación* 43 (January-April, 2007).

Fernández Bravo, Álvaro. "Los relatos de Viaje en América Latina." *Explora* MEC: Argentina, 2–16, 2007.

Fernández, Ronald. *The Disenchanted Island. Puerto Rico and the United States in the Twentieth Century*. Westport, CT: Praeger Publishers, 1996.

Figueroa Mercado, Loida. "Puerto Rico—Cultura y Personalidad." *Revista de Ciencias Sociales* 7 (March-June 1963): 93–102.

Fleming, Rachel. "Those Loose Ladies: An Examination of Scandalous Puritan Women in Massachusetts From 1635 to 1700." *Digital Commons at Salem State University*, 2015. https://digitalcommons.salemstate.edu/honors_theses/48.

Franqui-Rivera, Harry. "Why Puerto Ricans Did Not Receive U.S. Citizenship So They Could Fight in WWI." *Centro Voices E-Magazine*. Accessed November 9, 2020. https://centropr.hunter.cuny.edu/centrovoices/chronicles/why-puerto-ricans-did-not-receive-us-citizenship-so-they-could-fight-wwi.

Fry, Joseph A. "Imperialism, American style, 1890–1916"." In *American Foreign Relations Reconsidered, 1890–1993*, edited by Gordon Martel, 52–70. London: Routledge, 1994.

García Muñiz, Humberto. "La plantación que no se repite: Las historias azucareras de la República Dominicana y Puerto Rico, 1870–1930." *Revista de Indias* 65, no. 233(2005): 173–92.

García San Inocencio, Víctor and Víctor Rivera Hernández. 2015. *Derechos Humanos y Corrupción*. Report approved on July 24, 2015. San Juan: Comisión de Derechos Civiles de Puerto Rico, 2015.

García, Gervasio L. "Economía y Trabajo en el Puerto Rico del Siglo XIX." *Historia Mexicana* 38, no. 4 (1989): 855–78.

García, Gervasio L. "El otro es uno: Puerto Rico en la mirada norteamericana de 1898." *Los Americanos. Revista de la Universidad de Puerto Rico La Torre* Año 14, no. 53–54 (2009): 203–35.

García-Furtado, Laia. "The Joy of Always Being Emperifollá." *Elle*, July 30, 2018.

Gates Jr., Henry Louis. "Introduction: Writing "Race" and the Difference it Makes." In *"Race," Writing, and Difference*, edited by Henry Louis Gates Jr., 1–20. Chicago: The University of Chicago Press, 1986.

Geertz, Clifford. *The Interpretation of Cultures*. New York: Basic Books, 1973.

Gilman, Sander L. "Black Bodies, White Bodies: Toward an Iconography of Female Sexuality in Late Nineteenth-Century Art, Medicine, and Literature." In *"Race," Writing, and Difference*, edited by Henry Louis Gates Jr., 223–61. Chicago: The University of Chicago, 1986.

Golbach, Erich. "Protestantism-Capitalism-Sports." *Journal of Sport History* 4, no. 3 (1977): 285–94.

Gómez Navarro, Soledad. "La diferencia entre el desamparo y el consuelo: una reflexión sobre la muerte en el protestantismo y en el catolicismo." In *El mundo de los difuntos: culto, cofradías y tradiciones*, 9–20. San Lorenzo del Escorial, 2014.

González Cruz, José M. *Destilando caña: Resistencia y ron clandestino en la Isla de Puerto Rico*. Universidad de Brasilia, Brasil: Tesis de Maestría en Estudios Comparados sobre las Américas, 2014.

González, Dr. Guillermo. *The Governor's Suits. A Psychiatric Perspective of Puerto Rico*. USA: X Libris Corp, 2007.

Goodman, Alan, and Joseph L. Graves Jr. *Racism Not Race: Answers to Frequently Asked Questions*. New York: Columbia University Press, 2022.

Grabowsky, Jo-Ann and Thomas T. Frantz. "Latinos and Anglos: Cultural Experience of Grief Intensity." *Omega: Journal of Death and Dying* 26, no. 4 (1992–93): 273–85.

Grgurinović, Ivona. "Anthropology and Travel: Practice and Text." *Studia Ethnologica Croatica* 24 (2012): 45–60.

Gutierrez, Esteban, and Frank W. Fisk. "Annotated Checklist of Puerto Rican Cockroaches." *Transactions of the American Entomological Society* 124, no. 3–4 (1998): 333–54.

Guzmán Rubio, Federico. "Tipología del relato de viajes en la literatura hispanoamericana: definiciones y desarrollo." *Revista de Literatura* 73, no. 145 (2011): 111–30.

Hames, Gina. *Alcohol in World History*. London: Routledge, 2012.

Harley, David. Spring. "The Beginnings of the Tobacco Controversy: Puritanism, James I, and the Royal Physicians." *Bulletin of the History of Medicine* 67, no. 1 (Spring 1993): 28–50.

"How Mississippi Is Catching-Up—and Puerto Rico Is Not." *Puerto Rico Report*, August 2, 2017. https://www.puertoricoreport.com/how-mississippi-is-catching-up-and-puerto-rico-is-not/#.Xuob7UVKjIU.

Hughes, Geoffrey. *An Encyclopedia of Swearing: The Social History of Oaths, Profanity, Foul Language, and Ethnic Slurs in the English-Speaking World*. New York: Routledge, 2015.

Hulme, Peter, and Tim Youngs. "Introduction." In *The Cambridge Companion to Travel Writing*, edited by Peter Hulme and Tim Youngs, 3–10. Cambridge: Cambridge University Press, 2002.

Huntington, Ellsworth. "The Adaptability of the White Man to Tropical America." *The Journal of Race Development* 5, no. 2 (1914): 185–211.

Irizarry Álvarez, Femmy. "Las manos santas de Doña Mary." *Primera Hora*, April 11, 2015.

JanMohamed, Abdul R. "The Economy of Manichean Allegory." In *The Post-Colonial Studies Reader*, edited by Bill Ashcroft, Gareth Griffiths and Helen Tiffin, 18–23. London: Routledge, 2002.

JanMohamed, Abdul R. "The Economy of Manichean Allegory: The Function of Racial Difference in Colonialist Literature." In *"Race," Writing, and Difference*, edited by Henry-Louis Gates Jr., 78–106. Chicago: The University of Chicago Press, 1986.

Junta de Planificación de Puerto Rico. "Criminalidad en Puerto Rico: Serie Histórica 1900-2009." San Juan: Boletín Social, 2010.

Klein, Naomi. "Puerto Ricans and Ultrarich 'Puertopians' Are Locked in a Pitched Struggle Over How to Remake the Island." *The Intercept*, March 20, 2018.

Kuss, Malena. "Puerto Rico." In *Music in Latin American and the Caribbean: An Encyclopedic History, Vol.2*, edited by Malena Kuss, 151–88. Austin: University of Texas Press, 2007.

Ladd, Helen F., and Francisco L. Rivera-Batiz. "Education and Economic Development." In *The Puerto Rico Economy: Restoring Growth*, by Susan M. Collins, Barry Bosworth and Miguel Soto-Class, 189–238. Washington, DC: Brookings Institution Press, 2006.

Landy, David. *Tropical Childhood, Cultural Transmission and Learning in a Rural Puerto Rican Village*. Chapel Hill: The University of North Carolina Press, 1959.

Lapp, Michael. "The Rise and Fall of Puerto Rico as a Social Laboratory, 1945-1965." *Social Science History* 18, no. 2 (1995): 169–99.

LaRuffa, Anthony L. "Culture Change and Pentecostalism in Puerto Rico." *Social and Economic Studies* 18, no. 3 (September 1969): 273–81.

Learn, Joshua Rapp. "Survey shows U.S. citizens increasingly humanize animals." *The Wildlife Society*. January 15, 2020. Accessed July 7, 2021.

Leviatin, David. "Introduction." In *How the Other Half Lives: Studies among the Tenements of New York*, by Jacob A. Riis, 1–50. Boston: Bedford/St. Martin's, 2011.

Levinson, Julie H. "Beyond Quarantine: A History of Leprosy in Puerto Rico, 1898-1930s." *História, Ciências, Saúde—Manguinhos* 10, suppl. 1(2003): 225–45.

Levy, Patricia, and Nazry Bahrawi. *Cultures of the World—Puerto Rico*. New York: Marshall Cavendish Benchmark, 1995.

Lin, Judy. "Scholar Intrigued By How Societies Treat Their Elderly." *UCLA Today*, January 7, 2010.

López Cantos, Ángel. "La mujer puertorriqueña y el trabajo, siglo XVIII." *Anuario de Estudios Americanos* Tomo 57, no. 1 (2000): 195–222.

López Rojas, Luis A. *Historiar la muerte (1508–1920)*. San Juan: Isla Negra Editores, 2006.

Lorite Cruz, Pablo J. "Las exequias de niños en el catolicismo, fiesta 'alegre' a nivel iconográfico dentro de la muerte." In *El mundo de los difuntos: culto, cofradías y tradiciones*, 229–46. San Lorenzo del Escorial, 2014.

Luque, María Dolores. "Los conflictos de la modernidad: La elite política en Puerto Rico, 1898-1904." *Revista de Indias* 57, no. 211 (1997): 695–727.

Macdonald, Dwight. "Our Invisible Poor." *The New Yorker*, January 19, 1963.
Malavet, Pedro A. "Puerto Rico: Cultural Nation, American Colony." *Michigan Journal of Race and Law* 6, no. 1 (2000): 1–106.
Maldonado, Norman. "El Dr. Pedro Gutiérrez Ingaravídez (1871–1935) y el Instituto de Medicina Tropical." *Galenus* 43, no. 7 (December 2013–January 2014): 50–51.
Mari Mut, José A. *Fauna Casera de Puerto Rico*. edicionesdigitales.info. 2015
Mari Mut, José A. *Frutas olvidadas de Puerto Rico*. Puerto Rico: edicionesdigitales.info. 2014.
Mari Mut, José A. *Frutas y vegetales en los mercados de Puerto Rico*. edicionesdigitales.info. 2014.
Mari Mut, José A. *Insectos de Puerto Rico*. edicionesdigitales.info. 2015.
Mari Mut, José A. *Maderas de Puerto Rico*. edicionesdigitales.info. 2013.
Marqués, René. *The Docile Puerto Rican*. Philadelphia: Temple University Press, 1976.
Martínez-Ramírez, Héctor M. "Pentecostal Expansion and Political Activism in Puerto Rico." *Caribbean Studies* 33, no. 1 (2005): 113–47.
Mather, Cotton. *Ornaments for the daughters of Zion*. Cambridge, Mass.: Samuel & Bartholomew Green, 1692.
Maymí Hernández, Maritza. "De títeres a ciudadanos: Las representaciones de "los niños de la calle" y el deseo de gobernar (Puerto Rico, 1860–1920)." 17 (2006–2007): 59–90.
Mazrui, Ali A. *The Africans. A Triple Heritage*. Boston: Little, Brown & Co, 1986.
McClintock, Elizabeth A. "Should Marriage Still Involve Changing a Woman's Name?" *Psychology Today*, September 6, 2018.
Mejías Martínez, Kathiana. "A Christmas in Puerto Rico." *Cayey Students Write* December, 12–13, 2019.
Melgares Guerrero, José Antonio. "'Romper un hábito'. Costumbre penitencial que languidece en nuestros días." *Revista Cangilón* (December 1998): 5–8.
Memmi, Albert. *The Colonizer and the Colonized*. Boston: Beacon Press, 1965.
Mendoza, Eunice. *Machismo Literature Review*. Draft, New York: Center for Public Safety Initiatives of the Rochester Institute of Technology, 2009.
Metro Puerto Rico. "CENSO estima población de Puerto Rico es de 3.3 millones." *Metro Puerto Rico*, April 26, 2021.
Metro Puerto Rico. "Educación presenta su presupuesto para el año fiscal 2019–2020." *Metro Puerto Rico*, June 13, 2019.
Mintz, Sydney W. *Worker in the Cane, A Puerto Rican Life History*. New York: W.W. Norton & Co., Inc, 1974.
Mintz, Sydney W., and Eric R. Wolf. "An Analysis of Ritual Co-Parenthood (Compadrazgo)." *Southwestern Journal of Anthropology* 6, no. 4 (Winter 1950): 341–68.
Mohr, Eugene V. "Language, Literature & Journalism." In *The American Presence in Puerto Rico*, Edited by Lynn-Darrell Bender, 162–87. San Juan: Publicaciones Puertorriqueñas, 1998.
Molina Fumero, Gisela and Otilia Barros Díaz. "La Puertorriqueñidad. Nacimiento y desarrollo de una cultura de resistencia." *Estudios del Desarrollo Social* 7, no. 3 (2019), online.
Montaña, Servando, ed. *Antología de Nemesio R. Canales*. Río Piedras: Editorial de la Universidad de Puerto Rico, 2000.
Moral, Solsiree del. "Colonial Lessons: The Politics of Education in Puerto Rico, 1898–1930." *The American Historian*, (May 2018): 40–44.

Morales Tejeda, Aida L. "Santiago de Cuba: Miradas e imágenes urbanas en los relatos de viajeros." *Anales del IAA* (2016): 91–102.

Moscoso, Francisco. "La conquista española y la gran rebelión de los Taínos." *Pensamiento Crítico* 12, no. 62 (February–April, 1989): 2–16.

Moscoso, Francisco. *La revolución puertorriqueña de 1868: el Grito de Lares*. San Juan: Instituto de Cultura Puertorriqueña, 2003.

Munet, Frances. "Grieving and Death Rituals of Latinos." *Oncology Nursing Forum* 25, no.10 (1998): 1761–63.

Muñoz Jiménez, María Dolores. "El Rosario de Difuntos. El 'diálogo' con las almas del purgatorio a partir del caso de Quéntar (Granada)." *Gazeta de Antropología* 31, no. 2 (2015). http://hdl.handle.net/10481/36830.

Navarro-Rivera, Pablo. "Acculturation Under Duress: The Puerto Rican Experience at the Carlisle Indian Industrial School, 1898–1918." *Centro Journal* 18, no. 1 (2006): 222–59.

Negroni, Héctor A. *Historia Militar de Puerto Rico*. Madrid: Ediciones Siruela, S.A., 1992.

Norcliffe, Glen. "Women and Cycling: A Revisionist Interpretation." Paper presented at the 28th International Cycling History Conference, Mannheim, Germany, 2017.

Nuñez Meléndez, Esteban. *Plantas medicinales de Puerto Rico: folklore y fundamentos científicos*. San Juan: Editorial de la Universidad de Puerto Rico, 1982.

Oakland Tribune. "Porto Rico to Be Held Permanently." *Oakland Tribune*, July 21, 1898: 1.

Oppenheimer, Mark. "In God´s Name, or Baby 'Messiah', Competing Claims of Religious Freedom." *The New York Times*, August 16, 2013.

Ortíz Cuadra, Cruz Miguel. *Eating Puerto Rico: A History of Food, Culture, and Identity*. Chapel Hill: The University of North Carolina Press, 2013.

Pagán, Bolívar. *Historia de los partidos políticos puertorriqueños (1898–1956)*. Vol. 1. San Juan: Librería Campos, 1959.

Pedreira, Antonio S. *Insularismo*. San Juan: Imprenta Venezuela, 1942.

Pendergrass, Drew C., and Michelle Y. Raji. "The Harvard Crimson." *The Hardvard Crimson*, September 28, 2017. https://www.thecrimson.com/article/2017/9/28/the-bitter-pill/.

Pereira, Fernando. "Tras el rastro de las corridas de toros. El español Rafael Gómez Aguilar recopiló la historia del desarrollo de esta disciplina en la Isla, la que contó con un respaldo del público." *El Vocero*, June 27, 2019.

Pérez y Mena, Andrés I. "Cuban Santería, Haitian Vodun, Puerto Rican Spiritualism: A Multicultural Inquiry into Syncretism." *Journal for the Scientific Study of Religion* 37, no. 1 (1998): 15–27.

Pew Research Center. "Religión en América Latina: Cambio generalizado en una región históricamente católica." *Pew Research Center*, November 13, 2014.

Picó, Fernando. "Cafetal Adentro: Una historia de los trabajadores agrícolas en el Puerto Rico del Siglo XX." *Revista El Sol* 30, no. 1 (1986): 4–36.

Picó, Fernando. "La revolución puertorriqueña de 1898: La necesidad de un nuevo paradigma para entender el '98 puertorriqueño." *Historia y Sociedad* 10 (1998): 7–22.

Picó, Fernando. "Las construcciones de lo español entre los militares norteamericanos en Puerto Rico, 1898–99." *Revista de Indias* 57, no. 211 (1997): 625–35.

Picó, Fernando. *Puerto Rico 1898: The War after the War*. Princeton: Markus Wiener Publishers, 2004.

Pies, Ronald W. "Masks, Machismo, and the American Man-Child." *Psychiatric Times*, June 29 2020.

Pratt, Mary Louise. "Scratches on the Face of the Country; or, What Mr. Barrow Saw in the Land of the Bushmen." In *"Race," Writing, and Difference*, edited by Henry Louis Gates Jr., 138–62. Chicago: The University of Chicago Press, 1986.

Presser, Harriet P. "The Role of Sterilization in Controlling Puerto Rican Fertility." *Population Studies* 23, no. 3 (1969): 343–61.

Price, A. Grenfell. *White Settlers in the Tropics*. New York: American Geographical Society, 1939.

Pumarada O'Neill, Luis, y Rafael Pumarada. *Contexto histórico: Industria cafetalera en Puerto Rico, 1736–1969*. San Juan: Oficina Estatal de Preservación Histórica de Puerto Rico, 1989.

Quijano Seda, Gabriela. "Viven del sudor de la gente: producción y resistencia en la industria de la aguja en Puerto Rico." *Iluminuras* 14, no. 33 (2013): 262–73.

Quintero Rivera, Ángel G. *Salsa, sabor y control: Sociología de la música tropical*. México, DF: Siglo XXI Editores, 1998.

Ramos González, Carlos E. "La inviolabilidad de la dignidad humana: lo indigno de la búsqueda de expectativas razonables de intimidad en el derecho constitucional puertorriqueño." *Revista de la Academia Puertorriqueña de Jurisprudencia y Legislación* 10 (2010): 1–29.

Ramos Mattei, Andrés A. "The Growth of the Puerto Rican Sugar Industry under North American Domination: 1899–1910." In *Crisis and Change in the International Economy, 1860–1940*, edited by Bill Albert and Adrian Graves, 234–57. Norwich: ISC Press, 1984.

Ramos-McKay, Julia M. *Locus of Control, Social Activism, and Sex Roles in Puerto Rican College and Non-College Individuals*. MA Thesis, Amherst: Department of Psychology, University of Massachusetts, 1976.

Reyes Tosta, Mylord. "El aprendizaje del español y del inglés en Puerto Rico y sus influencias extranjeras." *Scientific International Journal* 10, no. 3 (2013): 44–53.

Rigau Pérez, José G. "El servicio de salud pública de los Estados Unidos en Puerto Rico, 1898–1918." 19 (2009–2010): 143–77.

Ríos Viner, Jessica. "Las curanderas: sanadoras en peligro de extinción." *El Nuevo Día*, April 2, 2007.

Rivero, Ángel. *Crónica de la Guerra Hispanoamericana en Puerto Rico*. Río Piedras: Editorial Edil, 1998.

Rizzo, Tracey, y Steven Gerontakis. *Intimate Empires. Body, Race, and Gender in the Modern World*. New York: Oxford University Press, 2017.

Roca, Angelina S. de. "Algunos valores prevalecientes en la sociedad puertorriqueña." *Revista de Ciencias Sociales* 1–2 (1963):121–40.

Rodríguez Centeno, María M. "Tiempos de crisis: Los campesinos y el café en Puerto Rico durante el cambio de siglo y la Gran Depresión." *Agroalimentaria* 11 (2000): 1–23.

Rodríguez, Alfonso. "Puerto Rico, tierra de toreo que resistió el cambio de soberanía." *La Vanguardia*, June 3, 2019.

Rodríguez, Camille. "Tradición de las Fiestas de Cruz." *El Visitante*, April 29, 2018.

Roman, Jesse. December. "The Puerto Rico Healthcare Crisis." *Annals of the American Thoracic Society* 12, no. 12 (2015): 1760–3.

Román, Reinaldo L. *Governing Spirits: Religion, Miracles and Spectacles in Cuba and Puerto Rico, 1878–1956*. Chapel Hill: The University of North Carolina Press, 2007.

Romberg, Raquel. *Witchcraft and Welfare: Spiritual Capital and the Business of Magic in Modern Puerto Rico*. Austin: University of Texas Press, 2003.

Rosa Nieves, Cesáreo. "El aguinaldo navideño en Puerto Rico." *Pedagogía* 3, no. 1 (1955): 97–110.

Rosario Urrutia, Mayra. "Cultura, poder y protestantismo: el desplazamiento de la industria del alcohol en Puerto Rico, 1898–1917." In *El Conflicto de 1898. Antecedentes y Consecuencias Inmediatas*, edited by Eda M. Burgos, 344–56. San Juan: Editorial de la Universidad de Puerto Rico, 2000.

Said, Edward. *Orientalism*. London: Routledge & Kegan Paul, 1978.

Sánchez, Luis Rafael. *No llores por nosotros, Puerto Rico*. Hanover, NJ: Ediciones del Norte, 1998.

Santiago-Valles, Kelvin A. *"Subject People" and Colonial Discourses. Economic Transformation and Social Disorder in Puerto Rico, 1898–1947*. New York: State University of New York Press, 1994.

Saunders, Nicholas J. *The Peoples of the Caribbean: An Encyclopedia of Archaeology and Traditional Culture*. Santa Barbara, CA: ABC-CLIO, 2005.

Schwartz, Stuart B. "Introduction." In *Implicit Understandings. Observing, Reporting and Reflecting on the Encounters between Europeans and Other Peoples in the Early Modern Era*, 2. UK: Cambridge University Press, 1994.

Senado de Puerto Rico. "Quinta Sesión Ordinaria, Vol. LV, Núm. 8." Diario de procedimientos y debates de la décimoquinta Asamblea Legislativa, San Juan, PR, February 8, 2007.

Silbey, David J. *A War of Frontier and Empire: The Philippine-American War, 1899–1902*. New York: Hill and Wang, 2007.

Silva Gotay, Samuel. *Catolicismo y política en Puerto Rico bajo España y Estados Unidos: Siglos XIX y XX*. San Juan: Editorial de la Universidad de Puerto Rico, 2005.

Silva Gotay, Samuel. *Protestantismo y política en Puerto Rico: 1898–1930*. San Juan: Editorial de la Universidad de Puerto Rico, 1997.

Smith, Bill Leon. "Animals Made Americans Human: Sentient Creatures and the Creation of Early America's Moral Sensibility." *Journal of Animal Ethics* 2, no. 2 (2012): 126–40.

Smith, Patricia K. "The Economics of Anti-Begging Regulations." *The American Journal of Economics and Sociology* 64, no. 2 (April 2005): 549–77.

Solomon, Richard. "Sexual Practice and Fantasy in Colonial America and the Early Republic." *Indiana University Journal of Undergraduate Research* 3 (2017): 24–34.

Sotomayor-Carlo, Antonio. "Celebrating the Colonial Nation in San Germán's Patron Saint Festivities, 1950's." *CENTRO Journal* 20, no. 2 (Fall 2008): 101–25.

Spurr, David. *The Rhetoric of Empire. Colonial Discourse in Journalism, Travel Writing, and Imperial Administration*. Durham, NC: Duke University Press, 1993.

Steinmetz, Katy. "From Messiah to Hitler, What You Can and Cannot Name Your Child." *Time*, August 12, 2013.

Steward, Julian H., Robert A. Manners, Eric R. Wolf, Elene Padilla, Sidney Wilfred Mintz, and Raymond L. Scheele. *The People of Puerto Rico*. Chicago: Board of Trustees of the University of Illinois, 1956.

Streets-Salter, Heather, and Trevor R. Getz. *Empires and Colonies in the Modern World. A Global Perspective*. New York: Oxford University Press, 2016.

Strong, Josiah. *Our Country: Its Possible Future and Its Present Crisis*. New York: The Baker & Taylor Co., 1891.

Suárez, Ana Lourdes. "Devociones, promesas y milagros. Aproximación a dimensiones de la espiritualidad en sectores populares." *Ciencias Sociales y Religión/Ciências Sociais e Religião* 18, no. 24 (2016): 54–70.

Suárez-Findlay, Eileen J. *Imposing Decency. The Politics of Sexuality and Race in Puerto Rico, 1870–1920*. Durham: Duke University Press, 1999.

The Social Issues Research Center. "The Flirting Report." Oxford, UK, 2004.

Thompson, Lanny. "Colonial Governmentality in Puerto Rico and the Philippines: Sovereign Force, Governmental Rationality, and Disciplinary Institutions Under US Rule." In *Rethinking the Colonial State: Political Power and Social Theory*, by Søren Rud and Søren Ivarsson, 21–46. Bingley, UK: Emerald Publishing, 2017.

Todorov, Tzvetan. *Nosotros y los otros*. México: Siglo XXI, 2013.

Torres Guzmán, Sandra. "Doña Chencha cura con sus manos santas." *Primera Hora*, January 4, 2016.

Torres Rivera, Edil. "Espiritismo: The Flywheel of the Puerto Rican Spiritual Traditions." *Revista Interamericana de Psicología* 39, no. 2 (2005): 295–300.

Trujillo-Pagán, Nicole E. "Worms as a Hook for Colonising Puerto Rico." *Social History of Medicine* 26, no. 4 (2013): 611–32.

Tunc, Tanfer Emin. "Manifest Destiny's Child: Mary Hazelton Blanchard Wade and the Literature of American Empire." *Children's Literature in Education* 48, no. 3 (2017): 245–61.

Tyack, David, and Elisabeth Hansol. *Learning Together: A History of Coeducation in American Public Schools*. New York: Russell Sage Foundation, 1992.

Urrego Ardila, Miguel Á. *Familia, biopolítica y cambio de orden colonial. San Juan de Puerto Rico, 1898–1930*. Morelia, México: Instituto de Investigaciones Históricas de la Universidad Michoacana de San Nicolás de Hidalgo, 2016.

Urrego, Miguel Ángel. "Cambio de soberanía y confrontación moral en Puerto Rico, 1898–1920." *Revista Mexicana del Caribe* 7, no. 13 (2002): 125–52.

Valera, Jr., Edmundo E. "Imperialism of Righteousness": The Influence of the American Protestant Social Gospel on Foreign Missions and Expansionism, 1890–1910. Doctorate Dissertation, Department of Theology, Fordham University, 1998.

W. B. F. *In the West Indies*. London: Arnold Fairbairns, 1905.

Wade, Lisa. "Before Love: Puritan Beliefs About Sex and Marriage." *The Society Pages*, February 15, 2013.

Wagenheim, Kal and Olga Jiménez de Wagenheim, eds. *The Puerto Ricans. A Documentary History*. Princeton: Markus Wiener Publishers, 2008.

Wallach, Jennifer Jensen. *How America Eats: A Social History of U.S. Food and Culture*. Maryland: Rowman & Littlefield Publishers, 2013.

Walsh, Ellen. "Advancing the Kingdom": Missionaries and Americanization in Puerto Rico, 1898–1930s. Doctorate Thesis in Philosophy, University of Pittsburgh, 2008.

War Department. *Report on the Census of Porto Rico, 1899*. Washington: Government Printing Office, 1900.

Weber, Max. *The Protestant Ethic and the Spirit of Capitalism*. London: Routledge, 2001.

Wodak, Daniel, and Sarah-Jane Leslie. "The Mark of the Plural. Generic Generalizations and Race." En *The Routledge Companion to the Philosophy of Race*, edited by Paul C. Taylor, Linda Martín Alcoff, and Luvell Anderson, 277–89. Routledge, 2017.

Wokler, Robert. "From l'homme physique to l'homme moral and Back: Towards a History of Enlightnment Anthropology." *History of the Human Sciences* 6, no. 1 (1993): 121–38.

Woloson, Wendy A. "In Hock: Pawning in Early America." *Journal of the Early Republic* 27, no. 1 (Spring 2007): 35–81.

Wood, Tana E., Grizelle González, Whendee L. Silver, Sasha C. Reed, and Molly A. Cavaleri. "On the Shoulders of Giants: Continuing the Legacy of Large-Scale Ecosystem Manipulation Experiments in Puerto Rico." *Forests* 10, no. 210 (2019): 3–18.

Wright, Marcus J. *Wright's Official History of the Spanish-American War*. Washington, DC: War Records Office, 1900.

Wyss, Jim. "Puerto Rico Tries to Save Cockfighting Industry, Defying Federal Government." *The Miami Herald*, December 18, 2019.

INDEX

Abbad y Lasierra, Fray Iñigo, 13
absentee corporations/absentee economy, 5, 53, 65, 128
Africa/Africans, 44, 52, 112–15, 171, 202, 209–10, 212, 223–24, 318, 336, 399n20, 403n4
African Americans, 24
agouti, 353
agregados, 60, 129, 134
agua de Florida, 194
aguinaldos, 222, 227–29, 401n2
Albizu Campos, Pedro, 87–88, 106, 389n18
alcohol, 15, 69, 159, 164, 236, 257, 329–33, 335
alcoholado, 194
alphabetization, 180
American exceptionalism, 13, 32
American investors, 4, 7, 54, 61–63, 65, 68, 72, 76, 90, 93, 98, 192, 200
Americanization, 4, 7, 30, 34, 97, 100, 107–10, 226, 298, 308–9, 314, 336
anemia, 63, 115, 135, 191–92, 195, 197–200, 206, 302
animal treatment, 336; animal abuse, 349, 351; animal cruelty, 237, 346–48, 350–51
animalization, 43
anthropology/anthropologists, 7–9, 29, 40, 45, 52, 54, 58, 110, 113, 119, 148, 156, 164, 257, 272, 324, 346
armadillo, 353
arrogance, 14, 21, 54, 105
Ashford, Bailey K., 23, 37–38, 44–45, 62–63, 124, 136, 197–200, 204, 207, 246, 274, 324

assimilation, 10, 29, 59, 97, 124, 305, 309, 324, 356, 405n12
Atkins, Grace W., 204
autonomy, 77, 93, 111; Autonomic Act of 1897, 77, 90
authority, 7, 15, 22, 45–46, 52, 78, 81, 85, 97, 124, 128, 146, 148, 155, 164, 166, 169, 171, 175, 181, 199–200, 209, 217, 237–38, 298, 314, 337, 361
ay bendito, 52–53, 264

babies, 70, 105, 113, 171, 193, 207, 215, 253, 262, 271, 286–87, 297, 299–300, 334, 344, 395n16, 397n22
Baldwin, James, 202, 399n23
banana stomachs, 302
bananas, 43, 69, 72, 134, 260, 291, 316, 318, 320–21, 324–25, 328, 338, 343
baptism, 172, 189, 218, 273
Baptist religion/ministers, 71, 174, 177, 180, 302, 329
baquiné, 212
baseball, 220, 237, 241–42
beans, 23, 30, 55, 62, 69, 129, 166, 193, 315–20, 325, 328, 335
Beard, A. F., 331
beauty, 14, 28, 50, 55, 57, 93–94, 104, 112–13, 115, 117, 123, 137, 156, 182, 224, 236, 245, 262, 268, 279, 281, 284, 287, 291–92, 322, 347, 354, 361
beggars, 23, 36, 65, 73–76, 103, 200, 222, 250, 345
bias, 6–7, 22–23, 87, 103, 164, 278, 356

421

422 INDEX

Biascoechea-Pereda, Miriam, 51–52
Blythe, Marion, 24, 29, 101, 121, 137, 139, 184–85, 202, 213, 215, 218, 222, 225, 227–29, 231, 266, 282–83, 301, 307–8, 317, 331, 343
bolita, la, 164–65, 169
bootlegging, 163–66, 169; *ron caña*, 164–65, 211, 396n11; *pitorro*, 164, 396n11
boxing, 220, 238, 242
Boyce, William D., 8–9, 21, 30, 38, 41, 78, 118, 131, 193, 196, 306, 309, 337
Brameld, Theodore, 51–52
bread, 41, 139, 156, 247, 251, 273, 303, 317, 320–21, 324, 327, 335, 343
Brown, Wenzell, 23, 30–31, 38, 50, 87, 98, 103–5, 116, 156, 162, 221, 248, 252, 254–55, 309, 342
Browne, Waldo G., 9, 44, 93, 130, 279, 357
bubonic plague, 195; Black Plague, 73
bullfights, 177, 236–37, 240, 242
burials, 170, 185, 209, 211–15

CAAM (*Colegio de Agricultura y Artes Mecánicas*), 123, 151, 175, 268, 294, 309
Calvinism/Calvinists, 131, 173, 210, 241
Cammann, William C., 74, 114, 281, 334, 351
Canales, Nemesio R., 302
capitalism/capitalists, 61, 69, 72–74, 90, 107, 131, 133–34, 136, 139, 173, 192, 200, 233, 241, 261, 269, 303, 336–37, 354
carnival, 90, 178, 229, 231–32, 288
Carpenter, Frank G., 26, 75, 235, 288, 326, 334
Carpenter, Vere C., 180, 183
carretera central, 326
casinos, 118, 218–19, 224, 236
Catholic Church/Catholics, 27, 46, 52, 108, 145–46, 149, 170–82, 184–86, 189–90, 209–15, 223, 226, 229, 232–33, 238, 242, 273, 329, 332
Catholic nuns, 31, 174–77, 179, 209
Catholic priests, 47, 140, 146–47, 151, 170, 172–77, 179, 181–82, 185, 187, 198, 225, 270, 273, 288, 347
Catholic saints, 136, 170–71, 176–79, 182, 210–11, 214, 227, 229–30, 242, 267

cemeteries, 176, 211, 213–16
centrales azucareras, 63, 206
Césaire, Aimé, 42, 44, 358
chaperone, 142–43, 151, 219, 287, 289–90
children, 9, 11, 14, 19, 21, 24–25, 28, 31–35, 38, 40–41, 43–46, 53, 55–57, 59, 62–63, 66–67, 69, 71, 74, 78, 88, 96, 103, 106, 109–11, 113, 119, 123, 125, 130–31, 135, 142, 144, 146–49, 151, 154–55, 159–60, 171, 178–79, 181–82, 186, 193, 197–99, 206–7, 211–14, 222, 225–30, 242, 246–47, 251, 257, 264, 266–67, 270–74, 276–77, 281, 286, 290–92, 296–314, 328, 331, 337, 340, 344, 347, 349, 354; homeless, 312–13; street, 312–13; wayward, 83, 312
Chillicothe Reform School, 314
Christianity/Christians, 12–14, 27, 73, 174, 178, 180–81, 183–84, 188, 227, 237, 346
Christmas, 28, 31, 179, 222, 225–29, 261, 316, 327–28, 401n2
Church, 13, 27, 46, 52, 108, 113, 145–49, 164, 170–78, 180–82, 184–89, 215, 229, 232–34, 281, 332
Church, A. M., 160, 223
churches, 27–28, 36, 123, 140, 171–72, 174–75, 177–79, 181–83, 185, 187, 189–90, 204, 210–11, 214, 225, 230, 278, 283, 285, 287
cigarettes, 34, 93, 133, 142, 151, 191, 260, 323, 334–35, 340
cigars, 93, 125, 142, 191, 260, 280–81, 333–35, 340
citizenship, 78–80, 308, 391n7
civilizing mission, 4, 10–15, 27–28, 31, 33, 36, 49, 78, 81, 96, 103, 108–9, 124, 126, 135, 182, 199, 305, 308–9, 335, 355, 358, 362
Clark, Victor S., 46, 78, 155–56, 168, 193–96, 201, 256–57, 265, 276, 282–83, 290, 293, 295, 305, 317, 322, 327
cleanliness, 78, 155–56, 168, 193–96, 201, 256–57, 265, 276, 282–83, 290, 293, 295, 305, 317, 322, 327
cockfights, 23, 29, 34, 99, 119, 131, 151, 172, 177, 233–34, 237–40, 242, 258, 346–47
cockroaches, 202
codfish, 55, 62, 316, 319, 324–25

coffee: drink, 31, 47–48, 74, 139, 142, 191, 211, 236, 249, 258, 261, 266–67, 315–17, 319–21, 324–25, 327–29; industry, 42, 60–63, 93, 114, 120–21, 124, 129–30, 135, 157–58, 197, 200, 276, 290–93; trees, 45, 62, 125, 130

colonial government, 4–5, 61–65, 68–69, 71, 74, 75–78, 81, 85–86, 88–89, 102, 107, 111, 119, 121, 124, 145, 146, 149, 157, 174, 176, 192, 194, 201, 209, 216, 233, 237, 241, 247, 294, 298, 304, 308, 309, 312, 345; colonial regime, 78

colonialism, 5, 7, 9, 13, 17–18, 36, 42, 45, 49, 54, 57–58, 71, 87–88, 91, 101, 107, 110, 111, 159–60, 174, 191, 337, 356, 358–59; colonialist, 16, 103, 170

colonization, American, 14, 113, 120, 126, 201, 314, 333, 335, 354, 356, 358

colonized, the, 3–4, 9, 12, 14–15, 17, 21, 27, 38–44, 50, 54, 57, 58, 75, 92, 102, 128, 138, 159, 169–70, 190, 201, 223, 244–45, 259, 261–62, 335, 340, 356, 359

colonizer, 9, 13, 15, 17, 38–41, 43–44, 57–58, 75, 128, 140, 169, 356, 358–59

colony, 3–4, 15, 17, 29, 36, 48–49, 53–57, 61, 67, 76–77, 80, 85–86, 89–92, 98, 100, 114, 120, 170, 181, 191, 233, 340–41, 353, 356, 358

Commonwealth, 86, 88; Estado Libre Asociado, 88–89

compadrazgo/compadre, 273–74, 341; *comadre*, 273

concubinage, 147–48, 173

Confederate money, 338, 406n2

Cooper, Jim, 32, 54, 73, 104, 110, 116, 118, 120, 123, 143, 151–55, 175, 208, 219, 224, 233, 251, 254, 268–69, 272, 277, 286, 289–90, 294, 301, 309–12, 334

coquí, 353–54, 407n15

Corridas de Júas festival, 184–85, 398n25

corruption, 78, 84–85, 87, 89–91, 140, 173, 332; influence peddling, 85; nepotism, 85

Creager, Charles, 41, 43, 96, 213, 222, 295–96, 337

criollos, 37, 95, 158; Spanish Americans, 39

Crowell, Katharine R., 28

cruelty, 34, 106, 185, 237, 346–48, 350–51

Cuban-Spanish War, 3
cucubanos, 354, 407n16
Cuisener, John, 8
curanderas/os, 205, 207

Dana, Arnold Guyot, 20–21, 61, 86–87
dancing/dances, 20, 40, 93, 116, 120, 131, 143, 160, 178, 203, 212, 218–19, 221–29, 242, 270, 272, 287–89, 327, 341; *bomba*, 223–24
Darwinism, Social, 13–14
daughters, 28, 57, 62, 86, 100, 121, 144, 153, 206, 213, 219, 246, 261, 270, 289, 294, 323
Davis, Richard Harding, 93
Dean, Corrine, 20, 24–25, 76, 107, 110, 237, 263
death/dead, 4, 21, 38, 43, 47, 50–51, 61, 65, 71, 90, 93, 142, 159, 171–72, 185, 191, 196, 202, 209–15, 217, 236, 238, 272, 274, 287, 313
defensive attitudes, 48, 51–52, 71, 122, 124, 160, 240, 246, 285
dehumanization, 41
Delano, Jack, 48, 64, 228, 255, 257–58, 267–68
Detweiler, Charles S., 174, 184, 187–89
Deusen, Elizabeth Knepple Van, 186, 206, 218, 220, 226, 230, 247, 292, 325–28
Deusen, Richard J. Van, 186, 206, 218, 220, 226, 230, 247, 292, 325–28
devotion, 8, 56–57, 100, 124, 131, 142, 147, 170–71, 177, 182, 187, 230, 245, 276, 287
diaspora, 357
dignidad, 52, 155, 247–51, 403n12
dignity, 47–48, 51, 61, 76, 121, 125, 129, 148, 247–48, 250–51, 265–66, 270, 317, 349
Dilla Alfonso, Haroldo, 218
Dinwiddie, William, 12, 43, 95, 161, 172, 194, 214, 236, 246, 255, 264, 291, 296–97, 299, 306, 320, 323, 334, 350
Disciples of Christ, 180, 188, 211, 328
discipline, 17, 46, 69, 114, 134, 167, 189, 208, 233, 270, 288, 304, 309, 312
divorce, 78, 146–47, 153, 175, 294
docility/indocility, 44, 46, 50, 62, 66, 201, 248, 255
dogs, 44, 216, 220, 298, 344, 352
domestic violence, 148

dominoes, 161, 234–35, 342
Douglass, Paul, 27, 133, 173, 187, 257, 347
drinking/drinks, 32, 52, 104, 144, 186, 203–4, 206, 219, 222, 226, 228, 230, 240, 251, 255, 261–62, 268, 315, 321, 327–34, 342
drugs, 48, 163, 198, 205, 245
drums, 222–24
drunkenness/drunks, 211, 234, 329, 331–32
Drury, Marion R., 187
Duany, Jorge, 119
duenna, 142–43, 278, 287, 293
Du Puy, William A., 82, 107, 256
Duggan, Janie Prichard, 103, 182, 202, 205, 214, 303
dwellings/dwellers, 42–43, 64–66, 69, 101, 121, 125, 133, 196, 228, 265, 293, 303; huts, 42, 46, 63, 71, 74, 124, 130–31, 135, 144, 150, 196, 213, 219, 258, 260–61, 265, 274, 283, 290–91, 293, 296, 304; shacks, 28, 42–43, 62, 121, 137, 179, 228, 234, 257, 267, 283, 290; thatches, 258, 291

earthquakes, 11, 20, 73, 76, 138, 186, 196, 203–4, 254; San Fermín, 196
Easter, 184–85
economy/economics, 4–5, 7–8, 21, 29, 32, 36, 50, 53–54, 59–60, 62–64, 67–70, 72–73, 75–76, 102, 118–19, 121, 127, 133–34, 136, 148–49, 156, 163–64, 169, 191–92, 196, 199–201, 209, 226, 238, 256, 261, 274, 276–77, 293–94, 297, 315, 330, 341, 346, 403n9
education, 4, 23, 26, 30, 38–39, 51, 56–58, 61, 64, 67, 69, 72, 78, 98, 107–8, 118, 125, 132–33, 136, 138, 168, 176, 181, 187, 189, 197, 199, 216, 240, 246–47, 264, 288, 294, 304, 306–7, 309, 312, 314, 336, 346–47
Edwards, Frank, 41, 43, 71, 99, 122, 142, 158–59, 168, 174, 209, 241, 331, 349
elections, 80, 82, 84, 86–90, 106, 125
elites, 42, 50, 58, 78, 82, 86, 93, 95, 99, 104, 116–17, 119–20, 122–23, 129, 131, 141–42, 144–45, 150, 155, 159, 187, 194, 214, 218–20, 224–25, 232, 234, 242, 246, 256, 270–71, 276–78, 280–81, 287–90, 292, 299, 318–19, 323, 329, 332–34, 337, 343–44, 347, 354

elopements, 145
emigration, 54, 66, 71–73, 76, 119, 127, 272
empires, 3–4, 9, 14, 17–18, 26, 38, 57, 64, 77–79, 91, 105–6, 111, 140, 170, 191, 340, 356–59
English language, 7, 30–31, 48, 51, 72–73, 86, 101, 107–11, 123, 145, 156, 246, 250, 263, 272–73, 305, 308–9, 311, 314, 321, 339, 385n2, 392n10
entertainment, 23, 101, 172, 177, 181, 218, 220, 231, 234–37, 239, 242, 266, 281, 287, 323, 342, 350
Episcopal Church, 180, 204
evil eye, 171, 205, 207, 399n29
exploitation, 13, 20, 49, 52, 65, 76, 85, 93, 98, 105, 122, 128, 130, 136, 192, 200, 216, 255, 294, 303, 329
extended family, 23, 149, 269–77
Ezraty, Barbara Tasch, 228

factories, 65–66, 74, 122
faith, 14, 17, 27, 47, 82, 135, 168, 174, 177–78, 182–83, 189, 205
faithfulness, 45, 147, 151, 153
Falcón, Rafael, 88, 154, 267
Fanon, Frantz, 9, 17, 42, 49, 96, 140, 159, 170, 201, 223, 358–59
fans, 278, 285–86, 299
fashion, 231, 256–58, 281–83, 286, 296, 397n17
fatalism, 46–51, 59, 96, 138, 206, 238, 354
fathers, 25, 34, 74, 142, 144, 149, 155, 160, 173, 179, 188, 209, 213, 215, 270–74, 277, 287, 291, 297, 304, 307
federal funds, 67, 76
federal government, 19, 21, 65, 71, 82, 88, 101, 194, 314
femininity, 98, 278, 281, 286, 288, 291
festival, 179, 186, 223, 229–30, 234, 333, 398n25
Fiala, Anthony, 137, 327, 338
fiestas, 160, 174, 218, 221, 327; Fiestas de Cruz, 186; Fiestas Patronales, 229–30
fights, 19, 52–53, 58, 67, 79, 84, 142, 150, 158–61, 167, 182, 247, 289, 337
Figueroa, Loida, 481

Financial Oversight and Management Board, 68
Fitzpatrick, Joseph P., 47, 116, 151, 270, 273, 348, 386n18
Flax, Herman J., 156, 178, 207, 276
Fleagle, Fred K., 50, 133, 192, 205, 274, 292, 313, 330, 386n18
flirtation, 100, 123, 131, 278–80, 284, 296
food, 21, 30–31, 34, 36, 58, 62, 64, 69, 71, 74, 95, 104, 110, 121–22, 124, 133, 136, 157–58, 163, 184, 192–93, 200, 221–22, 226, 228, 230, 239, 251, 261, 265, 268, 273, 296, 298, 302–3, 305, 307, 312, 314–20, 322–24, 327, 329–30, 335, 338, 344, 347, 351, 353, 357; Food Stamps Program, 67
Foraker Act, 61, 78
Forbes Lindsay, Charles H., 125
foreigners, 5–6, 8, 15, 18, 23, 26, 45, 55, 101–2, 105–6, 108, 124, 184, 188–89, 191–92, 205, 226, 255, 264, 271, 274, 278, 328, 353
Fowles, George Milton, 8, 39, 84, 117, 129, 140, 186, 234, 241, 252, 257–58, 282, 320
Franck, Harry A., 30, 37, 42, 49–50, 54, 85, 151, 196, 332
fruits, 10, 12, 43, 69, 70–71, 93, 107, 133–34, 136, 157, 204–5, 265, 268, 292, 298, 315, 318, 320–21, 325, 327, 335, 343–44, 348, 356–57
funerals, 176, 209, 211–14

gambling, 23, 118–19, 125, 131, 165–66, 172–73, 177, 186, 229, 233–36, 238, 240–42, 258, 332; tables, 219, 233–35, 327
García, Gervasio, 129, 134
garlic, 315, 317, 335
generosity, 5, 11–12, 21, 41, 48, 67, 94, 106, 124, 160, 186, 220, 228, 244, 260–67, 269, 274–75, 338; selflessness, 261
George, Marian M., 32–33, 137, 202, 239, 298, 304, 343, 344, 349, 351, 353
Golbach, Erich, 241
González, Guillermo, 44
gossip, 30, 47, 119, 141–42, 145, 152, 173, 178, 263, 344
grandfathers, 142, 270
grandmothers, 28, 118, 208, 270, 277, 290

gratitude, 69, 95, 103
Great Depression, 48–49, 64, 87, 159, 238, 303, 314, 332
Greater America: The Latest Acquired Insular Possessions, 236, 300
Greenfell Price, A., 10
Grose, Howard B., 27, 71, 105, 136, 146, 175, 177–78, 184, 244, 253, 301
Gruber, Ruth, 149, 168, 189, 203, 251
guava, 321, 325–27, 338, 343
Guernsey, Alice M., 128, 291, 305, 307, 312
güiro, 222, 401n12
Gunther, John, 49, 193, 303
Gutiérrez-Ingaravidez, Pedro, 45, 124, 136, 197, 199–200, 207, 246, 274, 324

hacendados, 34, 60–63, 120–21, 129–30, 274
Hall, Arthur D., 93, 177, 246, 256, 342, 351
Halstead, Murat, 98, 202–3
Hamm, Margherita Arlina, 9, 22, 24, 114–15, 121–22, 131–32, 143, 176, 194, 220, 225, 244, 266, 269, 270–71, 277–80, 282, 284–86, 288, 292–93, 299, 302, 315–18, 320, 322–23, 325, 327–28, 344–45, 353
hammock, 28, 125, 131, 135, 204–5, 229, 290, 298
Hancock, Ralph, 51, 66, 89, 139, 153, 190, 253, 344
Hannaford, Ebenezer, 43, 102, 328, 342, 349
Hanson, Earl Parker, 89–90, 163, 314
happiness, 28, 31, 48, 56, 71, 73–74, 84, 96, 125, 132, 136, 168, 200, 209, 212, 218, 224, 226–27, 243, 252, 254, 256, 259, 273, 279, 291, 296–97, 299–301, 306, 335, 351, 356
Harris, Alice, 14, 136, 163
Hazelton Wade, Mary, 32–34, 354
health, 8, 26, 33, 50, 58, 60, 67, 69, 76, 101–2, 132, 168, 171, 184, 191–96, 199–200, 204–9, 216, 241, 288, 301, 303, 321, 328, 332, 336
Hernández Colón, Rafael, 111
Herrmann, Karl Stephen, 94, 97, 133, 181, 244, 287
holidays, 111, 135–37, 171–72, 185, 218, 225–27, 229, 256, 308, 394n15
Holsinger, Justus G., 29, 47, 61, 65, 83, 137, 171, 206–7, 209, 211, 249, 251, 269, 337

homelessness, 61–62, 302, 312
honor, 12, 51, 141–42, 148–49, 151, 162–63, 179, 185, 210, 229, 238, 247, 257, 265–66, 270–71, 274, 286, 311, 323, 352, 403n4
hookworm/uncinariasis, 53, 62–63, 135, 197–200, 216
hope, 7, 27, 29, 31, 62–63, 65, 85, 96, 108, 125, 136, 234, 237, 239, 242, 261, 263, 267, 290–91, 335, 356, 358–59
horses, 3, 43, 97, 123, 129, 137, 165, 185, 203, 220, 236–37, 253, 266, 285, 288, 299, 334, 344, 346–52, 398n25, 401n11; ponies, 158, 342–43, 348–49
hospitality, 145, 160, 226, 260–66, 268, 274
hospitals, 12, 28, 61, 63, 180, 193, 201, 204–5, 208–9, 280–94, 303, 356; Presbyterian, 28, 204; Ryder Memorial, 204
hostility, 15, 66, 69, 102, 104, 159, 201
humor, 5, 48, 59, 98, 236, 255, 286
hunger, 24, 38, 44, 68–69, 74, 90, 142, 171, 191–92, 199, 221, 233, 255, 267, 300, 303, 308, 314, 345; starvation, 61–62, 69–71, 88, 125, 200, 255, 302–3, 314, 317, 345
hurricanes, 20, 47, 49, 61–62, 64, 73, 76, 121, 126, 138, 177, 193, 203, 303, 356; *Edith*, 203; *María*, 73; *San Ciriaco*, 61–62; *San Felipe*, 64, 193, 303
husbands, 32, 47, 144, 146, 148, 150–55, 157, 178, 213, 270, 276–78, 282, 287, 289–90, 292, 294, 296, 324, 333–34

Ickes, Harold L., 44, 282–83
ignorance, 9, 30, 34, 37, 41, 43, 71, 105, 124, 126, 172, 192, 196, 198, 200, 206, 244, 246, 248, 281, 287–88, 305, 332, 338
iguana, 353, 407n13
illegality, 23, 77, 157, 164–65, 237, 240, 332
illegitimacy, 142, 146–49, 151, 312–13
illiteracy, 53, 78, 85, 91, 167, 245–46, 264
immaturity, 14, 41, 336
imperialism/imperialists, 3–4, 12–14, 17, 21, 27, 32–33, 36–57, 58–59, 76, 97, 99, 107, 190, 237, 240, 340, 351, 355–56
impotence, 49, 358

independence, 3, 38, 41, 57–58, 64, 77–78, 86–89, 92, 106, 111, 134, 150, 288, 291, 341, 346, 357
indolence, 128–29, 133, 138, 172, 191, 220, 306
industrialization, 6, 14, 32, 37, 65–66, 72–74, 76, 81, 107, 134, 144, 163, 173, 253, 273, 276, 312, 315, 329, 333, 343
inequality, 7, 39, 69, 71, 76, 97, 122, 169, 190, 200, 259, 359
infancy/infants, 12, 66, 192, 207, 211–12, 227, 229, 239, 300–301, 303, 328, 334
infantilization, 40
inferiority, 9–10, 14–17, 21, 33, 39, 44, 50–51, 59, 80, 96, 134, 148–49, 245, 249, 261, 274, 277, 345, 403n4, 405n12
infidelity/adultery, 153, 156; extramarital affairs, 150, 153, 395n16
instruments, 222, 228, 270, 285, 295, 401n12
Insular Police, 41, 164–66, 346
insularism, 253
intelligence, 14, 60, 63, 79, 114, 117–18, 167, 184–87, 244, 246–47, 249, 259, 280, 305, 307–8, 349, 358, 389n18; smartness, 33, 219, 246, 305
Internal Revenue Service Code § 936, 68
invasion, US, 3, 6, 9, 14, 19, 26, 32–33, 60–61, 76–77, 80, 90, 92–93, 95–99, 107, 111, 113, 121–22, 129, 134, 136, 141, 145–47, 149, 155, 157, 160, 165, 173–74, 176, 180, 196, 198, 213, 215, 232, 240–41, 246, 254, 266, 276, 291, 304, 312, 328–29, 337, 339, 347, 353, 356

James, Arthur, 63, 135, 149, 161, 182, 184, 186, 206, 219, 229, 235, 242, 245, 262, 271, 339
JanMohamed, Abdul, 15
jíbaro, 37, 44–47, 51, 62, 105, 124–26, 128–29, 131, 136, 156, 170, 186, 199–200, 207, 240, 246, 256, 258, 260, 274, 316, 324–25, 332
Jiménez de Wagenheim, Olga, 358
Jones, Chester Lloyd, 53
Jones Act, 80, 164, 332, 396n10
Jordan, William F., 42, 132
journalists, 12–14, 19, 22, 24, 26, 35, 44, 47, 48–49, 51, 55, 65–66, 75, 82, 84, 86, 89, 112, 119, 137, 139, 149–50, 168, 172, 175, 178,

189, 194, 203, 207, 211, 235, 245, 247, 251, 253, 255, 258, 271, 286, 288, 299, 306, 313, 326, 340, 351, 358

Kellogg, Eva M., 32–33, 385n10
Kipling, Rudyard, 14, 387n41
kite fights, 235

laboriousness, 130, 135, 295
Landy, David, 160, 257, 272, 310
latrines, 197–99, 267
laws, 13–14, 23, 33, 45, 78–79, 89, 108, 117, 124–25, 146, 148–50, 159–64, 166, 169, 172, 177, 192, 195, 198–99, 206, 215, 226, 231, 233, 237, 244, 305–6, 312, 317, 343, 346–47, 361
laziness, 10, 23, 34, 43, 53, 69–71, 75–76, 124, 128–29, 131–33, 135–39, 172, 194, 198, 244, 264, 293, 295–96, 343; indolence, 128–29, 133, 138, 172, 191, 220, 306
Lehman, Tom, 88, 154, 267
leprosy/lepers, 200–201
Lindbergh, Charles, 86
Lions Club, 143, 219, 224
Lloréns Torres, Luis, 358
Locke, John, 8, 346
Lord, Everett W., 15, 30–32, 86, 264–65, 288, 319, 338
loudness, 41, 90, 96, 104, 211, 219, 225, 245, 252–53, 279
loyalty, 45, 63, 79–80, 85, 93, 155, 167, 175, 264, 273–74, 338

machete, 70, 129, 159–60, 167, 247, 258, 265, 340, 343
Macheteros, 46, 389n18
machismo/macho, 143–44, 149–51, 240, 395n16; masculinity, 150–52, 256
makeup, use of, 281–82, 296
malaria, 192, 206, 302; yellow fever, 192, 399n20
malnourishment, 43, 135–36, 192, 271, 302–3, 314; malnutrition, 64, 69, 76, 192, 199, 200, 209, 211, 302–3; undernourishment, 63, 192, 311, 318, 356
Manichean allegory, 15; Manichean world, 42, 140

Manifest Destiny, 13
March, Alden, 95, 102, 115, 194, 238
Marden, Phillip Sanford, 55, 109, 137, 233
Marketplace, 36, 113, 119, 172, 177, 203, 287, 292, 316, 325, 338, 341, 343–45, 349; Plaza del Mercado, 344
Marqués, René, 5, 21, 44, 261
marriage, 24–25, 32, 78, 117, 119, 141–42, 144–51, 156, 170, 172, 176, 270, 313
Mathews, George M., 181
Mazrui, Ali A., 336
McGuire, Edna, 242, 319
McLean, Robert, 79, 102, 198
medicine, 64, 121, 198, 200, 204–7, 221, 234, 290, 329, 333, 341
Melgarejo, Juan de, 208
Memmi, Albert, 9, 15, 17, 42–44, 75, 128, 261–62, 356, 358–59
Mennonites, 47, 65, 83, 88, 137, 171, 206, 249, 269, 336
middle class, 8, 27, 32, 47, 65, 67, 76, 100, 121–23, 144–45, 152–53, 167, 193, 214, 225, 276, 282, 288, 329, 336, 347, 350, 354
midwives, 207
Miles, Nelson A., 3, 26, 40, 96, 361–62
military government, 4, 61, 77–78, 165, 351
Mills, Job S., 28, 172–73, 184, 195
Mintz, Sydney W., 164, 324, 346
misery, 13, 43, 48–50, 61, 63–65, 69–71, 76, 135, 154, 221, 238, 255, 347
mission, 108, 166; American Mission Association, 331; American Mission for Lepers, 201; boards, 174, 204; missionaries, 4, 6–8, 12–13, 19, 24–28, 35, 38, 47, 61, 63, 65, 75, 78–79, 83, 101, 106, 113, 114, 116, 121, 132, 134, 136–38, 140–41, 145–46, 149, 151, 154–55, 161–62, 164, 170–74, 176–77, 180–84, 186–90, 192, 194, 198, 202, 204–6, 211–16, 222, 224–27, 229–31, 233, 242, 249, 253, 258, 262, 265, 269, 271, 282, 290–91, 302, 304, 306, 308, 312, 317, 320, 328–29, 331–32, 336, 345–47
Mixer, Knowlton, 42, 107, 161, 224
modernity, 9, 12, 33, 63, 66, 69, 72, 102, 110–11, 122, 124, 126, 144, 163, 173, 205, 224, 236, 241–42, 258, 270, 273–74, 276, 281, 287,

289, 294, 298, 304, 312, 319, 333, 344, 350, 354, 356
Mohr, Eugene V., 41
Monroe Doctrine, 13
Montesquieu, Charles de Secondat, baron of, 10, 133
Moore, J. Hampton, 12, 166, 283
Morales Tejeda, Aida L., 21
morality/morals, 14, 21, 33, 40, 43, 71, 73, 76, 79, 89, 91, 106, 131, 134, 140–41, 144–45, 148–49, 151, 155–56, 171–73, 181, 186, 229, 233, 237, 248, 277, 300–301
Morehouse, Henry L., 183
Morris, Charles, 119–20, 164, 333
Morton, C. Manley, 172, 188, 192, 194, 211, 317, 329
mosquitoes, 201–2
mothers, 16, 24, 28, 34, 36, 74, 106, 118, 144, 149, 150, 177–78, 181–82, 193–94, 203, 208–9, 212, 215, 219, 270–72, 274, 277, 287, 289–92, 294, 297, 300, 304, 306, 310, 334, 354
mourning, 185, 211, 214–15, 286
Muñoz Marín, Luis, 54, 72, 80, 88–90, 248
murders/killings, 58, 103, 125, 150, 163, 192, 238, 244, 318, 330, 347–48, 350–51
music, 90, 119, 221–32, 242, 252, 254, 261, 270, 293, 343, 352, 357

nationalism/nationalists, 33, 39, 54–55, 86–87, 240, 242, 389n18
Nationalist Party, 64, 87, 103, 106, 389n18
native pastors, 188
needlework industry, 64, 106, 276, 287, 291–92
Negroes, 20, 52, 87, 112, 113–20, 219, 224, 231–32
New Deal, 48, 64, 257, 267
noise, 105, 202, 221–22, 235, 251–55, 259, 299, 336, 342–44
novena, 214
nudity/nakedness, 11–12, 20–21, 29, 31, 43–44, 299, 301, 307, 314

obedience, 31, 79, 107, 124, 270, 303, 310, 332
Ober, Frederick A., 69–70, 141, 171, 239, 258, 278, 281, 300–301, 305, 329

Olivares, José de, 13–14, 22, 43, 69, 71, 75, 98–100, 114, 131–32, 135, 137, 143, 145, 147, 161, 201, 262, 279, 287, 291, 300, 308, 318, 331, 334, 340, 349
Oliver, William H., 17, 23, 43–44, 74, 96, 99, 102, 151, 157, 166, 216, 225, 234–35, 239, 261, 298, 302, 330, 338, 342
Operation Bootstrap, 65–66, 89
oratory, 87, 245
orphans/orphanages, 12, 49, 88, 180, 211, 272, 274, 312–13
O'Sullivan, John, 13
otherization, 39, 243, 259
overpopulation, 66, 72
oxen, 306, 346–47, 350–52

pasmo, 207
pawnbroking, 266, 341
peasants, 12, 23, 43, 60, 63, 69–70, 72, 94, 113–14, 119–21, 125, 128–29, 132–36, 171, 181, 186, 192, 197–99, 206–7, 227, 240, 247, 260, 274, 284, 293, 297, 324–25, 333, 336–37, 345, 347–51, 355
peddling, street, 293, 312–13, 342–44
Pedreira, Antonio S., 11
pendejo phenomenon, 50–53
Pentecostalism/Pentecostals, 175, 183, 189–90, 398n28; Evangelicals, 33, 186–87, 304
personalism, 82–83, 179, 247, 249, 251, 311
pests, 15, 20, 201–2, 217, 353
Petrullo, Vincenzo, 39–40, 46, 52, 54–55, 58–59, 103, 110, 118–19, 128, 134, 148, 156, 245, 337
Phillips, Henry Albert, 22, 88, 106, 138
Picó, Fernando, 121, 129–30, 160, 170
Pimpare, Stephen, 73
pitiyanqui, 358
plantains, 69, 124–25, 130, 133–34, 166, 265, 316, 318, 320, 325, 327, 335, 338, 343
politics/politicians, 3–5, 7–8, 12–13, 21, 32, 38, 41, 53, 57, 59, 64, 66, 70, 72, 77, 91, 108, 134, 140, 144, 191, 198, 201, 244, 293, 356
Popular Democratic Party, 65, 88–89, 125, 149

poverty, 5, 16, 24, 28, 30, 46, 48–49, 60, 64–65, 67–69, 71, 73–76, 78–79, 91, 96, 121, 128–31, 133, 135, 140, 148, 156, 162, 182, 189, 191–92, 200, 204, 209, 212, 216, 218, 238–39, 242, 255–58, 271, 273, 283, 291, 293, 296–97, 300–303, 306–7, 313–14, 328, 335; poor children, 74, 298–99, 302–3, 343; poor women, 141, 155–56, 290–91; poor workers/peasants/laborers, 20, 23, 34, 39–40, 42, 47, 49, 61–64, 66–67, 69–72, 74, 89, 116, 120–24, 126, 135–36, 142, 146–47, 152, 161, 164, 169–71, 181, 187, 193, 197, 200–201, 204, 206, 212, 214, 221, 227–28, 230–31, 233–34, 236, 247–48, 250, 258, 261, 267–68, 270, 274, 280–81, 306, 316, 318–19, 324, 328, 330, 337, 344–45, 347, 354–56

prejudice, 6, 22, 23, 35, 54, 105–6, 117–18, 119–20, 126, 167, 184, 187, 248, 282

Presbyterians, 60, 138, 180, 204, 213, 231, 246

prisons/prisoners, 48, 55, 100, 158, 166–68

Prohibition, 164, 332, 396n10; Temperance Movement, 329, 332, 346

promenade, 82, 178, 229, 232–33, 287

prostitution/prostitutes, 151, 155–56, 289, 332–33

Protestantism/Protestants, 27–28, 46, 75, 78, 113, 126, 134, 140, 146, 149, 155, 170, 173, 176–77, 179–84, 186–90, 201, 204, 210, 212, 215, 229, 233–34, 241–42, 269, 301, 304, 308, 329, 332, 345

Puerto Rico Reconstruction Administration (PRRA), 206

Puritanism/Puritans, 8, 13, 75, 129, 131, 140, 148, 173, 177, 224, 233, 241–42, 258, 268, 280–81, 283, 296, 300–301, 329, 333

quinceañera parties, 218

race/racial, 10–11, 13–15, 32, 41, 54, 57, 79, 81, 83, 91, 97, 101–2, 109, 112–17, 119–20, 122, 124, 126–27, 134, 138, 141, 161, 189, 219, 231, 248, 271, 278–80, 344

racism, 12, 87, 113, 117–18, 166, 170, 232; racial prejudice, 117–18, 120, 126; racial segregation, 112–17, 122, 126, 219, 231, 304, 329; racialism/racialists, 10–11

Rand, Abby, 110, 144, 150, 235–36, 240, 269, 316

Rand, Christopher, 118, 271

rats, 195–96, 202

rebellion/rebels, 45–46, 59, 88, 158, 188, 201, 297

Rector, Charles H., 191, 214, 244, 266, 344, 350

religion, 11–12, 27, 40, 81–82, 170–75, 180, 182, 187, 189–90

religiosity, 170, 173, 179

reputation, 45, 89, 124, 131, 141–42, 156, 288

resentment, 51, 55–56, 58, 81, 111, 116, 119, 128, 157, 167

resiliency, 31, 359

resistance, 24, 53, 110, 117, 119, 138, 148, 160, 169, 202, 205, 238, 240, 279, 329, 356–58, 361

respect, 11, 23, 38, 41, 44, 50–51, 56, 66, 79, 99, 116, 124, 132–33, 136, 141, 144, 147, 162–64, 175–77, 179, 181, 199, 202, 205–6, 209, 211, 222, 247–48, 250–51, 255–59, 265, 269, 270–71, 273–74, 299, 314–15, 335, 359

revolution, 46, 58, 73, 109, 254, 346; American, 346; Industrial, 73

rice, 23, 30, 48, 55, 62, 69, 74, 129, 166, 193, 254, 267, 280, 312, 315–21, 324–25, 327, 335, 337

Robinson, Albert G., 10, 68, 95, 97, 99, 131, 138, 166, 232, 256, 262, 325–26, 332, 339–40, 348

Rockefeller Foundation, 197, 200; Rockefeller Sanitary Commission, 62

Rollins, Frances, 32

Roosevelt, Theodore, Jr., 16, 39, 105–6, 166, 193, 303

Root, Elihu, 78

rosaries, 160, 177, 186, 211, 214, 400n46

Rossiter, Emanuel, 6, 40, 96, 158, 174, 210, 261, 279, 338, 352

Rousseau, Jean Jacques, 8, 386n31

Rowe, Leo S., 52, 150, 163, 231, 247, 259, 261, 273, 281, 286, 299, 319
rum, 20, 64, 104, 120, 151, 164–65, 186, 194, 204, 206, 211, 277, 329–32, 334, 341
Rush, Benjamin, 346

Said, Edward, 17, 243
sanitation, 78, 191, 194–96, 202, 345
Santa Claus, 226–29, 401n10
santería, 171
santiguadoras, 207
savagery/savages, 10–11, 14, 28, 71, 162, 335, 343, 358, 386n31, 403n4
Schloat, G. Warren, 32
schools, 12, 29–30, 33–34, 38–39, 66, 85–86, 107–11, 114, 117–18, 123, 126, 132, 136, 140, 152, 155, 160, 168, 174, 180–81, 185, 207, 221, 226–27, 241–42, 246–47, 264–65, 272, 281, 286, 291, 294, 299, 304–14, 345, 356; Sunday schools, 185, 227, 308
Schwartz, Stuart, 8, 22
Seabury, Joseph B., 16, 32–33, 46, 147, 192, 212, 221, 230–31, 239, 294–95, 298, 307–8, 342
seditious bands/*partidas sediciosas*, 158; *tiznados*, 158
segregation, racial, 112–17, 122, 126, 219, 231, 304, 329
self-determination, 49, 240
self-government, 78, 80–81, 83, 85, 91
sereno, 207
sex, 11–12, 98, 100, 119, 133, 141–45, 147, 149, 151–53, 156, 159, 191, 224, 276, 279, 280, 282, 289, 301, 305; premarital, 151, 289
Sherman, Thomas E., 173–74, 209, 215
shoes, 12, 28–29, 42, 62, 65, 135, 168, 188, 197, 199, 202, 225, 234, 256–57, 265, 284, 306–7, 310, 340, 353, 394n6
Siegel, Morris, 164
siesta, 131, 137, 139
Silva Gotay, Samuel, 13, 181
slums, 48, 63, 65–66, 257, 261, 282–83, 303; *El Fanguito*, 257; *Machuelito*, 48; *La Perla*, 65
smoking, 34, 151, 193, 208, 298, 315, 323, 333–34, 344

social classes, 115, 118–21, 124, 140–42, 188, 194, 199, 215, 230, 232, 234, 251, 257, 264, 282–83, 344
soldiers: American, 3, 6, 19, 25–26, 40–41, 43–44, 74, 93–100, 111, 113, 122, 142, 150, 155, 157–58, 166–68, 180–81, 196, 203, 210, 212, 216, 224, 234–36, 238–39, 241, 260, 280, 295–96, 298, 302, 328, 330–31, 334, 337–38, 348, 350–52; Puerto Rican, 54, 166–67; Spanish, 140, 157–59
songs, 130, 183, 186, 222, 279, 343
sons, 57, 62, 86, 107, 124–25, 142, 152, 173, 178, 182, 185, 246, 270, 277, 290, 307, 324
Spain, 3–4, 44, 56, 58, 71, 77, 80–81, 91–93, 111, 115, 125, 143, 148, 150, 170, 176, 179, 302, 305, 328, 361
Spanish culture/traditions, 27, 51, 109, 120, 150, 170, 177, 181, 209, 226, 229–30, 232–33, 236, 264, 278, 284, 309, 329
Spanish food, 317, 321–22
Spanish imperialism/Spanish colonization, 3, 9, 45–46, 49, 58, 61, 71, 77–79, 85, 89, 92–93, 111, 124, 128, 145, 149, 157, 169–72, 174, 179, 181, 201, 208, 216, 233, 304, 337
Spanish language, 20, 30–31, 39, 51, 65, 86, 88–89, 98, 105, 108–9, 125, 150, 173, 181–82, 228, 250, 263, 272–73, 280, 330, 340, 357
Spanish people/Spaniards, 37, 44–45, 57, 85, 92, 95–96, 115, 120–21, 157–59, 176, 262, 266, 348
Spanish-American War, 4, 6, 17, 92
Spencer, Herbert, 13–14
spiritism, 52, 171, 179, 183, 205
sports, 142, 144, 177, 220, 240–42, 288, 300; group, 240–41
Spurr, David, 13, 191
St. John's Festival/*Fiestas de San Juan*, 230
St. Peter's Day, 231
starvation, 61–62, 69–71, 88, 125, 200, 255, 302–3, 314, 317, 345; hunger, 24, 38, 44, 68–69, 74, 90, 142, 171, 191–92, 199, 221, 233, 255, 267, 300, 303, 308, 314, 345
statehood, 38, 57, 77, 407n1
sterilization, 54, 66, 76, 175
Stoddard, Charles A., 60, 141

stores/storeowners, 68, 71, 94, 98, 129, 158–59, 176–77, 182, 198–99, 227, 245, 252, 260, 273, 291, 293, 295, 325, 331, 336–41, 344–45
street peddling, 293, 312–13, 342–44
Strong, Josiah, 14
students, 30, 38, 73, 103, 106, 109–10, 118, 123, 175, 188, 208, 224, 227, 254, 268, 272, 286, 289, 303–11
Suárez Findlay, Eileen, 141, 147, 279
submission/submissive, 41, 44–46, 59, 96, 259, 298, 326
subordination, 11, 15, 17, 44, 52, 82, 166, 250, 270, 357, 359
sugar (food), 31, 267, 308, 315, 320, 324–25, 327, 330, 337, 354
sugar industry, 3, 20, 61–64, 72, 76, 92–93, 106, 120–21, 124, 134, 136, 164, 204, 223, 226, 324–25, 346
suicide, 104, 159, 215
Sundays, 32, 100–101, 109, 135, 158–59, 175, 177–78, 185, 224, 227, 232, 236, 238, 242, 256, 258, 285, 287, 308, 344–45, 397n8; Sunday school, 185, 227, 308
superiority, 9–10, 13–15, 17, 21, 26–27, 32, 39, 45, 50–51, 102, 105, 113, 119, 124, 135, 140, 156, 166, 168, 188, 247, 250, 261, 274, 290, 350, 356
sweets, 228, 321–22, 325–27, 343

tables, 104, 183, 190, 202, 219, 265, 267, 271, 316, 319, 321–25, 327; gambling, 219, 233–35
Taíno Indians, 44–45, 209
Tavener, Mary Hilaire, 23, 31, 90, 164, 179, 197, 207, 209, 333, 358
teachers, 19–20, 22–25, 30–32, 34, 38, 50, 72, 76, 85–87, 98, 103–4, 106, 109–10, 116, 120, 123, 143, 151, 154, 156, 164, 168, 175, 196, 207–9, 219, 224, 226, 233, 237, 246, 251, 254, 263, 265, 268–69, 271, 277, 281, 286, 288, 289–90, 293–94, 304–11, 314, 318, 331, 334, 341, 357; English, 196, 207–9, 219, 224, 226, 251, 271, 277, 286, 289, 294, 310, 334, 357
Three Kings' Day, 170, 179, 227–29

tobacco industry, 3, 42, 61–62, 64, 76, 92, 106, 120–21, 124, 136, 276, 290, 292; chewing tobacco, 334
Tocqueville, Alexis de, 13
Todorov, Tzvetan, 10–11
Tous Soto, José, 86
travelers, 6, 8–9, 11, 16, 19–21, 24, 29, 33, 73, 253, 269
trullas/asaltos, 227–28, 401n11
tuberculosis, 21, 63, 191–93, 302
Tugwell, Rexford Guy, 21, 36–37, 53–54, 57–58, 65, 78, 87, 125–26, 166–67, 195, 248–49, 257, 264, 303, 319, 354
Tydings Bill, 87–88

ugliness, 15, 105, 113, 142, 285, 353
"ugly Americans," 105
unemployment, 63, 66, 72, 119, 163, 191, 209
unincorporated territory, 4, 77
universities, 246, 270, 288, 294; CAAM, 123–51, 175, 268, 294, 309; Universidad Interamericana, 246; University of Puerto Rico, 151, 246
US Congress, 4, 16, 36, 60, 64, 67–68, 77–78, 80, 86, 88, 91, 111, 332; congressmen, 5, 79, 113; US invasion, 3, 6, 9, 14, 19, 26, 32–33, 60–61, 76–77, 80, 90, 92–93, 95–99, 107, 111, 113, 121–22, 129, 134, 136, 141, 145–47, 149, 155, 157, 160, 165, 173–74, 176, 180, 196, 198, 213, 215, 232, 240–41, 246, 254, 266, 276, 291, 304, 312, 328–29, 337, 339, 347, 353, 356

Valle Atiles, Francisco del, 260
Van Middeldyk, Rudolph A., 131
Vandercook, John W., 339–57
Verrill, A. Hyatt, 15, 20, 22, 79–80, 100–101, 105, 108–9, 168, 196, 201, 216, 221, 242, 252, 313, 341, 345, 357
Vespucci, Amerigo, 11
violence, 50, 52, 59, 64, 87, 91, 95, 97, 99, 117, 122, 132, 144, 148, 157–62, 166, 169, 184, 202–3, 223, 237–38, 240–41, 351, 357–58
Virgin Mary, 170–71, 178–79, 182, 210, 214, 229, 398n25
virginity, 141–42, 144, 151

visitor's economy, 68, 102
voting rights, 37, 80, 82, 85–86, 88–90, 248, 332, 396n10

Wagenheim, Kal, 44, 48, 53–54, 66–67, 73, 112, 123, 126, 144, 155, 165, 179, 203, 207, 211, 221, 226, 248, 316, 357
wakes, 170, 211–12
Weber, Max, 173
Wilcox, Ella Wheeler, 352
Wilcox, F. W., 42, 204, 346
Williams, Grace Petrie, 79, 102, 198
Wilson, Edward S., 82–83, 85, 103, 245, 305, 308
Wilson, James H., 3, 26, 113, 180
Winslow, Isaac O., 32–33
winter resort, 101–2, 111
Winthrop, John, 13
wives, 23, 39, 62, 94, 121, 129, 135, 144–46, 149, 151–55, 168, 171, 178, 199, 202, 234, 248, 250, 255, 257, 266–67, 270, 276–78, 289, 295, 303, 324, 333–34, 345, 349

women: American, 24, 32, 34, 154, 281, 288–90, 295, 329, 334; Puerto Rican, 19, 25, 28, 41, 43, 54, 63, 66, 70, 74, 96, 100, 113, 117, 119, 123, 131, 141–42, 144–48, 150–56, 160, 162–63, 165, 168, 176, 178, 181, 185–86, 189, 194, 198, 211, 213–14, 219, 223, 225, 230, 232–33, 236, 244, 256–58, 276–96, 304–5, 307, 323–24, 332–34, 337, 343–44, 347, 354; washerwomen, 21, 294–96, 307, 337
Wood, Leonard, 71–72
workers, 20, 37, 42, 60–61, 63–64, 69, 74, 76, 105–7, 120, 124, 130, 134–36, 139, 158, 170, 181, 184, 187, 192, 196, 198–99, 226, 247, 251, 258, 276, 284, 291, 303, 319–20, 324, 329–30, 332, 346; laborers, 10, 20, 50, 60, 62–63, 68, 70–72, 98, 114, 124–25, 129–30, 132–33, 135–36, 146, 159, 192, 197, 200, 216, 274, 329
World War I, 80, 196
World War II, 64, 155, 166, 178, 319

ABOUT THE AUTHOR

Dr. Ligia T. Domenech earned her BA in social welfare from the University of Puerto Rico at Río Piedras, and both her MA in Caribbean and Puerto Rican studies and her PhD in Caribbean and Puerto Rican history from the Center for Advanced Studies of Puerto Rico and the Caribbean (San Juan). She has over twenty years of experience teaching history, humanities, and social sciences at the University of Puerto Rico, the Interamerican University (Puerto Rico), Vincennes University (Indiana), Northern Essex Community College (Massachusetts), and UNI 3 (Uruguay). Dr. Domenech has published: *¡Que el pueblo decida! La gobernación de Roberto Sánchez Vilella, 1964–1968* (*Let the People Decide: The Government of Roberto Sánchez Vilella, 1964–1968*) (San Juan: EMS Editores, 2007), where she discusses the rough transition from populism to technocracy in Puerto Rico; and *Imprisoned in the Caribbean: The 1942 German U-Boat Blockade* (Indiana: Iuniverse, 2014). She has also written chapters for *Guerras irregulares en el Caribe* (*Irregular Wars in the Caribbean*) (México: Instituto Mora, 2019), *Island at War: Puerto Rico in the Crucible of the Second World War* (University Press of Mississippi, 2015), and

Puerto Rico en la Segunda Guerra Mundial: Baluarte del Caribe (*Puerto Rico in World War II: A Caribbean Bulwark*) (San Juan: Editorial Callejón, 2012). Originally from Isabela, Puerto Rico, she now resides in Montevideo, Uruguay, where she teaches and researches how Americans portrayed Cubans and their culture from 1898 to 1959.

www.ingramcontent.com/pod-product-compliance
Lightning Source LLC
Chambersburg PA
CBHW030601230426
43661CB00053B/1795